The
Juvenile Offender
Perspective and Readings

**DOUBLEDAY PUBLICATIONS
IN SOCIOLOGY AND ANTHROPOLOGY**

Consulting Editor
Charles H. Page
Professor of Sociology, Smith College

The
Juvenile Offender
Perspective and Readings

By
Clyde B. Vedder, Ph.D.
University of Florida

1954
Doubleday and Company, Inc.
Garden City, N.Y.

Library of Congress Catalog Card Number: 54–6239

Printed in the United States of America
At the Country Life Press, Garden City, N.Y.

FOREWORD

~~~~~~

NO social problem has wrought deeper concern in the United States and, in fact, throughout the world, than juvenile delinquency. Aside from the universal and natural feeling adults cherish for children, and more especially, frustrated and thwarted children, the knowledge that a happy and wholesome youth is the best guarantee for a future mature society, prompts lavish and unselfish expenditures of time, energy, and money in attempting to solve the eternal riddle of delinquency. Generations pass but the dilemma of aberrant juvenile behavior persists. Yet lethargy, apathy, discouragement, or a fatalistic cynicism cannot halt the impressive will of society to scrutinize the mysteries of human behavior, from the onset of birth through early childhood, adolescence, and adulthood in order to arrest or eradicate the development of unsocial or antisocial tendencies.

As one surveys the writings of those who, a hundred or more years ago, were dismayed when so many children fell by the wayside or ran afoul of the law, he is struck by the similarities of alarm of those days and the present. The term *juvenile delinquency* is not as old as the phenomenon we recognize and know; rather children of this category were referred to as "depraved," "headstrong," "wayward," or just "waifs and strays." Perhaps the first time the term was used was in 1823 when a group of New York educators and philanthropists formed a society for the prevention of juvenile delinquency and opened this country's first institution known as the House of Refuge. Yet over a hundred years earlier, Pope Clement XI had been distressed by the spread of young adult criminality and erected his Hospice of San Michele in Rome for the reception and treatment of incorrigible adolescents.

The number of books, pamphlets, reports, monographs, charts, statistical analyses dealing with the subject is prodigious. Yet despite this impressive array of literature, it is a fact that in this broad country there appears no journal or magazine exclusively devoted to the subject. The general public receives its ofttimes superficial or garbled knowledge of the juvenile delinquent from the slick paper magazine with its articles written primarily to catch the eye and titillate the imagination.

Yet no one familiar with the subject would minimize its seriousness. The anxiety felt for problem children is shared not only by law-enforcing officials, from the police to juvenile court judges, but by social agencies, recreation officials, civic and women's clubs, school officials, and informed parents as well. It is, in truth, a perplexity that dips into every home at one time or another.

But when we begin discussing specific phases of this universal problem, we discover numerous facets that stimulate sharp differences of opinion. Perhaps the first of these is the definition of the delinquent. There are many such definitions, some of which, like incorrigibility, are blanket terms. Equally enigmatic is the extent of this so-called delinquency. No adequate methods exist whereby anything more than an approximation of the extent of the problem can be assayed. Is there a true delinquent rather than merely a sporadic or situational violator? If so, can he be spotted in his early years by either his aggressive or otherwise emotional behavior or by physical constitutional traits? How can we treat the potential or incipient juvenile delinquent once he is spotted so as to divert his disapproved behavior patterns into constructive channels?

The student of this baffling problem has many questions to ask. The old truism that "the more one studies the problem the less sure he is" certainly applies to the field of juvenile delinquency.

The book of readings compiled by Professor Vedder, supplemented so judiciously by introductory comments to set the stage presented in each chapter, demonstrates that he is alert to the many phases of the problem. It is indeed a difficult task to extract from the plethora of articles written in the professional journals by experts just the right material that will interpret to the student and practitioner the seriousness and wide scope of the problem. But Professor Vedder has done a workmanlike job. He has included many of the very best articles available and in a very readable style has injected much of his own thinking on the subject.

The work has been prepared to supplement a textbook in the field. It meets a real need, primarily in colleges and universities where professional journals are either not available or appear only in single copies. It is doubtless the author's intention to bring together much of the best current material into the confines of one volume. In addition to college use, the style of the writers and the contributions they make to the field suggest a wide clientele among practitioners in the fields of psychiatry, social work, and education. In fact, many laymen, whether or not they be parents, will do well to avail themselves of this work.

Negley K. Teeters
Temple University

PREFACE

~~~~~~

IN the field of crime it has become apparent that adult law-breakers are drawn in large numbers from the ranks of youthful offenders—lessons in crime are learned early and, all too often, well. It is not surprising, then, that sociologists, psychologists, and members of related disciplines are applying their knowledge and their skills to problems of prevention of juvenile delinquency and rehabilitation of "delinquents."

Numerous techniques and facilities designed to cope with these problems have appeared in recent years. And there has appeared also a multitude of articles on delinquency by authorities and "authorities." Many of the former, the authoritative writings, however, are found only in professional journals and thus are read by few. To meet this situation, this book makes available in one place a number of carefully selected writings by specialists in juvenile delinquency. The selection itself, the author believes, results in a collection of materials especially useful for teachers and for their students. Today's students will be the specialists and authorities of tomorrow.

The arrangement of the readings reflects the principal divisions of the field of juvenile delinquency, indicated by the chapter headings. The readings in each chapter are preceded by a brief textual discussion written to serve as a general guide for the student. But the readings themselves, it must be stressed, make this volume especially useful for both collegiate and professional instruction.

The readings, of course, do not cover the field; juvenile delinquency is a dynamic and, fortunately, an improving professional specialization. Nor could any such selection be viewed by the specialists themselves as altogether satisfactory. Certain articles may be considered classics in the future; others no doubt will be superseded. Some excellent articles were purposely excluded because they are available in other collections of readings. And a number of contributions of "practical men" were purposely included so that the student might have at hand insightful observations that characteristically are not exploited in the classroom. This combination of contributions from administrative and academic specialists, it is hoped, will help to pave the way for greater cooperation and larger understanding in the controversial field of juvenile delinquency.

The author's largest indebtedness, clearly enough, is to those silent partners who made this book a possibility. These include the authors of the readings from the following publications and the editors of these journals, who granted permission for the use of the selections in this book: *Federal Probation, Journal of Criminal Law and Criminology*, the *1940 Yearbook* of the National Probation and Parole Association, *Sociology and Social Research*, *The Annals* of the American Academy of Political and Social Science, *American Sociological Review*, *American Journal of Sociology*, *Bulletin* of the American Association of University Professors, *San Francisco Chronicle* and "Wide World," *Social Casework*, and *Social Forces*. All selections are reprinted in their entirety; however, the majority of the footnotes accompanying the original works have been omitted.

The author has benefited—and believes that the book has also—from the numerous suggestions and criticisms, many of which could not be fully exploited, of Professor Herbert A. Bloch of St. Lawrence University and Professor Charles H. Page of Smith College.

For the time-consuming work of typing the manuscript, the author wishes to thank Louetta Young and Peggy Austin, of the Department of Sociology and Anthropology, University of Florida, who so diligently and faithfully performed their tasks. Grateful acknowledgment goes also to Marie R. Byrd for collecting, assorting, and typing the author's original notes; and to Louis J. Maloof for his assistance and encouragement in the preliminary stages of the preparation of this work.

Accolades this volume may merit belong to the authors of the readings. Shortcomings of the book, of course, are altogether the author's responsibility.

January, 1954   Clyde B. Vedder

CONTENTS

1 THE JUVENILE DELINQUENT

EVERY year thousands of American boys and girls get into trouble. Most of them, with little or no outside help, conform to society's rules and grow into good citizens; but others, too many of them, continue to pursue the practices that lead to delinquent careers. They are the professional criminals of to-morrow.

There is no need to dwell upon the current deep concern over "juvenile delinquents," as these young people have come to be known. Sometimes this concern expresses itself in such questions as these: Why does one boy steal a car and another refuse to commit any depredation? Why does one child become a thief and another in the same family a "pillar of the community"? Why does a son of a criminal father follow in his footsteps while his brother does not? Questions of this order that seek explorations of specific individuals' behavior are exceedingly difficult to answer without careful *psychological* study. Questions of another type—why, for example, are the delinquency rates of this group or that relatively high or low? how do certain cultural and social conditions stimulate delinquent behavior? why are rates going up or down? what is wise and realistic policy in coping with delinquency?—demand *sociological* answers. Some of these answers are developed in the pages that follow.

THE MEANING OF DELINQUENCY

A very difficult problem in studying juvenile delinquency is deciding upon an exact definition of the term itself. No two authorities agree in this matter. In a broad sense, juvenile delinquency refers to the antisocial acts of children and of young people under age. Such acts are either specifically forbidden by law or may be lawfully interpreted as constituting delinquency, or as requiring some form of official action. According to one authority, delinquency actually has many different meanings. There are *legal* delinquents (those committing antisocial acts as defined by law), *detected* delinquents (those exhibiting anti-social behavior, for example), *agency* delinquents (those detected who reach an agency), *alleged* delinquents (those apprehended, brought to court), and *adjudged* delinquents (those found guilty).[1]

In most juvenile research, the term "juvenile delinquent" denotes a child who has been *officially* acted upon by the courts or police officers. The age which the term "juvenile" covers varies in different states, ranging from the ages of sixteen to twenty-one, with the majority of states considering in-

[1] Lowell Juilliard Carr, *Delinquency Control* (New York: Harper & Brothers, 1941), p. 59.

dividuals as juvenile if they are under eighteen and over six. A Massachusetts law defines a juvenile delinquent as "a child between seven and seventeen who violates any city ordinance or town by-law or commits an offense not punishable by death." Under this law nearly every child within this age range is, or will be, a delinquent-by-definition.

THE NATURE AND CAUSE OF DELINQUENCY

Many approaches have been explored in an effort to secure information revealing the nature and causes of juvenile delinquency. Among these are the *legalistic* approach (the juvenile treated as an adult offender and based on the assumption that age is a correlative of increasing responsibility), the *individual* approach (a case study method), the *group* approach (a study of gangs and other youth groups, with implications for the delinquent or studies of delinquency in relation to social situations), the *cultural* approach (the effects of culture conflicts and culture contacts on the delinquent), and the *ecological* approach (the study of spatial and temporal relations as they are related to the physical setting).

The approach, however, generally followed over the years has been *hit-or-miss*. Authorities continue to attack with panaceas the problems of juvenile misbehavior which persist despite the rush to construct more playgrounds, swimming pools, and youth canteens, with the hope that these will alleviate the situation. Failure of one approach after another continues to breed more failure. Youth still comes before the bar of justice.

There sometimes seem to be nearly as many "causes" of juvenile delinquency as there are individuals who have studied the problem. Delinquency has been attributed to bad companions, adolescent instability, mental conflicts, extreme social suggestibility, early sex experience, love of adventure, motion pictures, school problems, poor recreation, excessive street life, vocational dissatisfaction, sudden impulses, bad habits, obsessive ideation, poor physical structure, ill health, or premature puberty. Yet most children have experienced one or more of these "causes" and have never become delinquent.

Many persons in the general public believe that juvenile delinquents are a special biological type, "possessed," "degenerate," or "moronic." But delinquency is not a disease. Delinquents are not necessarily sick persons, either physically or mentally.

Of course, real delinquents do exist. Moreover, it should not be forgotten that it will take more than semantic magic to solve the problem of juvenile delinquency. There *are* genuine delinquents. Realistic sociologists may not agree with the pious and frequently not insincere expression that "there is no such thing as a bad boy." But when a boy strikes and permanently injures an old man merely because he wants to steal some cigarettes from his shop, or when a boy attacks and injures a young girl merely to satisfy his own selfish desires—such a boy is "bad"—or perhaps there needs to be a new interpretation for "badness."

The complexity of "delinquency" is further emphasized by the fact that it may mean one thing morally, something else legally, something different practically, and another thing statistically. It seems impossible to define the term so that it will satisfy all interests.

Most delinquents who come before the courts are underprivileged children from impoverished, overcrowded homes in deteriorated neighborhoods, where they run in gangs from whom they learn to steal and to rob. Does one conclude from this that poverty, slums, and bad companions are the causes of delinquency? If this is so, then why is everyone who is poor and who lives in slum areas not delinquent? Many delinquents are malnourished and are undersized; they have physical defects or they are mentally deficient. Is delinquency then caused by a physical condition or mental deficiency? Again, if this were true, how to account for the many healthy, bright delinquents—the college graduates who are in the penitentiaries? One hears about the pernicious influence upon children's behavior of the radio, the motion pictures, and comic book crime thrillers. Still, a multitude of children are exposed to such items of popular culture every day, yet they never commit a delinquent act. A large proportion of delinquents come from miserable homes, broken homes, homes in which discord is rife. Can it be that the cause of delinquency is bad home environment? Then why does one child become a thief and another in the same family become a useful citizen? These questions, of strategic importance in the study of the causation of delinquency, are raised by Edith K. Lesser in a provocative discussion.[2]

To understand the delinquent fully it is imperative that information be secured concerning his physical structure, his intellectual abilities, his family background, his family relationships, his school, his neighborhood, his playmates, his interests and his activities. Even more important is the knowledge of how he feels and thinks about these things, because ultimately reformation must come from within.

Important as may be the information concerning the delinquents that come under the official custody of society, an adequate picture of juvenile delinquency is still unavailable. The recorded delinquency cases are only a known fraction of those actually existing. The majority of delinquents solve their own problems without the ministrations of the court, the clinic, or the psychiatrist.

It is generally agreed that no child is *born* a delinquent. Delinquency is acquired through the learning process. It is a form of social behavior. The alleged delinquency of youth is often the reflection of his adult surroundings—perhaps better said, the sum total of the transmitted patterns from these surroundings, and the influence of response-tendencies that help shape his personality. Juvenile delinquency may not be the real issue under discussion; it may well be adult personal and social disorganization.

Delinquency results, one writer stresses, when there is a relative absence in the individual of internalized norms and rules governing behavior in conformity with the norms of the social system to which legal penalties are attached. It results from a breakdown in previously established controls, and/or a relative absence of such controls, for example, from the apparent conflict in the social rules or techniques for enforcing such behavior in the social groups or institu-

[2] "Understanding Juvenile Delinquency," *Federal Probation*, XIII, September 1949, 56-58.

tions of which the person is a member. This writer concludes that delinquency may be seen as a functional consequence of the type of relationship established between the personal and social controls.[3]

READINGS

Peter Lejins in his article, "Pragmatic Etiology of Delinquent Behavior," suggests that the criminologists engaged in the study of the causes of delinquent and criminal behavior should not turn their backs on the analysis of the concept of cause. He stresses the belief that the juvenile acquires his delinquent behavior (which could be called conformist delinquency) through *conforming* with the behavior pattern in his group.

According to Jerome E. Bates in his selection, "Abrahamsen's Theory of the Etiology of Criminal Acts," Abrahamsen greatly minimizes the importance of such social factors as the broken home, evil associates, habits of thought, as determinants of juvenile delinquency. This article also brings out that each delinquent is unique despite surface similarities with other offenders.

Leontine R. Young in "We Call Them Delinquents" questions the commonly accepted theory that only by punishment and more punishment can "bad" children be made "good." Far too many in authority have forgotten that juvenile delinquents *are* children. Unless children are respected as individuals not much respect for adults may be anticipated.

Hertha Tarrasch in "Delinquency Is Normal Behavior" says that some form of delinquent behavior in children might be almost an expression of normalcy. Few adults would expect a child to be 100 per cent obedient, abiding by every rule and always doing what is expected of him. Every child has a delinquency potential, caused by strong selfish impulses which demand satisfaction and which are frustrated by social codes.

Pragmatic Etiology of Delinquent Behavior[*]

~~~~~~

By Peter Lejins. Professor of Sociology, University of Maryland, College Park.

ETIOLOGY or the inquiry into the causes of criminal and delinquent behavior is unquestionably the very heart of modern concern with crime and delinquency. (Though the fields of juvenile delinquency and adult criminality in many respects present separate problems, there are many areas in which considera-tions pertinent to the one apply also to the other, and often investigations significant for both have been made only in one of the two fields. Although this paper deals with causation of juvenile delinquency, where appropriate reference will therefore be made to both juvenile delinquency and adult crimi-

[3] Albert J. Reiss, Jr., "Delinquency as the Failure of Personal and Social Controls," *American Sociological Review*, XVI, April 1951, 196.

[*] Reprinted from *Social Forces*, Vol. 29, March, 1951, pp. 317–320. Used by permission of author and publication.

nality.) Any progressive action in handling the problems of criminality and delinquency has as its springboard an etiological concept, explicit or implicit. The only types of crime and delinquency control that can be operated without any reference to the causes of the undesirable behavior are control through the threat and execution of punishment for the forbidden act without any regard for the offender and control by erecting mechanical obstacles in the way of the potential offender. These latter methods, however, were the mainstays of the past centuries, and though they are still with us today, they have the connotation of necessary evils at best, while the fancy and the hopes of modern Western society are pinned on prevention and correction.

The Issue of Causes

But both prevention and correction of the offender as understood today presuppose knowledge of the causes of the objectionable behavior. One cannot rationally and purposefully prevent delinquent behavior, that is, remove the causes of its appearance, without having an explicit or implicit idea as to what the causes are. One cannot correct the delinquent, that is, put a stop to his already manifest delinquent behavior by removing the reasons for it, without having an explicit or implicit theory as to what the reasons are. The theoretical and academic criminologists have felt this need of the practitioner in the field of crime, and from the early days of systematic criminological writing and research until today the bulk of learned criminological discussion revolves around the issue of causes. Likewise the layman, to the extent to which he is a product of our rational industrial society, has a deep-seated concern for that which makes a criminal or delinquent behave the way he does. The average citizen of today is sufficiently imbued with the general tenor of his society to feel that if we know "how something works" we might be able to direct it according to our wishes.

The result of this preeminent concern for the etiology of delinquent and in general criminal behavior, is the tremendous volume of work which has been and is being done regarding this topic. The research, writing, and oral discussion of the causes of crime by both trained and lay people which started in the nineteenth century and went on increasing like an avalanche still continue and have reached vast proportions. To give an idea of the volume of literature now in existence on the subject, one may safely state that a lifetime is not long enough to familiarize oneself with the writing available on the subject of the causes of delinquency and criminality. Likewise it has become impossible even for a person specializing in the field to keep up with all the materials in all their ramifications currently appearing on the subject of the causation of crime and delinquency. So far quantitative studies of the published or currently appearing materials have been used only very infrequently as a method of measuring the extent of human concern with a certain topic. Were such a study undertaken, the interest of Western society in the etiology of criminal and especially delinquent behavior would be shown as occupying a very prominent niche.

Unfortunately it has to be recognized that this mass of research, writing and verbalization on the subject of the causes of delinquency and crime is presently in a state of utter confusion. It is the most bulky but at the same time the weakest part of criminology. It is the most crucial to the entire field; it offers some great promises, but it needs some magic transformation, perhaps a stroke of genius, to give it the structure of a scientific discipline. It is that portion of criminology which has led some of the most outstanding American criminologists to question the scientific character of the entire field.

Here are just a few outstanding examples: as recently as 1933 the distinguished scholars Jerome Michael and Mortimer J. Adler, in a survey of the field of criminology (*Crime, Law and Social Science*), were led to publish the conclusion that "There is no scientific knowledge in the field of criminology," and "we have no knowledge of the causes of criminal behavior." The dean of American criminologists, Professor E. H. Sutherland, a person who is perhaps less than anybody else in the field of American criminology given to dramatic overstatement, similarly finds it necessary to restate as late as the 1947 edition of his textbook *Principles of Criminology:* "Criminology at present is clearly not a science, but it has hopes of becoming a science."

One of the most outstanding examples of a position to which the present state of criminal etiology may lead is that taken by Professor Walter C. Reckless, who was led by the hopelessly confused state of criminal etiology to suggest giving up the search for the cause of criminal behavior and replacing the concept of cause by that of "differential crime risks" (an impossibility in accordance with the views of the present author, as can be deduced from the statement in the very beginning of this paper): "Perhaps the greatest influence retarding the progress of criminology has been the traditional emphasis on the study of the causes of crime."

Absence of Concern with Concept of Cause

One very peculiar situation in the field of etiology of delinquent and criminal behavior, which is, however, very seldom pointed out and discussed, is the almost complete absence of any concern on the part of criminologists with the concept of the cause itself. Now, the concept of cause has been the subject of attention of logicians, students of scientific method, and philosophers for thousands of years.

Many members of the specific scientific disciplines have also delved into it and have agreed on a definition of cause, at least an operational one, for their particular field. A tremendous literature on the general and specific concepts of causality testifies to the seriousness and extent of the effort. Yet the criminologists have on the whole proceeded in their etiological studies without too much worry, and often with none at all, about the meaning of the word cause. In most cases it is quite obvious that the term cause is used in criminology in its popular vague sense. Here, then, is clearly a case of extensive research with the crucial term of the hypothesis ill defined or not defined at all. How can one hope to produce scientific knowledge by verifying hypotheses which propose a relationship of cause and effect without having fixed what this relationship implies and means. In this respect, from the standpoint of scientific method, the field of etiology of delinquent behavior is as yet in a very naive and raw state indeed.

There are, of course, a few exceptions. For this country one might mention the following examples. Reckless' discussion, already mentioned, of the desirability of substituting the concept of categoric risks for the concept of cause; Sutherland's distinction between adventitious and systematic criminal behavior and the implications for the search of the causes of the two; Tappan's chapter on the "Problem of Cause" in his *Juvenile Delinquency*, with the distinction between proximate and situational cause, but especially, of course, the somewhat earlier monumental analysis by Michael and Adler that was already mentioned. Yet these sporadic attempts remain such and have so far not added up to a generally accepted interpretation of the concept of cause. In most cases the authors themselves, after some discussion of the concept of cause, proceed with the presentation of the conventional theories of causation built around the same old and vague concept.

The potential argument that the discussion of the concept of causes is not properly the task of the criminologist but should rather be done by a student of scientific method is, of course, invalid here. The same applies to the argument that it is up to a general theory of human behavior to work out the general frame of reference for the specific disciplines dealing with some one aspect of human behavior, that is, also for criminology. It is self-understood, of course, that the general theory of causation is a subject for the student of scientific method, and a general theory of human behavior is a subject for a general psychologist, social psychologist or sociologist. All this, however, does not relieve the criminologist of the duty of defining the concept which happens to be his main research tool. It is not being advocated here that the researchers dealing in special disciplines should put aside their specific interests and first work out the general theory of causation and a general frame of reference for the science of human behavior. But it should not be implied that the absence of agreement on the basic questions of the general theory of science relieves people in special disciplines of all requirements of scientific method. On the contrary, by working out specific problems in accordance with the rules of scientific method, they should be contributing to the development of a general frame of reference. This seems to be the rather universal process by which science grows.

Furthermore, the main trouble does not seem to be that scientific method does not offer the criminologist anything worth looking into on the issue of cause. On the contrary; there certainly are enough ingenious and worthwhile propositions about the use of the concept of cause in the field of criminal behavior that should be investigated and tested. It

looks much more like an absence of a tradition and custom on the part of the people working in delinquent etiology to be concerned with the meaning of the term cause, as well as complete illiteracy on the part of many criminological writers in the matters of scientific method.

An illustration may help drive home this very important point. In 1942 and 1943 respectively, two books about the concept of causation in the social sciences were published in this country: MacIver's *Social Causation* and Sorokin's *Sociocultural Causality*. Both authors are well known American sociologists, as a matter of fact, both belong to the very top of the contemporary sociological Olympus. Both authors deal with the very heart of the subject matter, which has been and still is of crucial importance to the criminologists. Both constantly use crime and delinquency causation to illustrate their points, and MacIver even uses crime causation as his star example of the causation problem in the social sciences. And yet not one of the ten books on criminology and juvenile delinquency which the author of this paper picked up at random from his shelf and all of which were published at least two years after MacIver's and Sorokin's monographs contains even the name of either of the two authors. And yet all ten deal extensively with the issue of causes. One should not imply from this illustration that this writer thinks that it is a must for a criminologist to refer to the said works of MacIver or Sorokin. But taken as a whole this situation is extremely indicative of the prevailing conditions. It points up a lack of alertness, a lack of constructive effort to approach the problem in the true spirit of scientific investigation, in short, a serious gap in the basic approach of criminology as a discipline to its most crucial problem, especially since criminology itself admittedly does not have much to offer on the positive side.

One of the main points of this paper then is that the criminologists engaged in the study of the causes of delinquent and criminal behavior should not turn their backs on the analysis of the concept of cause, but on the contrary, should make a sustained effort to state their hypotheses as clearly as possible in this respect and carry out their research within a clearly established frame of reference.

Pragmatic Theory of Causation

The concept of cause of delinquent behavior suggested in this paper might be referred to as a product of the pragmatic theory of causation. It is believed that this concept would best serve the purposes of theoretical organization of the scientific knowledge in the field, be most effective in directing further research, and be most meaningful as a frame of reference for treatment and prevention. The essence of this pragmatic theory of causation lies in the recognition of the fact that any happening, any event has as its precondition the total situation which preceded it. Man singles out of this antecedent situation some element or elements and declares them to be the cause or causes of the event. Different people select different items. But what are the criteria of this selection? The pragmatic theory of causation proposes that this selection should be done, and in reality most frequently is being done, on the basis of man's interest in influencing the course of events. Those elements of the entire antecedent situation which are most manipulable are declared to be causes, because they are the most meaningful, the most significant. There is no point in selecting as cause something that cannot be altered or manipulated in any way. Even if it is obviously an indispensable precondition, if it is out of man's reach there is no point in bringing it out and wasting energy on it.

When a bad fire is reported in a news-

paper today, one usually finds some mention of the causes. Antiquated fire extinguishing equipment, a poorly organized and slow functioning fire department, the combustible material of which the building was constructed, carelessness with fire, etc., all these are items which can be manipulated, changed, improved, and therefore it is meaningful to bring them out. Yet one can be sure that no one has ever read a description of a fire with a comment that the cause was the presence of oxygen in the air. If the oxygen were removed from the air, that would surely prevent fires and do so perhaps better than any other measure, but there is no point in talking about this as a cause, because nothing can be done about it. It goes without saying that in different societies and in different epochs, with different cultures and technologies, different elements of the antecedent situation might be most conveniently manipulable; hence the causal explanation will also differ. This would make understandable the changes in the causal interpretations as the civilization of the world changes. An excellent concise statement of this pragmatic theory of causation appears in Quincy Wright's *The Causes of War and the Conditions of Peace*.

Application of Pragmatic Approach

Now let us see if the pragmatic approach to the problem of cause will yield any positive results when applied to the etiology of delinquent behavior. An analysis of contemporary theoretical research into the causes of juvenile delinquency and practical attempts at treatment seems to indicate two major "manipulable" antecedents of delinquency. Two different situations seem to be giving rise to what we call delinquent behavior, and accordingly it is justifiable to speak about two basic types of delinquent behavior.

In one, delinquency seems to result from the child's learning delinquent behavior (growing into the delinquent pattern) from other members of his primary group, very much the same way as he learns other things. To use sociological lingo: the juvenile acquires the delinquent behavior as he does any other cultural trait of the cultural heritage passed on to him by his group in the process of socialization. I suggest calling this type of delinquent behavior con--formist delinquency, stressing the fact that the child becomes delinquent through conforming with the behavior pattern in his group. It is the fact that his group is at odds with the dominant part of the society that leads him into trouble. Again in sociological terminology: the delinquent's group happens to be the carrier of a "criminalistic subculture," and that results in his being considered a delinquent by the "law-abiding" society. The manipulable antecedents in such situations seem to be either the criminalistic subculture itself or the process of its being passed on to the juvenile. Consequently either a reorientation of the carriers of the subculture is recommended (the area projects developed by Clifford R. Shaw), or the removal of the child from the group (see Shaw's recommendations for the treatment of Stanley in the *Jack-Roller*). Sometimes an interpretation to the child of the situation seems to be the only feasible and effective method, so that he may see the situation from the point of view of the "right side of the fence."

The argument that this reference to the criminalistic subculture simply removes the question of the causes of delinquent behavior one step further, namely to the question of the causes of this subculture, does not hold. As just indicated, the process of passing this culture on to the juvenile offers great opportunities for "manipulation" and purposeful influence. Likewise the sociologists have good hypotheses regarding the origin of the criminalistic subcultures and there again is an opening for "manipulation." Thus the frame of reference supplied by the concept of conformist delinquency appears to be a significant one; to use John Dewey's terminology, it seems to offer definite possibilities for "the transformation of a problematic situation (which involves confusion and conflict) into a unified one."

In the other etiological type of delinquency the situation giving origin to delinquent behavior seems to consist of a conflict between the child and his immediate primary group: the family, the school, the neighborhood people, etc. As a result of this conflict a situation of extreme conscious or subconscious dissatisfaction with the status quo (a state of frustration) develops in the child. To get out of this, the juvenile makes desperate moves in various directions and occasionally becomes delinquent. A classical example of this type of interpretation is Healy's description of the main mechanisms leading to delinquency from such states of frustration. The manipulable antecedents of delinquent behavior in this type seem to be the various situations leading to frustration in the child and then again the possibilities of directing the energies of the frustrated child into socially acceptable rather than delinquent activities (substitute satisfaction, e.g. of a wholesome hobby, for criminal activities with a delinquent gang). In this situation the child appears as a rebel against his immediate primary group or some relevant members of it. He does not behave the way the adults in charge of him want him to behave, hence the suggested name for this type: non-conformist delinquency. Like the concept of conformist delinquency, it seems to offer a suitable theoretical tool for the reorganization of a problematic situation.

In all probability the conformist and non-conformist delinquent behaviors appear relatively seldom in a pure form, though ample illustrations are available in the literature. As elsewhere in the social sciences, these ideal type situations are useful tools of analysis in spite of the fact that the majority of actual cases is usually located in the continua somewhere between the ideal types. This dichotomy of ideal types is proposed as a valuable organizational principle for the contemporary analysis of juvenile delinquent behavior. In the light of the present practices of control and prevention of juvenile delinquency this type of analysis seems to be meaningful, and in turn the development of this frame of reference should strengthen our hand in contending with the problem posed by delinquent behavior.

The final test of this hypothesis is, of course, whether a different frame of reference can be shown to offer a better explanation and give more aid to these efforts of our society.

Abrahamsen's Theory of the Etiology of Criminal Acts*

By Jerome E. Bates. Formerly Field Consultant, New York City Youth Board; Assistant Director, Children's Center, Department of Welfare, New York.

THE ORIGINAL statement of Abrahamsen's theory is to be found in his book, *Crime and the Human Mind*, where he shows a great grasp and appreciation of the social and cultural factors involved in criminal behavior.

The interest of society in the reasons for anti-social behavior is of recent origin. Formerly society was mainly concerned with the apprehension and punishment of the criminal. Interest has now shifted from the fact of crime to the motivations behind criminal acts. The rise, especially within the last twenty-five years, in the efficiency of city, state and federal departments of probation and parole reflects this rising interest.

Motivation for Deeds

Just as society depends upon the individual so does the individual have certain expectations and anticipations with regard to society. The individual also has a world of reality which is unique to him and colored by his own consciousness which he has the ability to develop apart from what may be called "the real world." This process, this duality of realities, frequently results in the commission of acts which are not clearly understood by the actor. It is now well recognized that emotional considerations color the operation of intellectual processes and even interfere with them. Every deed has a secret motivation. There may be several motives operating, of which only one may be evident to consciousness. These processes are, of course, identical for anti-social as well as social behavior. The criminal is just as often unaware of the true motives for his action as is the ordinary person. To the layman, there seems to be no connection between the criminal and his crime. This becomes evident when one discusses a crime with the criminal's relatives. To cover their shock and confusion at the arrest of their kin they usually offer some rationalization or half-truth to explain his behavior, such as: "He must be crazy," "evil companions," "he needed money," etc.

The professionally trained worker interviews the offender and makes a complete psychiatric and social investigation

* Reprinted from *The Journal of Criminal Law and Criminology* (Northwestern University School of Law), Vol. XL, December, 1949, by Jerome E. Bates.

with the aim of answering the following questions: "Why did the defendant commit the Act?" "What personal needs and urges in him were satisfied by its commission?" Finally, "What steps need to be taken to adjust the defendant's psychological disequilibrium and also satisfy social demands for protection against his possible future aggressions?"

In seeking answers to these questions it should be kept in mind that the individual is strongly affected by his social milieu and is conditioned by all his experiences, past and present. These experiences, particularly those which were charged with painful emotion and have since been repressed, are of especial importance in understanding criminotic or neurotic motivations. In understanding criminality we must keep in mind the fact that criminality and neurosis are to be considered as two sides of the same coin. One difference between the neurotic person and the offender is that a neurotic person suffers out his past experiences whereas the offender *acts* out his difficulties. It should, however, be kept in mind that there are also criminals who suffer and suffer deeply, particularly because of their guilt feelings, which in many instances may be one of the reasons why a criminal commits his crime. People whose behavior is more conditioned by their inner conflicts than by their material circumstances are more numerous than is generally realized. Extensive statistics are not available as to this type of person, but lack of statistics does not preclude the assumption of their numerous existence. Any person professionally trained in psychology and related fields meets them daily, socially and otherwise, in surprising numbers.

Efforts to fix the etiology of criminal behavior in such social factors as "the broken home," "habits of thought," "incompetent or indifferent parents," "evil associates," "inadequate supervision," etc., have met with failure. Despite grandiose claims by many investigators no piece of research has as yet adequately demonstrated that criminal behavior is due primarily to the operation of one or more of the above social conditions or of others that could be mentioned. Each criminal is unique despite surface similarities with other offenders.

Examination of Offender's Past

Instead of talking about the influence of this and that factor, the broken home and so forth, I prefer to examine the offender's past for evidence of what I call "childhood emotional deprivation." In this manner we can account for the existence of those criminals (and normal persons) who had a broken home or what not, yet suffered no real emotional deprivation as they found adequate or compensatory satisfaction elsewhere.

If we agree with Miller *et al.*, that "frustration leads to aggression," then we can at least begin to understand the criminal act. Emotional deprivation, with its subsequent feelings of frustration and consequent aggressive reaction, if continued over a long enough period of time, may lead to anti-social behavior as a means of satisfying ego demands. The fact that a given person becomes a neurotic rather than a criminal depends, I think, upon the development in him of sufficient super-ego (conscience) by parents or others at the time he is suffering from childhood emotional deprivation.

A sudden loss of a job, a disappointment in sexual adjustment and numerous other precipitating factors acting upon a person predisposed to aggression because of emotional deprivation, may produce a criminal act. Few people turn to crime overnight. Careful and detailed psychological analysis of the offender and his social constellation usually produces evidence that he gradually became "sensitized to criminal activities," as Abrahamsen puts it, over a long period of time. At the same time one must remember that we all have criminal tendencies and the fact that we do not act on them depends on our entire psychological adjustment to our fellows and their property.

As time goes on and the sensitized person begins to repress the memory of his childhood deprivations, there arises a chronic feeling of anxiety-tinged, free-floating aggression. In the absence of restricting super-ego factors this person is the potential criminal who commits an overt criminal act under pressure of one or more initiating events. After the pattern of criminal behavior is set and reinforced by repetition, the criminal thus "has receptive traits in his personality which produce a criminal response."

Explanation of the Criminal Act

What, then, is the explanation of the criminal act? According to Abrahamsen, "Crime is a product of the individual's tendencies and the situation of the moment interacting with his mental resistance. Letting 'C' stand for crime, 'T' for tendencies, 'S' for situation, and 'R' for resistance, we derive the following formula: $C = \dfrac{T + S}{R}$."

Abrahamsen points out that the "T" factor is not simply "aggressive tendencies" since they are present in all men. "T" also refers to aggressive inclinations of an indirect nature; for instance, projections, rebellious hostility towards anyone, protest reactions, or excessive motor activity. A criminal act does not take place solely because of the release of repressed aggression, but may occur also because the offender has built up a defense of aggression which is expressed tangentially by projections, rejection of authority, protest reactions, etc.

Several investigations have disclosed that passivity often lies behind an act of criminal aggression, and might be regarded as being of an oral nature. Frequently, therefore, it is not the offender's aggression which is responsible for his

act, but an inner core of passivity. "This indirect aggression which harbors feelings of anxiety and insecurity, being related to the pregenital period, may show how deep-seated are the emotional elements. The main characteristic of aggressive action is that it has a main potentiality, that it is unacceptable and, therefore, often repressed by the ego, and that when aggressive action takes place it is frequently not understood by the individual." Workers in the correctional field who are aware of these mechanisms are, therefore, in a better position to understand the shame, confusion, and panic reaction displayed by some first offenders following their arrest.

"S," the situation, is an indeterminate factor in mobilizing the criminal act. As each person has a unique psychological make-up, it follows that only he can achieve a particular aim in a given environment.

According to Abrahamsen, personality reactions in criminals are by nature comparable to those found in a disease. He also claims that a higher incidence of psychosomatic disorders is to be found in the family constellation of the offender than in the family members of psychotic or neurotic patients. In discussing tension within the family of an offender, the author claims that the tension is quite different from that found in the family of a neurotic. It has been my experience to find that the hostility in the family constellation of offenders is more intense *in degree* than that found in the background of neurotics. It is also less masked, more open, and more apparent to the trained observer. Neurotics have been exposed as a rule to strong super-ego development, whereas one seldom finds a good amount of moral training in the backgrounds of offenders, particularly habitual offenders.

Abrahamsen makes only modest claims for the validity of his theory which impresses me as well thought out and useful as a working concept in criminology. The statement of it in mathematical form is merely a conceptual device, however, and no one should be lulled into a feeling of security regarding our knowledge of criminal behavior. Present knowledge in the field is still pitifully inadequate and treatment methods still more so. This occurs, I think, because mental life and processes are largely inaccessible except to psychoanalytic techniques. As a consequence, correctional workers, not possessing as a rule any considerable degree of psychological training, are apt to lay great stress on the function of environmental factors in producing criminal behavior. Hence occurs all the emphasis on the broken home, poverty, sibling rivalry, overprotection, overindulgence, and so forth. These factors are readily detectible and are often seized upon by probation officers as the "cause" of criminal behavior. The fact that millions of persons experience these social situations but do not become criminals is sufficient evidence to refute the environmentalists. They may, however, become neurotics or make a good social adjustment on a compensatory basis.

It is a rare probation department that carries on any real research, other than the compilation of environmental statistics of doubtful validity and reliability.

Research in the field of criminology has been undertaken only by foundations or isolated candidates for the Ph.D. degree in the social sciences. As pointed out by Reuben C. Brustuen, there is seldom any cooperation for research purposes between probation departments and nearby university graduate study divisions. Politically speaking, the presentation to the legislature of validated research showing the efficacy of more intensive treatment of probationers and parolees is a good plan to obtain the necessary funds.

Proposals for Crime Prevention

If we assume the general validity of the theory discussed here and if we agree that crime should be viewed as a social disease, then Abrahamsen's threefold proposal for crime prevention is relevant.

1. Basic treatment must start with maladjusted children if we are to overcome behavior problems in childhood.

2. Early detection and psychiatric treatment of potential offenders will reduce the number of criminals.

3. Research in the field of criminology might best be directed toward investigations of (a) the working of the mind of the criminal, and (b) the interrelationship between psychosomatic factors in bodily disease and criminal behavior.

We Call Them Delinquents[*]

By Leontine R. Young. Formerly New York School of Social Work; Professor of Casework, School of Social Administration, The Ohio State University, Columbus.

IN THE DRAB, scrubbed room, ironically known as a living room, a young boy sat sullenly apart from the group. Crouched on a stiff chair he looked like a crumpled puppet propped there by a careless child

until one looked carefully at his pale, unmoving face. It was a mask of desolation, a face on which despair and hate and fear had already set their seal of blank rigidity. His eyes stared back at you with

* Reprinted from *Federal Probation*, Vol. XV, December, 1951, pp. 9–13. Used by permission of author and publication.

the bleak and certain knowledge that you like all adults were a feared and hated enemy, an enemy so dangerous that even his hate and his fear must be veiled from you. Only in the blankness of a death mask was there any degree of safety for him, any hope of self-preservation.

You smiled at him knowing as you did so that it was meaningless, and your smile broke into nothing against that stony immobility. He was a juvenile delinquent, newly committed to a correctional institution, and this was the recreation period. As a visitor you dutifully watched the activities of the children but as a human being your eyes came back always to the masks, searching for some hint of what they concealed, poignantly aware of the human tragedy which had made that concealment necessary. You remembered that once, not so very long ago, each one of those masks had been born into the world with the capacity for laughter, for honest, natural human responses, for growth and creative development; and before your eyes the crime of wasted human talents, of the denial of warmth and color and productive life took shape and form.

Have We Forgotten They Are Children?

Some people still say in one way or another that some children are born good and some are born bad. Most people deny that in words, but their actions expose a strange compromise with their denial. In action they say these children we call delinquents have from whatever cause become bad; they are now different and set apart from other children; and only by punishment can we make them good again. If punishment does not succeed, there is no recourse but to go on punishing and isolating and paying the inevitable bill which mounts higher and higher in price. We have forgotten that these are children, that behind the delinquency is a person, that behind the mask is a hurt and miserable child—twisted by violence, stunted by hate and

blinded by fear, true—but nevertheless a child. We fear these children because unlike some other sick children they turn their hate and violence outward and damage others as well as themselves. Our concern arises in the first place not because they have been hurt and denied the chance for normal human growth nor because inevitably they further damage themselves but because they hurt and menace us. When they attack us, steal from us, threaten our safety and our possessions, we respond only to what they do, not to what they are nor why they do it. Even when we try to understand, try to help them, we so often fail and grow disillusioned because they do not listen to our admonitions, do not heed our advice, seem so indifferent to our standards. In easy discouragement we say that compulsion and punishment are after all the only way; and sometimes we speak bitterly of the folly of "coddling" children like this.

Have We Respected Them as Individuals?

Rarely do we, the adults, look first to ourselves and our own attitudes. We do not note that our concern is not for the child but for his behavior. We ask of him conformity, to be "good," but we do not inquire into his unhappiness. We set up rules and demand that he obey them, but we do not observe what insistent demands spring from his own needs nor do we see any need to take account of them. We frown upon his anger and his violence and tell him to put them aside as if they were worn-out toys to be lightly discarded. That hate and anger do not simply evaporate is a fact we disregard; that in his past the child has had real reason for the violence of his emotions we ignore. So often we ask in effect that he give up his delinquent behavior because it disturbs us, is unacceptable to us, but so seldom do we ask what we owe him, do we inquire how he has been cheated and attacked, what we can now give him. In fact most of the time we seem to proceed on the incredibly naive premise that a delinquent child is simply "bad" because he wants to be, because he enjoys being that way, and all we have to do is persuade or compel him to be "good." When he refuses to do so, we expect that by punishment we can make him see that being "bad" is really more painful in the final analysis than being "good." Perhaps after all we are guilty chiefly of an abysmal lack of imagination, of a tremendous blindness which sees only the effect of the delinquent's behavior upon ourselves and so rarely what it is really telling us of a child's unhappiness, revolt, and confusion.

What happens that transforms a sentient human being, that dynamic bundle of creative potentialities, into an attacker and a fortress, into the immobile puppet on a chair in a few short years? Take Bill. He was born into a slum family; unwanted because he was yet another mouth to feed, another body to care for, another voice to make demands upon a mother already overburdened with unremitting insatiable demands. His home was a tenement where the family of seven shared three rooms with the rats who made frequent visits and the insect life that could not be dislodged from the crumbling old building. There was neither space nor air, and the room where Bill slept opened only on an air shaft. Bill's father worked hard, but without education or special skills, he earned barely enough to keep his growing family fed and sheltered. Periodically under the weight of drudgery and worry he would get roaring drunk and explode his growing anger by beating up any of his family within reach. When he was sober, he was often sullen and morose; and frequently he struck the children as if he could in this fashion somehow redress the balance of his life. Bill hated and feared his father; understanding little of his father's frustrations and bitterness he knew clearly, however, that he was an unwanted responsibility to his father and a scapegoat for his anger. Bill learned early the power and tremendous advantages of size, but size to him meant only the opportunity to hurt and exploit. Of size and power that protected he had no experience. Bill's mother plodded through the days as if she were long since done with the business of feeling anything more than irritation and a chronic dull despair. She neglected the children much of the time and what little attention she devoted to Bill was withdrawn when a new baby came along to claim the dregs of her wavering affection. Bill learned early to look out for himself. With all the passionate egotism of any young child he fought for what he wanted; but carefully locked inside himself was the conviction that he was of no value as a person, that he had nothing of any account to offer, that he had no place of his own in the world. His experiences at school, in the neighborhood, and on the streets only confirmed that verdict, and he fought against it in the only way he could—by making trouble, by attacking others. He trusted no one, and it is dubious that the possibility of such a feeling ever entered his mind although unrecognized by himself he suffered constantly from the need and longing to do so. He hated and feared anyone bigger or stronger than himself because they were certain danger to his own survival, and very naturally the law and all its representatives were to him as a second father. They stood in the way of what he wanted and they waited only to punish and destroy him. The only law Bill acknowledged was the pressing demand of his own desires, and like the very small child these desires were direct, primitive, and urgent taking no account of obligations to others and hampered in their fulfillment only by outside forces. Where would Bill have learned about obligations to others, respect for law, the satisfaction of being an established and sharing member of an orderly society? No one had acknowledged any obligations to him; no one had respected him as an individual; no one had shared in happiness and generosity with him. And so Bill was one against the world, finding only a transient and superficial place in the sun with others like himself and knowing deep in his heart that the world was too big, too powerful for him and for those others he called his friends. He covered that knowledge with bravado, with defiance, with a mask of indifference and would have died before he admitted its truth.

Bill is one kind of delinquent—there are many. There is Jane who stole only to distribute her spoils to the other more unfortunate children around her. Even in the face of indisputable proof she always denied she had taken anything. Jane had spent her short life in six foster homes, and each had asked her to leave because she did not fit into the pattern of behavior they approved. She had not seen her mother in 5 years, and she had never known her father. She was secretly ashamed and frightened of what she did, but she could never explain why she did it and indeed she did not know herself. Instead she denied everything in the futile hope that by this means it would cease to exist and for the rest withdrew more and more into herself like a frightened small animal into a burrow. For all delinquents the behavior is much the same—they steal, fight, truant, run away from home, and in one way or another defy authority—but the persons behind the behavior and the reasons for it are different. One thing they all share in common—their distrust of adults who are bigger and stronger than they and the hurt they have received from those adults who should have protected and loved them. These children have learned in a hard and bitter school that weakness is an invitation to destruction, that confidence in a grownup is a passport to be-

trayal, and that the primary law of life is that might makes right.

How Can We Help the Delinquent Child?

For those who in whatever capacity seek to help these children, the great question is how to open the door of this warped, self-maintained prison and help them look out at a world that contains friends and laughter as well as enemies and hate. We know that this means an internal as well as an external change. The attempt to make people be good has always failed; the only possibility for change is to help them want to be good. Up to the present we have for the most part sought to impose by coercion those standards of behavior which society has learned from long experience are necessary to an orderly existence. Correctional institutions have attempted to suppress the child's violence and antisocial behavior, sometimes as kindly as possible, sometimes brutally meeting violence with violence. Without regard for the individual child's feelings or his ability to conform to these standards our efforts to "reform" him have often made demands that he could not possibly meet and we then have punished him for a failure that was from the beginning inevitable. All too often in fact we have asked of him a degree of suppression and conformity that no child could hope to meet successfully without damage to his own personality and that must become for any child abnormal. The result for the delinquent child is a reinforcement of the same old lesson—adults wish to punish not to help, to destroy not to build, to exploit not to protect. Even when the method is kindly the objective, because it is delusory, remains unjust. The child may submit helplessly to superior strength, may for a time give the appearance of "goodness," but he has merely gone underground usually to await more favorable opportunity. He learns quickly that it is not about him as a person and his happiness that we are concerned, but about his behavior and its effect on us, which is to say about ourselves. And thus we repeat the old lesson—"we do not care about you and what happens to you so long as you do not endanger us. If you do, we will stop you by force." Amazing that we should ever have expected that this could rehabilitate, could alter rebellion into co-operation.

What then can we do to help these bitter children who do menace us both as children and soon as adults? First we can care enough about them as people, as human beings of value to us and to our society, to try to reach them and help them before they are involved in serious trouble. Their problems and unhappiness are visible in school, in the community, in any place where there are eyes to see. Often they have already come to the attention of authority in minor ways, have sometimes come to the court, and they have been warned of coming punishment if they do not change their ways, and then they have been returned to their same old problems and unhappiness. In few if any communities, does there exist anything like even minimum facilities for helping children in this still preventive stage. The few clinics and youth agencies are overcrowded and often can offer only a fraction of the time, attention, and treatment needed to make more than a superficial dent in the problem. Even where such time and service is available, these agencies are largely dependent upon the wish of the child and his family to seek help. Nor can it be overlooked that to many disturbed children the offer of such help, in the beginning at least, wears the guise of a new trick by officialdom, a new and more subtle way of persuading the child to betray himself so that he may more easily be destroyed. He looks for the catch beneath soft words and is frankly skeptical of any adult who says he wishes to help him. As one girl in such a setting put it, "What are you people getting out of this? Just what is

your angle?" To convince such a child that there is no hidden "angle" takes time—often a good deal of time, patience, and most vital of all the opportunity to test and experience for himself over and over again the fact that this particular adult is honest, always means exactly what he says, and never betrays or lets him down. And in many cases this must be done without the co-operation and support of the child's family who often regard the whole business as an indirect attack upon themselves.

In all honesty it must be added that a number of the private agencies whose services should be available to these troubled children have been and are fearful of sharing in the responsibility for their care. Aware of the very real problems inherent in trying to help our delinquents they have too often evaded the whole issue and adopted a "leave it to the courts" attitude. This has been particularly true in those situations where the suspicion of the child and often his parents necessitates an active, seeking-out policy on the part of the agency if any real contact is to be made and any possible relationship established. In other words, if the child is to learn that there is such a thing as adult interest in him for his own sake the worker must take the initiative and prove that interest in action which can be bold, imaginative, and as flexible as the situation requires.

When a child has been brought into court for an initial offense and placed on probation, there is still the chance of preventive work. The probation officer, who has both the advantages and disadvantages of a representative of court authority, may be able to use that authority to great advantage if he can prove to the child that it exists to protect not to punish. And again his primary job must be giving the child the opportunity of trusting him. And again this takes time—much time, patience, skill, and great integrity. To the overworked, underpaid probation officer, who is the rule rather than the exception, this degree of attention for any single child is a wild-eyed dream lost from sight in the clamoring demands of an endless stream of cases. Bill becomes a case not a person and Jane a problem not a human being. So the opportunity for change is lost, and another embittered boy or girl goes his way to make trouble for himself and for others. No clearer proof of the public's basic indifference to its troubled, unhappy, rebellious young can be found than in this bow to a method of help which is then denied reality by its deprivation of the tools which would make it possible.

Our first and greatest need is to find and know our unhappy children early before they have been so damaged that irreparable harm has been done. This is a search for which the total community must be responsible—day care centers, schools, churches, courts, social agencies. And that search will never be conceded its true urgency until we face the tragic truth that just as a child can be irreparably starved physically so can he be stunted and warped beyond the hope of recovery in his emotional growth. If we are to make any genuine attack upon that greatest of all crimes—the waste of human happiness and with it the loss of its great gifts to the world—we have to start not when we are menaced but when the child himself is hurt. And secondly, when we find that child we need available the best facilities for his help that the limit of our knowledge can provide. We know so pathetically little, but sadder is the fact that we do not use what we do know.

We know now that a percentage of our delinquent children cannot be helped even by the best of community services so long as they remain in their current environment and in homes deeply damaging to them. At present we have little choice but to put them in large, so-called correctional institutions. With the best will in the world—and that will is not always present—these institutions cannot hope to know the individual child and his individual needs. Their only recourse is to establish a program, formulate standards of behavior, evolve a series of activities, and then either kindly or otherwise seek to compel the child to conform to them. What is left out is the one thing most important to and most needed by the child—understanding of him as a separate and individual personality and to be known and loved by some one person. At its root this is the great longing of every child, to be important to someone, to have his specific needs and wishes respected as worthy of concern, to know that in a world of the big and powerful he has a place of his own, that his own precious individuality is held inviolate. The delinquent child has by and large learned only the reverse of this. He has been educated to hate and fear. If he is to want to be "good" in our sense, we must give him the experience of being important to us, being wanted by us. In other words we have to re-educate. Instead of asking him to conform to the alien and impersonal demands of a large institution we need to create the small and flexible settings which can conform first to his needs and which will make only those requirements he is able to meet. He can be protected from himself and the community can be protected, but he can also be given a chance to learn that there are such things as friendship, understanding, and respect for himself and others. In fact, the key to much of our failure in helping our angry children lies in the fact that we have demanded that they obey our demands, meet our needs while we deny their demands and ignore their needs.

Do We Care Enough?

And finally, we need to stop seeing delinquents and start seeing children. Now we classify our children by the trouble they cause us. We will only begin to achieve real success when we become concerned with the unhappiness of any child and when we no longer isolate into one separate group those boys and girls who have expressed their inner trouble by hitting at the world. Now we stigmatize them, dig a gulf between them and the secure and law-abiding, create a hurdle over which they must climb to reach the distant rewards we dangle before their eyes. "What does a juvenile delinquent look like?" asked one man who knew them only through the newspapers. Naive the question is, yet not so strange. What does a label look like?—like Mary who ran around with any man who would buy her a cheap gift because her mother had deserted her and no one else had ever wanted her or like Bill who stole and fought because his father hated him and his mother had never cared?

This is the concern and the responsibility of the total community, not a select burden for any designated section of it. We may allocate labels—this one to the right and that one to the left—but the misery and bitterness of a Bill and a Mary belong to all of us. And to all of us belongs the decision—help for a child or punishment for a delinquent.

It takes money and time and thought and work and love and patience and that special creative something which looks through the eyes of the child as well as the eyes of the grownup to help our troubled children. Is it worth it to us? Or is the boy with a mask for a face right after all—we just don't care enough?

Delinquency Is Normal Behavior*

By Hertha Tarrasch, M.D. Director, Child Guidance Clinics, Rock and Jefferson Counties, Janesville, Wisconsin.

EVERY child has a delinquency potential for we all have strong selfish impulses which demand satisfaction and which are frustrated by our social codes. The capacity to master urges and needs, to tolerate pain and frustration for some future gratification and to conform with the standards of the external world, means emotional maturity. Only as a child can substitute some other compensation for immediate fulfillment of his antisocial and asocial impulses is he willing to give up or postpone them. If he does not find a proper compensatory mechanism, he follows these strong drives, which, under certain environmental influences, lead him into antisocial, that is, "delinquent" behavior.

Important Factors in Treatment

The child instinctively wants to imitate the mother and others about him. Parents whose standards are in contrast with society's demands will inculcate in their children similar ways of behaving. The cultural, moral, religious, and social patterns of a family are important in the child's growth. In many families deviations from the accepted social code are not very obvious, in fact may be hidden, and when children from such families get into trouble with the legal authorities it is difficult to understand why they have done so. However, careful investigation and study will prove that such a child has absorbed these undesirable standards early in life by imitation of his parents. We cannot therefore speak of a child's super-ego, his standard of conduct, as right or wrong. Fortunately there is in childhood and adolescence, and even in adult life still much flexibility and it is therefore possible to bring about changes in the pattern. The longer the

* Reprinted from *Focus*, Vol. 29, July, 1950, pp. 97–101. Used by permission.

original pattern has existed, the more difficult it is to bring about a change. Unconscious processes cannot be changed unless they become conscious.

Too many restrictions in the moral and religious area will create frustrations of a child's urges and needs and gratifications. This is another factor which must be understood in treating juveniles if we are to determine where correction is necessary. Detailed study of all these factors in a given child is essential because they influence diagnosis, choice of treatment, and prognosis.

A child learns by experience that if his mother unconsciously or openly rejects him and withholds from him warmth, affection, and love, she will give him attention when he forces it by misbehavior. He has learned that he cannot expect to get attention by good behavior. Deprivation creates pain within him and arouses tensions and frustrations which result in explosions such as temper tantrums and other aggressive behavior. In this way he develops mechanisms to force the mother's attention even though they may bring severe punishment. He takes revenge upon the mother for her neglect; his hostility is followed by guilt and the punishment she administers for his misbehavior relieves him of the tension and also of the guilt feelings he experiences. Thus a vicious circle is formed which develops a masochistic attitude in many children. When tension rises they have formed the habit of reacting by misbehavior calling for punishment and as they grow older these acts often take the form of delinquent behavior.

In treating such a child we find that he does not respond readily to a direct approach because it is too threatening to him and he is not able to identify himself with another parental figure, the therapist. Immediately the old pattern of behavior crops up and he challenges the therapist or the foster mother if he has been placed in another home just as he did his own mother. To give in to such

children is but to follow out a part of the established routine; neither will punishment help, since this too is but a part of the same routine. They will often, however, respond to group therapy and group living and develop a gradual identification with a group-parent such as a teacher in the school, a house parent in an institution, or a foster parent in a home where there are a number of children.

Consistent, firm, but kind handling is necessary to bring such a child to learn to accept reality and to conform to the standards of society. With the gradual acceptance of new standards the child may be able to change his super-ego, first by making unconscious processes conscious, and then by changing the conscious processes.

Any neurotic mechanism represents a partial arrest in the emotional maturation and ability to cope with impulses at various age levels and in harmony with reality. Deprivations of the essentials for physical development and maintenance such as food, water, and warmth, create tensions which are very obvious. The lack of these essentials results in immediate disaster, and the consequences of such neglect—illnesses—are easily discerned. Not only are the signs of emotional tensions much less easily read, but there has been little effort to educate the general public in the symptoms of this type of deprivation, with the result that their deleterious effects are not discovered early enough.

The delinquent child is often the victim of the unhappy marriage of his parents. If he resembles one of them the marital partner projects his hostility toward the mate on to the child. These are usually unconscious processes but not always entirely so, for we sometimes hear a mother say of her child, "He is lazy and good-for-nothing, just like his father." Thus a delinquent child may feel that it doesn't pay to be good since the parent to whom he is chiefly attached and whose approval is so essential for his emotional balance identifies him constantly with the negative characteristics in the marital partner. In nearly all the cases I have seen at the State Training School for Girls, where I am consultant, this factor is important. For example, if the delinquent girl's father is an alcoholic or "runs around," and the child has her father's personality, the mother will, when angry, accuse her of the father's undesirable traits. This naturally creates in the child a feeling not only of rejection but also of utter hopelessness.

Any feeling of segregation as in an institution, any locked doors or other like precautions to secure "conformity" will bring out rebellion in a child. No matter what other provisions are made with the intention of making them feel at home these restricting measures will remind them constantly of the old situation. We cannot expect good results with such management, in fact, we call forth more and more hostility and rebellion. If we want to change the delinquent's reactions towards the environment we shall have to change all the factors which have brought about the development of the faulty super-ego. We have to give such a child at least the opportunity to work up to equality with the outside world by a gradual promotion to those standards and not by the creation of special standards.

A non-delinquent child has been able to identify himself in some degree with an adult in his environment and to form a super-ego which conforms with reality, that is, with the standards of society. In the delinquent child the super-ego is usually not in harmony with reality. Therefore, in the treatment situation the non-delinquent will identify much more quickly and permanently with the therapist, representing reality, than can the delinquent child. There has been some sincerity and consistency in the non-delinquent's background, while we find persistent inconsistency in the home environment of the delinquent, so that it is very difficult for him to accept and believe in the consistent attitudes and treatment of the therapist or anyone else in his environment.

The Therapist and Rehabilitation

During the early period in the treatment of delinquents we often have to take decisions out of their hands because these children are not yet able to manage their impulses properly. We can give them responsibilities only in homeopathic doses until the super-ego is strong enough to take the normal amount. Relapses occur frequently if we let them make too many decisions too soon, because their judgment is defective. We often forget that judgment comes with maturation and is developed gradually. The growth of the delinquent child has been seriously hampered and he needs our benign help. He may conform for a longer or a shorter period but he then relapses and challenges the therapist. The slightest feeling of tension, of frustration brings out the old reaction, often violent, because these children feel "betrayed" and "trapped." That is when understanding and boundless patience are needed.

The initial phase of learning to trust an adult is much longer in the delinquent child because he has very little to build on. The therapist has first to eliminate the unwholesome factors and revise the completely distorted picture the child has about right and wrong, good and bad. While this is under way a new and wholesome super-ego has to be developed. The older the child, the longer this process takes, because the pattern has become so strongly fixed. This whole process of rehabilitation or reconstruction of a personality is never just a question of direct therapy but requires the cooperative teamwork of all persons involved in the particular case. To get this cooperation, complete understanding and education of all significant persons in the environment is imperative. Just as in any physical illness, the treatment is not the whole answer; the reality situation at home and in society has to coincide. The therapist seeks the cause of the trouble and endeavors to correct it, but meanwhile the child has to live in a home, has to be educated in school, has to consider the ties of his religion and has to make an adjustment to his environment in toto. The adults involved have to understand the cause of the emotional illness or they will not be able to accept such a child wholeheartedly. Once the child has begun to believe in the therapist and in the sincerity of those in his environment, and to accept consistency in handling and merited rewards and punishments, then rehabilitation proceeds as swiftly as in the nondelinquent child.

Parental Influence. Parents are for their children the Bible. What a mother or a father tells the child is at first accepted fully. But when children find out that parents are teaching them one lesson and expecting them to live up to it, while doing exactly the opposite themselves, they begin to wonder why there are two such different codes. According to our experience, parents of delinquent children rarely have a successful marriage. The emotional tensions are, it is true, often not easily apparent. That is why we frequently hear the remark, "I cannot understand why that child went astray, because his parents are such 'nice' people, so good and religious." A closer examination often reveals that this seemingly happy couple has considerable difficulty in keeping up their marriage and covering up their differences. Social, cultural, financial, and religious pressures often keep many impulses under cover.

To be sure, social pressure can also be helpful in certain cases where without them the parents would not cooperate. We cannot force a mother or a father to accept their child wholeheartedly, but if the community exerts such power that they fear to lose its respect, or the father fears for his job, or the mother for her acceptance in her social group, they are much more likely to cooperate with the social agencies in making plans for their youngster.

Children who have been openly and consistently rejected by a mother or a father can sometimes build up defense mechanisms because the situation is more or less a known danger. They suffer rejection and insecurity, but with a little help from the therapist they somehow learn to master the situation. The prognosis is much less hopeful when the rejection is not so obvious, that is, when a parent covers up his feeling and rationalizes it. In these cases the children are thrown into terrific conflict. A child depends so much on his parents that clinic treatment may, by increasing his anxieties, be more of a threat to him than a help. Good therapeutic results can only be obtained where parents are actively cooperative, or at least do not silently sabotage the clinic effort.

Influence of Sex. The problem children whom clinics and workers are most hesitant to treat are girls guilty of sex misbehavior. Agencies seem less afraid to deal with other antisocial tendencies in children, such as stealing. Therefore, we find more rehabilitation work being done with boys than with girls. Everyone seems to regard adolescent girls with their sex troubles as a special group. We forget the root of the difficulty, and do not see that sex misbehavior is just as much a compensatory mechanism for anxiety and insecurity as are stealing, lying, bed-wetting, or day-dreaming. Sex activity, which is a sudden physical relief, also forcefully relieves any kind of anxiety, at least temporarily, and in treating these young girls we should consider the basic difficulty and not solely its expression.

Both sexes want security, love, recognition, but for a boy between six and sixteen the most important thing is competition with other boys on a physical level, proving himself a man like the father or hero ideal—a man who can fight, who will later be able to protect his wife and children and be adequate as a husband and father. Anything which interferes with this ambition gives the boy a feeling of inadequacy and inferiority, no matter if it be lack of size, muscular strength, aggressiveness, or other factors. From the examination of many of these children in the clinic one comes to feel that what a boy fears most is to be called a "sissy" or other derogatory name which suggests that he is not sufficiently masculine. For the girl the most important question is, "Am I attractive enough to please boys? Can I compete with mother and with other girls on a feminine level so that the boys will like me and give me attention, so that I can get married and have children and be accepted in the group?" The sex-delinquent girl usually feels unable to compete with other girls, and gives in to sexual demands to prove she is adequate and able to compete successfully.

These two basic differences shape the antisocial tendencies of juveniles. A boy will express his difficulties by exaggerating the masculine angle or by trying to force it; the girl exaggerates the feminine qualities which for her naturally mean sex. It is not so much actual sexual gratification which the girl desires, but the physical affection and caressing which goes with it. The sexual act, usually demanded by the boy, is but the natural consequence of the preliminary wooing. To put such children in an institution means exerting even more pressure upon them. It only increases their feeling of inadequacy to the point where they may lose entirely the desire to strive for independence, competition, and acceptance, and they resign even before they start.

Kind of Therapy

We must not forget that the stigma (and in spite of our changing approach to delinquency it remains a stigma) of having been in a corrective institution cannot easily be removed. It puts the child immediately in a disadvantageous position notwithstanding the positive values there may be in the institution program. It is important, therefore, that we give the child every possible opportunity to cope with the situation before we add the irreparable trauma of institutional commitment. Unfortunately training schools may expend so much of their energy on custodial care that little opportunity is left for rehabilitative measures.

When a patient goes to the hospital with a physical illness, he receives medication and therapy directed specifically to his ailment. His physical disability is not treated with occupational therapy, vocational training, and disciplinary measures. We send our children to correctional institutions to be treated for an illness, yet when we investigate the care and treatment they receive for their emotional difficulties, we find a terrible lack. They get physical care, regimentation, and some vocational training, but little consideration is given the ailment which brought them there. Girls are taught cooking, sewing, and beauty culture, all of which could be given much more advantageously in their own communities. But most unfortunate of all the injustices we heap upon these children is the shame of having been in a correctional institution—a stigma they cannot hope to live down.

It is important to evaluate the dynamic factors in each child in order to make a prognosis as to response to treatment and the type of treatment which would be most effective. There are children—and of course adults in a larger measure—in whom ability to reconstruct their faulty super-ego formation, that is, to develop eagerness to live up to society's cultural, religious and ethical standards is practically nil. Many of the so-called psychopathic personalities probably fall into this category. Also, here belong many of the "over-institutionalized" children, those brought up in orphanages. We shall probably always need the carefully supervised environment of an institution for some cases, but to send every child for a minor or even a major offense to a correctional institution does more harm than good.

The decision as to what kind of therapy to use is most important. With some, individual deep therapy in combination with the development of a wholesome home environment (improvement of parents' attitudes, or a foster home) may bring the desired result. Others may be so unable because of their deep distrust to identify at once with either parent or parent figure, or with the therapist as a substitute figure, that the problem has first to be treated by superficial group therapy, such as is offered by the school working under clinic supervision. The school is the first socializing factor in the child's life. It is there he first meets with other children, has to adjust to a group, and learns to respect authority. We have cases where clinic treatment with individual therapy failed, but the school situation under supervision of the clinic succeeded. The teacher was accepted as a substitute parental figure and the child was able to identify with the group father. The schools are even more important in prevention by spotting early cases. Since many parents cannot face reality and do not care for advice, the school is the best source of identification of early cases. Every step should be taken to help teachers and educators understand and evaluate behavior difficulties so that they may direct such cases into the proper channels. Clergymen have also been of great help to our clinic. Positive results were frequently reached with their help. The more understanding we give them of the dynamics of personality difficulties the better therapists they will be.

Sending a child to an institution is the most expensive way of dealing with his problem. Only too often we take the line of least resistance and because a child has become a nuisance to the community, we take the easy way out, close our eyes to his needs, and send him away, thinking we have washed our hands of him. We hope the trouble is now removed. Perhaps it is for a time, but without proper study, investigation, and a wise handling of the whole situation, this child will continue to be a trouble and a burden. No change of personality will suddenly out of a clear sky take place in this confused, bewildered, belligerent youth. First we have to find out all the causes of his misbehavior. The remedy has not only to be applied to the child, but to the parents, the schools, and to the community. With the full cooperation of parents, schools, agencies, courts, and indirectly by legislatures, many of these problems could be treated at home, or by foster home or other placement.

I am not advocating the elimination of correctional institutions. If they could be made into havens of treatment and cure of the more severe emotional illnesses of children they could become of inestimable value. Like the legislators, the members of governing boards of the training schools need education in the dynamics of behavior for it is in their power to make of these correctional schools institutions of rehabilitation which in time would cease to stigmatize the children committed there.

Job for Citizen and Professional

At this point many persons will raise the objection that there are not enough professional persons to effect such a comprehensive program. This is only partially true, for every parent, every teacher, every nurse, every citizen is, so to speak, a potential therapist if proper use were made of their potentialities. This would mean that those equipped with the necessary knowledge and experience should be set to training all these groups in a clinical sense, not simply by lectures, but by practical demonstrations so that the individual members of the group could get a real understanding of the motivating forces of conduct.

That so little has been done in educating the public to the needs of children is partly due to the conviction of professional persons that the layman cannot understand the language of the trained specialist. If this is true it is our fault. We have not adjusted our language to him. We cannot expect to get cooperation if we hold interested citizens away from us by so-called "scientific" terminology instead of translating our material into plain English. The progress which has been made in the eradication of tuberculosis and venereal diseases as well as in maternity care has been due in large part to the education of citizens in these matters. The physicians who undertook the education did not hurl unintelligible terminology at their public. The scientist who cannot express himself simply is unfortunate indeed. His knowledge is useless to great numbers of people who need to have some of it.

√ Delinquency prevention through child guidance is one of our goals, but how can this development take place if our community is not to take part in the solution of their problem, if people are not first given information, then authority, so that they feel the service exists for them and not they for the service?

SELECTED REFERENCES

1. Lesser, Edith K., "Understanding Juvenile Delinquency," *Federal Probation,* XIII, September 1949.

In this article, Lesser raises provocative questions in juvenile delinquency which, so far, have successfully eluded specific answers. Stressed is the fact that reformation must come from within rather than from without the youngster.

2. Neumeyer, Martin H., *Juvenile Delinquency in Modern Society* (New York: D. Van Nostrand Co., 1949), Chapter 1: "Juvenile Delinquency as a Social Problem."

In this first chapter effort has been made to present all the approaches to the problems of juvenile delinquency and to inform the student what juvenile delinquency really is.

3. Carr, Lowell Juilliard, *Delinquency Control* (New York: Harper & Brothers, 1941), Chapter 3: "Delinquency Control as a Social Problem."

Here juvenile delinquency is described as the broadest gateway to crime, with supporting data on the volume and cost of crime.

4. Tappan, Paul W., *Juvenile Delinquency* (New York: McGraw-Hill Book Co., 1949), Chapter 1: "The Nature of Juvenile Delinquency."

Here is revealed a legal-sociological approach to juvenile delinquency that is clear-sighted and unsentimental. Tappan discusses the question: Can delinquency be measured?

5. Ellingston, John R., *Protecting Our Children from Criminal Careers* (New York: Prentice-Hall, 1948), Chapter 3: "Psychological Clues to Delinquency."

Ellingston, special adviser on criminal justice for youth to the American Law Institute, brings a fresh, incisive point of view to juvenile delinquency as he describes in detail the injustice of the traditional criminal administration and analyzes the fallacies on which it is based.

2 THE EXTENT OF JUVENILE DELINQUENCY

NOWHERE does the failure of crime control show up more clearly than among our youth. Even before World War II, according to one study, national statistics indicated that some two million of forty-three million boys and girls in the United States below the age of eighteen years came to the attention of the police annually. Youth plays a top-heavy part in the traditional crimes that feed the headlines and for which arrests are made. They frequently commit the familiar crimes against property, often with attendant violence, and their inexperience and lack of judgment make them relatively easy to apprehend.

The *Uniform Crime Reports* of the Federal Bureau of Investigation show that crime increased 1.5 per cent across the nation in 1950 in all offenses except robbery. Every five minutes during that year someone was feloniously assaulted or killed. About every fifteen seconds, hour after hour and day after day, a crime of desperate proportions—robbery, assault, burglary, rape, kidnaping, manslaughter, murder—is committed in the United States. For the first half of 1951, the FBI reports disclose even more crime over the nation. (Although the Bureau's *Uniform Crime Reports* provide the best source of information, about 40 per cent of the urban and rural communities are not represented therein, owing, in part, to the neglect and the apathy of law enforcement agencies.)

According to the FBI, one person in every six arrested in 1946 had not reached the age of 21. These minors made up half of all the arrests for auto theft, a third of all arrests for robbery, burglary and larceny; one in four was arrested for rape, and one in eight for murder. Convicted adolescents constitute a large group in the prison population. In New York State just before World War II, the youth between the ages of 16 and 21 formed over 35 per cent of all admissions to prisons, reformatories, and institutions for defective delinquents. Crime as a habit evidently is generally acquired in youth. J. Edgar Hoover, head of the FBI, informed the Boy Scout convention at the New York World's Fair in 1939, that criminals outnumbered the 1,200,000 Scouts in the United States nearly four to one.

Since 1926, the United States Children's Bureau has been gathering data on cases from reports from juvenile courts which voluntarily send them in. These courts are largely located in the north-east-central geographic division of the United States. Scattered throughout the country there are about 3000 courts which handle juvenile cases; and in the past quarter-century only about one-sixth of these have made reports. According to Sophia M. Robison, almost

26

one-fourth of these reporting courts are located in one state—Connecticut. In an article[1] Dr. Robison asks the pertinent question: How can it then be claimed that such figures are a reliable basis for estimating either the extent or the character of juvenile delinquency in the United States?

During 1948, 94,236 children's cases were handled by 399 juvenile courts reporting from seventeen states. About one-half the cases were conducted without formal judicial action. According to the United States Children's Bureau, if the volume of delinquency continues at the 1948 level, 275,000 delinquents may be expected to come before the juvenile courts of the United States each year.

AGE AND SEX

Age and sex factors are significant elements in juvenile delinquency. The sex ratio is approximately five boys to one girl. The girls tend to be concentrated in the same age periods as the boys, except that there are fewer cases of girl delinquents in the preadolescent period.

Uniform Crime Reports, which gives the arrests of all age groups, shows that the ages seventeen to twenty-one predominate in the frequency of arrests. Of the 831,288 fingerprint records examined in 1951, only 85,233 represented arrests of women, a ratio of approximately ten men to one woman.

MINORITY GROUPS

Adult attitudes of the larger community toward minority groups, particularly racial groups, add to the difficulties in dealing with juveniles. The tendency towards relatively high juvenile delinquency rates in certain minority groups may be explained by a number of conditions, including low economic status, bad housing, overcrowding, restricted employment opportunities, racial proscriptions, and intensified conflict between the older and newer generations.

In the years between 1880 and 1920, many authorities were concerned with the "criminality" of the immigrant or the children of the foreign-born. Since the passage of legislation in the early 1920's, which materially reduced the influx of immigrants, it must be recognized that most non-native Americans are past the middle years and their children are nearly all born in the United States. Studies conducted on the relationship between immigration and delinquency will rapidly become obsolete as first-generation, even second-generation immigrants tend to disappear from the scene.

The number of children of foreign-born parents reported delinquent has dropped since the curtailment of immigration in 1922. Until this time, native-born children of immigrant parents, growing up in areas of cultural conflict, made a substantial contribution to the number of recorded juvenile delinquents. In 1930, about two-fifths of the girls and one-half of the boys were of foreign-born parentage. Today, the vast majority of offenders of both sexes, over 70 per cent, are native-born of native-born parents.

Decrease in delinquency appears to occur in direct proportion to the assimilation of minority groups. The new marginal groups are those rural workers

---

[1] "Wanted—An Index of Crime and Delinquency," *Proceedings,* American Prison Association, 1945, pp. 203–212.

coming to such large industrial areas as Detroit, Chicago, and Los Angeles. On the labor market, the Negro might be considered the "new immigrant."

Negro convictions and imprisonment seem to be three times that of the white population when population proportions are equated. Negro children, because, in part, of the functions of bias, become delinquent officially at an earlier age than do white children. Negro rates of delinquency have mounted to quite large proportions during the last two decades. It is easier to arrest, convict, and incarcerate Negro children than white children. Frequently, Negro children are charged with offenses that would not be imputed to white children.

The social factors underlying Negro criminality are well stated by Davie as they affect and are affected by juvenile delinquency. He shows that in the cases handled by the juvenile courts Negro children appear more than three times as often as an analysis of the phenomenon would predict on a general population basis. In the distribution of offenses for which white and Negro children are brought before the courts, Negroes are more often guilty of stealing than of any other crime. A study of the disposition of these cases indicates that Negro boys are less likely to be dismissed for their offense than white boys and their commitment to an institution is more likely to occur. Cultural inferiority, economic pressure, and racial antagonisms play as important a part in Negro child delinquency as they do in adult crime.[2]

Delinquency rates then appear to be in part a function of ethnic discrimination. Hence it is not surprising to find increased rates of delinquency among the Spanish-American section of our population, and the Indian as well as the Negro elements.

RURAL-URBAN DIFFERENCES

It is generally believed that cities have higher rates of delinquency than rural areas. Crimes of petty theft tend to be concentrated in cities. Proportionally, more children are committed to correctional institutions as the density of the population increases. Various studies have tended to show rural delinquency to be somewhat less than urban delinquency per unit of population.

According to the *Uniform Crime Reports*, urban crime had an upward climb from 1947 to 1951. In most instances it was found that the larger cities had the highest crime rates. Although the chief concentration of offenses, both adult and juvenile, are in the larger urban areas, the next highest rates seem to fall in those rural areas converging about these urban areas. The more industrialized the rural areas the greater is the tendency to commit delinquent acts.

Rural crime in 1951 increased 5 per cent over 1950. Rural trends failed to coincide with urban trends in (1) negligent manslaughter, which showed a decrease in urban areas, and (2) crimes of rape, which decreased in rural areas. Rural delinquency, owing in large part to rapid progress in transportation and in communication and the resulting urbanization of the countryside, has been

---

[2] Maurice R. Davie, *Negroes in American Society* (New York: McGraw-Hill Book Co., 1949), pp. 258, 259.

increasing very fast. The lure of the city and mounting rural-urban interaction have not had a positive influence on farm youths. In 1952, rural crimes were 8.6 per cent above 1951, according to the crime reports covering 1,631 rural police agencies serving a population of nearly forty million. For some types of offense of a serious personal nature, the rural rates are equally high, and in some instances, even higher than urban.

As for criminal behavior at both juvenile and adult levels, indications are that rural areas have lower rates than the urban areas for most offense classifications. On the basis of available data, it is estimated that the urban rate for criminal offenses in general is about three times higher than the rural rate. It should be remembered, in considering this statistical contrast, however, that the rural reporting is not as complete as urban reporting. According to the FBI in some instances it appeared that the reports used in preparing rural data may have been limited to cases in which arrests were made. Although delinquency is still closely associated with urban life, rural trends toward delinquency appear to be increasing and are likely to continue because of rapid modern industrial and social change.

Rural children as a whole fare worse in health than do city children. Selective Service experience of World War II found this to be true also of educational and cultural advantages. Apparently, fresh air, sunshine, and green meadows are not sufficient to guarantee health or to reduce delinquent behavior.

It is difficult to make general estimates concerning the volume of juvenile offenses and the general trends since the beginning of this century. Some studies appear to bolster the opinion that the volume of delinquency for both sexes is increasing steadily. It seems that rural-urban differences are not as great in regard to crime and delinquency as in years past. As the processes of communication, mobility, and urbanization proceed, it is reasonable to assume that the gap in reported delinquency between urban and rural areas will continually diminish. From the available evidence it seems reasonable to conclude that little decrease in the extent and volume of delinquency can confidently be anticipated, but rather it might be expected that there will continue a gradual upward rise in the years that lie immediately ahead.

READINGS

The most reliable and comprehensive statistics on crime in the United States are published semiannually by the FBI in *Uniform Crime Reports*. O. W. Wilson in his "How to Measure the Extent of Juvenile Delinquency" relates this source of information to juvenile delinquency. He advances several worthwhile proposals that would render data on child delinquency more meaningful.

I. Richard Perlman, the well-known statistician, decries the lack of nation-wide data on the extent of children in crime in his selection, "The Meaning of Juvenile Delinquency Statistics." The strengthening of existing child services and the efforts by local, state, and federal agencies to prevent conditions that lead to juvenile delinquency are credited with reducing postwar delinquency.

In the selection, "Statistics Will Get You if You Don't Watch Out," this thought is discussed by Lurline V. Simpson in a humorous though nonetheless serious manner. If statistics are to be really useful, both their virtues and limitations must be understood.

In the article, "Negro and White Male Institutionalized Delinquents," Sidney Axelrad finds that the courts commit on a differential basis, in favor of the white group. At the time of the gathering of the case material for the study the author was a member of the Medical and Research Department, New York State Training School for Boys.

Jessie F. Binford in "Postwar Problems of Youth" discusses the problems of children who were adversely affected by family disorganization, mental illness, child labor, and alcoholism. The roots of juvenile delinquency, as Miss Binford says, do not lie only in the homes, the schools, and the churches of the nation. Because of the discrepancies between what juveniles are taught by these agencies and what they find existing in fact in our city life and government, many children have lost respect for integrity and authority.

How to Measure the Extent of Juvenile Delinquency[*]

By O. W. Wilson. Professor of Police Administration, University of California, Berkeley.

CONSIDERATION of the problem of juvenile delinquency immediately raises the question, "How is the extent of delinquency to be measured?" This question has been pondered an even greater length of time by those who have sought its answer in regard to general criminality. Some progress has been made in the latter field, and it would seem worthwhile, in seeking the answer in reference to the extent of juvenile delinquency, to consider the blind alleys that have already been explored in the search for a similar measure of general criminality.

Efforts in the latter field have produced an acceptable system for measuring the amount of crime. Although the system used is the best that has yet been developed anywhere in the world, it is not perfect. A study of it, however, may lead, quickly and directly, to a system for measuring the extent of juvenile delinquency, and thus avoid circuitous meanderings over paths long since abandoned in the search for an acceptable measure of general criminality.

Uniform Crime Reporting System

The method used in this country for measuring variations in criminality is the uniform crime reporting system developed by a committee of the International Association of Chiefs of Police under the able direction of Bruce Smith. It is based on the preparation by local law enforcement agencies of uniform monthly crime reports, and annual reports that show the percentage of crimes that have been cleared by the arrest of the perpetrator. These reports are voluntarily submitted to the FBI where they are tabulated and published semiannually with other information gleaned from fingerprint records also received from local and other agencies.

Before proceeding, it may be well to consider whether the juvenile delinquency information being sought is of the same kind as that being provided in the field of general criminality by the system of *Uniform Crime Reports*. Presumably the information desired is the

[*] Reprinted from *The Journal of Criminal Law and Criminology* (Northwestern University School of Law), Vol. XLI, December, 1950, by O. W. Wilson.

extent of juvenile delinquency, however the term may be defined. Should its extent be measured in terms of the numbers of juvenile offenders who have been dealt with by the police?—or by juvenile courts?—or made wards of juvenile courts?—or removed from their homes for purposes of correction? Or is the extent of juvenile delinquency best measured in terms of the number of juvenile offenses? The answers to these questions may be found through a review of the attempts to measure general criminality.

The total amount of crime serves as a measure of the extent of criminality. How else might it be measured? The blind alleys that have been explored include the number arrested, the number tried in criminal courts, the number convicted, and the number of inmates in penal institutions. Why go down these blind alleys once more? There is no better, more direct, more accurate measure of the extent of criminality of the people than in terms of the crimes that they commit. (The validity of this conclusion is so generally accepted that it seems unnecessary to discuss the extraneous influences that cause sharp variations in the numbers noted above. The extraneous influences include changes in law, policy, procedure, and public sentiment.) Since this is true, it seems equally true that the best measure of the extent of juvenile delinquency is in terms of the delinquent acts.

Do *Uniform Crime Reports* accurately and completely measure the amount of crime? They do not report all crime, but only the Part I classes (homicide, rape, robbery, aggravated assault, burglary, larceny, and auto theft) selected on the basis of the likelihood of their "being known" to the police. The Part II offenses include those less likely to be known to the police, such as drunkenness, traffic violations, and many others considered less serious, as well as some more serious ones such

as abortion, arson, and fraud. The Part II offenses are reported nationally only on the basis of arrests. The justification for this difference in treatment of Part I and Part II crimes seems apparent.

Since *Uniform Crime Reports* do not include all crimes, a question may be raised as to whether they provide a fair index of the crime total. The answer cannot be given categorically. Some contend that Part I crimes are committed by criminal failures, that the successful criminal commits "white collar" crimes which are more important than the Part I offenses, and that, in consequence, Part I crime is not a fair index of the total amount of crime. The problem of the juvenile delinquent, however, does not revolve about his participation in "white collar" crimes. In terms of offenses that are repugnant to the general public, that are of first concern to the police and the criminal courts, that fill our penitentiaries, and that result in juvenile difficulties, Part I crimes seem to be of immediate concern. Most persons think of criminality in terms of Part I crimes. It will be considered in the same light here.

From a practical point of view it seems, therefore, that the extent of Part I crime may be taken as an index of the amount of crime that is of immediate concern to all agencies in the administration of criminal justice. Further, the present impossibility of measuring accurately the amount of other crime makes the acceptance of this index a necessity.

Part I crime, then, is the best available measure of the extent of general criminality. Since this is true, it seems obvious that Part I crime committed by juveniles is the best available measure of the extent of juvenile delinquency.

Since Part I crimes are being reported and serve as a measure of general criminality, if it were possible to segregate those committed by juveniles, an equally valid measure of juvenile delinquency would be available. The problem is to ascertain which of all Part I crimes are committed by juveniles. This cannot be done specifically, but a juvenile crime index can be used which will serve the same end, i.e., provide a measure of the extent and changes in frequency of juvenile crime.

Although Part I crimes committed by juveniles may be either more difficult or less difficult to clear by arrest than Part I crimes committed by adults, it seems fair to assume that any variation in difficulty within a community will remain fairly constant. It is possible, therefore, to measure variations in frequency of juvenile crime by using an index derived by applying to the number of all crimes in each Part I class the percentage of "cleared by arrest" cases in that class that were cleared by the arrest of juvenile perpetrators. For example, if 40% of all "cleared by arrest" auto thefts were cleared by the arrest of juveniles, then the juvenile auto theft rate index would be 40% of all auto thefts in that community during that period.

Expansion Proposals

It is proposed that the system of *Uniform Crime Reports* be expanded to include annually the juvenile crime rate index in the community for each Part I crime. This should be divided into two parts: for offenses committed by persons 15 to 17 and 18 to 20 years of age, inclusive.

If this procedure were applied to each year group (a juvenile crime rate index for each year group would be feasible only in the large city) from 15 or 16 years onward, it is believed that the peak of criminality (as measured in Part I crimes) would be found near 17 years of age with annual decreases in the percentage of total Part I crimes committed by any one year group until the individual is prevented from further criminality by old age or the grave.

Since *Uniform Crime Reports* provide the best available measure of criminality, the adoption of this proposal would provide an approximately equally accurate measure of the extent of juvenile delinquency. If *Uniform Crime Reports* do not measure the extent of general criminality, then attention should be given to this general problem before proceeding further with the more specific one of measuring the extent of juvenile delinquency.

The Meaning of Juvenile Delinquency Statistics[*]

By I. Richard Perlman. Public Welfare Research Analyst, Children's Bureau, Washington, D.C.

Is JUVENILE delinquency increasing or decreasing in our country? How much?

These questions are frequently asked. Newspaper accounts are conflicting. Considerable publicity is given this subject, particularly in reports of shocking rises in delinquency rates. What are the facts about juvenile delinquency trends in the United States? Upon what do we base our opinions? There apparently exists a real need for clarification of the subject, for a better understanding of the available statistics, their values, and limitations.

Definition of Delinquency

Perhaps the greatest obstacle to any use of statistics on juvenile delinquency

* Reprinted from *Federal Probation*, Vol. XIII, September, 1949, pp. 63–67. Used by permission of author and publication.

is the difficulty of defining precisely what is meant by juvenile delinquency. Varying definitions are encountered. Each affects considerably any attempt to measure juvenile delinquency.

A definition of juvenile delinquency on a legal basis depends upon the applicable laws specifying the age of the child and circumstances under which an adjudication of delinquency can be made. Strictly speaking, only those cases of children adjudicated as delinquent can be included in this category.

If this legal definition of delinquency is assumed, a host of questions comes to mind. What about cases dismissed, frequently with a warning to the child or his parents, but without an adjudication of delinquency? What about the many cases of behavior, similar to the adjudicated cases, which are handled unofficially by probation staffs without actual court hearing? Examination of court reports shows that the proportion of dismissed cases and unofficial cases varies considerably from court to court. This variation becomes difficult to explain except on the basis of differences in administrative practices and philosophies of courts regarding unofficial handling of cases. What about the many cases of juvenile misbehavior not represented in juvenile court statistics either because the children are not apprehended by the police or because they are dealt with by the police or social agencies without referral to court? What about the varying legal definitions of juvenile delinquency and age jurisdictions set up in the statutes of the different states? These variations result in the statistical counting of a person as delinquent in one state who would not be so counted if he were in another state.

A similar observation may be made concerning the development of specialized courts for older adolescents. In states where such adolescent courts are used, the offenders will not be included in juvenile court statistics; in other states where juvenile courts serve older adolescents, similar offenders in similar age groups will be included.

Then, too, there are differences in community attitudes toward utilizing the court which consequently affect the statistics. In some communities the juvenile court is regarded as an agency to which cases are referred for service. In other communities the juvenile court is looked upon as the place to refer only cases in which judicial authority is thought to be needed. All of these factors point out the difficulties in measuring delinquency based on legal factors alone.

In recognition of the many objections to the legal definition of juvenile delinquency, another definition frequently used is "any such juvenile misconduct as might be dealt with under the law." Such a definition obviously implies that the misconduct may be classified as delinquency whether or not the case comes before the juvenile court for its adjudication.

The problems in measuring juvenile delinquency under so broad a definition immediately become evident. It would be necessary to secure data from all agencies dealing with children whose behavior problems *might* be dealt with by the law. This obviously is not feasible on a national scale.

Measurement of Delinquency

The lack of agreement on a clearly defined idea of what is meant by juvenile delinquency and the difficulties in obtaining data under some of the definitions postulated have led many to seriously question whether delinquency can satisfactorily be measured at all. There are others, however, who do not take such an extreme point of view. This latter group recognizes that while it may be impractical to obtain a precise measurement of juvenile delinquency, nevertheless, statistics that can be gathered—based on numbers of children who are dealt with by law enforcement and judicial agencies in the United States—are significant. Such children represent a portion of all children whose misconduct might be dealt with by the law. It is assumed, therefore, that changes in the number of children coming to the attention of law-enforcement and judicial agencies give some indication of changes occurring in the total group. This is undoubtedly a safer assumption for comparisons of year-to-year changes in national data than it is for local data or for inter-area comparisons, because of local changes in law or administrative practice that affect time series but are less significant in national totals.

The two series of statistical data currently being collected by federal agencies which are most frequently used in relation to juvenile delinquency are the juvenile court statistics collected by the Children's Bureau and the police arrest data based on fingerprint records reported to the Federal Bureau of Investigation in its uniform crime reporting plan. It may be helpful, therefore, to describe briefly these two reporting plans, their history, what they count, the extent of coverage, method of collection and some of the limitations of the data.

Other series of data are collected by federal agencies such as the statistics on federal offenders collected currently by the Bureau of Prisons and population of institutions for delinquent children collected at intervals by the Bureau of the Census. These other series of data, however, are less frequently used in relation to juvenile delinquency because they are restricted to so small a portion of the total group of children with behavior problems.

Juvenile Court Statistics

In 1926 the Children's Bureau initiated its plan for the uniform reporting of juvenile court statistics. The need for such a uniform reporting plan was first recognized by the Children's Bureau Committee on Juvenile Court Standards and later confirmed in 1923 at a conference held under the joint auspices of the Children's Bureau and the National Probation and Parole Association. The reporting plan was prompted by a desire to obtain a general picture of the volume of the work of juvenile courts in dealing with delinquent behavior and to have some assurance that the data collected would be based on uniform units of measurement and definitions. The data have been collected and published beginning with the calendar year 1927. Since that time the details of the uniform reporting plan have been modified several times in order to increase the usefulness of the reported data and to achieve greater economy in their collection and tabulation. The basic purposes of the plan—to stimulate the uniform reporting of juvenile court statistics and their use for interpretive and administrative purposes—have remained the same. At the present time the data are obtained on summary report forms transmitted by state agencies concerned with juvenile court or probation work (e.g., state departments of welfare, statewide juvenile courts, departments of probation and correction, etc.). These summary reports are based on individual court reports to state agencies. The data are now being published in the Children's Bureau Statistical Series.

The reports from the courts and states are voluntary and consequently are not nation-wide in coverage. At the present time they cover jurisdictions which include about one-third of the population of the United States. They are now heavily weighted by large urban areas located predominantly in the northeast region of the country.

The basic unit of count in the juvenile court delinquency statistics of the Children's Bureau is the juvenile delinquency case disposed of officially as well as unofficially by the court. One child may appear before the court two, three, or more times during the year and each appearance is counted as another case if a new complaint is filed and dealt with separately. Data on the number of delinquency cases disposed of include not merely the most serious offenses, but many types of alleged delinquency from the most serious to the most trivial.

As was previously pointed out, many children whose behavior may be classed as delinquent are not represented in juvenile court statistics, either because they are not apprehended or because they are dealt with by the police, social agencies, schools, or other resources in the community and are not referred to a court. Variations in administrative practices, differences in age jurisdictions, and the availability of other community resources also affect the number of children reported by different communities in their statistics. These limitations reemphasize the impracticability of using juvenile court statistics alone to make comparisons of the extent of juvenile delinquency in different communities or regions. However, juvenile court delinquency cases furnish an indication of the extent of juvenile misbehavior serious enough to need court attention. As such, statistics from a group of reporting courts where laws and organizational patterns have remained fairly constant over a period of years are significant. They also may be used as one indication of trends in the larger problems represented by juvenile misconduct. The larger the number of courts included in the reporting group, the better the general picture since atypical changes by a few courts do not seriously affect the over-all consolidated data.

Police Arrest Data

The only source of federally-collected statistics on police arrests are from the uniform crime reporting plan of the Federal Bureau of Investigation. This reporting plan was developed in 1929 by a Committee on Uniform Crime Records designated by the International Association of Chiefs of Police and a technical staff financed by the Laura Spelman Rockefeller Memorial. The purpose of the plan was to improve the accuracy and completeness of police statistics. It was recommended at that time that the Federal Bureau of Investigation be requested to handle the uniform crime reporting program. Beginning with 1930 that Bureau has conducted the reporting program. The data are published semiannually in its bulletin, *Uniform Crime Reports*.

The program is entirely voluntary in regard to the submission of reports by local and state police. It provides for two separate sources of data:

(1) Data from monthly and annual summary reports on offenses known to the police. Although the Federal Bureau of Investigation is planning a revision of its reporting to include data on the age of the person involved in the offense, to date these summary reports have not included this item. Therefore, they cannot be used as a source of police arrest data for children.

(2) Data from fingerprint cards transmitted to the Federal Bureau of Investigation by the police for persons arrested for violating state laws and municipal ordinances. The fingerprint cards show the age, sex, race, and previous criminal history of the persons arrested. These cards, therefore, are at present the only source of federally-collected statistics on police arrests of children.

Uniform Crime Reports states that the data compiled from fingerprint cards by no means represent all persons arrested since there are many persons taken into custody for whom no fingerprints are forwarded to Washington. This would be especially true for children because in many places children when arrested are not fingerprinted as a matter of law or public policy. In addition, the geographical coverage of the fingerprint reporting is undetermined and may change from year to year. The Federal Bureau of Investigation believes, however, that for many years practically all of the law-enforcement agencies throughout the country making arrests have forwarded fingerprint records regularly to its central clearinghouse for identification. Hence, while the figures may be an understatement since they are limited to those arrests where the offenders are fingerprinted, the Federal Bureau of Investigation believes that the trends reflected periodically do represent a reasonably reliable index to all arrests throughout the Nation. This, they feel, is particularly true since the same policies, in general, prevail year after year as to those who are fingerprinted.

Police Arrest Data and Juvenile Court Statistics

The limitations outlined for both the fingerprint arrest data and the juvenile court statistics indicate clearly that neither of these series purports to measure the extent of juvenile delinquency. Each, however, does provide an indication of changes in the number of children getting into difficulty with the law and, as such, may be assumed to have some relationship to changes in total juvenile delinquency. It might be expected, therefore, that, despite the limitations of each series individually, both would present a somewhat similar picture. This is precisely what we find when we examine the year-to-year changes indicated by the data from juvenile court statistics and the police arrest data in the chart below. The direction of changes observed are in accord with the general findings and opinions of consultants and specialists working with delinquent children.

The juvenile court data shown in the chart represent total delinquency cases reported by 76 courts serving urban areas of 100,000 population or over for which data were reported for the 10 years, 1938–1947 inclusive. The data on

COMPARISON OF DELINQUENCY CASES DISPOSED OF BY JUVENILE COURTS, WITH POLICE ARRESTS OF CHILDREN UNDER 18 YEARS OF AGE, 1938–47

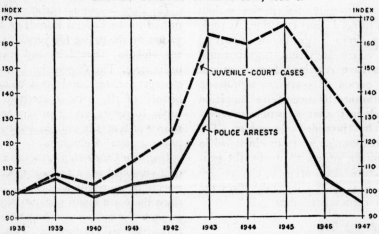

Sources:
    Police arrest data from section on fingerprint records in *Uniform Crime Reports* (annual bulletins) issued by Federal Bureau of Investigation.
    Juvenile court cases from data reported by the U.S. Children's Bureau on delinquency cases disposed of by 76 large urban juvenile courts participating in the federal-state juvenile court reporting system from 1938 to 1947 inclusive.

police arrests represent the total number of fingerprint records for children under 18 years of age as reported in the published *Uniform Crime Reports* for the same period.

We find that despite the fact that neither of these series represents a completely accurate measurement of juvenile delinquency and despite the differences in unit of count, extent of coverage, and geographic representation, nevertheless there is a remarkable similarity between the direction of changes indicated by the two lines. Both increased sharply from 1942 to 1943, both decreased between 1943 and 1944, both increased again in 1945 to the 10-year peak and both showed sharp decreases in 1946 and 1947. This striking similarity cannot be accounted for on the grounds that the police arrest data composed a large proportion of the cases referred to court. For as has been pointed out, the police data are based on fingerprint records and are therefore only a small proportion of those referred to court. As Edward E. Schwartz has pointed out in his article in *The Annals* (January, 1949)

The marked similarity in the movement of the two series, notwithstanding their differences in source and coverage, strongly suggests that they are subject to common determining factors. Nationally pervasive social forces which could well have affected both the number of arrests of children and the number of juvenile-court delinquency cases were operative for the period under consideration . . . . It seems likely, therefore, that statistics available on a national basis do indicate for the past ten years the direction of the large changes in the number of children who were in conflict with the law.

National Statistics

Juvenile delinquency statistics should be used constructively to stimulate nation-wide efforts toward providing services which will help keep children out of trouble. They are not useful if they simply furnish the basis for ill-considered statements about the children of this generation.

An important function of the national uniform reporting programs is the opportunity to assist states and localities to develop or improve data on problems concerning children and youth. In this way, statistics will become available to state and local authorities directly responsible for the administration of programs for children and youth, for their use in more effectively planning and operating these programs.

The presently collected federal statistics are used to provide an indication of changes in the number of children getting into difficulty with the law. They are limited to some extent by the weakness of data at the present time. Steps ought to be taken therefore to extend and improve the present series.

Some measures for improvement in coverage are already in progress. The Federal Bureau of Investigation data on juveniles, until recently, were limited to children arrested and fingerprinted and therefore included only a small portion of children arrested. That Bureau has just inaugurated a new report which will show the age, race, and sex of all persons arrested whether fingerprinted or not. This should do much toward improving their coverage of the data for juveniles. The Children's Bureau revision of its juvenile court reporting plan in 1946 emphasized state-agency collection of data. This revision was directed toward extending the coverage of its reporting to include greater representation from all geographical areas, especially rural.

Because participation in these uniform reporting series is voluntary, much assistance could be given by national police, probation and judges' organizations in interpreting the need for more comprehensive information on the problem of juvenile delinquency and in stimulating participation in the reporting.

In addition to extending and improving the data, steps need to be taken to help in the public interpretation and use of the separate series of federally-collected statistics. This need arises from the fact that police arrest data and juvenile court data each represent different stages in the handling of delinquent youth. Consequently, they do not agree in the extent of change from year to year although, as we have seen, they do agree in the general direction of change over a period of years. This lack of agreement in extent of change is what may be expected in view of the different data being collected and the different procedures used in collecting them. It furnishes some reason for confusion in the public's mind. Other causes of confusion result from a lack of understanding regarding the definitions used, the coverage of the reporting, limitations of the data, and so forth.

A Subcommittee on the Improvements of Juvenile Delinquency Statistics of the Federal Interdepartmental Committee on Children and Youth, arranged for by the Administrator of the Federal Security Agency at the request of the President, has considered ways to overcome this confusion as well as other methods for improving juvenile delinquency statistics. A report of this Subcommittee containing its recommendations has been completed and will be released in the near future.

The above comments are based on the assumption of a continuance of the present methods of collecting statistics relating to juvenile delinquency by federal agencies. In studying ways of improving the methods and types of data collected and the uses to which they may be put, two interrelated basic questions arise: (1) Can the data obtained from the various series be interrelated to provide indices more representative of total juvenile delinquency than now can be obtained from any one individual series? (2) Can it be established that one of the series of statistical data now being collected is the

most representative index of delinquency (not true measurement of delinquency) and that it should be used to the exclusion of all other series?

It does not seem feasible to determine the answers to these questions through a study of the national statistics. Intensive study of all available statistics in local communities of agencies dealing with behavior problems may prove more practical in arriving at the answers. For example, it may be possible in a local community to establish a complete register of all children known to all agencies who are considered to be delinquent. For this purpose the broadest possible definition of delinquency should be used. Any one component series of data (police, juvenile court, school, etc.) could then be related to this total group to determine which series most closely represents the total group. Several communities have already experimented with such a central registration and others are in the process of planning for it. Much more experimentation must be carried on in local communities before it can be hoped to obtain adequate conclusions regarding the interrelationships between the various series of statistical data relating to juvenile delinquency.

Conclusions

Nation-wide data on the extent of juvenile delinquency are not available. The juvenile court statistics and the police arrest data now being collected by federal agencies do furnish a crude indication of national trends in the number of children getting into difficulty with the law and as such give some insight into delinquency trends. Based on these data the number of children getting into trouble with law-enforcement and judicial agencies seems to have increased sharply during the war to a peak in 1945. The factors accounting for this increase were those relating generally to wartime conditions—the absence of one or both parents from the home, shortages of trained personnel to deal with children's problems, wartime anxieties and strains, migration of families, and unwholesome surroundings and associations of children in some types of employment. From the peak of 1945, children brought to court or arrested decreased sharply in 1946 and continued downward in 1947, following the end of the wartime conditions. The decrease may reflect also the strengthening of existing services to children and efforts by local, state, and federal agencies to prevent conditions that lead to juvenile delinquency.

Statistics Will Get You if You Don't Watch Out!*

By Lurline V. Simpson. University of Washington, Seattle.

"ALL Americans quote statistics," a foreign colleague once said to me. Then, eying me whimsically, he added, "I suppose even you know some."

That was many years ago, and if I knew any they didn't trouble me. They flitted harmlessly on the periphery of my world. They applied to someone else. Now, however, I know dozens and they are closing in upon me. How long can I escape?

"*One out of eight will die of cancer,*" proclaim giant posters, with the unlucky eighth (me?) graphically obliterated.

"*One out of six is suffering from chronic disease,*" reports the dignified and impersonal Medical Journal. Getting closer!

"*One out of every two persons will suffer serious injuries from accident during the year,*" predicts the omniscient public press, and proceeds to illustrate its findings with the catastrophic consequences from such routine activities as making beds and taking baths.

"*Four out of five have pink tooth brush.*" A near miss, especially since, in defiance of equally dire calculations and the blandishments of purveyors of artificial dentures, I still have my teeth.

"*EVERY faculty member has five-eighths of a child,*" shamelessly reveals the campus Daily, after completing one of its periodical "if so what of it" polls. Reflecting on some of the faculty children I have known, I am inclined to admit the plausibility of the figure while shuddering at its implications. For even the most generous and benevolent of the investigators have thus far neglected to provide my fractional if hypothetical offspring with a father. Does the administration read the Daily?

But hope springs eternal. Haven't some explorers discovered a spinsters' paradise in the preponderantly male communities north of the Arctic Circle? Or the salvation of technical respectability may lie in the social scientists' revelation of the sort of Mad Hatter's Tea Party suggested in the puzzling datum: "*Three out of every two marriages end in divorce.*" It behooves me to get on the mark and prepare for the next shift, or foredoom the already handicapped little stranger to serve the percentage of time in corrective institutions reserved for products of "broken homes."

I have not yet exhausted the statistics, or vice versa. Indeed, we now come to the versatile vices. "*Every man, woman, and child in the United States smokes five cigarettes a day.*" What does that make me? Possibly college professors have a special category, but I am becoming sensitive. How does one achieve

* Reprinted from *Bulletin* (American Association of University Professors), Volume 36, Winter, 1950, pp. 723–725. Used by permission.

status? Even the beneficent counts leave me untouched. *"The entire population of the country can ride in motor cars at the same time."* Yet, except when competing for the three cubic feet of space rightfully mine in municipal transit facilities, I dodge with the pedestrians.

Thus far I have lived a charmed life, the forgotten pawn, the exception to all rules. But this precarious existence divided between tight-rope walking and juggling with the forces of mathematical determinism is taking its nervous toll. The day of reckoning cannot be indefinitely postponed, especially as even my credit is becoming strained; is it not true that *"Each citizen of the United States owes a debt of $1789"?*

The cloud of malevolent little figures approaches threateningly closer, closer, CRASH!

At last I am taking my allotted motor ride, careening madly in an ambulance, dashing to give birth to my five-eighths, thoughtfully clutching the new-born's first day's quota of five cigarettes. "My child will have a better chance than his milk-fed mother," I vow before drifting into blessed oblivion.

Dimly I hear the specialists' consultation: "Erroneous diagnosis. Not parturition. Chronic pink tooth brush. Remove the patient to Room 219. Deposit $1789 in the office for incidentals."

Bells. The campus chimes? Oh, yes. I remember. Painfully I gather myself up from the floor, shake off the heap of final blue books, and mop up the red ink. What was that last statistic? *"One out of twenty will end his life in a 'mental institution' "?* Well, some might call the State University that. It is all a matter of definition—or is "semantics" the currently acceptable term? Has the Daily investigated how many profs use blue books as soporifics? I cram those remaining into my brief case, mechanically obey the printed exhortation to "Stop! Look! Turn out the lights!" and close the door of 219 behind me.

Negro and White Male Institutionalized Delinquents[*]

By Sidney Axelrad. Chairman, Department of Anthropology–Sociology, Queens College, New York.

A REVIEW of the literature from 1914 to date discloses that there has been no empirical comparison of Negro and white delinquents. There have been a number of studies dealing with the relative incidence of delinquency in different racial groups. Blanchard indicates that, in proportion to the population, there are about five times as many Negroes as whites in the city and state prisons of New York and that there are about five times as many Negro children arraigned as delinquents in the children's courts of New York City as there are white children in proportion to their relative frequencies in the total population. Robison, in her book *Can Delinquency Be Measured?*, concludes:

> There is a persistently higher percentage of Negro children in the delinquency category than would be expected on the basis of their proportion in the population. However, the dearth of Negro children under care in all but official agencies points to extreme differences in type of care available for white and Negro children.

* "Negro and White Male Institutionalized Delinquents," Sidney Axelrad, *The American Journal of Sociology*, Vol. LVII, May, 1952, pp. 569–574. Used by permission of author and publication.

From Robison's and other studies it is clear that many factors must be taken into account in evaluating court and other agency data relating to delinquency. The reasons that the court figures show such a disproportion of Negro children may very well lie in the relative paucity of other means of treatment (which would result in a greater proportion of Negro children being referred to the courts). Whatever the causes may be, it is apparent that there are differences in the incidence and treatment of Negro and white delinquents; but how the Negro and white delinquents differ, except in gross respects, chiefly a statement of court offenses, is not known. The present study is an attempt to determine what these differences are and to set forth some hypotheses for their origin.

Delinquency involves both an act and a social and legal evaluation of it. It is necessary to begin research in this area by excluding as many variables as possible. For this reason, and with the realization that the kind and number of generalizations might be narrowed, the study was confined to one state institution and only to children who had been committed by the Children's Court as delinquent. By selecting an institution that draws almost entirely from one city and from one court system, we exclude differences resulting from local conditions and legal and judicial variations.

Confining the sample to boys *committed* for delinquency results in the further elimination of other variables. If the study is confined to those committed to an institution as delinquents, the differences that might be expected to exist between those children who can be treated while they remain in their own homes and those who must be removed are automatically excluded.

The data presented were drawn from the case studies of 300 boys—179 Negro

and 121 white—who had all been committed to the institution between 1933

TABLE 1.*—AGE IN YEARS AT COMMITMENT

Age	Per Cent Negro	Per Cent White
10	1	0
11	2	6
12	19	14
13	22	29
14	27	43
15	23	8
16	6	0
Total	100	100

TABLE 2.—NUMBER OF PREVIOUS COURT APPEARANCES

Number of Previous Court Appearances	Per Cent Negro	Per Cent White
None	10	9
1	18	17
2	30	18
3	23	24
4	12	15
5 and more	7	7
Total	100	100

and 1934 as delinquents. They were all under the age of sixteen and over the age of ten at the time of commitment. Forty-two per cent of the group was white; 58 per cent, Negro. This ratio corresponded to that which prevailed in the institution during these years; the 300 cases constituted about 90 per cent of the institutional population at the time. Aside from the racial ratio, the only other selective factor was the adequacy of case records. Because only the better-studied cases were selected, the sample is possibly biased in the direction of including only the more serious problems.

We shall present the data as answers to two questions: (1) Did the Children's Court commit Negro and white children

* Number of cases in this table and in following tables, unless otherwise indicated, is 179 Negro and 121 white.

on a different basis? (2) Are there significant differences in background, family relationship, and family constellations between the two groups?

Selection for Institutionalization

The Negro group was almost two years younger than the white delinquents at the time of admission. The median age for the Negro group was 13.1 years; for the white, 15.0. The difference between the medians was 1.9 years, with a standard deviation of .19.

Negro children were younger than white at the time of first court appearance. The median age for the Negro group was 12.1; for the white, 12.8 (Table 1).

Negro children were institutionalized after a smaller number of court appearances than white children. The median number of previous court appearances for the Negro group was a little over 2; for the white, almost 4 (Table 2).

The same proportion, a third of each group, was institutionalized without previous probationary periods. But if we take as a base the number in each group who have had probation before institutionalization, a different picture emerges; almost 70 per cent of the Negro group were committed after one probationary period, only 50 per cent of the white; 27 per cent of each group had two probationary periods; but only 4 per cent of the Negro group, as against 23 per cent of the white, had more than two periods. Thus, there appears to be a tendency for the white delinquent to be afforded a larger number of probationary periods prior to institutionalization than is the case with the Negro delinquent (Table 3).

Seventeen per cent of the Negro children had been previously institutionalized in an institution for delinquents; 59 per cent of the white children had had previous institutionalization. If previous commitment is an indication of more serious delinquency, then it can be con-

cluded that the offenses of the white delinquents were more serious. However, it may also indicate the lack of resources other than the state institutions for the Negro delinquent; as stated above, the greater proportion of previous institutionalization for the white delinquent may be attributed to the existence of other facilities which can be used before commitment to the state institution has been made necessary. The length of prior institutionalization was almost the same; the median stay was 10.7 months for the Negro and 12.6 months for the white.

TABLE 3.—NUMBER OF PROBATION PERIODS

Number of Probation Periods	Per Cent Negro	Per Cent White
None	33	37
1	46	33
2	18	17
3	3	10
4	0	3
Total	100	100

The white delinquents have had greater prior institutionalization in homes for dependents—10 per cent for the Negro children, 19 per cent for the white—and the median time in the institution was double for the white children—24.5 months to 12.3 months. It is apparent that a Negro child will be committed with less previous institutionalization than the white child.

If we consider the formal charges on which these boys were brought before the court and for which they were committed as delinquents, some significant differences emerge. In both groups most boys were committed as a result of more than one offense, but differential treatment is still evident. Thirty-eight per cent of the Negro boys were committed on the basis of one charge, as against 28 per cent of the white boys; 37 per cent of the Negroes with two charges, as against 29 per cent of the whites; but from this point the proportion was reversed. Twenty-three per cent of the white delinquents had three offenses as against 17 per cent of the Negro delinquents, and 20 per cent of the white delinquents had four or more offenses as against 8 per cent of the Negroes. Of the major offenses, white children were committed for more serious offenses: burglary, 48 per cent white, 29 per cent

TABLE 4*.—OFFENSE OF DELINQUENTS

Offense	Per Cent Negro	Per Cent White	C.R.
Burglary	29	48	3.3
Larceny	24	49	4.5
Truancy	18	38	3.8

Negro; larceny, 49 per cent white, 24 per cent Negro (Table 4). White delinquents were more prone to be committed for truancy than the Negro delinquents, 38 per cent as against 18 per cent. This should not be understood to mean that the white children were less adjusted than the Negro. (Only those differences are discussed where the critical ratio is $\geq 3, P = .01$.)

Almost all the delinquents were school problems. It is probable that the community, or at least the school system, considers truancy in the white child as something about which it is willing to be active. Seemingly, it did not care so much in the case of the Negro child.

It may be concluded that Negro children are committed to a state institution as delinquents, younger, with fewer court appearances, less previous institutionalization, and for fewer and less serious offenses than white children.

The Neighborhood and Family

In considering the background and family constellations of the two groups of delinquents, it should be borne in

mind that delinquents are likely to have rather severe family pathology. We might expect differences of pathology in the two groups rather than absence of pathology in one of the groups.

The Negro children much more than the white delinquents came from areas characterized by high delinquency rates and high density. Much more than the white delinquents, they lived in neighborhoods that contain a majority of residents of their own racial stock (Table 5).

TABLE 5.—NEIGHBORHOOD OF DELINQUENTS

Neighborhood	Per Cent Negro	Per Cent White	C.R.
Urban	88	60	5.7
Rural	2	2	3.3
Delinquency area	50	22	5.3
Suburban	11	26	3.1
Congested	70	35	6.3
Dominant racial group same as child	67	30	7.0

Of the Negro children, only two were not Protestant. Of the white children, almost 60 per cent were Catholic, one child was Jewish, and the others were Protestant.

In American society it is normal for the child to live exclusively with both his parents. But only 18 per cent of the Negro children did so as contrasted to 46 per cent of the white delinquents. Eighty-two per cent of the Negro children came from broken homes; 50 per cent of the white children. But here again there is a difference: of the 60 white broken homes, 50 per cent of the separations were caused by death; of the 139 Negro broken homes, 37, or 26 per cent, were caused by death of one of the parents. Very clearly factors other than death are responsible for the proportion of broken homes among the Negro delinquents.

---

* These figures are computed on a total base of 296—Negro, 179; white, 117.

The Negro children came from families which were smaller than those of the white children if the size of the family is measured by the number of children in the family (Table 6). The median number of children in the Negro family was a little more than 3; for the white families, almost 6. But the distribution indicates even greater deviation. Eighteen per cent of the Negro delinquents were only children. Nineteen, or 58 per cent, of the Negro only children were illegitimate. In this group of delinquents the smaller size of the Negro family was not caused by the death of a parent but by the instability

psychosocial environment in which a child lives may be obtained in terms of the number of sets of parent figures with whom he has lived. For this study, each set was counted as a unit and defined as a home situation. Thus, a child who had lived only with both his parents prior to the present institutionalization would have 1 home situation; a child who had lived with both his parents, his mother alone, and had been previously institutionalized would have 3. The number of home situations other than the present institutionalization showed significant differences. The median number of homes for the Negro delinquents was 2.1; for the white delinquents, 1.0. The range for the Negro delinquents was

TABLE 6.—NUMBER OF CHILDREN IN FAMILY

Number of Children	Per Cent Negro	Per Cent White
1	18	3
2	18	4
3	19	10
4	13	19
5	10	15
6	7	14
7 and over	15	35
Total	100	100

TABLE 7.—STATUS OF CHILD IN FAMILY

Status	Per Cent Negro	Per Cent White	C.R.
Unwanted	17	4	4.0
Illegitimate	25	5	5.0
Stepchild	33	17	3.3
Foster-child	30	13	4.0

of the relationship between the parents. In this group, 25 per cent of the Negro delinquents were illegitimate, while only 5 per cent of the white children were.[1] Seventeen per cent of the Negro children were unwanted, 4 per cent of the white; 33 per cent of the Negro children were stepchildren, only 17 per cent of the white; 30 per cent of the Negro children were foster-children, 13 per cent of the white (Table 7).

A gross index of the stability of the

from 1 to 7; for the white delinquents, from 1 to 5. Analysis of the distribution indicates that 51 per cent of the white delinquents had been in only one situation; only 23 per cent of the Negroes. This is a difference of 28 per cent (C.R. 7.8). Thirty-one of the Negro children and 18 of the white had been in 3 situations, a difference of 13 per cent (C.R. 3.8); 17 per cent of the Negroes and 5 per cent of the whites had been in 4 or more homes, a difference of 12 per cent (C.R. 5.0).

Institutions are included in these situ-

[1] The census reports for 1930 of the number of illegitimate births of Negro children for New York indicate a figure of 6 per cent. This should be compared with the 25 per cent for our group. It may also be of interest to note that the figure for our group is higher than those reported for the cities of the deep South.

The average size of the Negro family in urban areas in New York is 2.6. Thus, the median number of children in the family of the Negro delinquent exceeds the size of the total family among Negroes. Families of this size are found only in the rural areas of the South. The median size of families of native white individuals was 2.9; for the foreign-born, 3.6. The median number of children in the families of the white delinquents was 5.

ations; and it should be remembered that the Negro delinquents had been institutionalized less often than the white delinquents. These differences point to a much greater instability of homes for the

TABLE 8.*—TYPES OF FAMILY CONSTELLATIONS

Type	Per Cent Negro	Per Cent White	C.R.
With both own parents	76	92	4.0
With mother and step-father	25	11	3.2
With mother only	49	21	5.5
With other relatives	37	10	6.0
In other family	18	4	3.9

TABLE 9.—DIFFERENCES IN PARENTAL FACTORS

Parental Factor	Per Cent Negro	Per Cent White	C.R.
Death or deprivation	59	35	3.9
Desertion	41	14	5.7
Discipline deficient	50	72	3.9
Immigration to America	27	2	7.3
Language handicap	2	41	8.5
Neglect	72	52	3.6
Racial difference	3	14	3.2
Rejection	66	46	3.5
Religious difference	1	9	3.3
Rural-urban shift	39	5	8.0
Separation	36	13	4.9
Sex immorality	54	31	4.0

Negro children than for the white delinquents.

The family constellations differed in the two groups of delinquents. The white delinquents tended to have lived more with both biological parents; the Negro delinquents either with mother and stepfather, with mother only, with other relatives, or in unrelated families (Table 8). In 26 per cent of the Negro

families the mother was the only person employed; this was true of only 5 per cent of the white families.

The family of the white delinquent was larger than the median for the New York City population; the family of the Negro delinquent was also larger than the average Negro family; and it exhibited instability as compared to the families of the white delinquent. It was likely to be mother-centered. This, according to E. Franklin Frazier, is a tendency found in the Negro family of the South and related to the form that the Negro family was forced to adopt during slavery and immediately following the days of abolition.

There are further differences. In contrast to the white delinquents, the Negro children came from homes where there was more death or deprivation of a parent, desertion, neglect, rejection, separation, and sexual promiscuity. Contrasted to the Negro delinquents, the white delinquents came from families where there was deficient discipline, language handicap, ethnic difference, and religious difference (Table 9).

Summary

The case records of 300 institutionalized delinquents—179 Negro, 121 white —were analyzed to determine whether the courts were commiting Negro and white children on the same basis and whether the two groups differed in family constellations. The study discloses that Negro children are committed younger, for less serious offenses, with fewer previous court appearances, and with less prior institutionalization. Negro children came from more unstable homes and from homes with a different kind of family pathology from the white delinquents.

* This table represents the significant differences in all the types of family constellations in which the delinquents have lived. Since many of the delinquents lived in more than one type, the total is more than 100 per cent.

Postwar Problems of Youth[*]

By Jessie F. Binford. Executive Director, Juvenile Protective Association, Chicago.

DURING this century, statistics have been compiled from case records, special studies, surveys, and reports of an ever-increasing number of social agencies, public welfare departments, juvenile courts, child guidance clinics, reformatories and prisons. We have undisputed facts, in terms of human lives, as to what constitutes the needs of all children. And yet, in 1912, the first White House Conference considered only dependent children; the second in 1919, did include child labor, health, and child welfare legislation, but it was not until the third, in 1930, that all those factors were considered which influence the childhood and youth of the 45,000,000 growing children in America—that is, childlife in its total aspects. In protective casework with children and their parents and the consideration of community conditions and the unnumbered influences which are so often factors in their individual problems, there evolves, I believe, more than in other social agencies, a picture of childlife in its total aspects.

Victims of Neglect and Deprivation

Some are so-called delinquents and criminals, but very few in comparison with those who suffer from such tragic neglect and deprivation that they develop health, conduct, and emotional problems. In their lives we see the "shadows that somewhere along the way between babyhood and childhood and through their adolescent years have forever darkened the bright promise of youth and may perhaps lead to delinquency and crime."

The brother and sister, only 10 and 12 years of age, who finally decided that he being a boy would run away, but that she would have to commit suicide to escape from the quarreling of their parents which they could no longer endure.

The 15-year-old boy who lost the sight of one eye and may become totally blind through his illegal hazardous employment on a railroad.

The 11-year-old boy, so typical of many of the children of divorced parents, who tried to help the judge determine the question of his custody with the simple obvious solution, "I want to be with both of them."

The 18-year-old boy who went to the police station at 2:30 A.M. in a very intoxicated condition, to confess a robbery he had just committed, and then in court heard the tavern keeper, who sold him whiskey illegally, discharged and himself found guilty.

The 12-year-old girl kept out of school, in the house all the time and denied all medical care subject, her mother said, to "spells" which were "from Heaven and God-inspired."

The 15-year-old girl who ran away from a wretched home and in another city easily found hospitality and companionship and employment in a tavern, and was later found by the police in a park, having been raped by one of her tavern friends.

The little girl, so disturbed in school and truant so often, found to be living in constant fear of her father, who was at that time on his 8th week of excessive

---

[*] Reprinted from *Federal Probation*, Vol. XI, October–December, 1947, pp. 7–11. Used by permission of author and publication.

drinking. To get away from his cruelty and abuse she was working on a newspaper truck from seven to nine each night.

The 13-year-old girl found by the police in an alcoholic stupor on the street, after she and two boys, 13 and 14 years of age, had been sold liquor by the owner of a liquor store.

The 18-year-old boy, now serving a long sentence in the penitentiary, who stabbed a man to death, after having been illegally sold liquor in four different taverns.

The 15-year-old boy, an illegitimate child, left alone so much at night that he roams the streets, steals, and has told the children in his school that he has a "G.I." knife hidden at home with which he is going to kill the next man his mother brings home to live with them.

The six children of a mother who is a religious fanatic, who never permits them any pleasure or recreation, and a father so ill and irritable from lead poisoning that he has become an excessive drinker.

The nine little children whose mother is mentally ill, with a long history of mental illness and poverty in her own family, so cruel that she pressed the hands of the 1-year-old girl on a hot stove. Their father, who also has a history of mental illness in his own family, is utterly incapable of coping with the wife's outbursts and accusations, except by beating her so severely that hospital care was necessary. All the children need medical care, they have special disabilities, they are shy and nervous and cruel to each other. This family lives in four small rooms.

The children whom you see testifying in our courts about their fathers or mothers who are being tried for contributing to their delinquency, and against adult sex offenders who on the streets or in theatres have committed sex crimes against them; in our divorce courts, where they break down because they do not want to accuse either parent. One always cringes when little children are asked "do you know what it means not to tell the truth?" and "what will happen to you or where you will go, if you tell a lie?"

David Ruge, the 16-year-old boy, who had never been a problem in his home or his school, but kept always to himself from the time he became conscious of his ugly, misshapen face. As he grew older, he had asked his mother about plastic surgery, but she had told him to "forget it—you have to be a millionaire to have anything like that done." Suddenly he committed the serious crime of writing an extortion note to his employer. The Juvenile Court transferred him to the Criminal Court and the Cook County Jail. His family could not raise the fee for the criminal lawyer to whom they appealed even by selling all their defense bonds. In despair they suddenly remembered their old neighbors of 20 years ago at a settlement. An attorney, one of our board members, defended David with the understanding and procedure he should have found in the Juvenile Court. The judge had to face public opinion which permits and often demands that juvenile offenders still be prosecuted and punished as adult offenders and delayed his decision. A veteran newspaper reporter caught the significance of this boy's crime and his story was copied by papers throughout the country. One thousand dollars was offered by a man in Ohio for plastic surgery if David could be released. Other contributions were sent in, even as small as $1.00 from an anonymous source with a letter "Dear David: I hope that your dream comes true." The best that could be done for David in the Criminal Court was to convict him and place him on probation. In the Juvenile Court he would not have had a criminal record. Today, the shadow in David's life has been dispelled. He is no longer inhibited and sullen, but confident and happy, for a famous surgeon has made him look like other boys.

From this mere glimpse of shadows that darken the lives of children, we begin to see that there is no one cause for their truancies, dependencies, delinquencies, crimes, mental and physical illness, and likewise no one remedy. At the same time, there evolves another picture: the "total aspects" of adult delinquency in neglecting to safeguard the rights and needs of all children. This picture changes from year to year, at least in the emphasis of those influences and conditions which recur the most often in the lives of children who need protection.

The Aftermath of War

The years of war have passed, but its scars remain and many will never be completely healed. We see them today in homes that were broken when mothers formed new attachments while their husbands were away, or who after working several years are unwilling to assume again the duties of home and motherhood; in the children who went to work and will never continue their education; in the migrant families, especially from the South who cannot adjust to urban life and have not found the economic security they expected; in the restless, neurotic fathers and young men who cannot become adjusted to homelife; in the many children who were boarded out and some deserted in the inadequate, unlicensed foster and mutual boarding homes, so many of which still exist. The war increased and intensified many old problems.

Inadequate Housing. In 1894 Jane Addams was writing about "the subtle evils of inadequate and wretched housing." Never have they been so acute as today. Thousands of families are living in old, condemned, overcrowded buildings, with inadequate cooking and toilet facilities, so alive with rats and vermin that parents sit up nights to protect their children; living under the con-

stant fear of fires and the threat of eviction, with no possible place to move.

It goes without saying that in such houses marital and parental relationships are strained and broken down, children become truants and delinquents, get sick and die. When you grope your way through dirty alleys and up rickety dark stairs and hallways, ever fearful of rats, into dark, barren cold rooms and face the sodden despair of parents, whose morale has completely broken down and see the neglected, sick, dirty, little children you think "can this be America?" And yet, even in places like these, children still cling to those more intrinsic values of affection and security, which home means to them. The little 10-year-old girl, who took a bottle of aspirin to kill herself to get away from her quarreling parents and a home infected with bedbugs, roaches, mice and rats, again threatened to throw herself on the railroad track if she could not go home when she was placed in a country boarding school for children.

Family Disorganization. The war has undoubtedly contributed to the appalling increase in divorces, almost every one of which involves the welfare and future of children. These children are forever deprived of a normal home, their loyalties are confused; they become the vehicle through which each parent so often vents his enmity against the other; they are subjected to the emotional strain of divided custodial rights and continued court appearances in relation to them.

Can anyone analyze the emotions of a 10-year-old girl who was not permitted to see her father, whom she adores, for 2½ years, during which a long legal battle was being fought to deprive him and her of their rights? Who and what can "adjust" a frail, nervous, restless little girl of 11 years, who is failing in school? She has to spend each weekend with a father who prejudices her against her stepfather, makes her jealous of her little halfsister and derides all the ideals of her very good and normal home with her mother and stepfather.

Mental Illness. Never before has mental illness been such a factor in causing conditions from which children must be protected. No words can portray what life means to the many children who are trying to live and grow up in the care of a feeble-minded or insane parent; subjected to cruelty and abuse, to physical neglect, kept out of school, often developing strange patterns of behavior because of association, living in constant fear of what happens in the most irrational moments of an insane person. Many of these families have long histories of mental illness for several generations. Fathers and relatives often refuse to consider commitment, not knowing what to do with the children. Psychiatric treatment at home presents insuperable difficulties for many of these parents, even examinations for commitment are difficult to carry through.

If it is true, as stated, that before the war "one in every 13 persons has either a sick or defective mind and today one in 10 has; that in the last 60 years sick minds have multiplied twelve times over, three times as fast as our wealth; four and one-half times as fast as our population and four times as fast as our school teachers" and that "it is youth that is cracking up the fastest," is it not perfectly obvious that with all our progress in science we are ignoring the most important fact—that life today is not adjusted to the sanity of human beings?

Child Labor. During the war years we lost many of the gains we had made over a long period of years in the prevention of child labor. It was more or less accepted as necessary, even in the most hazardous occupations. Conditions improved in 1946, but we cannot be complacent when more than 2,500,000 children in America from the ages of 14 through 17 years were still at work—one out of every six being 14 or 15 years of age. The important fact is that they are not receiving an education which seems to be completely forgotten by those who still use the old argument, "It is good for children to work. I worked when I was a boy."

Liquor Problem. From the very beginning of the Juvenile Protective Association, the sale and excessive use of alcohol have presented one of the greatest problems. In 1946, appeals made to us and our own investigations of community conditions challenge us with what has become a national problem, the sale and excessive use of alcohol. Two-thirds of the complaints we received on community conditions were about the illegal sale of liquor to minors in taverns and liquor stores. In a large percentage of our individual cases the excessive use of liquor by parents, especially mothers, and by minor boys and girls, stands out in great significance.

Illegal tavern conditions in Chicago have become so commonplace that they overwhelm all efforts of citizens and interested groups to get any enforcement of our laws. Our local liquor control situation is now so involved in city and state politics and has been mismanaged so long, that adequate control measures and their administration will require drastic changes to bring about any improvement. Our taverns are licensed indiscriminately, except for the endorsement of ward politicians. Many are centers for gambling, prostitution, lewd and obscene entertainment, so often controlled by syndicated interests. They have become social recreation centers in almost every neighborhood. They and the liquor stores violate our laws in selling liquor to minors. The taverns themselves and the alarming increase in excessive drinking are a great factor in broken homes; in the most utter neglect of children, in prostitution, and immorality; in the delinquencies and crimes of minors, even murder; in the increasing number of alcoholics, who appeal to us for the treatment which it is now impossible to offer them.

This problem must be studied in its total aspects. Realizing this, we took the initiative in organizing the Chicago Committee on Alcoholism, with Dr. Anton J. Carlson as Chairman. This group whose membership represents scientists, physicians, psychiatrists, social workers, business men, and religious leaders will not only study further the causes of drinking and promote treatment for alcoholics, but also, we hope, the business practices of the liquor industry and its political power in our law-enforcing departments and our legislatures.

Conclusion

Juvenile delinquency is one of the most popular and publicized subjects today. The most quoted statistics are those of the Federal Bureau of Investigation. Whether there is more or less is not as important, we believe, as the community conditions and influences which affect many more juveniles than are ever recorded in delinquency and crime statistics; business interests which violate protective laws in selling liquor, in initiating children in gambling habits; in selling them toy guns with which they simulate adult criminals in thefts and hold-ups; the alluring news stories and radio programs of crime and criminals which give them patterns for their games and codes for their behavior; the movies from which they get such false values in life and living.

The roots of juvenile delinquency do not "lie (only) in the homes, the schools, the neighborhoods and the churches of our nation," as President Truman said in his recent address to the National Conference for the Prevention and Control of Juvenile Delinquency. They lie in business interests which exploit youth

for profit, and in every city, state, and national law-enforcing department which fails to enforce protective laws. Today, children from good homes, schools, and churches, as well as those deprived of all children most need, are confused by the discrepancies between what they are taught and what they find exist in our city life and government. They have lost respect for integrity and authority.

Our varied services reveal the policies and practices of many public departments. We sincerely believe that it is impossible to take and keep any one of them out of political domination, as the schools or the police. We must have the same policy for all public services if anyone is to be secure and if they are ever to have the efficiency, integrity, and standards that will protect the welfare of those for whom they exist.

After her first few years at Hull House, Jane Addams said she "discovered that one of the great revelations of social work was the extraordinary pliability of human nature and that it is impossible to set any bounds to the moral capabilities which might unfold under ideal home, civic, and educational conditions."

Many parents and children are born into and live under conditions which most of us could never surmount. Some come through with endurance, courage, and fairly adequate lives, but, we must always remember, deprived forever of so much that life could have meant to them. As social workers and as citizens who support social work, we have become more understanding, intelligent, and scientific in response to all the complicated factors in individual lives. Our ultimate goal must be the adjustment of life to human needs.

SELECTED REFERENCES

1. Ellingston, John R., *Protecting Our Children from Criminal Careers* (New York: Prentice-Hall, 1948), Chapter 1: "The Unreality of Crime Control."

This chapter indicates the fact that most crimes go unsolved and most law-breakers are uncaught, particularly the major offenders. In the main, the prisons catch only the unimportant offender, and to a large extent only the young.

2. Teeters, Negley K. and Reinemann, John Otto, *The Challenge of Delinquency* (Prentice-Hall, 1950), Chapter 1: "Delinquency as a National Problem."

This introductory chapter substantiates the thesis that the crime problem is closely associated with children and older youth. The volume and extent of juvenile delinquency are well covered, and an interesting discussion of the delinquent personality is presented.

3. Elliott, Mabel A. and Merrill, Francis E., *Social Disorganization* (New York: Harper & Brothers, 1950), pp. 71–75.

This particular section has an excellent discussion of juvenile delinquency among the children of the foreign-born and the complicated world in which they live.

4. Neumeyer, Martin H., *Juvenile Delinquency in Modern Society* (New York: D. Van Nostrand Co., 1949), Chapter 2: "Extent and Distribution of Juvenile Delinquency."

Here Neumeyer gives the sources and inadequacies of statistical data as related to juvenile delinquency. A full discussion is provided on the relation of race and nativity to the distribution of delinquency as well as on the rural and urban differences that research has disclosed.

3 ECONOMIC CONDITIONS AND FAMILIAL FACTORS

MORE than any other factor influencing delinquency, the economic conditions of the nation and changes in these conditions seem to exert the greatest power. The business cycles react profoundly upon delinquency trends. These economic swings are especially important as they directly affect the economic conditions of families and communities.

Thus it is that juvenile delinquency tends to follow the business cycle—up in prosperity, down in depressions. Less crime is committed by young persons during depression periods in part because families devise "fun" at home. There is less money for outside recreation and more parental supervision, since adults are less likely to work on "grave-yard" and "swing" shifts at the factory. Moreover, there seems to be a greater reluctance on the part of the complainants to press charges against children committing offenses during poor times. Tradespeople, especially, are more lenient in overlooking delinquent acts because they realize that the child who steals food may be hungry. Budget slicing of police personnel also means fewer chances of detection and apprehension of delinquency behavior. Therefore, Carr, writing about the 1930's, states that the reduction of delinquency during a depression may be due to (1) changed attitudes, (2) decreased deviation pressures, and (3) increased out-of-court facilities.[1]

The contributions of poverty cannot be ignored in juvenile delinquency. Many child offenses against private property can be traced to economic causes, but usually causes other than sheer hunger or economic misery. To go through life forced to submit to an apparent substandard level of living is a dim prospect for most youth and sometimes will not be tolerated at any cost. Yet, in 1949, ten million families struggled to live on an income of less than $2000 per year, eight million individuals and families had an income of less than $1000 and five million persons who were able to work could earn no wages whatsoever.[2] Little wonder that delinquency was prevalent.

INFLUENCE OF STREET TRADES AND DOMESTIC SERVICE

One of the romantic stereotypes of life's success myth in the United States is the "little business man" newsboy who, unfortunately (rarely in fact) never becomes a business man. Actually, he runs afoul of the law more frequently

[1] Lowell Juilliard Carr, *Delinquency Control* (New York: Harper & Brothers, 1941), p. 57.
[2] As cited in Negley K. Teeters and John Otto Reinemann, *The Challenge of Delinquency* (New York: Prentice-Hall, 1950), p. 128.

than the nonworking child. It has been said that about 70 per cent of the inmates of Sing Sing prison once sold newspapers.

Street trades include street vendors, errand and delivery boys, as well as newsboys; the domestic service jobs include waitresses and housemaids. In the United States over 250,000 children under sixteen years old are employed in street trades and in domestic service. Domestic service constitutes an occupation of high moral risk for girls, not solely because of unprincipled male employers but also due to the cheaper types of commercialized recreation centers these workers characteristically frequent during their leisure hours. Domestic service has been termed an "occupational slum" since it is neither a profession, trade, nor a business. When working children are compared with nonworking children, from three to ten times as many children employed in the street trades and in domestic service become delinquent each year.

Contrary to public opinion, most children in the street trades tend to come from good homes which appear in the background of 65 per cent of the street venders and bootblacks, 78 per cent of the messenger boys, and 78 per cent of the delivery and errand boys, according to Carr.

INFLUENCE OF HOME AND FAMILY

It is generally recognized that juvenile delinquent behavior is influenced by the physical condition of the dwelling, the slum type of neighborhood, the housing shortage. Mental attitudes are affected by physical surroundings, and the care and love of the parent for the child may be subjected to a severe strain due to conditions of bad housing.

Every culture contains certain norms for home life. In the United States "normal" home life has been said to be characterized by seven fairly definite criteria: (1) structural completeness, (2) racial homogeneity, (3) economic security, (4) cultural conformity, (5) moral conformity, (6) physical and psychological normality, and (7) functional adequacy (emotional security).[3]

It cannot be overemphasized that a child's family is the most important influence in shaping his personality and character. In this profound primary group the child acquires his basic ideals and a sense of right and wrong. Here he first experiences social interaction and becomes conscious of standards, goals, values, and the formulation of judgments. Here he is a member of the cell-unit of society, the first stage upon which he learns to imitate his elders as he begins his awakening into a fuller knowledge of the world about him. Undoubtedly, therefore, the preeminent requisite for the prevention of delinquency is a stable and secure family.

Delinquency and delinquent recidivism are often viewed as a consequence of a defective home life, with accompanying inadequate religious and moral education. Many cases of delinquency are directly attributed to the failure of this primary group, the family, to provide the child with appropriate nondelinquent social roles and to exercise social control over the child, so that these roles are accepted by him.

---

[3] As cited in Carr, p. 110.

The Gluecks in their well-known study *Unraveling Juvenile Delinquency*, observed that delinquents as a group were to a greater measure the victims not only of less stable households but also of broken homes. To a much greater extent than nondelinquents, they had substitute parents—that is, foster or step-parents—or lived with relatives. In the affectional relations between the parents and the boys, the delinquents were much more the victims of the indifference or actual hostility of their fathers and mothers and were, in turn, less devoted to their parents than the nondelinquents. Both the mothers and fathers of the delinquents were less consistent and less kindly in their disciplinary practices. Delinquent children, that is to say, grew up in a family atmosphere not marked by the obedience to legitimate authority.[4]

It is generally recognized that broken homes constitute an underlying cause of juvenile delinquency, but the concept "broken home" does not have an adequate definition or a universal connotation. Broken homes are usually classed as those disrupted by divorce, separation, desertion, or death. The number of broken homes is not known and available statistical data on "broken homes" are by no means reliable. Moreover, a home may be broken by death, divorce, or otherwise, without inducing delinquent behavior. Most of the actual delinquents continue to come from homes that are not "broken" at all. The Wickersham Commission made a study of the parental situation of 40,503 children appearing in ninety-three different courts during 1919. Results of the study showed that 64 per cent of the children lived with both parents and only 36 per cent came from broken homes. Later studies have borne out these findings.

Illegitimacy may also induce deviant behavior, especially when the child is aware of his "fatherless" status. The stigma attached to this situation, rooted in traditional mores and reinforced by many adults in the name of "morality," all too often becomes a part of the child's own deep concerns. And this situation is further aggravated by legal conditions. The term "illegitimate" is stamped on the birth certificates of such babies in Iowa, Minnesota, New Jersey, Ohio, and West Virginia. In Illinois, Montana, and New Mexico the words "father's name unknown" are written on the certificate.

Although the information concerning sibling relationships and numbers of the family is inconclusive, it is known that the delinquent ratio is higher for girls who have only brothers than it is for girls who have only sisters. The order of birth may have some significance; but, contrary to the popular belief, the Gluecks report in the study referred to above, that lone children, first, and last children, are least apt to become delinquent. The inbetween's are more inclined to show danger signs—such as temper tantrums, profanity, obscenity, and, in 33 per cent of the cases, overt acts of delinquency—before they are eight years old. However, unlike the "rotten apple in the barrel," the delinquency of one sibling does not tend to spread to the other brothers and sisters.

The value of family life is so firmly established in our culture that numerous reformatory delinquents frequently attempt to construct some facsimile of it. Large groups of girls divide themselves into extended "families" and assume

[4] Sheldon and Eleanor Glueck, *Unraveling Juvenile Delinquency* (New York: The Commonwealth Fund, 1951), p. 133.

fictitious family names, headed by a "father" or "grandfather." Included in these groups may be both whites and Negroes. This system is sometimes highly organized; for example, in one female reformatory two separate "clans" existed and carried on a family feud akin to the historic feuds of the southern mountaineers. Perhaps these delinquents are seeking, in their own way, a stable family life which they never had.

Not infrequently a delinquent may have modeled himself after some family member who also may be delinquent. Though some children cry out in court, "I would rather die than go home," others have strong attachments to unworthy parents or to depraved relatives and crave to return to their "care." Frazier tells the story of one boy who committed burglary with an uncle. The uncle stole a watch and chain; the boy grabbed a raincoat and shoes. The uncle escaped the police; the boy was apprehended. The boy, however, accepted his punishment and did not betray his uncle.[5]

PUNISHMENT OF THE PARENTS

Because, directly or indirectly, relatives and parents are frequently abettors of juvenile misbehavior, many of the specialists working in the field would punish parents as well as children who are apprehended. Some social workers believe that juvenile delinquency is primarily parental delinquency. They propose that the parents be jailed or fined and forced to attend lectures on how to rear children. In fact, it has become almost a fad to ascribe the children's misbehavior to parental neglect or indifference. Judge Paul W. Alexander of the Domestic Relations and Juvenile Court, Toledo, Ohio, pursued a parent-punishing policy for over ten years. During this time he sentenced ninety-one parents to prison terms totaling over eighty years. From this experience he later concluded, however, that to punish parents accomplishes nothing for the children themselves.

Based on the alleged "growing sociological theory that a child takes the criminal path because his parents, unwittingly or not, have shoved him that way," the courts of Eugene, Oregon, have instituted a program which punishes parents up to $200.00 fine or one hundred days in jail. It is reported that one father had to pay $50.00 because his son caused continual trouble, and a mother was jailed for thirty days and fined $25.00 because her boy was found drinking in the streets. It may well be asked: will the mother, after thirty days in jail, be a better mother? Will her son respect her more and have confidence in her? Does the jail offer training in parenthood? Will the parent-child relationship be improved? Or is not such an attitude toward parents another community rationalization in an effort to wash its hands of its social responsibility? The problem child in court has probably long been the problem child in his home.

FOSTER HOMES

Almost a half century ago, the first White House Conference on Child Care (1908) recommended that every child should have a normal home—or its near-

---

[5] E. Franklin Frazier, *The Negro Family in the United States* (Chicago: University of Chicago Press, 1939), p. 271.

est substitute. Where efforts to preserve the natural home were not successful or seemingly possible, it was urged that children be placed in foster homes in preference to placing them in institutions.

Legally viewed, foster-home care refers to care of a child by adults not related to the child by blood or marriage or by legal adoption. It is a provision for dependent and neglected children, for children awaiting adoption, for those who are physically or mentally handicapped, or children who are delinquent. Although foster-home care has been practiced fairly extensively for many decades, the use of this procedure in the case of juvenile delinquents is of quite recent origin and is relatively restricted.

In the absence of long-tried experience and of conclusive information about foster-home care of delinquents, various opinions are expressed concerning the wisdom and efficacy of this procedure. For example, it has been argued, on the basis of some studies, that foster home prospects should be first offenders only, that is, should not include recidivists, and should be young in years, preferably under ten years. Experience with older children in foster homes, many of whom represent "failures" in the sense that delinquent behavior persists, suggests, at least, that these offenders tend to define the foster home itself as a "punishment" much as they regard assignment to an institution for delinquents. Certainly further investigation is needed in this area, but it must be agreed that a crucial element in correction is always to be found in the offender's own attitudes and sentiments.

READINGS

William W. Wattenberg and James Balistrieri point out in their contribution, "Automobile Theft: A 'Favored-group' Delinquency," that in contrast to young people charged by the Detroit police with misconduct, juveniles involved in automobile theft come in relatively higher proportion from good neighborhoods and favored ethnic groups.

Leontine R. Young in "Delinquency from the Child's Viewpoint" reviews the ramifications of familial relationships, particularly when rejection of a child by his own mother is experienced, with the resulting development of antisocial attitudes.

In the selection "Family Disorganization as a Causal Factor in Delinquency and Crime," Charles W. Coulter suggests that in treating family disorganization, society may be treating a symptom and not a cause of juvenile delinquency. There may be a more fundamental set of causes in our society that have escaped detection. In the meantime, as against the extremists among the modern educational pragmatists, there is the great necessity of strengthening the discipline and training function of the home.

Foster-home placement problems are discussed by Herbert D. Williams in his article, "Foster Homes for Juvenile Delinquents." He reviews the different types of foster-home care and says that, in general, the use of foster homes for children needing care away from their own homes has increased. Starting from the indenture of dependent children and coming down to the problems of the present day, he traces the history of foster homes.

Automobile Theft: A "Favored-group" Delinquency[*]

By William W. Wattenberg and James Balistrieri. Wayne University, Detroit

THE PURPOSE of this paper is to explore certain implications of "white-collar criminality." That concept, based largely on evidence dealing with adults, challenges the adequacy of some generalizations concerning crime and its causation. The point of impact of the concept lies in its assumption that the form of antisocial or illegal conduct rather than its frequency varies from social class to class in our society. If this is so, then there is need to search for factors common to the causation of delinquency or similar misconduct at all social levels rather than to accept without reservation the vast mass of research linking juvenile misconduct with neighborhood situations which in turn reflect the economic status of the adult population.

In general, the ecological findings are that delinquency rates are highest in those sections of a city where, among other things, rentals are low and the occupations are typically unskilled or semiskilled labor. The relative poverty of the population is associated with high transiency rates, substandard housing, and a breakdown of family and other controls. Often youth is also exposed to a conflict of cultures. This constellation of influences is assumed to give rise to a neighborhood subculture of which delinquency patterns are one aspect. This subculture transmits to youth a readiness to embark upon delinquent behavior.

Challenging all this is the contention that crime is culturally defined rather than culturally determined and that it is not the fact of criminality but the form of it which varies with socioeconomic level. Thus, we have burglars and embezzlers, holdup men and black-marketeers, prostitutes and fashionable mistresses. The antisocial conduct of the "lower classes" affronts the middle-class legal norms and so leads to prison terms and criminal records. The antisocial deeds of "respectable" folk are likely to draw much milder treatment. All this casts doubt on many research data by implying that we have not been measuring the extent of crime or of delinquency but only of the varieties we do not like. By such reasoning, no theory of delinquency or criminality can be adequate unless it explains the "white-collar" offenses as well as the more obvious forms of theft and violence. It is assumed that, if this were done, the present emphasis on relationship of socioeconomic variables to crime might have to be discarded.

For the field of juvenile delinquency, the existence of "white-collar" offenses is difficult to establish. We have fairly good figures on assaults, burglary, truancy, and similar offenses. However, the early manifestations of patterns which could develop into bribery, bucket-shop operations, and price-control evasions are not likely to draw police attention. Certainly, statistical evidence would be hard to get. Apparently the best we could do would be to assume that among juveniles there was much hidden misconduct analogous to adult "white-collar" crime.

An alternative would be to search for

* "Automobile Theft: A 'Favored-group' Delinquency," William W. Wattenberg and James Balistrieri, *The American Journal of Sociology*, Vol. LVII, May, 1952, pp. 575–579. Used by permission of authors and publication.

some class of offense which departed from the usual high correlation with socioeconomic or ecological variables. Then, by exploring the similarities and differences between the offenders thus identified and a run-of-the-mill group, we might find more clues as to causal factors common to antisocial character formation in privileged as well as underprivileged groups. To be most helpful, in this respect the offense must be sufficiently common and widespread so that it is not peculiar to a single neighborhood. Also, to avoid argument as to antisocial quality, the offense should be clearly illegal and generally condemned. Otherwise, we would be bogged down in claims and counterclaims as to whether or not the offenders were real delinquents.

Evidence of the existence of such an offense was turned up in connection with another investigation. In a study

age. Again, results were statistically reliable. This is significant because the largest recent foreign immigration to Detroit's transitional areas was from Eastern Europe.

The police explanation of the small proportion of Negroes involved in automobile theft was one of danger and difficulty. Veteran police officials said that colored youngsters were almost sure to be challenged by parking-lot attendants and thus were barred from some opportunity to take cars. Also, it was widely believed that squad-car crews were prone to investigate credentials of Negro young people driving automobiles. However, these explanations, even if accurate, did not account for the nationality differentials among white boys. Therefore, it was decided to dig deeper.

All investigations made by Detroit police of boys aged ten to sixteen in-

TABLE 1.*—RELATIONSHIP BETWEEN AUTOMOBILE THEFT AND RACE OF ALL BOYS INTERVIEWED ON COMPLAINT BY DETROIT POLICE, 1948

| | | Number | | Per Cent | |
Race	Total	Involved in Automobile Theft	All Others	Involved in Automobile Theft	All Others
White	2,774	230	2,544	88.5	70.5
Nonwhite	1,096	30	1,066	11.5	29.5
Total	3,870	260	3,610	100.0	100.0

* $X^2 = 38.29$; $n = 1$; $P < 0.01$.

of the complete police records of 1,170 boys all of whom had passed their seventeenth birthdays it was found that during the period when they had been ten to sixteen years old automobile thefts were proportionately three times as frequent among white boys as among Negroes. (The general ratio of delinquencies was two to one; automobile theft aproached seven to one; results were significant well beyond the 1 per cent level of confidence.) The same offense was proportionately heavier among boys of West European parent-

clusive for 1948 were secured and analyzed. These reports included some fifty items of information obtained by interview with the boys and their parents on such matters as housing, neighborhood conditions, family relationships, peer-group activities, and recreation. In all, data were available for 3,870 boys, of whom 2,774 were white. These records were carefully sorted, and all records involving any form of automobile theft were segregated. There were 260 such records. As shown in Table 1, the previously discovered tendency for automobile theft to be a "white" offense was thoroughly verified.

Significant Factors in Comparisons among White Boys

In order to avoid various possible distorting influences, such as the correlations between race and such variables as housing, employment discriminations and the like, it was decided to confine the remainder of the study to comparisons among white boys only. The 230 involved in automobile theft were compared on every available recorded item of information with the 2,544 charged with other offenses. In all cases the chi-square computation was employed to establish the degree of statistical reliability with which the null hypothesis could be rejected. A total of fifty tables was prepared and tested. Of these, nine proved significant at the 1 per cent level of confidence; five more, at the 5 per cent level. Thus, the number of tables showing statistical significance was more than five times chance expectation. For convenience, the statistically significant factors will be discussed below in terms of the clusters into which they fell.

Socioeconomic level. The automobile-theft group again met the requirements of the category denoted by the title of this article. As compared with the other boys in trouble, they were reliably more likely to come from neighborhoods rated "above average" by the police and ·less likely to come from neighborhoods rated as "slums." This was borne out by the more objective evidence of the ratio between the number of rooms in the dwelling unit and the number of persons occupying the unit. The proportion of boys from dwellings with less than one room per person was significantly smaller than for all other boys contacted by the police. There were other tables of inconclusive reliability which supported this general picture. In these the tendency was for the automobile-theft group to come from racially homo-geneous neighborhoods, to live in single-family homes, to come from homes not showing need of repairs, and to have only one parent employed.

On one socioeconomic item no relationship with automobile theft was found. When police were asked to classify the family income as either "adequate" or "inadequate," both the automobile-theft group and all other boys came from the same percentage of homes classed as having "adequate" income. However, fewer boys involved in automobile thefts had parents both of whom had to work to secure that level of income.

Age. As might be expected, automobile theft was largely confined to the older boys; it was relatively rare below the age of fourteen. Accordingly, a number of items in which chronological age was a factor were significantly related to the offense. These included reliable tendencies for the boys involved in automobile theft to be better developed physically, to have completed sex development, to be in the junior high school grades in school, to have records of previous offenses, to have laboring jobs, and to use some of their earnings to purchase their own clothing.

Peer-group relationships. This group also showed evidence of socializing well with other young people. The statistically reliable tables showed they were less likely to be classed by the investigating officers as social "lone wolves" and were more likely to be members of definite gangs with a reputation of either being rambunctious or engaging in organized theft. Although the statistical reliability was inconclusive, it seemed likely that they also got along well with their classmates in school.

Miscellaneous. There were three statistically reliable tables that do not fit into any of the three clusters described above. When police officers rated the attitude of the boys toward themselves, they were more likely to class it as "responsive." Also, in disposing of the cases, the police were more likely to be stern and either file an official complaint or otherwise refer the case to the juvenile court. This, of course, was an indication of the seriousness of the offense in the eyes of the police, even though they were not required to file delinquency petitions in such cases. The third significant table dealt with the degree of the parents' participation in their sons' recreation; for the automobile-theft group this was more likely to be ranked in the medium level of "occasional," as contrasted to "regular," on the one hand, or "seldom," on the other. Interestingly, this was the only item involving family relationships where statistical significance appeared.

More consequential for the purpose of this article were the similarities between the automobile-theft group and the less privileged other white boys involved in all other offenses. In the list below we give only those items not previously mentioned which failed of significance in the present series of comparisons but were found reliably linked to repeating among all boys interviewed by Detroit police in 1948.

1. Number and sex of siblings
2. Boys' expressed attitude toward home
3. Boys' expressed attitude toward parents
4. Boys' feeling of being "picked on"
5. Boys' appearance
6. Estimated intelligence
7. Hobby and sports interests
8. Membership in organized youth groups
9. Church attendance
10. Attitude toward school
11. Attitude toward teachers
12. School grades
13. Chores around home
14. Method by which parents gave boys money
15. Comparability of boys' recreational equipment with playmates
16. Attitude toward adult neighbors
17. Distance of home from nearest recreational facility
18. Parents' attitude toward boys
19. Parents' attitude toward police
20. Marital status of parents
21. Degree of quarreling between parents
22. Family ownership of a car

In summary then, we get the following general picture of white juveniles involved in automobile theft: they were more likely to come from relatively favored neighborhoods, to be older, and to have good social relationships with their peers. On indexes of family relationships, school adjustment, and religious training they were like a cross-section of all other white boys interviewed on complaint by the Detroit police.

Discussion

To some extent the above findings buttress the implied contentions of the writers on "white-collar" criminality. That is to say, there is here shown to exist at least one type of offense which is relatively less correlated with low socioeconomic level and neighborhood disintegration than the general run of juvenile offenses. This being the case, it is fair to argue that we need to look for formulations of causal influences beyond the customary "bad"-neighborhood factors. We have reason to assume that there may be other varieties of antisocial conduct which would not so swiftly be indicated by police or court statistics and which are sufficiently prevalent in good neighborhoods and among high socioeconomic folk to rule out their being dismissed as exceptions.

Interestingly, in the case of automobile theft, we are dealing with a group that is well socialized as far as primary-group relationships are concerned. These boys are not isolated, peculiar individuals. In the rubrics of the Hewitt and Jenkins study of clinic cases they are neither the quarrelsome, "unsocialized aggressives" nor the pathetically neurotic "overinhibited" children. Rather, they are similar to the "socialized delinquents" in all respects save residence in deteriorated neighborhoods.

There may be a possible systematic explanation in the general picture of this last-mentioned "type." On the basis of a very elaborate statistical analysis, Hewitt and Jenkins described this group as characterized by good ability to relate to people and by a conscience partially formed in the sense that it did not include the prohibitions of the wider society. The value systems of such individuals were quite responsive to the immediately present code of interpersonal relations pertaining to their friends but only weakly responsive to the more abstract rules codified in statutes and ordinances. Thus, if a boy's friends got pleasure from riding in automobiles, he would oblige in carefree fashion by borrowing a car. Similarly, if an adult with a similar value system found he could get along well in business by violating price controls or by bribing public officials, he would be untroubled by compunctions. However, if his immediate associates would react hostilely to such crude or dangerous crimes as burglary or physical assault, he would shun such behavior. Of course, in a "bad" neighborhood where such out-and-out criminality was tolerated, that might enter into his conduct. Much would depend upon the limits prevalent among his associates.

The common element in all this is a rather general type of personality structure. If such is indeed the case, the causes of all varieties of antisocial conduct having this quality are to be found in how that personality structure is formed. Hewitt and Jenkins believe they could trace it to a lax kind of family in which children are not rejected but rather have weak affectional relationships with their parents, who exercise little supervision over them. It is easy to see that such a pattern might be relatively prevalent where parents are bedeviled by a struggle for existence and are bewildered by the culture conflict found in slums. However, with some variation, it also could be found in better neighborhoods where parents are forever "on the go" or even where children are reared by a succession of servants.

Using methods very different from Hewitt and Jenkins, the studies conducted by the Committee on Human Development (Havighurst and Taba) of the University of Chicago in "Prairie City" led to a description of a very similar type of personality. In their reports it is called "the adaptive person." This "type" is described as having high "social intelligence" and as conforming easily to the expectations of whatever group in which it is found. Their case studies led them to believe that the family relationships were the important factor in its development. The relationships in the home were characterized as easygoing and the parents as having "broad and tolerant" moral views and as setting few restrictions on the social activities of the children.

Whether we accept the formulation of Hewitt and Jenkins or that of Havighurst and Taba, the principal point would be that a variety of permissive upbringing produces a personality "type" with little moral courage and a potentiality for engaging in antisocial behavior finding support among associates. Obviously, this is only a hypothesis, to be tested by carefully designed studies. In all probability, as our storehouse of scientifically verified knowledge grows, such a hypothesis would undoubtedly have to be modified. At best it would apply to only one of a number of patterns leading to delinquency and crime. It would hardly cover adequately all types of misconduct, delinquency, crime, and fraud.

It should be pointed out that even the admittedly incomplete hypothesis now being advanced hardly negates the theories built on statistics showing high correlations between delinquency rates and socioeconomic variables. Rather, it would offer an explanation of how some cases contributing to such correlations might arise. The tensions induced by relative poverty, culture conflict, and social pressures might interfere with the parents' supervision over their children or otherwise lead parents to be lax in a fashion which would produce in slum areas a relatively high proportion of young people prone to engage light-heartedly in the theft, violence, and immorality tolerated by the neighborhood's culture.

Summary

In this study 230 white boys charged with automobile theft were compared with 2,544 others in trouble with the Detroit police in 1948. They had good peer-group relationships, came from relatively more favored neighborhoods, but were otherwise similar to juvenile offenders in general. It was suggested that the common factor accounting for one general class of antisocial behavior regardless of socioeconomic factors was a personality structure which readily accepted the values of immediate associates but which responded weakly to the enactments of many of the larger social entities.

Delinquency from the Child's Viewpoint*

By Leontine R. Young. Formerly New York School of Social Work; Professor of Casework, School of Social Administration, The Ohio State University, Columbus.

"THIS business of growing up is terrible. I wish I could go to sleep tonight and not wake up until I'm twenty-one. Then it would be over and I'd be all grown up." The expression was naive, but the feeling behind it was desperately sincere. Jean was fifteen and the court commitment designated her a delinquent. Young as she was she had defied adults and their rules. She had gone her own way, angry and violent, running away from home, spending her nights at dubious clubs and dance halls, stealing now and then, recklessly inviting trouble from strange men who saw in her youth and defiance an invitation and an opportunity for exploitation. When her mother objected, she exploded in rage and screamed that she would do just as she pleased. Then the court stepped in and put a stop to her dangerous activities by sending her away to a small institution, with the vague hope that in some way she might be later returned to the community a more conforming and more responsible person.

What Adults Saw

Her behavior had frightened and disturbed the adults around her, and with good reason. Civilization is built upon law and order and the voluntary participation of people in creating and maintaining that law and order. We recognize the danger in violent defiance of the rules of organized society by our young people. Unfortunately in our alarm we often crack down blindly on these boys and girls, trying by punishments and superior strength to force them into line. Wittingly or not we act upon the old theory that some persons are born good and some are born bad. It is a theory which has the virtue of simplicity if not of validity. We pay dearly for that consoling simplicity, since we cannot teach cooperation with a law-abiding community by resorting to coercion and punishment. In our anxiety to suppress delinquent behavior we overlook the delinquent, the person behind the behavior. In our concern with what he does we

---

* Reprinted from *Focus*, Vol. 30, May, 1951, pp. 69–74. Used by permission.

ignore why he does it, what he is like, how all this looks to him.

The community saw Jean at best as a nuisance, at worst as a menace. Adults who knew her history were aware of course that she had not had an easy life, and they deplored the environment in which she was growing up. An illegitimate child, she had been reared by her aunt, who, she was told, was her mother. She knew her real mother as merely a cousin. Jean's "cousin" was scorned by the family, for she was an alcoholic, a prostitute, a hopeless failure. No one believed that Jean could possibly figure out that the woman in the role of mother was really her aunt and that the woman in the role of cousin was really her mother. To be sure the aunt had more than once said to her in anger, "You're just like your mother"; and relatives had warned Jean that if she did not mend her ways and behave herself she would turn out to be "no good, just like your mother." But the family did not think that these remarks would raise any questions of importance in Jean's mind. She was after all only a child and hence could not be expected to understand.

While the aunt tried to do her duty by Jean, she did not really want the girl. Jean was to her only an added responsibility, another chore in a life that was already overburdened with too much work and too little money. She resented the irresponsibility of Jean's mother and the additional demands of a child not her own upon her time, her strength, and her pocketbook. She took out this resentment on Jean from time to time, letting the child know that she was unwanted. Occasionally the aunt would feel conscience stricken over her rejection of the child, and at such times would indulge her. Such inconsistency did not, of course, make for discipline. As Jean grew older and became more openly defiant, rebellious, and antagonistic, the aunt became increasingly bewildered,

bitter at the child's ingratitude, and frankly anxious to be rid of her. The girl was going to be like her mother, and the aunt felt resentfully that her years of effort and struggle had been wasted. The child had always been difficult; now it was time to see whether the court could scare her into good behavior. It is not hard to understand why the aunt felt as she did and why she wanted to transfer Jean to someone else's authority. The situation was now beyond her control and Jean no longer paid any attention to anything she said.

What the Child Saw

How did all this look to Jean, the delinquent, the incorrigible? Ever since she could remember she had felt there was something wrong about her, something that made her different from the other kids. As a small child she had blundered into low-voiced conversations about her which broke off abruptly when her presence was noted. With the sharp and lucid insight of childhood she had early realized that the family regarded her as a burden, as an unwanted mouth to feed and body to clothe, as someone who did not really belong to them and for whom they had no real need or wish. If it seems strange to adults that a small child should be so sharply aware of this, aware of the things that the grown-ups deny to themselves, it is only because we so rarely listen to children. Like all children Jean had a desperate need to be wanted, to have a secure and definite place of her own, to be nourished and protected, to feel that she belonged to someone. She knew that she was not wanted in any such fashion, despite her aunt's sporadic efforts to appease her. Like all people she found little comfort in being an obligation. What she did not and could not know was why she was not wanted just for herself. And like every child she could find only one explanation—there must be something mysteriously, innately wrong with her.

Sometimes it is hard for adults to realize that a child may concern himself with such a question or arrive at such a conclusion. Actually the unwanted child will say this directly to the person he can trust. As Jean put it: "I decided I was just so bad nobody could love me."

Jean's fear and insecurity were strengthened as she came to realize that her aunt was not her mother, as she learned who her mother really was and recognized the attitude of the family toward her mother. As a young child she had heard the angry conversations about her "cousin," had observed the attitudes of the family, had watched her real mother visiting in the home. Under the circumstances it was not too difficult for her to arrive at the truth; but what she did not understand was the aura of mystery and shame that colored all conversations about her birth. Why didn't her mother claim her? Why did the family act as if she had from the beginning been a mistake? What was wrong with her mother and with her? To all of these questions she had no answer; only the fact of shame and concealed disgrace was definite. Once she confronted her aunt directly with a demand for the truth, but her aunt insisted that Jean was her own child. This lie did not convince the child; on the contrary, it added to her confusion and deepened her certainty that there was something wrong with her.

By the time she was adolescent Jean saw the world as a hostile camp. She did not understand adult rules but she was sure that their purpose was to restrict and punish her. She had no trust in adults; she viewed them as enemies who deceived her, secretly hated her, and sought to restrain her to certain ways designed to make her unhappy. This restraint, unpleasant as it was, seemed logical and natural to her. How else, she reasoned, can people deal with some one innately and hopelessly bad? Never having been treated with respect she had

little or no respect for herself. Regarding herself as already condemned she did not question the verdict; indeed, she secretly joined the adults in hating herself. In short, she agreed with her family that she was no good. But she was a fighter and she fought back against all adults, trying to take from them what she wanted, trying to make them pay for her unhappiness.

Why should anyone want to conform to the standards of a society which has already declared him an outcast? To the child, society and family are the same thing. Like so many delinquents Jean did not question the wisdom of adults, but she hated them because they had condemned her to self-hatred. Why then should she obey them or try to please them? She might with great effort win their approval of her behavior; she could not win their approval of her as a person. Jean fought in the dark, and her punches were wild. From the outside she was cocky, defiant, tough, indifferent to what anyone thought, determined only to have her own way. From the inside she was frightened, afraid both of what she was doing and of what might happen to her, confused, angry, and still wishing someone could like her, could care what happened to her. It makes a great difference which side of the window you're looking through.

What the Child Learned

To help a girl like Jean, we must know her not only as others see her but also as she sees herself. If we label her bad, punish her for her rebellion, we only confirm her delusions. For the truth is she is no more innately, constitutionally bad than any other human being. What she needed was someone she could trust and love, someone who cared about her as a human being and not just as an instigator of delinquent behavior, someone who was concerned with her happiness as well as her morals. When Jean was sent away to an institution, she found such a person. It wasn't easy because she went prepared to hate everybody and everything. Labeled a delinquent, she figured she was really finished and might as well make it as tough for everybody else as she could. She fought against kindness, respect, and consideration. Above all, she fought against love because love really upset her whole system of life. People don't find it easy to change the basic premise by which they live, even when that change promises the happiness they've always wanted. They're suspicious; they've been hurt before; they look constantly for the catch. As Jean remarked frankly, "What do you people get out of this? I can't figure your stake in it."

In the institution to which she had been sent, Jean met, for the first time in her life, strength that was concerned with protecting her, not punishing; that set limits and held to them no matter how she rebelled and yet respected her always as an individual with rights as well as responsibilities. This was authority as a friend, not an enemy. Wary of any such alien idea she tested it out thoroughly, finally smashing all the glass in the kitchen windows in one explosive display of temper. The staff refused to regard her as a menace, let her cool off, and held firmly to the demand which had precipitated the explosion. She had to pay for the damage bit by bit out of her allowance, not as punishment but simply, it was explained, because one can't smash up things in an orderly society without making restitution. After that, Jean began voluntarily to give up some of her destructive behavior to please an adult she cared for. For the first time in her life she had found someone she admired and wanted to be like. For the first time in her life she was ashamed of her outbursts of temper. That was when she said, with fifteen years of emotional confusion behind her, "This business of growing up is terrible."

Growing up is not easy for anyone; for children who have been hurt, who have to change their fundamental attitude toward themselves as well as toward other people, it is truly a gigantic task. To face yourself is one of the most difficult tasks in the world. Jean had to learn to respect and like herself; to see other people as potential friends rather than as natural enemies; to realize that external authority can be supplanted only by self-discipline; to understand that freedom is always the Siamese twin of responsibility, self-assumed and self-maintained; to know that blind rebellion is only a worse form of bondage. She had not only to give up her old way of life to please the person she loved but ultimately to accept that person's standards of behavior and make them her own. She had to be convinced that these standards were right and desirable for herself. It is no reflection on Jean to observe that she did not achieve complete realization of these goals. How many people do? But she is living a useful and self-respecting life and no court has seen her since.

The Problem

Each delinquent is trapped in his painful and dangerous conflict with authority. Because he has not been loved for himself, he loves no one. Because he has not been respected as an individual, he respects neither himself nor anyone else. Like the nondelinquent child, he forms an opinion of himself that is a reflection of his family's attitude toward him. When adults use their superior strength, not to guide a child to maturity but to break his will and spirit, the child has only this alternative—to submit and be crushed, or to fight blindly, bitterly and destructively. (In either case he proceeds from a premise of hate.) Ordinarily the delinquent chooses the latter course and comes to regard society as his natural enemy. To him authority is always depriving, punishing, hostile. He regards adults as policemen whose chief function is to take all the fun out of his life and force him to do what he does not want to do. Nevertheless he does not question the fundamental rightness of that authority. He assumes that his behavior is wrong; but since no one really cares about him or his happiness, he sees no reason why he should be especially concerned about the consequences of his behavior. He snatches at whatever pleasures come his way and feels little sense of responsibility for his actions. The concept of authority as a protective force that will relinquish control gradually along with growth in the child's personal responsibility is a concept totally alien to his experience and knowledge. It is a concept only dimly realized if at all by great numbers of adults whose own childhood experiences have blocked its normal fruition into emotional maturity.

For the delinquent child so violently in rebellion against authority a whole process of reeducation is necessary; and the child will submit to that process only for the sake of someone he loves and trusts. If he has been hurt badly, he may be unable to trust any one completely. Hate closes in but love opens out. He realizes that to show love for anyone places him in a vulnerable position, for it exposes him to the risk of being hurt again. To make that decision once he has been deeply hurt requires great trust and great courage on his part. The amazing thing is that so many of our deprived, unhappy children are still able to make that decision; the sad thing is that we give them so few opportunities to make it.

Consider this boy, for example. John, born out of wedlock, was deserted in infancy by his confused, immature mother. He spent the first years of his life in a large institution where he was fed, clothed and sheltered—but not loved. Literally no one cared whether as an individual he lived or died. As a statistic he was white, male, thirteen months and three days old—what has that to do with John, the little boy that lies in a crib and stares at the ceiling? Then he was moved to a foster home, but the foster mother became sick and John had to be moved elsewhere. By the time he was seven he was living in his eleventh foster home where, as in his other homes, his foster mother said that if he was good and behaved himself she would keep him. (She might just as well have said that she did not love him. The parent who says to the child "I will love you as long as you please me" does not love the child and thinks only of his own inflated egotism.) By the time he was fourteen John was a truant. He lied, he fought, he stole. A lonely little outcast, he lived in the world like a lost soul from another planet and with all the strength left to him he struck back at a society which had made no place for him. He rarely smiled or laughed, and only with small children did he occasionally relax and joke. Sometimes John seemed to like another person, but when that person left him, he didn't seem to care. To a doctor he came to know and have some trust in, he talked a little of how he had been "pushed around" from one home to another, how he had known that no one really wanted him, how hopeless he had felt because he belonged to no one. He admitted that he was not trying to help himself but explained angrily that no one had ever tried to help him. A short time after this talk, the doctor left the community to take another job. Deprived of the only person who had ever lent a sympathetic ear, John joined in a gang robbery, was caught, and was committed to a correctional institution.

John needs more than correction now. How are we to give him back his stolen childhood? How are we to teach him to smile, to know that life is not a prison, that all people are not his enemies? How are we to teach him now not to steal, not to hurt, not to destroy, when all he has known has been hurt and rejection? Can we ask John now to trust and love another human being? Can we expect him now to begin the task of becoming a part of a world he has never known? Can we require from him an almost superhuman effort? For most boys and girls whose experiences are similar to John's, these are demands that cannot be met. Therefore we shut them away from society because, by that time, they are a menace and we have no other choice. But we robbed them before they robbed us; we destroyed them before they sought to destroy us. The guilt lies upon all our souls.

We often see only the trouble a child makes; we fail to see his unhappiness. Defiance, recklessness and destructiveness we can observe in almost any small child who is frustrated and angered. With the little child we smile because we know his emotion is transitory and because his capacity to destroy is so puny in comparison to the violence of his feelings. The child deprived of love, security and adult direction has no chance however to overcome that violent hostility, no incentive to give it up for the greater satisfaction of approval and encouragement from those he loves. His power to hurt and destroy grows with the years, but there is no accompanying transmutation and sublimation of violent, primitive emotions, no concomitant capacity for self-control. We do not smile when the adolescent and the adult indulge those same emotions for now they have become dangerous. They are out of the individual's control, as they are with the little child. This adult may have grown physically and even mentally, but because he has remained emotionally an infant and an unhappy one, he has only expanded his capacity to hurt and damage. He still views everything and everybody from the standpoint of the small child but without the small child's healthy resiliency, his capacity for spontaneous, unques-

tioning love and faith and happiness.

With varying degrees of clarity the delinquent child senses that he has been cheated out of normal development; he realizes that he is too old to be out of control. The adolescent is particularly aware of this condition, an awareness which he loses unless someone helps him to check the sad and warped development of his personality structure. He realizes it often so much better than we do.

One bright girl of thirteen, a chronic runaway and truant, remarked astutely, "People always act as if I ran away just because I wanted to, as if I sat down and figured it was a good idea. That doesn't make any sense. I know when I run away that the police will pick me up in a couple of days and I'll be punished for it. I never really have a good time while I'm free. I'm always worried and afraid. I don't know why I go or what I'm going to do—all I know is that I have to go. I'd be a fool to do that on purpose, and I'm too smart to get myself in that kind of jam if I could stop it." Each of her escape attempts was a running away from something she could not tolerate—a mother who had hated her and beat her into insensibility, a mother who had warped her child's character until the girl feared and fled from every mother person. She was intelligent enough to know how each blind venture would turn out, but like the small child she could not control herself.

And then there was Marie, brilliant and dynamic, who had run around night after night with any man who came along, throwing herself away because she hated herself and everyone else. Breaking through her hostile shell she cried bitterly: "I hated you for locking me up, but you can't know how relieved I am at night to know that the door is locked and I can't get out. You knew I couldn't stop myself and I was terrified of what I might do, of what might happen to me. . . . In sixteen years I have never loved anyone, not anyone. Can you imagine how terrible that is, how lonely I've been?"

Conclusion

There is a time when for a little while at least our unhappy adolescents know that their only chance for self-control, for happiness in the future, depends upon the strength and understanding of an adult who can give to them some of the security, the love, and the guidance for lack of which they have remained emotionally stunted. They can grow up, hard as it is, if they still have the capacity to love and trust, and if they have someone who can transmute that capacity to

actuality. For the adult the relationship requires strength, understanding, infinite patience and the salty spice of humor. Most of all it requires real liking for the child, an honest investment of emotion with no guarantee of return. It means being, for a confused, miserable, angry child, a parent person who may help him to grow toward maturity, who may yet undo some of the harm already done, and give the love and the strength that have not been given/ It remains true and always will that the best cure for delinquency is prevention. But between now and Utopia we have only the faith and the hope that what hate and fear have done, love and confidence can undo./

Family Disorganization as a Causal Factor in Delinquency and Crime*

By Charles W. Coulter. Formerly, Department of Sociology, University of New Hampshire; Professor of Sociology, University of Rochester.

DELINQUENCY and crime have as many causes as any other type of human behavior. To catalogue such causes would be difficult and to list them in the order of their importance impossible. As the disorganized family stands well up toward the top of such a list we may be justified in re-examining its significance. By a disorganized family I mean one that is so disturbed that it does not function normally and smoothly. The disturbance may reach the proportions of dissolution by reason of death, illness, imprisonment, desertion, separation, divorce, war, or other associated causes. Or what is more significant, the family may remain intact and still be disorganized because of economic conditions, environmental pressures, occupational requirements, incompatibilities, irritations, unvocalized tensions, frustrations, and other psy-

chological conditions, habits such as drunkenness, vices—overt or concealed—and a host of other familiar causes.

I do *not* mean a family which experiences many or all of these processes in a minor degree. Outside death and divorce, all families do. Organization, disorganization, and reorganization are taking place in every family all the time. In proper combination they are normal, inevitable, and beneficent processes and are essential to health, growth, and progress.

A healthy family like a healthy body is a family which has what my associates in biological chemistry call metabolism; i.e., a favorable balance between the organizing process of anabolism and the disorganizing process of catabolism. Ill health follows the loss of balance as surely as night follows day. So the dis-

* Reprinted from *Federal Probation*, Vol. XII, September, 1948, pp. 13–17. Used by permission of author and publication.

organized family is one which is disturbed to the point where it does not function in a normal way. The point of dangerous imbalance varies between families and from the social viewpoint is somewhat arbitrary.

Delinquency Defined

For a definition of delinquency I presume I shall have to follow Burt and say: any act committed by a juvenile which is or may be legally punished. I do not like the term delinquency and I certainly do not like Burt's definition. Running a car over 45 miles an hour anywhere in my state is a delinquency, but I sometimes run over 45. Traffic on the open highway in my state normally moves at a 45–55 mile rate. When my grandson runs his bicycle on a stretch of sidewalk in Durham he becomes delinquent. But he does it. When my 8-year-old granddaughter lighted the firecracker she had bootlegged from Washington when she came to visit us and hoarded so that she could adequately celebrate the glorious Fourth she was delinquent but I did not stop her. What I am trying to say is that the term is vague and the definition is stuffy and cockeyed. Yet when I use the term delinquency you well know that I mean any extreme and dangerous antisocial variation in child behavior. Just that.

Such extreme or dangerous behavior is traceable to no single cause. There is behind it in the background always a *constellation* of causal factors. They may be as multitudinous as the stars in the Milky Way, as fugitive and intangible as the foot of the rainbow, but they are nonetheless real. To take one factor out of the blurred pattern of causes and examine it minutely is scientifically permissible so long as we keep clearly in mind that the particular factor we are dealing with is a functional part of the composite pattern.

Before estimating the effect of the disorganized family on the rate of delinquency, might I suggest that both the disorganization of the home and delinquency, which have increased at substantially the same rate during the past half century, may be symptomatic of a more fundamental set of causes in our society and that in dealing with them we may be treating the symptoms in both cases and not the causes at all.

I know that the delinquency rate has doubled since 1926, in spite of everything specialists in delinquent behavior have been able to do about it, and this is no criticism of the way they have done their job. I know that our divorce rate is now the highest in our history on the basis of any statistical measurement used for comparison, in spite of everything we sociologists have been able to do about it, and we don't consider that a criticism of ourselves. In 1946 there was one divorce for every 2½ marriages performed. In the City of Chattanooga (180,000 inhabitants) there were 3½ divorces to every marriage solemnized in 1946. Neither we crime specialists nor we sociologists need harbor any illusion that our jobs are going to be reduced or disappear. Properly understood, this situation and the prospect should not disturb us. The worst thing about it is the growing social hysteria that accompanies it. It is screamed from the pulpit and platform. It is emblazoned by the press. It is tilted at by the Jeanne d'Arcs in women's federations and by the St. Georges in men's service clubs but the rate steadily climbs. Few see it and deal with it sanely as the functional accompaniment of a more fundamental social disorganization. Many even condone the situation of which it is symptomatic.

Always in a transitional era, an era of industrial and political change, an era of war and threat of war, there is social imbalance. During the period of the English Commonwealth under Cromwell in 1652–1660 there was not an ecclesiastical marriage in England. The almshouses were full of neglected children and the prisons overflowed as never before or since in English history. It was estimated that one man in three was a criminal which is not surprising when we remember that stealing a sheep was a capital offense. The industrial and political system was shaken from top to bottom by the English revolution and the situation was aggravated by popular hysteria. No more lugubrious literature has come out of England than during that period. Yet England came through and for 200 years has been one of the most stable, prosperous, cultural, and law-abiding nations in the world.

Dr. Sorokin of Harvard recently characterized ours as the bloodiest century in the last 2,500 years. He insists that despite our protestations of peace we will be wading through blood, sweat, and tears for several decades to come. Yet the last 50 years have witnessed more scientific and industrial progress than took place in the previous 8,000 years of human history.

The physical, mental, and social sciences have made more progress than in any other similar period of history. We are in the midst of an era of upheaval, turmoil, and transition which are the concomitants of progress.

The social situation is more poignant and critical in America today than elsewhere in the world partly because this country is the focus of technological change and partly because of our popular but somewhat spurious idea of the meaning of freedom in a democracy. Law, order, and tolerance are the creed and ideal of our society from top to bottom. Success and personal freedom however are also a part of that creed. The infraction of law is easily rationalized when it interferes, or seems to interfere, with individual freedom or the achievement of success.

Sharp business practices and sharper labor tactics which are essentially rackets stalk unchallenged through the land.

Political graft, exploitation, adventitious group pressures, and surreptitious sex immorality—all technically illegal—are condoned or treated with a shrug of the shoulder meant to imply "It is none of my business," or "there is nothing I can do about it." With adult delinquency so rampant and flagrant, it is not strange or illogical that the child should rationalize his antisocial conduct and that we should have a wave of delinquent behavior.

Disorganized Homes and Delinquency

Now to get back to our specific topic —the causal relation of disorganized family life to delinquency.

There is some confusion in popular thinking about the contribution of broken homes to delinquency. Technically broken homes are those in which there has been death, divorce, separation, or desertion of one of the parents. Such homes are physically disorganized, not necessarily socially so. They popularly are thought to furnish a disproportionate number of delinquents. Statistically they do not. The range is roughly from 30 to 45 per cent.

As early as 1918 E. H. Shideler estimated that approximately 25 per cent of all American children came from broken homes. If less than 50 per cent of delinquents come from such homes the ratio of broken homes among delinquents and the general child population of the country could not be above 2 to 1.

Shaw and McKay, in their later and more intensive study of delinquency in Chicago, found the ratio 1.18 to 1 for boys and 1.49 to 1 for girls which shows the greater effect of the broken home on the deterioration of the girl than on the boy.

But N. D. M. Hirsh concludes that "the proportion of siblings who are delinquent in cases from broken homes is about the same as the proportion in cases from unbroken homes." And Marian Cambell finds that "neither school achievement nor conduct is affected appreciably by a break in the home after the immediate stress has passed."

The best evidence which I could multiply indefinitely, points to the conclusion that broken homes are not nearly so serious as a causal factor in producing delinquents as disorganized homes. It is not physical absence of the father or even the mother but a faulty human relationship which causes the child to go astray.

Homes from which Delinquents Come

The homes from which delinquents come are usually classified into five categories although not necessarily in this order:

(1) Homes with criminal patterns.

(2) Homes in which there are unsatisfactory personal relations because of domination, favoritism, nonsolicitude, overseverity, neglect, jealousy, a stepparent, or other interfering relative.

(3) Homes in which one parent has a physical or mental disability—invalidism, feeble-mindedness, blindness, deafness, psychoneurosis.

(4) Homes socially or morally maladjusted because of differences in race, religion, conventions, and standards, or an immoral situation.

(5) Homes under economic pressures —unemployment, low income, homes in which mothers work out.

It is my contention that families in such homes are measurably socially disorganized. They are the danger spots so far as delinquency is concerned, and our attention should be centered on such families not with the hope of completely eliminating the conditions but with the purpose of safeguarding the children brought up amid these hazards.

Homes with Criminal Patterns. Let us look at these types of disorganization briefly with a view to finding out what can be done to ease such home conditions. I have placed first, *homes with criminal patterns.* In Burt's classical study of vice and crime in England he found

five times as many delinquents from homes in which crime was present as in noncriminally-patterned homes. The Gluecks found that 84.8 per cent of the reformatory population of Massachusetts came from homes with other criminal members, and 86.7 per cent of all juvenile delinquents studied came from such homes. The New York Crime Commission in its study of truancy found that 83 per cent of those later charged with felonies had come from homes with criminal records. So a family's familiarity with crime is highly important in its influence on the aberrant conduct of the children. Crime breeds crime. Criminal homes breed criminals.

We are discovering more and more the significance of the somewhat intangible family attitudes and patterns of behavior in subtly conditioning the thinking and conduct of the child. If we would deal effectively with delinquency we must begin by purifying the polluted stream at its source.

Or to make my suggestion concrete, I would place under probationary supervision every home with a criminal pattern in which there are children. Probation has the organization. It has an increasingly complete coverage of all areas. It possesses the necessary techniques for doing that job. It sounds drastic and expensive but it would be financially justifiable in the long run and act not only as a safeguard but as a deterrent as well. It would bring home to people, who seem to overlook it, the fact that there is no individual delinquent. He is a part of a pattern and that pattern is subject to modification if the method is sufficiently drastic.

Homes with Unsatisfactory Personal Relations. The second type is that in which there are unsatisfactory personal relations—domination, severity, favoritism, jealousy, neglect, etc.

The child has the same wishes as the adult. He wants security, response, recognition, and new experience or some fun out of life. These are normal human socializing urges. Properly aligned and satisfied they make the world go around. They are part of the race's heritage. Where the satisfaction of these fundamental needs is denied him at home the child becomes frustrated, unhappy, feels he does not quite belong.

But no fundamental wish can be entirely blocked. It must find satisfaction some way; if not directly then obliquely. What is more natural for the unsatisfied child than to seek a situation or create it, socially or antisocially, in which he can maintain a favorable balance between the drive within and the satisfaction from without. Truancy is his protest against unhappiness. It betokens inadequacy or lack of understanding on the part of his teachers. In the gang he gets the recognition he fails to find at home or in the school. When the gang pattern includes pilfering and the willful destruction of property his proficiency in these acts is an achievement which brings him the recognition and personal satisfaction he fails to realize through socially approved channels. His behavior under these circumstances is just as normal as going to Sunday School. The process is the same in the home of the rich and the home of the poor. It is not a matter of economics but of social psychology. The consciousness of being loved, appreciated, secure, recognized as part of the expanded personality of the parent is more significant in the safeguard of the child than advantages in the economic field.

Only as the value of congenial home relations is re-emphasized, only as parents are made aware of the significance of the personal relations within the home can we hope for improvement of the delinquency situation in our society.

Or again to make my suggestion concrete, I would have discussion centers set up for parents in every city and hamlet in every state of the Union, looking to the building up of more wholesome family relations. I see it as an adult educational venture with the physician, psychiatrist, clergyman, social worker, nurse, probation officer, and socially-minded citizen participating.

A start has already been made in this direction in a number of states through the organization of community and district councils on delinquency. In New Hampshire, in June of 1947, for the first time under the auspices of the State Society for Social Hygiene such a clinical council held an institute for parents on methods of building up wholesome family relations. It is not the unique function of the organization to do this job but its board, under the chairmanship of a judge and with the membership of two doctors, a lawyer, a priest, a psychiatrist, a sociologist, and two members of the state legislature, felt that the job was so fundamentally important to the organization's function that it had to be done.

Expensive, you say. Initially, yes; in the long view, no. If an attack on parental ignorance and indifference is the answer to our problem of better living, some of the time and effort of these specialists is not too valuable to be earmarked for this purpose. Incidentally, the magistrate, the judge, and the probation officer would have an excellent reference clinic for the parents of recalcitrant children clearing the courts.

Homes in which Parent Has a Disability. The third type is that tragic home in which one parent or the other is blind, deaf, invalid, or suffering from some mental disorder. Here the home *is* disorganized. Outside of institutionalization, which it is desirable to avoid as far as possible, there is not much which can be done about it. Formally, the home has all the appearance of organization without its disciplinary and supervisory substance. The parents frequently are unaware, or only vaguely aware, of their inadequacy. There may be no lack of affection in the home, yet the children feel ashamed and apologetic, think of their homes as a necessary convenience and to the extent of their normal effervescence run wild. These are the sad facts recognized by every specialist in the field.

The busy medical practitioner, the busier district nurse, and the home teacher for the blind have on occasion looked in on such families and given service and counsel. Such service, however, is specialized and sporadic and touches only the fringes of the human problem.

This is a situation in which I could wish for the resurrection of the long extinct "friendly visitor" as she was called. In the earlier days of social work these public-minded lay people under the general direction of the welfare worker undertook the intimate supervision of such problem homes. They were in constant contact and provided friendly counsel and help. They were eyes to the blind, ears to the deaf, solace to the invalid, and an intelligent safeguard to the mentally disturbed. The overprofessionalized social worker has lost an effective ally and a valuable community champion as she has crowded the friendly visitor out of the picture. For this is precisely the type of home in which the friendly visitor is sorely needed. The service is unofficial, informal, unobtrusive, intimate, and friendly. It is the essence of social service.

Morally Maladjusted Homes. The fourth type is the morally maladjusted home due to differences in race, in religion, in standards, or to the presence of an immoral situation; in other words, a home of quarrelsomeness or immorality. It is not the fact that the parents are of different races, have different religions, conventions, or even moral standards that affects the child deleteriously, but rather that bickerings, irritations, suspicions, jealousies, and factions within the family are occasioned by the differences. Disunity replaces harmony. Instead of a refuge of protec-

tion, a haven of safety, the home becomes a place of tension, due to the child's apprehension of what may or may not happen. From such a home, as from the presence of veiled immorality (never entirely shielded from his shrewd young eyes), the child wants to get away as often and as long as possible. Such a home affords a dubious security for his budding spirit and drives him along the line of least resistance into the delinquent gang for the camaraderie a maturing personality demands. Here again I know of no panacea. Even the provision of adequate community recreational facilities and services is a poor substitute for a happy home. Such recreational services are being enlarged and perfected. That is part of our social trend. But they will have to be supplemented by parental training in the methods and techniques of building up wholesome family life, perhaps by such a community effort as I have already indicated, if we are to have any assurance of improvement in the delinquency situation which now threatens every community.

Homes under Economic Pressure. The fifth type of home is that under economic pressure. I have placed the economically maladjusted home last on the list of contributors. In many cases it is not, and in no case should it be, a contributor at all. Many of the most exemplary children come from the poorest homes. It is improbable that poverty is ever a direct cause of delinquency. Temporary financial reverses, temporary unemployment seem to have no statistically demonstrable effect—good or bad. Only where both parents work out and the child is left unsupervised, especially at night, does the delinquency pattern develop. Permanent unemployment or unemployability which determines the authority of the father and provokes filial disrespect is undoubtedly a contributor.

The recent rise in wage scales, the noticeable falling off of employment of married women in industry and the present planning to safeguard our economy against boom and depression, these together with social security, state medicine, A.D.C. and other recent public assistance programs, hold out for us the real promise of the complete removal of the economically maladjusted home from the category of contributors to our problem. If for no other reasons than this, in spite of the inordinate cost and the bungling, we are justified in encouraging the extension of these social safeguards.

Conclusion

In closing, may I re-emphasize one point which is implicit in every factor in our breakdown of the disorganized family as a cause of delinquency and crime. That is the necessity of strengthening by every means at our disposal the discipline and training function of the home. This is the crux of our problem.

Going back to Burt's study in England, defective discipline was present 6.9 times as frequently in the homes of delinquents as in those of nondelinquents. It was four times as important as poverty. The Gluecks found "unsound disciplinary methods" in the homes of 70 per cent of all delinquent children they studied.

The American home, so far as it fails, does so not through design or malignance, but through neglect, ignorance, and unwillingness to take the responsibility for directing its children. In a few cases is the discipline vicious or criminal. In most cases it is inadequate and inconsistent. Our problem of delinquency is basically a problem of educating, directing, training, advising with and safeguarding parents, and of impressing upon them their continued responsibility. Give us better, more informed and responsible parents and we will guarantee a reduction of the problem of delinquency and crime.

Foster Homes for Juvenile Delinquents[*]

By Herbert D. Williams. Director, Juvenile Welfare Board, Pinellas County, St. Petersburg, Florida.

CAN foster family homes be used for the rehabilitation of juvenile delinquents? If so, what kinds of homes are needed and where and how can they be found? What safeguards must be used to insure that efforts in this direction are successful? What experience have we to go on in the use of such homes? Which juvenile delinquents can be placed in foster homes? What kind of supervision is necessary for such placement? These are just a few of the questions which occur to anyone who is contemplating the use of foster homes for juvenile delinquents.

There has been an increasing accept-

ance of the importance of home life in social adjustment. Perhaps never before have the values of family life as determinants of the economic, social, civic, and other adjustments of adults been so generally recognized as now. At the same time there has been more understanding of the strengths and weaknesses of institutions and other forms of group care for juveniles. Better understanding of the personalities of delinquents as a result of the development of mental hygiene clinics, together with some research on the results of placement of children under various auspices also have helped to

* Reprinted from Federal Probation, Vol. XIII, September, 1949, pp. 46–51. Used by permission of author and publication.

improve treatment methods of all kinds —the use of foster homes is one of these.

There are different types of foster home care: the adoption home, the boarding home, the wage home, the free or work home. In its early beginning foster home care was limited almost exclusively to the adoption home, the wage home, the free or work home. In general, there has been an increasing use of foster homes for children needing care away from their own homes. This has been particularly evident in the case of dependent and neglected children. In New York State, for example, only 31 per cent of all children in foster care in 1911 were to be found in foster family homes, and only 8 per cent were in boarding homes. In 1942, 58 per cent were being cared for in foster family homes and 49 per cent were in boarding homes.

More recently the trend, as indicated above, has been in the direction of foster family boarding homes. For delinquents this is the most satisfactory type of home. The treatment and reclamation of the delinquent places an emphasis upon service under close supervision and requires more time and effort than is the case with less serious problems.

History of Foster Family Care

As Henry W. Thurston points out, foster home care resulted from the breakdown of the feudal system in England. The first step in the process was the indenture of dependent children, based in part on the previous apprentice system. It had for its purpose making some person or family responsible for the care of a destitute child. The only difference between indenture for the dependent child and the method used for giving industrial training was that in the case of the dependent child some advance was made to the master until the child was able to work.

The first organized efforts to use foster family homes for the care of children was limited largely to the care of destitute, abandoned, and dependent children. About the middle of the nineteenth century there was developed in the United States an ambitious program of placing children in homes in the Middle West. Children were sent out in large groups and were selected by families upon arrival at designated points. This was in the form of informal indenture. The adults to whom the child was given agreed, in most instances, to send the child to school, feed him, clothe him, and give him training.

Undoubtedly, some of the children placed through this method were what would now be called delinquent children, but most of them would be classified as destitute children who had no relatives, or whose relatives could not provide for them in their own homes.

The most ambitious effort in the direction of placing children in free family homes or work homes was that of the Children's Aid Society of New York. From 1853 to 1879 this society placed out some 48,000 children in western and southern states. These placements were completely informal and were subject to abuses. These became known and ultimately brought about many improvements in child placing. Among these were more careful investigation of the prospective home, employment of staff to visit the home and children, and the development of standards of record keeping.

It was 1866 before there was any suggestion that some children needed to be placed with families to whom board should be paid. This suggestion was made about the same time by the Massachusetts State Board of Charities and by the Boston Children's Aid Society. This society began to use boarding homes for children appearing in the courts charged with crime. From this early beginning Massachusetts has continued to use foster care in families to a great extent. In those states which used institutions for the care of dependent and neglected children the movement toward the use of foster families for problem and delinquent children was retarded.

The beginning of the twentieth century was marked by a tremendous upsurge in the manifested interest in children. The juvenile court movement began in 1899. This was followed by the establishment of Big Brother, Big Sister, Boy Scout, and other organizations interested in juveniles. Public opinion had been outraged by reports of abuses of children and demanded that something be done for their protection, and the prevention of delinquency. There also was a growing skepticism regarding the value of institutional care for neglected children. The relative merits of home care and institutional care were being debated. This had happened before, in the last half of the nineteenth century, and a mighty effort to remove the children from the mixed almshouses had resulted in the establishment of orphan asylums in this country. The results of placing children in these had been discouraging and again attempts were being made to discover more selective methods of treatment for different children. An appreciation of the need for "suiting the action to the needs of each child" which had been expressed by Birtwell of the Boston Children's Aid Society in 1888, and accumulated experience indicated that a variety of resources would be required if the individual needs of the child were to be met.

Prior to 1900 the main reliance had been on institutional care for the juvenile offender who required care away from home. However, with the development of the juvenile court there was an increasing emphasis upon removing the stigma of crime from juvenile delinquents. Children were to be treated differently from adults. They were to be retrained. The state assumed the role of parent for this retraining. Every effort was to be made to keep the delinquent

child from the adult criminal. This led to the establishment of juvenile detention homes and separate court building or courts for the juveniles.

Use of Homes for Detention

The detention homes were at first mostly juvenile jails or wings of existing jails. They still are in many places. There has been an increasing concern about confining children in the same buildings with adult criminals, but, while in many states it is against the law, children still are confined in common jails. Detention homes, where they exist, are still for the most part unsatisfactory, both as to plant and as to program. The opportunities for contagion, emotional upset, and the difficulties of developing any program for a large heterogeneous group of all ages and abilities, constantly changing, with varying periods of residence, have stimulated the search for a more constructive and satisfactory method of caring for children needing temporary detention care. Many children who can be cared for in their own homes and do not need to be placed in confinement are placed in detention care where a detention home exists. It becomes a catchall and destructive in its influence on children and on community attitudes toward children and their needs. Perhaps large cities need detention homes and can afford the costly type of care involved. But they need a number of varying types to fit the needs of the children requiring temporary care away from their own homes. For most cities and counties it is, in our opinion, an expensive and unsatisfactory way of meeting the situation. Several cities and counties have demonstrated that foster family homes can be found for the detention care of most children who need it. These boarding homes reduce the number of children kept in detention, minimize the contagion between delinquents, alleviate the emotional upsets, and provide a more wholesome and normal environment for the child being separated from his home.

There always will be some older adolescent delinquents who cannot be contained in a regular foster family boarding home. They are the aggressive, gang-minded, excitement seeking, chronic runaway types of individuals. In larger cities there will be several of these. In smaller communities the number will be very small. Because of the dramatic quality of their acts, they tend to overbalance the detention program in the direction of secure group custody—jail-like in type. It is surprising to find that most of the so-called "tough ones" respond to the warmth and acceptance of a good foster home. Where funds are limited it would seem better to provide foster homes for detention with not more than two beds in a home, spend the remainder on a more adequate child welfare program, locking children up only after they have demonstrated beyond the shadow of a doubt that such is required.

Evaluation of Foster Home Placement

It is a truism in the field of child welfare to say that the best place for a child is in his own home with his own parents unless the home is definitely destructive in its influence, and that he should not be removed from his home without every effort being made to develop whatever assets are present. The development of probation resulted from a recognition of this fact. It attempts to capitalize on the assets which exist in the home and in the individual to the end that adjustment to social living can be brought about in the environment in which the child will, in all likelihood, continue to live. For a long time it has been recognized that the best institutions fail to provide the best elements of a good home. They are artificial and, in the case of most institutions for delinquents, they operate in a vacuum so far as normal community contacts and living are concerned. This has led to the tentative use of foster family homes for some of the problem and delinquent children. With the development of mental hygiene clinics and better diagnostic facilities and techniques and with the development of more careful observation, supervision and recording, together with better evaluation of foster parents and families, the boarding home placement of children who present behavior problems or who have committed delinquent acts is fraught with less danger than was formerly the case.

The most ambitious undertaking in this field was, so far as we can learn, the efforts of the Children's Aid Association of Boston. The results of a study of 501 problem and delinquent children placed in foster family homes over a period of 10 years are reported in a book by Healy, Bronner, Baylor and Murphy titled *Reconstructing Behavior in Youth* (1929). They concluded that most delinquent children will make a better adjustment in carefully selected foster family boarding homes than in an institution, giving as a reason that the family life in a community setting offers a more natural environment and a better understanding of what society demands. They also emphasize the fact, substantiated by other experience, that a family home can be found for almost any child, regardless of his behavior problems or his offenses. Another emphasis which should be mentioned is that children do not fall into categories, such as dependent, neglected, truant, and delinquent. Careful study of children shows that there are no really distinct lines of demarcation or distinction between these groups. They have much more in common than is implied by such labeling.

As a result of these studies the conclusion is reached that approximately 85 per cent of normal children who have been labeled as delinquent, because they have committed delinquent acts and have been brought to the attention of the authorities, make a satisfactory adjustment in foster family boarding homes and cease to be delinquents. Apparently the type of offense committed, or the fact that the delinquent has committed one or more different kinds of offenses, has little bearing on the rate of success or failure. The one significant factor that increased the rate of failure was the presence of abnormal mentality or personality. This led to the conclusion that mentally abnormal delinquents and those classified as psychopathic personalities show little promise of success in foster family boarding homes. One rather surprising result of this study was that for the normal, successful placement for the older group—those between 13 and 18—was "only slightly less successful" than for those under 13. It is true that more abnormal personalities were found in the older group than among the younger group, but if these were excluded the results are as indicated above.

To sum up in the words of the authors:

First of all, we see plainly that delinquent children, even the severely delinquent, can be treated with great assurance of success through placing. For normal children, we have found no conditions or factors, whether of sex, age, heredity, or type of delinquency, that prove great obstacles to a favorable result. For normal personalities the chance of success is over five to one.

It is interesting to compare the results of this study with those of a study made by the State Charities Aid Association of New York (*How Foster Children Turn Out*—A critical analysis of 910 children who were placed in foster homes by the State Charities Aid Association). This study covered the period from 1898 to 1922 so far as placements were concerned, and reported that 77.2 per cent of those whose capability was known were capable—that is, were law abiding, managed their affairs with good sense, and were living in acordance with good moral standards of their communities.

At least two of the state training schools for delinquent boys, the New York State Training School for Boys in 1937 and the Illinois Training School for Boys, have tried using foster homes for the placement of certain children committed to them. Funds were made available to enable the school to place the child in a carefully selected foster family boarding home, instead of permitting him to return to a home which had proved to be destructive in its influence and which did not respond to the efforts of social workers while the child was in the training school. Sometimes the home was selected and the supervision was carried by a social agency, but in some instances, particularly in the case of the older child, the school found a suitable home and supervised the child and the home after the placement of the child. Both schools established divisions of foster home care in their social services or after-care departments. The difficulties of finding suitable homes and the extent of supervision required should not be minimized, nor should the valuable results achieved.

Basic Considerations in Use of Foster Homes

Perhaps the most basic consideration in the use of foster family homes for problem and delinquent children is the extent to which the personality and needs of the child are known. These can be determined only by a careful study of his life history up to the point where he is. Not only must his own actions and emotional life be studied, but the attitudes of the family toward him, his attitudes toward them, the kind of influences outside the home which have been playing on him and their effect on him; the kind of setting which brings out the behavior complained of, its psychogenesis, his relation to his father, mother, other relatives in the family. All are important. The child needs to be studied physically, and mentally to determine his assets and liabilities, his interests, peculiarities, the content of his inner mental life, the specific causes of his maladjustment. In other words, it is necessary to bring the whole child, with all that implies, into consideration before definite plans are made for his treatment. It may be determined that foster care should not be considered for this child because of his attitude toward his parents, or his need for group care in an institutional setting. There are still many problems to be solved in working out a more accurate set of criteria for the use of foster homes for delinquents as against institutional placement.

In general, foster homes work best for those who have a need for affection, individualized attention, who require closer and more intimate relationships with adults and those whose personal habits and attitudes are not such as to make them too conspicuous in a community. Other factors which determine whether the delinquent child should be sent to the institution instead of a foster home are inherent in the community resources when contrasted with the institution. Some children are in need of special educational tutoring and remedial work which may not be available in the community where a suitable foster home is located, but the institution may have such specialized services. This is also true of the psychotherapy which may be needed in a particular case. Some children may need to be placed in an institution to get the psychotherapeutic treatment required. Some neurotic children do better in a foster home than in an institution if psychotherapy is also available. Children who do not respond to casework treatment are not ready for foster home placement, nor are those with strong aggressions against parent persons.

Another group of children who may need institutional treatment as a prelude to foster home placement are those delinquents who because of poor standards, indulgence, and neglect refuse to accept discipline. Delinquents whose mental imagery is preoccupied with thoughts of sex perversions and who have been indulging in perversions over a rather long period of time should be placed with caution, if at all, in boarding homes. This is also true of the delinquent who finds it impossible to accept or give affection and loyalty and who has been variously described as psychopathic, narcissistic, or an individuated delinquent. As a matter of fact, successful treatment of this group, either in an institution or out of it, has been rare. Foster home care is not indicated for the delinquents who have an organic pathology of the nervous system, or who are psychotic, or who fall into the classification of the defective delinquent. What has been said above emphasizes that the successful use of foster family boarding care for delinquents implies the use of scientific diagnosis as a prelude to placement.

It should be said that there are some exceptions to what has been said above. Some foster parents have accomplished miracles with most unpromising cases. So much depends upon the degree of involvement of the child in the directions indicated. So much depends, too, upon the patience, understanding, and strengths of the foster parents.

Another important factor which must be emphasized is the selection of foster homes in which delinquents are to be placed. This involves a careful study of each person in the home. Also to be considered are the location (preferably suburban or rural), community educational facilities, recreational facilities, clinics, personalities of the persons in the home, the atmosphere of the home, the arrangement of the home, etc. Experience in the use of a home is the best guide in determining whether it will be suitable for a given child. Some experience with problem children by the foster parents is almost a prerequisite for placement of delinquents in a home. Training school cottage parents sometimes make excellent foster parents for delinquent children, if they meet personality and attitude requirements. They will have shown their capacity to absorb deviations from the norm, will have demonstrated their patience, understanding, and the warmth of their acceptance. Not only should there be a careful study of the home as indicated above, but there should be careful preparation of the foster parents for work with the problem child. Successful placement requires a continuing help to the foster parents.

It goes without saying that well-trained social workers are required to work successfully with delinquents. Not only must they have had formal training, but they must be fitted by personality and temperament to work with this more difficult group. Experience in working with children, including problem children, should precede work with delinquents. Above all, they must have patience, understanding, and an appreciation of the time required to overcome the attitudes and habits of long duration. They must be able to take disappointment and understand that progress toward the goal of social adjustment is filled with peaks and valleys of achievement. The social worker is perhaps the most important member of the team working toward the reclamation of the delinquent. She is the one continuing tie for the child throughout the process.

We have discussed the child, the foster parents and the social worker. The process of making them all work together is involved in the follow-up or supervision. The skill of the social worker will be expressed in the supervision which she gives to the situation. It is through her contact with the child and the foster parents that the attitudes and problems of the child become known. Her integrity and real interest will increase the likelihood of developing more meaningful relationships. The child's relationship to the social worker should be the same as that toward a good adult friend. He should not be reminded too much of the agency, nor should he think of himself as one of many cases. The social worker should be devoted to the child and his problems during the time of supervision. Frequent visits are necessary, especially in the beginning of the child's stay in a new foster home. Sufficient time should be allowed so that the social worker can follow through on any problems which present themselves. This means a small case load.

Conclusions

In an attempt to meet the needs of individual children, there has been increasing recognition of the necessity for developing various types of facilities. No longer is there insistence upon any one best method of taking care of all children presenting problems of social maladjustment. The conflict between the advocates of institutional care for all and advocates of foster home care for all has now given way to attempts to determine just what children need institutional care, for how long, what kind, and what children need foster care, what kind and how secured.

There has been an increasing use of boarding home care for a number of children presenting special problems. This is also true of those labeled as delinquent. Foster family boarding home care has been used for them in lieu of institutional placement, before institutional commitment, as an interlude with institutional residence, and following institutional placement. Some training schools for delinquents have had more than a decade of experience with this type of boarding home care. The results have been gratifying, despite the fact that some of that period was during and after World War II when housing shortage was acute and conditions generally not conducive to finding foster homes and keeping them.

The use of subsidized foster family boarding homes for detention care, for all except the largest cities, promises success, if properly supervised and subsidized. They are more economical, more normal, prevent contagion resulting from grouping all ages and problems together, give more individualized attention, and do less damage to the child. A few exceptional cases need more custodial care than can be given in any except specially modified homes. Careful selection of foster parents who have had experience with problem children, high grade supervision, and a small number of children in each home are essential for detention care.

The successful use of foster family boarding homes for problem and delinquent children requires that a careful study of the whole child be made and that placement be based upon a knowledge of the whole child and the home in which he is to be placed. Some children cannot profit by placement in a boarding home, no matter how good. This should be recognized and the child should be given the type of care best suited to his needs. Some knowledge has been acquired as to the types of personalities which can benefit from foster family care. This should be used. But much more research is needed to develop the criteria which we should have in prescribing various types of care, including boarding home care.

What has been said about the selection of the child also applies to the selection of the home in which care is to be given. Skilled caseworkers can evaluate homes and match them with the children to some extent, but experience with the homes is still the best method of determining what kind of problems they can absorb. Here again we need to do more research before completely satisfactory criteria for placement can be known. In the past two decades some real progress has been made in the development of supervisory skills in dealing with problem and delinquent children, but we still have many unanswered questions in this field. Temperament, training, and experience are the triad needed for success in this field. In addition, qualities of sympathy, understanding, and patience

on the part of the social worker are essential. Working with foster parents, who work with problem and delinquent children, requires something extra in the way of qualifications. This should be recognized in the compensation given. It will be a good investment.

Foster parents working with problem and delinquent children are required to give more time and go to more trouble than is the case for children with less severe problems. There is a growing acceptance of the idea that foster parents who give extra service should be compensated for this. Helpless children, those who require special diets, crippled children, fall into this group. Some of the problem and delinquent children also would qualify for extra service. The New York State Training School for Boys at Warwick, begining in 1938, paid slightly more than the rate for dependent and neglected children. Following the war this was increased considerably over what was being paid for dependent children.

Finally, some delinquent children of all ages can benefit from foster boarding home care. The number over 15 years of age will be less than those under that age, but the nature of the problem is more significant than the age of the child. It is easier to send a child to a detention home or to an institution than it is to take him home and make plans for him which include careful study and evaluation. Police authorities often have little patience with the length of time involved or with the process itself. Some social agencies prefer to accept good children who are not involved with the law and who do not present frequent emergencies. The problem and delinquent child has little respect for week-ends or for holidays, and sometimes interferes with regular office hours and routines. But, despite all this, it is possible to achieve gratifying results when careful selection of the home, the child, and the social worker is made.

SELECTED REFERENCES

1. Neumeyer, Martin H., *Juvenile Delinquency in Modern Society* (New York: D. Van Nostrand Co., 1949), Chapter 3: "Delinquency Trends in Contemporary American Society."

This chapter is recommended for a full discussion of delinquency in wartime and postwartime trends.

2. Tappan, Paul W., *Juvenile Delinquency* (New York: McGraw-Hill Book Co., 1949), Chapter 7: "Causes and Conditions of Delinquency — Social Variables in the Etiology of Delinquency."

More research has been devoted to familial factors in delinquency than to any other single influence. A complete discussion here includes poverty and unemployment as well as the family as factors in delinquency.

3. Maslen, Sydney, "Housing and Juvenile Delinquency," *Federal Probation*, XII, June 1948.

The contemporary housing situation and its relation to juvenile delinquency is ably demonstrated.

4 COMMUNITY INSTITUTIONS

IN THEIR fullest sense, "institutions" incorporate attitudes and reciprocal behavior patterns of groups of individuals, guided by established culture standards, and designed to fulfill specific human objectives and needs. The belief in public education, for example, profoundly rooted in American tradition and mores, has found expression in such specific institutions as the public school and the state university. One important function of these organizations is to implant common standards and forms of behavior.

Despite the general trend towards standardized behavior in this society, strong tensions arise in the community because of differences in value standards and modes of operation of the several institutions governing our lives. Inconsistencies within and between community institutions help to aggravate social problems, such as crime and juvenile delinquency.

THE SCHOOL AND DELINQUENCY

While the home is the first and most important influence in shaping the personality and character of the child, other environmental forces, such as the school, help to determine them also. The school is perhaps the most strategic community agency in the effort to prevent delinquency, since it reaches practically all children at a relatively early period of their growth.

One reason that this potential advantage of the school is not exploited fully is found in the intellectual diversity of the students combined with a fairly standardized program. The public school, it has been claimed, does a fair job with the pupil of average intelligence, a poor job with superior children, and practically no job with the dull group. Thousands of boys and girls quit school because they are offered little opportunity to learn anything which their limited mentality can grasp. Another complicating factor is the situation in which school administrators frequently lack the insight to deal effectively with disciplinary problems.

For many maladjusted and potentially delinquent children, school seems to be just another frustrating and unhappy experience. The school sometimes intensifies feelings of frustration and inadequacy, often generated in the family and play groups. And many pupils caught in these circumstances seek an outlet for their frustrations in truancy and delinquent behavior. Truancy has been called the "kindergarten of crime," for often enough the young truant, under the influence of older boys and girls, learns techniques of stealing and other forbidden activities during his stolen hours. An adequately conceived preventive program in the school could aid considerably, perhaps, in lowering the juvenile delinquency rate. The frequency of truancy and dishonesty in children in the schools before their first contact with the law suggests that an efficient visiting teacher or counselor program might have prevented some later delinquencies.

Of basic importance, however, in any school program is the realization that the school is working with growing personalities who enter the classroom with attitudes already shaped by the home and neighborhood environment. Children come into contact with their teachers and learning routines with likes and dislikes, fears and anxieties, unsatisfied cravings and unfulfilled desires. If schools fail to recognize these background conditions and to take them into account in their educational activities, some children will rebel against school itself and may take the first step toward delinquency.

Increasingly, the public schools have come to acknowledge these facts and are slowly broadening the scope of their interest and responsibility. Both the schools and the juvenile court recognize the fact that delinquency can frequently be prevented by redirecting the child's antisocial and destructive impulses. With the growing awareness of the need for such attention to be given the child, educators have increasingly stressed the need to provide individualized services for problem children.

As a force in preventing delinquency, the school has many limitations. Teachers do not necessarily agree on what constitutes "delinquency." Teachers, for obvious reasons, are primarily concerned with deviant behavior in the classroom. Many teachers emphasize actions that unsettle classroom decorum, while mental hygienists are more interested in such behavior symptoms of extreme shyness and suspiciousness. Most teachers undoubtedly recognize the recalcitrant, unyielding and perverse child, the bully, the promiser who never delivers, the constant eraser of written work, the pencil chewer, the devotee of obscene words, phrases or pictures written or drawn on the walls or sidewalks. The teachers' reactions to such behavior and their informed and understanding treatment of children who engage in these symptomatic acts are of vital importance in the prevention of delinquency.

The character of school work likewise must be considered in the effects it induces in children. What is the effect, for example of subjecting the child to laborious exercises far removed from the central experiences of his life? Reading about "innocent little lambs" (unreal creatures, at best), fairies, trips to the country, or the volume of rainfall in Tibet, for example, may have only negative impact on children raised in city streets. To these pupils delinquency offers thrills and excitement in contrast to uninteresting and confining school work.

It is expecting too much of schools, of course, to assume that they can overcome the influences of undesirable homes and community conditions. Yet a more developed preventive program in the school surely is one important weapon in the fight against delinquency. Most delinquent children come directly from the American public school room, where they have presumably been indoctrinated with the standards of a law-abiding society. The fact that this indoctrination is often ineffective presents a challenge to the schools and to the communities of which they are a part.

THE CHURCH AND DELINQUENCY

A satisfactory definition of the role of the church in preventing delinquency is by no means easy of formulation. Among the sources of the difficulty, one author stresses the following: (1) the lack of agreement upon the legitimate aims and methods of organized religion itself, stemming from sectarian controversy; (2) the confusion concerning the proper scope of religious activities in relation to the work of other institutions, involving seemingly artificial distinctions between the "sacred" and "secular"; and (3) the traditional view that the historic mission of the Protestant churches is to teach religious principles almost exclusively, depending upon their beneficial effects upon individuals for the solution of social problems.[1]

The difficulties, marked in the Protestant denominations, are not as manifest in the Catholic Church. The social teachings of the latter are rooted in authoritative and scholarly encyclicals and there is agreement concerning "secular" programs—a situation greatly abetting effective work in coping with delinquency. The Catholic Youth Organization, for example, has as a major objective the prevention of juvenile delinquency and works towards this goal with one of the most extensive and popular youth programs in the United States today. Both the Sisters of the Good Shepherd, dedicated to the correction of delinquent girls, and the late Monsignor Flanagan's famous Boys Town, Nebraska, have inspired similar programs among Catholics and non-Catholics.

Protestant Church activities are not nearly as extensive. The Northern Baptists, the Protestant Episcopal Church, various Lutheran bodies, and the Congregational Church, however, have instituted or, as is more often the case, sponsored programs directly designed to curb delinquency.

Carr believes that the role of the Protestant churches in this effort is handicapped by the preaching of "old-fashioned," individualistic, personal salvation; and where the need is greatest, church contacts are lowest. He further points out that the churches especially tend to follow the migration of the middle-class homes. Not infrequently some church leaders convey the impression that active interest in delinquency problems is "worldly" and "belittling." Ultraconservative administrations have driven Boy Scouts out of church basements and slashed young people's work budgets to increase expenditures on the choir. Ministers have been called, supposedly to enlightened churches, for the express purpose, as one church official put it, of "ending this infernal monkey business," namely, the somewhat noisy presence of groups of youngsters in the church parlors on weekdays.[2]

Sunday School and church training do not seem greatly to deter juvenile delinquency. From the available evidence to date there seems to be little relationship between Biblical information and the different phases of conduct by juveniles, delinquent or otherwise. This is true regardless of denominational

---

[1] Philip M. Smith, "Role of the Church in Delinquency Prevention," *Sociology and Social Research*, XXXV, January 1951.

[2] Lowell Juilliard Carr, *Delinquency Control* (New York: Harper & Brothers, 1941), pp. 370–373.

category or regularity of attendance by young people. Such evidence probably warrants the conclusion that there has not yet been devised part-time, religiously-oriented, character-building programs for young people that will adequately substitute for the day-by-day relationships of parents and children. This conclusion does not mean that the churches cannot be more effectively used than has been the case to date in the prevention and control of delinquency.

RECREATION AND DELINQUENCY

Delinquent behavior tends to increase after school hours and after suppertime hours, because primarily of lack of adult supervision. Children sometimes fill in leisure hours with lawless activity and most juvenile crimes are committed during the hours which are unsupervised. Moreover, the provision of facilities for so-called wholesome recreation does not seem to alter this situation in any large measure. There are high delinquency rates, at times, in areas containing social centers, swimming pools, youth centers, and settlement houses.

Nevertheless, it has been stressed by at least one authority that energetic young people may get into trouble when searching for entertainment. Professor Ruth Cavon, for example, notes that boys arrested for building a shack in the park were not malicious; neither were the children who burglarized sports equipment from a country club, nor those who stole a motor boat ride on the river, nor those who sneaked into the moving pictures without buying tickets. In their hunt for recreation, they became court cases.[3]

Sometimes more drastic consequences are in store for youngsters seeking entertainment. Juveniles may actually be killed as a result of indulging in certain forms of "play." For example, in the game of "Chicken" (played by a group in a moving automobile) the driver speeds the car faster and faster until one of the group finally is scared into telling him to slow down; this one is labeled as "chicken." Such puerile activities of young people have been aptly called "teenicide."

Youthful recreation suggested by the radio, television, motion pictures, and comic books may at times lead to delinquent behavior, particularly in the case of susceptible youngsters. With this possibility in mind, one national radio hook-up banned until after 9:00 P.M. all programs which might encourage the adolescent generation to participate in criminal acts. Such approaches probably serve, at least, to encourage many children to wait up for the broadcast. *Time* (March 3, 1952) reports that a group of San Francisco mothers similarly interested in the possible effects of the mass media, observed children's television shows for four hours, recording thirteen murders and assorted killings, and sluggings, six kidnappings, five hold-ups, three explosions, three instances of blackmail and extortion, three thefts, two armed robberies, two cases of arson, one lynching, one torture scene, and one miscarriage. In a half-hour serial, the mothers clocked 104 gunshots; in another serial death was "shudderingly described" fourteen times in twenty minutes. What kind of behavior will result from exposure to this type of entertainment?

Various attempts have been made to answer this question. For example, in

[3] Ruth Shonle Cavon, *Criminology* (New York: Thomas Y. Crowell Co., 1950), p. 114.

1932, by means of questionnaires and written accounts of personal reactions, Herbert Blumer and P. M. Hauser undertook a study of the motion pictures and delinquency (*The Movies, Delinquency and Crime*). They obtained information from 874 delinquents and 878 grade and high school boys and girls. Their conclusions showed that motion pictures seem to have a deleterious influence on 10 per cent of the males and 25 per cent of the females. Motion pictures, of course, depict the good and virtuous as well as the bad; and some of the best literature, not excluding Shakespeare, contains references to "evil" behavior. According to Judge Camille Kelley of Memphis, in approximately fifty thousand cases which came before her, less than six could be blamed on the motion pictures. Whatever the hunches, not very much is yet known about the impact of motion pictures, radio, and television.

The comic books and comic strips have also been cited as exercising an undesirable influence upon those children who avidly read them. Comics are read, according to some estimates, by four out of five children over six years of age. They appear in some fifty million copies of daily papers. About forty million comic books are sold every month. Their specific influence, however, is not clear—although dramatic cases are occasionally brought to the attention of the public. Thus is read the story about two twelve-year-old Oklahoma boys, who, stimulated by a comic book strip, stole an airplane, flew it 120 miles, and brought it down without mishap. They said they had learned how to fly by reading the funnies.[4] In the December 6, 1948, issue of *Time* is the story of two Canadian boys, eleven and thirteen years old, accused of murder and robbery. At the hearing they said that they got their ideas for their crime from the forty to fifty comic books they were accustomed to reading each week. The presiding judge commented: "I agree as to the influence of the literature these boys have been subjected to. A concerted effort should be made to see that this worse than rubbish is abolished in some way." Most adults probably sympathize with this plea. But there seems little doubt that the influence of comic books has been over-emphasized frequently by adult authorities and by juvenile offenders themselves.

To be sure, illegal conduct, adult and juvenile, is often undeservedly glamorized by the motion pictures, by radio and television, and by the comics. There can be no quarrel with those who decry this situation—or with those who condemn the tabloid publicity that so often gives crime and delinquency a kind of prestige. But the causes of delinquency and the reasons for its persistence are many and complex. Mass media and recreational institutions play their part. The effective control of delinquency and its abatement, however, call for inclusive measures that meet the community organization and the life of the individual at many points.

READINGS

Arthur C. Johnson, Jr., in "Our Schools Make Criminals" discusses the implications of the "proper influence and treatment" given to some children who

---

[4] Reported in Negley K. Teeters and John Otto Reinemann, *The Challenge of Delinquency* (New York: Prentice-Hall, 1950), p. 188.

need guidance and assistance. Too many children are not dealt with sympathetically and yet firmly; schools can help to make criminals.

In "Who Are Our Truants?" Alfred J. Kahn stresses the difference between nonattendance at school and truancy. He says that an effort must be made to understand the individual absentee and the underlying causes of his truancy.

John Otto Reinemann in "The Truant before the Court" emphasizes the growing awareness of the desirability and the value of "spotting" the potential delinquent at the earliest stage of his development. This responsibility undeniably rests with the juvenile courts, school authorities, and other character-building agencies.

Church attendance and juvenile behavior are discussed by William W. Wattenberg in his article, "Church Attendance and Juvenile Misconduct." He concludes that church attendance is only a part of a way of life which generally reduces tendencies toward juvenile misbehavior. Whether a person is inclined to agree with him or to disagree with him is less important than the realization that here is a viewpoint which deserves serious attention.

The comic book phenomenon as it is related to juvenile delinquency is analyzed by John R. Cavanagh in "The Comics War." While the matter remains debatable, there still seems to be insufficient evidence showing that reading about crime actually produces criminals. Certainly there are particular incidents showing this association, but no general conclusions can be drawn as yet. However, the comics have been called the "marijuana of the nursery." In his article Cavanagh summarizes the psychodynamics involved, the aggressions, the fantasies stimulated in young minds, and other such psychosociological aspects of the comic books.

Our Schools Make Criminals[*]

By Arthur C. Johnson, Jr. Formerly Educational Supervisor, State Prison, Attica, New York.

For several years I have suspected that our schools condition some criminals—that for many school-age children, present educational practices backfire in their social intent. But I couldn't put my finger on the how and why of it until I visited a children's court recently. There I saw a little tike start out along a road which had begun in his school classroom and which probably will end at a prison gate. I know, for after twenty years equally divided between public and prison educational work, I know both ends of that road.

The youngster made a brave pretense at toughness—apparently the only test of manhood he knew—but behind the attempt was just a frightened boy. I have seen this same reaction in youthful offenders too often to be fooled by it. "Your Honor," a court investigator testified, "I know this case well. John's teacher and the principal of his school agree that he is a confirmed truant and trouble-maker, who refuses to respond to proper influence and treatment."

I have read hundreds of juvenile case histories without realizing that a second-

* Reprinted from *The Journal of Criminal Law and Criminology* (Northwestern University School of Law), Vol. XXXIII, July–August, 1942, by Arthur C. Johnson, Jr.

hand opinion may become prosecutor and jury for what in effect constitutes a criminal trial. There could be no defense —John *was* a truant, and he certainly appeared to be a trouble-maker. The judge sealed the fate of the sullen lad. "John Doe, Jr., on the evidence, this court has no alternative but to declare you a delinquent under the law, and commit you to (institution named) until such time as the authorities there are convinced that your attitude and conduct have changed. That is all."

Consistent in his role of tough guy, the kid glared at the judge and snarled, "A'right, send me away an' see if I care! I'll show 'em I c'n take it."

What a perfect start for a criminal career!

On the objective evidence, no one could take exception to the court's finding—it was too late for compromise in this case. But experience told me that, taken in time, John *could* have been saved.

In some such manner 18,000 youths a year are herded into institutions for corrective treatment—over one-half committed as habitual truants from school and incorrigibles. Many times that number are placed on probation—for the courts *do* compromise, whenever possible. *Why do so many boys run away from school?*

Negative School Influences

Personal contact with over 7,000 prisoners made me ponder the investigator's statement: ". . . refuses to respond to proper influence and treatment." To what "influence and treatment" had John been subjected in school? What constitutes "proper" influence and treatment *for John?* We can answer rather definitely for an average child, but John was not an average child or he wouldn't have been in court. Had his teacher and principal actually tried to supply proper influence and treatment—had they worked with John to help *him*—or was he merely

the nuisance-discard from a class and school? That these are valid questions is shown by actual statements by other Johns:

(1) "The teacher tried to make me wear better clothes like the other children. I finally told her to go to hell and walked out. I swore then that I would have better clothes if I had to steal them and I did."

(2) "I had a stutter. I was put in a class with a lot of screwballs. My pals kidded me and I quit."

(3) "My mother was going nuts and I was worried about her. One day the teacher called me crazy too. I never went to school regular after that."

(4) "I was fired from school because I wouldn't study my history. When they brought me back and tried to make me study history again, I started to skip school."

(5) "I just couldn't recite in class. The teacher nagged at me and to avoid trouble I left school."

(6) "I don't know why I ran away from school. I couldn't get along in a crowd, that's all."

(7) "I was put in a class with a lot of dumb clucks. It was too much for me and I quit."

(8) "One day I got to school late and was told that if I couldn't get there on time, not to come at all, just to spoil the class record. I took them at their word."

Equally obvious end-products of illy considered school "influences" are to be found in any prison. If these boys had been handled sympathetically and understandingly at the right time, many would not, today, be where they are.

In the past, I always accepted the occasional trouble-maker as an inescapable headache for the school. I now know that the school was frequently an even greater headache for that child. For as I better understand the attitudes which underlie antisocial behavior, I see that they often hinge on little things for which the school alone was at fault.

It is so easy to dodge embarrassing issues by treating the problem boy as a discipline case, waiving all personal responsibility by turning him over to the social worker and the courts. These are too often so concerned with opinions of other and untrained observers that they have neither time nor opportunity to study the boy, his personal problems, the real causes for his sorry plight. Altogether too many youngsters are being *judged* bad and, in their youth and pliability, in fact are being *made* bad.

The juvenile institution is, in the main, a tardy answer to America's dilemma of delinquency—side-stepping the real issue, extravagant in taxpayer dollars, and utterly wasteful in ultimate human values. We must counterbalance the effect of delinquent influences while the child is most susceptible to them, not create them ourselves.

Result of the School's Failure

That it is a school problem is clear. In a group of 634 consecutive prison commitments, 258 were recidivists of whom 194, or 78 per cent, had truancy as the first entry in their crime ledger. Of the 376 first offenders, 231, or 61 per cent, got the same start. On their own admission, 140, or 67 per cent of the remainder, had been off-the-record truants. *This is a serious indictment of our schools.*

It is a present problem. Of these 565 truants, 67 were under nineteen; 182 were between nineteen and twenty-one; and 197 between twenty-one and twenty-seven years old when last committed.

It has been said that of every one hundred boys of school age, eighty are average, healthy, normal youngsters. Being slow mentally, ten have to be "pushed." Highstrung and rebellious against restraint, the remaining ten become behavior problems and "must be sat on." *It is with this ten per cent that the school fails.*

Hark back to our own schooldays for a picture of the boy who must be "sat on." There was a John in our class. For any of many reasons, this boy was made to feel alien—a misfit in the group. He got less consideration than we. Sooner or later, he accepted our attitude as a challenge and reacted accordingly. Reaction followed one of two characteristic patterns: either the boy started an indiscriminate bedevilment of teacher and pupils alike; or abandoning the social approach, he became moody and sullen, subject to violent outbursts of temper on the slightest provocation. Either attitude required ever increasing effort to maintain itself. Failing to reach goals gratifying to his bruised ego, John eventually ran away from what he realized had become an untenable position. And with him into truancy went the rankling acknowledgment of personal defeat—to be compensated for at any cost.

In this sequence of attitudes and conflicts lies the germ for a fixed manner of behavior—abandonment of the conventional self and the adoption of a reputational personality. The expression, "I may as well have the game as the name," sums up the whole distorted outlook. Continued, it may lead to delinquency and crime.

Left to his own resources, John will grow up conditioned to a tempo of excitement and social insecurity, antagonistic to the humdrum, nomadic, agitative —a mentally maladjusted individualist for whom the term psychopathic personality applies. In everyday language the psychopath is a bundle of nerves; emotionally unstable, impulsive, self-centered, non-cooperative, hence socially embarrassing. He is intelligent, but he rarely uses his intelligence to his own ultimate best interest and frequently employs it to antisocial ends. Thirty per cent of present prison populations possess these abnormal personality traits.

One prisoner—always in trouble, even in prison, told me: "I believe in all or nothing. When held down, my mind is never at peace. The reaction is dissatisfaction with my lot and a desire to wreck whatever barrier suppresses my will."

Disgruntled with the world about him, he would wreck it—but he succeeds only in wrecking himself. This is a characteristic psychopathic reaction.

No one can say with certainty what underlies the condition. It appears to result from external maladjustments "exploding" to form internal conflicts or neuroses which often baffle the combined knowledge of all the sciences. It appears, at least partially, a by-product of the age in which we live—one dedicated to speeds which in a generation have stepped man from the horse and buggy into the stratoplane. One father aptly expressed it in the statement: "I put my son on a merry-go-round and forgot to take him off." Unless we master the speeds we are creating, they must destroy our children. This is our basic social problem.

Of 196 instances of prison adjustment and discipline, 92 were definitely psychopathic and 63 showed closely related conditions. We may assume that 155, or 79 per cent of the group were from that ten per cent of boys who "must be sat on."

The Job Ahead

The potential trouble-maker forms but a small yet constant group in the school population. With native intelligence, instinctive cleverness, personal courage; he is tense under the lashing of emotional stress, perpetual restlessness, easily aroused antagonism—an unnatural blending of positive and negative character traits readily discernible to the observant. In our prisons, penitentiaries, jails, and juvenile institutions are thousands of these boys—now adult social outcasts. In our schools and yet to enter school are other thousands, boys as they once were, doomed to travel the same road to the same end, unless the school of tomorrow does something for them which, today, it is not doing. We can't lump the intelligent but unstable John with "a bunch of screwballs" and "dumb clucks," and expect to cure all by the same process.

Very little attempt is being made by the school to correct the existing situation. Only a handful of American communities have planned crime prevention programs originating there. The school is the one agency contacting all children in the traditional setting and natural manner essential in such a program. From his first day at school, the overly restless and emotional child must be identified and quieted, before his character is set and he becomes a *mis*-behavior problem—antagonisms developed, rebellions established, emotional barriers erected—a case for correction not prevention.

Dropped in their laps by the times, schoolmen have a vital situation confronting them. They must not approach it by assuming that techniques of demonstrated value to the normal boy will correct deficiencies in John. And John must not be made a scapegoat to rationalize their failure. We need a new approach to a new problem having aspects in common with experience.

Prevention involves occupational therapies peculiar to each boy. The effect of causes behind abnormal behavior must be neutralized by activities of individual interest and occupational worth. Education, as such, must be so organized and motivated as to appear but the integral part of a desirable whole. The larger purpose must be met whether one single other thing, now deemed educationally essential, is accomplished or not. With so much at stake, we can't afford to quibble over ways and means for doing.

Trade Training Not Enough

Historically, trade schools developed with one eye on the academic misfit. Many still function primarily as first aid in the cure of the delinquent. Vocational training has a very real place in the education of a run-of-the-mine boy. It would seem to be twice as valuable for our John. But prison experience demonstrates that a skilled trade—circumscribed with personal repressions and occupational restrictions as it is—may pyramid mental and social unrest in the emotionally un-stable. Here is the training-conditioning underlying a flat refusal to do mainten-ance work.

"I guess I was a trial to my teachers. Fi-nally the principal had me transferred to the vocational school. I was put in the carpentry class, but I didn't like it and got out by the simple method of refusing to work. I did the same in the print shop. When I found the plumbing shop just as bad, I ran away and have been on the loose ever since. That kind of work tied me down too much."

Vocational educators confuse the crea-tion of desirable habits of work with trade training, on the false assumption that the one may be secured only through the other. Too often they fail to realize that the prospective trainee must be guided into employment on the eco-nomic level at which he may adequately maintain himself, and therein they fail as teachers.

The utilization of vocational activities and materials for therapeutic purposes is not new. A few schools have developed outstanding programs based on this con-cept. Their methods and results have been so publicized that they need not be repeated here. Even the casual visitor will recognize the vitalizing personality of one man or woman as being responsible for the success of each.

At one such school, I was greeted with:

"See what (the principal) let's me do! No one ever let me do things like this before. So what? I'm always in trouble. I ain't any more."

At another I heard:

"Gee! It's swell here and I'm doing fine. I ran away from home to get out of going to school—but this ain't no school, mister, get that straight."

This hard boiled little egg didn't realize that he *was* in a school. How different from most juvenile institutions, where escape is a matter of almost daily occur-rence!

If there is a recipe for effective educa-tional work with boys who "must be sat on," it is contained in those words: "but this ain't no school, mister, get that straight."

We may summarize a crime prevention program: it is one of sympathetic under-standing and guidance—not impersonal and mechanized techniques of the labo-ratory now so commonly substituted for it. The first step with each boy is to "get under his skin," not "in his hair." Men and women who can attract boys becom-ing hardened to life and suspicious of motive must be brought into the work. Our job is to establish emotional con-trol, create habits of humility in thought, consideration in action, responsibility in performance—all attitudes of approach, *not necessarily skills for doing.* We will succeed only when we apply the simple formula of individual persuasion by per-sonal example, *and apply it in time.*

We have streamlined our economics. But the human cycle is constant—we can-not streamline human conduct or cor-rect faulty behavior by production line methods.

Who Are Our Truants?*

By Alfred J. Kahn. New York School of Social Work and Research Consultant, Citizens Committee on Children of New York City.

IT HAS become fashionable to discuss truancy as a symptom of more serious problems. Many, perhaps most, schools continue despite this to act on quite

* Reprinted from *Federal Probation*, Vol. XV, March, 1951, pp. 35–40. Used by permission of author and publication.

different principles. The fact is that sophisticated psychological explanations which stress basic causes are not necessarily more helpful than formulations which, with finality, describe as causes such things as "sheer orneriness" or "lack of character." The concept of truancy as a symptom is useless unless followed through with a particular organization of attendance programs and with an attempt to understand the individual absentee and his truancy.

Invariably at this point in the discussion someone refers to the magnitude of the nonattendance problem and asks how one can be concerned with the causes of absence of *individuals*. We are reminded, for instance, that in urban areas of the United States roughly 12 per cent of all pupils are absent from school on a given day. Such questioning frequently stems from the widespread misunderstanding of the nature of serious truancy and its place in the total nonattendance picture.

Nonattendance and Truancy

Most nonattendance is not truancy, but this is seldom remembered when the functions of attendance bureaus or departments of school systems are discussed. While there are no large-scale systematic studies of causes and reasons, a recent partial estimate (*Absent from School Today*, Metropolitan Life Insurance Company, 1949) tells us that only about 13 per cent of all school absences have nonmedical causes. Further light is shed on the nature of the problem when we learn that in New York City approximately 400,000 referrals a year to the Bureau of Attendance represent about 100,000 children. (Children are now referred after 5 days of unexplained absence.) In this department, between 65 and 70 per cent of the absences so referred are considered after investigation to be lawful and about 30 to 35 per cent unlawful.

The lawful absentee is the child whose excuse is acceptable according to the criteria of a given school system. The unlawful absentee is the child without an explanation, or the child whose explanation is unacceptable. Those in the latter category who have been absent without the knowledge and permission of their parents are, technically, our truants. Data being currently compiled by the Bureau of Attendance in New York City will soon provide more exact statistics, but it is a fair estimate that not over 15 per cent, and probably closer to 10 per cent, of referrals to the Bureau represent truancy.

The categories of "lawful," "unlawful," and "truant" may seem clear in their definitions, but there are strong grounds for suspicion and some proof that individual children often are misclassified when their absences are evaluated. For instance, some parents who permit unlawful absence are more willing than others to provide their children with contrived excuses; therefore, what should technically be counted as unlawful absences may be recorded as lawful. Other parents are willing to give their children "excuses" for unlawful absences which have taken place without their permission. Thus, what should be listed as truancy is considered as lawful absence.

Some parents who have language difficulties or who come to large cities from backward rural areas do not understand our schools and their rules. Therefore, some lawful absence may be recorded as unlawful.

Once these considerations are introduced, it can be understood that whether a child becomes known as a truant depends on more than his own act. Such variables as the nature of the parent's relationship to the child, the value with which a particular cultural or social group rates school attendance, the understanding parents have of our school system, and many other factors are very important in evaluating all attendance data.

The truants whose absence is "covered up" are seldom identified, and their numbers are not known. We are unable to discuss them or their problems except to suggest the possible pathology in parent-child relationship where this occurs regularly. The other group of truants, who make up 10 or 15 per cent of the children referred to attendance authorities, represent in themselves a substantial total, and they must be understood.

What causes their truancy? What is known about the problem? Data are incomplete, but it is possible to make some broad statements on the basis of case analysis and limited statistical studies. Before summarizing what is known as well as some of the more useful hypotheses, we should like to note that school systems have, despite limited systematic knowledge about truancy and other nonattendance, large volumes of statistics. These statistics reflect not efforts to understand the phenomenon but, rather, what we have called "statistics anxiety."

Statistics Anxiety

School systems are frequently subject to "statistics anxiety" in relation to attendance. The background of this state is readily understood. Principals often find that their performance is evaluated, in part, by the school's attendance standing and they, in turn, bring pressure to bear on teachers. State financial aid is sometimes tied, as it is in New York City, to average attendance figures. What is more, and this too must be said, it is easier to concentrate on the quantitative measures of school "accomplishment" than on the less tangible qualitative measures of a dynamic education for children.

These and other forces give us our weekly, monthly, and annual attendance rankings. Schools award or withhold stars to children, banners to classes, and prestige to principals as attendance rates go up or down a few percentage points. But they seldom face basic questions. School systems seldom ask what the harms are in the pressure, and they seldom properly concentrate on the small group who require attention: the children whose nonattendance is a sign of trouble or danger, an indication of a need for help.

How many children who are ill (and who may spread infection) attend school daily because they fear to spoil the class attendance standing? No systematic data are available, but all school personnel can cite illustrations. How many parents adopt the mood of the school's attendance pressure and ignore legitimate reasons for keeping a child at home? No statistics are compiled, but we know of cases where children were deeply hurt by such lack of understanding of their needs.

Those who create the attendance-rate pressures ignore the overwhelming evidence that, once the community has established, via its values, its traditions and its educational law, children of certain ages should go to school, the vast majority of eligible children do attend regularly. Most parents want their children to attend and co-operate with school programs. Although New York City attendance rates have fluctuated, they have changed very little since World War I. Furthermore, attendance rates do not rise as we add more attendance officers to our staffs.

We have every reason to believe that it is not pressure to attend which makes the substantial difference in attendance rates (lawful and unlawful) but such generally unstudied variables as: the weather; epidemics of childhood diseases; ethnic and cultural backgrounds (how parents of a given background value education); economic conditions (employment opportunity for teenagers); the mood of the times (wartime declines); the competence of the given teacher (variations in attendance rates in a given school); and the total school mood and program.

Those studies which have been made suggest that fuller analyses of these items (and such others as school size, grade placement, nature of the curriculum, social and personal problem areas) would point the way to dealing with attendance problems. If the concentration were less on regular series of comparative statistics and more on the analyses of such factors as those listed, we would have new insights not only into truancy but also into many other school problems and needs.

Inevitably such substantial attempts to understand attendance and nonattendance would focus the problem properly on the individual child and what school means to him. Only such study, within school systems, conducted by staffs which understand children, could shed important light on truancy. And only such understanding brought to bear each time a child is absent, whether or not the absence is labeled as truancy, can tell us what needs be done.

Meanings of Truancy

Most nonattendance need not be a source of concern. Many absentees are ill, must stay home because of special family situations, or are absent for transitory reasons. The arrival of the circus or the fleet, the beginning of the baseball season, or an unusually good day for fishing keep some children from school. Others take time off to explore a new intellectual discovery. These are all technically unlawful, but normal and understandable reasons for occasional absence which do not worry us. However,

. . . for a group of children . . . exact size unknown, absence is one symptom of mild or severe disturbance. This group has rightly become a source of considerable concern. We must know about the meaning of the serious nonattendance for these children before we can say clearly what kind of help they may need—and what, therefore, must be provided within the school system.

When we examine the absences of these children, we find that they sometimes tell of superficial problems which may be cleared up spontaneously or which may become worse if not dealt with. At other times, the nonattendance reveals serious and deep pathology requiring immediate treatment.

From the point of view of the individual, what is behind the act of unlawful absence? Who are our truants?

As stated, we have only partial insight into truancy. However, statistical research and case studies do justify stating some basic concepts important for teachers and for attendance workers. If these concepts can provide the framework for training and development of skills, school personnel will be in a position to do a great deal to prevent serious maladjustment and to decrease individual unhappiness. What is more, the approach to the truant in a mood to help and understand him will further deepen our knowledge of the significance of truancy.

Truancy and External Situations

First, teachers, school social workers, guidance counselors, attendance workers, and psychologists identify the truancy or other unlawful absence which can be described as a situational reaction. The lack of warm clothing on a cold, wet day, an unusual acute family problem, a parent's decision that the child must undertake a special errand, or the "dare" of one's friends are technically unlawful but cause little concern if they are not repetitive; they can occur in normal family situations.

At times (and we believe quite often), school conditions are at the core of these absences. A too complicated or a too dull curriculum will result in absence; some children find the classroom frustrating and confusing; to others, school contains less challenge than self-initiated activity while unlawfully absent. Students are particularly responsive, too, to the classroom behavior of those teachers who really do not like children and do not enjoy teaching.

Even when we meet what seems at the surface to be a simple, transitory home or school problem resulting in nonattendance, we cannot assume at once that the transitory external problem is all that is at stake. Different children, in what seem like similar circumstances, react differently. Furthermore, exploration of these reactions often reveals that something more than the external problem is involved. Therefore, the discovery of an environmental or family problem should not be taken to mean that we necessarily understand the unlawful absence. We must still seek explanation of why the specific child acts as he does. Only this approach can separate the simple transitory problem from that which is more serious.

The fact that truancy may be the reaction to an external situation thus does not always mean that it is not serious—or that it will remain external. For, the frequent inability to attend school because one's father is intoxicated and causes a disturbance in the morning may lead to such humiliation as leaves its mark on the personality. The lack of a white shirt for school assembly or any similar problem may set off a chain of reactions as the child experiences teacher criticism or wonders about his family inadequacy. Soon, undesirable methods of handling problems become part of the child's characteristic behavior, quite apart from the specific situation. At this stage, removing environmental causes and adjusting home problems is no longer enough.

Truancy and Behavior Disorders

From the above it can be seen that there is no sharp delineation between the transitory situational experience and the problem which reflects personality damage. A child's truancy may begin as an understandable reaction to a passing incident at home, at another time be a healthy protest against a bad school situation, and may at still a later date develop into an escape from a fantasied problem.

The child's verbal explanation of the truancy (or his parent's too) may be far from the true reason—sometimes because he does not know the reason. He may say that he preferred to go swimming or that he hates the teacher, but case studies show that these are often not the real causes. For, we must recall that school means different things to different children. To some it is a place of comfort, security, new experience. Children who have had, in their lives, trouble in relating to others, accepting authority, finding security, cannot see school as a friendly place. Anxiety, or deep discomfort may keep one child away, but his own lack of grasp of the real problem, of necessity, makes his explanation superficial. Hostility to adults may motivate another to give false excuses. We tend to react more sympathetically to the anxious and the fearful, but the problems of the hostile (whom we usually punish) may be as serious and as little under control.

Available evidence tells us that many truants are the children called *behavior disorders*. These are the children who are raised by inconsistent, unloving, rejecting, overprotecting parents whose own upbringing or daily problems block better relationships. Since such children experience too little real security and affection, they lack sufficient motivation to accept, as their own, society's demands and codes of right and wrong. Their lives are full of frustrations. Some of these represent material and physical deprivation. Other frustrations are experienced because these children have little tolerance for rules and limits. They react by hitting back, literally and figuratively, at their families and the rest of the world. When young, they are often known to be enuretic, runaways, children with eating problems (common to many children but problematic if prolonged or accentuated). As they grow older, these children may become defiant and aggressive. They have difficulty in accepting routine; they are often serious truants.

These are many of the aggressive truants whose hostility and defiance engender an impulse to punish. Yet such a reaction does little but to prove to them that adults are their enemies and that their view of the world is correct.

Help must be given before the antisocial patterns are firmly fixed in the personality. Such help must take the form of providing the security, love, and acceptance which parents could not give. When thus gratified, the child becomes able, in a belated socialization, to accept society's rules.

Psychoneurotics

The largest group among the "disturbed" unlawful absentees are psychoneurotic children who are amenable to treatment. The neurotic patterns resulting in nonattendance may take many forms, but the most significant early one seems to be the *school phobia*. The crucial point about the school phobia is that it is a situation in which another emotional conflict is embodied in the school phobia. The child refuses to go to school because he fears something terrible will happen if he goes. Fear is usually involved—either a fear of school or a fear of pupils, often a fear of failure in school work and fear of the separation from the mother essential to going to school. Numerous signs of anxiety are seen on school days (vomiting, dizziness, perspiration, choking, pains without an organic basis).

It would take one too far afield to attempt to sketch how an emotional conflict involving one's family and feelings about oneself can become embodied in a fear of school; but psychiatrists and others with clinical experience are able to sketch the process very exactly and point to a relatively high rate of cure as some evidence of the correctness of the view.

There is general agreement that the child suffering from school phobia should be returned to school as soon as possible. The attention one receives as a result of one's malady, the reactions in those concerned, the anxiety caused, the relief of being away from a source of discomfort, all become in themselves satisfactions reinforcing the initial phobic reaction. The problem of handling, however, requires considerable diagnostic skill because the extent to which one can use pressure to return to school, the point at which one can require return through compulsion if necessary, must be determined by very subtle weighing of the factors causing the conflict. Also to be considered is the ability of the child to tolerate further anxiety.

Nonattendance, where it derives from school phobia, must therefore be handled through a plan providing for early diagnostic appraisal and decision whether early return to school is desirable. If it is decided that he should be in school, such a child requires the help of an understanding teacher.

Psychotics and Others

There is, among maladjusted adults, a vaguely defined group of individuals known, according to different diagnostic schemes, as psychopaths, character disorders, neurotic characters, etc. (which may refer to the same or different conditions). Many of the individuals come to attention when they ignore society's rules, or act aggressively; some are unusually clever and glib. It would not be within our scope to enter into the problems of proper diagnosis of these individuals except to say that they often are found in our prisons, guilty of a wide range of offenses. When studied, many of these prove to have been truants when young, but they constitute only a small part of our truancy problem. What is more, they are seldom clearly identifiable before adulthood.

Truancy also may be part of the severe mental illness, *psychosis*, of which schizophrenia is the most common type. There is considerable psychiatric controversy as to whether this illness is found in infants or in children of elementary school age, but it is identifiable (exact rates are unknown) among children of junior high school and high school age. For the schizophrenic, there is a blurring of the boundaries between the real and the imaginary world. The sense of his own individuality is also partially lost. Of necessity, all of this reflects itself in school attendance and adjustment. When the developing schizophrenic truants, he often cannot explain his absence nor is he aware of the rules for obtaining an excuse. It is of crucial importance that he be identified early so that a psychiatrist may make a treatment plan. The dangers of lack of identification are real and possible consequences serious. In one large school system (this incident is not unusual), an attendance officer forcibly placed a truant in school for several successive days without attempting to understand why, each morning, the youth seemed to be in terror of going to school. On a final climactic day the boy fled and was chased over slum roof-tops, endangering him and others. Later, when other procedures had led to proper psychiatric examination, the boy was diagnosed as schizophrenic.

Truancy and Delinquency

In many, perhaps most, jurisdictions, habitual truancy is considered juvenile delinquency, as defined by law. But this is not the issue in the minds of those who work with children when they ask about the connection between truancy and delinquency. The real question is the relationship between such "less serious" delinquency as truancy and "more serious" violations of the law.

The timing and the nature of the help given are crucial in deciding whether a child whose truancy is a reaction to a particular *transitory or chronic home or school situation* later becomes more delinquent.

It is likely that of the truants who are absent for *psychoneurotic* reasons, relatively few are involved in other delinquencies (or at least no more than in a cross section of nontruant pupils). The psychoneurotic has very severe inner controls and conscience and is ordinarily a conformer.

On the other hand, many children with *behavior disorders* are aggressive and noncomforming. Truancy is one of their most commonly used patterns. Whether they engage in other unlawful activity depends in part on whether we ignore the early signs, in part on other sources of satisfaction and help. Thus, while some behavior disorders become serious delinquents, many do not.

Substantial numbers of so-called psychopaths, neurotic characters, character disorder cases, etc., are delinquents. However, these diagnoses can seldom be made accurately in cases of children of school age. Furthermore, these groups constitute a small proportion of all truants.

Although we know this much about the different emotional meanings of truancy, the tendency remains in much of our society (and therefore in many schools) to proceed as though all truants are or will become serious delinquents. Authorities react to the truancy by hitting back or other punishment. Such measures, we well know, usually accomplish nothing positive for delinquents or for anybody else. In addition, punishment, deprivation, or anger may well cause serious damage to some of the children described.

The major considerations for those in child-helping services are the following:

(1) Many (probably most) truants never become serious delinquents.

(2) More truants than nontruants are potential delinquents.

(3) The major importance of truancy is that it identifies a child who may be in trouble. Unless understood and helped, his problems and delinquencies may become more serious.

An Approach

Truancy must be seen as one of many symptoms which call our attention to children in trouble or need. It is easy to understand that our reactions and handling of children in difficulty have traditionally reflected the nature of their bids for help. We have sympathized with the physically handicapped child and with the one who told us he was afraid of school. We have punished the truant. But it is known that anxiety or phobia, compulsion or aggression, enuresis or truancy, may all be surface signs of other trouble. Having, in many fields, given up treating symptoms per se, we must act similarly with respect to unlawful absence.

The program that such an approach implies must be developed in detail with a view to the needs and resources in a given situation. Child guidance experience provides us with certain basic principles. We know that we waste money and effort, in addition to endangering a child's future development, if we are concerned only with getting the physical body of the absentee back to school. We need a program which meets absence through efforts to comprehend its meaning. The attendance program should be part and parcel of a general child-helping program in the schools and not a thing apart. This must follow from the recognition that the difficulties bared by absence are often no different than those revealed by learning problems, restlessness, nail-biting, or withdrawal in the classroom. Only as we see truancy as an early danger sign, marking a challenge to the child-helping services, can we move in attendance work from the medieval ages of statistics anxiety and punishment to the modern maturity of promoting personality health and development.

The Truant Before the Court[*]

By John Otto Reinemann. Director of Probation, Municipal Court of Philadelphia.

IN PRACTICALLY all juvenile court laws the term "delinquency" is defined so as to include truancy, thus establishing the jurisdiction of the juvenile court in such cases. The Pennsylvania Juvenile Court Act (in conformity with the Standard Juvenile Court Law) contains provisions for the care and treatment of that type of delinquent "who is habitually truant from school or home." Jurisdiction of the juvenile court in Pennsylvania extends to the eighteenth birthday.

Compulsory school age, according to the Pennsylvania School Law, begins with the time parents elect to have the child enter school (which is usually at the age of 6, and may not be later than at the age of 8 years), and ends when the child reaches 17. The compulsory attendance requirement does not apply to children who are 16 or over and are regularly engaged in lawful employment and who hold a proper employment certificate. Also, children who have been examined by an approved mental clinic or a certified psychologist and found to

* Reprinted from *Federal Probation*, Vol. XII, September, 1948, pp. 8–12. Used by permission of author and publication.

be unable to profit from further school attendance may be exempt.

Only such truancy cases are referred to the juvenile court (Juvenile Division of the Municipal Court of Philadelphia) by the Board of Education in which all efforts on the part of the school personnel, including their staff of counselors and attendance officers, have proved unsuccessful. In those instances in which the child's absence is exclusively the result of parental neglect, the case is prosecuted by the school authorities in the Magistrate's Court where fines, in a graded scale for repeated offenses, may be imposed.

In all other situations in which the truant behavior is centered in the child's maladjustment (though this in itself often is a result of parental inadequacy), the case is presented to the juvenile court. Here, too, a screening process takes place; cases where the truant child seems to be merely beyond parental control can be disposed of after an informal hearing by referees at the House of Detention for Children who have the power to adjust cases, continue them for a progress report from the probation officer or the Board of Education, with a view of adjustment at the later hearing. In 1946, a total of 132 truancy cases were thus informally disposed of, and the appearance before the referee and the close supervision by the school attendance officer brought about salutary results.

In more serious cases, particularly those where placement or special court service, such as probation or medical probation, is indicated, petitions are filed by the Board of Education for a formal court hearing. In 1946, a total of 220 such cases were handled, and they formed the basis for the present study.

Scope and Method of Study

The immediate impetus to the study was the growing awareness of the desirability and the value of "spotting" the potential delinquent at the earliest possible stage of his development. Realizing that truancy has often proved to be a warning signal for impending delinquency, a joint responsibility rests upon juvenile courts, school authorities, and other character-building agencies, to study the truancy phenomenon and to draw practical conclusions from the results of such investigations.

The cases referred to above were selected as the basis for the study because 1946 represented the first full-time peace year and the abnormal conditions created by the war-time employment of many children of school age had terminated. Further, the 220 cases were chosen because their disposition through formal juvenile court hearing required thorough investigations and examinations by the court's probation and medical staffs, and thus these case records contained valuable social and medical data. The very detailed findings of the school authorities which often were incorporated in their petitions also were available.

For the excerpting of these records a questionnaire was devised covering identifying data, social and family history, school history, and court history.

The cases which formed the group under study included 220 children of whom 163 were boys (113 white and 50 nonwhite) and 57 were girls (40 white and 17 nonwhite). Their most frequently represented ages were 14 (33 per cent) and 15 (31 per cent); only 9 per cent were past 16. Of the total of 4,468 delinquents whose cases were disposed of through court hearing in 1946, these truancy cases constituted less than 5 per cent. If we confine our comparison to those under 16 years of age, we arrive at a ratio of 201 truants to a total of 1,950 delinquents, or about 10 per cent. Occasionally, in this study report, the total number of delinquents will be used as a control group.

It should be pointed out that the 220 children, whose cases formed the basis for the study, were referred to the court for truancy exclusively; the source of referral in all cases was the Board of Education. In many of the other delinquency cases, poor school attendance also was observed, but truancy did not constitute a major factor in their delinquent behavior.

Findings of Study

ENVIRONMENT

Size of Family. The average number of children in the family was five. In 14.1 per cent of the cases there were 3, in 17.3 per cent there were 4, and in 14.1 per cent there were 5 children. In 37.2 per cent the number of siblings was six or more. Within the group under study there were 8 pairs of siblings, in 4 instances two brothers each, and in 4 instances each a brother and a sister.

Marital Status of Parents. The marital status of the parents is presented in Table 1. It appears that broken home conditions existed in 65 per cent of the cases. This is a considerably higher percentage of broken homes than in the total delinquency group where it was 47. Death of one or both parents had occurred in the families of 38 out of the 163 boys, or in 23.3 per cent of the cases, while in the total delinquency group the corresponding figure was 19 per cent in boys' cases.

Marital difficulties in the home of the children had become so serious in 28.6 per cent of the 220 cases that they led one of the parents, mostly the mother, into the Domestic Relations Division of the Municipal Court. This Division attempts to bring about reconciliation between husband and wife in cases of separation or desertion, and if this cannot be achieved it imposes and enforces the payment of support orders by the husband for his wife and children.

Home Conditions. The data on the physical aspects of the home were based on observations of the school attendance officer and the court's probation officer. They took into account the type of house or apartment, number of occupants and rooms, general cleanliness, adequacy of furniture and plumbing facilities. Physical home conditions were rated as "good" in 31.8 per cent; as "fair" in 28.6 per cent; as "poor" in 31.3 per cent. No data were available for the remainder of the cases studied.

Neighborhood. Neighborhood conditions also were evaluated in the attendance officers' and probation officers' reports. In 17.7 per cent they were rated "good"; in 48.6 per cent "fair," and in 33.6 per cent "poor."

Employment of Mothers. In 30 per cent of the cases the mother was employed, full time or part time.

TABLE 1.—MARITAL STATUS OF PARENTS

Marital Status of Parents	Total	Per cent of Total	White Boys	Nonwhite Boys	White Girls	Nonwhite Girls
All cases	220	100	113	50	40	17
Parents divorced . . .	8	4	6	—	2	—
Parents separated . . .	49	22	16	17	9	7
One parent deserted . . .	15	7	8	5	2	—
Father deceased	33	15	16	7	9	1
Mother deceased . . .	16	7	7	3	3	3
Both parents deceased . .	5	2	3	2	—	—
Parents not married . . .	13	6	2	7	2	2
Father in prison . . .	1	1	1	—	—	—
Father in state hospital . .	3	1	2	—	1	—
Parents married and living together	77	35	52	9	12	4

SCHOOL HISTORY

Types of Schools. The overwhelming majority of the 220 children, namely 201, were enrolled in public schools; 18 attended parochial schools of the Roman Catholic Church, one was registered in a private school. Exactly one-half of the group attended elementary school at the time the truancy petition was filed by the Board of Education, the other half was in junior high school, including 6 children attending vocational high school.

Grades. Forty-six children (or 21 per cent of the total) were assigned to special classes and special schools for orthogenic backward and orthogenic disciplinary pupils. There were 10 children who were not assigned to any class or for whom data regarding their school grades were not known. The ages and grades of the remaining 164 were compared with the ages and grades of the total school population. The school census served as source material indicating which grade the normal pupil of a given age attends. Using this means of comparison, it was found that while 11 truants were aged 9 to 11 inclusive, 38 of the truants attended grades 2 to 6; 34 truants were 12 or 13 years old, while 78 were enrolled in the corresponding grades 7 and 8; 111 truants were 14 and 15 years old, but only 47 had reached corresponding grades 9 and 10; 8 truants were past 16 years of age, but only one was in 11th grade. In other words 71 were retarded in their grade assignment. To these must be added 27 children who were in special classes or special schools due to backwardness (without grade assignment). All told, there were 98 out of 210 children (for whom assignment was known), or 47 per cent, who were retarded in school.

COURT HISTORY

Previous Court Referrals. Recidivism was found in 77 cases, or 35 per cent of the total. It should be pointed out, how-

ever, that 46 of the previous court referrals were concerned with minor delinquency charges and were "adjusted" or "dismissed" by the court. In the remainder of 31 cases, probation or commitment to foster homes and institutions was ordered. In 24 instances, or 11 per cent, the previous reason for referral also was truancy. It seems noteworthy that the percentage of recidivism of this group of 220 truants was considerably less than the percentage of repeaters among all children referred to the court for delinquent acts during 1946, which was 48 per cent.

Siblings' Delinquency. In 134 cases, or 61 per cent, 1 or more siblings previously had been referred to the court for delinquency; in 64 instances, or 29 per cent, truancy was the reason. It seems significant that a rather large proportion of the siblings of the truants had shown delinquent tendencies, as compared to the truants who themselves had been referred to the court before. It probably denotes a certain atmosphere of delinquency in the home of the truants.

Physical Status. Physical examinations revealed that 87 children (or 39.5 per cent) suffered from minor defects (such as infected or enlarged tonsils, carious teeth, defective vision, etc.), while 75 (or 34.1 per cent) had major troubles including 17 cases of heart disease, also hernia, obesity, asthma, nephritis, venereal disease, epilepsy, etc.

Intelligence. Table 2 shows the intelligence quotient of the 220 truants. It was arrived at through psychometric tests given by court psychologists immediately preceding the court hearing. About 44 per cent of the children had intelligence quotients of 85 and below. This percentage was very close to the previously mentioned figure for retardation in school (47 per cent). It compares favorably with the total delinquency group in which children with an I.Q. under 85 represented 56 per cent.

TABLE 2.—INTELLIGENCE QUOTIENT OF 220 TRUANTS

Intelligence Quotient	Total	Per cent of Total	White Boys	Nonwhite Boys	White Girls	Nonwhite Girls
All scores	220	100	113	50	40	17
60 and below	9	4	5	3	1	–
61 – 65	7	3	2	3	1	1
66 – 70	12	5	2	8	–	2
71 – 75	18	8	11	3	2	2
76 – 80	30	14	17	8	3	2
81 – 85	21	10	10	5	3	3
86 – 90	33	15	17	3	8	5
91 – 95	21	10	12	2	7	–
96 – 100	27	12	17	5	4	1
100 – 105	11	5	4	2	4	1
106 – 110	8	4	5	1	2	–
111 and above	11	5	6	1	4	–
No data	12	5	5	6	1	–

Reasons for Truancy as Recorded in the Court Investigations. Table 3 shows 15 factors contributing to truancy in the order of their frequency. The compilation is based upon the observation of the probation officer who investigated the case prior to court hearing. In exactly half of the cases two principal causes were given, and therefore the total of all reasons given is 330. The percentages are, of course, figured out on the basis of the 220 individual cases. Out of the seven first-ranking reasons four refer directly to some inadequacy in the family home, with "lack of supervision by parents" ranking first with 21 per cent, and "broken homes" second with 19 per cent. It should be stressed that this list of contributory causes is based upon the subjective judgment of the investigator; several of the factors might be overlapping.

Court Dispositions. Court dispositions resulted in 21 discharges, or in 10 per cent of the cases. Cases were continued for further report from the school authorities in 37 cases, or 17 per cent, mostly in order to give the youngster a chance to attend regularly. Probation was ordered in 66 instances, or 30 per cent; 54 boys, or 25 per cent of all truants, were committed to schools for truants,

TABLE 3.—MAIN REASONS FOR TRUANCY AMONG 220 TRUANTS AS RECORDED IN COURT INVESTIGATIONS

Reasons for Truancy	Frequency	Per cent*
Total	330	–
Lack of supervision by parents	47	21
Broken home	43	19
Parents unable to control child	39	18
Child's dislike for school in general	38	17
Indifference of parents .	23	10
Child wants to work (or is working illegally) .	23	10
Mother is working . .	21	10
Inadequate home . . .	18	8
Child associating with poor companions . .	16	7
Child disturbed . . .	16	7
Child mentally deficient (middle or low grade moron)	15	7
Mother sick	13	6
Child sick or physically handicapped . . .	9	4
Child's dislike for particular school . .	5	2
Father frequently absent	4	2

* Based on 220 truants rather than frequency of reasons given.

one maintained by the Board of Education, the other by the Roman Catholic Church. Twenty-four children, or 11 per cent, were committed to other institutions for delinquent children, and 10 to institutions for dependent children and child-placing agencies. The remainder of the dispositions consisted of the issuance of bench warrants, commitment to a hospital and to the custody of a relative.

Subsequent Court History. The court history subsequent to the disposition of the truancy situation, covering a period from 1 to 2 years—i.e., from the time of the court disposition to the time of this study—shows that truancy continued in 29 cases, or 13 per cent of the cases. This included 18 cases of children on probation. Forty-three other children were involved in one new offense other than truancy; 14 were involved in more than one offense other than truancy. In other words, 26 per cent committed one or more new offenses other than truancy. Satisfactory adjustment was noted in 134 instances, or 61 per cent.

Conclusions

The following summary findings with reference to environment, school history and court history might be listed:

Environment

1. The truant children of the group studied came, on the average, from fairly large families.

2. In almost two-thirds of the cases broken home conditions prevailed, a larger proportion than found in the total group of delinquent children.

3. About one-third of the physical home conditions and a little more than one-third of the neighborhood conditions were evaluated as "poor."

4. In 30 per cent of the cases the family income was so low as to compel the mother to secure full- or part-time employment.

School History

5. Almost one-fourth of the truant children were assigned to special classes, special schools, or were not assigned at all.

6. Almost half of the truant children were retarded in school.

Court History

7. Siblings of the truants had been referred to the court for delinquency in 61 per cent of the cases. In 29 per cent of the cases they had been truant.

8. Only in 26.3 per cent of the cases were the findings of the physical examinations entirely negative.

9. There were less children with low I.Q.'s in the truants' group than in the total delinquency group; but even so, 44 per cent had I.Q.'s of 85 and below.

10. Inadequacy of the family home, and particularly lack of supervision and broken home conditions, ranked first among the factors contributing to truancy.

These results of the study in Philadelphia tend to corroborate the findings of similar investigations undertaken in other communities. Much has been written about the school's responsibility to be on the alert for the presence of the above listed symptoms, inherent in the truancy picture, as "tell-tale" signs of potential delinquency, so that preventive measures can be taken at an early time.

Suggestions for School and Court

What is the juvenile court's role with respect to the truancy problem, particularly in relation to the school authorities? Being constituted as a court of law, the juvenile court is only secondarily a preventive agency. It can function solely after some form of delinquent behavior, in this instance habitual truancy, has been ascertained.

From the experience in Philadelphia which is duplicated in many other communities, the following observations might be noted:

1. Any effective program of controlling truancy is predicated upon a close co-operation between the board of education and the juvenile court and a clear understanding about the limits of their

respective functions. The juvenile court can expect from the school authorities that a thorough and conscientious job of screening has preceded each referral of a truancy situation to the court and that, consequently, only those cases are brought to its attention which cannot be handled satisfactorily within the school system itself. The school can expect from the juvenile court that truancy cases referred to it are not considered to be of less importance than other cases involving offenses which are on the criminal statute books. Truancy as a symptom of deep emotional disturbances frequently calls for a more painstaking study and a more intensive plan of treatment than does an occasional stealing episode. It would be a violation of the spirit of juvenile court legislation and practice to measure the importance of a case in terms of types of offenses rather than the seriousness of the behavior disorder.

2. Co-operation between court and school, in individual cases, means a full exchange of information regarding the personality of the child, his family background, his school history, and other social and medical data known to either of the two agencies.

3. It has proved of great value to have a representative of the school authorities attending all juvenile court hearings, including nontruancy cases, and to give him an opportunity to present his appraisal of the case and to make recommendations for its disposition.

4. Despite the best intentions toward constructive co-operation, reactions such as "the other agency passes the buck" or "does not do enough," are bound to creep up occasionally. A good way to avoid confusion and combat misunderstandings of this kind is to invite a representative of the school authorities to explain their functions, limitations, and problems to the probation officers of the juvenile court, and vice versa.

5. Plans for so-called "parental schools" (i.e. institutions for truants), if they are needed in the community, especially in urban areas, should be the result of common deliberation between school and court representatives.

These are some suggestions to implement real co-operation between court and school. The writer does not consider this list as exhaustive; nor does he overlook the equally important co-operation and co-ordination of services between the school, the court, child-placing and family welfare agencies, recreational groups, child-guidance and mental hygiene clinics, churches.

Since this report deals with the truant before the juvenile court, it has been felt that special emphasis should be laid upon the two agencies which are primarily involved—the school and the court. Their common problems are based on individual and social inadequacies, their common methods are direction and guidance with a constructive use of authority, their common aim is the welfare of our youth.

Church Attendance and Juvenile Misconduct*

By William W. Wattenberg. Wayne University, Detroit.

As is true of so many reports concerning delinquency, various authorities disagree as to the relationship between church attendance and juvenile mis-

* Reprinted from *Sociology and Social Research*, Volume 34, January, 1950, pp. 195–202. Used by permission.

conduct. Moreover, such scientific studies as have been made show inconsistent or contradictory findings.

In 1948 J. Edgar Hoover stated flatly: "In practically all homes where juvenile delinquency is bred there is an absence of adequate religious training for children. . . . Most of them have never been inside a church."

By contrast, in 1944 William Kvaraceus, on the basis of facts gathered concerning more than seven hundred delinquent boys and girls brought to the Children's Bureau of Passaic, New Jersey, while he was Director, declared that 54 per cent of them attended church regularly and 25 per cent seldom or never. The remainder were irregular in attendance. He also found that there was no significant difference between percentages of church membership among delinquents and the entire population of New Jersey.

A much more carefully developed study (Carr-Saunders) in England gave still other results. A comparison of 276 London delinquents with 551 nondelinquents from the same neighborhoods found 29 per cent of the delinquents and but 39 per cent of the nondelinquents regularly attending religious institutions. A similar study in provincial towns found 41 per cent of the delinquents and 51 per cent of the nondelinquents to be regular in church attendance. In both city and country there was a clear difference of 10 per cent favoring the church attendance of nondelinquents.

At this point we must issue a caution concerning the way the whole question is approached. Some are likely to approach such an investigation as though the value of religion were being questioned. To them, figures and opinions such as have been cited are used to "prove" that it is either effective, ineffective, or partially effective.

To those interested in reducing the toll of delinquency upon young lives, the questions to be asked would be phrased differently, something like these: With how many youngsters in trouble do religious bodies now have contact? What part is religion playing in the lives of those with whom such contact exists? What can be done to make this contact more vital in helping the young people to develop more consistently social patterns of behavior?

Statistics gathered by the Crime Prevention Bureau and the Boys' Juvenile Bureau of the Detroit Police Department throw some light on the answers to the first two questions. Beginning in August 1946, all boys picked up for offenses were interviewed to obtain answers to questions concerning their environment, home conditions, and their own characteristics. In addition, in most cases their homes were visited by police officers. Among the items upon which the officers gathered information was the relative frequency of church attendance.

The findings for the first group of 2,137 boys are shown in Table 1. It will be seen that a considerable pro-

TABLE 1

CHURCH ATTENDANCE OF BOYS INTERVIEWED ON COMPLAINT BY DETROIT POLICE, 1946

Frequency of Attendance	Number of Boys	Percentage of Boys
Regular	931	43.56
Occasional	546	25.54
Seldom	339	15.86
Never	302	14.15
Not stated	19	.89
Total	2,137	100.00

portion were credited with regular church attendance. The percentage was lower than that found by Kvaraceus, somewhat higher than that reported by Carr-Saunders, and vastly greater than that estimated by Hoover. If the "regular" and "occasional" groups are combined, the churches can claim some marked degree of contact with roughly two thirds of the boys in trouble in Detroit.

These results are subject to some question. First, there is a good possibility that some boys and their parents were

The original group of 2,137 was followed in 1947 as far as the records of the Crime Prevention Bureau would permit. Those who were in trouble again numbered 672. It can be fairly assumed that these repeaters included the more seriously delinquent boys. The group of 1,465 nonrepeaters, on the other hand, included many who had been minor offenders in 1946 or who had learned to stay out of trouble successfully for at least one year. Table 2 shows the relative percentage of church attendance for these two groups.

TABLE 2

CHURCH ATTENDANCE OF REPEATERS AND NONREPEATERS

Frequency	Total	Number Repeaters	Nonrepeaters	Per cent Repeaters	Nonrepeaters
Regular	931	254	677	37.8	46.2
Occasional	546	182	364	27.1	24.8
Seldom	339	131	208	19.5	14.2
Never	302	100	202	14.9	13.8
Not stated	19	5	14	0.7	1.0
Total	2,137	672	1,465	100.0	100.0

Chi-square equals 16.75.
Degrees of freedom equals 4.
P is less than 0.01.

intent upon making a favorable impression and therefore claimed a higher regularity of church attendance than the facts warranted. Accordingly, the findings should be discounted to some extent. The internal evidence of the data, however, indicates that falsification of the replies was far from universal; as we shall see, there were some distinct differences between the boys reporting regular attendance and those reporting they seldom or never went to church.

More serious, the percentages mean little unless they can be compared with those prevailing in the general population. There was no possibility of making the necessary survey with the resources available. An alternate possibility, however, was available and could be used.

The chi-square calculation, shown at the base of the table is merely a statistical device for calculating the probability that differences of this kind might be due to chance factors. For those not trained in statistics it will suffice to state that where, as in this table, P is less than 0.01, the statistical odds are better than 100 to 1 that a repetition of the study with another group, similarly selected, would yield substantially the same results.

The table shows a clear connection between church attendance and the likelihood that a boy in trouble with the police once will be in trouble again. Boys claiming regular church attendance were 37.8 per cent of the repeaters but 46.2 per cent of the nonrepeaters. On the other hand, those reporting they seldom went to church were 19.5 per cent of the repeaters but only 14.2 per cent of the nonrepeaters. In blunt police terms, a boy who goes to church regularly is a better risk than one who does not do so. Yet churches still have substantial con-

ance: (1) whether or not the boys' parents were living together and (2) whether the police officers had rated the neighborhood as "good," "average," or "poor." Table 3 presents the tabulation for all boys for whom information on the three factors was available.

TABLE 3

RELATIONSHIPS BETWEEN CHURCH ATTENDANCE, CHARACTER OF NEIGHBORHOOD, AND INTACTNESS OF HOMES OF BOYS INTERVIEWED ON COMPLAINT BY DETROIT POLICE, 1946

Frequency of Church Attendance	Good Neighbor- hood	Broken Homes Average Neighbor- hood	Poor Neighbor- hood	Good Neighbor- hood	Unbroken Homes Average Neighbor- hood	Poor Neighbor- hood
Regular	32	96	52	119	236	95
Occasional	20	87	61	44	129	57
Seldom	9	60	29	16	86	37
Never	11	45	28	28	80	35
Total	72	288	170	207	531	224

Chi-square equals 78.27.
Degrees of freedom equals 6.
P is less than 0.01.

tact with a significant number of even the repeaters.

There is, of course, the possibility that the clear relationship found is not necessarily one of cause and effect but that both the church attendance and the relative immunity to repeating may be products of some other situation, such as family morale, good neighborhood conditions, and particular patterns of upbringing. It is also very probable that, for example, the religious beliefs of the parents might lead them to keep a home intact rather than to break it by divorce. By the same token, they would be concerned to see that their sons received a religious background. In such cases both the intact home and the religious instruction might combine to strengthen the boy's resistance to delinquency.

There were two items of information gathered by the police which one would expect to be related to church attend-

As the chi-square test shows, a very high and statistically significant relationship does exist. Further analysis reveals that this is due to high concentrations in 2 of the 24 subgroups: (1) boys living in unbroken homes in good neighborhoods and claiming regular church attendance, and (2) boys living in broken homes in poor neighborhoods and reporting occasional church attendance.

The first group includes a relatively high number of cases because in the general population in good neighborhoods unbroken homes and high church attendance are very frequent. This concentration, therefore, is probably a reflection of general conditions rather than of forces making for delinquency.

The second group, however, does deserve close attention. Here, we are probably dealing with a complex of interrelated causal factors. In some cases, for example, the backing of a home may force the mother and children to move into a poor neighborhood where the conditions may weaken family morale and result in a backsliding in religious observance; all of the factors may play a part in the delinquency of the boys. In other cases, lack of religious belief may make a family living in a bad neighborhood so susceptible to the neighborhood's disrupting influences that the parents separate and the boys become delinquent; the delinquency and the separation are both reactions to the way the boys on the one hand and the parents on the other regard themselves and their obligations to each other. Other and even more complicated interactions are possible.

To try to untangle such interlocking patterns of cause and effect is not possible at this stage of the game. What we can say with confidence is that church attendance is part of a cultural complex involving family solidarity and neighborhood standards which is definitely related to juvenile misconduct. We can also say that religion is most likely to produce shifts in misconduct among young people living in poor neighborhoods or suffering the handicaps of broken homes.

A careful analysis showed that low church attendance was concentrated in homes broken by divorce rather than those broken by death.

There was one other type of analysis which we could make from the facts available. In most cases, the records showed the offense charged against the boy. Therefore, it would be possible to see whether boys claiming regular church attendance were more likely to avoid particular types of misconduct. Another way of putting the matter is to ask whether regular church attendance tends to immunize boys against particular temptations or pressures.

Table 4 presents a summary of one analysis of this sort. In the table the frequency of offenses for boys claiming regular church attendance is compared with that for boys whose attendance was reported as occasional, seldom, or never. The ratio between the two groups was 10 to 13. There was no very strong difference in this ratio for any group of offenses; the strongest was a ratio of 10 to 20 in the case of robbery, but numbers here were quite small. The chi-square calculation confirms the general impression that no conclusively strong relation-

TABLE 4

RELATIONSHIP BETWEEN REGULARITY OF CHURCH ATTENDANCE AND OFFENSES CHARGED AGAINST BOYS INTERVIEWED ON COMPLAINT BY DETROIT POLICE, 1946

Charge	Total	Regular Attendants	All Others	Ratio Regular : Others
Assaults	45	20	25	10 : 13
Sex Offenses	48	24	24	10 : 10
Robbery	25	8	17	10 : 20
Burglary	263	105	158	10 : 15
Larceny	468	207	261	10 : 12
Auto thefts	96	50	46	10 : 10
Drunk	26	12	14	10 : 11
Disorderly	90	33	57	10 : 18
Traffic offenses	42	19	23	10 : 12
Miscellaneous	604	260	344	10 : 13
Total	1,707	738	969	10 : 13

Chi-square equals 9.26.
Degrees of freedom equals 9.
P is less than 0.50 but greater than 0.30.

ship exists. The influence of church attendance on juvenile misconduct lies, then, in lowering the general likelihood that a boy will get into trouble rather than in specifically strengthening resistance to particular offenses.

There is always the possibility that in a case like this, where apparently no relationship exists, the negative results really mask relationships which do exist in various subgroups. Therefore, a final series of analyses was made of the relationships between church attendance and offenses for each type of neighborhood and for each type of home: (1) unbroken, (2) parents separated, (3) parents divorced, (4) mother dead, (5) father dead, and (6) both parents dead.

With one minor exception, all results were inconclusive. The exception was a tendency for sex offenses to be high where the father was reported dead and there was regular church attendance. The police officers who collected the information say that in many of these cases the boy was really born out of wedlock and the mother camouflaged the facts by reporting she had a husband whose absence was explained by death. In such instances, especially where the mother was quite religious, the whole area of sex would receive a special attention from the mother and possible mishandling of education in that area could acount for the warping which showed itself in sex offenses. If this is true the causal factor is the mother's guilt rather than the boy's attendance at church.

The significant fact, however, is that all the other analyses were inconclusive. This would seem to bolster the previous findings that church attendance is part of a way of living which generally reduces tendencies toward juvenile misconduct.

The Comics War*

By John R. Cavanagh. Senior Medical Officer and Psychiatrist, U. S. Naval Disciplinary Barracks, Portsmouth, New Hampshire.

PITY THE POOR parents perturbed by the profound proclamations of psychiatrists and psychologists (and many others) concerning the menace to their children from reading the "Comics"! They cannot see the harm themselves, in fact the daily comic book session comes as a welcome relief from the children's usual turbulence. However, trained as we are from childhood to accept the authority of science, such a paragraph as this one written by Agatha Shea (Chicago Public Library) must be very disconcerting.

Every now and then, when tragedy enters into the life of some boy or girl, investigation leads back to the youth's reading of the comic books and their incitement to crime and the community is, for the time being, alerted to the daily menace of our children. Sometimes our cities are moved to take legal action against the publishers and purveyors of this unfit reading matter for children, but at its best such action is necessarily slow and not always immediately effective. In the meantime children continue to buy and read these crime and sex ridden booklets, and the home too often pays little heed until one of its own boys or girls becomes the victim or perpetrator of a crime. I have talked with hundreds of Chicago parents on this subject and find them all gravely concerned. They point out, and rightly, that banning unsuitable comic magazines from the home only means outside reading and borrowing with

* Reprinted from *The Journal of Criminal Law and Criminology* (Northwestern University School of Law), Vol. XL, June, 1949, by John R. Cavanagh.

perhaps a little added excitement in the circumventing of authority. What then can be done about this ever present problem? Must parents sit with folded hands while their children's morals and ideals are broken and a perverted view of life is left on impressionable minds?

Such statements are doubly disturbing to parents who have read a well thought out article in *Child Study*, a journal which they have always considered authoritative in its field, which stated unequivocally: "There is no competent evidence that reading about crime makes criminals. The motivation towards unsocial acts lies much deeper than any casual contact with ideas printed on a page."

Again, may I repeat, pity the poor parent! He is bombarded daily with a prolific literature on this subject which is almost completely bereft of logic and facts but replete with questions and exclamation marks. Little factual evidence has been produced that the comics are harmful. A small number of cases have been produced in which comic book reading has preceded or accompanied the commission of a crime. Actually, does this prove anything? This is the *post hoc ergo propter hoc* form of argumentation which even the freshman student of dialectics has learned is a fallacious one. If it is true as we are told, that 40,000,000 comic books circulate each month and that each one has several readers, should not their harmful effects, if any, be more evident? Emotionalism sells better than intellectualism, and makes better copy.

There is no need to prove that the comics are popular. This fact is already known. How popular they are is little short of amazing. There is no question but that they are big business today. It is difficult at first to grasp the fact that a reliable source indicates that in 1946 the monthly circulation was 40,000,-000. This is especially remarkable when we realize that the first of the modern

comic books was published in 1933. It is further estimated that each comic book is read by several people and that 75 per cent of all comic books are purchased by children out of their own funds—an outlay of $300,000 a month or $3,600,000 per year.

While we are on the statistical angle of the subject I should like to present just a few more figures, derived from Waugh's book entitled "The Comics," an excellent history of the comic book from its beginning to the present day.

(1) Between the ages of 6 and 11, 95 per cent of boys and 91 per cent of girls buy comics as a steady diet.
(2) Between the ages of 12 and 17, 87 per cent of boys and 81 per cent of girls use comics regularly.
(3) Between the ages of 18 and 30, 41 per cent of men and 28 per cent of women retain their interest.
(4) After the age of 30, 16 per cent of men and 12 per cent of women read them.
(5) During World War II, the *combined sales* of *Life, Readers Digest,* and *The Saturday Evening Post* were exceeded by the comic books by a ratio of 10–1.

If the comics are as bad as we hear they are, something should be done about them. What we need, however, are fewer exclamations and more facts. Up to the present there have been more references to the harmful effects of the comics in the popular press than in the professional literature. So far we have been in the position of scooping the water out of the tub with a cup to keep it from overflowing rather than turning off the water. My plea is to investigate first why children like comics and secondly to determine, if possible, how harmful they really are.

It is good medical practice to seek the cause of the disease before attempting a cure and it is good teaching practice to begin where the children are. I should like, therefore, to offer an explanation of the psychodynamics of a child's interest in the comics. Waugh has a simple explanation for this which has much truth in it. He states: "Then to a child, the comic book goes directly at the business of satisfying you in the most sensible possible manner. No long-winded introduction—the action starts right off—and that's what you want, you want things to happen very fast, and, of course, in pictures where you can see it all; and then they are in bright, gay colors, not like the silly, gray newspapers grownups read." Unfortunately the full explanation is probably not so simple.

For those who are unfamiliar with the psychodynamics of aggression and phantasy, I should like to review briefly some of the facts concerning them before proceeding further.

Aggression

Aggression has been defined as a primary human characteristic necessary for survival in the struggle for existence. There is a tendency, even among those who should know better, to confuse this term with other words of similar meanings such as hostility, hate and sadism. These terms are not synonymous with aggression and should be distinguished from it. Hostility means a feeling of ill-will or enmity. Sadism is the derivation of pleasure from the infliction of pain on another person of the opposite sex, and hate is a feeling of intense aversion. On the other hand, aggression is sometimes an expression of anger and, depending on the milieu, it may manifest itself in more than one way. For example, it may show itself clinically merely as self asertion, or as an attempt to destroy the object or person who is the cause of the aggression or who has deprived the subject of something or who has something he wants. This sounds like a dangerous and undesirable trait to possess, but as indicated in the definition, it is universal among us. In its socialized form it is seen in the competition of athletics or business. This trait is so important and universal that

many have considered that it is inborn —an instinct as important and as essential as the better known instinct of self preservation. Recent investigators are more inclined to view it as an acquired characteristic in spite of its universality. As an acquired trait aggression may arise from one of several possible causes the most important of which is unquestionably frustration. Other common causes are insecurity and feelings of inferiority. If frustration is an important cause of aggression its presence in children is readily understood because childhood consists of a series of frustrations of greater or less degrees. We should bear in mind that aggression may be a response not only to actual but anticipated frustration. The wide distribution of aggression is attested by Percival M. Symonds who states: "Frustration is universal and so far as frustration is necessary, aggression, as a response to it, is equally necessary . . . When a mother asks 'Is it necessary for my child to be aggressive, to be impolite to other children, to insist on having his own way' one can only answer that these tendencies are not only common and universal, but, in fact, necessary and inherent."

It is obvious that we cannot, or at least should not overtly display our aggression (desire to attack or destroy). Such expression is definitely frowned on in our present stage of civilization and the mature adult attempts to disguise or suppress any emotional expression. Even children who are more forthright in the expression of their feelings recognize the necessity of disguising their aggression because of the inevitable punishment which would follow its expression. Each age, however, has its own favorite method of showing displeasure with the way things are going. The small child may scream, cry, hit, bite or have a temper tantrum, the child in school may refuse to eat, get poor marks, destroy property, be insubordinate or insolent. The adolescent may steal, tease, swear or be sarcastic. Each age has its favorite method of expression but they all mean the same, *viz.* anger against someone or something. Spanking is an aggressive act on the part of the parent against the child. As pointed out before not all aggressive behavior is antisocial behavior. It may be sublimated in many ways and show itself in a socially acceptable form in contests both scholastic and athletic. All business contacts are of a similar nature. Our aggressive feelings may be sublimated in a variety of ways.

All children are subjected to frustrations. Ideally a child's frustrations should be repeated and small. This is the essence of good child training. Such repeated small exposures are not likely to build up a larger store of aggression than the child is able to manage through his normal outlets, as during play or other competition. It is only when a child's aggressive tendencies become greater than he can handle that it is likely to result in fear and anxiety on his part and may then manifest itself in antisocial behavior or in a neurosis.

The above discussion may be summarized thus: (a) Aggression results from frustration, insecurity and feelings of inferiority and is universal in children. (b) The usual outlet for this feeling is in rough aggressive play or in misbehavior. (c) In some cases, unless aggression is drained off, it may pile up and result in a neurosis or gravely anti-social behavior.

Phantasy

Before drawing any conclusions from the above discussion I would like to take up another phase of the child's psychological existence. This is his phantasy life. Phantasy, or as it is better known, daydreaming, is a normal phase of the child's development. It has been defined as the mental anticipation or *substitute* for the actual fulfillment of a wish. It serves many useful purposes during the child's period of development in giving him substitute satisfaction for his thwarted desires, in giving him relief from the pressure and painfulness of reality, and it serves also as a defense against unacceptable behavior. He is, by this means, able to escape from the guilt which he would otherwise develop from any overt misbehavior by phantasying the situation in the role of a spectator. For those who have repressed their own childhood phantasies it may be well to emphasize that the daydreams of children and adolescents are consistently filled with episodes of crime, violence and death or such erotic trends as love and marriage. Punishment and cruelty play a large part in their phantasies. These thoughts have been present in the minds of children since history began. The comic books do not place them there.

Phantasy and play acting are a normal phase of the child's development and it is only when the daydreams are based on anxiety that they tend to be exaggerated and may be carried over into overt activity. Phantasy becomes harmful when it serves as a means of escape from reality and thus becomes an end in itself. For example, if an adolescent would rather daydream about having a date than to actually have one, it is pathological.

Psychodynamics

It is apparent, therefore, that the normal aggressive reactions find release in the phantasies stimulated by the comic books which thus become the means by which children are able to work off their hostility towards their parents and others without the development of guilt which they might otherwise feel. They may thus displace onto the characters in the comic books the aggression which would otherwise be too dangerous to show overtly or even to imagine. Many have commented on the quieting effect of the comics, the "marijuana of the nursery," usually in the belief that this is harmful. It seems more likely that the child is merely projecting himself into the story and releasing his aggression in the realm of phantasy rather than finding it necessary to be noisy, troublesome or to indulge in other overt aggressive behavior. For the normal child such conduct is not harmful or detrimental. For the neurotic child it could be detrimental but not necessarily so, and in any case he will be equally harmed by the radio or movies.

Another element which probably contributes to a child's interest in the comics is the Gestalt factor. This refers to the fact that we normally view things as wholes. Adults more readily grasp the full meaning of written words because they have more associations to each word as a result of their experiences than a child could possibly have. A child reads a sentence and frequently fails to grasp the full meaning because the finer shades of meaning escape him. All of us, even to the present day, prefer books with pictures. We like to see the author's concept of the hero or heroine; we like maps which help us to follow the action. The child likes pictures which help him to grasp the meaning of the words, to give him a better Gestalt—a better view of the whole meaning. Educators might learn a lesson from this for the higher grades. We already teach children to read by showing them the pictures which represent the word they are learning.

Objectionable Comics

The prevalent attitude seems to be that all comics are objectionable. This is certainly not the case, and if you read the "fine print" almost everyone who writes about the comics admits this. Unfortunately, the average reader is not concerned with the ordinary, work-a-day writings. His attention must be caught and retained. If it is not, many of our daily article writers will be out of work. So, in order to retain an audience it is necessary to highlight the unusual, the bizarre, the sensuous, the anxiety producing factors. The facts are there, but the usual, the ordinary have slight sales value and consequently must be softened in the interest of the stimulating, unusual items.

There are comics which are undesirable. These are in the minority. The group known collectively as "jungle adventure comics" typify this class. Within the group all of the features are displayed which have been considered objectionable. Here are found the scantily clad females, the chained females and the sexually suggestive situations which are the comics' most objectionable feature. However, such pictures and situations become significant principally when viewed through the repressions of the viewer and seem to arouse little anxiety in the well adjusted reader.

Conclusions

From the tone of this paper it might be concluded that the writer is attempting to prepare a "White Paper" for the comics. This is not the case. He is merely suggesting that we stop trying to hold back the tide with emotionalism and that we approach the problem realistically. The arguments being so vigorously vocalized against the comics are the same ones used against the movies in their early days. Fortunately the movies are still with us and play an important part in education. The more we write about these "sex ridden" booklets the more adults are going to purchase them. Actually they are not as salacious as many writers would have us believe. Young children, contrasted with mature folk, are not interested in sex as suggested by posture and scanty clothing. The comic book publishers, being business men, give their public what it wants.

I should like to digress for a moment to suggest that some of the vehemence against the comics is aroused in those adults who have trouble in handling their own aggressiveness and whose conscious or unconscious conflicts are stirred into action by what they see there. Be that as it may, parents who develop a distaste for comic books for whatever reason, are not helping their children to deal with them in a realistic manner. It would be much better if they inquired into them, find out what their children like about them and why they find them so absorbing. Any undesirable comics would disappear off the news stand if parents took sufficient interest to look over the comics their children read and to direct their reading.

I conclude these remarks with the following observations:

(1) No one has conclusively demonstrated that the comic books are detrimental in any way.

(2) Campaigns to eliminate them are useless and serve only to release the aggressive feeling of the crusaders.

(3) No normal child under the age of 12 is likely to be harmed by them. Neurotic children need treatment and would be equally affected by the movies or the radio.

(4) Normal adolescents may be harmed by certain types of comics especially the "jungle adventure" type.

(5) Parents are the best judges of what their children should read. If parents supervise their children's reading of comics the undesirable ones would soon disappear.

(6) The argument that children waste time on the comics, which could be better spent needs further study.

(7) More study should be devoted to eliciting the facts about the comics.

(8) There will always be objections to everything but most of the objectionable features of the comics would be remedied if the publishers would adhere to a few simple rules among which I would like to suggest:

(a) Law enforcement officers should not be made to look ridiculous or silly.

(b) References should be omitted to petty crimes or crimes committed against or by children.

(c) Pictures should be omitted of scantily clad women, of women being tortured by men or of chained women.

(d) The contents of the book should be reflected in its cover.

SELECTED REFERENCES

1. Lesser, Edith K., "Understanding Juvenile Delinquency," *Federal Probation*, XIII, September 1949.

This article well illustrates the sociological truism that delinquency is learned behavior, particularly in reference to the educational milieu. The continuing responsibility of the school is justifiably stressed.

2. Taber, Robert C., "The Potential Role of the School Counselor in Delinquency Prevention and Treatment," *Federal Probation*, XIII, September 1949.

As a comparatively recent innovation in the educational process, the increasingly important role of the school counselor is presented, a role designed to be effective in both the prevention and treatment of delinquency.

3. Ellingston, John R., *Protecting Our Children from Criminal Careers* (New York: Prentice-Hall, 1948), Chapter 27: "The Unsolved Problem of Leisure Time."

The necessity of supervision during leisure hours of children to help reduce youthful delinquency is discussed in a forthright manner. Fun and enjoyment are no longer "sinful," and the steady increase of the hours relegated to recreation makes this area peculiarly significant.

4. Teeters, Negley K. and Reinemann, John Otto, *The Challenge of Delinquency* (New York: Prentice-Hall, 1950), Chapter 6: "Cultural Factors and Delinquency."

The authors present a most interesting as well as informative discussion of juvenile delinquency as it is affected by the press, the movies, radio, comic books and comic strips.

5. Blumer, Herbert, and Hauser, P. M., *The Movies, Delinquency, and Crime* (New York: The Macmillan Co., 1933).

For students particularly interested in the effect of the motion pictures on young people—and the relationship to delinquency—this study will be helpful and of consequence.

5 SPECIAL PERSONALITY AND BEHAVIOR PROBLEMS

JUVENILE delinquency is usually symptomatic of an underlying disorganization of the individual's personality or of his social environment or of both. It is not a disease or a clinical entity. Juvenile delinquency is a descriptive term referring to asocial and antisocial behavior.

Delinquency is not necessarily the overt manifestation of basic personality disorganization. Although the available evidence is not conclusive, it is possible that there is not an appreciably higher percentage of emotionally maladjusted boys in reform schools than among those on probation, in detention homes, or in the general population. On various personality tests, reformatory groups do not suffer much by comparison with noninstitutionalized youth. The stereotype of the juvenile delinquent as a mentally or emotionally "deficient" should be discarded.

In *Unraveling Juvenile Delinquency*, a recent study in a distinguished series of investigations by these authors, the Gluecks present a pattern (possibly extreme) of a "dynamic" offender which is diametrically opposed to the frequently held image of the delinquent—the weak, skinny, pasty-complexioned, who skulks about in a furtive manner smoking the inevitable cigarette. They describe this "typical" juvenile delinquent as follows:

> The delinquents, as a group, tend toward the outline of a solid, closely knit, muscular type, one in which there is a relative predominance of muscle, bone, and connective tissue. . . .
>
> On the whole, the delinquents are more extroverted, vivacious, impulsive, and less self-controlled than the non-delinquents. They are more hostile, resentful, defiant, suspicious, and destructive. They are less fearful of failure or defeat than the non-delinquent. . . .
>
> It is evidently difficult for them to develop the high degree of flexibility of adaptation, self-management, self-control, sublimation of primitive tendencies and self-centered desires demanded by the complex and confused culture of the times.[1]

Very likely this description approaches the misleading view of a counterstereotype. Yet it serves as a warning that any fixed notion of the delinquent as a "personality type" does not square with the facts. The latter call for a conception of the juvenile delinquent prohibiting distinctions on the basis of psychotic and psychoneurotic traits. This does not mean that psychological and psychiatric knowledge is unimportant in understanding and working with

---

[1] Sheldon and Eleanor Glueck, *Unraveling Juvenile Delinquency* (New York: The Commonwealth Fund, 1950), pp. 274, 275, 278.

delinquency. Certainly the specialist should have technical competence in the field of personality disorders to plan any program of rehabilitation for the delinquent. This very competence provides child guidance clinics, whose personnel utilize techniques developed in medicine, psychiatry, psychology, and social work, one of the principal tools essential for effective work.

PHYSIOLOGICAL FACTORS AND PERSONALITY

Personality disorganization may be aggravated by various physiological circumstances. Consider the case, reported a few years ago, of the sixteen-year-old offender, bald as a cue ball, who faced the court charged with burglary. The judge being convinced that the conspicuous hairlessness played a part in the boy's delinquency, had him fitted for a toupee and released him to relatives in another county, rather than commiting him to an institution. The restoration of a more normal appearance may account for the fact that no further trouble from him was reported. Similar physiological "stigmata" have been witnessed in court cases—such as a very large nose, eyes of two colors, acne, a club foot. And there seems little doubt that these "deformities"—as defined by the youngsters themselves and by some of their fellows—often play an important role in encouraging individuals to "fight back" by delinquent acts. Such physical characteristics may induce special psychological difficulties within individuals and self-conceptions that are socially unacceptable and individually and socially harmful.

NEUROTIC AND PSYCHOTIC FACTORS AND PERSONALITY

Because of the seemingly irresistible nature of their acts, the crimes committed by neurotic and psychotic offenders are only incidental to the satisfaction of the inner urges that are imperious in their demands. Offenders with psychoneuroses are usually persistent offenders. Neurotic categories would include various forms of hysteria, those having obsessions (of blindness, deafness, of being followed), and those driven by compulsions indicated by the manias, such as pyromania (compulsive fire-setting) and kleptomania (compulsive stealing). In addition are the phobias (abnormal fears) and the philias (abnormal loves). The neurotic, unlike the psychotic, is more of a nuisance than a danger to himself and others. Outstanding traits include his marked inefficiency and his inadequacy in adjusting himself to his environment, as well as deep feelings of uneasiness and guilt. The neurotic's misbehavior is an act of compromise, so that any direct attack upon his misconduct is apt to be futile. Arrest, conviction, and imprisonment only tend to reinforce his own feelings of inferiority. But neurotic or psychotic personality conflicts, it should be remembered, do not lead *inevitably* into crime. Most criminals, in fact, are not maladjusted mentally, and most psychologically maladjusted persons are not criminals.

The truly psychotic offender is divorced from reality. He has little insight into himself or into the conditions responsible for his crime. The paranoic, for example, may burn the house of one who is "working against him," or he may murder his enemy's entire family, even his own, as he labors under delusions of grandeur or persecution. The schizophrenic is most likely of all psychotics to commit a crime. Paranoid schizophrenics may murder because they have heard the "voice of God" commanding them to do so. The encephalitics have the highest specific relation to crime, resulting sometimes in grotesque suicide, self-mutilation, and violent destruction of property. Senile dements engage in crimes of rage and temper and sex offenses against children. Paretics (those reaching the terminal stage of syphilis) sometimes commit assault and murder. Manic-depressives may pass worthless checks in the manic phase or commit suicide during the depressive phase. Juvenile offenders, when psychotic, are most apt to be schizophrenic; significantly, schizophrenia was formerly known as dementia praecox.

The number of cases that fit the different neurotic and psychotic categories depends in part upon the particular clinic or psychologist involved. Diagnoses in the field of psychiatry, not being an exact matter, are highly variable, sometimes diametrically opposed. For example, one or more psychiatrists may testify for the prosecution in an insanity plea and find the defendent "sane"; in the identical case, other psychiatrists for the defense may find him "insane."

On the other hand, American jurisprudence has failed to keep step with dynamic psychiatry. This lag helps to account for the fact that it may be decreed that one offender is a "neurotic" and thus not insane, while another is a "psychotic" and therefore *ipso facto* not responsible for his acts. But what is the difference, it has been asked, between a schizophrenic who walks around naked because "voices" have told him to do so and the exhibitionist who, without hallucinations but through some obscure and irresistible inner urge, feels driven to expose himself in public? Insofar as basic motivations are concerned, is one more or less "insane" than the other? Fairly frequently questions of this order face officials and others who deal with juvenile delinquency itself.

Ideally, of course, competent clinicians in the juvenile delinquency field should decide whether the offender should be treated as a "mental" case or not. The crime's very nature, especially if it is of a bizarre type, may reflect emotional disorders of the culprit and as such should be thoroughly investigated by professionally competent personnel. For the jailing or imprisonment of compulsive offenders, including, for example, many homosexuals, is not only a cruel measure from a humanitarian point of view but precludes the type of remedial work essential for adequate correction.

MENTAL RETARDATION AND DELINQUENCY

Probably the greatest impetus to the American "feebleminded school" of delinquency came from the writings of H. H. Goddard, who many years ago suggested that all criminals and delinquents are feebleminded, that the criminal type is really a species of feebleminded, and due to personal and social pressures may be driven into crime and delinquency for which persons of this type are "fitted by nature."[2] The inadequacy and misleading nature of such views is, of course, now an elementary lesson in social science. However, even today many people believe that there is a high correlation between feeblemindedness and

[2] H. H. Goddard, *Feeblemindedness: Its Causes and Consequences* (New York: The Macmillan Co., 1914), p. 37.

delinquency. Furthermore, there is considerable confusion generally in properly distinguishing between mental disease and mental deficiency. And in some cases, there is no clear-cut distinction between the two phenomena, since they both may be found in one individual.

Retardation of development is a basic characteristic of the feebleminded—they take longer to walk, to talk, and even their dentition is delayed. Most mentally retarded boys and girls have poor memories and tend to be creatures of habit.

Mental defectiveness, though rarely an immediate cause of unlawful behavior, is nevertheless associated with it. Usually more suggestible than the average youth because they lack developed critical faculties, the feebleminded appear among serious delinquents much more frequently than in the general population. About one in eight seems to be the ratio of the number of feebleminded children among all the cases brought into court as defendants. Within a year a total of about twenty-five thousand feebleminded boys and girls will appear in court.

Feeblemindedness does not cause delinquency, but mental deficiency and delinquency tend to be correlated in court statistics. One reason for this correlation, in all likelihood, is the fact that the brighter children in many instances not only are saved from the reformatory experience, but also quite frequently manage to avoid detention, court arraignment, or even arrest by the police.

THE PSYCHOPATHIC DELINQUENT

The *psychopathic* delinquent seems to be in a psychiatric no-man's land, "psychopath" being a wastebasket term to explain human behavior that is adjudged not to be normal, neurotic, psychotic, or feebleminded. Unlike psychotics and neurotics, psychopaths appear to have no irresistible inpulse to commit delinquencies, no delusions, no hallucinations, no memory defect, and no organic disease of the central nervous system. For this reason, they are usually held legally responsible for their unlawful acts.

The outstanding characteristics of the psychopath are impulsiveness, irrationality, superficiality, and the inability to foresee the consequences of his own action. His dream life appears to have a unique quality, the dreams themselves being almost completely free of guilt so commonly found among neurotics. Recent studies indicate the probability that the personalities of adult criminal psychopaths have reached only the pre-adolescent stage of development. Verified knowledge, however, about the psychopath as an identifiable single "type" is still quite skimpy.

Nevertheless, in the field of delinquent and criminal behavior, characteristic traits of the psychopath are discernible. For example, he will commit fraud and theft for astonishingly small amounts. His crimes usually reflect no planning, not even discernible rewards. The psychopathic child may smash his own toys. Psychopathic delinquents often commit offenses for what appear to be silly, trivial reasons. These traits are illustrated in a recent textbook by accounts of three seemingly senseless, probably psychopathic crimes. One fourteen-year-old boy strangled the baby he agreed to tend as a baby sitter. A seventeen-year-old Oklahoma boy killed his girl because she refused to go out with him. A Chicago boy killed his young sweetheart while they were witnessing a gangster movie—and insisted he did not know why he did this. These crimes seemed to lack discoverable motives, and brought their perpetrators no financial gain whatsoever.[3]

The "typical" psychopath appears to commit quite unrelated crimes, apparently for the "hell of it." The juvenile psychopath may drown chickens or goats in the local mill pond while being truant from school. He may pour acid on a puppy's tail, or stab another child. Such individuals have been called "morally insane" or "social imbeciles," for they seem to be unable to learn from experience.

Placing the psychopathic boy or girl in a reformatory, jail, or a house of correction, contributes little to his (or her) rehabilitation. Hospitalization and psychiatric treatment are indicated in these cases. However, psychopathic offenders are seldom reformable, at least with present methods, and if they commit criminal acts persistently, it is often argued that they should be permanently segregated for their own benefit and for the protection of society.

ALCOHOLISM AND DELINQUENCY

Alcoholism is a morbid condition resulting from the inordinate or persistent use of alcoholic drinks, rendering the victim mentally ill and afflicted with a body allergy. This condition should not be confused with occasional heavy drinking. The alcoholic constitutes a special problem in crime and is an excellent example of the repetitive offender. Dipsomania is not, in principle, a police problem, but in the absence of other agencies to cope with it, nearly 50 per cent of police time is expended on "drinking" cases. Drunkenness is the charge in about 60 per cent of all police arrests in Milwaukee, a large number of whom are probably alcoholics, and produces between 70 and 75 per cent of all admissions to the Milwaukee House of Correction.

Sufferers from such conditions as alcoholic hallucinosis, alcoholic delusional psychoses, or polyneuritic psychoses, to use the technical terminology—itself suggestive—may find their way into criminal behavior in much the same manner as the drug addict who commits a crime. The alcoholic seems to be driven by inner compulsions beyond his control, the crime or the deed being only incidental to the psychic condition. Thus the need for professional psychiatric aid is strongly indicated in cases involving actual alcoholics. Considerable drinking among young and older people alike is not necessarily indicative of alcoholism.

It is difficult to determine the extent and intensity of juvenile drinking. Many high school boys and girls consume alcoholic beverages, irrespective of socio-economic status. Both the extent of drinking among minors and the number of delinquencies committed as a result of intoxication are in the realm of guesswork. According to the annual reports of the Los Angeles Police Department,

---

[3] Negley K. Teeters and John Otto Reinemann, The Challenge of Delinquency (New York: Prentice-Hall, 1950), p. 517.

only from 1 to 3 per cent of juvenile arrests during 1940–1946 involved the charge of drunkenness. There is considerable recidivism among some juvenile offenders due to alcoholic liquor. But persistent alcoholism, it should be stressed, is more than likely to be symptomatic of some unresolved emotional conflict than merely the desire to experience the euphoria that often accompanies drinking.

On both the juvenile and adult level, alcoholism constitutes a serious problem. Not only are many crimes committed by persons while under the influence of alcohol but alcoholic intoxication is itself legally a misdemeanor. And drinking, of course, results in much "disorderly conduct." Adult drinking often contributes to the neglect of children, and the lack of adequate parental supervision in turn frequently stimulates a child's initial act of delinquency.

DRUG ADDICTION AND DELINQUENCY

If drinking and alcoholism represent severe problems in the lives of many young people, an even larger departure from conventional mores is the practice of drug addiction. Addiction is itself "delinquency"—as witness the "blue-grass commitment" by which an individual may incarcerate himself in Kentucky by admitting that he is addicted to the use of narcotic drugs. In such instances, probation may be granted, provided the individual submit to the treatment made available at the Hospital for Narcotics maintained by the federal government at Lexington.

Because of the expense involved in obtaining narcotics, drug addiction is related to other forms of delinquency; in many instances, the addict must steal in order to obtain the necessary funds to support the drug habit. Many young people may steal from their own homes, appropriating books, jewelry, clothing, radios, and the like, in order to convert them into cash they can use to purchase drugs. Juvenile addicts sometimes buy and sell drugs on a commission basis in school hallways and lavatories, or they may become "mules," acting as messengers or delivery boys, intermediaries between the user and peddler of drugs.

There is a strong tendency to exaggerate the "tie-in" between crime and delinquency and drug addiction. The "crazed" drug addict on a crime rampage is a fairly familiar stereotype reported in the press. Yet out of 5,200 drug addiction cases which appeared in the Chicago court—the only one of its kind in the world—there were only 158 "boosters" (shop-lifters), 58 "guns" or "cannons" (pickpockets), 191 burglars, 206 larcenists, 195 murderers, 46 purse snatchers, 47 confidence men, and 7 sex assaulters. The balance, 4,292 persons or roughly 90 per cent, were charged *solely* with drug addiction.[4] These figures are consistent with other findings that indicate that relatively few addicts are prone to crimes of violence or, for that matter, engage in *habitual* criminal behavior of any sort.

It is difficult to ascertain the extent of juvenile addiction. In the past it has been a convenient "whipping boy" for social reformers, "do-gooders," crusaders, and sometimes authorities themselves; and it is always good copy for

[4] Cited by Lois Higgins, Bureau of Crime Prevention, Chicago, Illinois, in her address to the American Prison Association, Biloxi, Mississippi, October 24, 1951.

the tabloids. It is more than a possibility that the threat of juvenile drug addiction has been overemphasized. In the first nine months of 1951, the *Uniform Crime Reports* show that only 1,856 individuals of over fifteen million persons under twenty-one were arrested in connection with the use of drugs. The deputy commissioner of the United States Bureau of Narcotics stated at that time that, with reference to teen-age addiction, the figures are no longer rising. Very likely, however, rates in some cities have been increasing within recent years.

Drugs used by the juvenile include marihuana, heroin, cocaine, morphine and opium, among others. One of the easiest and cheapest drugs to procure is marihuana which is not habit-forming in the physiological sense, but which is certainly habit-forming psychologically. A real danger in marihuana-usage is the fact that its effect upon individuals is unpredictable, affecting the same person differently on various occasions. Furthermore, marihuana serves as a stepping stone for the jaded drug user to try something different; hence he may graduate to heroin or cocaine. Heroin is most often preferred, although it is expensive, and accounts for approximately 60 per cent of drug offenders appearing before the Chicago drug court. Cocaine is the luxury item of the drug trade. Cocaine tends to induce revery rather than the depraved acts sometimes reported in the press. Cocaine users have conspicuous habits—an itchy nose and a general air of furtiveness. Morphine tends to impart to the user a feeling of increased mental and physical vigor. (Morphine sometimes actually benefits particular individuals, such as the chronic alcoholic or the psychoneurotic.) Each of these drugs, perhaps costly cocaine to the least extent, is used by some American youths; and the behavior thus induced has become a part of "normal" juvenile life in some circles.

Most remedial programs of the past and many of the present tend to be punitive in character. The conviction that "there ought to be a law" is still widely held. But with the passage of each restraining law, the price (and profit) tends to rise, which financially benefits the peddler of the drugs. One reason for the punitive attitude toward drug users is because, in the United States, drug addiction is relatively prevalent in the "underworld" and is thus associated with crime and its correction, in contrast to drug addiction in Europe which is viewed as primarily a problem for the medical and allied professions.

There are hopeful signs that in the future remedial programs will tend to become more realistic, especially as research findings are made available to those in charge of such programs. Alfred Lindesmith, one of the many social scientists working in this area, has made worthwhile contributions to a better understanding of the drug addict and has done much to invalidate the commonly accepted stereotype so familiar in sensational literature. The drug user, Lindesmith points out, does not spend much of his time in a dreamy stupor; as a rule, he does not even maintain the delusion of being carefree and happy. He is rather a miserable and harassed person, as anyone who knows addicts is aware.[5]

---

[5] Alfred R. Lindesmith, "The Drug Addict as a Psychopath," *American Sociological Review*, V, December 1940.

Both alcoholism and drug addiction are related, at least in some instances, to the sexual activities of adolescents, which likewise have been highly publicized in the tabloids of today.

SEXUAL PRACTICES AND DELINQUENCY

The breakdown of traditional sexual mores and the drift and diversity of changing opinion about sexual morality affect individuals in different ways. Although contemporary sexual attitudes appear to have become highly liberal, as compared with the views of our forebears, it is not at all certain that modern youth is as profligate as "public opinion" sometimes appears to suggest. Differences in sexual orientation and practice, however, may reflect differences in socioeconomic and class standards. For example, Dr. Winston W. Ehrmann's survey at the University of Florida, a five-year study of college youth, indicates that 61 per cent of the men and 91 per cent of the women "draw the line" within conventional moral limits in their current dating behavior. This finding is fairly consistent with Kinsey's surveys of the sexual practices of American men and women, in which he reports class and educational differentials which indicate that sexual intercourse itself is engaged in at an earlier age and more frequently among the less educated who, however, tend to avoid the "petting" preliminaries that are so marked among college youth.[6]

While early sexual demoralization is not uncommon in the careers of delinquents, *official* charges of sexual intransigence do not appear with high frequency in the public records, except in the case of female offenders. In the most recent Glueck study, only 3.6 per cent of the cases studied, all male, had been officially charged with sex offenses as compared with 59 per cent who had records of burglary and 58.4 per cent charged with larceny. The low incidence of sex offenses in this study is attributable in large part to the fact that most delinquencies committed by girls are sexual in nature, whereas those delinquencies committed by boys and young men are mostly nonsexual.

The relatively small number of cases brought before the courts for sex offenses is primarily a reflection of current court practice and community attitudes rather than an accurate index of the extent of sexual irregularity. The courts are apt to be indulgent of the male offender in respect to sexual lapses but severe in the handling of girls who have actual or suspected records of sexual freedom.

Partly as a reflection of the contemporary cultural accent on sex, the public is easily titillated by accounts of sexual escapades—a fact which the newspapers have capitalized. Consequently, many notorious sex cases have tended, and still tend, to overemphasize sex as an offense.

In some disorganized areas and families, the opportunities for sexual exploitation of young boys by adult homosexuals are quite extensive. Influenced by promised financial rewards, boys have been known to aid and even to seek out older males who prefer them as sex objects. There is also the problem of females who use youngsters for normal as well as deviational sexual gratifica-

---

[6] See A. C. Kinsey, W. B. Pomeroy, and C. E. Martin, *Sexual Behavior in the Human Male* (Philadelphia: W. B. Saunders Co., 1948), Chap. 10.

ich is often known to the police of metropolitan areas. How-
n and juvenile delinquency are far from synonymous. It must
that sex deviation is widely practiced among nondelinquents.
present evidence, it may be asserted that sex or sex deviation
auses nor is the cause of juvenile delinquency.

---

rt discussion of special personality and behavior problems as they
o delinquency, the treatment has been necessarily sketchy due to
omplexity of the subject matter. Reactions to such problems in most
are emotionally toned—not only among readers but also for those
professional task is to write of such activities. Moreover, each of the
discussed above deserves far lengthier treatment than the preceding
discussion. But there is a growing number of able works in these areas.
e of them are listed at the end of this chapter.

READINGS

A moot question since H. H. Goddard's time, the relationship between intelligence and delinquency is discussed by Harry Manuel Shulman in a paper titled "Intelligence and Delinquency," which was read in 1950 to the International Congress of Criminology in Paris.

Karl Birnbaum presents one approach to juvenile delinquency in "A Court Phychiatrist's View of Juvenile Delinquents." Delinquency to the juvenile in trouble does not mean the same thing as it means to an adult not in trouble. Insight is provided into personality types, particularly the mentally defective and the psychopath. As brought out in this article, diagnostic caution is urged.

Ray H. Everett raises the perennial question regarding prostitution in his article, "Can We Regulate Prostitution?" Juvenile sex misbehavior usually rates headlines and the increasing number of amateur prostitutes is a matter of grave concern. No doubt the best long-range weapon against prostitution is wholesome, honest sex education in the home, school and church.

Intelligence and Delinquency*

By Harry Manuel Shulman. Director of the Community Service Division, The City College, New York.

THE STUDY OF the relationship of intelligence and delinquency began with the early 19th century neo-classical criminal justice doctrine that since crime was a rational choice of conduct, mental defectives in common with infants and the insane, were not legally responsible for their actions. While the medical differentiation of mental defectives from the insane was accomplished during the early part of the 19th century, it was not until the late 19th century that scientific standards were established for the measurement of degrees of mental ability

* Reprinted from The Journal of Criminal Law and Criminology (Northwestern University School of Law), Vol. XLI, April, 1951, by Harry Manuel Shulman.

and for the determination of mental defect, despite man's observation since time immemorial of the individual variability in mental ability. These were tests for general intelligence, the product of research by a whole school of psychologists, but attributable directly to the researches of Alfred Binet, of France.

The application of these early crude intelligence tests to samplings of institutionalized offenders in prisons, reformatories and juvenile training schools and the finding that a very large proportion of those tested could be diagnosed as mental deficients, led to the single-factor theory of mental deficiency as the greatest cause of delinquent conduct. Thus Harry H. Goddard, one of America's most distinguished adherents of the psychological school of crime causation, was impelled to state, as late as 1919, that "It is no longer to be denied that the greatest single cause of delinquency and crime is low-grade mentality, much of it within the limits of feeble-mindedness." A similar declaration was made by Dr. William Healy, while Dr. Charles Goring, the English investigator into Lombroso's claims, declared more conservatively that defective intelligence was a vital constitutional factor in the aetiology of crime.

While there was substantial agreement as to the facts, there was considerable divergence as to the interpretation of the test findings, leading to such theories as: (1) the mental defective is a type of "born criminal," i.e., the "moral idiot"; (2) feeble-mindedness is a hereditary unit-character following Mendel's law, accounting for the preponderance of male defective offenders; (3) the feeble-minded characteristically commit dangerous crimes of assault and sex assault; (4) feeble-minded individuals commit crimes, in the absence of inhibiting social factors, because they lack the capacity to grasp the social values of their culture, including its social and legal definitions of right and wrong; (5) the feeble-minded cannot foresee the consequences of their actions, hence cannot be deterred by the threat of punishment laid down for crimes; (6) feeble-minded are suggestible, and so respond to the criminal leadership of brighter persons; (7) feeble-mindedness in individuals reared in families and neighborhoods where delinquent example is common, leads to delinquency.

Thus the elaborations of proponents of this single-factor theory ranged from the biological to the bio-social. The biological concept of the mental defective as a moral idiot or a Mendelian criminal type preceded in historical sequence the bio-social view of the mentally deficient offender as a product of social interaction. During the early decades of the 20th century there was still a predisposition to think fatalistically of mental deficiency, delinquency and dependency as inevitably associated phenomena. Even Sumner, in his brilliant source-book on the *Folkways,* published in 1906, was willing to associate these three groups as the submerged tenth at the bottom of the social class ladder.

Today, the concept that mental deficiency is necessarily a product of a tainted heredity is no longer accepted as wholly true. Evidence exists that perhaps one-half of all mental deficiency is the effect of non-germinal toxic and mechanical damage during the intrauterine period and at birth. Mental deficients are found among all social classes and in every parental occupational and educational level. Nor is the concept any longer accepted that mental deficients must necessarily be behavior risks. Together with the awareness that mental deficiency occurs in all levels of the population, it has been discovered that under proper conditions of child rearing and supervision, the mental defective may become a docile and obedient personality, with useful occupational potentialities. A perhaps contrary trend of thought is seen, however, in the growth in many American jurisdictions, of the practice of voluntary sterilization of defective delinquents, and in the spread of legislation authorizing this practice.

Despite a changing outlook upon the relationship between mental defect and delinquency there remain a number of questions regarding which it is essential to have scientific evidence, such as: (1) The proportion of mental defectives among delinquents compared to the general population; (2) significant differences in general mental ability between delinquents and the general population; (3) criminal patterns and tendencies toward recidivism among defectives compared to non-defective offenders; (4) the relationship between level of intelligence and treatability. We will consider these matters in the following sections. First, however, we shall seek a somewhat clearer view of the nature of general intelligence, of mental deficiency, and of the concepts and procedures involved in their measurement.

The Testing of General Intelligence

Whereas no adequate concept of the nature of intelligence has yet been constructed, owing to a conflict among psychologists as to the priority of general intelligence or of specific intelligences (such as social, mechanical, musical intelligence, etc.) there is agreement that general intelligence is the capacity to learn from experience. Binet constructed a scale to test the growth in this ability, based on the observation that in childhood and youth growth in learning ability parallels physical growth. In the absence of any objective criteria for the measurement of learning growth, Binet depended upon empirical trial and error, devoting fifteen years to the discovery of a scale of mental tests of increasing difficulty, correlated with the chronological age of his subjects.

Out of this experimentation came the year-level general intelligence scale. Tests were assigned to a year-level when 75 per cent of the subjects in an age-group successfully performed the tests. By assigning a given number of sub-tests to each year-level, and a given amount of year-level credit to each sub-test, it became possible to establish a *mental age*, consisting of the basal mental age below which all tests were passed, plus year-level credit for all succeeding tests passed. By comparing the mental age with the chronological age of the child and multiplying this ratio by 100, it became possible to establish an intelligence quotient, or IQ. Thus a child of 12 years, chronological age, with a mental age of nine years, had an IQ of 9/12 x 100 or 75, while a child of the same age with a mental age of 15 years, had an IQ of 15/12 x 100 or 125.

Successive tests of child population samplings by other psychologists disclosed that tested general intelligence assumed a normal or bell-shaped curve, with half of the IQ's falling within the range of 90 and 110, the remainder being almost equally divided above and below this range. Terman classified intelligence ratings into the following mental ability levels: Above 140, "near" genius or genius; 120–140, very superior; 110–120, superior; 90–110, normal or average; 80–90, dull; 70–80, borderline mental deficiency; below 70, mental deficiency.

Problems in the Testing of Intelligence

Despite the proliferation of individually applied verbal tests for general intelligence, their standardization in nearly every tongue and their application to millions of school children, certain fundamental problems in intelligence testing remain unsolved. Among these are: (a) the nature of the normal learning curve, (b) the constancy of the IQ and (c) the nature of the mental functions which the tests presume to measure.

The form of the learning curve is related both to the constancy of the IQ and to the determination of a mental growth cessation point, to serve as the enumerator of the equation for the determining of the IQ among children above that chronological age. The determination of that point is of very real significance in the diagnosis of mental defect, especially when mental deficiency must be established as a legal entity for purposes of differentiated social treatment. There is evidence that the growth curve in learning ability reaches its maximum somewhere between the fourteenth and sixteenth year, and then declines sharply. Thus examiners have variously taken chronological ages between 14 and 16 to represent adulthood, for intelligence testing purposes. As a result, a given mental age will fluctuate in IQ according to the adult year level chosen. Until there is arbitrary uniformity in defining this mental growth cessation point, the percentages of mental deficiency established for either general populations or delinquent samplings will be noncomparable. It was suggested by many psychologists that 15 years be arbitrarily set to represent adulthood for mental growth purposes, and the majority of child guidance clinics now adhere to this standard.

The labeling of children as to their mental ability by means of the IQ assumes the constancy of the IQ; that is, that the future mental growth of a child is predictable in terms of his rate of mental growth up to the time of testing. The evidence to date is that within a probable error of perhaps 2.5 points in either direction, *under conditions of constant cultural stimulation,* the IQ does not vary with age. But such factors as serious illness, or irregularity in exposure to learning situations, or other factors that affect opportunity for learning, do appear to affect the learning growth rate, and the IQ. Thus, there is evidence that children transferred from inferior to superior cultural environments appreciate in their learning rate, and gain in IQ, and that children returned from superior to inferior cultural environments tend to regress in learning rate and in IQ to the level previously established in the inferior social environment.

The product of learning growth known as "native" general intelligence is thus not alone dependent upon nature, but on nature and nurture. As a result, general intelligence must be viewed as a product of biosocial interaction. This introduces the problem of the significance of cultural differences in the determination of intelligence levels. This factor is of significance for the relation between intelligence and delinquency. Since the accurate measurement of general intelligence is dependent upon constancy of cultural stimulation, factors tending to differentiate the cultural background levels of delinquents and non-delinquents would lead to the under-estimation or over-estimation of the intelligence of one group or the other. Thus a finding as to the relative mental status of delinquents and non-delinquents requires holding constant the factor of cultural stimulation. Since this has not usually been done, a finding that delinquents are inferior in tested general intelligence to non-delinquents does not necessarily prove that intelligence and delinquency are causally related but only that the same antecedent factors that contributed an inferior nurture to the group from which the preponderance of delinquents were drawn, also led to the preponderance of that culture level in juvenile court arraignments.

The desirability of disentangling the functions of nurture and nature in learning potential, so that "native" potential may be measured, has led to the suggestion that culture-free mental tests be devised. Whether culture-free tests, if they could be devised, would successfully elicit the full measurement of intelligence potential is questionable. Motivation has ordinarily strong cultural reference, and especially for delinquents, the necessity of arousing full response to an intellectual situation probably involves the utilization of culturally familiar motivations, since among delinquents there is a disproportion of emotionally disturbed children. (Furthermore, the emotional tensions accompanying the usual situations within which delinquents are psychologically tested—prior to court adjudication or upon admission to a juvenile training school—probably lead often to blocking of full participation in the test situation.)

A final comment on the role of culture in the testing of general intelligence must stress the desirability of the homogeneity of culture backgrounds among delinquents compared with non-delinquents for mental status. Since delinquents are drawn disproportionately from urban areas, from among industrial groupings that include disproportionately numbers of children of ill-educated, bilingual and low-socio-economic status parentage, they should be compared in general intelligence, not to the whole child population, nor even to the total urban child population, but to samplings drawn from the same races, ethnic origins, socio-economic levels, and residence areas. These fundamental needs must be kept in mind in evaluating the available evidence on the intelligence of delinquents.

The General Intelligence of Juvenile Delinquents

We have said that the earliest studies of the general intelligence of juvenile delinquents emphasized their retarded mentality as a class. Studies of more than 200 American samples of institutionalized delinquent children, on a literal translation of the original Binet-Simon scale, in connection with the knowledge that practically no institutionalized feeblemental age, led to the conclusion that at least one-half of juvenile delinquents were mental defectives.[1]

Recent examinations, however, have tended to a reduction in the proportion of alleged mental defect among juvenile delinquents, in part as a result of newer tests having a higher mental age "ceiling," that permitted the testing of superior individuals, in part the greater skill of examiners and the use of more effective techniques for achieving motivation, and in part the extension of tests to broader samplings of juvenile delinquents to include non-committed as well as committed cases.

A study in 1928–29, of all the mental tests reported on criminals and delinquents, comprising some 350 reports on approximately 150,000 offenders, showed a decrease from an average of 50 per cent of delinquents diagnosed as feebleminded in the period 1910–1914 to an average percentage of 20 per cent in the period 1925–1928. The wide variation in test results was regarded as reflecting differences in test methods and scoring rather than differences in mental abilities of offenders.

Comparison of Intelligence Levels

Attention has been directed during the two past decades to a comparison of the intelligence levels of juvenile delinquents as compared to the general juvenile population. Samples of juvenile delinquents, drawn for the most part from court-arraigned cases, have been

---

[1] Mental retardation has been referred to by two terms, *feeble-mindedness* and *mental deficiency*, each having a somewhat different meaning. Mental deficiency refers only to mental test level. Feeble-mindedness refers to an inadequacy in personal social adjustment —to get along in school, make an independent living, manage one's own affairs, etc.—without special assistance or supervision. An individual may be mentally deficient as defined by test, yet capable of self-support and adequate social adjustment in a congenial social environment, and hence, not feeble-minded. The writer recalls a juvenile training school graduate who by test was mentally deficient, yet who out of his experience in the institution powerhouse, invented a fuse with a handle that minimized the danger of shock, and established a paying manufacturing enterprise around his invention.

found to be lower in tested general intelligence than the child population series upon which the major intelligence tests were standardized. Terman, in standardizing the revised Binet, found that approximately 50 per cent of his one thousand unselected American school children fell between an IQ of 93 and 108 and that the remainder fell above and below in equal proportion. Only .33 per cent had IQ's below 65 and only 2.6 per cent had IQ's below 75. In comparison, Healy and Bronner, in their 1926 court sample, reported 13.5 per cent of their cases as mentally deficient, Burt reported 8 per cent of a London, England, court sample as mentally deficient, and Merrill reported 23 per cent of 1,731 Los Angeles court delinquents as mentally deficient with IQ's below 70. Merrill, however, pointed out that her sample contained an unknown proportion of Mexican-born and Mexican ethnic stock children of presumed bi-lingual backgrounds. In a second California court sample of 500 cases from a territory having a more homogeneous ethnic stock, she reported 11.6 per cent as mentally deficient.

Relatively similar findings have been reported for other delinquency samplings, some more selective and others less selective than total court intake. Kvaraceus reported 10.4 per cent of all public school problem children referred for guidance care as mentally deficient, with IQ's below 70. Sheldon and Eleanor Glueck reported 13.1 per cent of a sample referred by the Boston juvenile court to the Judge Baker foundation clinic for diagnostic study as mentally deficient. The New Jersey Juvenile Commission found 13 per cent of New Jersey children committed to juvenile training schools to have IQ's under 70.

Zeleny, after equating the procedures of different examiners, concluded that the ratio of delinquents and general child population in respect to mental deficiency was about 1.2 to 1.

Somewhat similar findings were reported for differences in *average intelligence* among delinquents and non-delinquents. Kvaraceus found an average intelligence quotient of 103 among unselected Passaic, New Jersey school children compared to an average IQ of 89 among 761 problem children referred by schools to a central guidance service. Eleanor Glueck, comparing 1,000 clinic-referred juvenile delinquents with 3,638 school children, found that only 41.6 per cent of the delinquents had average intelligence or better (IQ's over 90) compared to 79 per cent of the school children.

Intelligence of Groups Given Selective Treatment

Whereas contemporary interest in the relation of general intelligence and delinquency has continued unabated, instead of seeking a causal explanation of delinquency in intellectual inferiority, the tendency has been to explain the established test differences between delinquents and non-delinquents as a product of social selection. That is, inferior mentality is coming to be viewed as one of a series of attributes that characterize children whom society has selected out for formal adjudication as delinquents through the differential operation of the machinery of juvenile justice.

There is evidence that not only are juvenile delinquents non-representative of the whole child population for social status, but that the selectivity of the delinquent group increases proportionately with the degree of authority applied to their handling. Thus they are found to be drawn in disproportionate numbers from (a) lower socio-economic groups, (b) Negroes, (c) foreign-born parentage, (d) groups disproportionately high in indices of mental disorder, dependency and adult crime. Those dealt with unofficially, either through the courts or through the public and private child guidance facilities of schools and community appear to represent a group from higher socio-economic status than those officially arraigned or committed to juvenile training schools.

There is further evidence that the selective social characteristics of the officially arraigned delinquency group is accompanied by differential tested intelligence; and that as more selective screening takes place among the arraigned group, in terms of the severity of the subsequent controls applied, the greater the tested intelligence differential. Thus William C. Kvaraceus, in New Jersey, reported an unselected sampling of Passaic school children as having an average IQ of 103, and all public school children referred to a special service division of the Board of Education for child guidance care as having an average IQ of 89. Maude A. Merrill, in California, reported an unselected sampling of 2,904 children in the general child population as having an average IQ of 101.8 and a court sampling from the same area of 500 consecutive arraignments as having an average IQ of 92.5.

As one progresses from court arraignment to training school commitments, the average IQ drops. Merrill cites evidence that with the 1916 Stanford Revision of the Binet scale, the average IQ of court samples reported in the literature is around 85, and for institutional commitments, around 82.

There are two possible interpretations of these findings: (a) that greater maladjustment accompanies lower intelligence, resulting in the application of more extreme social controls; (b) that the greater maladjustment and the lower tested intelligence among official cases are both dependent upon inferior antecedent cultural backgrounds of delinquents as compared to general population samples.

The first interpretation leads to the conclusion that since a disproportionate number of severely maladjusted institutionalized delinquents tend to be dullards

there is a correlation between mental backwardness and the social conditions within which delinquency is encouraged. From this conclusion it is an easy step to the view that mental dullness and social breakdown, as measured by such terminal indices as dependency, delinquency and crime, are closely related phenomena.

The cultural interpretation rejects the adequacy of the initial findings, arguing that the very tests used for the measurement of general intelligence are discriminatory against the delinquent group. They are not culture-free tests, but tests depending largely upon skill in language expression, vocabulary, breadth of reading, exposure to conceptualized discussion, etc., involving a high level of training in the use of written and spoken English, and presuming an exposure to comparable linguistic cultural material in the family, among both delinquents and nondelinquents. But since we already know that a disproportionately large number of delinquents are of low socio-economic status, whose parents suffer from the handicaps of limited schooling, partial or total illiteracy, and bi-lingual or foreign language speech, it may be inferred that their social backgrounds are not comparable to those of the general child population. Hence the general intelligence test results are not explicable by any fancied relation between intelligence and delinquency, but by a real relationship between court arraignment and low socio-economic and culture status.

Research evidence bearing upon both types of interpretation is at hand from studies of the differential intelligence levels of public school children in high and low delinquency areas. Shulman has shown, for New York City, that the tested intelligence of children in high delinquency areas tends to be lower than that of school children in low delinquency areas. In a recalculation of data from a series of group intelligence tests conducted among public school pupils by the Board of Education, he found that in five public schools in high delinquency areas, the median IQ's ranged from 88.5 to 98.5, with an average median of 91.5, while in seven public schools in low delinquency areas, the medians ranged from 95 to 115.5, with an average median of 103.5. Thus between the low delinquency areas and the high delinquency areas there was an IQ difference averaging 12 points favoring the low delinquency areas. Similar findings, based upon extensive study of the same source data were reported by Julius Maller.

More pertinent to a cultural interpretation were the findings of Allison Davis, who devised a test for the measurement of untaught responses to problems in daily life outside of school. In an experimental study of school children from varying socio-economic backgrounds, on standard intelligence tests, and on the test for daily life problems, he found that whereas on ten standard tests there was an average difference of nearly 8 points in IQ between the high and the low socio-economic groups, favoring the former, these differences vanished when the tests for daily life problems were applied. He concluded that the standard tests did not truly measure the problem-solving potentialities of children from low socio-economic backgrounds.

Delinquents and Matched Control Samples

Whereas apparently significant tested intelligence differences, usually without calculation of statistical significance, have been found between arraigned delinquents and the general child population, the controversy as to the role of native and cultural factors in the results has led some authorities to suggest that comparisons of delinquents and non-delinquents in samplings in which socio-economic status is held constant might be helpful in resolving this problem.

In this connection, Lichtenstein and Brown are reported to have found among 658 grade school children from a high delinquency area, 10 per cent with IQ's below 70. Use of this figure as a control percentage for the general population in a high delinquency area would not be unfavorable to the theory that delinquents are of the same tested mental potential as non-delinquents when equated for socio-economic background. Some of Merrill's findings lend additional weight to this theory. Among 300 delinquents of both sexes compared to 300 non-delinquent controls from the same communities and public schools, she found an average IQ for the controls only slightly and not significantly higher (89.3–86.7) but on the other hand she found among the delinquents almost twice as many IQ's below 70 as among the controls.

However, the findings of other investigators controvert this point of view. Cyril Burt's delinquents and controls from the same districts and public schools in London showed differences favoring the controls, with 1.2 per cent in the defective group (IQ's 50–70) compared to 7.6 per cent in the delinquents, a ratio of better than six to one; and IQ's above 115 among only 2.5 per cent of the delinquents and 8.5 per cent of the controls, a reverse ratio of better than three to one. Charles, comparing Kuhlman-Anderson IQ's for 528 reform school boys with a public school group of the same socio-economic status found that among delinquents, 29.5 per cent of white boys and 47.3 per cent of Negro boys, had IQ's under 70, compared to 1.16 per cent and 3.48 per cent, respectively, for the public school groups.

A difficulty in equating culture backgrounds in terms of socio-economic status or area of residence is that within the same area of residence, as pointed out elsewhere by the writer, or within the same income group, there are significant familiar variations in culture level. A stricter measure of cultural homogeneity is afforded when delinquents and non-delinquents within the same families are compared for general intelligence. Healy and Bronner, in 105 court-arraigned delinquency cases, compared to a like number of non-delinquent siblings matched closely for age and usually for sex, found differences slightly favoring the non-delinquents. Their data sought to exclude mental defectives and were therefore valid only for IQ's above 70. Their findings (figures for delinquents given first) were: IQ above 110, 13–17 per cent; 90–110, 52–57 per cent; 72–90, 30.8–22.6 per cent. These differences were not calculated for significance. Shulman, in a smaller matched sample of siblings, found that for 28 pairs, delinquents averaged IQ 75 and non-delinquents IQ 86. Thus, both studies favored the theory that delinquents tend toward lower tested intelligence than non-delinquents, when equated for culture level. It is suggested that in the interest of a resolution of this question of the relation of intelligence and delinquency, further studies concern themselves with the intelligence of delinquent and non-delinquent siblings, with emphasis upon the analysis of those physical and emotional factors that might affect learning, mental growth and motivation to maximum test output.

General Intelligence and Type of Offense

Since the publication of Goring's study on the English convict, there has been an interest in the relation of intelligence and type of offense. Forgery and fraud have been associated with higher levels of intelligence and crimes of violence with lower levels. Findings of this type, based on adult samplings, are as pointed out by Merrill, of limited significance for juvenile delinquency, since legal offenses are not always descriptive of juvenile behavior. Thus, in 500 cases

of children's offenses, she found only eight cases of forgery. It could also be pointed out that many other forms of offense have their origin in the economic and cultural roles of adult life and their presence in adult criminal statistics affords no basis for use of similar categories in dealing with children.

Merrill has traced certain relationships between type of juvenile offense and intelligence level. She found intelligence positively correlated with forgery, lack of parental control and malicious mischief; and negatively correlated with sex offenses, truancy and vagrancy. Stealing, comprising a majority of the cases in her sampling, was found to have no significant relation to intelligence. It is possible, however, that a refinement of the categories of theft, to reveal differential theft patterns, would have been productive of more significant results.

Luton Ackerson, in a sampling comprising nearly 5,000 cases, found that for children ages five to 12.9 years, the offenses of stealing, fire-setting, forgery or check-raising, incorrigibility, truancy and escape from an institution, increased with IQ increase. However, since his entire sample had a low median IQ, the results are not too significant. Certain of his findings were very interesting. He found a greater tendency to gang membership among IQ's from 40 to 99 than among problem children with IQ's over 99. He found, among girls ages 13–17.9 years, a higher proportion of sex delinquency, including unmarried motherhood, among low IQ's. It should be pointed out that since none of his correlations exceeded .30 they are not statistically significant, even though suggestive of further avenues of exploration. Ackerson's findings on the sex offender may be taken together with those of Alexander Tendler, that on a test for impulsiveness (the Porteus Maze) unmarried female sex offenders who did not become pregnant, achieved scores superior to those who became unwed mothers. Thus the young unwed mother is described by these findings as tending toward lower general intelligence and greater impulsiveness than either the sex delinquent girl who avoids pregnancy or the non-delinquent girl.

Qualitative distinctions have been made between the offenses of individuals of different intelligence levels. David Abrahamsen, speaking without specific reference to children, has remarked that the offense chosen is typical of the individual who commits it; thus an individual with a low IQ will usually commit a simple theft such as breaking in through a window and taking some insignificant object, or stealing a car, leaving it and running away.

John Levy made the observation that bright children tend toward personality problems and dull children toward conduct disorders. Among more than 700 children with IQ's above 80 referred to a child guidance clinic, personality problems increased with IQ from 25 to 53 per cent, and conduct problems decreased from 32 to 12 per cent. He sought to equate out the socio-economic factor by comparing 50 bright children (IQ's over 110) from the lowest socio-economic group with 70 dull children (IQ's 80–90) from the highest socio-economic group and found that socio-economic differences did not modify the trend of his findings.

In this connection, the findings of Allison Davis and Robert J. Havighurst are significant, that middle-class families tend to rear their children more rigidly than do lower-class families and that differences in socio-economic status are more important in rearing than those of race. Thus the rearing practices of middle-class Negro mothers tended to approximate the tightness of control by middle-class white mothers as opposed to the relative permissiveness of the lower socio-economic group of mothers in both races.

It is possible that the common factor operating in both the Levy and Davis-Havighurst findings was differential general intelligence, with higher parental intelligence tending to be correlated with strictness of rearing and lower parental intelligence with permissiveness in rearing. If this were so, the anxieties resulting from the frustrations of strict rearing might have explained the greater number of personality problems in bright children, and the contact with delinquency attitudes and experiences that would result from laxness in rearing in lower socio-economic areas might have explained the greater number of cases of conduct disorder among dull children.

The writer has pursued this line of reasoning further, pointing out that the differences in types of adult crime characteristic of lower and middle classes—the former tending to assault and theft, and the latter to fraud—may be in part a function of differences in childhood rearing. The lower-class child, reared permissively, but frustrated in his status aspiration in a democratic society, and subjected to temperamental and culture clashes in his family environment, may react to his frustrations by conduct disorder, while the middle class child, reared strictly, but with less frustration of his status aspirations, may react to frustrations in opportunity for self-expression and to temperamental and culture clashes in his family environment by anxiety and personality problems. Thus the lower class child may behave as though the social order has many loopholes and few restrictions, and the middle-class child as though society has few loopholes and many restrictions. Such behavior would be consistent with differential criminal behavior in adult life, with the poor tending toward crimes involving outbursts of hostility and aggression—thefts and assaults—and the middle-class tending toward crimes involving tension maintenance and the application of an extensive range of conventional protective practices—namely, fraud.

Intelligence and Recidivism

The relationship of intelligence and recidivism, *i.e.*, repetition of offenses, has been given some attention. In the United States, roughly one-quarter of all children arraigned as juvenile delinquents had previous arraignments. This proportion is much higher among Negro children. The proportion for girls is roughly one-half the rate for boys of the same race.

Criminologists have reported that among adults, low IQ's contribute an excessive proportion of offenders who tend to become recidivist about as frequently as other offenders and to be as successful on parole. The findings for children are inconclusive. Cecil W. Mann and Helene Powner Mann found among 428 child recidivists lower IQ's (average IQ 78) than among 1,731 unselected delinquents (average IQ 84) arraigned in the Los Angeles juvenile court. The Gluecks found recidivists to deviate in the same direction. But Merrill found no significant difference between recidivists and single arraignments, while R. A. Lane and P. A. Witty found no difference.

The problem of recidivism has been approached by some investigators in terms of the normal curve for intelligence. Haggerty, among others, has reported that while deviants from the normal curve, *i.e.*, both superior and dull children, tend to higher incidences of behavior disorder than children of average intelligence, the bright group tend to "unlearn" much of their maladjusted behavior between the ages of 9 and 13 years, whereas the dull either continue or increase in the extent of their maladjustment with age increase. In this connection, the finding by Tendler is pertinent, that in a psychiatric child guidance clinic, among matched groups of children, the bright group responded to case work treatment more effectively than the dull group.

Ackerson has studied the effect of intelligence on frequency of offense at different age groups. He found the same results as Haggerty, that bright children tended to a reduction in the frequency of their offenses, compared to dull children. He reported that among pre-adolescents under the age of 13, there was an increase with IQ (to IQ 110–120) of frequency in 154 types of problem incident, but among adolescents ages 13–18 years, the increase in frequency of problem incidents was only among the low IQ's, 70–80, particularly with respect to conduct disorder. Thus the findings of Haggerty, Tendler and Ackerson, while each having a somewhat different orientation, all indicate that bright children tend toward a reduction in their behavior problems with age increase, with or without treatment, while dull children tend toward an increase in behavior problems with age.

Social Intelligence and Delinquency

The material up to this point deals with the relation of *general* intelligence and delinquency. General intelligence has been thought by many psychologists to be a poor indicator of social adjustment. The tendency has been to limit the prognostic use of tests of general intelligence to the prediction of educability through formal classroom instruction in the content of academic education, and to seek the prediction of social *recidivists*, for purposes of social intelligence research. The primary behavior disorder, the personality disorder, the assaultive group, and the matured predatory group, may have varying levels of social intelligence corresponding to the varying degrees of social participation involved in different types of delinquent activity. There is a possibility that training school admissions are heavily loaded with predatory offenders whose antisocial experience has included considerable group association and delinquent gang membership. Such delinquents may have had considerably greater experience in group participation than others, and may test higher on tests for social intelligence than isolate offenders.

Mechanical Intelligence and Delinquency

In addition to general and social intelligence, psychologists have distinguished a number of others in the hierarchy of capacities, of which for our purposes perhaps the most important is mechanical intelligence. This series of qualities, which includes the capacities for form perception, effective hand-eye co-ordination, and an understanding of mechanical relations, is of prime importance in a technical society. A number of tests, some involving actual manipulation of mechanical objects, and others requiring only paper and pencil responses, have been standardized, including the Stenquist Mechanical Assembly Test, the Mc-Quarrie, the Minnesota, the O'Rourke, etc. In addition, numerous tests exist for the measurement of specific motor performances. These tests have demonstrated that general intelligence and mechanical ability are largely independent capacities, the correlation between them rarely rising above plus .40.

Early tests on delinquents gave rise to the hope that here was a quality in which the problem individual might find compensating superiority to the well-adjusted child, and thus a basis for constructive education and training. Several experimenters found delinquents slightly superior to non-delinquents in mechanical ability, and others found no significant differences between the two groups. Slawson found the performance of delinquent boys at the House of Refuge and the Hawthorne school practically on a par with that of New York City school children, on a paper-and-pencil group form of the Stenquist. The writer, on a small sample of 22 pairs of delinquents and their non-delinquent brothers, found the delinquents as a group superior to their brothers, as well as to unselected school children, on a mechanical assembly form of the Stenquist, adjustment through other tests. Thus Miss Chassell, in an extensive survey of the literature on the relation of intelligence and morality, found correlations between plus 0.10 and plus 0.39, none high enough for statistical significance. Such findings do not wholly thrust aside a relation between inteligence and morality, since the findings demonstrate a positive relationship, but the correlation is too low to be predictive.

The term *social intelligence* refers to the capacity for social adjustment and maturity in social relationships as differentiated from the ability to learn from experience. That is to say, an intelligent person may through his general intelligence learn to profit from experience, but not necessarily in the direction of benefit to society. The adequate study of social intelligence has been retarded by a lack of research in this area, resulting in a lack of well-standardized tests for social intelligence. In part, this has been due to a lack of reference points for the measurement of social development. Child psychology has been relatively successful in tracing the social development of the pre-school age group, but beyond this age our knowledge of the individual process in social development is extremely sketchy and based very largely upon doctrinaire speculative theories.

Chief among the very few social intelligence scales is the Vineland Social Maturity scale, a year-level scale standardized for the estimation of level of social performance through the observation of social behavior in the areas of personal hygiene, household duties, purchasing, employment, social relations and civic life. In the belief that this scale might disclose delinquents to be socially immature, in the light of their ego-centricity, it has been used by some investigators. The scanty evidence is conflicting, and not helpful. For example, N. N. Springer, testing 80 white and 50 Negro delinquents, found that social maturity level tended to be correlated with IQ, so that bright delinquents tended to be socially mature as measured by the scale. The social maturity of first offenders and recidivists was related to their mental levels. Thus, from this study, it would appear that any tendency toward social immaturity among juvenile delinquents would be a function of their tendency to vary from the normal for general intelligence. This area will have to be studied much more before adequate generalizations can be made.

It may prove to be necessary to treat statistics of delinquents in more qualitatively descriptive categories than merely *first offenders* and although they were inferior to their brothers on the average, for general intelligence and school achievement.

Belief in the relative adequacy of delinquents in mechanical ability, as compared to general intelligence and academic school achievement led to a movement during the '20's for the use of trade and vocational education as a delinquency rehabilitation program. School problem youths together with other academic failures were shunted into trade and vocational schools. This program has been generally abandoned, with recognition among educators that competence in trade and vocational careers calls for good intelligence, stable temperamental and personality characteristics, and adequacy in mathematical and language skills, in addition to good mechanical ability. The frequent mental dullness, emotional instabilities, and reading and writing disabilities of a large proportion of delinquents make them poor risks for industrial training. Today, delinquents are recommended for trade and vocational education only on the basis of individual diagnostic study and counselling.

A Court Psychiatrist's View of Juvenile Delinquents*

By Karl Birnbaum, M.D.

MAJOR PROBLEMS in the handling of juvenile offenders in court are presented by cases that are not psychotic but plainly pathologic; they are diagnostically labeled mental defectives, defective delinquents, constitutional psychopaths, or sexual psychopaths.

The difficulties in these cases cannot be ascribed simply to the undeniable fact that the medicopsychiatric approach to the delinquent essentially differs from the legal and juridical one; for the practical work done in and by the juvenile court has sufficiently proved that these seemingly incompatible points of view can be very well reconciled in the best interest of both the child and the community.

The difficulties have to be sought rather in the nature of these pathological types themselves. Yet that does not at all mean that the factors which are of importance in understanding and appraising the average young offender can here be discarded. On the contrary, it is just the combination of the pathological and the "natural" factors that makes the picture of these pathological juveniles more complex and its interpretation more

* Reprinted from *The Annals* of The American Academy of Political and Social Science, 261 (January 1949), pp. 55–63. Used by permission.

complicated. It therefore seems not superfluous to point here in advance to those two cardinal determinants which are found in every structural analysis of youthful delinquents: the immature mind from within and the environment influences from without.

The mental immaturity, or more specifically the immaturity of the personality, has to be considered a constant central element in each group of these pathological juveniles. The specific features of an incompletely integrated and organized personality structure may somewhat vary in the diverse phases of childhood, puberty, and adolescence; but unless the juvenile is controlled and guided, his emotional instability, the lack of inner balance and self-control are sufficient to make him more or less unfit to find his way in a social world shaped by and adapted to the mentality of the adult.

Less easy to assess in pathological youth is the influence of the external factors such as commonly presented in the textbooks of criminology under the heading of economic, social, and cultural causes of delinquency. What difficulties may result in specific cases can easily be deduced from a single statement of a noted expert in this field: Cyril Burt lists more than 170 distinct conditions as adverse causes which may contribute to juvenile delinquency.

Individual Analysis

Even without further details, it then appears obvious that merely to offer a diagnostic label is not enough for the clarification of a pathological juvenile case. But to add simply a schematic enumeration of all the external factors involved would not suffice, either. Rather, a systematic, discriminating analysis of every individual picture is indispensable. It must not only show the special significance, position, and role which the various dynamic forces have in the complex interplay of factors, but also explain how these agents operate in the particular psychological configuration and sequence that finally leads to delinquent behavior and personality patterns.

This analytic procedure will thus clear up the points that matter most in pathological as well as in normal cases, namely, what the delinquency means to the young offender himself and what aims it serves in the dynamics of his inner life. In particular, it will become apparent what sort of personal needs and desires he seeks to satisfy by his delinquent acts, what obstacles or dangers he tries to escape, what inner or outer conflicts he strives to overcome, what frustrations or deprivations he attempts to compensate. All this together—but not the diagnosis alone—tells us what kind of offender the pathological youth really is, what we have to expect of him in the future, and what points of attack he offers to break down his antisocial propensities and build up a socialized personality.

Thus, indeed, a very worth-while task is set before the court psychiatrist. The trouble is that there are no ready patterns to be applied in every case, that every individual has psychological dynamics of his own, and—what is worse—that for a full insight into these psychodynamic mechanisms and processes one is dependent on a branch of scientific psychology that only in the last decades has made the necessary inroads into long neglected sectors of psychic life. All these general drawbacks play a part in the problems of the special types here to be dealt with.

The Mental Defective

The mental defective, in spite of his frequent appearance in court, is not too troublesome an object so long as one has to do with outspoken cases of lower and lowest grade. Idiots and imbeciles, for instance, can in most cases easily be disposed of by placing all the emphasis on the intellectual defect as a criterion that is readily discernible, fairly measurable, and capable of standardization. With the I. Q. at hand, giving general directions for proper handling, no further difficulties might come up except that a rigid admission policy of institutions, based too exclusively on fixed upper and lower limits of the I. Q., tends to cause placement difficulties.

The matter is different in cases in which the intellectual defect is not sufficiently marked to dominate the psychological picture and to explain the delinquent behavior. The figure of these mental defectives of borderline or slightly subnormal level would appear in a false perspective if seen in terms of intellectual deficiency to the exclusion of any other aspects. In these cases the fundamental fact has to be borne in mind that the arrested mental development which underlies the pathological condition is affecting all sectors of psychic life and thus entails temperament, emotions, will, and drives no less than memory, comprehension, judgment, and so forth. From this angle, the person with merely slight intellectual defect may be considered, as it were, a pathological variant of psychic immaturity, and, as such, requires focusing the attention on its particular character make-up.

In simple cases with a primitive personality, one may do sufficient justice to the mental defective by limiting the characteristic to a few basic elementary traits such as energetic or unenergetic, active or passive, steady or unstable, impressionable or irresponsive, and the like. But other cases of greater forensic significance resist such a simplification of the character picture. Apart from the general fact (to be elaborated in a later context) that every character, normal as well as pathologic, represents a complex psychological structure with traits of diverse origin, it is the inevitable and hardly dissoluble combination of the natural, transient, mental traits of the developmental period and the persistent trends of pathological immaturity that confounds the picture of the mentally defective juvenile and easily misleads the examiner. With the normal traits of adolescence superimposed on and exaggerating those of the defective personality, the aspect of the delinquent youth may appear more serious and somber than the facts warrant. This erroneous view can sometimes be corrected only after many years of slow maturing, when the surprising part which the physiological immaturity had in the former delinquency picture ultimately becomes apparent.

The Defective Delinquent

In the center of forensic interest are, of course, those mental defectives who are characteristically named defective delinquents. They are singled out by law as particularly antisocial individuals who need confinement and training in specific institutions.

The question of what constitutes a defective delinquent has been and still is controversial, not merely because judges, psychiatrists, psychologists, and staff members of training schools look at him from different angles, but also because his nature itself is dubious. Certain it is (a merely negative statement) that the defective delinquent is not simply a defective who is delinquent or a delinquent who is mentally defective. But what are his positive criteria?

If one surveys the greater number of the inmates of institutions for defective delinquents as they appear in court before commitment or after discharge, one cannot find a uniform, clear-cut type. They vary not only in their intellectual equipment but even in those attributes which appear more relevant to the concept of the defective delinquent. Among them are first offenders as well as recidivists; individuals with a short or a long history of delinquency; active, aggressive types, and merely undisciplined, weak characters; boys whose delinquent inclinations seem to come directly from innate personal qualities, and others whose antisocial tendencies mainly reflect acquired habits. What might here stand out as common traits—a defective mentality and an inferior personality as manifested in all kinds of social maladjustment to family, school, and community life—might at best suffice for a descriptive characterization but not for the recognition of a specific pathological type.

Now, no doubt the defective delinquent is not a genuine, scientifically well-established type, but a psychiatric-legal term; therefore one had better derive his specific properties from the underlying legal concept.

Taking as basis the Pennsylvania law and especially the respective articles of its Mental Health Act of July 11, 1923, we find as fundamental statements (a) that the defective delinquent is a mental defective but not insane and (b) that he has criminal tendencies.

Criminal tendency. Starting with the latter, more problematic, characteristic, the criminal tendency is explained as "the tendency to repeat offenses against the law or to perpetrate new ones as shown by repeated conviction—a tendency to habitual delinquency." According to this definition the diagnosis of a defective delinquent could and should be made only in cases of repeated offenses and convictions.

This, certainly, is for all practical purposes a very helpful suggestion, but can the court psychiatrist always strictly follow it? It would, for example, contradict the concept of a genuine criminal tendency if he ascribes this attribute to those emotionally disturbed children who, frustrated in the home in their natural desire for affection, belonging, or emotional security, time and again relapse into delinquent behavior. On the other hand, the examiner would probably not hesitate to recognize such a criminal tendency in a first offender if the picture of the delinquent youth or the delin-

quent act itself showed a marked preponderance of such specific "criminogenic" traits as aggressive drives, explosive temperament, coldness of feeling, and the like.

Of special importance in juvenile cases is another question: Should a true criminal tendency be attributed only to active, aggressive, antisocial individuals, inclined to serious crimes against person and property, or also to the more asocial-parasitic types—the shiftless, passive, weak-willed, habitual delinquents with their minor offenses of vagrancy, begging, petty larceny, and so forth? The present general practice in juvenile courts seems to be to consider both groups as suitable for training in an institution for defective delinquents, and, indeed, both types are to be found there, with the active anti-social type somewhat prevailing. One can admit in the first place that the active juveniles with inherent readiness for aggressive crimes require the specific training in this kind of institution, but that is no reason to exclude the others, whose weakness of moral resistance, of will and character, equally needs such disciplinary treatment.

Mental deficiency. The other criterion of the defective delinquent, mental deficiency, gives occasion for special contemplations. The law demands as basis for the diagnosis the presence of both intellectual defect and criminal tendency; it does not require that an inner connection between both factors exist or be proved. As a matter of fact, mental deficiency is not inseparably connected with criminal propensities, nor is there any unequivocal correspondence between the grade of the mental defect and the seriousness of the delinquency. There are low-grade feeble-minded persons without any antisocial inclinations, and conversely there are persons who show a very moderate intellectual deficiency but an outspoken readiness for criminal actions.

The latter group leads directly, without demarcation line, to the individuals with normal dull or low average intelligence who could make a fair social adjustment were it not for their inferior character qualities, which constantly get them into trouble. Cases of this type may also appear more or less suitable subjects for institutions for defective delinquents, but they are not acceptable, since their I. Q. is too high. (An I. Q. of 75 is usually the upper limit.)

This dilemma raises the question if, from a practical angle, it would not be better to broaden the definition of the defective delinquent to include every individual who, on account of defective intelligence, defective character, or both, shows inherent criminal tendencies. Such a wider concept would not only eliminate useless controversies in cases with questionable intellectual defect, but would have the greater merit of taking care of the psychopathic juveniles, who seem to be somewhat unsatisfactorily handled, although they notably contribute to habitual criminality.

The Constitutional Psychopath

The court psychiatrist is usually in a quandary when the question of the juvenile psychopath comes up. There are many cases which are suspected to belong to this pathological type because the personality of the young defendant or the offense itself appears uncommon, exceptional, or otherwise psychologically conspicuous. Yet there are relatively few cases in which the diagnosis can be verified beyond any doubt. That is not due simply to the controversial concept of the constitutional psychopath, though that often complicates the matter. At any rate, for all practical purposes one can apply a fairly plain and workable definition which states:

1. The psychopath belongs to the borderline group midway between the normal and the psychotic person.
2. His cardinal characteristics are to be found not in the intellectual sphere but in the province of the personality, in anomalies of temperament, instinctual drives, emotions, will, and character.
3. These abnormal traits are constitutional; that is, innate and (probably) hereditary.

But even with such a simplified concept at hand, one is not relieved of all difficulties in the individual case.

Personality traits. First of all, looking at the personality picture, one finds not the innate traits in their original form and isolated from others, but complex psychological structures in which those constitutional, primary elements are combined and even amalgamated with secondary, acquired traits, or are presented in the special shape which external influences of the life history have given them. Even in juveniles, with their character development still unfinished, it is not easy to discriminate between innate abnormal endowment and later reaction formations due to experiences during the formative years.

Apart from that, the external appearance itself as reproduced in the descriptive picture of the case does not aid as much as one might expect in ascertaining the diagnosis. The so-called psychopathic traits of character differ from the normal ones in degree and not in kind, and there is no way of exactly measuring whether a trait is within or without the limits of normalcy. From a pratical standpoint, that means that, in general, personality traits, even if suggestive of psychopathic nature, give no absolutely reliable and cogent criteria.

This holds true especially in juvenile cases. There is, for instance, such a resemblance between specific psychopathic and typical adolescent traits that such findings as emotional imbalance, lack of self-control, or dominance of primitive impulses lead diagnostically to no useful result. Augmenting the difficulties, even the differences in degree become irrelevant, since some youngsters show the natural traits of juvenile immaturity in an exaggerated form without any indications of an underlying psychopathic constitution to account for it.

This similarity between psychopathic and juvenile traits is not surprising, since the psychopathic personality, after all, is likely to be a special pathological form of psychic immaturity, the outcome of a moderate developmental disturbance which affects not so much the basic intellectual elements of the mind but rather the subtler structure of the character. Be that as it may, in these dubious cases the court psychiatrist is faced with an alternative not to be disregarded, since the proper handling depends very much on whether transient traits of the adolescent period or permanent trends of a psychopathic constitution are involved.

Social criteria. Admitting that the character traits in general are not specific enough to serve as criteria of a psychopathic personality, we can hardly expect more from the so-called social criteria, that is, those asocial or antisocial trends which traditionally are interpreted as reflections, if not proof, of the innate "vicious" tendencies of a constitutional psychopathic inferior. The forensic psychiatric practice demands greater reserve in this respect. Take for instance one of those impressive cases in which we find an unusual combination of outspoken antisocial trends, early manifested in childhood, intensified and enlarged in adolescent age, with constant relapses in spite of previous experiences and no proper response at all to corrective measures. There always is an open question whether the whole picture has factually a mere constitutional foundation or rather is in the main acquired, resulting from all those various criminogenic influences in home, family, and neighborhood to which children of the underprivileged classes are often exposed during formative years.

Moral qualities. No less caution should be observed in interpreting the moral qualities of a juvenile and especially in attributing to him that innate total lack of any moral feelings that marks him at once as prototype of a psychopathic antisocial personality, a kind of "born criminal." Not only is the proof of the innate nature of this alleged absolute moral defect mostly inconclusive, but even its actual presence is often not sufficiently demonstrated. As a fact, it is hardly possible to verify beyond doubt the absence not only of the higher socioethical sentiments but of so elementary and basic human traits as natural sympathetic feelings towards others. What commonly passes as proof, namely, the appearance of aggressive, destructive, brutal, cruel behavior in children, may be adequately explained in terms of natural childish traits such as carelessness, unorganized or misled overactivity resulting in reckless actions, thoughtless experimenting motivated by curiosity, and the like.

The Offense. Similarly questionable is the attempt to use the offense itself and its psychological and other concomitants as cogent evidence of a psychopathic perpetrator. However grave, strange, perverse, repulsive, and opposed to all normal feelings the criminal act and the subsequent behavior may appear, there should not be any recourse to the label "psychopath" as diagnostic makeshift unless all other motivations and causes are excluded. Impulsive discharge of strong drives, explosive relief of pent-up emotional energies, excessive aftereffects of emotionally overcharged experiences, uncurbed reactions to frustrated passions, and similar uncommon psychological occurrences are absolutely compatible with normal character make-up, though not the rule. To be sure, the crux of the matter is that these particular dynamic forces and mechanisms often enough operate just within the framework of a psychopathic constitution; they have grave consequences because of the pathological reaction tendencies of the psychopath.

Deceptive attitudes. Finally, as a last complication, it should not be overlooked that the juvenile offender, subsequently exposed to the legal consequences of his doings and the psychological atmosphere of the court, may present an external aspect that is far from reflecting the real personality, not to speak of the basic innate traits. This surface picture, dominated by the momentary psychological reactions to the whole situation, may easily deceive the examiner unless he is looking for what is behind it.

There are in the first place the various forms of self-defense and self-protection which, consciously or instinctively set in motion, may suggest psychopathic trends. A defiant, antagonistic, aggressive attitude may be mistaken as expression of psychopathic antisocial inclinations. Cold indifference without any signs of remorse, compassion, or other emotional responses may appear as pathological lack of any natural human feelings, while in fact it is due to a psychogenic stupor, a temporary blocking of emotional reactions and expressions.

Further contributing to the distortion of the external picture of the personality are the diverse kinds of deceptive behavior which are used—partly intentionally—partly instinctively—to meet the forensic situation. All these reaction forms—telling lies, play acting, and, if need be, malingering—are found especially in psychopathic cases; they do not make it easier to ascertain what kind of person is hidden behind the false façade.

Diagnostic caution. All these pitfalls should warn the court psychiatrist against too hasty and generous labeling of a juvenile delinquent as a constitutional psychopathic inferior, thus stamping him as an unreformable moral defective, a prospective habitual criminal, a potential murderer, and what else this ominous diagnosis seems to imply. If this caution is not observed, it may happen that the subsequent development refutes both the somber diagnosis and prognosis. After the stormy course of the critical adolescent period, the individual may have ultimately, though belatedly, reached a stability, a dependability, and a maturity which no longer fit the previous picture.

But there is no cogent practical reason to enforce a diagnosis in doubtful cases. Even with the diagnosis left undecided, full justice can be done to these juvenile offenders. An exhaustive analysis, neither overdrawing nor disregarding the pathological elements, simply presents the personality, as it is, with its positive and negative sides, its assets and liabilities, and thus furnishes all the material for a constructive handling of the individual case.

The Sexual Psychopath

The juvenile sex offender poses problems of a special kind, requiring separate consideration. They are, of course, in the main related to the particularities of the juvenile psychosexuality. But even the position of the sexual factor in the sociocultural life plays a part. The present-day overconsciousness and overawareness of sex compels the court psychiatrist to be very critical of the information related to him as so-called sexual misbehavior of children. The tendency to overrate and misinterpret juvenile behavior, however harmless, in a sexual sense sometimes furnishes monstrous pictures of youngsters, depicted as sexually overprecocious, excessively oversexed, and affected with all sorts of sex perversions, especially with homosexuality and sadism.

Sexual immaturity. At the examination of the defendant himself, difficulties immediately arise if one loses sight of the basic fact that juvenile sexuality has a psychology of its own which does not admit of measurement, evaluation, and judgment of its manifestations in a way that might be appropriate to the sex behavior of adults. What in the sex conduct of children appears unnatural, perverse, abnormal, or psychopathic, mostly finds its full explanation in the very nature of their sexual immaturity.

This is doubtless true of sex misbehavior of younger children where sex play of any kind directly reflects natural infantile traits such as sexual curiosity, imitation of grownups, playful experimenting, and so forth. It is equally true of the more significant sex activities of adolescent sex offenders, where the whole range of sex delinquency, from indecent exposure to molesting little girls to sodomy and violent attempts at rape, can be traced back to the characteristics of a typically immature psychosexuality.

What this immature sexuality means can be made clear in a few words: The sex drive is not yet fully differentiated and organized; it still lacks the distinctive trends of the mature sex instinct, since its connection with the natural biological objects and ends is not yet firmly established; and finally—most important—the sex impulse is not yet integrated in the total structure of the personality; and therefore is not properly balanced and controlled by the regulating forces of reason and socio-ethical sentiments.

Most of these cases concern accidental sex offenses in which the causal connections are apparent, and the psychological configuration at once reveals the nonpathological origin of the delinquent act and—by implication—the sexual normality of the juvenile delinquent. In other cases the picture seems more complicated, since relapses and persistence in the deviant sex behavior seem to indicate a more deep-seated and inherent propensity. Yet here too, one can ascertain without difficulty that a natural psychological process has led to natural results, namely, to some kind of sex habit. The juvenile, if and when frustrated in the adequate gratification of his sex needs, is looking for and indulging in substitute or compensatory forms of sexual satisfaction. A follow-up soon

proves that no constitutional pathology is involved. With advancing maturity and suitable sex opportunities available, the false patterns of sex behavior are abandoned and replaced by more natural and socially acceptable ones.

Pathologic constitution. The true problems begin when the suspicion of an underlying psychopathic constitution compels the examiner to answer the question whether or not an individual is a sex psychopath. That happens especially when the juvenile, instead of following the natural course just mentioned, and giving up the apparent sex habit, continues acting at this immature, infantile level and ultimately incorporates the perverse tendencies as an integral part in the structure of his personality. Though on the surface it looks as if merely external factors—in particular influences of early life which have left a lasting impression on the forming of the sexual personality —do account for the situation, closer analysis reveals rather that the real cause of these fixed sex deviations lies in a pathologic sexual constitution. It incapacitates the individual to outgrow the infantile stage of psychosexuality and to develop mature forms of sex functioning. This persistence of an immature—undifferentiated and unorganized—sexuality belongs to the cardinal characteristics of the sex psychopath. It furnishes the proper subsoil in which, precipitated by suitable sex stimuli, sex perversion thrives. Among the pathological sex offenders, this type of sex psychopath stands out for its practical importance. Its representatives are to be found especially among the exhibitionists, the homosexuals, the bisexuals, and the individuals with sex propensity towards children.

Reserve needed. The greatest reserve must be used when juveniles are charged with homosexual offenses. To attribute to a young person, without further proof, innate homosexual inclinations and accordingly mark him as a constitutional sex psychopath would contradict not only our general knowledge of juvenile sexuality but also our special experiences in the juvenile court.

Some justification for such an assumption may exist in exceptional cases. They show signs of a deviating physical organization, a female or intersexual type of bodily build, endocrine physical abnormalities, and the like, which seem to indicate that the sex perversion is at least organically founded and part of a general constitutional psychophysical pathology. But even in these cases a more plausible explanation would be that a constitutionally infantile psychosexuality has obtained a homosexual shape by specific environmental influences of the formative years.

Needless to say, a juvenile must not be called a sex psychopath merely because he shows traits suggestive of a psychopathic character and because these character traits (such as emotional instability, over-impressionability, psychic imbalance) are essential determining factors in his sex delinquency. That a juvenile psychopath on account of his general character make-up commits or has the tendency to commit sex offenses does not make him a sex psychopath.

A last problem may come up in certain serious cases of juvenile sex offenders under the influence of sensational publicity and excited public opinion. Should the youth be considered a "criminal sexual psychopathic person" in the sense this term is used in some criminal codes (e.g. Michigan or Illinois)? This special type of sex offender—analogous to the defective delinquent—has been singled out for specific handling, to meet more effectively the menace of certain abnormal individuals who seem to have an inherent disposition and tendency to commit sex crimes.

The question is not whether such a specially defined medicolegal type should be in general recognized, but whether it is needed in dealing particularly with sex offenders of juvenile age. This can be answered in the negative, for various reasons. Contrary to the common opinion and the lasting impression made by every single case, grave sex offenses are relatively infrequent among juvenile delinquents, and the probability of relapses is, as follow-up studies show, surprisingly slight.

Apart from this, the special provisions for handling all kinds of delinquents are so ample in the juvenile court and the judicial dispositions so flexible that proper care can also be taken of more serious sex cases. They seem in part to be suitable subjects for institutions for defective delinquents. Yet it shall not be denied that these juvenile sex offenders generally need a more psychiatrically oriented treatment than that accorded them up to now.

The question of proper treatment—not only of the sex delinquent but of every juvenile delinquent individually—remains open. It includes so many far-reaching problems that it could scarcely be touched in the context of this short paper. No ready-made answers can be given in these cases which altogether ask for individual solution. But since better understanding of the individual leads to more efficient practice, this attempt at an analytical clarification of dubious cases may serve as one of the preliminary steps for a constructive treatment of juvenile offenders.

Can We Regulate Prostitution?*

~~~~~~

By Ray H. Everett. Executive Secretary, Social Hygiene Society of the District of Columbia.

"HIGH school girls seek spending money in vice district." That was the headline of a news item which shocked many American parents a decade or so ago. After school hours, went the report, some youngsters in their teens would detour from their homeward paths, stop for an hour or two at certain brothels and serves as members of the "oldest profession." Payment was far higher than any they could get for other types of work. As for the hazards involved, how could children be expected to realize them? If the girls gave any thought to the matter, their reasoning might well be as follows: "Surely if these resorts were dangerous, our city officials, the police, and our parents wouldn't permit them to operate."

But, overlooking the heavy toll of delinquency and disease exacted by commercialized prostitution, some sincere citizens believe it should be legalized in the United States. "We may as well be realistic," they say. "We will have this business whether we like it or not, so why not regulate and tax it as we do other businesses?" And this viewpoint is strengthened by statements of some old-time police chiefs, physicians, and even an occasional minister. In the words of one notable proponent, "The only practical solution is legalized prostitution under rigid police and health supervision."

Legalized Prostitution

But these advocates overlook the fact that their proposed "solution" has been tried for decades—tried and found wanting. One after another, the European countries have given up legally regulated prostitution for the best reason in the world—the system *didn't* work. Redlight districts, despite carefully devised regulations, always have been centers of crime and disease. No legal code ever enacted has been efficient enough to control the traffic in women and children which goes hand in hand with tolerated prostitution. Nor have health regulations been invented which are sufficiently ingenious to control the activities of the death-dealing habitué of the vice districts, the tiny but potent spirochete of syphilis.

France was one of the nations where the system had been tried for many years. "How does it work?" we once asked a famous French physician. "It doesn't!" was his response. "Neither commercialized vice nor venereal infections are controlled by our present program."

Under this regulation system, you recall, the police are charged with the licensing of girls and women who wish to pursue the ancient profession. They are registered and given cards which must be shown on demand. "Much like the licensing of automobile drivers in an American city," commented our Parisian informant, "but with far less effective results." It is easy to understand his criticism when you consider statistics on regulation in Paris.

Approximately 6,000 prostitutes were registered with the police of that city. But there were about 60,000 unlicensed ones over whom the police had no routine supervision. In other words, 1 out of 11 received some measure of "regulation." The remaining 10 were free

* Reprinted from *Federal Probation*, Vol. XI, October-December, 1947, pp. 39–42. Used by permission of author and publication.

lances, plying their trade clandestinely. If caught, they were subject to arrest, detention, and compulsory enrollment with their registered sisters.

How effective can such a system be considered? A system that reaches less than 10 per cent of the class intended to be controlled. Legally it surely is the weakest of links; medically it is farcical. For even the 6,000 who were licensed formed a continually changing array, but few of whom accepted police restrictions without attempted evasion. M. le Docteur Rist, member of the Paris Academy of Medicine, made the following comment in an address to his colleagues: "It is rare indeed that a prostitute, after a certain time, does not come to shun police control. Yet they (the police) would have us believe that inspection of these 6,000 licensed prostitutes and the removal from circulation of those who are diseased, plays a paramount role in the battle against the venereal diseases, while 60,000 unlicensed ones escape all medical control! It is absurd."

Now a few words more on this question of health protection may not be amiss. Defenders of legalized prostitution make loud and repeated claims that their program aids in the control of syphilis and gonorrhea. But does it? The evidence of health authorities says "No." Regarding the situation in Paris, we refer again to Docteur Rist's commentary. It declared that "all doctors who have studied the question in good faith—and many among them were once convinced advocates of regulation—know full well that licensed houses are an important source of syphilitic and gonorrheal infection. The medical examination of prostitutes, especially when it is done in the licensed houses, is usually a farce, pure and simple." This same verdict applies in the United States.

Rist's condemnation of vice regulations shows that the system has improved but little in the past 35 years. For it was that long ago when the famous American scientist, Abraham Flexner, was sent to Europe by the Rockefeller Bureau of Social Hygiene to study and report on Continental methods of control. His book, *Prostitution in Europe*, remains the classic critique in that field, and it has few equals as a scathing indictment of attempted regulation measures. Wherever the system has been tried, he says, "it has failed—and failed miserably."

Yet it is this same outworn failure that would be given a trial in the United States if its proponents had their way. The delusion still persists that, by some legal magic, a civic disgrace in every other country where it has existed can be made a civic asset here. These advocates would change our laws so as to permit the business of prostitution to operate in a single section of a community. That is, they would attempt to concentrate it under legal sanction or toleration. Unfortunately for the success of this theory, they cannot concentrate the disease, graft, and social decay which inevitably accompany such a system. No—these dire results permeate the whole life of the community. They reach out into the homes; they promote juvenile delinquency; and they foster corruption in police and other official circles.

Prostitution a Business

Commercial prostitution is a business. Its operators count on large profits. Their patrons demand novelty and glamour. Immediately there arises that question of recruits, "the younger the better," as procurers will tell you. Brothels—whether legalized or winked at—constantly require fresh faces and bodies to replace their human stock in trade when it becomes shopworn. Whose daughters will they be?

Along the same line, to bring the problem home, whose sons will become patrons of the vice section? For, just as the prostitution padrones are not overly scrupulous in securing inmates for their resorts they are not too finicky regarding the ages of their customers. What though the law may exclude minors! Laws, in red-light philosophy, are made to be evaded.

Comes, too, the question of real estate values. Within the "district," property rents are high. A few landlords make large temporary profits. But property in the adjacent areas crumbles in value because decent citizens have no desire to live near a section where crime, drunkenness, and perversion hold sway.

The argument sometimes is advanced that legalized prostitution "protects innocent women and children" by providing a recognized resort for adventurous Don Juans and Casanovas. On the contrary, you will find more so-called "sex crimes" committed in communities where commercialized prostitution has gained a strong foothold than in those where antiprostitution laws are vigorously enforced.

Another point raised by those who advocate a segregated district is that, unless such a district is provided by law, commercialized prostitution spreads throughout the community. This "scatteration" depends largely on the attitude of local police and public. If these two forces are united in constant and vigilant opposition to organized prostitution, there will be no widespread epidemic—and the occasional case, though unpleasant, is not a major source of community danger. But studies have shown that cities having a legalized or officially tolerated prostitution district, also have a higher percentage of scattered prostitution. They find themselves in the same situation as Paris with her 6,000 licensed professionals, as contrasted with her 60,000 members of the demimonde who thumb their noses at the police and their regulations.

Prostitution a Health Menace

Yet another hazardous item in the legalized vice program is the false sense of security it instills in patrons. Its farcical health supervision does not give the protection that is expected. Not only are the male customers exposed to infection, but there is the later possibility of grave danger to marital partners. They share the risks though having had no share in the escapade that caused it. Perhaps the following true incident will illustrate this point. It relates to a cultured wife and mother. She and her husband were friends of ours many years ago. They lived in an American city where prostitution was tolerated and attempts made to render it safe. Inmates of the red-light houses were given medical examinations periodically, and each "madame" would proudly boast of the healthfulness of "my girls."

After militia drill one night, this husband, with a number of comrades, took a trip "down the line." Despite the district's health supervision, he contracted syphilis and transmitted it to his wife. It is such cases as this—and they number a host—that have made health authorities almost unanimous in denouncing official efforts to make prostitution safe by medical means. They have seen many experiments made. And as Flexner said, all have failed and failed miserably.

Formerly some police officers favored "regulated vice" because, as a chief once declared, "When you want to find a criminal, the first place to look is in the redlight district." There he often could be assured of the company of fellow thugs, and a hideout until he could skip town or the trouble blew over. Among the inmates and hangers-on he would find a choice assortment of such kindred spirits as procurers, forgers, marital renegades, and the ever-present dope peddlers. Narcotics helped the menacing crew to forget their troubles. Unfortunately, however, weak minds often are ready tools for any kind of criminal undertaking when they are "hopped up" by narcotics. Altogether, one would hardly classify this motley assortment of underworld dwellers as civic assets!

White slavers and the white slave traffic are melodramatic subjects. For centuries they have been discussed sub rosa and with bated breath by good citizens of many countries, but little effective action was taken to curb their dealings. Acknowledged as universal public enemies, the traffickers continued to carry on a world-wide business transporting their human merchandise to and from all points of the compass. And in all the years, where have they found the biggest and most profitable customers? What patronage has made it worth their while to violate the edicts of state, church, and society in order to supply fresh prostitutes on demand? These two vital questions can be answered in three words, "the licensed brothels." Legalized prostitution means licensed houses; and licensed houses mean an open market for white slave exploitation. Yes, those who hope to improve social conditions in some American comunity by securing the passage of laws permitting prostitution are playing directly into the hands of the world's most malignant racketeer—the white slave "procurer."

Reports of the League of Nations

If you have the slightest doubt regarding this tie-up, read the reports of two commissions of experts assigned by the League of Nations to study the vast network of white slavery which extends to all shores of the seven seas. A noted law-enforcement specialist from the United States, Bascom Johnson, was named director of investigations. Associated on the commission were scientific men and women from North and South America and from European countries—diplomats, physicians, lawyers—trained minds, impartial and accurate observers. Their purpose was to learn how and where the prostitution traffic was carried on, who were its major profiteers, who its major victims, and why it had been allowed to become so sinister an international problem.

The first commission, called officially "The League of Nations Special Body of Experts on Traffic in Women and Children," visited and studied conditions in 28 countries of the Americas, Europe, and North Africa during 1926. In 1927 these experts reported the following conclusions concerning licensed brothels:

The existence of licensed houses is undoubtedly an incentive to traffic, both national and international. This has been established by previous enquiries and is admitted to be true by many governments as a result of their experience. The enquiries made by us not only confirm this fact but show, as other observers have remarked, that the licensed house becomes, in some countries, the center of all forms of depravity.

Even stronger was the denunciation of the second commission which reported in 1932 the results of its studies in the Near and Far East. It reads:

Taking all considerations into account, the Commission holds that the principal factor in promotion of international traffic in women in the East is the brothel and in the chain of brothels which are at the disposal of the trafficker, particularly the brothel in the place of destination of the victim. The most effective remedy against the evil, therefore, is in the Commission's opinion, the abolition of licensed brothels in the countries concerned.

Incidentally, the Commissions' investigators often took their lives in their hands while making their "undercover" investigations. No quarter would have been given by the vice racketeers whose criminal activities were under surveillance. A few murders, more or less, would not weigh heavily on the consciences of the ring leaders and their henchmen. For, in the course of their work, they were used to indulging in such crimes as seduction, assault, forgery of passports, fake weddings, and the like, whenever violence or trickery best served their purposes. All these activities and many more are carefully analyzed and described in the authentic, scholarly language of diplomacy used in League publications. But you will find their "traffic" reports far from dry reading.

Among other interesting facts disclosed in these publications, we find that Sweden never has permitted licensed houses; Norway abolished the system in 1890 or thereabouts; and Denmark abolished it in 1901. "Why," you may ask, "are these three countries singled out?" In reply, we would call your attention to the statement that these three make up the trio of nations which were so tremendously successful in fighting the world's great health menace, syphilis, prior to World War II.

In Sweden, syphilis was a vanishing disease. In Norway and Denmark its ravages were reduced year by year until its victims numbered merely tens rather than thousands. These three countries, too, are famed for their fine social welfare laws and their well-rounded programs of infant and maternal health supervision. Is it not significant that these nations long ago resolved that licensed prostitution has no place in sound public health and social welfare programs!

A great majority of the world's nations have followed the example of this trio and have abolished prostitution as a legally recognized institution. In most of the remaining countries, the abolitionist forces are growing daily in numbers and strength. Those persons who favor the old regime are inclined to scoff at leaders of the opposition and to classify them as "crusaders" and "reformers." Human progress has seen many scientific and social welfare leaders similarly designated.

But the two most striking testimonies we have seen on the prostitution question were delivered by hard-headed soldiers—men who scarcely could be assailed as visionary idealists. The first, credited to that outstanding British hero, Earl Kitchener of Khartoum, old "K. of K." as the Tommies called him, declared: "I have found that it pays us better to try to make men moral than to attempt to make immorality safe."

The second statement, written by General Pershing, was made after the American Army had tried all systems, from maintaining its own segregated districts or stockades, to strict law enforcement. Here is the verdict of this great leader:

Many of us who have experimented with licensed prostitution or kindred measures, hoping thereby to minimize the physical evils, have been forced to the conclusion that they are really ineffective. Abraham Flexner has argued the case so convincingly that on the scientific side it seems to me there is no escape from the conclusion that what he terms 'abolition' as distinguished from 'regulation' is the only effective mode of combating this age-long evil.

After all the evidence is in, we may well conclude that legalized prostitution does not have a logical leg to stand on. The prostitution racket with its exploitation of subnormal mentalities, its incitement to white slavery and perversion, its spreading of syphilis and gonorrhea, and its callous disregard of social decency, is not a line of business in which any modern community can afford to share. Good laws and vigilant enforcement may not eliminate commercialized prostitution, but they can keep it down to a minimum. And, when you think it over, that's about all we are able to accomplish with other offenses against public welfare.

Sex Education the Best Weapon

Fundamentally, of course, the best long-range weapon against prostitution is wholesome, honest sex education in the home, school, and church. Though old taboos die slowly, there has been considerable progress along this line during the past quarter century. For example, the author of this essay now finds it easy to use the expression "human reproduction" in talking to any audience whereas, in the 1920's, to avoid blushes of embarrassment on listeners' cheeks, the accepted oratorical detour was "passing on the torch of life from generation to generation."

Even now, however, the three logical sources for sound sex education and guidance spend far too much of their respective time arguing over which should have the major responsibility. On this question we would trail along with the District of Columbia Congress of Parents and Teachers. Here is the statement outlined by that organization's Resolutions Committee at the Thirty-Fourth Annual Convention, May 13–14, 1947:

We believe that the responsibility for sex education is three-fold; the home should be the logical place for dealing with the more intimate aspects; the church should help in the ethical and moral aspects; the school should help by laying scientific foundations through courses in elementary science, health and physical education, biology, and home economics.

Even when some such program is in full bloom, the biological whimsy that made the two sexes in their present forms assures us a sufficiency of social hygiene problems. But the right kind of sex education, used as an integral factor of character training, will reduce the incidence of sexual promiscuity and promote healthier, happier marriage, parenthood, and homebuilding.

SELECTED REFERENCES

1. Gluckman, Robert M., "The Role of Psychiatry in the Understanding and Treatment of Juvenile Delinquency," *Federal Probation*, XV, September 1951.

It is to be hoped that in the near future many of the social problems will be alleviated, if not solved, by the disciplines of sociology and psychiatry as they function together. The psychiatric contributions to understanding juvenile delinquency are well covered in this article.

2. O'Keefe, Daniel, "Mental Hygiene Facilities for the Juvenile Delinquent," *Federal Probation*, XII, June 1948.

The importance of a competent clinic which utilizes the various techniques of medicine, psychiatry, psychology, and social work in the treatment of juvenile delinquency is ably demonstrated here.

3. London, Louis S. and Caprio, Frank S., *Sexual Deviations* (The Linacre Press, 1950), pp. 45–51; 588–637.

These two sections of this book in dynamic psychiatry are highly recommended, for herein is cleared up much of the current confusion in the etiology and psychopathology of criminal behavior.

4. Carr, Lowell Juilliard, *Delinquency Control* (New York: Harper & Brothers, 1941), Chapter 4: "Why Maladjustment and Delinquency?"

In this chapter the interrelations of the individual, the community, and culture are presented. No punches are pulled as Carr answers the question: Why delinquency?

5. Cleckley, Hervey, *The Mask of Sanity* (St. Louis: C. V. Mosby Co., 1950).

In the author's opinion, this is the most outstanding book written on the psychopathic personality. Chapter 19 illustrates significant variations in the psychopathic syndrome.

6. Cavon, Ruth Shonle, *Criminology* (New York: Thomas Y. Crowell Co., 1950), pp. 240–50.

In this section Cavon has an unusually well organized presentation of the differences and similarities among psychopaths, neurotics, and psychotics as they relate to crime.

7. Landis, Judson T. and Mary G., "Our Teen-Agers: How Good Are Their Morals?" *Collier's*, March 15, 1952.

A spirited defense is made of teen-agers, the vast majority of whom are not involved in delinquency.

6 JUVENILE GANGS

GREGARIOUSNESS is a persistent feature of human relationships. It is a common trait manifested in "consciousness of kind" and the hunger of the social person for comradeship and in his fear of aloneness. Juvenile gangs are phenomena of gregariousness, to be sure. But they illustrate much more about society and culture than this universal trait. And their study also reveals some important factors in the development of delinquency.

JUVENILE GANGS AND THE SOCIAL STRUCTURE

Juvenile gangs, both their frequency and the type of behavior in which their members engage, reflect the social structure of the community. Studies made in recent years have documented, for example, the extent to which the class system of the local city or town determines the associations of people in general, including the grouping of youth in cliques, bunches, and gangs. Both the well-known investigations of "Yankee City," a New England town of some seventeen thousand population, and of "Elmtown," a larger midwestern city near Chicago, reveal that adolescents generally intermingle, fraternize, and form informal but cohesive groups largely along class lines.[1] When it is kept in mind that the norms of behavior deemed socially appropriate in the United States are largely those established by and reinforced by the "middle classes," the class restriction of youth groups can be seen to play an important role in the determination of conduct, delinquent or otherwise.

The most clear-cut illustration of the influence of class and neighborhood influences is to be found in the larger cities. For many years it has been observed that socially and physically deteriorated urban areas are marked by both high delinquency rates and numerous juvenile gangs, many of which engage in antisocial and criminal conduct. A quarter of a century ago an impressive contribution to the understanding of juvenile gangs was made by Frederick M. Thrasher. Professor Thrasher studied 1313 gangs containing twenty-five thousand members, concentrated around Chicago's Loop—the central business district. He concluded that gangs are characteristically found in geographically and socially interstitial areas, often in a section where expanding industrial plants encroach upon the city's older residential quarters. At the time of the study, this "delinquency area" was concentrated around the

[1] See W. Lloyd Warner and Paul S. Lunt, *The Social Life of a Modern Community* (New Haven: Yale University Press, 1941); A. B. Hollingshead, *Elmtown's Youth* (New York: John Wiley & Sons, 1949).

business district. Numerous subsequent studies have borne out Thrasher's findings: that in such divisions of the city lack of family control and of adequate community recreational facilities encourage youth to form their own play groups and gangs, which, without proper guidance, may establish their own norms of behavior, including delinquent behavior.

Of course, not all city gangs bring about delinquency. Cliques of various sorts, male and female and mixed, arise in all sections of the city and in smaller communities as well. But there seems little doubt that in those areas where deprivation is greatest and where the "Gold Coast" symbols of affluence are physically nearby but socially distant, there exist the most compelling encouragements for youth to engage in law-breaking activity.

Even in these sections of the community no two gangs are alike. But there are basic similarities in their leadership hierarchies, their group loyalties, their search for adventure and excitement, and their oftentimes first-hand knowledge of the underworld, whose representatives they may admire. That the latter factor is widespread is suggested by Thrasher's findings: of the 1313 gangs, 530 were characterized as "delinquent" or "criminal" and only 52 gangs were described as having no demoralizing effects on their members.

GANG ACTIVITIES

Delinquent behavior, as viewed by the members of the gang themselves, is not always "demoralizing"—often quite the contrary. Oftentimes respect in the group and hence self-respect depends upon some degree of prowess, or at least willingness to engage, in acts defined as delinquent by outsiders. And often these acts have their origin in play itself. This situation is illustrated by the groups of boys who "went stealing" for recreation, as reported to Clifford Shaw during a famous study he conducted several years ago.

> When we were shoplifting we always made a game of it. For example, we might gamble on who could steal the most caps in a day or who could steal in the presence of a detective and then get away. We were always daring each other that way and thinking up new schemes. This was the best part of the game. I would go into a store to steal a cap by trying one on, and when the clerk was not watching, walk out of the store, leaving the old cap. With the new cap on my head I would go into another store, do the same thing as in the other store, getting a new hat and leaving the one I had taken in the first place. I might do this all day and have one hat at night. It was fun I wanted, not the hat. I kept this up for months and then began to sell the things to a man on the west side. It was at this time that I began to steal for gain.[2]

This quotation also suggests the role played by group pressure in determining behavior patterns in gang life. Delinquencies, as well as nondelinquent acts, are commonly committed by youth operating in small groups; the "loner" is relatively a rare case. For in the age demarcation of the gang, internal group pressures and loyalties tend to compel the more youthful and less prestigeful members to engage in behavior patterns established by the bolder and older

---

[2] Clifford Shaw, *Delinquency Areas* (Chicago: University of Chicago Press, 1929), p. 35.

leaders. And these leaders, if they live in certain areas of the city, often find *their* models rooted in local tradition, tradition giving sanction to delinquency and crime.

And here is seen the gang functioning as an important educational agency. If members of these quite natural boyhood (and girlhood) associations learn how to play marbles or stickball they also learn other and less innocent group-ways. For the gang may teach—and quite effectively in this school of deeds—how to "roll drunks," steal from railroads or buildings, "boost" from stores, fight gang "wars," and so on. All of these, in a word, may be part of the group's way of life.

Usually originating in play groups, the juvenile gang gains group solidarity in its conflicts with school, police, and larger community. Crime techniques are often disseminated and may themselves symbolize the gang's uniqueness and its value for its members. Group identification and morale are further enhanced by the adoption of a special language: the members may be "on the bop" when looking for a street fight, they may be heading for a "session" when going to a dance, or may be imbibing "Sneaky Pete" when drinking a mixture of gin and wine.

The activities of delinquent gangs, particularly in recent years, have constituted a serious civic problem in large cities. World War II witnessed the growth of many "combat" gangs, some of which were responsible for such crimes as "mugging," rape, homicide, and various types of petty racketeering. In the 1920's Thrasher reported forerunners: the "Murderers," whose members stole from delivery wagons, broke into boxcars, and stole automobiles for joy rides; the "Dirty Dozen," an especially aggressive gang that deliberately provoked ethnic groups as well as rival gangs and "earned" its money by bootlegging and stealing. In more recent years, these patterns are repeated—with the gangs acquiring more lethal weapons, including knives, guns, knucklers, and chains. And these weapons, unfortunately, have been put to use quite frequently by teen-agers as reports in such cities as New York, Chicago, and San Francisco reveal.

This grim picture, however, should not lead to the conclusion that all or most members of juvenile gangs prey upon society without compunction. According to one study, of those youth brought into juvenile court only about 10 per cent should be classified as vicious, hardened, habitually delinquent. This minority includes the youngsters who adopt delinquent behavior as a career and the gang as a medium of "protection, comfort, and training for effective operation."[3] And these are the young people who so frequently become "hardened criminals" in later life.

GANG "MORALITY" AND ORGANIZATION

Much has been written of gang "morality." And certainly it is true that the juvenile gang, like other close-knit small and intimate social groups, has its own social norms, its own "code." A large part of this code, as publicized by

---

[3] Lewis J. Doshay, "The Challenge and Solution of Juvenile Delinquency," *Journal of Clinical Psychopathology and Psychotherapy*, VI, April 1944.

such motion pictures as "Knock on Any Door," is supposed to be expressed by the slogan: "Live fast, die young, love all the girls, hate all the cops, and have a good-looking corpse." While this is no doubt a somewhat misleading expression of the gang's code, it is clearly the case that, in order to survive in a hostile world, the gang must follow a fairly severe set of rules. And of central importance in the gang's code is the insistence upon loyalty to the group. Thus the adult criminal principle of "Never squeal or burn your partner" is matched in the juvenile gang by the rule "Don't rat." The obligation to follow the rule is supported by a privilege: it is better to take a beating at the hands of the police than to disclose gang information, and in turn the members of the gang will do as much for *you*.

The code of the gang is closely related to another of its essential components: its system of internal organization, usually informal but none-the-less effective. Almost all juvenile gangs (like their adult counterparts) develop a hierarchy of control, descending from the recognized leader down through such positions as "war-general," "light-up" man (in charge of the arsenal), the funny one or jester, the "dumb" one, the "goat"—names used by the members of a corner gang in an Italian neighborhood, reported in *Street Corner Society* by William Foote Whyte. Both the "officials" of juvenile gangdom and the group loyalties holding the gang members together, it should be noted in passing, are sometimes exploited by local political machines, as Whyte brings out in his study, for their own ends. For here are already well-organized potential henchmen at the service—for a price—of local "bosses."

Not only is the gang marked by internal organization, but its "working" relations with outside groups, including other gangs, are sometimes quite extensive. Many juvenile gang members, for example, "graduate" to more mature law-breaking groups. In New York City, it has been reported that older gangs often have junior auxiliaries or "Tiny Tims." Very young boys, serving their apprenticeships in these junior groups can look forward—much as Cub Scouts look forward to more senior status—to becoming regular members of gangs with such picturesque names as the "Forty Thieves," "Swamp Angels," "Slaughter Housers," "Hudson Dusters," "Musketeers."

Quite frequently the gang's name illustrates its ethnic composition. When it is remembered that lower-class residential areas are often also the living-centers of concentrated ethnic groups, "racial" and national and religious, it is not surprising to learn that juvenile gangs themselves take on an ethnic stamp. Thus in New York, among other gangs, are found the "Gestapos," "Bombinos," "Latin Counts," "Puerto Rican Eagles," and "Irish Dukes"; in Detroit, the "Little Jewish Navy" and "Purple Gang"; in Los Angeles the "California Daylighters," who, at times, terrorized "enemy" ethnic groups.

One should not conclude, however, that juvenile gangs are always stamped by ethnic alikeness or that all spring from the most deprived sections of the population. Some gangs contain representatives of two or more ethnic groups, for example, several in New York City, in a sense, are little "melting pots," and the members of many others come from families considerably more affluent than "lower class." Similarly delinquency is not restricted to the latter groups by any means. According to Louis P. Spitz, head of the Juvenile Delinquency Board in Reno, delinquency is fairly widespread through that community (Reno is probably not an especially representative city), involving at times children of Reno's "best" families. Delinquency and juvenile gangsterism, then, are not merely problems of concern to welfare officials who work among families on "the other side of the tracks." As community concerns, however, it must be remembered that middle-class children not only have much greater opportunity to channel their energies in law-abiding group activities but also rarely, as compared with their more deprived peers, become deeply enmeshed in either the temptations of the criminal world or the police agencies organized to cope with that world.

GIRLS AND GANGS

Delinquency and gangism are not, of course, confined to the male sex. However, somewhat in keeping with the persistent tradition of male superiority, girls in juvenile gangland seem to play special and somewhat subordinate roles. Nor do boy juvenile gangsters, especially when they have attained adolescent years, reject female fellow-members. To the contrary, girls are recruited into gangs. Many become members voluntarily and apparently with enthusiasm, though some enter only under threats of physical violence. Sometimes the membership of these female auxiliaries is indicated by secret symbol, such as a spider tattooed on the left hand, attesting affiliation with "The Spiders" of Los Angeles, or a red dot used by "The Cherries" of the same city. Or the girls may have designs "carved" on themselves, especially if they are defined by the boys as subsidiary members. It has been reported that parents who object to their daughters joining gangs run the risk oftentimes of juvenile revenge, such as the slashing of the tires of the family automobile, its ignition wiring being torn out, or the filling of the fuel tank with sugar or sand. But it is probably true that most girls who find their way into youth's gangdom do so without the aid of such dire measures. Girls no more escape the compelling circumstances of their lives than the boys themselves.

What are the functions of the girl gangster? In some degree, of course, she is the juvenile counterpart of the much-publicized "moll" of adult "mobsters." Gangsterettes are often expected to submit to the sexual advances of the boy members; young girls, not infrequently by force, are initiated into "adult" sex practices. They sometimes assist boys in gang fights, illustrated a few years ago by girls using their then-popular high pompadour arrangement of hair to conceal such weapons as knives and finger-nail foils. Girls have been used by gangs in New York City to waylay leaders of rival groups—the traditional "decoy" technique. These seem to be the principal activities of even those girls who organize their own female gangs—the "Robinettes," "Chandeliers," the "Shangri-la Debs," and so forth. Thus Bernard summarizes:

Only rarely does the girl gang function without affiliation. In the great majority of cases it exists as the auxiliary of some boy gang, to which it gives fierce loyalty. One important duty is to act as weapons carriers to the boys, who thus escape seizure and charges. The girls also supply alibis, claiming that a suspect boy was with them at a "session," or in bed at the time of the crime's commission. Principally, however, the young ladies act as camp followers, supplying the lads with such sex as they require—and fulfilling duties as lures and spies.[4]

Juvenile girl gangsters have come into the public limelight especially since the years of World War II. Around Naval bases and Army camps, for example, they have at times been used by their civilian companions as bait to lure service men into out-of-the-way places, where the latter were "rolled" and robbed. Apart from the publicity given to such cases, it appears that the number of female gangsters has been on the increase in recent years. Gang offenses among girls between the ages of fourteen and seventeen, in 1948 and the first six months of 1949, ran almost 10 per cent higher than during the peak delinquency war year of 1943. In spite of their subservient position in boys' gangs and the fact that their own gangs are usually viewed as auxiliary to the male groups, these young women are reported to be more difficult to handle than the boys themselves. New York police have been reported to comment, for example, "These junior gun-molls are tougher than the guys."

THE APPEAL OF THE GANG

Why do young people join gangs? Several of the background factors already have been indicated. But an important part of the picture of juvenile gangism would be missed if the fact were overlooked that gang activities, from the viewpoint of young people themselves, are fun. Everyone values recreation and an important function of gang affairs, both law-abiding and law-breaking, is to provide recreation for its members.

Ruth S. Cavon reports (in *Criminology*), the case of one small gang of boys, all under eleven years of age, who persistently stole equipment and contents from unlocked cars—whether they had "use" for the loot or not. Their real gain was derived from the excitement and anticipation of their final act: leaving in the cars small printed cards reading "Lock Your Car. The Nighthawks." Imagination was at work here. Sometimes imagination and the youthful search for adventure leads to serious violations of the law, as illustrated by this story from *Life:*

> In Bakersfield, California, six youngsters ages 8–13 and a dog named Butch left their slum district called "Billy Goat Acres," and set out on foot for excitement. When they got hungry, they broke into a fruit store, then smashed some windows in a used-car lot, found an unlocked car, and started West across the Tehachapi Mountains, but after 20 miles, sideswiped a truck, blew out two tires, had to abandon the car. They found another in a rancher's garage, but 104 miles later near Los Angeles, they skidded into a soft shoulder, had to leave the car, but in a matter of moments, picked up another car. But this time the owner called the police.
>
> At 95 miles an hour they roared onto Los Angeles' Sepulveda Boulevard followed by two radio patrol cars; the cops opened fire and after eleven shots, the car

---

[4] William Bernard, *Jailbait* (New York: Greenberg, 1949), p. 93.

stopped. Police approached warily, guns drawn against what they fully expected was a carload of adult desperados. Out popped the unhurt and tousleheaded members of the Billy Goat Acres mob.[5]

The search for fun, then, often leads to delinquent acts. These acts may become established in patterns of behavior receiving at least some sanction from the adult world, even from certain of its more prestigeful members. When, for example, during World War II, one newcomer to a gang objected to stealing tires on the ground that, according to press and radio, such behavior was akin to treason due to the rubber shortage, the leader, one Knifey Joe, replied "G'wan home, punk. Treason! Look at them big shots and politicians riding around on new tires and getting all the gas they want. Don't be a sucker!"[6] When the prevalence of more immediate law-breaking adult models who inhabit the local breeding-grounds of delinquent juvenile gangs, including often enough members of the youngsters' own families, are considered, it is not surprising that illegal patterns of behavior are taken up by youth groups—sometimes in the cause of "play."

Many boys and, increasingly, girls idolize and imitate great outlaws of the past, from Robin Hood to the James brothers. And in juvenile gangs there is often hero worship of outlaws of the present, the adult gang leaders. The fact that so many of these youngsters are poverty-bred and slum-fed helps to account for the "big-shot" ideal. Moreover, under these conditions, there are numerous handicaps facing youth, disadvantages of descent, limited education, sometimes even illegitimacy or physical disability. But, in keeping with the ubiquitous success norms of the greater society, the aspirations of these young people call for rapid advance up the social ranks, if possible. And in the minds of some of them—those especially impressed by the "big-shot" models—social barriers can be hurdled and fame and fortune achieved quickly by adopting the ways of the criminal or near-criminal world.

The appeal of illegal and extra-legal short-cuts to "success" complicates and aggravates the problem of the delinquent juvenile gang. People coping with this problem—parents and social workers and community leaders—often couch their appeals to follow conventional and legitimate paths in terms of abstractions that do not compete successfully with the concrete and immediate and "real" lures facing young people who are growing up in "delinquency areas." These areas, moreover, encourage attitudes of bitterness and cynicism, so frequently found among gang members.

If youthful aspiration is to be constructively channeled, if the glamor of the big-time criminal is to be lessened and legitimate means of achievement are to be followed, if cynicism is to be replaced by confidence in socially constructive values, and if the juvenile gang is to be just that and not a breeder of delinquency—if these goals, essential in an adequate reform program, are to be achieved in any substantial degree—social science and the community must join hands in a more concerted and realistic effort than has yet been made.

---

[5] By permission, from *Life* Feb. 11, 1952. (c) *Time* Inc.

[6] Reported in Pamphlet No. 300, Children's Bureau, U. S. Department of Labor, 1943.

READINGS

James R. Dumpson in "An Approach to Antisocial Street Gangs" discusses the success enjoyed by a privately financed welfare council in New York, which managed to infiltrate into four of the most troublesome juvenile gangs in central Harlem—the "Jaybees," the "Gay Blades," the "Royals," and the "Knights." Sex offenses were minimized and gang warfare was stopped. Only four workers participated in this experiment; hence a permanent group of workers might go far in solving permanently the city's gang problem.

Another experiment concerned a two-man project designed to develop techniques for dealing with nonconformist juvenile gangs not easily reached by social agency programs. This is reviewed by Ernest G. Beier in his article, "Experimental Therapy with a Gang." Extraordinary patience was necessary to build up the requisite rapport to conduct sessions of group therapy, some of which were characterized by the boys pouring out feelings and thoughts for which the group had been unprepared. A follow-up study of the group, though contemplated, has not been made at the time of publication.

The underlying reasons why boys are attracted to gangs are portrayed by Sam Glane in "Juvenile Gangs in East Side Los Angeles." Carefully considered are the inherent difficulties in trying to reach the gang and the recognition that only through coordinated community-wide efforts will the juvenile gang problem ever be solved.

For their article, "Gang Membership and Juvenile Misconduct," Wattenberg and Balistrieri studied the records of some 5878 adolescent boys contacted by the Detroit police. They concluded that socioeconomic indices had greater value in predicting recidivism in the case of gang members, while family indices were of greater value in the case of nongang members.

An Approach to Antisocial Street Gangs[*]

By James R. Dumpson. Formerly Consultant on Delinquency and Correction, Welfare Council of New York City; Child Care Consultant, The Federation of Protestant Welfare Agencies.

ONE OF THE concomitant phenomena of the social and economic disruption of the recent war was the marked rise of delinquent behavior on the part of teenage youth in this country. Particularly in our urban communities, a dramatic and disturbing series of outbreaks of warfare was observed among teen-age groups or clubs disdainfully called gangs. During

1945 and 1946 in New York City, violence among "conflict gangs" reached an all-time high. From September 10 to September 19, 1946, a 9-day period, three youngsters were killed in gang warfare in one neighborhood of the city.

Action was deemed imperative to protect the community and its members. The Prison Association of New York

[*] Reprinted from *Federal Probation*, Vol. XIII, December, 1949, pp. 22–29. Used by permission of author and publication. See also Paul L. Crawford, Daniel I. Malamud, James R. Dumpson, *Working with Teen-Age Gangs* (New York: Welfare Council, 1950), 162.

called on the Welfare Council of New York City as the central planning and co-ordinating social agency in New York to "formulate a definite program of action" for the amelioration of antisocial activity by gangs. Despite considerable discussion about the causes of juvenile delinquency, few efforts had been made to examine empirically the methods being used to prevent and control delinquency. The Council called together a committee of experts in the field of youth services, and after months of careful analysis and study, the committee recommended the operation of an experimental project with street gangs designed to formulate methods for developing and extending suitable programs of treatment. The project was to operate for a 3-year period in two of the most seriously affected areas of the city. Limitation of funds finally confined the effort to one area, and in the spring of 1947, the Central Harlem Street Clubs Project was set up.

In reporting on the Central Harlem Street Clubs Project, the writer, at the outset, wishes to acknowledge the contribution of the entire staff of the project in the presentation of the material on which this paper is based. However, the writer personally takes responsibility for the form in which it is presented, and particularly for the evaluations that are set forth.

Basic Assumptions and Objectives

There are multiple causative factors underlying individual delinquent behavior, and an examination of causation of antisocial group behavior similarly indicates many contributing factors. The degree to which any one factor contributes to antisocial behavior, whether individual or group, may be negligible. As stated by Harry Manuel Shulman, "It is the cumulative impact of a large number of these factors that constitute the multiple causation pattern and, at the same time, the complex treatment

problem of the delinquent situation." The aggression and hostility of the delinquent reflect his neglect, his lack of affection, his rejection by his family, neighborhood or community. Devastating economic and social conditions play a major role in the breakdown of the family which in turn results in emotional deprivations and frustrations that drive the individual to behavior which we call delinquent. Racial, religious, and class prejudice, topped off by a stereotyped and depersonalized school experience, contributes further to his feelings of rejection and to the influences of unsatisfying interpersonal relations in a home that frequently is emotionally demoralized.

The Committee on Street Clubs, in its analysis, defined the following as causal factors in the antisocial club behavior which they studied: (a) The glorification of violence and "commando" tactics during the war years; (b) The tension resulting from an intensified emphasis placed on racial differences; and (c) The deep-seated frustrations as the result of political, social, and economic discrimination on racial, religious, or nationality basis in our country or city.

The recreation and leisure-time agencies in the area were not equipped, either by stated function or structure, to cope with the street gang situation. A survey revealed that not more than 10 per cent of the total adolescent age group in the area studied were participating in adult-sponsored leisure-time activities. Even where attempts had been made to reorganize programs in an effort to attract a greater proportion of the teen-age group, it has not been possible to integrate into total agency programs those autonomous street gangs which already had developed patterns of aggressive antisocial behavior. The complex cultural and socioeconomic factors underlying the street gang pattern dictate that an approach to the situation cannot be anchored in a recreation program. No amount of adaptation of services on the part of leisure-time agencies alone can prevent or control juvenile delinquency. To seek the answer in recreation is to deny the subjective meaning of anti-social behavior. The prevention and treatment of delinquent behavior requires the utilization and co-ordination of *every* available and known resource in the community. It must use effectively the knowledge and skills of every discipline that relates to man in society. It must be a total community approach.

We have learned that punitive and repressive methods will not control the street gang situation. Such methods on the part of the police and other community agents have tended to heighten existing tensions and to increase hostile activity. Authority has its proper place in treatment and control, but must be used as part of a total plan which is geared to the individual and his needs. Brutality and ruthlessness on the part of the police merely fan the flames of hostility of gang members and serve to strengthen the unity of the group out of its felt-need for protection and retaliation.

The committee agreed that existing approaches were not meeting the needs of street gang members. Experimentation with an approach that would involve in a positive manner the total community and all of its resources seemed indicated. The approach used recognizes that the street gang is a normal expression of the needs of adolescents to emancipate from adults and to establish themselves as independent individuals. By its very nature, the street gang has constructive potentialities. It is a medium through which the adolescent can gain a security which arises from acceptance by one's social group and also one through which capacities for group loyalties, leadership, and community responsibility can be developed.

The objectives and goals of the project

as set forth by the Committee on Street Clubs may be stated as follows:

1. Reduction of antisocial behavior among street gangs through redirecting antisocial behavior into socially constructive channels.

2. The development of a local area committee composed of persons having an active interest in the area and concerned about our problems. The purposes of this committee would be to sponsor the project at the area level, be responsible for developing and utilizing local resources for meeting the needs of the street gangs, and to stimulate further community action toward the removal of forces acting as hindrances to wholesome living in the neighborhood.

3. The determination of the validity of the project method as an approach which may be adaptable for use by other areas.

In order to achieve these goals, it is necessary to structure a process that provides a dynamic relationship between the boys and the workers. The project must help the people of the area to focus their interest and constructive efforts on the problems which adversely affect wholesome living, and to provide them with skill in finding ways of solving these problems. Finally, if the project method is valid, the techniques employed should be defined for use by other areas and communities faced with the street gang problem.

Working directly with the various street gangs in the neighborhood are five area workers, one of whom is a woman, who are responsible for direct contact with a gang and who, through the skills and understanding of casework, group work, and community organization, attempt to help the gangs and their members to find satisfaction in socially acceptable club activities. The research director has the responsibility of recording the operations and of evaluating the results of the project. The area director, working with the Council's Consultant on Correction and Delinquency and the Committee on Street Clubs of the Welfare Council, provides the administrative direction of the entire project. The woman worker devotes her skills and efforts to the girls who are directly related to the boys in the clubs.

The Street Gang Structure

During the two years of the project's existence, relationship has been established with four of the area's most aggressive, antisocial gangs and contact has been established with the girls related to them. Each of these gangs has a history of violent gang warfare, weapon carrying, stealing, rape, and the use of narcotics. Truancy, drinking, and tangles with the police have been prevalent among the boys, whose age group is from 11 to 23, and many of whom have been in one or more correctional institutions.

Except during mobilization for gang warfare, the structure of the gangs is generally loose and organized for a face-to-face relationship and the protection of its members. The largest gang has approximately 100 members; the smallest about 35 members. However, the boys travel in groups of two or three and it is unusual to see more than 10 or 15 members together at any one time or place. Basically autocratic, the gangs can be divided into two distinct groups: leader and leadership clique consisting of five or six boys, and the members. The gang is broken up into various special interest groups for activities, and while membership in these gangs varies, there is a tendency for the leadership clique to play a dominant role in them and to determine the nature of most of their activities. The gangs also have what the boys call "divisions." These usually are based on age groupings, have their own organizational structure, and serve, by a kind of vertical mobility, to perpetuate the gangs. The club officers' titles are functionally descriptive and seem to indicate the roles their holders have in gang warfare. Usually there is a "president," "vice-president," a war counselor, assistant war counselor, and occasionally a "light up"

man. This latter boy usually carries the pistols and initiates the war by "shooting up" the rival gangs.

Newspaper and magazine articles and recent glorified films on the gang have given a distorted picture of the frequency of the groups' participation in antisocial behavior. The experience of the project indicates that only a small part of the boys' time is spent in such activities. Participation in sports, attendance at the movies, parties, dances, "bebop" sessions, and "bull sessions" take up a much larger part of their time. Just "hanging around" and visiting their girl friends are important activities of all the gangs.

The so-called "street gang" may be one of three types: (1) A group whose principal activities are antisocial. This is the "criminal gang" whose sole function and activity is antisocial in nature. (2) A group which occasionally engages in antisocial activities. This is a normal social unit of adolescents. Under appropriate external stimuli, it may engage in antisocial activity. (3) A group which, as a unit, does not engage in antisocial activities although individual members of the gang may follow a confirmed pattern of delinquent behavior. Although our experience during the 2-year period has been with four of the city's most notorious gangs, it is my judgment that the so-called "street gang" is a combination of the last two types.

The Project Area

The section of New York in which the project is working is one of the most depressed, underprivileged areas in the city. It is an area of inadequate health, educational, and recreational facilities; overcrowding; poor housing; and low economic status. The people, for the most part, react to segregation and racial discrimination with hostile and tense feelings which underlie many of their attitudes toward the value system of the community at large. The violation of conduct norms among adults is an ever-present reality. Charges and counter-charges of bribery by the police and of police brutality are part of the daily flow of events. The setting for the average child is one of poverty, value conflict, bitterness, anxiety, fear, and anti-sociality. However, there has been no evidence of any sympathetic attitudes on the part of adults toward interclub warfare among the teen-age groups. Indeed, in most instances, many of the adults have characterized the boys involved in gang warfare as "trouble-making hoodlums," and this has been of real concern to many of the boys. As the boys have come to engage in constructive social activities, there has been an increasing measure of co-operation on the part of the adults. Their mixed feelings about the conventional institutions and values of the larger community, and the realities of segregation and discrimination present a real problem for effective organization for local community action.

Relations with Street Gangs

The operation of the project began officially with the appointment of the area director on April 14, 1947. For the first 3 months, the director's work consisted largely of a survey of the cultural, ethnic, economic, and social aspects of the neighborhood; charting the movement and respective areas of operation of individual gangs; and establishing a relationship with the leadership of the gangs and the indigenous adult leadership in the neighborhood.

The approach in establishing a relationship has been informal and no attempt has been made to interfere with the boys' accustomed ways of carrying out their activities. In fact, identification was built up through able participation by the area workers in those activities which had special meaning for the boys. It was found helpful to have an extra package of cigarettes on hand as the boys were always "bumming" them

from each other. Acceptance of the director by the gang can be noted by the following type of incident which is quoted from an area worker's process record:

> When one of the boys would ask if he got the cigarette from the director, frequently the answer would be "Yeah, man. He is a citizen," or by the statement, "No, man, he ain't no cop . . . we cased him."

The relationship with the first gang, the Royal Counts, was sufficiently established to enable the director to obtain their co-operation in fixing up the project office. Throughout the cleaning period, questions were asked of the director as to how the place was to be operated. The presence of office furniture seemed to have motivated many of these questions. They were answered frankly and directly, and the aims and purposes of the project were discussed freely. After the confidence and interest of this group had been secured, the boys were transferred to the first area worker at the end of three months. Through utilization of similar techniques, another area worker was able to establish a relationship with the Lords. In this case, the worker formed a close relationship with the janitor who cleaned the project office and who had been purposely selected to do this job because of his thorough knowledge of the neighborhood. Through the janitor, the worker was introduced to a key member of the Lords. Their interest in the Dodger baseball team, a picture at the neighborhood theatre, and invitations by the worker to accompany him on errands, laid the foundations for at least a beginning relationship. It paved the way for casual visits by the worker to their hang-out. Here he usually found the boys either boxing or sparring. He decided that their expressed interest in baseball was an attempt to please him or may have been a reflection of his anxiety to rush the job of acceptance. In order to extend the relationship, therefore, he attempted to use the medium of boxing instead of baseball.

A third worker made his contacts in a block where the existence of a street gang had been established. The worker was in need of housing and asked many people on the block for help in finding a place to live. In this way, he became acquainted with people of all ages. As was the practice with the previous workers, after just "hanging around," drinking coffee, playing the juke box, this worker became known as "one of the boys." He was included in conversations and challenged to pitch pennies, and to play football with the boys. Through these contacts, which were purposefully initiated by the worker, he gradually gained the acceptance of the members of the street gang. The following excerpt from his process records gives a picture of the background and atmosphere in this particular situation:

Edward (the candy-store proprietor) has a small juke box in his store, and I have played it quite often, frequently as a means of extending my stay. On four occasions, I asked the fellows to help me choose some decent numbers. After that they changed the numbers I punched to play records of their own choice. They don't do this secretly, but openly and with good humor. They stand around the juke box and talk about dates and dances—but I seldom, if ever, see them with a girl. They are usually together. Even on Saturdays and Sundays. When they enter the store and I am there, they greet me along with anyone else in the store whom they know. On the several occasions that I have entered the store to find them there, they continued talking or doing whatever they were engaged in. On one occasion, one of the fellows asked me for a cigarette and on another occasion they approached me en masse and asked if I did not want to hear "Let Me Love You Tonight,"—I laughed and played the record for the umpteenth time.

The workers experienced numerous frustrations and anxieties in developing relationship with the boys. Although constantly assured that there were no "deadlines" to meet and no rigid schedules to which they must adhere, they always looked eagerly for the first signs of real acceptance. But these signs, at least in the minds of the area workers, were painfully slow in appearing. Sometimes, in the midst of a conversation which had all the opportunity to deepen the relationship, the boys suddenly would move away leaving the worker alone. The worker might approach a group hoping to join in the conversation, and the boys would become silent. Months later, the boys would tell the workers that they originally suspected them of being policemen or similar representatives of the law. They had watched carefully for any clues that might confirm their suspicions. Finally, through real acceptance of the boys and their group, a conviction about the constructive potentiality of the club, and through his understanding, warmth, skill, and unending patience, the worker was able to establish a relationship in varying degrees with the members of the club. (The term "club" is used hereafter in reference to the street gang with which a working relationship has been established by the area worker.)

The Role of the Worker

What to do with the relationship has presented one of the most difficult questions in the project, for we are learning that this relationship has been structured differently from the usual casework relationship. We are only now beginning to define the quality of this relationship and to distill the area worker's role in its dynamics.

In working with the boys, the workers usually follow the initiative of the boys. They participate in games, bull sessions, block parties, "be-bop jumps," card playing, or just "hanging around." Recently, boys of several former conflict groups have gone on weekend camping trips, and other similar intergroup activities are planned. The workers see club members almost every day, usually in the afternoon or evening, and spend from 15 to 25 hours a week with them. Usually, they see from 4 to 12 boys in a contact. Sometimes they see only one boy in a contact; sometimes as many as 50. The contacts take place wherever the boys hang out—the street, the candy store, the pool room, at the boys' homes, and now, with growing frequency, at the project office.

We do know that the area worker's role varies with the needs of the group. At times the boys ask them to arbitrate a dispute, to give help in securing a job, or advice on personal problems. The worker's word is not law and the boys freely accept or reject the worker's opinion as they see fit without being rejected by the worker. In a discussion of antisocial behavior, the worker's role also varies. Frequently the worker will listen without expressing approval or disapproval. Sometimes he will ask questions to learn more about the boys' attitudes or behavior. At other times he will disapprove openly of their behavior and give his reasons. If the total situation warrants, the worker may initiate a group discussion and utilize group interaction. Or he may await an opportunity to discuss the situation with an individual boy in terms of that particular boy and his ability to use more intensive help. The area of antisocial behavior is the most difficult to handle. The worker must use great skill in defining his difference from the boy and at the same time maintain a horizontal relationship with him. Skillfully, he must determine the motivations of the boys' behavior, determine the leadership in the situation, and manipulate the situation so as to provide substitute satisfactions for the real goal of the antisocial behavior. In all of this, however, his identification with the boys and their needs must never blind him to his responsibility to the larger community. While he can never betray the confidence of the boys, he constantly must interpret to the schools, the police, and to the entire community constructive ways of meeting the needs and frustrations and hostility which their behavior represents. The worker must recognize and accept his own limitations in the helping process and assist a boy to move on to the use of specialized services in the community when the need is recognized and the boy is ready to use it. Gradually, very gradually, he must help the boys make the fullest use of the facilities in the community and at the same time help the agencies understand and accept this boy. Many of the leisure-time agencies are having to accept the hit-and-miss kind of participation by the boys as they test and retest the realness of their place in the agency after they have accepted the worker's suggestion that they use the agency's facilities.

The worker is called upon to assume responsibilities which other club members are unable or unready to assume. When the boys show an interest in some project, the worker usually helps in the planning and takes on responsibilities just as any other club member. He helps get equipment, permits for block parties, and secures tickets and passes from the police for events that the boys previously had rejected. Gradually the worker transfers responsibilities to individuals in the group, and himself takes on fewer and fewer responsibilities. To illustrate, one area worker writes in describing a second block party:

A significant change that is apparent is the contrast between the amount of responsibility that the boys took upon themselves at the first block party and at this block party. At the first block party I had to get my hand into a great many things and the boys waited for me to do things before they would start. This time they took on responsibilities without waiting for me. I just had to carry out my duties as a member of the group rather than as the supervisor.

At this block party, Fred took the responsibility for running the record machine; Leon asked the fellows not to shoot fire crackers; he had signed the permit for the party and therefore felt a keen responsibility for conducting it without unhappy incident with the law. Harry took chief responsibility for drawing up a list of the refreshments to be purchased, making the purchases, and supervising all of the boys who helped to prepare and sell the refreshments. Spike's feeling of responsibility was exhibited in his helping out where needed and checking up on all phases of the activity. Jim, an older boy, got a number of his friends to assist the boys in selling raffle tickets and took the responsibility for borrowing a large lamp from the owner of the barber shop and setting it up to provide light for the party.

The worker suggests new ways of doing things that are leading to a greater democratization of the clubs. The boys are experiencing the satisfactions of successful efforts and cherish the "rep" they are achieving in the community, which gives them the status they previously sought in daring and dangerous antisocial activities.

Community Self-Help

One of the unique objectives of the project is to offer assistance to the community in dealing with the problems of the area and meeting the needs of the boys. Chiefly, this involves the development of resources and the stimulation of local community action toward the removal of hindrances to wholesome living in the area. Not only has it been necessary for the staff to gain the acceptance of the boys in the clubs. The adults in the community were as suspicious and mistrustful of the area workers as the boys were. During the first 18 months' operation, the staff had to build the kind of relationship with the people in the area that would allow them to use the skills it has in community organiza-

tion. Efforts are being made to develop an area committee—parents, interested local citizens, and representatives of the four clubs with which the project is in contact. The area committee will attempt, on a local level, to engage in social action designed to effect changes in the neighborhood that contribute to juvenile delinquency. It will attempt to create an atmosphere in which the boys and the potential constructive value of the street club are accepted. It will set in motion the creation of a spirit of cooperation between the boys and the adults and a feeling on the part of the boys that they are "somebody," that they are valuable as individuals and in groups and have a worth-while contribution to make to the local community. The area committee receives guidance and direction from the staff using, however, whatever indigenous leadership there is in the neighborhood. It will receive the full support of the influential Committee on Street Clubs as programs are developed in matters of housing, police activities, health and welfare facilities, employment opportunities, educational facilities, and the elimination of adult criminal activity in the neighborhood. Progress in this area is painfully slow and considerable interpretation and support are necessary.

A professional advisory committee, made up of representatives of agencies and organizations in the local community, is attempting to supply services that are needed and to assist the agencies in meeting the needs of the boys and community as defined by the project staff. Plans are being considered by the committee as to how the techniques developed by the project may best be used by existing agencies after the project has terminated in 1950. The regional division of the Welfare Council of New York is working with the project staff, the area committee and the professional advisory committee in an effort to achieve the fullest co-ordination and the best arrangement of existing services, and to identify areas of unmet need.

Research

Space does not permit a detailed exposition of the research plan. The answers to two basic problems were assigned originally to the research director: (1) Is the area project effective? (2) Why is the project effective or ineffective?

Evaluating the effectiveness of the project involves a determination of the extent to which desired changes occurred in club members and the extent to which these changes can be attributed alone to the project's influence. Determination of the answers to the second question involves the formulation of the methodology developed in working with street clubs during the 3-year operation of the project. It will be necessary to define the methods which were followed by positive change, negative change, or no change at all. We shall want to compare those club members who change most with those who change least. It is hoped that research will indicate the extent to which such environmental influences as the socioeconomic conditions of the area, police practices, etc., seem to influence club members. And finally, we hope to be able to define the personal qualities and professional equipment necessary for an effective area worker. The area worker records his contacts by means of chronological process records. Following this, he answers an interpretation questionnaire designed to help him think through the significance of his experience in preparation for the next contact. He also prepares a review of his records each month as an aid to judging his progress, the effectiveness of his methods, and the most appropriate procedures for the future. Volumes of process records are being analyzed by the research director in order to provide an analysis of various change categories, an evaluation of the workers' techniques,

and the boys' response to them. From this material, research is able to provide a current evaluation out of which the staff is able to refine and reformulate techniques and methods of operation. Research also will allow us to state the success or failure of this approach to street gangs and help determine its usability in other communities facing a similar situation in the control of juvenile delinquency.

Preliminary Evaluation

Any assessment of accomplishments of the project must, of necessity, be tentative. Even now, we have not perfected the tools for measuring the effectiveness of this project approach to antisocial street gangs. And when this is done, we will be faced with the limitation that is set by not having any precise accounting of the extent to which the boys engaged in various activities at the beginning of the project. Nor can we be sure that we are securing now a complete picture of their activities. Even though the boys tell the area workers a great deal, we cannot be sure that they can and do "tell all." Finally, change is a gradual process. If the workers are putting into their relationship with the boys a content that allows the boys to experience a reorganization of any part of themselves, we may not be able to measure the full effectiveness of the project for some time yet to come.

Despite these limitations, we are able to make certain tentative judgments about change in the clubs and to isolate positive results in several of the change categories:

1. The boys are spending increasingly more time in constructive and satisfying activities. Behind these activities are hours of joint planning and sharing. Through these activities, we have helped the boys release much of their potential initiative, leadership, and resourcefulness in socially acceptable and individually satisfying endeavors. They have

gained some status in the group and in the community from these activities which they formerly sought in antisocial behavior. They have begun to gain a sense of individual worth and are developing an interdependent relationship with the adults in the community including the heretofore despised policemen.

2. Certain forms of antisocial behavior have decreased. Since the beginning of the project none of the clubs has engaged in interclub warfare although there have been incidents in other sections of the city. Concomitantly, there has been a marked decrease in intergang warfare among the gangs which occupy territory immediately adjacent to that of our clubs. There has been less measurable decrease in the use of narcotics, sex activities, individual stealing, truancy, and drinking. It may very well be that these forms of antisocial behavior for some of the boys are symptomatic of deep personality disorders and are not amenable to the approach of the project. However, there is evidence that the boys have a greater awareness of a new value system and, in individual instances, are consciously striving to identify with the value system of the area worker.

3. The ability of these boys to establish a relationship with a mature, warm, accepting adult has been unquestionably established. This accomplishment augurs well for their use of the only medium through which help may be offered to these boys in order to effect any substantial change.

4. Relations within the group have improved. The leaders are less autocratic and the opinions of the club members are more consistently sought. There is evidence that intragroup dynamics are beginning to operate in a broader democratic framework.

5. The boys have been helped to recognize the availability of facilities in the community which more satisfactorily meet their needs. Their use of the facilities of the Police Athletic League, the gymnasia of public schools, camping facilities, and their willingness to test their acceptance by the group work and leisure-time agencies indicates that success is being realized in broadening the boys' horizons and enriching their day-to-day experiences.

6. Here and there existing recreational agencies have been helped to accept these autonomous groups and to gear their programs to the boys' interests and needs. Considerable reorientation needs to be done in this area before the boys are ready to use the agencies and before the agencies are prepared to accept the boys.

7. Finally, several agencies in the city have begun to adopt this project's approach for their program in an effort to reach groups of boys similar to those in the project. In one instance, a group of extension workers from a group work agency is working with street gangs in the immediate area of another agency. In another instance, two recreational workers in the public schools have been released from the after-school program to work with two street gangs that recently caused the death of one boy and seriously injured another. A project in still another area of the city, under one of our regional councils, using the approach of the Central Harlem Project, has been completed successfully and the report is now being written. The program of the New York City Youth Board to prevent and control juvenile delinquency will include a group of workers who will use the approach of this project in working with street gangs in various parts of the city.

We are convinced, at this point, of the soundness of this approach. There remain many limitations to overcome and many problems to work through. As yet, we have not fully defined the function of the area worker, the specific equipment he needs to bring to the job, and the extent to which the area worker must use the disciplines of casework and group work. There yet remains the task of isolating, in a demonstrable way, the various techniques used by the area workers, testing the effectiveness of each of these with the various types of boys in the street gangs and the motivations of their participation in the antisocial activities of the gang. Then we will need to find the ways of adapting these techniques for use in existing or new agencies as a way of working with antisocial gangs.

Finally, if we are to prevent, control, and treat delinquency, we must all find a way to use, in every appropriate setting, the knowledge and skills we have concerning human behavior. We have not begun, as a profession nor as a society, to use all that we know about mental hygiene, social improvement, and change in our efforts to meet the challenge of juvenile delinquency. More than new agencies, more than new techniques, more than greater emphasis on psychiatry and sociology, group work, recreational facilities, or additional institutions, is our need to develop a broad, comprehensive program of child welfare in every community that utilizes every bit of knowledge and skill presently at our command. We shall need constantly to test and retest the things we do in that program. As we develop research in every phase of child welfare, we shall have a valid basis for change in experience and practice. Then, and only then, shall we meet the needs of children at home, in school, and in other areas of community activity. Then we shall effectively prevent and control the individual and group expressions of juvenile delinquent behavior.

Experimental Therapy with a Gang[*]

By Ernst G. Beier. Head, Mental Hygiene Department, Syracuse University.

A TWO MAN project, designed to develop techniques for dealing with nonconformist juvenile gangs not easily reached by social agency programs, was undertaken in upper Manhattan two or three years ago with the financial assistance of G. Howland Shaw, president of the New York City Welfare Council, and the American Philosophical Society. Two different techniques were tested, the second of which is described here. An attempt was first made on the activity level of the boys, the worker trying to expose the gang to a new environment. Rapport had been established by a friendly entrance into the lives and activities of about fifteen boys, ranging in age from fourteen to seventeen, in their street corner hangouts, and on their own level of entertainment, such as crashing movies. Afterwards more constructive activities like photography, weight lifting, and building their own clubhouse were encouraged. This part of the project has been reported by Bradford Chambers, the other half of the project team. Let it suffice to say here that the effects of careful introduction of acceptable activities to these boys was successful only as long as the workers were present. As soon as the adults withdrew the old gang activities were resumed. It became apparent that the boys sought the respect of the workers rather than a set of new activities.

Group Tests

Realizing this motivation we undertook the second phase of the project in an attempt to reach the gang through

---

[*] Reprinted from *Focus*, Vol. 30, July 1951, pp. 97-102. Used by permission.

group therapy. Here we were primarily concerned with the psychological structure of the boys' behavior, rather than with their gang activities. We thought that our good relationship with the boys could be utilized in an attempt at group therapeutic work, as lasting changes could be hoped for only when the boys no longer conceived of themselves as misfits who could not be respected and were in conflict with authority.

The gang's habitat was a community in transition, a slum district with rapid population changes characterized by racial conflicts of long standing. These conflicts had grown in intensity with the accelerated migrations of Negroes and Spanish speaking peoples from bordering Harlem. The most difficult task in dealing with a gang in this area, to establish rapport with them, was already accomplished. The psychologist had been previously introduced to the boys as a friend. It should be noted that, against all expectations, this introduction almost immediately broke down barriers. It seems that the delinquent boy, not unlike the rejected child whom Spitz pictures, clings to the stranger once he feels he can trust him.

After several visits the psychologist suggested that the boys might like to take certain tests. These tests, given in January 1948, substantiated previous observations, generally speaking. In the Rorschach tests the majority of the members showed extraordinarily few signs of phantasy or inner life, nor did they show signs of affectivity. Negativistic attitudes and estrangements from people were prevalent. The boys had built up such strong inner defenses against their hostile and repressive environment that their own thinking and imaginative faculties had been seriously crippled. A sentence-completion test, dealing more directly with immediate behavior mechanisms, also underscored their definite lack of sensitivity, their devil-may-care concepts, their profound hopelessness as to

their own place in society. The following are sample responses to items on this test:

When I think of the past few years, I feel rotten.

When I only would, I never had a chance.

When I have free time, I don't do anything.

When I wonder what I would really like to do, I forget it.

After this initial testing project the worker asked the boys if they cared to come to the university for some meetings in which they could discuss anything they wanted to discuss. The boys agreed and a date for the next meeting was set.

Group Sessions

The group therapy sessions which followed the tests were held in the Guidance Laboratory at Teachers College, Columbia University. The meetings were recorded, but unfortunately the recordings were not clear. The attendance gradually increased from three in the beginning to nine at the twenty-eighth session. The worker had previously told the boys that if they wanted to come, he would keep certain hours free every week for them. At the first meeting he repeated this statement, expressed his pleasure that the boys had come and added that they were to use this hour in any way they chose.

The three boys who showed up at the first session listened attentively and then suddenly agreed to use the hour any way they chose. One boy placed a chair on the table, and then sitting upon it directed traffic for the other two who ran around the room shouting and yelling. Another boy sang into the microphone (the members agreed that the hour should be recorded) and made obscene remarks, all the while glancing over his shoulder apparently to see the worker's reaction to his behavior. It was clear the boys were testing the limits of the freedom he had promised them. After some twenty minutes they calmed down.

The discussion that followed revealed the intensity with which the boys entered the session, the kind of personal problems which faced them, and the therapeutic techniques used. After the boys became quiet enough to talk the time was monopolized by Boy A. He had strong therapeutic needs and immediately began to discuss his mother's accidental death. He told of a New Year's party when he had refused his mother's demand that he go to a nearby store to buy a quart of liquor. Upon his refusal, his mother, already intoxicated, went herself. She never returned. The boy and his father searched for her later that night, and not finding any traces of her whereabouts, they concluded that she had gone to the home of some friends. The next morning, she was discovered in the snow, frozen to death. As far as the boy could make out, his mother had drunk the whiskey she had bought, and heavily intoxicated, she was unable to find her way back. He repeated his story over and over again. Although he had always been hostile toward his mother, or perhaps because of this fact, he thought himself responsible for her death. Here is an excerpt from the conversation:

Boy A: She sure pushed me around all the time. You couldn't do a thing to please her.
Counselor: That made you feel pretty hopeless.
Boy A: Sure, I was going to the dogs. I think even the army is better. You need some discipline.
Counselor: You wish somebody would tell you what to do.
Boy A: She never did. She never did do nothing for me, so I didn't get her the liquor. She had to go herself. She never got me anything when I wanted something of her.
Counselor: You feel you had a right to refuse . . .
Boy A: I didn't know what would happen, so I let her go. I just said, you go yourself.
Counselor: You are bothered to think that maybe you should have gone.
Boy A: Ya. (pause)

The speed with which Boy A took advantage of therapeutic opportunity perhaps can be explained by the pathetically eager response to counseling typical of the neglected.

In later sessions it was observed that the group situation had a particularly contagious effect on the members. As Boy A seemed to obtain relief by talking out his problem, other boys found it easier to express themselves. While Boy A was talking about his feelings toward his mother, other boys would interrupt to tell of equally strong feelings of their own. They were resentful if A did not give them an opportunity to relate their experiences. At such times the worker had difficulty in relating to all members without favoring any particular one. Thus Boy B kept interrupting Boy A, and only when the worker restated A's anger at the interruption and B's displeasure over his inability to get a word in, did A give B the chance to speak. Boy B without much hesitancy discussed his father, who came home drunk one night a week and showed violence towards the boy's mother and kid brothers. On one such occasion B had taken it upon himself to "put a damper on my old man's crap," and knocked his father out. He then dragged his father to a bed, hitting him once more to keep him quiet for the rest of the night. Boy C told of a similar traumatic situation. Several years previously this boy had been so severely beaten by his father that the latter was arrested and jailed. Naturally the boy dreaded his father's release. He told of his anxieties and his sleeplessness, and how he worked himself into such an agitated frame of mind that when his father finally did get out of jail, C threw a pan of boiling water at him. The father then left home and never returned.

Disturbed relationships were discussed, not only with parents but also with others in authority symbolically representing the parents. An example from the eighth session:

Boy A: Teachers! (spits out)

Counselor: You sure don't like them.

Boy B: They're no good, don't give a damn for you.

Boy C: Remember what's her name, when you said a word in class, she threw a ruler at you.

Counselor: That sure made you feel pretty mad.

Boy C: Nobody likes these teachers.

Boy B: You should have seen them in my last year. You always could get them mad.

Counselor: That was one way of paying them back.

Boy A: Sometimes they got so mad, policemen were called in.

Counselor: They didn't give you much of a chance.

It became clear again and again that the boys could only participate in discussions after tensions *within* the group had been recognized. This recognition of the feelings the boys had toward each other, an analysis of group transferences, seemed to weld the boys into the kind of group in which therapeutic gains could be expected.

Throughout these sessions the therapist's aim was to help the boys progress in the therapeutic situation at their own speed, and not to hasten the process by structuring the discussions. The boys took varying lengths of time to enter the discussions. The same probing and aggressive activities which had characterized their reactions at the first meeting continued with diminishing intensity in successive ones. Besides being limit-testing, this behavior may also be seen as an expression of the boys' resistance to meeting their problems. They were coming face to face with some aspects of their lives that they had not recognized before. The worker discussed this resistance with them.

On two occasions, however, the worker experimentally introduced techniques designed to structure the hour from the very start by suggesting specific topics. At the beginning of one session the therapist asked the boys to tell what they would do "if they possessed all the money they wanted and could spend it freely." This structure set off a discussion, and so-called resistive behavior was not apparent. It was interesting to note the dearth of imagination in these boys. One remarked that what he most wanted was a million dollars so he could build a house with a pool table in every room. One thought just of getting married, and some would use the money simply to invite members of the gang to their homes. Another would buy a factory merely to increase his already limitless fortune. It is questionable whether this suggestive structuring was worth while from the therapeutic standpoint. The worker had taken over the posing of the problem, the boys actually accepted *his* problem, and the slow pace in imagination may have been due to this fact.

A second try at structuring the session was attempted with the introduction of the topic of sex. Aware that these boys were experienced in sexual play and intercourse with their gang "debutantes," the therapist brought up this question for discussion. Again the attempt to structure the session was definitely a mistake. The boys listened quietly to the worker, but after he finished they followed their own thoughts and brought up other problems. In later sessions sex was discussed much more easily because their comments stemmed from their own need. They were ready to talk about it.

After about fourteen sessions and after discussion of a great many personal problems, a notable change occurred in the appearance of these neglected boys. They began to dress neatly, to shave and have haircuts. This was a rather sudden development. Even the elevator operator at the university commented on these improvements. One afternoon, after the fifteenth session, when the therapist accompanied the boys to their old corner restaurant hangout, one boy remarked, "Oh, Christ, back to this damn place again." The others echoed this sentiment. It was as if they were beginning to see themselves in a new perspective. They had always pictured themselves as "rough and ready guys," and their lives as going the way things were meant to be. But now they no longer seemed bound by this inevitability; they were beginning to wonder just why they had to live that way. The old hangout had now become "this damn place." It seemed as if the therapeutic process of the preceding months had in a way broadened their concepts of self, had begun to give them a feeling that alternate choices were possible.

At the end of the sixteenth session, five of the boys worked out plans to start their own business enterprise—polishing cars. They mimeographed sheets of paper announcing their organization and attached these notices to cars parked in the neighborhood. Although their independent business spirit did not last long, it was an indication of their need to build a different world according to the new concepts of themselves.

After the twentieth session attendance began to wane. Some members had obtained jobs and often could not make the hour. Four boys had joined the armed services. By the twenty-eighth session all except one boy had secured full time employment. A boy who had seemed unable to enter into the group discussions was recommended for individual therapy. From a theoretical point of view, it might be said that during these sessions the boys were helped to withdraw from the battleline of their fight with an authority symbolic of the parental conflict they had experienced. They no longer saw themselves as individuals violently resisting a hostile environment.

Analysis of the Process

Analysis of the group sessions led us informally to some tentative conclusions:

Voluntary attendance. A great deal of attention has to be paid to the *initial* rapport between the worker and the boys. Rapport was established here by aproaching the gang in its own haunts, and the original worker spent considerable time with the boys before therapy was attempted. With persistence it seems at least possible to contact a rebellious gang. Rapport would be even more important in dealing with groups of delinquents who are under official supervision. With us the boys attended the sessions voluntarily and the relationship had to be built up with extraordinary patience. However, both workers hold the opinion that therapy in involuntary settings may be possible.

Size of group. When therapy began the gang had eleven members, nine of whom at one time or another attended the sessions, so not all the members of the gang were reached. One, the former group leader, left because of loss of status. The workers found that best results were obtained when the meetings were attended by not more than six boys.

Selection of group members. Some workers suggest individual therapy before they permit members to enter groups. Age, education, type of problem, and other criteria have been considered as other factors in selection. I believe that more evidence should be collected on this point and that none of these criteria as yet sanction the exclusion of any individual.

Monopolizing. When some member of a group has particularly strong therapeutic needs, he may monopolize the hour. The therapist is often able to check this by directing analysis and discussion. Individual therapy, probably with another counselor, seems also a sound recommendation. If the group counselor gives individual therapy to one member, care would be indicated to avoid the charge of preference.

Structure of topic for discussion. It seems best not to structure the topic as it limits the range of discussion. Also, responsibility for finding a topic for discussion can be a therapeutic experience for the boys. Behavior that seems to the observer remote from the purpose of the group is often of great significance.

Factions. Crises often develop when two factions arise within the group. Here the worker has the difficult role of clarifying the feelings of each faction without taking sides, being at the same time mindful of the tensions that develop within the group.

Social contacts on the outside. It was inevitable that the problem of outside social life would arise, as the gang was already a social group, making frequent contacts with each other outside the session. Intimate personal problems and thoughts expressed during the therapy hours were inevitably discussed by the members when they met together after the session. This carry-over may be viewed as beneficial to some extent because of a cumulative effect on possible behavior changes. On the other hand, such rehashing of group discussions was also disadvantageous. One boy left the meetings and the gang itself after the fifth session. He had brought up personal matters during the therapeutic hour

that afterwards were used against him by the others. The boy had stated that he did not want to get married, and had expressed this feeling so vehemently that the other boys labelled him a "queer." The reason for this negative effect lay in the suddenness with which therapy started. The boys poured out feelings and thoughts for which the group had not been prepared.

Conclusions

It would be difficult to say how closely the changes observed in these boys were related to the group therapy sessions. One cannot be certain as to what the boys would have done without this experience. A follow-up study of the group, though contemplated, has not been made to date. The difficulties in setting the proper experimental design with an equated group are obvious. Further research is needed to establish the specific value of group therapy with a juvenile gang. However, those of us who were associated with this project believe that after our work was terminated the boys were happier and better adjusted individuals.

Juvenile Gangs in East Side Los Angeles*

By Sam Glane. Parole Officer, California Youth Authority.

FREQUENTLY in the last few years newspapers have headlined the activities of juvenile gangs in East Side Los Angeles when violent acts were committed. Several months ago the Los Angeles County Youth Committee and the Metropolitan Welfare Council of Los Angeles delved into the problem of these gangs and elaborated on their playground origin—a matter which was given some publicity in editorial comment. More recently still, the activities of "wolf

packs" and "rat packs" were widely publicized.

Beyond question, youngsters are attracted to neighborhood gang groups because their own homes lack attraction. Many disorganized families have created such a problem in East Side Los Angeles. Cultural conflict between alien-born parents and children of Mexican descent and American birth is common here. To quote a school attendance and child welfare supervisor: "The parents, by and

* Reprinted from *Focus*, Vol. 29, September, 1950, pp. 136–141. Used by permission.

large, are still law-abiding and docile, whereas the children feel they can get nowhere with their docility." Other factors in the disorganized family group include low economic status due to discrimination against minorities, overcrowding, disrupted family relationships, sporadic emotional outbursts in the home, and a consequent trend toward amoral social conceptions. All of these difficulties drive the adolescent and his younger brother out of the home to find release from the psychological ghetto in which his family is confined.

The minority group is constantly discriminated against and is denied opportunities and advantages in the community. Delinquency rates in which children of a minority group figure, therefore, can be misleading. Inspector Robert W. Bowling, head of the Los Angeles Police Department's juvenile division for many years, in a recent report indicating that a disproportionately large number of Mexican-American juveniles were arrested over a ten year period, explained that underprivileged areas suffering from official neglect and the lack of sufficient private preventive programs, have also received heavier policing and consequently have yielded more arrests. Discriminatory police and court treatment of Mexican-American defendants has also been charged as in the case of twelve youngsters sent to San Quentin for the alleged murder of another youth, whose convictions were appealed and later reversed.

The Neighborhood Gang

Play groups crystallize into neighborhood gang groups. Conflict in congested areas may originate over territory, loot obtained through the commission of overt delinquent acts, play spaces, or the privilege of exploiting groups or individuals. Oftentimes conventional opposition to a gang's unsupervised activities can fan antagonism into flame. By coordinated action the members of a gang acquire a "we" feeling, and the loosely organized street corner society has been formed. Such attitudes have a significant effect on the youngsters concerned and determine their entire future conduct in social goups. Certainly the social values of the youngster's own group mean more to him than the seemingly unnatural values attached to approved behavior patterns. He belongs to a predatory assemblage and his conduct is adjusted acording to the significance attached to it by his fellow adolescents and pre-adolescents. He seeks only their approbation.

These play groups are not systematically organized, although natural leaders emerge and are looked up to with great respect, even in the classroom. Intimate relations develop on the basis of common interests and desires. Traditions are originated through such practices as identical tattoo marks on the face, hands, and arms, and fraternity-like initiations. Although as a rule gangs exist in all stages of organization, most of those on the street corners of East Side Los Angeles have been loosely organized, but through years of association have developed strong loyalties. Frequent incidents giving rise to conflicts among these youngsters have served only to consolidate them into more tightly knit groups.

School administrators in the area hope to provide supervised activities for the children so that they will be less strongly attracted to gang life. A good beginning has already been made there in the construction of a large gymnasium building to serve also as a recreational center. It will be open evenings just as the school playground now is so that boys and girls need not "roam around looking for excitement elsewhere." School observers think the gangs tend to be clannish by neighborhood, that their membership changes continuously, and that some gangs become completely inactive. Thus the Marianna Cherries, boys of junior high school age, were the only group with the audacity to recruit members outside of their own district. They were also the group with the least respect for school authority.

Many of these children of sub-marginal families, who join their "shoot-the-breeze" associates for the relief of tensions, comprise what has been appropriately termed street corner society. As William Foote Whyte says in a book of that name:

The nuclei of most gangs can be traced back to early boyhood, when living close together provided the first opportunities for social contacts. . . . The gangs grew up on the corner and remained there with remarkable persistence from early boyhood. . . . Frequently movement out of the district does not take the corner boy away from his corner. . . . On any evening on almost any corner one finds corner boys who have come in from other parts of the city or from suburbs to be with their old friends.

They all find acceptance by joining the corner clan and develop a deep sense of loyalty to the group in their own immediate neighborhood. They evince hatred toward "outsiders," look for retaliation if one of their own particular clique has a grievance, and exhibit a lust for blood revenge which sometimes does not stop short of serious injury or even murder. Mexican-American adolescents are prone to give vent to a blind fury of passion on certain occasions. These conflicts are most frequently intra-racial among our East Side youngsters.

A deputy probation officer who covers the area in the investigation and supervision of juvenile probationers finds that very seldom is there concerted effort of a gang as a whole. He points out that individual matters may be handled jointly by a few who are looking for revenge or have entirely personal reasons to pursue certain activities while they cloak themselves in their activities in the name of the gang. In general there is no organized

aggression in these gang activities, and interracial tensions come out only when gang boys are in a confined situation. Several instances, however, of organized gang aggression are on record in the juvenile court of Los Angeles county.

A patrolman of the "gang detail" has been operating one of three radio cars specially assigned to investigate gang activities. He is familiar with the well-known hangouts or informal meeting places and keeps posted on members of the various gangs and the changing leadership, such as it is. He attributes many of the conflicts between rival gangs in the eastern part of the city to such differences as a dispute over a girl, who may dance with or become interested in a boy from a district outside the gang's recognized teritory, or over other aspects of territorial control. Leaders, in his opinion, attain their position through "pulling something and getting away with it without being apprehended." Also, the "strong-arm boys or those with cunning character" can secure this king-pin status through force or shrewdness.

Names of the gangs are often colorful. A few are: Big First, Little First, Whitefence (including Cherries and Monsters), El Hoyo, Flats, Gallardo, Little Eastside, State, Hazard, Little Hazard, Wabash, and Hunter. Several of these gangs have assumed the name of the street area in which their members reside or meet. Meeting places include street corners and vacant lots patrolled by radio cars.

There have been no homicides lately in the East Side which could be directly attributed to gang fights. This is surprising when one learns of the number of shootings or knifing attacks that occur within a year's time, of the guns and other deadly weapons which turn up following routine police shakedowns, and of the number of youths brought before the juvenile court for "assault with a deadly weapon."

One juvenile gang member may be

"jumped" or attacked by a rival gang, either because he happened to be going through foreign territory or because as has been suggested he has taken a girl friend from a rival gang's territory home from a dance, or just for intimidation. One boy needed several stitches in his cheek because he was ambushed, attacked and stabbed in the vicinity of a dark corner lot. He was unable to name a single one of the assailants, since they were complete strangers to him as he was to them, and he could not distinguish a single identifying characteristic in the poor light. Another youngster, temporarily in a block controlled by rivals, was attacked by several "Flats" boys because he happened to live in "Whitefence" territory. His nose was broken and he was knocked unconscious by a blow which necessitated emergency medical care in a hospital. The same boy was later shot at by members of the rival gang. Removal from the community was the only safe course for him. In still another case, various methods of physical torture were used on a youth to induce him to become one of a gang. As a rule, fear is the instinct most frequently aroused, and force or intimidation is employed to induce fear. Many of these street corner clusters are constantly on the lookout for an explosive situation involving neighborhood pride or an impulsively conceived pretext for a brawl with similar groups in other parts of the city, and attempted interference with their activities by conventional groups merely increases their hostility.

The Influence of Pals

The magnetic power of the juvenile gang for its individual members cannot be explained simply, as it is made up of complex factors. An emotional need may exist for identification with others in similar situations whose interests and desires have not been satisfied by the home, the school, the church, or other conventional social institutions. Leisure time spent loafing around the neighborhood corner or malt shop, will develop friendships whose common urge leads to delinquencies. However, "pals" who are bad company for each other cannot be considered the sole cause in the delinquency situation, as many parents of delinquent youngsters would like to believe when they rationalize their own shortcomings. Demoralization in the individual can certainly occur even after the abolition of the gang, but the gang greatly facilitates tendencies toward delinquency by giving prestige to already existing patterns of unwholesome conduct. In group solidarity gangland members assimilate modes of thinking, feeling, and performing typical of the delinquent.

Many boys who have returned from a forestry camp or one of the Youth Authority training facilities with every intention of avoiding further gang alliances may be physically assaulted, shot at, or forced by more subtle methods into renewed group identification for self-protection. The gangland boy's status may be enhanced in a highly delinquent area by his antisocial background. Sometimes a desire for a sentence to San Quentin is expressed by a youth awaiting adult court adjudication, so that on release he may boast of having been to the "Big House."

Psychologically the juvenile gang member is conditioned by the approbation of those with whom he is identified, and his attitudes, social concepts, and behavior are certainly determined by the anticipated reactions of his companions, regardless of what conventional society and its institutions may expect of him. He will adopt the vices practiced by his companions, although they may be detrimental to his own character or to society as a whole. Truancy from school may be encouraged in him because an activity requiring absence from school is being planned by the gang, although truancy is not a recognized gang activity as such. Smoking may be encouraged in spite of the state law prohibiting sale of cigarettes to minors. Drinking of intoxicating liquors or use of narcotics may be the order of the day. There always seems to be an adult around to buy these prohibited items for the minors desiring them. Unfortunately such adults are rarely apprehended.

Gambling with cards or shooting craps is another commonly practiced vice. The use of profane language is frequently carried over into the home and the schoolroom, as evidenced by complaints from parents and teachers. Vulgarity and obscenity, stimulated within the gang, may result in premature sex experiences. Such practices usually spread to the entire group, which exercises a powerful social pressure against the individual member who may have compunctions in regard to them.

Gang Activities

Just what are the activities in which a juvenile gang indulges? Boys and girls who have known each other over a period of several years look for a variety of experiences to give them the excitement and stimulation which has been lacking in drab home settings and the humdrum existence of limited environments where there is never enough money for a family vacation. Commercial entertainment can be only an occasional motion picture show for those who have the price. Consequently, gang boys shoot craps with a substitute for money if this precious medium of exchange is not to be had, pass around cigarettes when a member has persuaded an adult to purchase them, or share a bottle of wine.

When they need cash several boys band together to commit a delinquent act. Money dishonestly obtained frequently goes into the purchase of intoxicating beverages and narcotics commonly shared by the gang as a whole. Such joint vices result in strong group consciousness and identification with antisocial elements. The next step may be banding together to commit rape, assault, or car theft. Sometimes these bonds are of an overnight or temporary nature as many of these groups are loosely bound together. Also, some of these street-side "clubs" will show a flare-up of activity and then become quiescent for a long period of time. The inactivity can sometimes be attributed to the fact that leaders or "rifas," as they are known in Spanish, have been taken out of circulation and placed in one of the forestry camps maintained by the probation department or in one of the training schools or state camps operated by the California Youth Authority. Law enforcement authorities have increasingly turned to the Youth Authority for assistance in preventing further delinquencies of parolees.

Some gangs in the area may be quiescent while one may flare up with intense activity demanding investigation by the juvenile officers. Often jealousies arising out of a dance or other social event result in serious injuries to both sides. A feud may originate privately among a few and develop into a group conflict resulting in bitter hatred and hostility sometimes lasting for years. Usually some specific incident brings rivalry to a critical stage. Retaliations and return raiding trips involve the use of knives, clubs and loaded revolvers.

Prowess in a fight maintains the status of a gang in the neighborhood. There is a never-ending struggle for existence and for the preservation of play privileges, property rights, and the physical safety of members. Cycles of conflict become more intense as one incident leads to another. When embryonic gangs are threatened with disintegration, conflict may result in gang reorganization. On the other hand, disintegration of one circle of this artificially created society may result in replacement by another, spontaneously organized. Conflict, flight, and escape provide the zest of commonly shared interests.

Approaches to the Gang Problem

Our knowledge of the nature of the juvenile gang unfortunately is insufficient to provide us with a solution, perhaps largely because the gangs themselves are the results of complex social, economic, and psychological elements. Congested neighborhoods, substandard shacks and dwellings in unsanitary areas, and below-subsistence incomes cannot be rectified by waving a magic wand. Social workers are constantly faced with disillusionment by the very nature and immensity of the social problems giving rise to these delinquent and pre-delinquent groups.

Community resources for physical and mental health, welfare, and recreation are frequently unknown to those needing them most except by referrals through schools, churches, probation and parole officers, social workers and juvenile police officers. The Los Angeles City Recreation and Park Department has recently concentrated upon these deteriorated areas for playgrounds, swimming pools, and youth centers, some still in the planning stage. The Catholic Youth Organization has established the Santa Maria Center where communitywide participation has been encouraged. The Community Service Organization has recently unified social groups. Its aim has been to decrease inter-neighborhood hostilities among parents and open fighting among youths, by building a non-partisan civic action program. Impetus has been given this group by the recent election of the city's first Mexican-American councilman in eighty-five years.

Several self-help groups are bringing to the attention of local government officials the need for better housing, fair employment practices, health clinics, public services and inter-cultural unity throughout the city. People living in sub-marginal areas, through a gradual lessening of group prejudice and of social and economic pressures, hope for the elimination of the tensions and frustrations which basically lead to the formation of juvenile gangs.

Hostility between the police and the Mexican community was characterized recently by Beatrice Griffith in her book *American Me:*

The condition of mutual antagonism between the Mexican community and the Los Angeles police creates a dangerous situation that is inimical to peace in the community. . . . The police, too, feel their insecure position, for they know that under such conditions it is almost impossible for them to be impartial and fair in their law enforcement. . . . In the face of incontrovertible evidence of police injustice, refuge is commonly found in the presumed incorrigibility of the Mexican lower class.

The local police station recently sponsored a group picnic to which close to a thousand youngsters were invited by the police. The police training academy for rookies has included lectures by competent Negro and Mexican-American spokesmen looking toward an increased appreciation of diverse cultural contributions to the American melting pot. An attempt is being made to bridge the language gap, and planning with a citizens' committee to work on harmonious community relations is under way as part of the public relations program of the police department.

The schools can help with the gang problem by bringing obvious antagonisms and misunderstandings quickly to the attention of understanding principals and counselors. These school officials should not be imbued with a desire for applying discipline, but with a hope that differences may be settled through reasoning and arbitration based on calm discussion of complaining and accused groups. A more realistic educational approach, both with regard to general dissemination of intercultural understanding and vocational preparation and proper training in the high school grades for the use of leisure time is needed. Adult evening classes can help to bridge the cultural gap with the younger generation.

Wherever continuous outside leadership has been provided to the street group the delinquencies of these loosely organized neighborhood societies have been minimized or eliminated. But after all is said and done, we still have to come back to the individual approach. A special unit of the Los Angeles Youth Project is working with underprivileged youth who tend to be excluded from regular agency programs because of personal maladjustments. Encouragement by trained group workers for these individuals to take part in organized activities under supervision helps them to overcome their feelings of personal inadequacy, their sense of not belonging, their ignorance of working together cooperatively, their attitude of ridicule toward agency programs.

The local coordinating councils have helped to focus public attention on redirecting the activities of potential and actual delinquents into wholesome and socially acceptable projects. Recognition that delinquency prevention is a public responsibility is growing. The Community Services Division of the Los Angeles County Probation Department has a Group Guidance Unit director who supervises the "hand-to-hand" encounters, literally speaking, of a carefully picked and trained group work staff with some of the gang groups. The philosophy of this unit embodies recognition that delinquency is rational, meaningful, and purposive as far as the delinquent child is concerned.

Boys previously resistive to supervised organizational membership acquire a degree of socialization which makes it possible for them to transplant the group consciousness of the gang to a club under guidance along socially acceptable channels.

Coordinated communitywide efforts are called for to solve the juvenile gang problem. Cooperative measures for the improvement of the complex social, economic, and resulting psychological problems are being attempted. All available resources and an awakened civic consciousness must eventually diminish the many factors which result in delinquent behavior and unwholesome antisocial gang activities. Furthermore techniques are still being perfected in social redirection through the individual approach. Recognition of the needs of less integrated minorities can lead to measures which supplant the hazardous security of a lonely corner gang.

Gang Membership and Juvenile Misconduct*

By William W. Wattenberg and James J. Balistrieri. Wayne University, Detroit.

THERE has long been a fascination about those young people, mostly in their teens, who form groups which challenge society. Popular interest is evidenced by the avid consumption of highly dramatized articles on gang life and gang warfare. Scientifically, there is a puzzle to be solved: How can we account for those young people who prove able to make a seemingly fine social adjustment in groups of their peers but nevertheless get in trouble with the larger social organizations? There have been quite a few attempts to work out theoretical struc-

* Reprinted from *American Sociological Review*, Volume 15, December, 1950, pp. 744–752. Used by permission.

tures of the dynamics involved, but very few good research studies have appeared.

Opinions of Researchers

A number of workers tackle the problem first by assuming that membership in groups is a sign that something is wrong in the lives of the boys or girls concerned. There is no agreement as to who or what should be blamed. In *Street Corner Society*, W. F. Whyte points out that home plays a very small part in the daily routine of a full-fledged gang member. In a study of Mexican-American gangs in Los Angeles, E. S. Bogardus attributed gang formation to a sense of differences due to language difficulties, academic problems in school, contrasts in child-control methods, race discrimination, and low economic status. C. Himber is inclined to blame broken homes and weak religious ties, as well as social conditions. Going somewhat more deeply into personal factors found in gang leaders, M. Van Waters sees rejection in school, church and social clubs as putting youngsters in the position where the gang is their only road to prestige and status. The other gang members are likely to fill or give promise of filling psychological needs not met by the adolescent's own parents.

The larger proportion of writers either explicitly or implicitly assume that it is normal for pre-adolescents and adolescents to join groups. F. Redl goes even further and states that pre-adolescents have a deep need to form cliques and gangs among themselves. As a sociologist, C. B. Spaulding sees the gang as necessary to satisfy wishes for response and security. In accord with practitioners of group therapy, P. Rosenthal found that the gang setting permitted disturbed youngsters to work out some of their conflicts.

On the question as to why gang members go in for misconduct, the differences are very wide. A. S. Beckham, for example, believes that suggestibility is higher in such groups, due to such factors as broken or disturbed homes. Retardation in school, he feels, increases their willingness to accept suggestions of truancy. S. M. Robinson, N. Cohen, and M. Sachs attribute such phenomena as gang warfare to aggressive tendencies arising out of homes where there was hardly any family life but where there was fear of the parents. An answer more typical of sociologists has been given by D. B. Harris who states that delinquent gangs arise in areas in ecological transition and largely take on the standards prevalent in such areas.

Simple and appealing as this sociological explanation may be, a number of child-guidance workers and psychiatrists are emphatic in the belief that it is far from the whole story. W. Healy and A. Bronner point to their findings on delinquents who came from families in which there were non-delinquent siblings, which reveal that the delinquent in 91 per cent of the cases was extremely disturbed emotionally, largely because of poor relationships within the family. They regard the delinquent's lack of social restraints as a product of poor ego-ideal formation, due to lack of affectional identification with a good parent.

R. Topping has given a somewhat fuller picture of what she calls the "pseudo-social boy." She regards gang membership as possibly an attempt to compensate for a sense of effeminacy or of physical or mental inadequacy. On the basis of clinical experience she declares that many such boys show a lack of warm, wholesome attachment to other members of the family. Specifically, she notes there is often a dependent attitude toward the mother and an indifference or resentment toward the father. The causative situation within the family is held to be sufficient family acceptance to promote socialization but insufficient supervision and adult influence to build a strong sense of values. She further notes the possibility that such gang members may come from large families.

Findings from Objective Research

Those studies which are built around reports of more or less objective research, as contrasted with the ones which are primarily speculative or are based on clinical experience, show almost as wide a range of findings, which are supplementary rather than contradictory. The best known study, that of F. M. Thrasher, documents the sociological viewpoint. He came to the conclusion that delinquent gang membership was the outgrowth of a situation-complex involving inadequate family life, poverty, deteriorating neighborhoods, ineffective religion, poor education, and inadequate recreation. The gang was held to arise to fill the needs thus left unmet; the social setting determined the nature of the activity. As a statement of position, Thrasher's work was admirable; as a compilation of evidence, disappointing. The methodology is vague and the documentation weak, if delightful. One even runs across such romantic footnotes as "unpublished study of an experienced boys' worker in gangland," and "interview with a railroad detective."

Somewhat less inclusive are the manipulations of statistical data more familiar to the pedestrian psychologists. W. C. Kvaraceus found that in a group of 761 delinquents referred to the Children's Bureau of the Passaic Board of Education only 23 per cent of the boys and 33 per cent of the girls engaged in solitary misdemeanors. He found that only 7.9 per cent of the total group, however, had any affiliation with any recognized recreational activity. Working with 100 boys, aged 12 to 16, on their first commitment to the Indiana School for Boys, B. S. Atwood and E. H. Shideler found that delinquents had a higher degree of social participation than non-delinquents. A study of activities rated by six judges

gave rise to the conclusion that these boys were more extrovertive.

The techniques of multiple-factor analysis were used by Hart, Jenkins, Axelrad and Sperling in a study of personality traits of 300 delinquent boys. They found a factor which they labeled "street gang activity." The elements in the factor pattern which they presumed to be causative were neglect by parents and the disorganization often associated with immorality of the parents.

Hewitt and Jenkins Report

In many ways, the most promising report is that which L. E. Hewitt and R. L. Jenkins made (*Fundamental Patterns of Maladjustment*, 1946) on the basis of trained observers' analyses of 500 child-guidance clinic case histories. These were reduced to ratings on a series of items, and the degree of association between the items determined by tetrachoric correlation. The correlations were further studied to determine the existence of clusters or syndromes. One of these they called "socialized delinquent," and pointed out its similarity to Topping's "pseudo-social boy." A tetrachoric correlation of .63 $\pm$ .07 with a situational cluster of parental negligence plus exposure to delinquent conduct was found. In this pattern there was often physical inadequacy in the homes; the houses needed repair; the families were large; one of the parents was dead; there was parental alcoholism; and, above all, a general lack of supervision. In their discussion of this finding, Hewitt and Jenkins parallel Topping as well as Healy and Bronner in their use of psychoanalytical dynamics. They see the boys as coming out of the family situation with a weak super-ego structure and ready to identify with the delinquent patterns found among their older siblings or playmates.

Hypotheses. As their major hypothesis the authors accepted the position that the combination of a home typified by weak supervision or discipline and a surrounding neighborhood having a high delinquency rate or its concomitants was a primary causative influence in shaping the personality structure of adolescent boys who would engage in unlawful actions and, at the same time, make a good adjustment in gangs of their peers. If one were to use the adjective "anti-social" in relation to their conduct, the group under study would be anti-social toward larger social entities but not primary peer groups. From the basic hypothesis, the following corollaries which could be subjected to statistical test were derived.

1. *In a group of boys, all having police records, those belonging to gangs would show a higher proportion coming from poorly supervised homes and from unfavorable socio-economic conditions.* It is assumed as amply demonstrated that in large American cities neighborhoods which have populations low in the socio-economic scale generally have high delinquency rates. Level on the socio-economic scale would be indicated by such objective criteria as condition of housing, family income, and family possession of automobiles. The strength of home supervision could be evaluated in terms of such direct or indirect indices as a boy's grooming, the measures by which he was given spending money, and the extent of parental participation in his recreation.

2. *The differentials between gang and non-gang boys on items reflecting socio-economic conditions and home supervision would be sharper among boys repeatedly in trouble than among those whose police records were limited to a single incident.* It is assumed that repetition of a course of conduct is an indication of strength of the personality structure leading to the behavior. Accordingly, boys who are repeatedly in trouble can be considered more delinquent than those who showed no such consistency in "misconduct." Just as the degree of de-

linquency is a variable, so are the other factors under study. If a causal relationship exists, then we would expect to find that the differences between indices to home situations and neighborhood conditions for gang members would be sharper among seriously delinquent boys than those whose tendencies in that direction were light.

3. *Items reflecting weak home supervision and poor neighborhood conditions would be more highly predictive of repeating among gang boys than non-gang boys.* If a factor is causative, then its presence should be predictive. Thus in a group of boys arrested for the first time, those who belonged to gangs and showed most evidence of coming from weak homes and bad neighborhoods would be more likely to become repeaters. Moreover, such items should have a higher predictive value for gang boys than for those in whose behavior patterns other factors are operative.

Procedure. To test these propositions, use was made of the records of some 5,878 boys between the ages of 10 and 16, inclusive, who were "interviewed on complaint" by Detroit police officers in 1946 and 1947. When a complaint was lodged against a boy, he was interviewed and his home visited by specially designated Crime Prevention Bureau officers. On the information thus obtained, a "history sheet" containing some fifty items on home conditions, neighborhood situations and other matters of interest was completed. The data were coded and punched on IBM cards so as to be available for statistical manipulation.

Among the facts recorded for each boy was whether or not he was a member of a neighborhood gang. This was considered to be a group of four or more boys who spent their spare time regularly with each other. The police officers' judgment on this matter was based not only on interviews but also on such observations as they made in the course of precinct duties. On the basis of their recorded judgment, therefore, it was possible to divide the population on the basis of gang membership into two groups: 2,737 gang members and 3,141 nonmembers. This cannot be considered a simon pure dichotomy. What can be said with confidence is that our gang member group is more highly saturated with boys having a strong tendency to take part in gang behavior than the non-member group.

The records available covered the last five months of 1946 and all of 1947. The 1946 group could be divided into two groups according to whether or not they were in trouble again in 1947. On this basis, a three-way classification of the entire population could be made: 1,462 boys with records only in 1946; 670 repeaters with records in both years; and 3,746 new offenders in 1947. Here, again, the grouping was not a pure one. However, we can safely assume that the 1946 repeater group is more highly saturated with serious delinquents than either the 1946 non-repeaters or the 1947 new offenders.

To test the several corollaries to the principal hypothesis these groups were paired in different combinations. For each item recorded on the history sheets, a table was prepared and submitted to the chi-square test. Both this procedure and the data had been previously tested, as reported in other studies and found to be useful. Three sets of pairings were made. To test Corollary 1, all gang boys were compared with all non-members. To test Corollary 2, a similar pairing was made within the 1946 non-repeaters, 1946 repeaters, and 1947 new offenders, and the three sets of results compared with each other. To test Corollary 3, a comparison was made between the results of a 1946 repeater vs. non-repeater pairing for gang members and for non-members. In all, some 354 chi-square computations were made. Of these, 104 permitted rejection of the null hypothesis at a one per cent level of confidence.

In making the analyses, where a table showed statistical significance at the one per cent level it was further broken down to determine which cells contributed a total of 6 or more to the chi-square total. In effect, this meant that such a cell if incorporated as one of the four in a two-by-two-fold table would give rise to a statistically reliable result. In this way we could list not only the items which had a statistically reliable association with either gang membership or repeating, whichever was under study at the time, but also could point out which categories in that item had contributed to the result.

In preparing all tables, the "not stated" category was treated as any other. That is to say, failure of the police to secure an answer was considered as a category within each item. This had the statistical effect of increasing by one the degrees of freedom and thereby raising the chi-square total required to reach any given level of P. At first glance this may appear to cause an overly conservative evaluation of the results. However, previous experience with these data had indicated that the "not stated" categories could be psychologically significant. As will be seen, in this study they proved repeatedly to be of value.

Findings. The results of the overall comparison between gang members and non-members are given in Table 1. Only those items on which a statistically significant relationship was found are reported. For each of these, all categories yielding a contribution of 6 to the chi-square total are listed in the second column if they are associated with gang membership and in the third column if with non-membership.

It should be noted that the factor of repeating is not included in the table. The item was submitted to the chi-square test and for it the null hypothesis could not be rejected with confidence (P was greater than 0.30). In view of the size of the population under study, this can be

TABLE 1. ITEMS SHOWING RELATIONSHIP WITH GANG MEMBERSHIP AT ONE PER CENT LEVEL OF CONFIDENCE

	Category Associated With:	
Item	Gang Membership	Non-Membership
Parental participation in boy's recreation	Occasional	
Marital status of parents	Marriage Intact	Separated, both dead
Boy's chores around home	Few	Occasional
Allowance	Money given "on request"	None given, "Not stated"
Boy permitted to drive family car		"Not stated"
When parents are at home	Evenings	"Not stated"
Alcoholism in Family	Father	"Not stated"
Chronic illness in family		"Not stated"
Congeniality of family		"Not stated"
Boy's expressed attitude toward mother		Disliked, "Not stated"
Boy's expressed attitude toward father		"Not stated"
Boy's appearance		Neat and clean
Boy's recreational equipment		Not comparable to playmates
Father's age	Over 45	Under 45
Mother's age	Over 45	Under 45
General rating of neighborhood	Average	Good
Condition of home	Substandard	Modern
Racial homogeneity of neighborhood	Mixed	
Type of home	Flat	Rooming house
Nature of nearest recreational facility		Vacant area
Parents' employment		"Not stated"
Parents' income		"Not stated"
Type of entertainment boy prefers	Shows and sports	
Nickname	Has one he doesn't resent	
Attitude toward adult neighbors	Poor, Indifferent	
Attitude toward police in interview as judged by police		"Honest"
Attitude of parents toward police	Antagonistic	

taken to mean that these two variables are substantially unrelated.

Inspection of Table 1 reveals a pattern somewhat different from what one would expect if the major hypothesis and the first corollary were adequate. The items and categories distinguishing gang boys in general do not fit a picture of weak supervision or poor home relations so much as they would one of normality. On only three items do we find evidence of poor or inadequate home ties: (1) The boys receive funds on a hit-or-miss basis rather than as a definite allowance or as compensation for work done around the home; (2) the boys are required to perform few chores; and (3) the fathers were more likely to be alcoholics.

By contrast, the non-gang group shows distinct evidence of disturbed family relationships. Most striking is the highly differentiating significance of "not stated" replies. These would indicate either an emotional blocking on the item or a defensive secrecy. All told, the non-members showed a statistically significant tendency to be high on "not stated" replies for ten family items ranging from expressed attitudes towards parents to policy regarding use of the family car.

There was also direct evidence of emotional tension in the homes: (1) This group was high in number of separated parents, and (2) boys who openly expressed dislike for their mothers. In addition, there was a picture of some deprivation: more boys in this group (1) received no money from their parents and (2) had less recreational equipment than their friends.

On indices of socio-economic status the evidence somewhat more closely approximates the predicted situation. The gang members were more likely to come from substandard homes and racially mixed neighborhoods, which at the time of this study in Detroit (before the Supreme Court ruling on restrictive covenants) tended to be less well-to-do. The non-gang group had a higher proportion of youngsters living in good neighborhoods. The group living in rooming houses was 170, of whom 116 belonged to no gang.

On those items representing a rating of attitudes and peer group activity the gang boys conformed to the popular stereotype. They seemed to be out-going individuals who enjoyed popular commercial recreation, boasted nicknames, were hostile to adult neighbors and evasive with the police. In this latter attitude they appeared to have some support at home from their parents.

For several relationships stressed in other publications the results were inconclusive. Failing to pass the chi-square test at a one per cent level of confidence were such items as size of family, number of brothers, and frequency of church attendance.

In a second series of tabulations, a similar comparison between the gang and non-gang groups was made separately for each of three classifications of boys: (1) 1946 non-repeaters; (2) 1946 repeaters; and (3) 1947 new offenders. According to our second corollary, differences on items reflecting neighborhood conditions and family supervision should

have been more marked among the 1946 repeaters than either of the other groups, which were weighted more heavily with mildly delinquent boys. The results however, were inconclusive, if not negative. There was not a single interview item that discriminated at a one per cent level of confidence between gang members and non-members among the 1946 repeaters which was not an equally clear indicator for the 1946 non-repeaters, 1947 new offenders or both. By contrast, there were several items which attained a one per cent level of confidence in distinguishing gang members from non-members in both of the mildly delinquent groups but not in the repeaters. In view of the strong influence of N in the calculation of chi-squares and the fact that the 1946 repeaters were considerably smaller in number than either of the other groups, some such effect could be expected. To discount this influence of group size, we arbitrarily ruled out all instances where the P for the repeaters was less than .50. There still remained six items which were significantly related to gang membership among both the 1946 non-repeaters and 1947 new offenders but not among 1946 repeaters. On one of these, even the sign of the differences was reversed: more gang members than non-members among 1946 repeaters lived in rooming houses, although the reverse was true for the other groups. For the remaining five items, the direction of observed differences was the same in all three groups, although too slight among repeaters to approach statistical reliability. These five items were: father's age, boy's appearance, allowance, type of entertainment preferred by boy, and racial homogeneity of neighborhood.

It will be noted that none of these items is central to the major factors being studied, although three (boy's appearance, allowance, and racial homogeneity) are considered indirect indices.

On the third series of comparisons, the results were much more clear cut and

TABLE 2. ITEMS PREDICTIVE OF REPEATING AT ONE PER CENT LEVEL OF CONFIDENCE FOR GANG MEMBERS BUT NOT NON-MEMBERS

Item	Category Associated with:	
	Repeating	Non-Repeating
Size of Home	Inadequate	
Parent's Income	Inadequate	

interesting. Taking the gang members and the non-members as separate populations, we studied the phenomenon of repeating. For each population we compared the 1946 non-repeaters with the repeaters. Theoretically, if different causal factors were operating, the list of items predictive of repeating would not be the same for gang members as for non-members. As a glance at Tables 2 and 3 will show, this was definitely true. There were only two items which reliably predicted repeating among gang members but which failed of reliability for the non-gang boys. Both of these are clearly indications of poverty and low socio-economic level.

TABLE 3. ITEMS PREDICTIVE OF REPEATING AT ONE PER CENT LEVEL OF CONFIDENCE FOR NON-MEMBERS BUT NOT GANG MEMBERS

Item	Category Associated with:	
	Repeating	Non-Repeating
Number of sisters	Three or more	
Attitude toward father	Dislikes	
Boy's appearance	Slovenly	Neat and clean
Church attendance		Regular
Money received from parents	"Not stated"	
Racial homogeneity of neighborhood	Mixed	
Participation of parents in boy's activities		Regular
Family addiction to alcohol		None

A striking contrast is the list of eight items which although not reliably predictive for the gang boys were statistically significant for the non-gang boys. Of these the following six are clearly related to family conditions: number of sisters, boy's attitude toward his father, his appearance, his willingness to talk about the amount of money received from his parents, their participation in his activities, and alcoholism in the family. The seventh item, regularity in church attendance, may also be linked to family morale. Only one item, living in a racially mixed neighborhood, is definitely socio-economic. This one item may be of considerable theoretical interest.

Discussion. The results of this study indicate that the initial hypothesis was not wholly adequate. This is not too surprising when we recollect that the statistics and observations from which it was formulated were all based on youngsters who turned up either at child-guidance clinics, juvenile courts, or correctional institutions. By contrast, the population included in the present study is relatively normal. Only about ten per cent of the group were referred to the juvenile court. The boys covered in this study did belong to gangs and did engage in misconduct but not in as extreme a degree. Also, they were a more representative sample than boys who go before juvenile courts or are sent for clinic treatment. The latter group is selected or, rather, is the residue left after parents have used their influence, neighbors have relented, or youngsters have appealed to arresting officers. That findings in the population now under study differ somewhat from those in a residue group is to be expected in the same way that a study of factors linked with "intelligence" might be different in a relatively normal group as contrasted with one limited to feeble-minded children. This may account especially for the failure of the second corollary.

The main modification of the initial hypothesis seems to be in the evaluation of the family influence. The socio-economic factors held up well. However, the family picture of the gang boys is less like neglect and more like low-tension or easy-goingness. More significant, the way in which the non-gang boys appeared to show evidence of emotional upset due to strong tensions or deprivations at home suggests that the two sets of influence, familial and socio-economic, are not equal in effect but are dynamically related. It looks as though the social forces are limited in their play upon the individuals by the previous effects of the family factors.

An attempt to construct a theoretical formulation of the dynamics which could account for the findings runs head-on into difficulties in interpretation. The picture of the family life of many of the gang boys has been described as easy-going. The question which must be settled, and upon which the data cannot throw light, is whether or not this picture is objective truth on the one hand or is merely the manifestation of some defense mechanism, or both. For example, it is within the realm of probability that boys who had won emancipation would not be aware of family tensions. In this case, part of the differences between the groups would be symptoms or reflections of deeper but undefined present personality differences. The predictive value of those symptoms could remain prognostically valid, in the same sense that an intelligence test score or a Rorschach response can be a good indicator even though its full psychological import is debatable.

If one could assume that the data may be taken at face value, it is possible to account for them if we assume that those segments of personality structure which result from the interaction of the growing child with his parents would be more likely to be characterized by tension if the family itself was under high tensions.

The resultant rigidity in this portion of his psychological life space would strengthen the barriers within it and impede locomotion. Consequently his activities would be relatively more influenced by such an area of strong boundaries and high tensions than by the less developed areas. The predictive value of the family influences would therefore be great. An incidental finding adds weight at this point. It will be recalled that the only social index included in the list of factors which predicted repeating by non-gang boys but not by gang boys was a racially mixed neighborhood. E. Frenkel-Brunswik has demonstrated that ethno-centrism is linked with that type of rigidity which is also correlated with the presence of anxiety and a past history of being subjected to child-raising methods involving use of fear techniques. The findings for the gang boys would give the reverse of the dynamics. The sectors of personality structure formed by low-tension family interactions would have relatively weak boundaries and great flexibility; the development of the individual would be more free in the direction of social, peer relations. The effect of immediate situations would have relatively greater weight in determining action patterns than the carry-over of past family situations. Therefore, the socio-economic influences could be expected to have higher predictive value.

It must be emphasized that the basic data in this study are mass statistics and the findings deal with differences between groups in which there is considerable overlap. Therefore, it would be wildly inaccurate to assume that dynamic patterns such as those described above typify all gang boys or all non-gang boys. Undoubtedly there are many other factors operating in each specific case. At best, the patterns described might be assumed to be the common elements for the portions of each group which gave rise to the differences.

Practical Implications. The results of this study, if verified by others dealing with the same phenomena, have certain very important practical implications. There is the possibility that the difference in pattern of predictive factors might call for a new approach to prediction in criminology. As L. E. Ohlin and O. D. Duncan have pointed out, current formulae used by parole boards and others yield results little better than chance expectation. It may be that this is because all such formulae are applied without modification to an undifferentiated group. To use an old analogy, they may be trying to use the same set of measures to evaluate the ripeness of oranges and watermelons. Possibly it will be necessary to construct several different prediction tables to use with delinquents and criminals having different dynamic patterns. Dichotomization based on gang membership is not being suggested here, but rather a fuller study based on factors which underlie the patterns we have found and others which might be indicated by work along the lines of Hewitt and Jenkins.

There is also the possibility that these findings might provide a clue to treatment strategies. It would seem offhand that where delinquency could be traced to tensions arising out of early family history, individual psychotherapy would be indicated and an environmental attack contra-indicated. On the other hand, where delinquency resulted from a too free interaction with the peer culture or a poor neighborhood subculture, the unit of treatment or prevention would appear to be the social group or the neighborhood.

Summary. This study dealt with the records of some 5,878 adolescent boys contacted on complaint by Detroit police. Those boys who belonged to gangs differed from non-gang boys in showing evidence of coming from easy-going homes and living in socio-economically low neighborhoods. The non-gang boys displayed indications of coming from tense or depriving families. In predicting repeating by these boys, socio-economic indices had greater value in the case of gang members, and family indices in the case of non-members.

SELECTED REFERENCES

1. Tappan, Paul W., *Juvenile Delinquency* (New York: McGraw-Hill Book Co., 1949), Chapter 7: "Causes and Conditions of Delinquency—Social Variables in the Etiology of Delinquency."

    In this discussion, attention is called to the fact that exposure to unwholesome companions who carry habits and attitudes of law violation may easily spread delinquency patterns. Gang war incidents are related in dramatic manner.

2. Ellingston, John R., *Protecting Our Children from Criminal Careers* (New York: Prentice-Hall, 1948), Chapter 2: "The Social Roots of Crime."

    The pervasive influence of a lawless society is advanced as a partial explanation for much unlawful behavior of youth as well as the major role played by the delinquency area.

3. Neumeyer, Martin H., *Juvenile Delinquency in Modern Society* (New York: D. Van Nostrand Co., 1949), Chapter 7: "Companionship and Juvenile Gangs."

    In addition to a comprehensive presentation of the importance of gangs as viewed sociologically, Neumeyer's analysis of the "Zoot-suiter" is one of the best in the literature.

4. Thrasher, Frederick M., *The Gang* (Chicago: University of Chicago Press, 1927).

    This study, over many years, was concerned with 1313 gangs containing about 25,000 members and is a "classic" in the field of juvenile delinquency.

5. Whyte, William Foote, *Street Corner Society* (Chicago: University of Chicago Press, 1943).
6. Von Hentig, Hans, *The Criminal and His Victim* (New Haven: Yale University Press, 1948).

7 APPREHENSION AND DETENTION

IT IS estimated that there are more than a billion laws, including both felonies and misdemeanors, on the statute books in the United States; there are more laws than people—about six for every man, woman, and child. As laws increase in number, violations tend to increase. And there often appears to be a growing spirit of contempt for the law enforcement system, on both adult and juvenile levels. During World War II, parents sometimes boasted, in the presence of their children, of patronizing the black market. It is difficult to control behavior merely through legal taboos.

In many delinquency areas of urban communities, lawlessness has become almost a tradition that is handed down from one generation to another. Owing to the pervasive nature of the "spirit of delinquency," detection and apprehension are exceedingly difficult, for more often than not the police receive little cooperation from the citizens in urban delinquency areas.

The law itself recognizes only the chronological age of the offenders, ignoring the mental, emotional, and physiological ages as if they had no existence. Legally, responsibility for one's acts is presumed to increase with the years. Witness the differential treatment accorded the juvenile delinquent, the young adult offender, and the adult offender. From one viewpoint, the law ignores children completely, for they are not even mentioned in the Constitution of the United States.

Paradoxically, civil law holds that anyone under twenty-one years old is legally incompetent to enter into contracts. He may not hold or dispose of property; and yet let him commit a crime and the only question asked by the law is "Does he know right from wrong?" If the answer is affirmative, he must pay his "debt to society." He may be sent to jail or prison, or even executed for his crime, although according to the civil law of the state he may not be responsible enough to marry or to drink alcoholic beverages.

Such inconsistencies constitute one of the many reasons why there is so much disregard for the law in general, particularly in reference to the activities of juvenile delinquents. They know they live in an adult world in which there are different standards of morality for young people and adults. The mother pleads a "sick headache" to avoid playing bridge, but the child is punished for telling a little "fib." This "double standard" is one reason why adulthood seems so attractive to children.

THE POLICE AND YOUTH

When police deal with the juvenile by handcuffing and jailing him they aggravate a resentment he may have against society. Also the manner in which the police handle child offenders may determine in a large measure the juvenile attitude toward legal authority. Occasionally the police officer takes the attitude that the violation is a kind of personal affront, and may testify against the boy to "get even." Enlightened police administrators recommend treating juveniles with consideration in order to gain their confidence and respect. Certainly no policemen should resort to vulgarity, profanity, or obscenity—yet such behavior on the part of the "guardians of the law" is by no means rare.

The policeman often dispenses monitory justice (warnings). Typically he settles and decides more violations than he takes into court. He "judges" thousands of cases every year—such as petty thefts, breaking windows, and starting fires on the part of gangs in alleys. Because he is often the child's first personal contact with the law, he should conduct himself with dignity, impartiality and competence.

In keeping with this principle, the University of Southern California's Delinquency Control Institute designs courses of study to help the police officer understand the causes, treatment, control, and prevention of juvenile delinquency. He is taught how to approach young people and how to interview them, so that they may see in him a source of help rather than a threat. Many specialized courses are given at Northwestern University's Traffic Institute and Yale University's Bureau of Highway Traffic. Perhaps the most outstanding illustrations of this type of training are to be found in the Federal Bureau of Investigation's educational activities at the National Police Academy and in the preservice police training programs pioneered by August Volmer and now regularly scheduled at nearly a dozen colleges and universities, including the University of California and Michigan State, San Jose State and Fresno State Colleges.[1]

Many sincere but misguided efforts have been accorded the juvenile offender. Formerly, he was fingerprinted and photographed; now under a protective program which is followed in many communities, even his name is omitted when the crime he commits is reported by the press. However, inasmuch as the professional criminals often come from the ranks of juvenile delinquents, a reversal, in part at least, of the present "protective" trend seems to be in order. Proponents of fingerprinting juvenile delinquents believe that it is the best method of identification, that it helps to protect the innocent, that it completes the records and enables the FBI to include nation-wide juvenile delinquency statistics in their *Uniform Crime Reports*. Fingerprinting, it might be argued, constitutes no more a stigma than going to juvenile court.

Some police departments have made an effort to counteract juvenile delinquency by establishing junior police systems in which youthful members be-

---

[1] See, for example, Donal E. J. MacNamara, "Police Training in Prevention of Crime and Delinquency," *Journal of Criminal Law and Criminology*, XLII, July–August 1951, 263.

come subject to call at any time. Juvenile police duties include such activities as assisting in traffic details near schools, churches, even down-town corners; attending regular meetings; learning the type of conduct appropriate for a police officer. This type of program has been tested in various communities, including Decatur and Mattoon, Illinois, and considerable success has been reported. Youthful members conduct themselves as "officers and gentlemen" or face dismissal from the junior police group.

In any consideration of official methods of delinquency prevention, mention should be made of the program of preventive activities of the New York police department. The recreational program of the Juvenile Aide Bureau in New York works through the Police Athletic League (PAL), which has been in existence since the early 1930's. PAL's chief aim is to substitute wholesome recreation for antisocial activities, thus helping to prevent incipient misbehavior. PAL has over one hundred thousand members of which 15 per cent are girls.

Adding women to the law-enforcement agencies has greatly improved police efficiency—even in such detailed matters as estimating the ages of girls, when required. In California the police are not permitted to transport females between the ages of five and eighteen except in the presence of a woman. Interrogation of girls and women is conducted with a woman present. Although policewomen have been appointed since 1910, and there seems little question of their positive contribution to police work, there remains considerable prejudice against them. Instead of "checking" on the night-time activities of boys and girls on the streets, for example, policewomen may be restricted to clerical duty and other desk activities.

Police departments have also established juvenile bureaus specializing in handling juvenile delinquency cases, variously called Crime Prevention Bureaus, Youth Guidance Bureaus, Special Services Bureaus. This type of agency was initiated in 1913 when Portland, Oregon, established the first juvenile bureau in the United States. Despite forward-looking programs such as these, adaptation of similar agencies and techniques and, in general, progressive police work in the youth field have been disappointingly slow in the majority of the communities in the United States.

JAIL AND DELINQUENCY

A picturesque and revealing definition of a jail is that given by a one-time jail inspector for the federal government:

> Jail: An unbelievably filthy institution in which are confined men and women serving sentences for misdemeanors and crimes, and men and women not under sentence, who are simply awaiting trial. With few exceptions, having no segregation of the unconvicted from the convicted, the well from the diseased, the youngest and most impressionable from the most degraded and hardened . . . A melting pot in which the worst elements of the raw material in the criminal world are brought forth, blended and turned out in absolute perfection.[2]

---

[2] Joseph Fulling Fishman, *Crucibles of Crime* (New York: Cosmopolis Press, 1923), pp. 13–14. Used by permission of collaborator, Vee Perlman.

Many jails have improved since 1923 when Joseph Fishman wrote of the then-current conditions of jails throughout the nation; but a substantial number continue to fit his description.

Daily some 750,000 men, women, and children are compelled to drag out their hours in the idleness of a narrow cell or a common pen of the local jail. Jail thus fails to serve law and order and becomes a laboratory of delinquency and degeneracy. The judge who assigns an offending person to a jail to "teach him a lesson" is either cynical or ignorant or possibly both.

In spite of forbidding stipulations in state laws, at least fifty thousand children are detained in jail every year. One western state maintains a statute prohibiting the detention in jail of children under twelve years old; yet it was revealed in 1947 that in a period of nearly four years three local jails, all in one county, built up a record totaling 1,430 days of child-incarceration. Only two states, Connecticut and New Hampshire, claim that their jails are never used for children; rather they maintain detention homes. Despite the maintenance of child detention homes, thousands of youngsters are jailed every year in communities having some of the best detention facilities in the United States.

Children are assigned to jail in most communities, however, because there are no other places to detain them. And here they are all too often subjected to disgraceful conditions. In one community, for example, girls who had been charged with truancy were discovered sharing quarters with experienced prostitutes; and in another community, twelve-year-old boys and girls were held with adults in a dirty jail from June to August, waiting for the juvenile court to reconvene after the summer vacation.[3]

Cases such as these underscore the fact that the jail, presumably an aid in the maintenance of law and order, frequently has the opposite function of serving as an educational setting for delinquency and crime. And sometimes the lessons are taught with telling effect, abetted by such procedures as the inmate-created "kangeroo court." This tribunal, termed by one authority a "perverted form of self-government," is headed by a "judge" who is usually one of the worst prisoners. Penalties are brutal and the "court" imposes fines of a few dollars on newcomers called "fish" for "breaking into jail." One young inmate who died while in a western county jail, due to epilepsy according to the jail physician, lost his life in fact because a degenerate nineteen-year-old kangeroo court "judge" had severely beaten him for threatening to report the sexual assault and tortures practiced upon him.[4] Until conditions permitting such occurrences as these are changed, the jail system will continue to labor under the opprobrium the "Shame of America."

The jail was originally instituted as a place of detention until trial. It still fulfills this function, of course, as a temporary abode behind bars for men and women. But the jail also often imprisons, and sometimes for long periods of time, impressionable children and youth. And the lessons learned in jail

---

[3] John R. Ellingston, *Protecting Our Children from Criminal Careers* (New York: Prentice-Hall, 1948), p. 185.

[4] *Ibid.*

guarantee, in some cases, at least, the launching of careers in delinquency and crime.

DETENTION OF THE DELINQUENT

Juvenile court philosophy maintains that young people should be detained in special quarters prior to their appearance in court. *Detention* refers to temporary care of children removed from their homes pending investigation and the court's decision. *Shelter care* refers to emergency and temporary out-of-home care of children where physical restraint is not necessary, contrasted with detention which involves security features to insure the child's safekeeping.

Detention means different things to different children, depending upon the child's previous experiences and life patterns. For most boys and girls held by the law, detention connotes food and shelter. For others, it suggests indiscriminate contact with other detainees. Not infrequently, it is a degrading experience, especially where untrained personnel treat detainees as inferior persons. Moreover, detention usually means idleness—time wasted in so far as any rehabilitative efforts are considered. Detention has been described as the weakest link in the rehabilitation process.

A survey conducted in 1945 by the National Probation and Parole Association revealed a failure of some official agencies to obey their own state laws in providing detention homes rather than jails for juvenile offenders. The survey showed that for the most part detention homes were understaffed, overcrowded with children, and inadequately supervised by untrained officials. There are fewer than 150 detention homes in the United States. In the fifty-eight counties in the state of California only thirty-two have separate children's facilities, which is approximately 20 per cent of the entire nation's detention home facilities. Some detention homes throughout the nation are maintained as "show places" rather than as establishments for constructive community services. Too many officials are not deeply concerned with the welfare of their charges, since they apparently feel the youthful offenders are headed for the reform schools anyway.

On the positive side, detention homes offer excellent possibilities if proper attention is given to such items as the physical plant, location, administration, personnel, services to the child, information to the court, length of detention, and planning for detention facilities. There should be emphasis on cheerfulness, livability, and ease of maintenance. Ample room should be provided for indoor and outdoor play and game activities. Detention homes should be located within or near so-called "delinquency areas" and certainly not close by the local jails. The *services* to the child in a detention home that realizes its important function in the corrective process should include good physical and custodial care, medical examinations, psychological and psychiatric tests, child guidance and casework, and recreation and religious teaching.

Theoretically, the purpose of detention is to provide the child material and psychological security while authorities are studying his case and gathering information concerning his background. But there is a wide gap between the theory and practice of detention. Institutional confinement of any sort probably has some deleterious effect upon children whether they are "normal," emotionally disturbed, or delinquent. Detention, as it is exercised today, in a large measure, seems a relic of retributive penological thinking that disregards the possible consequences of detention for the child himself.

Today, as in 1945, when the National Probation and Parole Association made its survey on the nation's detention facilities, in many detention homes the staff is underpaid, untrained, and unqualified; knowingly or unknowingly, its members may even act as delinquency seducers. For many children detention is a bitter experience as they await their juvenile court hearing which sometimes drags on for weeks or even months. Unfortunately, the general public has only a meager understanding or appreciation of what the detention home is attempting to accomplish for youth in trouble. For this, as well as other reasons, community education is indicated as both desirable and necessary before the opprobrium of detention is removed.

READINGS

The police officer who works with juveniles requires special training, according to Donald Imler in his article, "Training Peace Officers to Understand and to Work with Youth." He outlines the curriculum of the Delinquency Control Institute to indicate the breadth and comprehension of this program at the University of Southern California.

One of the earliest cases involving a juvenile and the police was the classic incident of Charles Ross, who was kidnaped on July 1, 1874, and whose fate still remains a mystery. In Cynthia Lowry's report, "The Charles Ross Case," early police ineptitude and inefficiency in a large measure accounted for the fact that no solution or perpetrators were ever found.

Austin H. MacCormick attacks the jail problem in the United States as it relates to children confined therein in his article, "Children in Our Jails." Particularly, he takes the public to task for failing to be aroused at the revelation of indescribable physical and moral conditions. There seems to be a widespread feeling that the usual jail inmate is a dirty and depraved person. Improved facilities are suggested and standards for detention facilities with inspection and enforcement power are recommended.

In another article relating to children in jail—"Keeping Children Out of Jails: It Can Be Done"—Austin H. MacCormick and James H. Dooling say that it *is* possible to keep children out of jail. The Osborn Association, in collaboration with the National Jail Association, launched a campaign in 1948 against the widespread practice of confining children in county jails, 97.3 per cent of which have been rated below sixty on a scale of one hundred by federal jail inspectors. Education must be the chief mode of attack.

Henry J. Palmieri in "The Child in Detention" stresses the belief that the child must be studied from many angles; and unless a proper approach is utilized, officers may obtain only a fraction of the complete story about the child. The time spent in detention by the child is sometimes an excellent opportunity for the officials to establish a sound relationship with him. It will better enable them to become acquainted with the roots of his delinquency.

Sherwood Norman, an authority in the field of child delinquency, outlines certain goals in "New Goals for Juvenile Detention." Whatever the size of the detention home, personnel must be capable of meeting three basic program objectives: good physical care and custody; a full, varied, and creative activities program; and guidance through intensive casework. The effectiveness of the detention period will depend upon the way in which these objectives are met.

Training Peace Officers to Understand and to Work with Youth*

By Donald Imler. Director, Delinquency Control Institute, University of Southern California, Los Angeles.

THE American boy is taught in civics class that every citizen incurs responsibilities as well as rights. This civic responsibility should be shared by everyone in an effort to make this a better country in which to live. It seems logical that the administrator in the police field in accepting his combined right and duty to uphold and enforce the law also obligates himself to accomplish much in the fields of delinquency prevention, repression, and in the co-ordination aspects of community organization.

There is varied opinion throughout the country as to just how far into the treatment field the police should go. Most administrators agree that the police do not belong there. However, if the function of the treatment is not being handled adequately by probation, parole, and other social agencies, then police administrators feel that they are morally obligated to encourage the improvement of these services through the community organization process or perform the function themselves as a last resort if all community-wide efforts fail. They also realize that even if there are adequately functioning treatment agencies their officers, especially those assigned as juvenile officers, are engaged in treatment. This is by virtue of their

daily contact with juveniles, parents, and their problems, because everything that happens to a juvenile beginning with the first police contact is part of a larger treatment program.

The Juvenile Officer

The juvenile officer, while doing a very highly specialized job, at the same time handles a wide variety of matters. He also has wide latitude in his power of disposition. Depending primarily on his own judgment he may, (1) refer a case to a social or welfare agency or the probation department for informal handling, (2) petition the juvenile court to safeguard the welfare and interests of the child and society, (3) transfer the case to another public agency already having jurisdiction, (4) place the juvenile on report and arrange a suitable program of activities and supervision, or (5) he may counsel with the juvenile and his parents regarding the future conduct of the juvenile and may then release him to his parents.

This wide latitude of operation involves the exercise of sound judgment and requires deep understanding of a multitude of fundamental human problems. The scope of the problem is widened since in many departments the

* Reprinted from *Federal Probation*, Vol. XIII, March, 1949, pp. 42–44. Used by permission of author and publication.

juvenile officers are responsible for the investigation and disposition of adult offenders against juveniles. They are in a fine position to effect the public relations program of chief administrators due to the type of contact they maintain with both individual citizens and civic groups.

The juvenile officer is many things to many people and possibly his most important job is that of being the key man in determining the course of many human lives. Burdened with this responsibility then it is not logical that an untrained person could handle the job successfully. When a new officer is sworn in and given a badge he is a policeman in name only. It is the matter of his indoctrination with which we are concerned.

The grave responsibilities this implies give rise to the matter of personnel training problems and the question as to how the specialized training is to be obtained. In the larger departments screening of new juvenile officers is being carried on. The Los Angeles Police Department is now giving advanced training to new juvenile officers who have graduated from the regular officers' training course.

Many other departments, large and small, endeavor to cope with this problem of specialized training. The concensus is that all in-service training programs fall short with respect to the delinquency field. Probably the most complete supplement is the Delinquency Control Institute at the University of Southern California.

Delinquency Control Institute

The Institute, which was established in 1946, is the culmination of more than 2 years of planning by California peace officers and University staff members. Peace officers had long felt the need for specialized training in understanding and working with youth. The practical approach of the peace officers and other allied groups was merged with the academic approach of the University to formulate challenging objectives and a course of instruction.

The objectives of the Delinquency Control Institute are to

1. Provide an adequate training program in delinquency control for law-enforcement agencies

2. Provide in particular for California law-enforcement agencies (a) 60 trained juvenile officers each year; (b) heads of juvenile bureaus in local enforcement agencies; and (c) leaders and instructors familiar with the best delinquency control practices

3. Offer an integrated curriculum of the best police principles, practices, and procedures, appropriately supplemented by pertinent knowledge in related fields

4. Quicken and stimulate law-enforcement agencies through intimate contact with practitioners and academic leaders

5. Provide, through field work, observation and practice in the techniques of delinquency control

6. Carry on research and inquiry into the problems of delinquency control so that the Institute's curriculum will keep pace with knowledge in the field and

7. Make the information developed by the Institute available to law-enforcement agencies anywhere.

The Institute offers annually three terms of 12 weeks each extending from September through June. The program consists of a full-time schedule with regular classes Mondays through Thursdays. Fridays are devoted to supervised field work in local bureaus and other allied facilities. The student has an opportunity to increase his understanding and improve his techniques through actual participation in the routine work of the co-operating juvenile bureaus. The Institute's supervisor of field work and the various juvenile bureau supervisors aim to make the field work as meaningful and as practicable as possible for the student.

Upon successful completion of the course, college credit to the extent of 12 units is available to those properly qualified and accepted by the University. Each person completing the course also receives a certificate as evidence of satisfactory completion. Attendance is limited to 20 students for each 12-week term. Sixteen of these students are selected from among peace officers employed in either police or sheriff's departments; the remaining four students come from the following groups: parole, probation, or district attorney's staffs, attendance officers, and social workers. All sections of the State are fairly represented. Students from states other than California are also welcomed.

Applicants fill out the application form with the consent of the chief of police, sheriff, or other chief administrator, who is requested to add his own letter of recommendation. These applications are forwarded to the Director of the Delinquency Control Institute of the University of Southern California at Los Angeles. They are then considered by a special committee of law-enforcement officials and members of the staff, and recommendations are made to the University admissions office. It is expected that candidates in attendance at the Institute will have their regular salaries paid by the jurisdiction from which they come. Juvenile officers may attend under benefits of the G. I. Bill. Section 352a of the Political Code of California reads as follows:

Attendance at training schools. Payment of expenses. All officers and employees of a city or county, when attending special training schools to which they have been ordered by the legislative body of the city or county, may be paid from the respective city or county treasury their traveling and other actual and necessary expenses incident to attendance at such schools.

Full scholarships are available for each student selected. Living expenses are borne by each student personally except for officers from northern California where an interested foundation has made grants for the purpose of defraying living costs.

The Institute's Curriculum

For administrative purposes, the Institute has been placed in the School of Public Administration. The original concept, policy, and plan, however, are the result of interdepartmental and interagency consultation with the College of Letters, Arts, and Sciences, the School of Law, the School of Education, the Graduate School of Social Work, and the School of Public Administration. Thus, specialists in sociology, recreation, education, law, social work, and administration have aided those engaged in professional practice in the creation and operation of the program.

The curriculum covers several courses of study:

1. *Social Treatment Aspects of Delinquency Control*—Current social service programs for dealing with delinquents, with special emphasis on philosophy and practical application

2. *Special Police Techniques*—Interpretation of medical reports, narcotics, hypnotics, scientific crime investigation, case preparation and law of evidence, applied criminal psychology, interviewing and detention

3. *Conditioning Factors in Juvenile Delinquency*—Personality factors, family, companionship, population, cultural conflict, economic, physical environment, and community as factors, the effect of law-enforcement and observance, and the treatment of offenders

4. *Delinquency Prevention Techniques*—Community organization as an approach to crime prevention, methods, and techniques of preventive action

5. *Administrative Aspects of Delinquency Control*—Administrative techniques applied to police problems in delinquency control, co-ordinating, organizing, staffing official and nonofficial

agencies dealing with delinquents, statistics, analysis, and records

6. *Techniques of Learning and Teaching*—Procedures in the use of the library, note taking, outlining, and summarizing, as related to the field of delinquency control, systematic consideration of the techniques of instructing adults in small or large groups

7. *Legal Aspects of Delinquency Prevention*—Law and codes, law enforcement, judicial structures, the community and the law

8. *Field Work*—Under supervision in local law-enforcement departments and allied agencies to develop philosophy and skills in delinquency control

9. *Public Speaking*—Training in techniques of presentation of information concerning delinquency control to public groups, and

10. *Personality Development*—A study of current thinking in the field of psychology and psychiatry.

Police Service Training

Police administrators are deeply concerned with the problems they face in their efforts to professionalize the service. Even the rookie patrolman looks forward to the day when police will be considered in the same professional class with lawyers, doctors, engineers, and educators. However, before this can come about standards must be raised, a code of ethics universally established, the body of knowledge concerning police activity must be made available, research must be engaged in to establish these, and practice must be refined through the training of both neophytes and experienced officers.

The complexity of modern police work poses a serious problem; that is, the danger of overspecialization. Should it not be pointed out that no department can hope to specialize or particularize its activity without first establishing fundamental procedures and training its personnel in the basic principles of police work. This is the same principle by which the medical profession does not recommend that the medical student start his preparation to become a specialist until he has received training in the broad field of medicine. Just as a physician would decline to perform an intricate brain operation unless he had the specifically required training so neither would a police administrator attempt to set up a full program of crime prevention without training and skill in this field.

Law enforcement has more than a passing interest in what happens to children. On the one hand the taxpayer demands dollar for dollar returns and one of the most efficient ways to spend the tax dollar is on crime prevention and youth welfare. An administrator who is public relations conscious will recognize immediately the value of youth programs and what administrator would not enjoy his position much more today if he had the opportunity to work with and train the past generation rather than arrest and prosecute it. In view of this impossibility the only logical move is to see that prevention programs are set up, co-ordinated and administered.

This is a field of endeavor requiring specialized knowledge and skills. Every police administrator and planner as well as the juvenile officer in the field should have this training. It is now being offered free to those who are interested at the Delinquency Control Institute at the University of Southern California.

IT HAPPENED 75 YEARS AGO THIS WEEK—

The Charles Ross Case[*]

By Cynthia Lowry. Associated Press Staff Writer.

A Little Boy Was Kidnaped, Before There Really Was Such a Word, and the Mystery Goes On.

ONCE in a while—a few times in a century—a crime is committed or a mystery with criminal overtones pops up that seizes the imagination of a nation.

They can be counted almost on the fingers of one hand: the Crater case, Lizzie Borden, Dorothy Arnold. And, of course, the kidnaping of little Charlie Ross 75 years ago.

The Ross case has grown into a classic mystery. A dying man confessed his part in snatching the golden-haired boy. Another man served seven years in solitary confinement as an accomplice. Scores of men—one as recently as 10 years ago—have proclaimed themselves the missing Ross boy.

What happened to him? Even now, little more is known than his father found out on a warm, sun-bright day, July 1, 1874. Four-year-old Charlie Ross drove happily off with two strange men in a buggy. He never returned.

Charles Brewster Ross was one of the seven children of Christian K. Ross, a prosperous but not wealthy Philadelphia merchant. On the tragic day, Ross quit his store early because he'd promised Charlie and an older son, Walter, 6, some sand for their sandbox and some firecrackers to set off on the Fourth of July.

Mother Away

The father felt more than usual responsibility for his children that day be-

cause his wife, slightly ailing, had gone off for a short rest in Atlantic City.

But neither Walter nor Charlie was around when he returned to the spacious house in suburban Germantown. A servant said both boys had been playing in front of the house. A neighbor told him she had seen the boys climb into a buggy with two men and drive off.

An hour later, Walter turned up in custody of a Mr. Peacock who had found the boy wandering alone in Kensington, eight miles away.

"Where's Charlie?" Ross asked.

"He's all right," Walter told his father. "He's in the wagon."

Then was drawn from him the story of the two strangers who had been cultivating the little boys for several days, chatting and giving them candy. On that July 1, the men had returned and suggested the boys accompany them to "Aunt Susie's" and buy firecrackers. Without hesitation, the little fellows climbed trustingly into the wagon. In Kensington, Walter had been given a quarter and told to go buy firecrackers. When he quit the store, buggy, men and Charlie had gone.

Police Skeptical

After some time passed, Ross went to police with the story. Kidnaping was almost unheard of—the word wasn't even in use—and the police refused to take it

[*] Reprinted from *San Francisco Chronicle*, Sunday, June 26, 1949. Used by permission of "Wide World."

seriously. Finally, the worried father put an advertisement in the Philadelphia Ledger:

"Lost on the first instant, a small boy about four years of age, light complexion and light curly hair. A suitable reward will be paid on his return to E. L. Joyce, Central Station, corner of Fifth and Chestnut streets."

Joyce was a police officer. Ross used his name because Mrs. Ross, still in Atlantic City, knew nothing of the affair. But on July 5 came the first of a long series of communications from the kidnapers.

"Mr. Ros," it said in part, "yu money can fetch him out alive and no other existin powers. Dont deceve yuself an think the detective can git him from us for that is imposebel."

The police still were unimpressed—Ross took the letter to them in spite of a warning not to—but two days later another letter arrived, demanding $20,000 ransom and threatening the father with the murder of his child.

At this point, the police woke up and plunged into a frenzy of misdirected action. They threw a cordon around the city, conducted a house-to-house search, and picked up every child who answered even vaguely to Charlie's description. Meanwhile, Ross went ahead with an advertisement indicating his willingness to comply with the kidnapers' demands.

Communications between the two continued for some time with the distraught father alternately accepting police advice in refusing to pay for the release of his child and accepting (still by advertisement) the criminals' terms. Their letters stopped for a solid week after police offered a $20,000 reward for their capture and conviction.

Explicit Instructions

Finally a note came from New York giving explicit instructions for payment of the ransom money. Ross followed instructions—but with a secret police escort and with a bag which did not contain the required cash. He traveled on the back platform of trains between Philadelphia and New York and Albany, looking in vain for the predetermined signal to toss the bag on the tracks. Later, it appeared a newspaper had published an erroneous report Ross was in the West following a clue. This, it was believed, led the kidnapers to abandon the plan they had arranged.

There followed more exchanges which led nowhere. Finally, New York City police stepped in. Chief of Police George Walling was visited by a man who said that two men calling themselves Johnson and Clark had, some time before, approached him with the idea of abducting one of the Vanderbilt children at Throg's Neck, Long Island.

Chief Walling investigated and found Johnson and Clark were aliases for William Mosher and Joseph Douglas. He obtained samples of Mosher's handwriting and compared them with the ransom note. They checked, he said. But no one could find the pair—Mosher had broken jail some time before in New Jersey. Finally he got in touch with Mosher's brother-in-law, a man named Westervelt who had been dismissed from the police force a short time before.

Walling promised Westervelt he would be reinstated on the force and receive the $20,000 reward for the return of Charlie. Westervelt agreed, but later events indicated he continued to help Mosher and Douglas. Meanwhile Ross, senior, had suffered a complete nervous breakdown. He had also broken with the Philadelphia police and hired Pinkerton men to investigate.

Sky-High

On December 14, 1874, the case was blown sky-high.

At 2 A.M. on that morning, in the Bay Ridge section of Brooklyn, a householder named J. Holmes Van Brunt was awakened by a ringing burglar alarm. His son Albert investigated and reported a light in the unoccupied house of his uncle, 200 yards away. Accompanied by two hired men, father and son waited outside the house until two men emerged. Shots were exchanged. One of the burglars was killed instantly and the second was mortally wounded.

The dying man identified himself as Joseph Douglas. His dead companion was William Mosher.

"We stole Charlie Ross," he told the Van Brunts.

"Where is the child?" he was asked.

"I don't know. Mosher knows."

When convinced Mosher was dead, Douglas merely said Charlie would be returned safely within a few days. He died seconds later.

Young Walter Ross identified the bodies as those of the two men who had taken him and Charlie for the buggy ride. But no Charlie Ross turned up.

Westervelt was convicted as an accomplice. Although he served seven years in solitary confinement he never confessed.

The search went on all over the world. Ross spent more than $60,000 trying to find his son. He estimated he had examined more than 200 children in the vain hope one of them might be Charlie.

Children in Our Jails[*]

By Austin H. MacCormick. School of Criminology, University of California, Berkeley.

IT WOULD seem impossible that there could be found in American county jails any nook or cranny into which the spotlight of publicity had not been turned, or that any new scandal could be brought to light in what have been appropriately termed "the worst of our penal institutions." From John Howard's day to the present, reports on jail conditions have been an almost unbroken record of neglect, filth, and corruption. The occasional public scandals that throw a lurid light over some jails usually result in no more constructive action than removal of a jailer or two and temporary correction of conditions under which brutality and graft have flourished.

No report on jail conditions, hair-raising in tone or sobersided, has yet aroused the American public to demand deep-search and far-reaching action. Such a demand has not resulted, for example, from exposure of the iniquities of the fee system, under which it is financially profitable for local officials to keep as many prisoners in jail as long as possible and to spend the minimum amount on food and other necessities, or from revelation of indescribable conditions of moral and physical filth, or from unemotional inspection reports showing that in most of our jails prisoners are thrown indiscriminately together: those with contagious diseases with the well, the insane with the normal, the old with the young, the hardened with the unsophisticated, the guilty with the innocent.

Jail Conditions

Within the past four years, however, the spotlight has again been turned on our jails and has brought to light a specific situation so shocking that an insistent and sustained demand for its correction might have been aroused if

* Reprinted from The Annals of The American Academy of Political and Social Science, 261 (January 1949), pp. 150–157. Used by permission.

it had not been for the preoccupation of the public with the problems of war and the postwar period. In 1944 and 1945, a series of articles on the general subject of children in jails, by Vera Connolly who has a reputation for being careful of her facts, appeared in national magazines having a combined circulation of many millions. (*Woman's Home Companion, Reader's Digest, Collier's*) They revealed that thousands of children, some of them as young as eight or nine years of age, are confined every year in county jails in the United States for periods of a few hours to several months, usually under abominable conditions.

In preparation of her articles the author visited a number of jails in the company of a federal inspector and studied starkly revealing inspection reports. After years of writing on all types of subjects, including some very sordid ones, she was shocked by what she saw more than by anything else in her professional experience. Her indictment of the appalling conditions under which she found children confined contains such examples as the following:

The women's and girls' cell block was a flight farther up. . . . It smelt sickeningly. The toilet was foul. Mattresses were caked with dirt and stained. Roaches ran up and down the walls. . . . Into this hole are thrown girls whose major offense may have been running away, staying out after curfew, playing hookey, or having been deserted by their parents, and they share it with hardened prostitutes, other adult female offenders, and the insane. . . .

In another jail "a boy of ten, found by an inspector, beseeched pitifully: 'Mister, please get me out of here. I'll be a good boy.' The child seemed to be a chronic school truant. The jailer referred to him as a 'habitual criminal.'"

Miss Connolly found it common practice for girls of 14, 15, and 16 to be locked in "on top floors of partly-wooden fire-hazard jails that had no night jailer, no matron and only intermittent day service." In one of these a girl about 15 had been entirely alone for more than a month and when the visitors arrived

she sprang up and burst into tears. "Don't go, talk to me," she begged. We stayed awhile. "First there was a crazy woman in that cell over there," she told us. "Mumbled all day and at night she'd use her bucket and then knock it over and the smell would make me sick. I was glad when they took her away. But now I wish anybody was here. Anybody."

The Problem

These articles, which were undoubtedly dismissed by many as mere horror stories for reader consumption, had a sound basis not only in the author's firsthand observations but also in the voluminous federal inspection files to which she had access. The seriousness and the extent of the problem were also given unquestionable confirmation by the thorough study made during the past few years of juvenile detention facilities and practices in twenty-two states in various parts of the country by the National Probation and Parole Association. On the basis of this study the association's representatives estimate that 50,000 to 100,000 children are confined each year in our county jails. That a closer estimate cannot be made is due to the fact that jail population records are often incomplete, inaccurate, or entirely lacking.

There is no central clearing agency to supply figures on the number of children throughout the country detained annually, in jails or otherwise. Indeed, there are comparatively few states that require such reports from county officials. There are enough figures available, however, to indicate that the estimate cited above is by no means exaggerated; it may even err on the conservative side. In Arizona, for instance, Federal jail inspection reports showed that 1,752 juveniles had been detained in ten of the fourteen county jails between July 1, 1945 and June 30, 1946. Records of the other four jails were so poorly kept that it was impossible to tell how many children had passed through their portals. In two of the three city jails, 698 children had been held. The third city jail refused to permit inspection of its books. In every jail where girls were committed they were thrown in with women, and twelve jails reported that their efforts to segregate boys from men were "fruitless."

In Oregon, where the law is positive in prohibiting confinement of children under 14 in the same quarters as adults, inspection disclosed that it was common for 11- and 12-year-olds to be so held. Only 19 of 38 county jails had separate detention quarters for boys, and only three actually segregated girls from women offenders. Some 2,247 juveniles were jailed in that state in 1945, a figure that worked out to the alarming rate of 78.8 per 10,000 children.

Reports to the National Conference on Prevention and Control of Juvenile Delinquency show that for some urban counties in the United States the number of children detained in jails annually runs as high as 1,000 or more, and that single states have jailed as many as 4,000 juveniles in one year. About 75 per cent of these children may be released within a week and more than 90 per cent within a month, but many cases have been reported "where children rotted in jail three, five, six months or more, waiting for something to happen."

It would undoubtedly be possible to arouse strong public opinion against the confinement of children in jails, but if one seeks to arouse it, he must be prepared to indicate what form of action would be most effective. Would it be best to make an attack on the specific problem of children in jails, or using that as a means of creating public interest, to make an all-out attack on jails as a whole and all their abominations?

Anyone who considers the latter approach must be realistic and face the fact that it would not be a task of cleansing one Augean stable, but more than three thousand. The latest inspection reports of the Federal Bureau of Prisons show that 3,029 (97.3 per cent) of the 3,111 jails and workhouses throughout the United States inspected by the Bureau since 1930 were rated under 60 on a scale of 100. The Federal rating is a composite score on sixteen items that cover every phase of jail administration and operation.

Reform Resistance

Of all types of penal and correctional institutions in America, the aptly named common jail has more successfully than any other resisted the efforts of progressive penologists and public-spirited citizens to reform it. Such organizations as the American Prison Association and its affiliate, the National Jail Association, are continually seeking to raise jail standards, and what progress has been made redounds largely to their credit and to that of the Federal Bureau of Prisons. The latter, through its jail inspection service, has exerted definite pressure for improvement, especially where it has been able to apply a dollar-and-cents lever. A jail has to meet the Bureau's minimum requirements to get and stay on its so-called "approved" list and thus be assured of income from boarding Federal prisoners. There were only 648 city and county jails that met the Bureau's minimum requirements in 1947, and some of these were used solely because, bad as they were, they were the best facilities available. Many county officials, when told that Federal prisoners will be removed from their jails if conditions are not improved, are unable or unwilling to make improvements, and say so bluntly. The Federal authorities are then frequently forced to continue to use these jails or to transfer their prisoners to others that are no better.

During the fiscal year 1947 the Federal Bureau of Prisons inspected 539 jails and reported that "a considerable number seemed no better and no worse than when last inspected, but fully as many had become worse as had improved." The answer to this unhappy balance lies in public apathy and the fact that professional penologists tend to shrug their shoulders and regard the jail problem as one that defies solution short of the millennium.

Reasons for Inaction

The public apathy is largely grounded on lack of knowledge of jail conditions and a widespread feeling that the usual jail inmate is a dirty and depraved person who deserves little sympathy and is not worth trying to help. The public is only now beginning to realize, for example, that alcoholics, who make up the bulk of the jail population, are sick persons who need, and in large numbers will respond to, scientific and socialized treatment.

The attitude of defeatism among penologists, on the other hand, is based on knowledge of jail conditions and how they have resisted reform. The penologists know that the sheriffs and jailers who man the jails are under political control and that jail personnel from top to bottom is continually changing as the wheel of politics turns. Too often it happens that one appointee, totally ignorant of proper jail standards and jail administration, is succeeded by another and another and another, all equally ignorant. Some years ago the Federal Bureau of Prisons found that between January and October of one year 297 new sheriffs had taken over duties in connection with the management of jails which the Bureau was using for Federal prisoners and which it was circularizing with helpful material. At that time there were 979 jails on the Bureau's "approved" list. The turnover throughout the country may be greater or less than this, but the above

figures mean that even in the somewhat better jails, approximately one-third of the Bureau's effort to raise standards through the officials was discounted at the start. Any attempt to approach the problem of jails in general or children in jails on the county or community level would face the same handicap. County commissioners as well as sheriffs have to stand for re-election, and in cities a new mayor too often means a new jail administrator.

Method of Attack

In view of these considerations it does not seem realistic to approach the problem of children in jails indirectly by attacking the entire jail problem, or to attack either problem on the local or county level. To inform, convert, and stimulate to effective action the people and officials of over three thousand counties, many of them poor, sparsely populated, and in remote rural areas, by direct action would be a virtually impossible task. Pin-point precision bombing has its place in warfare, but the solution of a social problem of such immensity and complexity as this is not a matter of quick destruction but of painfully slow and laborious construction.

The wisest decision would be to make a direct attack on the problem of children in jails, as a phase of the general situation that not only cries for correction but also would command public attention more quickly than any other phase, and to approach the problem on the state level. For the reasons given above, the local approach is impracticable. Because of the dual difficulty resulting from what would be deemed Federal interference with county and state rights at the same time, an approach on the Federal level would also be impracticable. The state level thus emerges by elimination, and it could be argued on many other grounds that it is the best level on which to seek action with respect to this particular problem.

Disregard of Law

If the citizens of any state were aroused to action, the first solution proposed would undoubtedly be: There ought to be a law against jailing children. But there are laws. Practically every state has some adaptation of the Standard Juvenile Court Act, and jail detention of children is forbidden by statute in 28 states and the District of Columbia. The sorry truth of the situation is, however, that the laws "are more honored in the breach than in the observance."

A high official in the Department of Public Welfare in one such state cited the juvenile court statute which forbids that "any juvenile under fourteen years of age be incarcerated in any county jail or police station prior to the time of his trial." There is wanton disregard of the letter of this law as well as its spirit, and open violations of statute are countenanced by the very juvenile court judges who should see to its enforcement, this official asserted. He added:

Despite the fact that another section of this same statute states that anyone who knowingly violates this statute is liable to a fine not to exceed $100, I have heard of no one questioning the manner in which the law is disregarded or suggesting the imposition of the penalty provided for those who do so.

It is obvious that arousing an insistent public clamor to keep children out of jail is not enough; that the passage of laws against this practice is not enough; that if there is such a law there must be not only teeth in it but teeth that bite.

Alternative Facilities

On the other hand, it would be unfair as well as ineffective to demand that children be kept out of jail without providing authorities with facilities other than jails for the care and custody of children who must be detained temporarily. Most judges, it is safe to say, do not want to send children to jail. Many county com-missioners, sheriffs, and jailers know their jails are unfit places for children and would prefer not to have them there, but do not know what else to do with them. A recent report of the Federal Probation Service indicates that there are approximately 145 public detention homes for children in the country. More than one-third of these are within the borders of only three states. There are also the detention facilities provided by private or quasi-public agencies; but of about seventy such institutions, more than a score are in one state. In states where welfare departments are efficiently operated, the use of boarding homes augments other facilities for the detention of children; but in few states are such arrangements widely available.

To shock the public into demanding that children be kept out of jails is justifiable only if, at the same time, it is made perfectly clear what difficult practical problems county and local officials face. We must indicate to the public and to the officials themselves what types of detention facilities have been found satisfactory.

Standards for Detention Facilities

Approved standards for juvenile detention facilities have been worked out and are available in convenient form in manuals published by the National Probation and Parole Association and by an officially sponsored California committee (Advisory Committee on Detention Home Problems). These manuals, based on thorough study, contain plans and specifications of buildings of various sizes, and describe the programs that should be carried on and the personnel needed for these programs.

These manuals point the way to progressive action that could be taken immediately by cities and populous counties. Their problems are made easier by the fact that trained personnel is usually available and that transportation to courts and other agencies is not a difficulty. Rural communities and counties that have only an occasional child to detain obviously cannot set up elaborate facilities. They can combine with other jurisdictions, however, to establish a regional detention home that meets acceptable standards. Problems of transportation, especially in mountainous areas, are difficult but not insuperable. Certainly almost any amount of effort or cost should be expended rather than continue to confine children in the small, filthy, and neglected jails usually found in rural areas.

Where neither local nor regional detention homes are practicable, county commissioners and sheriffs should make a contract with a responsible local couple to care for one child or more on a per diem basis, and should get local welfare officials to act immediately in the cases of children who can be returned to their own homes, placed in boarding homes, or cared for in a welfare facility.

It must be recognized that these last-named methods are not always advisable: in the case of juveniles charged with murder or other serious offenses, for example, chronic runaways who live in some distant locality and cannot be trusted to remain in an ordinary home, and so on. If children must be detained even for a brief period at a jail, then there should be a secure room or two in a part of the jail completely separated from adult prisoners, or attached to the jailer's office or to the quarters in which his family lives.

One must also be realistic on the subject of age, and realize that some boys and girls, especially where the juvenile court age limit is high, are mature and sophisticated and far from childlike in their attitudes and actions. Many a boy or girl may be legally a child but physically, emotionally, and even mentally an adult. Some 18-year-old boys are big, vigorous, and dangerous, and cannot be trusted in insecure custodial facilities. Some girls of that age are even worse

problems than the boys. If one were to differentiate on the basis of age, it would probably prove wise to make a particular effort to seek proper provision immediately for children under 16, or under 14 at the very least, at the same time taking steps to do so as soon as possible for all those of juvenile court age.

It would be illusory to expect that there could be an immediate ironclad and absolute prohibition against jailing anyone within the juvenile court age limit. The Panel on Juvenile Court Laws at the National Conference on Prevention and Control of Juvenile Delinquency recognized this when it recommended certain revisions to the Standard Juvenile Court Act. In the matter of detaining children the panel wished the model act to be as strong as possible, but realistically practical. It recommended that the following proviso be attached to the section prohibiting jailing: "except that when no other detention facility is available and when the judge or director is not available, a child may be placed in jail or other place of detention for adults, but in a room or ward entirely separated from adults confined therein."

Inspection and Enforcement Power

The most effective step on the state level would appear to be to secure passage of legislation giving the state department of correction or department of public welfare the power of inspection of all city and county jails under a law which places rigid restrictions on jailing children. At the present time, only about a dozen states have laws providing for such inspection by a state department or agency, and not all of them can be held up as inspiring examples. When the head of a department with this inspection power is conscientiously determined to make such a law work, however, it can bring noteworthy results. In North Carolina, Dr. Ellen Winston, commissioner of the State Board of Public

Welfare, reduced to a near-minimum the number of children held in jails, and did this within a relatively short period.

Before Dr. Winston took office it is difficult to say how many children were being detained in North Carolina jails, legally or illegally. The laws of that state provide that no child under 14 may be confined in jail, and a child of 14 or 15 may be so confined only if charged with a felony the penalty for which is ten years or more in a state penitentiary. A Federal Bureau of Prisons report of a few years ago stated that the laws were not being enforced at the time, and the North Carolina jails had "generally low standards." Dr. Winston went to work first by publicizing the law and then by using her department's inspection powers to enforce it. The state Department of Public Welfare can and does require reports from sheriffs and county superintendents of public welfare with regard to conditions in the jails and the number, sex, age, and other characteristics of prisoners. Dr. Winston stated recently:

Through monthly jail reports we are able to pick up all children who have been detained in jail. We immediately write to the superintendent of public welfare in the county concerned and ask for a full report. The superintendents of public welfare requested that we send copies to the sheriffs and chiefs of police so that they will be informed we are following up on the situation. . . . The net result of all our activities is that we have reduced the number of children held in county jails to about 25 or 30 each month, approximately half of whom are held legally under the existing statute.

A number of other states have made a forthright and vigorous attempt to prevent the detention of children in jails and to improve jails in general. New Jersey passed a law in 1946, effective in 1947, prohibiting the confinement of any juvenile up to and including the age of 16 in a county jail, police lockup, or other place of detention for adults, and permitting the detention of those 17 or

18 years of age in such places only if they are completely segregated from adults. The juvenile court upper age limit is 18. Prior to this law's becoming effective, the State Department of Institutions and Agencies, headed by Sanford Bates, exercised as strict control as possible over the detention of juveniles through its Division of Community Services and Delinquency Prevention and its jail inspection service. In 1946 the reports for 17 counties, excluding four large metropolitan counties with juvenile detention facilities, showed that of 2,492 juveniles held in detention awaiting action, only 235 (less than 10 per cent) were held in jails or similar institutions.

Legislation

One of the first pieces of legislation sought by Richard McGee after becoming Director of the California Department of Corrections was a law giving the department authority to inspect jails and power to enforce acceptable standards. The bill failed of passage by a single vote, but is practically certain to pass at the next legislative session. One of the problems the Department of Corrections and the California Youth Authority are determined to solve is that of juvenile detention.

In the state of Washington in 1947 a Legislative Interim Committee on Juvenile Delinquency recommended the passage of a Youth Protection Act and establishment of a Department of Youth Protection and Institutions. This department would be responsible, among other functions, for providing detention care for all children requiring it, and seeing that "no children be detained in jails or lockups." The proposed legislation became involved in a partisan political fight and was defeated by a narrow margin. It was supported by many of the leading judges of the state, but did not receive the unanimous support of the rural judges. One of the sponsors of the bill stated after its defeat that "jail detention of children will not be eliminated until there is some type of state-wide program in a position to provide strategically placed detention facilities throughout the state."

The last two years have seen in three states new legislation that will undoubtedly result eventually in significant action on the entire problem of juvenile detention and especially on the use of jails for that purpose. In 1947 Minnesota established a Youth Conservation Commission and Wisconsin a Youth Service Commission, with a division in the State Department of Public Welfare as its operating agency. In 1948 Massachusetts created a Youth Service Board. All of these new services are patterned, with some modifications on the model Youth Correction Authority Act developed and sponsored by the American Law Institute.

Campaign for Public Interest

Although, as was stated above, the approach to the problems of children in jail must probably be on the state level and from there to the local and county levels, there is need of a carefully planned and patiently executed campaign on a nation-wide basis to arouse an informed public interest and bring into effective working relationship officials and civic groups who can stimulate and guide their states, counties, and communities to constructive action.

Such a campaign has recently been launched by the Osborne Association. The Osborne Association has been making surveys of prisons and juvenile institutions for over twenty years, but has not until now undertaken intensive work in the jail field. A foundation grant has been obtained, and assurances of the support and co-operation of the National Conference of Juvenile Agencies and other national organizations interested in various phases of the general problem of child welfare have been given. The sponsoring associations realize that the task will be a long and difficult one, and they are prepared to conduct a long-range campaign. They believe the hour has long since struck when we should have attacked our jail problems instead of accepting them, and that the duty and responsibility of getting children out of jail can no longer be shirked on the grounds that it is too onerous, too perplexing, or too formidable an undertaking.

Keeping Children Out of Jails: It Can Be Done*

By Austin H. MacCormick. School of Criminology, University of California, Berkeley; and James H. Dooling.

In 1948 the Osborne Association, in collaboration with the National Jail Association, launched a campaign against the widespread practice of confining children in county jails, 97.3 per cent of which have been rated below 60 on a scale of 100 by federal jail inspectors.

The shame of our aptly named common jails has been tolerated far too long by a public that at best can plead ignorance—the lamest of all excuses—by public officials to whom the jail is usually only another pawn in the political game, and by professional penologists who state frankly that the "jail problem has got us licked," but, in truth, have never given it a real fight.

Jails have been exposed *ad nauseam*

* Reprinted from *Federal Probation,* Vol. XIII, September, 1949, pp. 40–45. Used by permission of authors and publication.

and the public has proved that it has a strong stomach. It will not be enough to excoriate sheriffs and jailers, even when they keep a 10-year-old boy for weeks in a cell in which nobody should put a pig. The best ones will say "What else am I to do?" The worst ones will say "So what?" All too many have little concern for what happens to children or anything else so long as they hold their jobs. Education in many cases is as unprofitable as excoriation; sheriffs do not stay around long enough to learn. Since last November (1948), 550 new sheriffs have come on the scene in our 3,000 counties.

Education, nevertheless, must be our chief mode of attack. It must be education in not more than two-syllable words, education that gets down to bedrock principles and procedures. And before we start educating county commissioners, sheriffs and jailers, we need some educating ourselves. What they want from us is not glittering generalities but common sense solutions of specific problems, not merely what they should do but how they can do it, not merely demands to get children out of jails but advice on where to put them.

To learn some of the practical answers to the problem of the child who must be detained, pilot studies have been undertaken in two states, one Northern and the other Southern, that are making an earnest effort to solve the problem. In New Jersey, where the full co-operation of the State Department of Institutions and Agencies and its Division of Inspection has been given, the study is nearly completed. In North Carolina, where the State Department of Public Welfare is similarly co-operating the study is also in progress. Through these and other studies in carefully selected areas it is hoped to assemble information that will serve as a practical guide to county officials. It should prove especially useful to probation officers and others charged with child-caring responsibilities, who often are faced with the job of finding a place in which to detain a boy or girl who otherwise will be thrown into a jail that is unfit even for adults.

Public Interest through Education

Education also must be the first step toward securing public interest and action. By education, however, we do not mean steaming up the public to hasty and perhaps unwise action by heart-rending tales of children cringing in terror from crazy or drunken cellmates. The public, as well as the officials, must be told what to do, what methods people have found practicable. Our aim must be to bring about a sustained—not sporadic—public interest and intelligent —not hysterical—public action.

So much has been written and so much more said about detaining children in jail that we run the risk of assuming everyone recognizes it as bad practice and, therefore, it will only be a matter of time before this abuse is ended. We would be just as wrong to assume that, since everyone knows you should not cross a busy street against a red light, there will soon be an end to jaywalking. Safety education helps but, even where there are laws against it, most people keep on jaywalking unless the laws not only have teeth in them but teeth that bite. New York City, with the world's largest municipal police force, is one of the worst cities in the country for jaywalking. In Washington the pedestrian waits for the light to change because, if he does not, he will get a ticket and a fine.

During the past 50 years every state and territory of the United States has adopted juvenile courts or some form of special, socialized procedure for dealing with delinquent juveniles. Certainly within that time the red light against jailing a child should have flashed everywhere. As a matter of fact, 28 states and the District of Columbia have posted signs: "Observe the lights; it is against the law to jail children." Other states have contented themselves with framing warnings, some loosely worded and others more exact, but all unmistakable in their intent. Unfortunately many of the stop signals carry explanatory signs saying, in effect, that it is all right to cross against the light if you are in a hurry, or have too many other things on your mind, or think nobody is looking.

The result is that by the most conservative estimates this country still jails some 40,000 children a year, a number equal to all the children in the State of Delaware between the ages of 10 and 17! Furthermore, if we accept the more realistic estimates of 50,000 to 100,000— and we seem safe in doing so—it means we jail annually the equivalent of the entire 10- to 17-year-old population of a city the size of Pittsburgh, San Francisco, Denver, Atlanta, or Cincinnati.

Attitudes of Probation Officers

It would scarcely seem necessary to marshal again the arguments against jailing juveniles. All of us are aware that such malpractice is a negation of the principles of the juvenile court and most of us are fully conscious of the contaminating and degrading influences of the average jail on adults—not to mention children. It seems hard to conceive that anyone, particularly a probation officer or one attached to a juvenile court in any capacity, could take the "hard-boiled" attitude on this question. But there are such officials, few as they may be. Not long ago we met such a person: a chief probation officer and referee for the juvenile court of a populous county in a progressive state. It was a county lacking neither in financial resources nor in education, nonetheless it had been the custom for many years to lock up juveniles in the combined jail and workhouse. There was a state law of the type that permits jailing juveniles if they are *segregated* from adults. One of the county commissioners has fought consistently for a special detention facility for children and has had the support of many civic and fraternal organizations. But he has not had support from the source that should be the most concerned; he has again and again come up against the roadblock of the juvenile court staff itself!

"Why spend a lot of money fixing up a fancy place for these kids?" the chief probation officer wanted to know. "Most of them come from dumps and if you make it too easy for them they'll get so they want to go to the detention home for a vacation. Bars don't bother kids like that and, anyhow, they're always kept separate from the older prisoners."

As it developed, the "segregated" section for juveniles at the workhouse-jail consisted of a room over the wing of the women's jail—a room with double-deck beds. There were two girls in the room. Were there any others being detained? No, the matron explained, that was all. What if there were others—what if there were boys, too? "Oh, we'd fix up a place for the girls over here somewhere, and the boys would go over there—" motioning vaguely toward the men's wing.

In the men's section an attendant was asked where they segregated boys. He looked baffled for a moment and then replied, "You mean juveniles? Oh, we keep them in a special room—over there." Did he mean the room over the women's wing? "Yeah, that's the one," he said. But, it was pointed out, there were already two girls there. "We hardly ever have boys and girls at the same time," he countered. And if they did have? "Well," he said thoughtfully, "one night, come to think of it, we did have a 12-year-old like that, so we fixed him up with a cot in the bullpen. He was lonesome, poor kid, and the older prisoners comforted him."

The county commissioner who had been such a thorn in the side of the probation chief recalled that case. "I went in there at 10 o'clock that night and took the boy home with me," he said. "When I brought him to the next juvenile court session there was hell to pay, but I threatened to keep right on doing the same thing every time I heard about it."

"That's the kind of stuff you're up against," the probation chief commented. "A lot of busybodies are butting in all the time and interfering with the way we handle the kids. It's no wonder so many of them keep going bad until we have to send them along to the reform school. There's absolutely no sense in mollycoddling kids. I've found that out."

Happily there are not many professional workers in the juvenile field with the extreme point of view of the officer cited, but the number of those who fear "mollycoddling" is startling. Some call it just that, and others are more cautious in explaining that "what we want to avoid is pampering."

Purposes of Detention

It might be well at this point to pause and ask ourselves why we detain children in certain cases. Certainly it is *not* so we can either mollycoddle or pamper them, though if the truth were known most of them could stand a little kindness and decency for a change. We detain primarily because we want to make certain that a runaway will not run away again before his case is disposed of, or because whatever the child calls his home is not a fit place to remain in, or because he would be in danger of getting into more trouble if not placed under control until a wise solution to his problem can be worked out. Sometimes detaining a child is a slap at indifferent or neglectful parents. Whatever the reason for detention, the common jail does not satisfy the requirements. To a vast number of officials throughout the country, however, it apparently does, else we should not have such a staggering number of children jailed every year.

Such persons seem to be satisfied with keeping children in "cold storage" until the court is ready to act. Unfortunately the figure of speech is not an accurate one, for there is too much spoilage in the process. We are dealing here with living, thinking, human beings—pretty well mixed up in their thinking at that—and not with a side of beef or a sack of potatoes. Even if we were dealing with the latter, we would not leave them long in a filthy, vermin-ridden vault. And with a human being in jail we not only have spoilage to think about but the jail stigma he will carry the rest of his life. Finally, jailing a child means that if the juvenile court treatment is to be anything more than a fruitless formalism, we have begun the way best calculated to make the child unreceptive and unresponsive to it.

We must recognize that detention is more than a cold-storage process; that it is in itself the first step of whatever treatment we propose for the juvenile offender. Even if his be one of those cases which have been filling folders for years, detention can be a time when we learn something new and significant of his reactions and behavior. It can furnish the first real opportunity to find out what makes him tick, removed from the environment that contributed to his delinquency.

Scope of Detention Period

The detention period—always considering it as temporary detention—is not the time for deep therapy, short of an emergency, but there is no more reason why detention care should neglect the principles of first aid for the delinquent than there is for being content to push a hit-and-run victim off the highway and let him lie unattended until the ambulance arrives.

Detention, properly carried out, aims at many more things than merely holding the delinquent in a controlled environment, though it must first of all do that. Its broader scope is to administer whatever restoratives for body and spirit are possible and feasible and, by utilizing this opportunity to study the child to supply the juvenile court with something more than the name, address, age, and offense charged. Confinement in a common jail can serve none of these purposes.

Youth House in New York City has cared for 12,977 boys in a 4-year period. It has been criticized by people who should know better for considering its function to be treatment as well as detention, although its critics know that the staff of this detention facility includes persons who are fully trained in treatment techniques. Recognizing that it is dangerous for places of detention lacking trained personnel to attempt intensive treatment, we agree with Frank J. Cohen, the executive director of Youth House, who sums up his principles in the following words:

If we have come to accept the use of the detention home for the temporary care of children as a step in the rehabilitative process, we will have made great progress . . . . If we have come to the recognition that once a child is received in a detention home he is in a treatment process, whatever that may entail, we shall have made considerable strides over that which is implied in the mere physical holding of a child.

Methods of Detention

Once having conceded that jails defeat the aims of proper detention and that whatever "treatment" takes place there is likely to be of the baneful type, there invariably rises the question: "What if we have no detention home? Where can we put the child except in jail?" Certainly the jailer who honestly asks that question cannot be expected to supply the answer and, in many cases, neither can the sheriff. As a rule both hold their jobs directly or indirectly at the pleasure of the county commissioners and have to get along with what physical plant there is unless the commissioners

choose to loosen the county purse strings.

It would be an exceptionally powerful and conscientious sheriff or an exceptionally courageous and gifted jailer who could conduct successfully a one-man campaign to get proper detention facilities if his commissioners were opposed, or even lukewarm about the question. On the other hand, the probation officer who has his heart in his profession can readily muster the progressive forces of the communities he serves. He is the good right arm of the juvenile court and commands the confidence of the court. If the court makes a stand, county commissioners will have a hard time justifying inertia or opposition to safeguarding the wards of that court.

For any county there is always an answer to what can be done with children needing detention; there is no county so poverty stricken that it must jail them. If one has the energy and interest to hunt for them, there are always respectable and reliable couples who can be induced to accept a child or two on a boarding home basis for a modest per diem fee. If there are too many cases for such a method, or suitable homes are not available, there is the regional detention facility plan by which two or more adjacent counties share the expenses of a common home. If long distances make this method impracticable, there is always a room or two in a county-owned building—a courthouse or a hospital—that can be adapted to detaining children. The boarding home method may not always be ideal and the other methods may not always be most convenient, but they are far and away better than the quick and easy solution of the jail.

State Supervision

All these considerations, however, lead back to the question of how to assure ending jail detention. If one is realistic about it, the answer is the same as the answer to getting the color-blind, the short-sighted, the opinionated and the heedless pedestrian to obey the red light.

The problem of children in jails cannot be attacked effectively on the local or county level alone. It virtually would be impossible to inform, convert, and stimulate to action the people and officials of over 3,000 counties, and approaching the problem on the federal level would be deemed interference with both county and state rights. The state level of approach thus emerges by elimination. The state must be the policeman who sees that the red light is not ignored.

The most effective step on the state level would appear to be to secure passage of legislation giving the state department of correction, or state department of public welfare, inspection and supervisory authority over all city and county jails, under a law which places rigid restrictions against jailing children. The very fact that, although 28 states and the District of Columbia had strict laws against jailing juveniles, last year only Connecticut and New Hampshire claimed *never* to use jails, is evidence enough that red lights and warning signs alone do not suffice.

New Jersey Legislation. New Jersey has shown what can be done. With enactment of its Juvenile Court Act of 1929, detention of children was prohibited "in any prison, jail, lockup, police station, vehicle or *other place where the child can come in contact with any adult convicted of crime or under arrest and charged with crime.*" As in many other states which have similar statutes today, the intent obviously was to forbid all detention of juveniles in jails. The closing phrase was interpreted by some counties, however, to mean that detention was permitted in segregated sections of jails: that is, if a child did not physically come in contact with adult prisoners. In order to close this last loophole, the legislature passed an amended law in 1947, effective July 1, 1948, which stated flatly: "No child

under the age of 16 coming within the provisions of this subtitle (Juvenile and Domestic Relations Court) shall be placed in any prison, jail, lockup or police station."

Commissioner Sanford Bates of the Department of Institutions and Agencies transmitted to state and county administrators his interpretation of the Act and the basis on which he would enforce it. It was:

First, that actual propinquity should be removed between adult and child prisoners and second, that the child should not be stigmatized by having it said or understood or thought that he went to a place commonly recognized as a jail or building where adult prisoners are sent.

The matter did not rest there. Commissioner Bates has a Division of Inspection within his department. From the day the amended law was passed his inspectors in the field stressed the date on which it would become effective, not alone explaining how but why it would be enforced. It would be a little less than the truth to say that all counties were in accord after the new legislation any more than before it. The fact remains, however, that none had the excuse that the meaning of the law was not quite clear, or could argue that only occasionally was it necessary to jail a child under 16, or that it agreed with the law but would get around to establishing other detention facilities some other day. New Jersey found it necessary neither to club nor to threaten: it was enough that there was a state agency *to see whether or not children were being held in jails contrary to law.* Counties knew there were sanctions if it came to a test.

North Carolina Approach. New Jersey is not alone in its recognition that the power to end jailing of children must stem from the state level. The North Carolina State Department of Public Welfare for years has given leadership to the drive against confining children in jails. Its approach has been one of a broad educational nature, emphasizing the philosophy that the temporary emergency care of children is a function of child-serving agencies (specifically juvenile courts and departments of public welfare) and not the responsibility of law-enforcement personnel. This approach, through publications, speeches, state conferences, annual institutes, and consultant services, has been directed not only toward those serving in the child welfare field but also toward the county law-enforcement personnel. It has resulted, in practically all of North Carolina's 100 counties, in an acceptance of the tenet that the disposition, including temporary care, of children apprehended in delinquent behavior becomes the immediate responsibility of juvenile court or public welfare personnel.

Statistics on the detention of juveniles are compiled from data received monthly from county jails and juvenile courts. There has been a marked and consistent decrease in the detention of children in jails since 1936, with the exception of the past 3 years in which there has been a leveling off, presumably as a result of improved recording techniques developed by the present Commissioner of Public Welfare, Dr. Ellen Winston.

In cases of detention of children in jails, the county superintendent of public welfare is immediately asked for a full report. As a further step, sheriffs and chiefs of police are sent copies of such correspondence so that, as Dr. Winston puts it, "they will be informed we are following up on the situation."

Action of Other States. There are other heartening signs on the horizon. When Wisconsin, in 1947, established within its State Department of Public Welfare, a Youth Service Division to accept juveniles and minors from appropriate courts for supervision and in-

stitutional care, it required by law that the state department assist counties in setting up proper detention facilities for juveniles. Minnesota's Youth Service Commission and the Massachusetts Youth Service Board established in 1947 and 1948, are required to concern themselves with problems of detention as well as of training and treatment. California is likely this year to pass a measure, which had strong support in the last legislature, that would give the State Department of Corrections jail inspection authority and power to enforce acceptable standards.

Sherwood Norman, consultant for the National Probation and Parole Association and an expert in the field of juvenile detention, has cited Connecticut as offering "the most encouraging plan" for juvenile detention, as "it operates three regional homes, serving the entire state."

Standards for Detention Facilities

Approved standards for juvenile detention facilities have been worked out and are available in convenient form in manuals published by the NPPA and by an officially sponsored California committee. These manuals, based on thorough study contain plans and specifications for buildings of various sizes, and describe the programs that should be carried on, as well as the personnel needed for the programs.

They point the way to progressive action that could be taken immediately by cities and counties where either a local or regional detention home can be established. In small and remote counties we shall have to utilize boarding homes and other methods referred to earlier. But once we have authorized the state to take leadership in this all-important problem, we shall be in a position to set up red lights and to stop those who wilfully or heedlessly run through them. It may even be that some day we shall not need the policeman at the crossing, but he is badly needed now!

The Child in Detention*

By Henry J. Palmieri. Chief Probation Officer, Juvenile Court, Richmond, Virginia.

OVER and above the need for adequate staff, program, equipment and building, important as they are, there is a less tangible factor which must be recognized as an essential part of any detention home. To the detention home comes a variety of youngsters with as many reasons for coming as there are children—the defiant child, the chronically disturbed child, the recessive child, the over restricted girl and boy, the handicapped child, the victim of sibling rivalry or a broken home or gangster associations. Who is delinquent in these cases? The child? The parent? The community? Asking "Who?" won't solve the problems, but concentrated, cooperative effort in the community will.

How are we effectively to meet the needs of this group of children, all of whom have given us by their behavior a signal that they are in trouble and need help?

Custody alone is not enough. We know from sad experience that it will not successfully meet the situation. A boy or girl, detained for whatever reason, must go on living,—and living, to be satisfying, must have wholesome spiritual, physical and emotional outlets. None of these can be served separately. They must be offered as a part of a whole program arranged to meet the various and changing needs of the individual child. Otherwise we help to develop in him a lopsided and ineffectual personality.

We must set about to secure a clear understanding of the underlying causes of his behavior. We can start by helping the youngster to absorb the shock created by placement in the detention home. For many children this first contact with the law is crushing. In this situation all the old problems reappear, causing a great amount of anxiety. This trying time, however, is sometimes a golden opportunity to establish a sound relationship with the child. Once this has been done, there will be a better chance to get at the real causes of his behavior.

To understand these causes, the child must be studied from many angles. We find boys and girls bursting with a desire to tell all, but we also find boys and girls who are unable or unwilling to talk. This means that we get a part of the story or none at all unless we are skilful in our approach. When we do get the necessary information, including the child's feeling about his present situation and his ideas about it, success is more apt to follow in handling his entire problem. In the course of his stay we ought to learn what he thinks about himself and his present environment, the people in the detention home, the people with whom he lived and those with whom he formerly associated. Unless we can get some idea of his inner feelings about his behavior and the reasons for these feelings, we shall not accomplish much with the youngster while he is in detention. There are other things we must learn about him too. We certainly should know something about his family and how it has affected the child. Something about his school, his church affiliation, and most important of all, how satisfying these experiences were in his life.

* Reprinted from *Focus*, Vol. 28, January, 1949, pp. 22–23. Used by permission.

His likes and dislikes are important and they also serve as an index to his personality makeup. We must learn enough to prevent further behavior problems. We must not wait to see what he will do next.

The study of the individual child should continue during his stay in the detention home. A constant effort must be maintained to learn his mental ability, emotional maturity, cultural background, special interests and abilities. We must know why he failed to use his potential capacities, or in using them why he didn't develop into a more acceptable person. This information is negotiable even beyond the use made of it by the court; it can be used to advantage by any agency which may at some time have dealings with the child. To deny, ignore, or fail to include this service in a detention home program is to disregard the emotional health of the children detained.

Any agency dealing with children who are serious behavior problems must have workers able to recognize overt behavior for what it is and to go about the job of finding out the real motivating forces. This is especially true in detention homes where time is usually limited and all effort to help the child must be concentrated in a few days or a few weeks.

Advances have been made in our detention homes but we must look ahead to greater integration of education, religion, recreation, medical and social services which will permit us to more adequately meet the spiritual, physical and emotional needs of the children in our homes. There is no hocus-pocus method of knowing, understanding and helping a child in trouble. We must know what we are doing and do it knowingly.

Children in detention are not canned goods or automobiles which can be shelved or stored. Handling children under such conditions is a delicate time- and energy-consuming job requiring all the skilled assets of the best staff.

New Goals for Juvenile Detention*

By Sherwood Norman. Detention Consultant, National Probation and Parole Association, New York.

OLD CONCEPTS of detention grew out of the notion that delinquent acts call for retaliation. A youngster who appears to be a tough customer must be shown that "we can get tough too." The fact that between 50,000 and 75,000 children are still held annually in county jails and police lockups, most of which are substandard for adults, is evidence enough that the old concepts persist. But further evidence can be found in detention homes where life is a deadly adult-controlled routine and conformity is secured by deprivation of privileges or threat of isolation. These detention homes have little concern for the development of the child's personality. "The children are with us too short a time," we are told. Physical care and custody are the primary objectives in the county jail, in the typical detention boarding home and in the detention institution whose purposes seldom reach beyond spotless linen and lifeless routines. The idea is to hold the child in suspension and do nothing until an investigation is

* Reprinted from Federal Probation, Vol. XIII, December, 1949, pp. 29–33. Used by permission of author and publication.

made and the court decides on the treatment. No wonder detention has been referred to as a necessary evil!

New Concept and Standards

A different concept of juvenile detention is gaining momentum in this country. It is based on the fact that a child cannot be held in suspension; that detention may be more destructive than helpful unless the "storage-only" concept is abandoned in favor of beginning the process of rehabilitation at the point of arrest. The new detention offers individual and group therapy and, where available, clinical diagnosis. In the new detention each child finds acceptance regardless of his behavior and thus his attitude toward authority is reinterpreted.

From the standpoint of the court the prehearing period is an investigating, fact-finding period. Therefore the detention home should have much to contribute regarding the nature, needs, and potentialities of the child. To the youngster the prehearing period is a suspense period which represents society's retaliation for his behavior. Anxieties, bitterness, and resentment either burst forth or are driven within the child where they may strike back at society later. Probably at no time in life is a boy or girl in greater need of *an intensive period of skilled guidance, constructive activities to replace periods of idleness, and good physical and psychological care*. At no one time is the court in greater need of more information about the child with whom it must deal.

New concepts of detention care for children hold that these needs must be met whether on a level which a community of 10,000 can afford or with all the professional services available in a city of over a million. We insist on good physical hygiene. It is time we insisted on good mental hygiene. Administratively this calls for skilled personnel and a per diem cost which in some jurisdic-

tions may legitimately exceed the cost of hospital care. Organizationally it means a far more closely co-ordinated relationship between the police, court, detention home, probation officers and, where it is available, the clinic. Until these agencies unify their objectives we can hardly expect consistent interpretation of authority to the child nor reliable information about the child's real needs to the court.

Planning for a detention home cannot be satisfactory unless the purposes it is to serve are made crystal clear. In the light of the purposes set forth above, planning involves three major considerations: (1) The use to be made of detention by the police and the court; (2) The location, design and construction of the building; and (3) The personnel and program.

It is safe to say that no detention home and children's court in the country yet measures up to reasonable standards in all three of these equally important factors. Few detention homes and children's courts excel in more than one. But standards will never be raised unless we aim high and accept compromise *only as a step towards higher standards*.

The Use of Detention

The extent to which children are detained differs widely in communities of comparable size and delinquency potential. There is no doubt that on the whole we detain far too many children. Excessive detention is due partly to misunderstanding the proper function of detention and partly to a lack of co-operation by the court and the police in their control of admissions.

Juvenile detention is the temporary care of children who require secure custody prior to court action or return to another jurisdiction. This means children who have committed delinquent acts or present a dangerous likelihood of running away or committing further offenses if allowed to remain in their own homes pending court hearing. The care of children removed from their homes for reasons of health, neglect, or dependency is not detention care according to current interpretation. Arrangements should be made for the care of these children in foster homes or special institutions by the department of welfare through its children's services or by private agencies until public services have been developed. Dependent and neglected children should not receive care even under the same roof with youngsters who need physically secure custody.

The care of children removed from their homes as a disciplinary measure is not detention care. This practice, sometimes used by probation officers as a whip to keep their probationers in line, is not good casework and may violate the child's constitutional rights. The use of detention as punishment or retaliation may sometimes result in immediate conformity but has little to do with solving the child's basic problems. Instead it confirms his delinquency status, subjects him to further contagion in the detention home, and acts as a salve to the probation officer's conscience.

Excessive detention of children by the police "for investigation" can be overcome by a closer working relationship between the agencies concerned. When probation and police officers come together on a casework basis such abuses will be avoided. A change in the juvenile code could help bring this about. Will C. Turnbladh, executive director of the National Probation and Parole Association, recently stated:

The latest revision of the Standard Juvenile Court Act, prepared by a special committee of the National Probation and Parole Association, provides that the jurisdiction of the juvenile court attaches from the time a child is taken into custody. This is an attempt to reach through the widespread problem of indiscriminate detention in two practical ways:

(1) Through centralizing in one agency in the community; i.e., the juvenile court, the responsibility for detaining and releasing children instead of expecting several, or in some communities, upwards of 40 different law enforcement agencies to exercise this function for the court, and

(2) By providing a legally defined basis for the development of liaison and uniform clearance between the law enforcement agencies and the juvenile court—probation service in all matters affecting the detention of children.

The care of children committed by the court is an improper use of detention, except for the briefest period while awaiting transfer. A boy or girl who has been committed should be turned over to the agency responsible for him as soon as possible. The practice of allowing committed children to linger in detention for days and weeks before transfer is unfair to the child, unfair to the detention home, and psychologically unsound. The detention home is not a place for longer term treatment. It is a diagnostic and first aid station from which the youngster should be removed as soon as there has been sufficient social study for the court to decide on the longer term treatment and the child prepared for the new experience.

The Control of Admissions

Far too little attention is paid to the control of detention admissions. There are three phases of admission control, the first in the hands of the police. A united court-police policy can be achieved only through a sharing of objectives. The police or sheriffs in some towns lock up every youngster they refer to the court. In other communities less than 2 per cent referred to the court for formal action are detained. In many large communities the skill with which a child is handled and the likelihood of his being detained depend upon which officer happens to apprehend him. However, where there is in the police department a juvenile or youth bureau in charge of all police cases involving children (not just minor ones), court and police objectives can better be coordinated according to noncriminal procedures and fewer children will be detained.

The second step in admission control comes at the point of court jurisdiction. The child detained on authority of the police is either continued in detention or released on authority of the court. The mechanics of this process is often responsible for unnecessary detention. This decision to detain a child should come from the court on the recommendation of a probation officer or caseworker, not a clerk. A probation officer or intake worker should interview the parent and in some cases the complainant *as soon as possible* to determine whether the child should be detained or returned to the custody of his parents. When police bring children directly to the court rather than to the detention home during court hours, much unnecessary detention is avoided.

In a number of cities the police routinely call a probation officer before detaining a child, regardless of the hour. In other communities the judge reserves the right to authorize detention or release without delegating his authority to a caseworker. Hence, a number of children who might have been released by a probation officer are detained until the court can hold a preliminary hearing. Of course there always are cases where children need to be detained during the course of police investigation, but as previously pointed out a cooperative working relationship between the police and the court can allow for contingencies.

If the decision to detain or release is based on the best interests of the child, detention will not be used primarily as a convenience to the police or the probation officer. The judge needs to be alert to see that children are not left in detention because it is easier to interview them there. Some communities planning to enlarge detention facilities or to "build for the future" would find it less costly if they enlarged and improved their probation staffs. Many youngsters, otherwise detained, could remain in their own homes under the closer supervision of a caseworker, a procedure which should always take precedence over detention where possible.

The third step in detention admission control concerns the release or detention of children during the course of the prehearing period. Most courts make the decision to detain as early as possible in the prehearing period and right or wrong this decision sticks. There are a growing number of jurisdictions, however, where detention is used more flexibly. For example, John is detained at first because the relationship between himself and his parents is so strained that he would undoubtedly run away if he were not held in custody. However, during the course of his detention in which casework has been active with the boy and his parents, attitudes change to the point where John would be a good risk if released. Likewise, when the response of a youngster to casework supervision in his own home pending hearing is so unsatisfactory that running away or further delinquency is likely to result, then detention may be called for.

In communities where children are rarely detained, even though their offense is serious, runaways or further offenses during the prehearing period are as infrequent as they are for adults released on bond. Detention if used wisely need no longer be a panic reaction to the child's offense.

Types of Facilities

Of the many types of facilities used for detaining children the jail ranks at the bottom of the list and the specially designed and constructed detention home at the top. It may be argued that if the use made of detention and personnel and program are of such importance, what difference does it make if a youngster is detained in the local jail with a kindly jailor? It is further argued that some of the boys and girls are close to criminal court age and in states where juvenile court jurisdiction stops at 16 would be detained in jail anyway.

These arguments are just as spurious applied to juvenile jail detention as to the juvenile court law itself. Whatever the age of the child under juvenile court jurisdiction, the law protects him from criminal procedures. From a legal standpoint alone it is inconsistent to use the jail for detaining children. From a common sense standpoint it defeats the very purpose it is supposed to serve—the protection of society. The psychology of the iron bars spells defeat and failure for the youngster, not the help and guidance which the children's court is supposed to give.

A juvenile detention home must be neither jail-like nor threatening in appearance. It should be homelike, yet it should detain. Modern architecture and modern detention screens (which resemble fly screens but are practically impenetrable) can make this possible. A community which has been jailing children for years without appreciable expense may hesitate to spend 75c to $1.00 per capita to construct satisfactory detention facilities. This is particularly true if only a few children each year will occupy it. The only common sense solution is regional detention homes, state-operated, according to approved standards and supplemented by local boarding homes. This plan is best in conjunction with a statewide juvenile court. However, for the average county wishing to abandon the use of the jail or jail-like detention there are four alternatives:

The Specially Constructed Home. The specially constructed detention home is the best solution because it combines secure custody, homelike appearance, varied indoor activity areas designed to assure constant supervision, and other important features. The following types are recognized.

The family type home is designed as a home for a man and wife with facilities for up to eight children.

The single unit home may or may not have resident staff. It is designed for from eight to sixteen children.

The two unit or multi-unit home has separate living and sleeping quarters for two or more groups of children, each group not exceeding a maximum of fifteen.

The Converted Residence. The converted residence is a house owned or rented by the administrating agency and remodeled for detention purposes. The building should be of brick, stone, or masonry with fire resistant features. A frame house is not satisfactory if there are to be locked doors and screened windows. However, frame houses with fireproof additions for sleeping rooms can be used if security in the building is not expected in the day time, nor the sleeping quarters used as lockups. Remodeling usually consists of (a) security provisions: changing casements, installing screens, keying locks alike, replacing doors, etc.; (b) supervision provisions: knocking out partitions, rearranging rooms, eliminating narrow halls, installing large glass panels in walls to provide adequate activity space and proper visual control; (c) new construction: addition of rooms, small building in outdoor play area for school shopcrafts, etc., one or more fireproof wings for sleeping quarters.

The Boarding Home. Boarding homes for detention can be used for most children who need to be detained provided skillful boarding parents can be found and given adequate subsidy and supporting supervision. In small counties boarding homes can prevent jail detention for all but a few youngsters. They have the advantage of providing a substitute home, individual attention, and lack of delinquency contagion through large groups. For some delinquent children the boarding home is ideal. For others it is questionable. However, it must be kept in mind that detention is for children who require secure custody. Almost everywhere that boarding homes are used for detention some youngsters must be held in a secure detention facility.[1] These are the boys and girls who are in greatest need of skilled treatment and good detention care. Are we to relegate them to the jail and, in effect, write them off as hopeless? Some boarding homes have held youngsters by building strong rooms; but creating a jail cell within a home is no solution. Detained children require constant supervision and activity leadership which few boarding parents are willing to provide. Boarding homes, not being designed for the purpose, are usually badly arranged from the point of view of supervision so that children are shunted off into a room by themselves and spend many hours in "waiting room activities."

The Combination Facility. Combining detention with other facilities by providing rooms in a courthouse, county office building, hospital, county home, training school or other institution may be better than using the jail but is not recommended except as a stop gap measure. Combining detention care with any of these facilities interferes with the proper function of both, has never proved satisfactory and often results in a children's lockup without proper space, equipment, staff, or program.

A more satisfactory combination is the children's court and detention home. The advantage of this is that probation officers can be close to the children detained and see them frequently during the detention period. Children need not be transported from the home to the court as when the home is separated. Moreover, the building of a detention home can often be financed with greater ease if the juvenile court is included in the project. However, there is something to be said for keeping the court building separate and apart from the detention home since they represent two separate functions. Except in small jurisdictions, it is difficult to avoid the institutional atmosphere of a dwelling which is part of an office building used by the public.

The job of providing satisfactory detention care is so difficult that even excellent personnel is thwarted at every turn if the arrangement of rooms and construction of the building are inadequate. The only really satisfactory solution is new construction, provided up-to-date principles of detention home design are observed.

Program and Objectives

The detention home building may be the most up to date and intake may be carefully controlled by the court yet because of limited staff and program little more than human storage is provided. Adequate personnel means adequate program. Only together can they meet the needs of the detained child. Since county authorities are seldom willing to allow an adequate budget and since the working conditions are rarely good it is difficult to obtain qualified personnel. If detention is to pull out of the "storage only" stage, basic attitudes toward detained children and toward those in charge of them must change

---

[1] Erie County (Buffalo) New York has used boarding homes for years but one of them is actually a detention home with security features and a capacity for eight children. Others hold up to four children. The large supervisory, casework, and teaching staff which makes this plan workable is seldom considered when Buffalo's "boarding home" system is referred to. On a per diem basis it is fully as expensive as a good detention home and of course it should be.

and active citizen committees demand altogether different standards.

Whatever the size of the detention home, personnel must be capable of meeting three basic program objectives: good physical care and custody; a full, varied, and creative activities program; guidance through intensive casework. In the smallest family type detention homes these must be met by one or two individuals with help from outside professional sources. In the larger homes, professional casework and group work services should be employed as part of the staff. In either case, the effectiveness of the period of detention will depend upon the way in which these objectives are met.

Physical Care and Custody. High standards in the provision of food, rest, cleanliness, and exercise do not add up to good physical care if the ingredient most needed by the child—a warm acceptance of the child himself—is missing. This cannot be taken for granted. It must be genuine, fresh with each new child, and it must be continuous. Overwork and shortage of staff must not crowd it out. It is particularly important in the role of substitute parents who dispense the food, shelter, and clothing, for these elemental things are closely related to being wanted.

Secure custody defines the boundaries within which physical care must be given. While detention personnel need to be alert at all times, there is no place for the constant suspicion which destroys the relationship between the child and his supervisors. Whatever the physical setting, the fundamental basis for security lies in the relationship between the child and his supervisors, in a number of detention homes where children are taken out of the home to use community health and recreation facilities, the need for security can serve to create mutual trust and confidence. This is not inconsistent with a secure building which helps to remove temptation from

the child and strain from the staff.

Activities Program. The value of a full school and activities program in the detention home is disputed only where it doesn't exist. It is impossible to build up confidence in a youngster and to stress his assets without providing activities which have meaning for him. The utmost imagination must be drawn upon and mental, physical, and social activities involved. An increasing number of small and medium-sized detention homes have found it both practical and desirable to mix boys and girls in the program. The formula is small groups, constant supervision of the participating variety, and a full activities program. Physical activities should be vigorous and ample space and equipment provided for big-muscle exercise.

Arts, crafts, and music are program *essentials* which should not be confined to a school period. When a child creates something for himself or his family his achievement produces a sense of personal worth at a time when failure seems immense. Some youngsters, taught to use tools for the first time in the detention home, have carried this knowledge back to their homes where healthy new interests replace subversive activities. The best resources within a youngster are drawn upon when he loses himself in creative work. The effect is therapeutic for the child and, in revealing interests and potentialities, has diagnostic value for the detention staff and the court. Homemaking activities have their place, but even though it may break the ice for a new youngster to stir the soup, reliance upon housekeeping duties is no solution.

Bull and gripe sessions amongst detainees can be a most destructive influence when they are under cover. When made legitimate and participated in by the staff, collective thinking can turn into constructive discussion with elements of group therapy. The sophisticated delinquent tends to lose his status in the group when healthy activity and open discussion are encouraged. This takes young, vigorous, intelligent leadership.

Detention homes whose supervisors remain aloof and herd groups through a formal program to keep them busy only impress the youngsters with a system which has basic disrespect for them. A good program provides for choice. To remove a youngster suddenly from perhaps a too free world, and then take away every shred of independent action to ease supervision is no demonstration of respect for him as a person.

The fact that a child is detained for a short time and that regular classroom work cannot be duplicated is no reason for failing to provide school activities. School work in the detention home provides structure for the child's day and a sense of continuity which makes for less disruption when he returns to his own school. Teaching in a detention home affords an opportuity for intensive individualized help in academic skills and in crafts. It has often proved of greater value to the child than regular attendance (or truancy) in his own school for the same period. Public school home teachers, preferably trained in special education, are meeting the needs of some small detention homes, while in New York City the public school administration has established its own special schools within the detention homes. In some detention homes the school forms a source of activity stimulation to the home's personnel. The detention home school teacher serves as a tie between the troubled child and his school, and assists the court and probation officer by uncovering specific problems and attitudes in connection with school which may not have been previously known.

Guidance through Casework. The job of long term planning with the child belongs to the probation officer and should be part of the prehearing procedure whether or not the child is detained. In small communities where probation caseloads are low and qualified probation officers have a close relationship to the detention home, immediate guidance can be given on a day-to-day basis if called for. However, where the detention home reaches the size of a small institution or where probation officers are overloaded or unqualified, such an arrangement is less practical.

The detained child's need for guidance is not something which can wait until a busy probation officer comes around. Moreover, a probation officer cannot know the many situations which arise within the detention home. In some courts no casework is available to the child at all until the court orders an investigation or places the child on probation. The need for casework with respect to the child's adjustment to detention can be seen in forms of duplicity, rationalizing, uncontrolled aggression and other attempts to escape his predicament. Every detention home makes use of some form of guidance whether by inflicting a punishment or through the kind of intelligent counseling which helps a child gain insight into his own problems. At no one time is skilled casework so desperately needed. The child's self-analysis and his interpretation of authority are at stake. Rather than leave the job to the superintendent several detention homes with outstanding programs have recently added professionally trained caseworkers to their staffs. Their responsibilities fall into four overlapping areas:

1. Helping the child to face the realities of his immediate situation.

2. Assisting the child and the detention home by resolving behavior situations through casework and redirected activity rather than through punishment.

3. Serving as a focal point of inservice training for the supervisory staff.

4. Serving as a channel of interpretation between the child in the detention

home and the probation staff, the clinic and the court.

The child in need of detention is a child in need of clinical study and skilled observation. Thus a good detention home will serve as a short-term study home. When there is a close working relationship and a clearly understood division of function between the caseworker in the detention home and the probation officer making the social investigation, there is mutual support, not conflict.

Personnel

To achieve good physical care and custody, a full, varied, and creative activities program and guidance through intensive casework depend on small groups and a high calibre of staff. The smallest homes cannot expect to employ professional staff but they can offer sufficient salary to attract intelligent individuals who can understand the unhappy, resentful, and often aggressively unadjusted child, accept his personality, and live with him in a constructive relationship. Professional help often can be secured on a consulting basis. For example, menus can be checked by a qualified school dietitian and assistance in the handling of behavior problems by a trained caseworker or clinical psychologist.

Detention supervision requires warm personality, abundant good humor, intellectual curiosity, and a strong constitution. A detention home worker must be a well-adjusted person himself and able to take the anxieties and aggressive compulsions of the disturbed child in his stride without the need for retaliation. Tact, resourcefulness, and imagination are "musts" to keep detained youngsters constructively active and to prevent mental and social deterioration.

Properly staffed detention institutions with personnel operating on a 40 to 44 hour work week should expect to employ from 75 per cent as many workers as the normal maximum child population. A lower proportion than this almost invariably results in mass custodial care with only a token activity and guidance program. The ratio will not be as high in small detention homes employing resident staff.

It is impossible for those without experience to grasp the many duties involved in operating a small detention home. Even the simplest housekeeping duties become unbelievably complicated in a house full of detained youngsters, whether or not they assist with the work. Ordering groceries, planning, cooking and serving meals, cleaning, emergency repair work, laundry, mending clothes, seeing parents, conferring with probation officers and other workers, record keeping, bookkeeping, answering telephones, admitting new children at any hour of the day or night, clinical examinations, first aid and nursing when necessary, personal and group interviews and discussions with children, creative activity work with the youngsters, these are the major duties. Although there may be days when there are no children in the home at all, these days are unpredictable. There may be months when there is no let up. It is important, therefore, to provide proper relief to the extent of at least twenty-four or thirty-six hours a week and occasional evenings. If a man and his wife are employed it should be possible for them to go out together without constant anxiety over the management of the home in their absence. No less than one month's vacation with pay should be given.

Jail Detention and State Responsibility

Small communities with populations of under 50,000 seldom are able to afford proper detention care for their children. While the situation may be relieved somewhat by the use of boarding homes for certain youngsters, there is little likelihood of a satisfactory family type detention home being constructed for the purpose. There are persons so skillful with difficult children that they have been known to detain for the court all youngsters placed in their care without the use of physical restraints, but *such people are extremely rare.*

We might as well face reality. The jail detention of children will never be abandoned in this country unless the state constructs and operates specially designed, strategically located detention homes. These homes would supplement the local boarding home by taking only those children who require secure custody. State subsidies where tried have seldom been successful. In Virginia, for example where the state offers to pay almost the entire cost of operating a detention home, counties show a shocking indifference to juvenile detention.

There are isolated instances of inter-county co-operation in the sharing of detention facilities but this method of establishing regional detention homes cannot be relied upon.

Regional detention centers operated by the state according to high standards and supplemented by local boarding homes are the only hope of ridding ourselves of the blight of detaining boys and girls under juvenile court jurisdiction in jail. Ideally these detention homes would be located in the same general areas as regional child guidance clinics. Ideally, too, they would be affiliated with a statewide juvenile court system as they are in Connecticut. However, we need not wait for a state juvenile court to meet a very urgent problem. If we care for our children we will act now.

SELECTED REFERENCES

1. Braude, J. M., "Boys' Court: Individualized Justice for the Youthful Offender," *Federal Probation*, XII, June 1948.

Much is rightly made of the paradox of the social order that permits a youth to die on the gallows or on the battlefield, yet is not considered socially mature enough to vote. Well illustrated are discriminatory and contradictory aspects of civil and criminal laws.

2. MacNamara, Donal E. J., "Police Training in Prevention of Crime and Delinquency," *Journal of Criminal Law and Criminology*, XLII, July–August 1951.

A comprehensive survey of recognized institutions that prepare the student for a career in police and custodial professions.

3. Ellingston, John R., *Protecting Our Children from Criminal Careers* (New York: Prentice-Hall, 1948), Chapter 21: "New Police Methods with Children."

An unusually good discussion appears here relative to the policewoman's role in juvenile delinquency. Various types of juvenile bureaus specializing in handling juvenile cases are also presented.

8 THE JUVENILE COURT AS AN INSTITUTION

JULY 1, 1899, marks the official birth date of the juvenile court. On this date the law became effective in Illinois which established the first juvenile court in the city of Chicago. This was the first recognition of a separate area of legal control for juvenile behavior. By the middle of the twentieth century every state but one had passed some type of juvenile court statute.

From the beginning the movement was influenced by the juvenile court philosophy, an ideology sponsored chiefly by humanitarians and social scientists and a sprinkling of judges. This philosophy placed emphasis upon treatment consequence rather than upon behavior circumstance, the prevailing viewpoint of the criminal court. At the beginning, conflict arose in the legal profession as to whether or not the proposed policy of the juvenile court philosophy would violate the child offender's constitutional rights. Because of this conflict (and also because of the limited facilities of most juvenile courts) this philosophy has never fully materialized. Many criminologists now believe that the juvenile court is the principal experimental proving ground for changes in the entire crime-control system.

THE FUNCTION OF THE JUVENILE COURT

When the first juvenile court, in Chicago, began to function, it exemplified what Roscoe Pound described as "personalized justice." Destined to affect before the law not only the juvenile field but also the whole scope of human relationships under the law, it may be viewed as a twentieth-century approach to an age-old problem of human rights and responsibilities.

The underlying purposes of the juvenile court are two-fold: (1) to remove the child offenders from the ordinary criminal courts to equity courts, which consider the doer rather than the deed; and (2) to have this juvenile court render protection and treatment to *other* children needing both. Admirable as these purposes are in principle, they often fail to be carried out in actual practice.

In the juvenile court idea have been combined virtues of both the old common law and equity. Common law had established that children were not criminally liable if they were seven years old or under at the time of their offense. The juvenile court extended this earlier age limitation to 18 years old in most jurisdictions. Founded on the principle of *parens patriae*, namely, that the state must exercise guardianship over a child when the parents are unable or unwilling to discharge their full responsibility to him, the juvenile court, as a court of equity, avoids any stigma for a child which a criminal court contact might place upon him.

Juvenile courts are the least understood and the most misunderstood of all the nation's tribunals. Their distinctive philosophy, procedures, and approaches are features which few people appreciate; this is one reason why they have not been able to live up to the expectations of the public. Despite their existence for more than a half century, too many people still believe that juvenile courts are places where "bad" children are punished.

Endeavors to curtail the functions of the juvenile court have been attempted through legislation and court decisions. Restrictive legislation is usually proposed by persons who consider the progressive methods of juvenile court procedure as a scheme of "coddling" youthful offenders. Teeters and Reinemann cite a characteristic example of such assaults—the 1935 drive in Chicago (the court's birthplace!) to amend the law establishing the juvenile court so that all children above ten years of age and charged with felonies would be tried in adult criminal courts. The Supreme Court of Illinois, in considering the case of a fifteen-year-old girl charged with murder, declared that "it was not intended by the legislature that the juvenile court should be made a haven of refuge." Federal Judge William H. Holly characterized this statement as having decided that Cook County's juvenile court had no legal status, that it existed merely by license of the county's criminal court. The Chicago *Tribune* in an editorial in May, 1939, demanded that the criminal court assert its constitutional jurisdiction over young offenders. The editorial stated that the function of the criminal court is to punish offenses against the law—the juvenile court was not inflicting punishment. It also said that the present maximum age for juvenile delinquents was too high. Such actions and statements have greatly handicapped the development of juvenile courts.

Relatively untouched, however, is the principle upon which juvenile courts were established: that children under eighteen years of age have not reached the state of intellectual and emotional development which make them fully responsible for their acts. But there are qualifying provisions, for example, that if the juvenile's act is sufficiently repugnant, the court can decide that the child is responsible after all and should not be tried by the juvenile court. The latter may then refer the case to the adult criminal court. Recently such a decision was handed down in the courts in Miami, Florida. The offender, a sixteen-year-old boy, received a five year prison term from the judge of the adult criminal court. The Jacksonville *Times-Union* on February 5, 1952, reported that this was the first case under the new Juvenile Court Act (which permits the judge to send to adult criminal court juveniles whom the judge considers "obstinate") in which a juvenile offender was tried by criminal court. Such cases, it should be noted, have not greatly lessened the over-all trend to utilize the juvenile court process.

THE JUVENILE COURT JUDGE

Juvenile court literature frequently stresses the view that the assumptions, terminology, and procedures of the criminal court are obstacles to the rehabilitation aims of the juvenile court. Allegedly, a major reason for this situation is that the typical juvenile court judge has had criminal law training and experience which strongly influence the way he plays the role of juvenile court judge. Because many judges assigned to the juvenile court find it difficult to shed the formality and atmosphere of the criminal trial when they hold juvenile court sessions, they often arraign the child at the bar as if he were a hardened criminal and often use the probation officers as if they were prosecuting attorneys. They sometimes think exclusively in terms of guilt or innocence.

Too many judges must rotate in assignments to juvenile court or must devote the major portion of their interest elsewhere; therefore their interest in the welfare of children can not be sustained. For example, one study indicates that in one juvenile and domestic relations court the judge claimed that 70 per cent of his time is spent on divorce cases, while the remaining 30 per cent is not devoted entirely to juvenile offenders. In another court, the judge stated that he was required to give as much as 85 per cent of his time to matters *not* concerned with juvenile delinquents. And in yet another jurisdiction, the responsibilities assigned to the court were expanded into so-called "family" matters to the extent that even prostitution cases were included.[1] In one western state the writer knows of a situation where judges rotate the juvenile court assignment every six months. Some of the judges in this court have boys report to their offices in groups of four and lecture to them on the advantages of conforming to the rules of society! These same judges work without trained probation officers; they rely upon volunteers to do the social case work—which means little more than a routine signing of the "book" by the offender. The situation illustrated by these cases is hardly consistent with the modern accent on professional specialization.

Juvenile court judges are either elected or appointed by state or federal executives. In either system of selection, political influences often determine the outcome, and there appears to be an enormous variety in the qualifications considered for the assignment. Before the passage of the Juvenile Court Act in Florida in 1950, for example, the governor could appoint anyone as judge of the juvenile court as long as the person possessed "high moral character." For the judgeship of this juvenile court an appointee was not required to be either a lawyer or a social worker, nor to have special educational training or any experience in court. He merely had to be eight years older (or twenty-five years old) than the children he supervised and must have survived three summers of Florida sunshine![2] This, of course, is an extreme case and has been rectified by recent legislation. In 1941 the state of Missouri adopted a plan for its selection of juvenile court judges which plan has found favorable acceptance and is endorsed by the American Bar Association. Under this "Missouri Plan" the judge is appointed by the governor from three names submitted to him by a commission. The appointee, virtually "on probation" for twelve months, then

---

[1] Gustav L. Schramm, "The Juvenile Court Idea," *Federal Probation*, XIII, September 1949, 19.

[2] Roger J. Waybright, Chairman, Drafting Committee for *A Juvenile Court Act for Florida*, "Explanation and Presentation," Jacksonville, Florida, 1950, p. 18.

runs for election for a full term, his success dependent upon popular vote.

Because he is "low man on the totem pole" in the judicial hierarchy the office of the juvenile court judge does not, as a rule, attract top-level personnel. And the short tenure of office in many jurisdictions often discourages qualified men and women from seeking this job. At the same time, the judge's position is of central strategic importance in the juvenile court, combining the role of dispenser of justice with those of chief administrator, policy maker, and public relations official. In these capacities, he occasionally represents a curious picture of the juvenile court. For example, in the case of the two boys who pushed over about forty tombstones in Reno (reported in *Gazette*, July 14, 1948), the judge, for their punishment, ordered that twice weekly for several weeks each boy had to "patrol" the cemetery every evening, in addition to righting the tombstones. Another judge, in Brooklyn, delivered the following lecture to a seventeen-year-old boy charged with soliciting alms for textile strikers:

> What you need is for me to have you in a two-by-four room. What I would do to you! I'd blacken your eyes and give you some real American spirit and do for you what your parents should have done. We spend billions in this country for schools and what have we educated here—a mongrel and a moron! I have six kiddies myself and my oldest girl is ten. She knows who God is and the laws of the country. Down at my house we have a cat-of-nine-tails. I show it, and that is all. Get out of this courtroom. You are not fit to be here.[3]

Many such cases could be assembled, illustrating the extent to which highly personal views may color official decisions of the judge. The judge of the juvenile court may be solicitous or he may be vindictive; he may be as impersonal as law itself or he may be highly personal. This great latitude surely calls for men of professional training and of *judgment*—if there are to be effective judges of the young offender.

Of course, many juvenile court judges are highly capable, performing admirably even when greatly handicapped by limited funds and facilities. These superior officials characteristically concentrate on the offender's possible rehabilitation, not his punishment—"what are we going to do *for* him, not *to* him." They generally maintain an informal atmosphere in court; typically their speech, sympathetic and mild, reveals their quest to *understand* children. And, above all else, understanding the youth before him should be the judge's governing goal.

This discussion of the juvenile court judge should not overshadow the fact that the judge himself is by no means the only potential weak spot in the juvenile court system. Perhaps of equal importance are the problems resulting from the failure of state and county agencies to provide the facilities necessary for carrying out the functions of the court efficiently. These are problems directly confronted by the judges themselves. But they should become the concern of all citizens who are interested in the improvement of an institution so important in the lives of our youth—the juvenile court.

---

[3] Reported in Nathaniel F. Cantor, *Crime, Criminals, and Criminal Justice* (New York: Henry Holt & Co., 1932), p. 209.

READINGS

In "The Juvenile Court in Retrospect" Charles L. Chute, a long-time National Probation and Parole Association executive, reviews the progress of the juvenile court since its inception and characterizes its establishment as one of the great landmarks in child welfare development. Six worthy objectives are listed for the serious consideration of students of juvenile delinquency.

Gustavus Leovinger in "The Court and the Child" shows how the work of a juvenile judge can be disappointing, depressing, or rewarding. Inevitably situations will arise beyond judicial skill to help and beyond judicial wisdom to solve.

David Bogen in " 'Justice' versus 'Individualized Treatment' in the Juvenile Court" believes that a practicable and effective policy for the juvenile court must take into account the merits and limitations of both of these contrasting theories. What is needed is an enlightened "justice" which will protect the community's rights.

Walter H. Beckham has enjoyed the rare privilege of presiding over a busy juvenile court for nearly twenty years without a single appeal from his rulings. In "Helpful Practices in Juvenile Court Hearings" he gives an account of the practices that have made such an enviable record possible.

In "If I Were a Judge" Charles H. Boswell discusses the type of juvenile court he would have were he a judge. His guiding principle would be the maintenance of the court for the convenience of juveniles, parents, witnesses, and attorneys rather than for the convenience of the judge.

William Healy, a physician, is a pioneer in the orthopsychiatric approach to problems of juvenile delinquency. His "Thoughts about Juvenile Courts" stem from genuine experience. A preeminent leader in the juvenile delinquency field, he believes that the juvenile court is here to stay, representing as it does, justice for youth.

So much has been said and published criticizing the juvenile courts that Harrison Allen Dobbs has written specifically in their defense in his article, "In Defense of Juvenile Courts." He emphasizes the fact that the court was no fly-by-night happening and not the result of selfish and sentimental drives. However, the situation faced by the children's tribunal is a challenging one. Careful thought and action are required if the juvenile court movement is to go forward and not backward. In the future this young social institution certainly might make more lasting contributions to children's welfare.

The Juvenile Court in Retrospect*

By Charles L. Chute. National Probation and Parole Association, New York.

THE FIRST HALF of the twentieth century is near completion. The "terrible twen- tieth century," as Churchill called it, al- ready has seen two world wars and thus

* Reprinted from *Federal Probation*, Vol. XIII, September 1949, pp. 3–8. Used by permission of author and publication.

far has attained scant success in establishing peace and comity among nations.

But let us look at the brighter side. The progress of science in these 50 years has been phenomenal. We are developing a science of human understanding and behavior. Democracy and popular rights have advanced in many countries. In our own special field of delinquency control there have been great advances. Social work and the medical sciences have come to the aid of our courts and institutions. Probation work, after its experimental beginnings in New England, has been extended all over the country. It has been developed in all the federal courts. Parole has been established. Correctional institutions have been improved, though they still have a long way to go for effective crime control and prevention. Last but not least, the juvenile court has been developed from scratch.

The Passage of the First Act

July 1, 1899, is an important date. On that day the law became effective in the state of Illinois which established in Chicago the first juvenile court in the world. Probably no single event has contributed more to the welfare of children and their families. It revolutionized the treatment of delinquent and neglected children and led to the passage of similar laws throughout the world. It has been acclaimed by legal experts like Dean Roscoe Pound as "the greatest advance in judicial history since the Magna Charta," and by sociologists as the embodiment of a new principle: that law violators, the antisocial and maladjusted, especially among children, should be treated individually through social and protective processes, for their own protection and that of society, instead of by the punitive and retaliatory methods of the criminal law, which always have failed to repress crime. The juvenile court was the first legal tribunal in which law and the sciences, especially those which deal with human behavior, were brought into close working relationship.

The act established the first separate court to deal with all cases involving dependent, neglected, and delinquent children under 16, providing for the appointment of a special judge by the Circuit Court of Chicago, with unpaid probation officers, a separate court room and noncriminal records. For the first time, children who violated any law or ordinance were defined as delinquent, to be dealt with not as criminals but as wards of the court under its equity powers and procedures.

The Committee of the Chicago Bar Association (which approved the act for passage) summed up the purposes of the new law in the following words:

The fundamental idea of the juvenile court law is that the state must step in and exercise guardianship over a child found under such adverse social or individual conditions as develop crime. . . . It proposed a plan whereby he may be treated not as a criminal, or legally charged with crime, but as a ward of the state, to receive particularly the care, custody, and discipline that are accorded the neglected and dependent child, and which, as the act states, "shall approximate as nearly as may be that which should be given by its parents."

Events Preceding the Illinois Act. Many events in Illinois and in other states led to the passage of the first act. In many sections there had been a growing concern over the plight of children tried in criminal courts no differently from adults and confined in jails and prisons. The first important event was the establishment of special institutions for child offenders, beginning with the New York City House of Refuge in 1825 and later, similar publicly-supported reform schools in Massachusetts, Pennsylvania, and other states. Then came acts in a number of states providing for separate hearing of children's cases in the regular courts. In 1869 Massachusetts passed a significant act requiring the courts to give written notice to the visiting agent of the State Board of Charities before committing children. It was made the duty of the agent to attend "the hearing in person or by deputy, in behalf of the child." The Board was authorized to provide for children in family homes. This is probably the first time that a social worker was given legal status as a court officer. Later, in a few states, separate sessions, separate records, and detention apart from adults were required for juvenile offenders.

Probation, based on the common-law power of courts to suspend or defer sentence, had been developed extensively in Boston by devoted volunteers like John Augustus. The success of this work with both adults and children led to the passage of the first probation law of 1878, limited to Boston. Two years later this was followed by an act authorizing all cities and towns in Massachusetts to appoint probation officers; and in 1891, appointment of probation officers was made mandatory for all courts of the Commonwealth. The use of probation was unlimited either as to the offense or age of the offender. Vermont, following the lead of Massachusetts, adopted a probation law in 1898, and Rhode Island and Minnesota in 1899. But the greatest impetus for developing juvenile probation throughout the nation came with the passage of the juvenile court laws.

Organizations behind the Act. In Chicago it was the social and civic organizations—notably the Chicago Woman's Club and the Catholic Visitation and Aid Society—that first urged a juvenile law. The Woman's Club actually had a bill drafted in 1895 for a separate court for children and a probation department, but their legal advisors told them it was unconstitutional, and they abandoned it. They and many other organizations kept up the agitation. Hull House, under its peerless leader Jane Addams, interested itself in the plight of the thousands of children then in the jails.

The Illinois State Conference of Charities devoted its entire program in the fall of 1898 to "The Children of the State." Dr. Hastings H. Hart, Superintendent of the Illinois Children's Home and Aid Society, was a speaker and urged getting together on a juvenile court bill. The co-operation of the Chicago Bar Association was sought and they appointed a committee to prepare a bill that would secure the support of all interested agencies. Judge Harvey B. Hurd, the chairman, enlarged his committee of five lawyers to include representatives of social and civic agencies. Dr. Hart was appointed secretary and prepared the first draft of the juvenile court bill. It underwent much revision at the hands of the lawyers but finally was approved as the Bar Association bill and was introduced in the legislature by Representative Newcomer. After a hard fight, during which some compromises were made (especially in omitting a provision for paid probation officers), it passed on the last day of the legislature.

The first judge of the Chicago court was Richard S. Tuthill, assigned from the Circuit Court. He was succeeded in 1904 by Judge Julian W. Mack, who was active in developing the court and became a nationally-known exponent of the juvenile court movement.

Spread of the Movement

Following the success of the Chicago court, the movement spread with amazing rapidity. In Denver, Colorado, the famous Judge Ben D. Lindsey independently organized a juvenile court in 1899 under a so-called "school law" with limited jurisdiction over delinquent children of school age. A juvenile court act similar to that of Illinois was passed in Colorado in 1903. Judge Lindsey, despite his shortcomings, became the best-known proponent of juvenile courts throughout this country and Europe. One of his greatest contributions was the securing of the first act in 1903 giving jurisdiction to the juvenile court to deal directly with parents and other adults contributing to delinquency or dependency under either chancery or criminal procedure. The court thus became the first juvenile and domestic relations court. His court developed private confidential hearings and encouraged families and even children to bring their problems directly to the court.

Within 5 years after the passage of the pioneer act, juvenile court laws had been enacted in ten states: California, Indiana, Iowa, Maryland, Missouri, New Jersey, New York, Ohio, Pennsylvania, and Wisconsin. Some of these laws resulted in specially organized courts in only one or two cities. The court was still in an experimental stage. All the earlier courts had administrative weaknesses, particularly in not providing adequate probation staffs. Some of the courts were handicapped by limited jurisdiction and the retention of criminal procedures. They suffered also from political pressures and constitutional attacks, but 10 years after the enactment of the first juvenile court law the constitutionality of the statutes had been well established. A number of cases had been brought to the highest state courts and it had been held by overwhelming weight of authority that juvenile courts are not criminal in nature and hence are not unconstitutional because of informality of procedure, deprivation of jury trials, or other provisions guaranteed under state constitutions to persons charged with crime.

Within the first 10 years 20 states and the District of Columbia adopted juvenile court laws. By 1920 all but three states had them; and today every state has such a law—though in some it is limited and imperfect.

Juvenile court laws or many of their provisions have been followed in most European countries, beginning in England with the passage of the Children's Act of 1908. A League of Nations study in 1931 showed at that time that juvenile courts or some substitute for them were established in 30 foreign countries.

Age Jurisdiction

The National Probation Association published its first *Standard Juvenile Court Act* in 1925 to carry out the juvenile court standards adopted jointly by the Association and the U. S. Children's Bureau in 1923. The act sought to give the juvenile courts exclusive jurisdiction up to 18 years of age in all types of children's cases needing court action. In recent years a number of states have raised the jurisdictional age limit from 16 to 18, so that today 29 states, the District of Columbia, Alaska, and Hawaii have the 18-year age limit.

Perhaps the greatest defect in juvenile court laws has been their failure to provide complete jurisdiction over children. Twenty-one of our states (almost half) permit some offenses, either all felonies or only capital offenses, to be excluded from juvenile court jurisdiction or to be shared concurrently with other courts. This is inconsistent with the original purpose of the juvenile court, which seeks to treat all children who are in need of care and protection, regardless of the offenses committed. In a few states the intent of the law to give exclusive jurisdiction over children has been thwarted by Supreme Court decisions. Illinois is one of them, its Supreme Court having ruled as late as 1935 that the criminal courts have a prior jurisdiction in criminal charges against children over ten years old. Apparently only a constitutional amendment can alter this.

State-wide Juvenile Courts

Another unmet need in most of our states is for uniformity of standards between the many local courts and for state-wide coverage so that all children in need of care may have protection. To that end, one of the most important developments has been the extension of state-controlled juvenile court systems. Such a system, with judges appointed by a state juvenile court commission, was first established in Utah in 1908. Later, administrative control of the courts, including the division of the state into districts, appointment of judges, and supplying of staff, was taken over by the State Department of Public Welfare. Five district juvenile court judges (four of them full-time) serve the entire state and they are fairly adequately paid. All of them have full-time probation officers. Every child in need of court care can be reached by these courts.

In 1941 Connecticut became the second state to establish a state juvenile court. Three full-time judges are appointed by the governor for overlapping terms to serve the entire state. An adequate number of probation officers, state paid and under a merit system, as in the other two states having this system, serve in district offices. This state plan superseded that which had long been in existence whereby city police courts and justices' courts all over the state handled children's cases, frequently without adequate facilities.

The third state to establish a statewide juvenile court was Rhode Island in 1944. One state court with two full-time judges replaced 12 district court judges—all handling children along with criminal and civil court work.

State juvenile courts are being discussed today in other jurisdictions, especially in Virginia and Florida. There are numerous advantages. First, they make it possible to provide efficient juvenile court service for all children, including those in the rural districts which have seldom been adequately reached. Second, they make possible the appointment of qualified full-time judges and probation officers, assigned to districts. Utah has demonstrated that a state

court plan is adaptable to large rural states as well as the smaller, more populous ones. It is only a matter of larger districts and more traveling for the judge and his officers. It is to be hoped that the plan will be explored further and tried out in other states, especially those which have never been able to develop rural or state-wide services.

The Probation Staff

From the beginning it was realized that no juvenile court could function without an efficient probation staff. Most of the earlier courts did not provide paid probation officers but tried to get along with volunteers or with the assistance of workers from other agencies, as many rural courts must do today. It was soon discovered that the juvenile court needed its own full-time social service staff, at the same time utilizing the assistance and co-operation of the representatives of a great many welfare agencies.

In Chicago, because the original act made no provision for paid probation officers or for a detention home, a citizens' committee, known as the Juvenile Court Committee, was formed. Mrs. Joseph T. Bowen (still active and interested, although now over 90 years old) succeeded Julia Lathrop as chairman in 1900. With the aid of the Chicago Woman's Club, the first paid probation officer was provided. One of the earliest reports on the needed qualifications for juvenile probation officers had this to say:

They must be men and women of many sides, endowed with the strength of a Samson and the delicacy of an Ariel. They must be tactful, skillful, firm and patient. They must know how to proceed with wisdom and intelligence and must be endowed with that rare virtue—common sense.

The Juvenile Court Committee continued to raise the salaries of probation officers until the number of probation officers had reached 22. They were carefully selected. Timothy D. Hurley was appointed by the mayor to the law department of the city and assigned to the court as the first chief probation officer. In 1905 the legislature amended the law to provide for payment by the county of the salaries of probation officers. They were at first under the county civil service system, but later, by an unfortunate court decision, were excluded. However, the court established its own plan of qualifying examination, which since has been continued.

Although there has been progress in many states in increasing the number of probation officers, and raising their training requirements, we still have a long way to go before probation work can be considered a profession with minimum educational and training standards. It is now generally agreed that probation officers and other court staff should be appointed through qualifying examinations. Best results have been obtained when they have been selected under regularly organized civil service or merit boards. In many of our larger cities the qualifications for probation officers correspond with the standards set up some years ago by the National Probation and Parole Association; namely a college education or its equivalent, and, if possible, training in a graduate school of social work. Equally important, the officer needs qualifying experience—at least 1 year of casework, preferably in a child welfare agency under good supervision. And of course, even more important, he needs those personal, psychological, emotional, and character qualifications essential for dealing effectively with children and families.

Such officers must be adequately paid. There has been encouraging progress in this direction. A study which we made in 1938 revealed the average salary of full-time probation officers throughout the country was less than $2,000 a year. Today it is approximately $3,000 —a minimum under present standards for this work.

Adult Jurisdiction

Departing from the earlier laws, many of which limited the jurisdiction of the court to dealing with children only, the great majority of the states today give the juvenile court extensive jurisdiction to deal with adults who contribute to child delinquency or neglect or who commit offenses against children. Many of the courts today have become in name, as well as in fact, domestic relations as well as juvenile courts.

The first family court, as distinguished from a domestic relations court with limited adult jurisdiction, was created in 1914 in Hamilton County (Cincinnati), Ohio, as a division of the Court of Common Pleas. For the first time divorce and alimony cases as well as all cases under the juvenile court act were brought under one jurisdiction. Most of the work with children is delegated to a large probation staff. Judge Charles W. Hoffman has been a leader in the movement for the establishment of such courts. After 35 years he is still judge of the court which he developed. Similar family courts were subsequently established in six other large counties of Ohio, as well as in Portland, Oregon, and Omaha, Nebraska. Domestic relations divisions, with jurisdiction over family cases, but not including divorce, were provided in the juvenile and domestic relations courts established throughout the states of New Jersey and Virginia. We have many experiments in operation throughout the country, but no one plan as yet can be urged as a model for all states. But it is clear that the future developments will be increasingly in the direction of bringing together into one court, with specialized staff and procedure, all court problems relating to the child and the family. Children cannot be treated without reference to their family background; and families cannot be dealt with without regard to the protective care of the children.

The Federal Juvenile Offender

Although by 1938 nearly every state had juvenile court laws, no solution for separate, noncriminal treatment of delinquent children brought before the federal courts was reached until the passage of the Federal Juvenile Delinquency Act that year.

With the passage of the Federal Probation Law in 1925, children had been placed on probation in an increasing number of cases but only after grand jury indictment and criminal trial. In 1932 Congress passed the act authorizing the transfer of juvenile delinquents from the federal courts to the juvenile courts in their home communities provided those courts were willing and able to receive them. The statement of President Herbert Hoover in signing this bill is noteworthy:

This measure is an important step forward in that it sets an example through its recognition by the federal government of the principle that even the relatively small number of juveniles in the federal system should be handled on a modern scientific basis. It is also a recognition by the federal government of the juvenile court as the proper place for the handling of the cases of all the juveniles, and is an acceptance of the principle that juvenile offenders are the product of and the responsibility of their home community.

After the passage of this act it was found (and unfortunately it is still true) that in many areas juvenile courts are lacking or ill-equipped to deal with delinquent children. In 1937 approximately 2,500 children's cases were still being tried in federal courts. The federal courts do not have equity procedure, and full juvenile court procedure is impossible therein.

The Federal Juvenile Delinquency Act authorizing informal hearings for children under 18 and, unless they are placed on probation, their commitment to the custody of the Attorney General for placing in federal or local institutions for juvenile delinquents or in boarding homes, has been effective in many cases. However, it is not as satisfactory a solution as the treatment of children in their own communities under full protective procedures of a good juvenile court. With the further extension of juvenile courts on a state-wide basis, the need for federal handling of children's cases should be reduced to a minimum.

Coordination of the Court with Other Agencies

There are unsolved problems as well as great inconsistencies in the matter of the relationship of the juvenile court to other agencies. It is agreed that the court is only one of many agencies dealing with child problems, and that its distinctive function is to deal with cases needing authoritative treatment and the enforcement of the state's parental powers. But other cases, and as many as possible (including most of the dependent and some of the neglected and minor delinquency cases), may better be handled preventatively by public and private welfare agencies. The juvenile court is an integral part of every community program of services to children. It is an administrative treatment agency as well as a judicial agency. It is the duty of the juvenile court, both through the efforts of the judge and his trained staff, to cooperate with community organizations and to use community facilities to the fullest possible extent. It also should assist in developing and strengthening such organizations.

Objectives for Future Efforts

The establishment of the first juvenile court was one of the greatest advances in child welfare that has ever occurred. Like all reforms, it was developed by the pioneers before the general public had grasped its significance or was prepared to accept its implications. There are still too many who are not ready to do so today, and that is the main reason why we have not yet realized all the ideals of the founders. Experience in the past 50 years, and especially in the last 35 years during which the writer has been privileged to play an active part in the promotion of juvenile courts, would indicate that future efforts should be directed to the following objectives:

(1) *Exclusive jurisdiction for juvenile courts in all cases of children who need the authoritative treatment of the state.* The authority of the court to deal with all children under 18 who are delinquent—at least originally—should be established, if necessary through constitutional amendments.

(2) *Improvement of court staff.* A workable plan should be developed for removing not only the staff but also the judge from political pressures. Provision should be made for nominating qualified judges, with assurance of independence and continued tenure of office. Probation officers and other social and technical staff members should all be appointed under civil service or other effective merit systems. Standards and salaries for such work should be raised.

(3) *The services of juvenile courts should be available to all children, especially to those in rural areas.* Wherever feasible, efforts should be made to develop state-administered juvenile courts because of their many advantages in uniform procedure, improved staff and facilities, and complete state coverage. In all courts, state aid (financial and supervisory) should be sought for the extension and strengthening of juvenile court services.

(4) *More uniform extension of the powers of the court, and more use of its present powers, to deal with parents and other adults who contribute by acts or neglect to the delinquency of children.* Further experiments should be developed in the unified family court, dealing with all problems relating to the family and children under a socialized procedure, and with courts for adolescents and youth up to 21.

(5) *Juvenile courts should seek greater co-operation and co-ordination with other social agencies—public and private —with the schools, the police, and citizens' groups.* Competent agencies—such as specially equipped police juvenile aid bureaus, school adjustment services, child welfare agencies, both public and private —should be encouraged to handle as many cases as possible in the first place. Through adequate intake and adjustment services in the juvenile courts, all cases should receive the kind of treatment which their individual needs require.

(6) *The juvenile court, through its judge and entire staff, must participate in community movements for the development of co-ordinated agencies for child and family welfare and for the prevention of delinquency. It must seek to strengthen its services through interpretation of its vital work to the public.*

The Court and the Child[*]

By Gustavus Loevinger. Judge, District Court, St. Paul, Minnesota.

IT IS IDLE to begin this paper by repeating well-worn phrases about the reasons for establishing juvenile courts or what they try to do. If I did I might put myself in the position of the inquisitive young man who asked Luther Burbank one day, just to make conversation, what he was then working on. Burbank said

* Reprinted from *Focus*, Vol. 28, May, 1949, pp. 65–69 . . . 91. Used by permission.

he was trying to cross an eggplant with a milkweed. The skeptical young man exclaimed: "What in the name of heaven do you expect from that?" "Why, custard pie, of course," was Burbank's unsmiling answer. A good many people still expect something almost as spectacular from juvenile courts. They want the judge to take a delinquent, and by some legerdemain, turn him out a hybrid between a wisdom-loving half-adult and a virtue-loving half-child.

Probably every juvenile judge would like to divert the adolescent who seems to have so much initiative, energy, and persistence in the pursuit of deviltry, into socially more acceptable channels of action. And when he sees that the delinquent is obviously the product of a delinquent home or a delinquent environment, his inability to discipline the parent or to eliminate the communal "poison spot" makes him feel frustrated. His first impulse is to wish for power over those whom he considers responsible. It appears to me at least debatable whether he should have or should exercise such a power. It is not difficult to foresee that if, incident to a juvenile court hearing, the judge could convert it into a trial of parents or tavern-keepers or poolroom operators or dancehall attendants for contributing to the delinquency of a minor, the whole judicial atmosphere might be changed, and the practice and procedure would have to be altered. The hearing, instead of remaining an investigation, would frequently become an inquisition; instead of an impartial inquiry into the condition of the juvenile it might become a contested court trial with the judge as the accuser; instead of frankly admitting misconduct, the child, probably cautioned or coached, would admit nothing and involve no one; instead of getting confidence and cooperation from parents, relatives, and friends, one would be likely to find them on guard against being incriminated or incriminating anyone. While the lack of

power to punish criminally those who may be morally and even legally responsible for the delinquencies of the youth, has its disadvantages, it seems to me that the separation of juvenile court jurisdiction over the delinquent from adult court jurisdiction over the contributor to the delinquency, is on the whole more salutary than harmful in spite of the feeling of helplessness it leaves in the juvenile judge at times.

This, of course, is not saying that there should not be changes in the laws for the protection of juveniles; or in the laws for improvement of juvenile courts; nor that there should not be greatly increased facilities put into the hands of juvenile judges with which to make diagnoses or to administer treatment. These problems are not discussed because they are not the subject of this paper although they may be intimately connected with the administration of juvenile justice.

Problems of City and Country Judges

At this point it may be pertinent to refer to the two kinds of juvenile courts in this state. In the three large cities they are a division of the district court with district judges presiding. For brevity, I'll refer to these hereafter as "city judges." In the 84 other counties of the state the juvenile courts are a division of the probate courts with the county probate judges presiding. I'll refer to these hereafter as "country judges." Admittedly the city judges have probation officers, social welfare workers, and medical, psychological, and psychiatric services available, at least to some extent, while all these are almost entirely denied to the country judges.

It is questionable whether in the handling of the individual delinquent in court this handicap of the country judge is not offset to a considerable extent. For illustration, the St. Paul judge must hold anywhere from 10 to 50 delinquency hearings each week of the year. Probably most country judges do not hold as many as 50 hearings in an entire year. A report of the Youth Conservation Commission on delinquency states that for the period from January 1 to April 1, 1948, 413 offenders under eighteen years of age were chargeable to Ramsey county while 237 were chargeable against the 64 rural counties which made reports. It is clear that the country judges, with a few exceptions, have a relatively small number of delinquents to handle in a year.

For the most part, the people involved in a juvenile offense are not known personally to the city judge. It is not unreasonable to suppose that the opposite is true of the country judge in many cases. The amount of time a city judge can spend on a case is apt to be greatly limited. The country judge is, presumably, rarely under pressure to dispose of a case in a hurry so as to get through the day's work. The city judge must diagnose and prescribe on the reports and impressions of social workers and probation officers. The country judge, with his personal knowledge and contacts, may have first-hand information. The city judge rarely has time to do any personal follow-up work. The country judge may, if he chooses, and he very often does, handle his own probation and social work.

These differences indicate that the problems of city and country judges in some aspects are different. Let us refer again to probationary and psychiatric help. To furnish these services to country judges on a county basis would seemingly involve a tax burden which the citizen would not assume. Even on a regional basis it would be heavy. The dilemma of the country judge may be comparable to that of the young man in New York City who asked his clergyman whether he thought a young man earning only $25 a week could live a good Christian life, to which the clergyman replied, "Young man, that's all he can do." The country judge will be sure to have a good "staff." He'll be it. It is likely to be a long time before the judicial aids now necessaries to the city judges will cease to be anything but luxuries for the country judges. Perhaps in the not too distant future a local probation officer will be recognized as a necessity as much as a local sheriff; and a local psychiatrist as much as a local health officer. Perhaps the requirements of district, probate, and municipal courts can be pooled with schools and local public welfare agencies to make these services available.

Relationship of Judge and Delinquent

Almost completely within the control of any juvenile judge is his personal relation to the delinquent, the way in which he handles each case in his court. On this aspect of the work of the juvenile judge, it matters little whether the scene is laid in a metropolitan center or a rural village.

When a juvenile is brought into court, the judge from then on is a part, a very important part, of the "environment" of that juvenile. If the judge's attitude toward the delinquent is wrong, then the judge himself may even become an obstacle to straightening out the juvenile. Moreover, if the judge's attitude is wrong, the likelihood that his diagnosis and his prescribed treatment will be right is greatly reduced. It is difficult to exaggerate the importance of the judge's attitude toward his task in the juvenile court.

Attitude. It has become commonplace to say that the judge's attitude toward the delinquent must be "scientific." The phrase "scientific attitude" is at times overworked. But many judges still fall short of being scientific in their attitudes. It may be difficult to define a scientific attitude, but the judge who has it will want to know first of all what sort of a delinquent the child is. Is he an "objective delinquent" whom I would de-

scribe as one who is such as a result of
observable environmental influences to
which his conduct is directly traceable;
or is he a "subjective delinquent" whom
I would describe as one who is such as a
result of subjective or psychological impulses of which the delinquent is not
conscious and which may have been
acquired in infancy? The judge with a
scientific attitude will avoid a hasty or
superficial diagnosis. He will not confuse
the issue, what sort of a boy or girl is
this juvenile, with the issue, who is to
blame. He will not fail to follow up
every clue, exhaust every resource, accept help from every quarter and make
use of every available device. He will be
open-minded on every modern method
for judging personality and for predicting future conduct. He will try to
familiarize himself with advances in the
understanding of adolescent psychology
and of probationary practices. It is probably not necessary to say he will welcome any information obtainable from
school records, church records, IQ tests,
multi-phase personality tests, aptitude
tests, medical examinations, psychiatric
examinations, social case histories, local
welfare records on the family, and similar
aids whenever any of them are available.

I doubt whether any of you will say
this is too high a standard to set up for
juvenile judges. Nor is it too high from
the standpoint of the welfare of the
child. The judge should at least have as
much intellectual curiosity as the student
who wrote to the National Probation
and Parole Association recently and
asked: "Would it be possible for you to
send me material on crime in the home,
crime in the church, and crime in the
Sunday school?" Had she used the word
"delinquency" perhaps there might be
some material available or at least room
for an argument.

Technique. But even a right attitude
may be rendered ineffectual by the
failure to use an effective technique. It

is now almost universally recognized that
juvenile court hearings should not be
held in the conventional courtroom with
the judge sitting on a high bench, with
the witness in a witness chair, and with
the juvenile and his parents standing
in front of the bench as in criminal arraignments. It is quite generally recommended that the hearing should be held
in a place more like a committee room.
Preferably the only persons present
should be the judge, the boy or girl, the
parents and immediate relatives, and the
witnesses to be questioned. The probation officer, if there is one, is also usually
present. If some social worker knows the
family, he or she is often in the room.
Sometimes the family minister is at hand.
The public usually is excluded. Every
one is seated except that sometimes
witnesses stand while telling their story.
It may often happen that the judge may
send everyone out of the room while he
talks alone with the child or a parent.
Clerks, bailiffs, and courthouse attachés
generally should not be around. A policeman should ordinarily be limited in his
attendance to a case in which he is a
witness.

In general, the customary trappings of
court procedure should be avoided. It is
rarely necessary that witnesses be sworn.
The juvenile should not be "arraigned"
and asked, "Are you guilty or not
guilty?" The presence of lawyers ought
not to be encouraged. Cross-examina-
tion, as in a court trial, should not be
allowed. All the questioning of the child,
the parents and the witnesses should be
done by the judge. The questioning
should, for the most part at any rate,
be in an ordinary tone of voice to bring
out facts and not in an accusing tone,
inferring fault or blame.

Atmosphere. Perhaps at this point it
may be proper to say that one of the
first objectives of the hearing should be
to establish a friendly relationship between the judge and the delinquent or at
least to break down the hostility with

which the juvenile frequently comes into court. Unless and until this is done there is little hope of getting at the true nature of the child or of getting his cooperation in carrying out a curative program. Sometimes the judge himself is surprised by the direct friendliness of a child who has been prepared for the hearing by the probation officer. When I was presiding in a juvenile court, a probation officer was so successful in explaining to a boy the interest of the court, that young August came into the courtroom wearing a broad grin and with extended hand greeted me with "Hello, Gust." Not to be outdone by his cordiality, I shook hands with August and inquired, "Well, how are *you*, Gust?" By this time the probation officer was so affected that he had to stuff a handkerchief in his mouth and rush out to hide his convulsive laughter.

Even when, as sometimes happens, the boy is openly and brazenly defiant, the judge must not indulge himself in "righteous indignation." He should recognize that the youth may feel that everybody is against him, that he is about to be "railroaded" to a "reformatory," and that he "hasn't a chance." The judge must recognize that because of his age, his lack of experience, his immaturity, and perhaps either because of his unfortunate environment or because of psychological factors, the juvenile, whether adolescent or pre-adolescent, can hardly be blamed for lack of understanding, for fear, for rebelliousness, and for an impulse to shield himself by denials, evasions, equivocations, and even falsehoods. It is often tactful, before coming to the discussion of the incident which brought the boy into court, to begin a conversation about something which is to his credit. It may be the way his hair is combed, something he is wearing, or something meritorious he has earned or done. It may be something inconsequential as an inquiry as to what he had for breakfast. This unexpected informality

may disarm him and invite his confidence and good will. When he has almost forgotten where he is or why he is there, the judge may say quite casually: "Tell me, how did you happen to get into this mess?" and follow this up with questions in the tone of voice one would use in asking the price of bread rather than in the demanding, commanding, or condemning tone of authority. Paraphrasing an ancient author, "a soft question turneth away wrath." In this way, the judge can usually get enough of the facts so that other witnesses to the alleged offense will not be needed.

It may be that the offense charged is very serious or even revolting. Few extenuating circumstances may appear. Even so the judge, however strongly he may condemn the offense, must try to maintain a relationship with the boy, inspiring him with faith in the fairness and good will of the court. A hostile child can rarely be helped. A hostile judge can rarely be helpful. The boy should feel that the judge won't let him down if he tries to make good, that the judge is against wrongdoing but not against the wrongdoer.

Language. Reference has been made to the tone of voice. No less important is the language used. The judge may have to characterize a specific act as "dishonest" or "cowardly" or "unfair." On the other hand, he should avoid using the phraseology of the criminal code in dealing with a child. A child is not "arrested," he is "taken into custody"; he is not "imprisoned," he is "detained"; he is not "convicted," he is "adjudged"; he is not "sentenced," he is "committed"; he is not being "punished," he is being "disciplined" or trained. He is not sent to a "reformatory" or even a "reform school," but to a "school" or a "home" or a "camp." He is not charged with a "crime" or found "guilty" of a crime, but he is adjudged a delinquent, or it is determined that he committed a delinquent act. What he did should not be termed a "burglary" or a "theft" or an "assault" but should be described in ordinary language which implies something socially or morally wrong.

Even more important than to avoid description of the act of a child as a crime is to avoid pinning on him a criminal label or even a label implying a bad character. A judge might be pardoned if he told the delinquent that on October 1 he "stole" $10 from a neighbor, but the judge should not label the child a "thief." The judge under provocation might say, "I think you lied to me yesterday about this," but he should not say, "You are a liar." The judge might say, "In taking this money you betrayed your employer's confidence in you," but he should not characterize the boy generally as "untrustworthy."

There are sound legal, sound moral, and sound psychological reasons back of this emphasis on the language to be used by the judge. By statute the proceedings in a juvenile court are not criminal, and the finding that the child committed the offense charged is not a conviction of a crime. Morally it must be constantly kept in mind that society admits that the juvenile is not a free will agent who has deliberately chosen to violate the law. It recognizes that the acts, attitudes, and acquired characteristics of a child are the result in part of his home environment, and in part of his social influences to which he has been subjected, and that, as to these factors of his delinquency, he cannot be held responsible. So when the judge, in talking with a juvenile, instead of characterizing by some appropriate adjective the particular offense known to have been committed, generalizes by labeling the youth with a bad character trait or a vicious fixed habit, he may not only be doing the boy an injustice, but he may be defeating the whole purpose of the proceeding by antagonizing him and erecting a barrier between them. Here again, the importance of the judge's language

in a hearing must not be underestimated.

Diagnosis. Having determined that the child did the acts charged in the petition, it is important for the judge to determine, if he can, whether the boy is an "objective delinquent" or a "subjective delinquent." There is no infallible guide to a correct diagnosis. But if the judge recognizes that delinquencies may be caused on the one hand by deep-seated psychological maladjustments and on the other by observable environmental influences, he will be on the lookout for these differences, and he will be more and more able, with experience, to recognize some of the symptoms in each group.

Some judges not only treat the juvenile as though he were a diminutive adult but set up standards of behavior to which few well-adjusted adults could adhere. There are still some juvenile judges who seem to feel that, having given the delinquent a good "calling down" after the hearing, and told him how he must behave thereafter, they have discharged their duty to the child and the rest is up to him. A substantial number of judges would include the parents in the "calling down," and would assume that having told the parents their faults, the judge has no further responsibility. Unfortunately, these judges are rather unrealistic in their attitude toward adolescents and toward parents.

Most parents learn in the course of time that training an adolescent in the amenities of social intercourse and of an orderly home regimen is a task taking years of time and infinite patience. Somebody has said, "The first half of our lives is ruined by our parents and the second half by our children." This cynicism is offset by Mark Twain who said: "When I was a boy of fourteen, my father was so ignorant I could hardly stand to have the old man around. But when I got to be twenty-one, I was amazed to see how much he had learned in seven years."

The judge who expects immediate and permanent results following a "good talking to" given an immature, undisciplined, misguided, poorly oriented youngster who happens to be brought into juvenile court, has probably forgotten his own adolescent years. Judge Vincent Hollaren of Worthington puts it this way: "For a judge to engage in a mere bawling-out, and to then fling a set of rules at the youth and *dare* him to make good, borders on sadism."

Probation Conditions. All this adds up to the caution, don't be merely a "moralist." Don't expect to "convert" either the youngster or his parents by a sermon. And don't be a "perfectionist." Make the conditions of probation such that there is a reasonable probability that they can be carried out. If these terms are violated, as you may likely find that some of them will be, you may express your disapproval and disappointment, but don't treat the boy as a lost soul or an irresponsible outcast or an irretrievable derelict. Probably he is still not far from normal. Perhaps the boy who seems to make a perfect record simply didn't get caught. Take for instance smoking. It's a bad habit for the young. It should be discouraged. But abstinence from smoking as a condition of probation may be next to impossible to keep. Similarly, fixing an early hour to be at home every evening may simply invite violations. Separating two delinquents who have a bad influence on each other may be very desirable, but if their association is likely to be unpreventable, then something other than merely forbidding it must be thought up. Another not uncommon condition is to require the child to attend church regularly. This may have the opposite effect from what is intended. Compulsory church attendance may identify the church with a punitive institution. It may symbolize the coercion of outside force rather than inward consent. It may make the youth hate the church. The judge should have this possibility in mind in imposing religious sanctions as a part of the probationary terms.

This naturally leads to another suggestion. Many judges say to a child: "I'm giving you just one more chance"; "this is your last chance"; "if you don't make good now, it's just too bad." There undoubtedly are times when the patience of every one has been tried by a refractory youngster to the breaking point. What the judge might like to do is to take him to the nearest woodshed. But a verbal ultimatum, especially in the early part of the probationary period, is generally ill-advised and more likely to put the judge than the juvenile on the spot. The judge must either make good or suffer a setback in the opinion of the child, his parents, and his associates. A delinquent may require many "chances" and much encouragement before he "recovers" from his tendencies. Sometimes it is a matter of outgrowing them. This may take months or years. Take the type of "incorrigibility" involved in insolence and disobedience in the home. This may be a normal evolutionary process aggravated by parental misunderstanding of adolescent drives. But ultimatums won't, and perhaps shouldn't, cure it.

Commitment. How can the judge decide between commitment to an institution or probation? There is no fool-proof guide. A judge can only use his best judgment. In some cases he is driven to desperation by the repeated offenses of the delinquent on probation. The local setup may leave him no real discretion. The city judge may have an intermediate institution such as a county school for boys or girls, or the parents may provide psychiatric treatment in the home or disciplinary supervision in a private school. If the boy is before a country judge, a county school is not available, and if the parents are poor, a private school is usually out of the question. A commitment to a state school may then be inescapable, but it may still be wise to stay the execution of the order to see if the threat has any restraining effect.

Relationship of Judge and Parent

Nothing has been said about handling parents who appear to have contributed to the child's delinquency. The subject of parental responsibility and the retraining of parents for their tasks is too important and too involved for the brief treatment which the limits of this paper allow. Here again, it is at least doubtful whether a "tongue-lashing," as the reporters like to call it, does any good. Usually the child returns to the parental roof during or after probation or after an institutional period. Much of the effort of the judge, the probation officer, or the training school is lost unless the cooperation of the parents can be obtained, and cooperation is more likely to come with a friendly than a hostile attitude. Parent and child must both be worked with.

The practice of handling cases of doubtful or minor delinquencies informally is to be encouraged. It will happen that a child may be haled into court for something he considered a prank. Not every offense committed by an exuberant or excitement-seeking youth is proof of a delinquent disposition. Before a boy is found to be a delinquent, either a course of antisocial conduct or a clear case of antisocial attitude should be evident. In a fair number of cases a device sometimes used effectively is the postponement of an adjudication of delinquency after a petition has been filed. If the child makes good under supervision, the petition may later be dismissed. In some cases such a course will wean the youngster away from conduct and companions tending toward delinquency. Parents and children both will appreciate the kindly consideration and sympathetic understanding back of such treatment.

Conclusion

The work of a juvenile judge can be disappointing and depressing. It can also be rewarding. Inevitably situations will arise beyond judicial skill to help and beyond judicial wisdom to solve. Inevitably others will arise which might be handled more effectively if the judge had adequate funds or adequate facilities. But most cases will present problems and opportunities for service which, while they may tax the ingenuity and inventiveness of the judge, will yield to patient perseverance and to sympathetic treatment. In them he must find satisfaction for his often unrequited devotion and for uncompensable services beyond the call of duty.

"Justice" Versus "Individualized Treatment" in the Juvenile Court[*]

By David Bogen. Superintendent, Juvenile Hall, Los Angeles County.

THE STORY is told of a prisoner who was sentenced to be hanged and who when asked if he had anything to say replied, "Judge, this is certainly going to be a lesson to me!" Many people, nowadays, consider that not only hanging, but also the less violent types of punishment, are rather unsatisfactory as educational procedures. They contend that punishment per se is essentially wrong; that our

* Reprinted from *The Journal of Criminal Law and Criminology* (Northwestern University School of Law), Vol. XXXV, November–December, 1944, by David Bogen.

penal system is an outworn relic of the past, and that punishment of criminal offenders should be abandoned in favor of the more modern and scientific approach of individualized treatment.

Those who advocate individualized treatment for criminal offenders feel that the commission of a crime indicates some underlying problem in the life of the offender and that the thing to do is to study the individual and his environment and to correct the causal factors which resulted in his wrong doing. Two people might commit the same offense for entirely different reasons and it follows that the treatment prescribed for them should be different, even though the offense was the same. From this point of view the offense represents a symptom of underlying causal factors and the aim is to treat the causal factors rather than the symptom; the individual rather than the offense.

This doctrine is diametrically opposed to the basic principles of criminal justice upon which our criminal laws and penal practices are based. Our traditional conception of "Justice" calls for the equal treatment of all who commit a given offense. When in 1764 Beccaria expounded this principle in his famous essay on crime and punishment, it was hailed by intellectual leaders of the time as a great step forward from the injustices and abuses which then prevailed. Up to that time, the theory that criminals should be punished according to "the degree of criminal responsibility" prevailed. Penalties were not fixed for various types of offenses, but were largely left to the discretion of the judge. As a result it frequently turned out that men of wealth or station who committed grave crimes were leniently dealt with while poor miscreants without influence in the community were harshly punished for trivial offenses. Beccaria held that punishment should be based upon the seriousness of the offense, regardless of who committed it, and that

the punishment should be prompt, sure, and as lenient as possible consistent with the protection of the community.

Criminal courts have in general adhered to the fundamental principle of punishment based upon the offense, and sentences have, for the most part, been determined by criminal statute fixing the penalties for particular types of offenses. In the juvenile court, however, these statutory penalties do not apply, and the doctrine of individualized treatment has gained widespread influence. Leading authorities in the field of juvenile delinquency urge that juvenile offenders be "treated" rather than punished and that such teatment be based upon the needs of the individual and not dictated by the offense.

Two assumptions are tacitly implied in this point of view. The first is that modern methods in the diagnosis and treatment of delinquency are sufficiently effective to bring about a successful adjustment in all or most of the cases which come before the juvenile court. The second assumption is that by adjusting the individual the welfare of the community will be adequately protected. Actual experience with cases of juvenile delinquency is apt to throw some doubt upon these assumptions.

For example, John M., a fourteen year old boy, is arrested for burglary. Thorough study of the case, including psychiatric examination, reveals various personal and environmental factors affecting the boy's behavior and on the basis of individualized treatment it is decided to allow the boy to remain at home under supervision of the probation officer. In so doing, the court has no assurance that this boy will not commit further lawless acts. Thus it happens that John is again arrested for burglary. This time, it may still appear that the best plan for re-adjusting the boy and overcoming his delinquent tendencies is to continue to work with him in his own home. The citizens whose homes have been burglarized may object to such a plan, but the program of individualized treatment calls for concentration upon the welfare and development of the boy and theoretically should not be affected by the degree to which the rights of others have been injured, nor by the attitudes of the community. Thus a court which seeks to follow the doctrine of individualized treatment may continue to treat a case in the community in spite of two or three violations of probation before resorting to placement away from home.

Another boy, Richard K., arrested for a petty theft, may, on the basis of individual study, appear to require institutional care. In this case placement in a correctional type of school for a period of a year might logically be prescribed, even though the boy has not committed a very serious offense. But here again, the court cannot be certain that Richard would not have refrained from further offenses if left at home on probation, nor that his conduct will improve after the period of training in an institution.

There is a further consideration which cannot be ignored. If commitments are made solely upon the basis of individualized treatment and without reference to the gravity of the misconduct which brought the child before the court, the public can have no assurance that partiality, favoritism, personal prejudice, or errors of judgment have not entered into the decision. Moreover, even in those cases where the treatment has proven successful in so far as the individual is concerned, it may be that the effect upon the community is not satisfactory. John M., for example, might have influenced other boys to join him in delinquent conduct when he violated probation, even if he eventually learned to obey the law himself. If he responded to the treatment plan at once, and did not commit any further offenses, the fact that he remained in the community after committing a burglary might still

prove undesirable. Other boys in his school and in the neighborhood would learn about the situation and the fact that a boy arrested for burglary was apparently not subject to any penalty for his offense might encourage others to look upon such acts as more of a prank than a dangerous violation of law.

Without entering into the question as to the effectiveness of deterrence and exemplary punishment, however, it would seem that the prescribing of any treatment so drastic as removing a child from his home and parents requires some safeguard against partiality or error. Existing techniques and facilities for diagnosing and treating delinquency have not proven sufficiently accurate or effective to alone provide a sufficient basis for such placements. Thus we find that in practice the more severe types of treatment are resorted to only in cases where the child has committed an offense sufficient to justify such a serious move. In other words, the juvenile court theoretically renounces the idea of dealing with the child on the basis of the offense but yet turns to the essential principle of "justice" when it comes to an important decision.

The interplay of the two conflicting doctrines, "individualized treatment" and "justice," may affect the juvenile court work in several ways. Some juvenile courts seek to "mete out justice" without any attempt to utilize the new techniques and principles of individualization. Others may actually adjudicate cases on the basis of the offense and merely rationalize their orders to fit the terminology and ideology of "individualized treatment." Still others may try to disregard the aspect of "justice" and handle cases as much as possible on a strictly individualized basis. As pointed out above, the latter course cannot be fully realized and too often results in a vacillating and inconsistent policy.

It is the opinion of the writer, that a practicable and effective policy for the juvenile court must take into account the merits and limitations of both of these contrasting theories. "Justice" cannot be safely disregarded, nor should the importance of individualization be under-estimated. There is a place for both in dealing with juvenile delinquents. If we substitute the word "treatment" for "punishment" in the doctrine of Beccaria and remember that he insisted upon the maximum of leniency consistent with public safety, we may still find it an equitable and flexible guide for juvenile court policy.

Youths who commit violent and serious offenses must in fairness to the community be taken into custody and segregated under treatment and observation until it is reasonably safe to release them. Others who commit less dangerous offenses but persist in such conduct, must likewise be cared for in a segregated environment. The point at which such segregation becomes necessary will depend largely upon the policy of the court, but must, in general, be determined by the overt conduct of the subject which is, after all, the ultimate test of his adjustment in so far as delinquency is concerned. This means that there is

an objective basis for segregating the child; a basis that is essentially immune to the suspicions of partiality or prejudice, and which is generally acceptable to the community.

At the same time there remains considerable scope for individualization. Delinquents who do not require segregation (first offenders, minor offenders, etc.) and who are eligible to remain in the community can be treated in whatever manner seems best adapted for the individual case. But individualized treatment should not end there. Within the institution, segregated delinquents need not be treated uniformly. There too, treatment may be oriented about the individual rather than the offense which caused him to be segregated.

What is needed then, is not the complete rejection of "justice" which has been so eloquently demanded by those who feel that the offense should not in the least control the disposition of juvenile court cases, but rather an enlightened "justice" which will protect the rights of the community and yet leave scope for modern individualized treatment within the limits which the behavior of the individual permits.

Helpful Practices in Juvenile Court Hearings*

By Walter H. Beckham. Judge, Juvenile and Domestic Relations Court, Miami, Florida.

BECAUSE it has been my rare privilege to preside over a busy juvenile court for over 15 years without a single appeal from any of my rulings involving delinquent children having been made, it is suggested that I might make some appropriate observations on helpful techniques in such cases. I feel that whatever success I may have had as a juvenile court judge may be ascribed in large

measure to "humanizing" my court procedure, and recognizing emotional and psychological factors in dealing with parents and children.

Before becoming a juvenile court judge I practiced law for several years but, like most lawyers, had very little experience with juvenile court practice. Consequently, when I became judge of a juvenile court my first thought was

* Reprinted from *Federal Probation,* Vol. 13, June, 1949, pp. 10–14. Used by permission of author and publication.

to conduct the court so as to make it "look" and "act" like other "regular" courts. I soon learned, however, that juvenile courts, or hearings involving juveniles, are and should be entirely different in many ways if best results are to be obtained. Such a court is, in fact, more a court of human relations than a court of law. Recognition of this by the judge, even in little things, often may determine the difference between success or failure in a given case, as measured by final results with the juvenile and parents involved.

The Place for Hearings

Let us start with the place of hearing. It should be the judge's chambers and not a public courtroom in which large groups of disinterested people and curiosity seekers may sit and hear the proceedings. The old-fashioned "police court" type of hearing should be abolished in hearings involving juveniles. The judge's chambers should be clean, bright, and cheerful, with inspiring pictures on the walls depicting happy family and child life. The furniture should be clean, comfortable, and in good condition, with an easy chair or two, especially for mothers with young babies. The judge's desk should be on the floor level with other chairs in the room, which should be arranged in a semicircle, like a round table conference, with the probation officer sitting at one end of the judge's desk and facing the judge, the child and parents, and the witnesses. The child and the parents should be seated together directly in front of the judge. Other properly interested parties and witnesses should be seated farther back in the room. If there is a large group of witnesses, they should be seated in another room and called in as needed. No smoking should be allowed and everything should be quiet, neat, and orderly. Parties involved in other cases should remain outside the judge's chambers, in the main courtroom,

or in some comfortable, quiet reception room, to be called into the judge's chambers as a group only when the case in which they are interested is to be heard.

The Voice and Attitude

A gentle, pleasant voice and friendly demeanor on the part of the judge and probation officer are highly important. It helps if the judge will nod and smile pleasantly at the parties in the case as they come into the room to be heard. Whenever possible, the court should avoid having officers in uniform and carrying pistols or "billies." The judge, or his probation officer, should take an interest in seeing that everyone is comfortably seated and quiet before the "hearing" (instead of "trial") begins. Everything should be done to avoid formality and to suggest ease and friendliness among those present. This allays the fears of parents and children, many of whom are facing a judge or court for the first time and usually are upset and worried. The law in some states does not require that the witness be placed under oath, or that the record be stenographically reported. This practice should be encouraged. It should be understood that a juvenile court proceeding is not a trial of anyone on criminal charge but, according to the laws of most states, is an "investigation" into the conduct of a young citizen to determine not whether punishment should be inflicted, but what action or program should be adopted for the welfare of the child.

Terms, Pleadings, and Procedure

Official papers in the case, such as the petition, complaint, or affidavit, as far as is legally possible should avoid the use of criminal court terminology, or language that appears in criminal court indictments or informations, but should recite in simple narrative form what has taken place and also show the actual conduct of the juvenile. In keeping with this, the case should be entitled "In Re: Johnnie Jones" instead of "*State of* —— v. *Johnnie Jones*," unless actually otherwise required by law. In conducting hearings, all parties should remain seated. The probation officer should open the case by reading the complaint, or petition, which describes in a few clear statements the case involving the juvenile, and then supplement the written pleading by his own personal statement of further knowledge of the facts gained from visits to the child's home, school, and community, usually known as the social background report or social investigation. This report also should include the previous court record of the juvenile. (In some jurisdictions the probation officer is required to present the complaint at the court hearing.)

In conducting hearings, if there is an official present from another court, or another probation officer present for the purpose of giving testimony, it is good practice to receive their testimony first and allow them to be excused in order that they may attend other duties. They will appreciate the promptness in which they were called, and in the future will be glad to co-operate without having to be legally summoned. Judges who give no thought to the element of time, and unnecessarily require witnesses to remain in attendance through lengthy hearings, may never expect to get their full co-operation or voluntary attendance again. Witnesses should be allowed to remain seated in the room and not called up to sit on the "witness stand."

After the probation officer has made his statement, he should present to the court those persons who are to give testimony in the case and their testimony should be received informally in the form of a general or narrative statement, under the friendly guidance of the judge who should do most of the interrogating. By following such procedure the judge may avoid a lot of technical details which may not be relevant to the case. If the judge will question witnesses fully in the beginning, indicating the line of testimony in which he is interested, usually any lawyer in the case will not have many questions to ask when the judge has finished. This will save the time of both the court and the lawyer.

After the probation officer has finished presenting his side of the case, the judge with a friendly smile and sympathetic voice should then ask the juvenile to tell his side of the story. If the juvenile is reluctant to talk, or is slow in responding, the judge, in order to establish friendly relations, should make a few typical inquiries about other things rather than the case before the court, such as what hobbies the boy is interested in, what he does at home, "does he have a dog," and similar questions. If the juvenile continues to be hesitant or defiant, the judge should simply and patiently explain that it is a welfare proceeding and not a criminal court, and that the purpose is to help and not punish.

Testimony

At the beginning, it is always helpful for the judge to find some opportunity to say something nice or complimentary about the juvenile, even commenting on a fine physical appearance, if nothing else. This presents an unanticipated approach to the juvenile who is expecting to be "bawled out." But when he finds the judge is saying something nice about him he immediately feels that "here is a judge who knows something" and is fair.

After the juvenile has made his statement, the parents should be asked for theirs. The judge should then ask the interested parties in the room for any statement or comment they wish to make from where they are sitting without being called up to a "witness stand." In general, it is found to be a good policy to let those who come to the hearing tell their story without too many interruptions, and without too many objections unless, of course, their remarks should go beyond all reasonable bounds. This policy helps those who come to the court "unlettered in the law" to go away feeling satisfied that they "had their say" and that the hearing was fair, and also usually means co-operation with the order of the court in the future.

Where circumstances warrant, the judge should hold a conference with the juvenile alone. "Grilling" the child on the witness stand should be discouraged. A child's testimony about his parents' conduct should be given in private. Lawyers usually will agree that the child's testimony should be taken by the judge alone.

If testimony is likely to be derogatory to the character of the parents, the child involved should be excused from the room. The court should never tear down the respect, love, and faith a child may have in his own parents, regardless of their behavior or misconduct. I have known judges to ignore this rule and allow all of the unpleasant facts of a mother or father's misconduct to be detailed in the presence of an unsuspecting and cringing child, including the unfortunate practice of letting a child know for the first time that he is an adopted child.

Inasmuch as there is no prosecution for criminals involved, and the niceties of proof which might be required in a criminal case are not required in a juvenile court, testimony should bring out the facts on a general basis rather than developing all the unsavory details. Filthy, vulgar, or obscene language actually used should, as a general rule, not be permitted, but the witness instead should be allowed merely to state in general terms the character of the language used, such as "obscenity," "profanity," "filthy." This same practice likewise should be used in commenting on sex offenses, and the particular occurrence should be described in general language —such as "improper sex relations," "forced immoral relations," or "having improper sexual intercourse"—rather than detailing all of the sexual acts which took place. Discussion of sex offenses always should be in refined language, and not in the language of the street. The showing of a child to be delinquent is merely painting a general picture of misconduct, or misbehavior, and does not have to conform to technical rules or proof as is required in specific criminal cases. Requiring this better type of language in the taking of testimony keeps a hearing on a higher plane, avoids embarrassment, and accomplishes the same purpose.

Such names as "kid" and "brat," or other opprobrious terms, never should be used in describing children, either in pleadings or in the testimony, but the child always should be addressed by his given name and the parents should be addressed as "mother" or "father." When the judge speaks to the parents, it is well for him to say: "Mother, do you have anything to say?" or "Father, do you have a statement you wish to make?" Children know their parents by such names and it immediately creates a sense of responsibility and affection in the minds of the parents and children. The judge should insist upon respectful language throughout the hearing.

Relations with Juvenile and Parent

From the start of the hearing the judge should play for the good will and co-operation of all the participants, especially the juvenile and his parents. This will help to obtain their approval of the court's final decision. Where possible, the judge should be liberal with praise and commendation and later should explain to the parents and the juvenile their law violations, responsibilities, and obligations. I find that "preaching" to parents and children about being good and obeying the law helps, but threats of jail and punishment fail to accomplish any good purpose. On the other hand, presenting the law as a "friend," or suggesting that the juvenile is a "partner" in his government and that he should help support it by not breaking the law, has good results. The use of "threats" of imprisonment for long terms and ending up as a criminal is not as effective as pointing out to the juvenile the value of good character and becoming successful in the world as a good citizen. The juvenile should be taught to be good because it is right and fair to the other fellow to be good, rather than being good because of being afraid to be bad. Mention of the family's church relations and encouraging him to be loyal to his religious belief often helps.

Before the court renders a decision, the probation officer and parents should be given an opportunity to make a recommendation, or offer a suitable plan for disposing of the case.

In rendering the decision, the judge should carefully and patiently explain to the juvenile what the court intends to do and why the court believes it is the best thing to do. He also should ask permission of the parents to enter the order he has in mind. Even though they do not have to be consulted, and they do not at first agree, they appreciate this inquiry from the judge and leave the court more favorably impressed with the sincerity and practicability of the judge's decision. I have had many parents and juveniles come to me at the close of a case and thank me for the disposition given—even though it may involve sending the boy or girl to a state home or school—simply because I had properly paved the way for them to accept the decision as being for the best interests of the juvenile. The judge who "snaps out" a hasty, vague order, and rapidly calls "next case," loses an opportunity.

Before announcing his decision, it is a good policy for the judge also to indicate to the juvenile and the parents what the court can do of a more serious nature; then, when the court does something considered by the family and the child to be less embarrassing or serious, the decision will be accepted promptly as a fair one, and as mild in comparison with what could have been done.

In committing to institutions or foster homes, the court should carefully explain where the place is, what kind of an institution or home it is, the visiting hours, and other helpful details. Presenting the pleasant features and opportunities of the institution to which the child is committed allays the fears of the parents that the child is being sent to some "terrible" penal institution. Commitments, of course, should be explained as being made for the improvement of the child, instead of for punishment. The better practice, if it can be carried out legally, is to make such commitments for indefinite duration, explaining to the juvenile and to the parents that the release from the institution will be made just as soon as the character and conduct of the child has improved satisfactorily and a report and recommendation for his release have been received.

Relations with Attorneys and the Public

In most juvenile proceedings lawyers are not required and the majority of cases are heard without them. Parents very properly may be told that it is not necessary to have a lawyer, but that they are welcome to employ one if they so desire. If a lawyer is engaged he should always be welcome and treated with the utmost courtesy. It should be remembered that in most cases lawyers usually have had very little experience in juvenile cases, and are likely to apply criminal court tests in the admission of evidence and strict constitutional rights. Within limits, the judge should allow lawyers to make a good showing for their clients, and then patiently explain to the attorney that juvenile court procedure is by law somewhat different than criminal court procedure. If the judge will deal tactfully with the attorney, even complimenting him on his work in the presence of his clients, the lawyer eventually will accept the juvenile court approach and will assist the judge in developing a welfare program for the juvenile. Some courts make the mistake of resenting the appearance of lawyers in cases, are inclined to believe they are trouble makers and, because of the multitude of questions they desire to ask, consider them as wasters of time. Some probation officers are inclined to give lawyers the impression they are not wanted in court. This is a great error. If lawyers are friends of the court and the probation officers, the court will experience considerably less trouble, will have fewer appeals, and will obtain better results on procuring the co-operation of the parents. Lawyers are usually men of family, with children of their own, and of high ideals, and if the welfare and protection of the child are emphasized by the judge, they usually will take his lead and can be most helpful to the court in developing a proper disposition of the case. Even if the court decides against the lawyer's contentions, it is well for the court to compliment the lawyer by stating that the case was well presented, that the lawyer did everything he could for the child and the parents, and that the court regrets that it cannot follow entirely the lawyer's recommendation. This practice creates a most appreciative and friendly feeling on the part of the attorney toward the court and will pay great dividends in future relations.

A helpful technique in dealing with the public is to try to operate the court for the convenience of the juveniles, parents, and witnesses rather than for the convenience of the judge. For instance, on taking office, I changed the time for hearing from morning hours to afternoon hours, wherever possible, in order to permit parents and children to come to court without too much interference with the household duties of the mother, and the child's school attendance. I found this was highly appreciated.

Important witnesses present should be called on first and allowed to leave. If possible, the court should receive the testimony of the outside witnesses at the beginning of the case and then inform them that they need not stay if they have other responsibilities. In following this procedure witnesses usually leave without being irritated by a long wait.

Fingerprinting of children for registration with law-enforcement agencies and publicizing the case in newspaper stories generally should not be done. Newspaper publicity will be embarrassing in future life, especially if the child makes good. Parents should be informed that every effort will be made by the court to avoid publicity. They, in turn, will have more faith in the court as a welfare agency and friend.

Probation

As previously pointed out, it is well for the court to lead up to the decision to place the child on probation by reciting the much more serious dispositions which could be made, such as commitment to an institution. Placing the child on probation then seems to be "giving him a break." The judge should explain to the child in detail what being on probation means, and the requirements expected of him. It is best to have probationers report on Saturday morning, or at a time not in conflict with school or outside jobs.

Reporting on probation should not consist of merely coming in and signing a card, but should be an occasion for the juvenile to discuss his activities and school, home, and community behavior during the past week. Failure to report on probation should be promptly followed up by a visit to the home or a telephone call to the parents. Big brothers and other well-meaning citizens who are interested in children and wish to help the court may be invited to sit in with the probation officer on the day children report and assist the officer in counseling with them.

When children are to be released from probation there should be something like a small "graduation" ceremony. A parent should be present. The officer should bring the child and parent before the court with a report and recommendation for his release from probation. The officer should praise the child for completion of his probation, and the judge should congratulate him, and the parents as well, and impress upon them the seriousness of the child's getting into trouble again. The judge should encourage the child to preserve the good record made on probation, express the hope that he will continue to do well, and invite him and the parents to come back to the court for any further assistance they might need. The child and parents usually will be very thankful to the court and will shake hands with the judge and express appreciation to the judge and the officer for their help and understanding.

When there is a large group on probation, it often is helpful to have all report at a given hour at which time some outstanding citizen or official on law observance may talk to them on good character and good conduct. Parents also may be invited and usually will be glad to come. A series of talks may be arranged prior to release from probation. At the conclusion of the series the "graduation" ceremony may take place.

Conclusion

A juvenile court judge should be active in all community and civic affairs involving child welfare and activities related to the work of his court. He should be interested in the field of prevention and should encourage the establishment of those community facilities which will help to prevent delinquency and make the community a better place in which to live and rear children. Some courts find it helpful to organize a Juvenile Council similar to Parent-Teachers Associations for public schools. Such a council should have representation from all groups, including churches of all faiths, and should be entirely nonpolitical and nonpartisan. Its purpose would be to furnish a united community to assist the juvenile court in developing new laws, new facilities, and worth-while activities in the field of prevention and parental education.

Although the juvenile court judge should not permit the publication of names and pictures of parents and children appearing in his court, the judge may well use all available publicity channels to interpret and promote the work of the court and to suggest needed community activities and facilities. The use of an occasional "human interest story" of a unique nature is regarded as legitimate and proper provided all names and identifying data of the child and the family are deleted or changed.

In my opinion, the greatest qualification a juvenile court judge can have is a genuine love of people. He must have a real interest in their problems, and an understanding and sympathetic heart.

If I Were a Judge*

~~~~~~

By Charles H. Boswell. Chief Probation Officer, Juvenile Court of Marion County, Indianapolis.

ROSCOE POUND, Dean Emeritus of Harvard Law School, made the statement that "It seems to me significant that the two outstanding achievements of American criminal justice—the juvenile court and probation—have to do primarily with *preventive justice*." The work and interest of judges, particularly juvenile court judges, have made these two achievements possible. Without the help of the judiciary the juvenile court movement never would have succeeded. As it is, corrective justice is fast becoming a reality in most communities. Judges have set as their goal a dynamic justice for youth which concerns itself with the correction and prevention of delinquency rather than a system which remains static and inoperative until youth falls within the machinery of criminal law.

During recent years my experience in the correctional field has been in the probation department of a juvenile court. Thus, as my ideas are expressed on the subject of this article, it will be well to remember that I also know, by being a personal witness, that in most large cities the juvenile court judge is the most harrassed of all judges. He is subjected to great pressures by law-enforcement officers, politicians, complaining neighbors, distressed parents, and self-styled authorities in the correctional field. His telephone rings day and night as people call upon him to serve the community at all hours. In practically all communities, he is underpaid and seldom can look forward to even a modest retirement pension plan.

The quarters assigned to his court are usually dark, dreary, dilapidated quarters. The job of the juvenile court judge is believed by many to be the most difficult and vexing as well as the most important of all judgeships. With these thoughts I shall consider mainly those practices which hinder further development of the juvenile court movement and which create problems for the court's staff. Probation officers have told me, when I have discussed the subject matter of this article with them, that many of the contemplated recommendations would be applicable to other courts. Judges are the last group of people who would want to rest on their laurels; rather they are individuals who want to improve their performances. For that reason I was happy to accept the assignment of writing this article.

Operation of the Court

If I were a judge, my guiding principle would be that the court be operated for the convenience of juveniles, parents, witnesses, and attorneys rather than for the convenience of the judge. Probation officers' chief complaint about judges is that they do not start court on time. It is the duty of a court to assist its clients in the solution of their problems and not to add to the burdens of the distressed people the court is called upon to serve. However, it is far too common for clients, attorneys, witnesses, and probation officers to be forced to spend 2 or more hours waiting in the courtroom for a case to be called. In a midwestern

* Reprinted from *Federal Probation*, Vol. XV, March, 1951, pp. 26–30. Used by permission of author and publication.

city recently a mother of nine children wept as she explained to her probation officer that while waiting for the case of her delinquent son to be called she was worried about what three of her younger children would do for lunch since she would be unable to return home by noon. The case of her 15-year-old son had been scheduled for 9:30, and she had been told that the hearing would not last more than an hour. The hearing judge arrived in court at 10:45 instead of at 9:00, which was the usual starting time for court sessions. After arriving, the judge found it more important to visit for almost a half hour with a visiting politician prior to taking the bench. The distressed mother was so upset over the lateness of the hour that she was unable to concentrate on the proceedings. An immigrant whose understanding of the English language was not good, she needed to have a hearing under almost ideal conditions in order to benefit by it.

Often court hearings fail to serve their purpose when clients, other interested parties, and attorneys have been upset by long, unnecessary delays. In the correctional process as well as in business our services are more effective if we render them with promptness and consideration for the needs of others. Time is an important asset for all people, and it is wrong for any judge to waste it needlessly. One attorney, after waiting for more than an hour for a juvenile court referee who was obviously late arriving at court, remarked: "This is just plain bad manners for the referee to keep people waiting. It is worse than keeping guests waiting who have been invited to his home."

Approach of the Judge

If I were serving as a judge of a juvenile court, once a hearing begins I would attempt to convey the impression that I was a friendly, interested, and sincere person. Everything possible would be done to avoid formality and to make the interested parties realize that they were among friends. Often this can be accomplished if the judge will smile and greet the interested parties in a pleasant manner. This form of greeting will make both parents and children less fearful and more willing to express themselves freely in the court hearing. Throughout the hearing particular care should be exercised that anything which smacks of criminal court procedures be avoided; for example, the word "hearing" rather than "trial" should always be used in a juvenile court. Furthermore, legal terms which are confusing to children and their parents should be eliminated, and all aspects of the hearing should be explained in simple, clear, and concise language.

As a judge, I always would keep in mind the element of time during the hearing and would not require witnesses to remain in attendance through lengthy proceedings when it was unnecessary. By being considerate of all parties the court will be in a much better position to gain their full cooperation and voluntary attendance in the future. The wisdom of calling professional people, such as medical authorities, as soon as possible is apparent. By following this procedure, the court impresses witnesses by these personal considerations and they are spared the inconvenience of being away from their business or profession for a long period of time.

"Don't's" for Judges

When I discussed this article with probation officers attending the Indiana Probation and Parole Association's annual meeting held in May, 1950, one chief probation officer suggested that it might be helpful if I listed some important "don't's" for judges. Judges understand the importance of "don't's" when discussing certain forms of behavior with juveniles and adults and this probation officer explained that surely judges would understand a list of "don't's" from their friendly and interested critics. This proposal has merit in that it is a simple and clear way of letting judges know what probation officers are thinking.

No Politics. My first "don't" to judges would be: Don't play politics in court! Juvenile court judges, to my knowledge, seldom respond to political pressure exerted to keep a child or an adult from a correctional institution. However, strong, narrow, partisan politics often raises its ugly head when appointments to the professional staff of the court are being considered. In Indiana unreasonable partisan politics have really been the curse of many courts employing probation officers. A recent penal survey made by the National Probation and Parole Association stated:

In most counties visited, the probation officers said frankly that their positions were political and that they expect to be turned out of office when a judge of the opposite political party comes in. Some of the judges also stated frankly that they choose their probation officers for political reasons. A judge in one of the larger counties says that since he is an elective official he must appoint probation officers who control votes. In other counties where the judges have not taken this position so frankly, the probation officers nevertheless have admitted that their appointments were political. This prostitution of probation to the uses of party politics has been one of the most, perhaps the most serious obstacle to the improvement of probation service in Indiana.

Judges should consider carefully one of the late Chief Justice Charles Evans Hughes' last public utterances when he stated, speaking of appointing probation officers: "There is no room here for mere place hunters or political derelicts." Playing politics with the welfare of children and their families is the worst kind of practice which a court could follow.

Judges throughout the country will be interested in knowing what another judge has to say on this subject. In his paper entitled, "Speaking as One Judge to Another," Judge Paul W. Alexander explained that there was a way out:

But are we forever doomed to endure the curse of politics in the juvenile court? Isn't there somebody, somewhere who can do something about it? Yes, there is. And we don't have to look outside the courts! It's the judge himself! And I don't mean simply by his raising his voice and inveighing against the iniquities of the machinery in whose cogs he appears to be so inexorably caught.

There are case histories to show that it is still possible for a lawyer to be elected to the juvenile court without having his hands tied by political obligations to reward the faithful and in spite of positive campaign promises to make his professional appointments strictly on the merit basis regardless of party affiliation, creed or residence. (I have learned that one of the unpardonable political sins is to employ a nonresident. The way to lick that is to bring in such good ones that their popularity offsets the job hunter's wrath.) And there are case histories to show that a judge can be re-elected in spite of his refusal to reward the faithful (who probably thought he was just kidding and couldn't possibly have meant what he said) and in spite of his having distributed his patronage strictly on the merit basis. In short, there are case histories to bear out the truth of the old maxim that "After all, the best politics is a good job well done."

No Derogatory Testimony. The second "don't" involves a practice in some courts which is most disturbing to anyone who has ever witnessed it. This matter involves permitting children to air testimony which is derogatory to the character of the parents or permitting children to be present when parents are being told of their shortcomings in candid terms by the court. Therefore, it is important to the success of any court not to participate in a practice which may weaken the confidence, love, and faith a child may have in his parents, even though those parents may have been guilty of gross neglect. Nothing can be more cruel for children than to require them to listen to a detailed description of their parents' failings.

No Hostility. Do not respond to a hostile child with hostility would be my third "don't" if I were a judge. Children are sometimes brazenly defiant at the court hearing, but it is never wise for a judge to become infected by the anger or belligerence of a juvenile. The understanding judge realizes that this hostility is more often than not generated by fear and frustration. Under the best of circumstances it is difficult to help a hostile child, and we all know that a hostile judge can rarely be helpful. It is desirable for a juvenile to feel that the judge will not let him down if he does succeed in making good and that while the judge is against wrongdoing, he is not against the wrongdoer. Unfortunately all judges do not realize that when a juvenile is brought in for a court hearing the judge becomes a very important part of the environment of the juvenile. It is truly tragic when the attitude of the judge toward the delinquent fails to show understanding, for then the judge becomes an obstacle to the rehabilitation of the juvenile offender. There is little chance, when the judge's attitude is improper, for the court to prescribe the correct plan of treatment. It is virtually impossible to exaggerate the importance of the judge's attitude toward his task in any court.

No Sermons. Another important "don't"—don't rely on a mere scolding or "bawling out" to accomplish much with an immature, misdirected, and unhappy youngster who is brought before you in court. Any judge who depends on lecturing to accomplish the results for which juvenile courts were established is defeated before he starts. It is unreasonable to expect to reform parents or change youngsters by a sermon. While making an address in Indianapolis recently, Judge Gustav L. Schramm of the Allegheny County Juvenile Court in Pittsburgh stated that "Many children appearing before me in juvenile court have been given 'hell' by experts without results prior to their referral to court. For that reason it seems futile to me to pursue the same course of action."

In his article, "Helpful Practices in Juvenile Court Hearings," Judge Walter H. Beckham describes the positive approaches which a judge can make in assisting the children and parents who appear before him. The following paragraph from Judge Beckham's article gives us a significant clue to follow in our efforts to establish an effective juvenile court program:

Before becoming a juvenile court judge I practiced law for several years but, like most lawyers, had very little experience with juvenile court practice. Consequently, when I became judge of a juvenile court my first thought was to conduct the court so as to make it "look" and "act" like other "regular" courts. I soon learned, however, that juvenile courts, or hearings involving juveniles, are and should be entirely different in many ways if best results are to be obtained. Such a court is, in fact, more a court of human relations than a court of law. Recognition of this by the judge, even in little things, often may determine the difference between success or failure in a given case, as measured by final results with the juvenile and parents involved.

No Unreasonable Probation Conditions. This leads us to our fifth "don't." Don't demand that either youngsters or adults meet unreasonable probation conditions. Any judge who believes that delinquent children in their middle and late 'teens should remain in their homes after dark has forgotten his own adolescent years. Requiring youngsters to be home early every evening is only extending an invitation to youngsters to violate their probation conditions. It is also unrealistic to expect to separate two boys who live next door to each other or to expect a 17-year-old boy to give up smoking when he has had the habit for over 2 years. The condition of requiring youngsters to attend church is also one frowned upon by probation officers. This kind of requirement tends to associate the church with a punitive institution. Of course, we all want youngsters to have religious experiences, but compulsory church attendance is not the way to achieve that goal. In fact, it is more likely to turn the youngster away from church than it is to get him to seek the aid of church leaders of his own volition. Probation conditions can be made positive and reasonable in nature. Casework services always will be more successful if the conditions are kept at a minimum.

No Threats. In many courts one finds trained, experienced, and intelligent probation officers who make thorough studies prior to the submission of reports to their judges. For that reason it is highly desirable that judges *do not* fail to utilize to the fullest extent the information which their probation officer has acquired about a given case. Most progressive juvenile courts now favor a prehearing conference between the judge and the probation officer before juvenile cases are heard. This is the best way of insuring a meaningful hearing for both the juvenile and his parents. If this practice is followed, it will be unnecessary for the judge to thumb through a summary prepared by the probation officer while the juvenile case is being heard in order to be informed on the situation before him. By reading the summary carefully and consulting with his probation officer prior to the hearing, the court is placed in a good position to render a valuable and needed service at the time of the hearing. Furthermore, if they care to do a little research on their own, judges will learn to value more highly the advice and recommendation of their probation officers than the advice of well-meaning attorneys, expensively-dressed parents, close friends of the judges, or other in-

terested parties who have not approached the problems of the juvenile with the same objectivity which characterizes the work of a well-qualified probation officer. Too many judges have permitted carefully developed probation plans to be upset by attorneys whose only real interest in the case is their fees. Some judges have learned how much respect and confidence they build up in their probation officers when they are treated as professional people whose interest in the success of the court and the welfare of children is as great as the most competent members of the bar.

Probation officers believe it unwise for a judge to use a correctional institution as a threat or as a club over the head of the juvenile offender. Nothing is really accomplished by these threats because in the majority of cases the juvenile understands quite well how far a court can go in permitting him to retain his freedom in the community. These threats when used are as futile as a judge's advising a juvenile with an I. Q. of below 80 that he could make grades of "A" and "B" in school if he would only try.

No Admonishments. A "don't" which logically follows the one of not using threats has to do with the expectations of some courts for youngsters and their parents "to make good" overnight. This expectation has led some judges to admonish children by saying, "If you don't stay out of trouble, it will be too bad for you when you appear before me again." It is not possible for probation officers to repair in a short time the damage which has been done to a child over a period of 15 to 16 years. Often a year or two is required for a qualified probation officer with adequate community resources to help juveniles work out their problems satisfactorily. This means that there may be a return to delinquent conduct on the part of juvenile offenders from time to time before the probation plan succeeds. Fortunately, most of these violations will not constitute a menace to the community's welfare. Furthermore, it often appears wiser to give juveniles more than "just one chance" on probation than it is to use a correctional institution where the juveniles' problems are more likely to become intensified rather than corrected.

Other "Don't's"

Other "don't's" can be summarized briefly:

Don't fail to participate in the development of community facilities which will help to prevent juvenile delinquencies and make the community a better place in which to live.

Don't overlook the advisability of using citizen groups in the strengthening of the court's own program.

In the course of protecting children and their parents from unfavorable publicity, do not fail to use human interest stories which will not damage the clients but which will point up unmet needs in the community, such as poor housing, no mental hygiene facilities, a dearth of recreational resources in highly-delinquent areas, and others.

Don't make the mistake which one judge made of requesting the probation officer to make a recommendation in open court when the court knew from the social investigation that commitment was recommended by the probation officer. In this instance the probation officer made his recommendation but the judge continued the boy on probation! You can imagine what kind of rapport the probation officer had with this particular juvenile.

Don't use the detention home for children needlessly, and do not permit other community agencies to use it as a dumping ground. Some social agencies have to be prodded when they permit children active with them to spend months and months in detention when satisfactory plans could have been made after a short period of detention if "detention cases" had been given priority.

Do not expect your probation officers to be able to accomplish a full and adequate social investigation overnight. The social study is a time-consuming matter, and the probation officer will be happy to devote more than a normal working day in making the services of your court successful. Judge, your competent probation officers are as desirous as you are to complete the assigned social investigations promptly, and you can help them by not keeping them waiting for an hour or longer the next time they have cases scheduled for court.

If the recommendations suggested in this paper were carried out by all juvenile court judges, the phenomenal growth which has characterized the juvenile court movement would continue, and the services of the court would be progressively more effective.

Thoughts About Juvenile Courts[*]

By William Healy, M.D. Director Emeritus, Judge Baker Guidance Center, Boston, Mass.

WHAT HAVE BEEN the accomplishments of our juvenile courts in these last 50 years? That seems a fair question. Lest there be apprehension that the question itself implies criticism of the original idea underlying the first juvenile court law in 1899, certain historical facts should be clear.

* Reprinted from *Federal Probation*, Vol. XIII, September, 1949, pp. 16–19. Used by permission of author and publication.

The records show that the splendid group of women who began years earlier to urge the framing and passage of such a law expressed no conception that the social ills and the handicaps and personal deviations of childhood and adolescence which make for the development of delinquent trends would be solved by the mere establishment of a new type of court. Nor, though recognizing and pointing out that youngsters under the prevailing procedures of jail incarcerations, criminal trials, and sentences to penal institutions were being inducted into criminal careers, was there a semblance of a promise that the adjudication of young offenders under the new law as juvenile delinquents would speedily or in large numbers reform them.

No, in the feeling behind the agitation for new procedures even the matter of how criminals were being made appeared secondary to the oppressive knowledge that children were not being treated with civilized fairness. Not yet fully responsible human beings in any adult sense, very often the victims of society's own failure to protect them from baleful influences, they were subjected to unsavory exhibitions of retributive punishment. Seemingly after long delay, as we look back upon more than 50 years of interest in penal reform, arose the urgent demand for justice for youth.

Principles Underlying First Law

In 1898 the Chicago Bar Association, on the strength of many reports and resolutions received, appointed a committee of members and laymen to survey facts and conditions and draft a State juvenile court law. One can imagine what a great stimulus to the argument for better treatment for delinquents came from the findings that in the previous year no less than 575 juveniles charged with offenses had been held in the Cook County Jail and that every month about 100 boys had been sentenced to the House of Correction, the city prison.

The law as drafted was readily passed by the Legislature and became effective July 1, 1899. To be sure, some provisions had been made in other states, as in Massachusetts, to deal with young offenders apart from the regular trials in adult criminal courts, but this Illinois law was the first explicitly to affirm that the case of a juvenile was to be heard under chancery practice. Then, if found to be a violator of law, the juvenile was not to be convicted, but rather adjudged a delinquent and thereupon became a ward of the State to the extent that the court could prescribe treatment and duration of treatment for him.

On more than one occasion, strange as it may seem, the constitutionality of this law was assailed as not being in accord with the legal provisions of the criminal code. These were critical times for the court but the legislative mandate creating it was upheld by the Supreme Court of Illinois. Everyone except those few who perhaps in some measure held to the ancient concept of the *lex talionis* acknowledged the more civilized fairness of the new law. This was amply proved by the rapidity with which similar laws were enacted in other states and other countries.

The Juvenile Court Judge

It was early discerned that it was possible to overemphasize the value of the machinery, as it were, of the juvenile court. The eminent jurist, Julian W. Mack, in an eloquent address at the twenty-fifth anniversary of the Chicago court spoke of this and added that we may think that because this finer conception of dealing with young offenders is provided for by the law everything connected with it must in practice be equally fine. People are inclined to believe "that every judge of the juvenile court must necessarily be a fine fellow, filled with the wisdom of the ages, capable of dealing with all the children who come before him." Incidentally, I am sure that Judge Mack, who himself did much for the court and sometimes sat on the bench, would have insisted that his legal training and experience had not fitted him to be a successful juvenile court judge. The enacted law definitely stated that the treatment of delinquent wards of the State "shall approximate as nearly as may be that which should be given by its parents." *Should* be given: from such an idea came the phrase *in loco parentis* and the stipulation that the court shall act as a wise parent.

Soon the question of personality qualifications for a judge of the juvenile court came to the fore, as it has since with many a juvenile court committee throughout the country, with, of course, never a possibility of exactly defining the proportionate desirable blending of empathy, firmness, intelligence, and familiarity with modern knowledge of the bases of human behavior. Parenthetically, it may be interesting to note that one of the questions frequently brought up is whether the man under consideration has children; for if not, it is argued, what does he know about children? However, by this time we have learned that an unusual proportion of juvenile court judges, proved able and devoted, have been childless or even unmarried, and the psychology of this is rather obvious.

I have had the opportunity of observing the work of many judges throughout the country and a few abroad, sometimes sitting on the bench with them. But this latter afforded little or nothing of value to the court any more than did the largely footless hours when by request during three years I sat as "friend to the court" in Chicago—mainly footless hours except when the offender before us had been studied in the clinic. Magic is nowhere produced by the juxtaposition of a psychiatrist and a judge. One everywhere found that judges, just the same as the rest of us, hold on to some perhaps

minor preconceptions and prejudices, but in general most to be noted over the years has been the steady growth of appreciation of the values of scientifically conducted studies of young offenders.

But appreciation really began as early as 1912 or so, when certain forward-looking judges came to see for themselves what such studies brought out. What they absorbed showed in their future court work—Edward Foote Waite of Minneapolis; Charles W. Hoffman of Cincinnati, who came before he took his seat on the bench; Frater of Seattle who went away saying, "hereafter no prescription of treatment without prior diagnosis" and who quickly established a definitive Department of Diagnosis in his court; and Harvey Humphrey Baker of Boston whose visits led later to the founding of the Judge Baker Guidance Center. By now the demand for such studies of young offenders has grown beyond the present possibilities of fulfillment.

Systematic Study of Outcomes

Many times during 40 years of contact with juvenile courts I have commented on the absence in these courts of scientific or business-like evaluations of the results of decrees from the bench for some general or specific treatment of an offender. Occasionally figures on recidivism are gathered, but without attempt at interpretations. What enterprise in industry, science, or business would continue a project aimed at some goal without correlating results with methods used and with discoverable blockings of the project? A physician, like a judge, prescribes treatment, but should we not consider him a weak member of his profession if he failed to ascertain whether it proved to be the right remedy; if the patient was not improved was the treatment competently carried out, or what otherwise militated against cure.

Failures with offenders do not reflect

on the aims of the court, but one may fairly ask if it is not the court's responsibility to undertake researches to show—and sometimes to make public—what factors make for favorable outcomes and, more particularly, what blocks successful treatment of its wards. With information obtained by a well-trained probation officer and the data from study of the delinquent available, commonly recognized inimical conditions and circumstances may be more or less clear.

But what about the standards of the social group to which the young offender belongs, social and ethical attitudes in thinking and acting, which are readily sensed by him? Some sociologists are making much of this nowadays as a usually uninvestigated powerful influence which very considerably determines behavior tendencies. Delinquency, they say, is a learned type of behavior, learned in association with those who define such behavior favorably and largely in isolation from those who define it unfavorably. By using a little imagination it will be seen that this theory of causation has wide ramifications and can be of importance for research.

Among subjects for investigation may be the effects upon the attitudes on youngsters of police methods of handling cases. And there is the perennial topic of what detention among other offenders, even in a physically well-equipped detention home, does to a delinquent. Then what are the weaknesses of the court's own implementation for treatment? Finally, in these short suggestions arising from my experience, I ask: Is it not the court's business to make it clear to itself, and perhaps to the public, unfitnesses and possibly positively deleterious influences of the regime of any institution to which the court has to commit young offenders? If it is the court's genuine aim to do the best for those whom it takes in charge, a lot of research is indicated.

My colleague, Dr. Bronner, felt so strongly the lack of information about even the bare facts of outcomes that in the early twenties we directed a research into the after careers of cases studied at least 7 years earlier for the court in Chicago. (Again this was under a grant from Mrs. W. F. Dummer who financed the first 5 years of our clinical research.) There were appalling findings: For example, of 470 traceable boys 13 had committed 14 homicides; 157, practically all committed earlier to juvenile correctional institutions, were or had been in adult penal institutions. These findings were published together with much other revealing material drawn from our case studies. It made a sizeable volume and perhaps included too much or did not deal with the facts in popular form; anyhow it did not attract much attention and, so far as we know, had no influence in modifying procedures or methods of treatment.

The Gluecks' later compilation of data (in *One Thousand Juvenile Delinquents*, 1926) from our studies for the Boston court worthily received wide comment, particularly in connection with their published follow-up of these cases. How much influence for the good these studies have had is hard to say.

It was once suggested to me by a man prominent in social work, with opinions of his own on the subject, that I with data in hand should loudly proclaim that juvenile courts are failures. Of course I was quite unwilling; besides the record of successes there are to be recognized certain achievements of the court that cannot be measured in terms of statistics. When Grace Abbott, former head of the United States Children's Bureau, published her criticism of juvenile courts in *The Survey* (May, 1936) and offered her plan that other social agencies acting in conjunction with neighborhood councils should be developed to undertake the treatment of juvenile delinquents, I again disagreed in spite of seeing something of the sort very effectively at work in Denmark. Until we progress much more in our cultural attitudes we need the strength of the law and of the court, with all its shortcomings, behind us in our efforts to deal effectively with juvenile delinquents.

The Achievement of the Juvenile Court

Occasionally the value of juvenile courts is challenged because there is no evidence that delinquency has decreased since they were established. In answer to this it may be said that no statistics are available showing that delinquency in proportion to the growth of population is or is not diminishing, though we must grant that it remains a major problem. Then along the same line is the argument that in family life and under the law the abandonment of dire punishment for delinquency has led us to reap the rewards of softness. Again, such an opinion lacks validity because it has no body of facts to support it.

The juvenile court can only very indirectly be held at all responsible for the continued occurrence of delinquency as a phenomenon. One can only say that it is in a position to know or to learn about the environmental settings that tend to engender delinquent behavior and that it might well be considered the court's duty to inaugurate measures that would stir public sentiment, official action, and social agency endeavors to improve conditions and neighborhood attitudes in delinquency breeding areas. The point that there are such areas was made with clarity by a boy sent by the court to our clinic: "You can't do anything for me, doctor, and the court can't. Would you be the yellow kid of our street when the gang yells, 'Come on, let's get some dough'? I'll betcha in a couple of months I'll be in court again." And he was.

The juvenile court is here to stay; it is a public social agency that has hardly begun to embrace its opportunities or even realize its possibilities for being a great social force in the American scene. In places where the court has developed into a family consultation center, or has turned its detention facilities into an institution for clinical study and treatment, or where modernly trained personnel are enlisted in probation service and utilize innovations of proved worth, or in places where, for therapy as well as diagnosis, the court functions in close cooperation with the clinic, distinct advances have been made.

But I would insist that attempted treatment of the delinquent, commonly conceived to be the purpose for which the court exists, consists only too often of disjointed efforts. There is immense need for outreaching, better and closer cooperations and coordinations. The ordinary working relations between those who have studied the case, those who undertake treatment either with the delinquent on probation or under the charge of a social agency, and officials of a correctional school, are so meager that they represent the antithesis of well-ordered scientific integration of effort. Perhaps it cannot be otherwise except under the auspices of an established Authority which shall conduct all steps and features of the study and treatment of the young individual who as a delinquent is a ward of the State.

The great achievement of the juvenile court so far has been, to my mind, the founding of a social institution which respects the dignity and potentialities of children and adolescents. Its concern for their welfare has gained for it the admiration and affection of our public. Best of all, from the standpoint of progress in civilization, it represents justice for youth.

In Defense of Juvenile Courts*

By Harrison Allen Dobbs. Professor of Social Welfare, Louisiana State University, Baton Rouge.

AMERICAN culture patterns encourage building up rather than tearing down, and we thrive because of this quality. Ideologically, to defend is, to us, more sensible and profitable than to offend; that is, wherever this can be plausibly done. This is true of social institutions generally, of the juvenile court particularly.

Reasons for defending the juvenile court movement are easily found. Four especially significant ones are chosen for emphasis. They reveal the climate in which this brief paper is written.

1. This year concludes a half-century of service by juvenile courts. It marks, also, for the writer a quarter century of growthful relationship with this welfare activity; retrospection is prompted.

2. The juvenile court concept is defendable from diverse angles, but all related. This permits an holistic rather than a segmentalized approach to this assignment. In the light of current psychological thinking such method has distinctive validity.

3. There are pragmatic advantages in viewing and meeting social problems positively. There are in this instance many potential strengths. These should be brought to the fore. Stressing the weaknesses of juvenile court practices would be a less fruitful process.

4. A dialectic viewpoint should be emphasized. The understanding, debating, and utilizing of opposites and dissimilarities can become a productive process socially. It is possible that counterideas may be favorably fused.

Usefulness can be enhanced more this way than by our giving up, defeatist-like, what basically it stands for and what the original charter intended. At this stage in juvenile court history, reconstructive possibilities should be more recognized and respected.

The plan of this paper called for formulating five postulates, and briefly clarifying and substantiating each one. This allows focusing on influential facets. Each has psychological and sociological meaning. However, the set, as a whole, has greater pertinence and weight than a consideration of the segments shows.

It is postulated that

1. The juvenile court occupies today a unique place in an essential social institution in community welfare, and that this position can be made more vital.

2. The constitutionality of the juvenile court has been well determined and sustained, and that this is of considerable moment.

3. From the viewpoint of the treatment which juvenile courts provide certain cases, its services have scientific validity.

4. There are psychological gains, which accrue nation-wide, when urgent social problems are met categorically, and that American children have benefited by having this specialized court service set aside for their use.

5. Thus far, public understanding of juvenile court functioning (and support for it) has been so restricted that a full

---

* Reprinted from *Federal Probation*, Vol. XIII, September, 1949, pp. 24–29. Used by permission of author and publication.

demonstration of its worth to individuals and groups has yet to be made.

What is set forth next does little more than provocatively outline feasible defenses. There is much that still must be studied and interpreted. More empirical study of its structure and function should be carefully followed through.

The welfare of many persons, children and adults alike, is at stake in this challenging matter. We are confronted with an urgent social problem, regarding which something more ought to be undertaken. In addition to offering defense, the five aspects that follow infer commonplace ways and means for making general improvement. It is reasonable to believe that the place that the juvenile court now holds nationally can be securely advanced.

A Unique Social Institution

The juvenile court was no fly-by-night happening. It was not all the result of selfish and sentimental drives. Quite the opposite, this special service was purposefully conceived. Distinguished legal and social work authorities intelligently fostered it.

These leaders determined to find more suitable ways to provide help for children with special needs. Whenever the early history of the juvenile court is reviewed, quantity and quality of forethought that went into its timely creation impress one. This origin must not be carelessly dismissed.

The juvenile court should hold its distinctive place as long as human needs persist which called for its creation at the close of the last century. Until a surer approach for meeting these is known and accepted, publicly thoughtful persons can have little question about its essentialness, on a social institution basis at least.

It has the right to occupy socially a prominent, secure position. That is, it has this justification, according to criteria of the cultural anthropologists—the

group of scientists who study historically social institutions and inform us about their start and values.

The establishment of the juvenile court in 1899 was, from the anthropological viewpoint, a definite attempt to implement, by means of social organization, what could no longer be done by individuals. At the time of its beginning, there were many boys and girls who were dependent and neglected, and many with conduct disorders. These frequently lacked proper care and training. Something additional in the way of an effective service was demanded.

Public insistence mounted throughout the nation. Steps had to be taken to augment the threatened welfare of the children and society itself. It was natural that new laws were enacted almost simultaneously by several states to institute a different kind of social organization. This was to answer, at least in part, individual and social problems then prevailing. Thus, the juvenile court movement pragmatically started.

The framework of any juvenile court can be empirically examined with profit. If creditable accomplishment is discovered, the essential characteristics that every sound social institution must possess can be identified. It has a distinguishing *charter* which was decided upon legislatively. It uses its own *personnel*. While norms that juvenile courts follow vary in their number and reach, these are always in evidence and are of great import. Courts have and use, as does every social institution, *maternal apparatus. Activities* are defined and intently planned so that the institution functions usefully; that is, reaches the *goals* for which ends it was created. These are essential qualities and give the juvenile court status as a valid social institution.

It is not difficult to see how such a system of organized activity has a great personal and social effect. When considered this way, the worth of the juvenile court cannot be neglected by a well-functioning society. This is especially so in a nation concerned with the fullest happiness, welfare, and usefulness of all its members.

There is a general belief, today, that the work of culture is not done by any community as a whole, nor by individuals. The crux of social effort is what small groups do. It is maintained that the juvenile court is a social manifestation of this organized, functional kind.

The juvenile court has a specific purpose. Up until now, at least, it is largely unparalleled in structure and function. A strong defense of it may be made on the basis of the fundamental usefulness it still has to certain individuals and groups. It has remained a serviceable social institution.

Constitutionality Factor

Laws represent crystallized public opinion of an important nature. Favorable court decisions that pertain to these crystallizations substantiate still further the need and reliability of collective viewpoints. This whole matter of its legal derivation invites scrutiny by serious juvenile court critics. Significant traditions have been carefully embodied in juvenile court law.

The enacting of juvenile court legislation all over the nation was, in itself, a real advance. However, more is shown by what the Supreme Court, of the States of the Nation, has ruled regarding the legality and appropriateness of juvenile court procedures. These rulings have given to it a rich heritage and a judicial impregnability, hard to upset.

Transition, legally and socially, from punishment concepts to those assuring social treatment (as the determining factor in what shall be done individually with cases of juvenile violators) is of tremendous, lasting importance. Legal decisions sustaining a greatly altered social attitude, many of which have now been made by distinguished jurists, have

become impressive and decisive. Their weighty opinions are poignant today throughout the United States and even the world.

Sociological and psychological issues that these authorities analyzed, and the nature of their arguments, furnish us presently an instructive backlog of evidence, much too pertinent and precious to be foregone even if fashions change. It is fortunate that foundation stones like these are in so securely. They guarantee strength and significant durability to what was at the beginning a social experiment.

The juvenile court venture that moved far ahead the old principle of *parens patriae* was a bold one. The State had long acted *in loco parentis* for destitute and needy children. However, still further to extend the concept of the State serving in the place of a child's parents was a far-reaching step. It excluded a great number of boys and girls from the perquisites of criminal law. It included them courageously in chancery planning. This was a momentous measure to introduce and extend.

Then, to have this innovation well authenticated by critical legal judgment makes the juvenile court movement rank unusually high in soundness and acceptability; that is, compared with certain other attempts at social change. The movement was immeasurably strengthened thereby. It may grow even more so, as time passes.

The jurisdiction of the juvenile court is contested in some places, and for some children's violations. Nevertheless, there is general agreement that these are mostly minor limitations and exceptions. On the whole, there is little legal debate today about the social help a competent juvenile court provides especially to well-selected necessitous cases. Its fundamental worth to such children is established now, beyond all doubt.

This paper will indicate later that there remain many administrative hazards. There is considerable functional uncertainty in juvenile court practice yet to be faced. Here, however, the main point has been to emphasize that, in its theory, juvenile courts have the green light to forge ahead. Fortunately, legal stumbling blocks have been mostly removed.

Many pertinent questions still arise. These call for thoughtful consideration. Why would it be unwise socially to dissipate these hard won gains? Has fullest advantage been taken of the sure, judicial foundation the juvenile court presently has? Should increased effort be made to assure its exclusive use in all children's cases where adjudication is required? What jurisdictional and administrative changes could augment its total efficiency? Communities have certainly made real progress in various directions. However, still more is demanded before final goals are reached.

The foolishness of abandoning midstream a reasonably good ship is not hard to discern. This is so, even if it seems at the moment not to be moving ahead altogether satisfactorily. The challenge should be to make its operation and advance much more certain and better serving. There is much in juvenile court activity which illustrates effectively this simple analogy.

If there were nothing else in its favor, the thorough determination of constitutionality furnishes proof of the sound position that the juvenile court has currently. This advantageous condition should never be slighted in defending its intrinsic worth.

Essential Services

In 1899, when the juvenile court movement began, there was extreme social need for the kinds of service that this new facility was to institute and supply. In 1949, scientific light on juvenile delinquency and its treatment shows that there remain case situations where the special approach to problems, like the juvenile court can make, is still desired. Psychiatric research and practice verify this point convincingly.

The place of authority in treatment need not be debated here. Its grave misuse has been discussed with justifiable alarm in the social casework field for a long time. Only recently has much professional attention been given to the distinctive part its proper use can have in helping children. Dynamic psychology has had much to do with this new conception.

It is apparent, at this time, that there has been undue veering away from what can be crucial aid in abetting certain delinquency problems; that is, if this help were more satisfactorily utilized. The better understanding of individual personality and the importance, in some instances, of authoritative guidance presently gives the treatment of children by juvenile court workers a heightened respectability.

Its status, as an essential social institution (with the unique charter, norms, and activities it has) can be still more potent. This aspect of its particularized functioning will be given greater heed when the selection of cases needing treatment in an authoritative setting is assured competent attention. Having loose intake policies seems today an influential weakness of many juvenile courts.

In some communities the responsibility and opportunity of the juvenile court in this particular field of social treatment is already more recognized and is being more diligently safeguarded. Results show the worth, more and more, of giving optimum juvenile court service only to those children actually requiring a form of legal and social care that it, alone, is able to provide.

The cluttering-up of juvenile court services with nonessential activities is costly and detrimental. This is especially so when the giving of necessary help, promptly and adequately, is greatly impaired thereby. Only where there is carefully controlled selection of cases on a highly discriminative basis can there be the assurance that the unique children's services, which the community depends upon a juvenile court to supply, will be successfully planned and furnished.

Two additional examples of a specific kind are suggested here to substantiate further the current validity of juvenile court concepts. Each in itself, if fully explored, gives additional cause for more nurturing, socially, of its services. Without these there will persist serious gaps in community organization for needy children.

The first of these has to do with matters pertaining to guardianship. The seriousness of changing a child's guardian is evident. It is a process usually requiring careful legal determination. It needs careful social effort to back it up. It is complicated in nature, both sociologically and psychologically. When it shall be done and where the new substitute-parent responsibility shall be lodged are serious questions, both individually and collectively. It could easily be perilous not to have a specialized judicial body handling this influential problem. Because of its categorized value and the availability of staff to give required professional service, the juvenile court, where it has had the proper chance, functions well in this particular matter. Effort of this sort should appropriately be extended rather than curtailed.

The second relates to giving some children protection from careless and violating adults. Contributing to the dependency or the delinquency of a child is a heinous offense, whatever its reason. It often has aspects that necessitate the use of intelligent authority for its probing and checking.

Here again the juvenile court, in its *parens patriae* role, is a suitable, effective agent for the State to use in exercising its authority for everyone's betterment.

Too little genuine use has been made of juvenile court services in protective ways, at least not on the best possible basis. In involved situations affecting children, a special court has a very realistic contribution to make. The juvenile court has done much already, but it could do much more in this direction.

Use of Categories in Social Organization

Specialization affords great advantages as well as influential limitations. Whether or not specialization is to be lauded depends upon the particular directives being sought. This principle applies in the social welfare field as elsewhere.

Much evidence, however, can be solicited historically to show that whenever social organizations, planned for individual and group welfare, become suitably specialized functionally, unusual progress is customarily realized. The progressive categorizing of community care for the welfare of needy children provides a telling example of this influential thesis.

What our having provided special courts to help meet children's problems wrought socially typifies excellently the value of a categorical approach. One of the most persuasive arguments proving that there is value in the juvenile court program is that which is being discussed here. Its categorical nature has been of great and lasting significance.

Because of its reasonable founding, a well-defined functional province was marked out. Therein legal procedures, which pertain to children's welfare especially, possess unusual characteristics that are wide-reaching in range and influence. These distinctive qualities rest on a certain kind of social philosophy. This is very different in nature and intent than that determining the usual handling of cases under the criminal code. This basic difference is a very important one. Philosophically, the juvenile court had a treatment purpose, and this necessitates the use of changed methods and new facilities.

The social and psychological significance of having procedures of this novel sort was increasingly observed. There quickly began to develop paralleling auxiliary services for further aiding these needy children. These extensions now make an impressive array. Particular contributions they give to social welfare become increasingly useful and requested.

Some starts can be traced exactly to the direct and indirect impacts which the juvenile court movement has had on total community planning. Thus, the purposeful categorizing of court services for children brought about naturally far-reaching results. This is especially so in case diagnosis and treatment.

Three illustrations are presented briefly to illustrate this point. These progressive ways for aiding children socially have resulted, to a considerable degree, because the juvenile court required special assistance and modified resources. The persistence of community leaders, sponsoring the improvement of court services, has been effective. Their supportive effort became influential socially.

1. The *child guidance clinic* was conceived and begun so as to better individualize the treatment of children in juvenile courts. These clinics were first attached directly to the court itself. The baffling problems referred there gave initial impetus, material, for scientific study and goals. Nevertheless, the juvenile court was, and still is, one of the cornerstones on which the guidance movement is built. Only a categorical agency like the court, would press so urgently the establishment of new social institutions to assist children in need.

2. The wide-spread program for *mother's pensions* was begun as a juvenile court adjunct. This new social service within the court paved the way for national *aid-for-dependent-children*

legislation. Financial provisions for the support of dependent boys and girls might have appeared eventually regardless of the juvenile court. However, it is certain that action came quicker, advances were more general, and acceptance by citizens was heartier because the pioneering juvenile court demonstrations proved the necessity and efficacy of public assistance for children.

3. *Juvenile detention,* now an integral part of community social service, is another social institution which is an outgrowth of juvenile court philosophy and practice. The quartering of children in jails was a serious social menace. The public was finally awakened to their responsibility and supplied custody so as to comply with the requirements of juvenile court acts. Further refinement of the detention program brought special residential facilities for the observation and scientific study of children with complicating problems. The juvenile court, acting in a highly categorical fashion, pointed the way and ardently urged these newer developments. It saw firsthandedly the importance of such facilities, and profited greatly by their establishment.

As a matter of actual fact the juvenile court, because of its specialized interests and methods, focused up successfully the necessity of attacking social and psychological problems where they start. It is not unreasonable to claim for the juvenile court movement much of the credit for mental hygiene programs and their multiple aspects.

Many children come to profit from exploratory experiences with a categorized few. Prevention rather than treatment is more to the front. Juvenile court usefulness in this particular respect may yet be only partially expended.

Dire Influence of Community Neglect

No social institution can do what it is supposed to do if it is denied the personnel and material apparatus required for carrying on its particular activities. The carefully determined goals its charter proclaims are reached only when the interest and planning of communities are consistently backed up with both moral and financial support. In the case of the juvenile court, generally speaking, this has certainly not been so.

A very persuasive reason for believing ardently in the juvenile court movement is the unusual accomplishment record it presents, despite strangling restrictions imposed upon it very frequently. Annual reports of juvenile courts country-wide reveal few instances where the quality and quantity of service given is commensurate with the nature and extent of children's problems that the community foisted upon them.

There is a good deal in these statistical data which reveals that oftentimes communities tend to use their juvenile court as a community scapegoat. This is a ruse that public opinion experts tell us people commonly utilize, consciously or unconsciously, to lessen guilt feelings. A special, kindly service is wanted to mend partly what has ruthlessly been allowed to fall to pieces. Court workers are expected to redo completely and quickly what society has been undoing in children for a very long time. This philanthropic gesture lets us, as citizens, rest more easily, at least momentarily.

Condemnation would be less deserved were last-minute aid given constantly and in adequate ways. This, however, is far from happening. It is doubtful if there is a single juvenile court in the country prepared to cure socially ill children with the precision and efficiency that characterizes the pediatrics ward of first class hospitals.

Regretfully, the service most courts give has only the slightest resemblance. It often is not a matter of not knowing what to do rehabilitatively. It is rather on account of the meagre staff afforded. The limited provisions made available for therapy preclude real helpfulness.

Society allows, much too generally and readily, unsatisfactory practices and standards in juvenile court activities. How many people care whether juvenile court jurisdiction is clear and certain? How often are judges and referees selected because of extra competence to deal scientifically with the psychological problems as well as legal ones? What is known about the experience and training of the probation staff? How much heed is given to the efficiency and fitness of physical facilities used? How well selected is each juvenile court case? What aids are provided to assure correct diagnosis and treatment? Is there sufficient time and thought to probe each child's problem?

The less than creditable condition of much juvenile court practice gives clear proof that what happens today to children in court concerns most citizens very little.

Only occasionally does one hear the protests of individuals or organizations. Consequently, outmoded principles of a hurtful laissez-faire kind commonly prevail. This stays so at great social cost and loss when individual outcomes are fully evaluated. Neglectful, near-sighted conditions like these hurt individuals and groups immeasurably.

Basically, the blame for limited juvenile court success rests on the public. It is not on philosophy nor functioning; not on court officials; not on unchanging children and families. Those of us who want so much from this children's court for almost nothing ought not be too critical of its poor performance. We allow and actually encourage this by our blind spots, indifference and escapist attitudes.

The juvenile court is a social institution we wanted and built, and still need on occasions. If it crumbles, the fault will plainly be ours. If it improves and extends, society must carry its part more trustworthily. Can public enthusiasm and belief that started it be revived and utilized? If not this way, then are there others to use so as to increase its present strength?

Conclusion

The situation we face here is a challenging one. Careful thought and action are required if the juvenile court movement is to move ahead and not backward. It is claimed reasonably that the concepts underlying it are defensible on a number of grounds. But more data should be assembled promptly to bear out this statement empirically.

It would be well for supporters to stress more the excellences of this specialized court than its limitations. Its essential service for children should be considered more as an integral part of total welfare planning. Consideration should gainfully be given to lessening materially the range of its present ac-

tivities. Society should be helped to understand how serious the results are of its own delinquent acts. Some new experimental methods might be introduced profitably.

Children are much too important to American well-being to be at all neglected or ever hurt. Every social help that we have must be utilized intently so as to extend their welfare and happiness. Court aid has real consequence.

The juvenile court is not an outmoded friend to children, nor one to be distrusted. It is not one emphasizing doing things that are harmful. Few children, in not many places, have so far experienced fully the worth, the ability, and other positive qualities inherently in it. It is interesting to speculate on what this young social institution, at its very best, might contribute to children's welfare in days to come.

SELECTED REFERENCES

1. Killian, Frederick W., "The Juvenile Court as an Institution," *The Annals* of The American Academy of Political and Social Science, 261, January 1949.

One of the best treatments of the origin, growth and development of the juvenile court.

2. Davis, F. James, "The Iowa Juvenile Court Judge," *Journal of Criminal Law and Criminology*, XLII, September–October 1951.

The result of a survey conducted to test the attitudes of juvenile court judges on their philosophical approach to the cases appearing before them. Only a small percentage of the sample tested retained the bias of the "criminal court" approach.

3. Dobbs, Harrison Allen, "Realism and the Juvenile Court," *Focus*, XXXI, July 1952.

The handicaps that have plagued the juvenile court are analyzed as well as the inability or unwillingness of the general public to understand or appreciate the juvenile court.

4. Rubin, Sol, "The Legal Character of Juvenile Delinquency," *The Annals* of The American Academy of Political and Social Science, 261, January 1949.

The theoretical purposes of the juvenile court are carefully considered in relation to the court's functioning on a practical level. Despite more than half a century of practice and progress, there still remains a sizable gap between theory and practice in the juvenile court.

9 TRENDS IN THE JUVENILE COURT IDEA

SINCE 1899, when the world's first juvenile court was enacted in Cook County, Illinois, this social institution has been gradually expanding. The development of probation theory, originated by John Augustus in 1841, lent itself to the spreading philosophy of the juvenile court. Also contemporary humanitarian influences made themselves felt in the reduction of capital penalties and cruel and unusual punishments.

In 1870, Massachusetts enacted a law requiring separate hearings for children in Suffolk County. In 1877 a similar law was approved in New York, and included certain provisions to prevent children from associating with adult offenders. In 1892 New York provided for special trials for those under sixteen. In 1898 Rhode Island enacted legislation similar to that of New York. In 1899 Colorado under its school laws began a system of special handling of the child with the innovation that truant officers or teachers might act as his supervisors. Thus the legislative beginnings of the juvenile court idea were fairly widespread during the last quarter of the nineteenth century.

Juvenile courts increased rapidly, Wyoming being the last state to establish such a court in 1945. Previously, in 1938, the federal government had passed a juvenile court act which provided for the treatment of the youthful offender, not as a criminal, but as a child in trouble. Juvenile courts are today still in the process of evolution, and new procedures and techniques are being developed.

INCREASE IN COURTS AND OFFENSES

Juvenile court business is becoming big business. The total volume tends to increase yearly. In 1937 the Children's Bureau reported that 462 courts serving 36 per cent of the population of the United States processed about one per cent of the nation's seventeen million children between ten and sixteen years of age. During 1937 these courts, in thirty states and the District of Columbia, reported 78,688 delinquency cases, about one-seventh of them girls and the remainder boys.

Because of the incompleteness of numerical data, only a general approximation of delinquency and juvenile court activity during World War II and the postwar period can be given. But most studies have shown that child offenses began to multiply during World War II, the rates of increase varying by states and by counties. Since 1943, courts have reported a continuous decline in girls' cases, but boys' cases registered an increase in 1945, following a decline during the preceding year. After a peak at the end of World War II (1945), juvenile court delinquency cases dropped in number each year from 1946 through 1948, a phenomenon which seems to be related to the improvement of the conditions associated with war. In 1949, for the first time since the end of the war, juvenile court delinquency cases reversed their downward trend and increased by 4 per cent over the previous year. That year it is estimated that almost three hundred thousand children, or about twelve in every thousand between the ages of seven and seventeen, came to the attention of juvenile courts because of delinquency.

Most juvenile courts have jurisdiction over actions involving dependent and neglected children. There was an over-all decrease of 8 per cent in the dependency and neglect cases between 1946 and 1949, probably as a result of the high level of employment and general prosperity during the postwar years and the elimination or improvement of many war-associated conditions. Of the total number of children's cases handled by the 413 courts reporting in 1949, about 24 per cent were dependency and neglect cases. The median age was six and a half years for these, while for delinquency cases the median was fifteen and a half years. The United States Children's Bureau estimates that if the volume of delinquency continues, even on the 1948 level, at least 275,000 children each year may be expected during the next several years to come before the nation's juvenile courts.[1]

APPEARANCE OF THE CLINIC AND THE COUNSELOR

Most delinquent children can be reclaimed; but their reclamation or correction demands continuity of treatment of each child as an individual. Extension of the functions of the juvenile court will materially enhance this endeavor. Some juvenile courts function with the assistance of guidance clinics or counselors. A typical child guidance clinic which works with a juvenile court combines the skills of the psychiatrist, psychologist, and social worker, makes a diagnosis of each offender, and serves as a consulting agency to the juvenile court. The counselor serves as an assistant to the juvenile court judge, as he does the preliminary work of interviewing the juvenile offender, as well as contacting all persons concerned in the case. His recommendations as to final disposition of the case are usually accepted by the busy juvenile court judge. Many juvenile courts, however, function without the assistance of a guidance clinic or a counselor. Because of lack of funds and personnel facilities, many judges must attempt to combine many functions in one office—a severe handicap to proper remedial work.

Moreover, officials of clinics and juvenile court judges are not always in harmony. Some officials are of the opinion that the clinic should concern itself with the cases that come from the public school, the home, or social agencies, and lean to the opinion that accepting court cases injures the reputation of the clinic, due to the delinquency aspects involved. For example, the clinic may recommend treatment for dependency, neglect and personality problem cases; but in delinquency cases, the juvenile court judge decides on the appropriate treatment necessary. Ideally, of course, the judge, the probation officer, the

[1] United States Children's Bureau, *Juvenile Court Statistics,* 1937; 1946–1949.

psychiatric social worker, and the psychologist should learn to work together for the sake of the child.

Another problem is posed because many parents appear unwilling or unable to understand the function of the clinic. Sometimes both the parents and the child consider the referral to the clinic as part of the punishment rather than a method of treatment. This attitude, often a consequence of inadequate education of the parents, may also hamper successful treatment.

One of the more recent adjuncts to the juvenile court, referred to above, is the much-needed counselor. The counselor tries to solve the problem first. Actually in many communities, the quality of the juvenile courts are in large part a direct reflection of the capabilities of the counselors attached to them. The counselor should have an extensive acquaintance in the community, particularly among those who control the purse strings. Like the judge, he should have an understanding of and sympathy for both adults and children.

EXTENSION OF THE JUVENILE COURT IDEA

In specific areas the juvenile court idea has been extended. These areas include the establishment of adolescents' courts, youth correction authorities, and family courts. In addition, the pervasive influence of the juvenile court is reflected in the procedures of some of the criminal courts.

Various agencies have been instituted to cope with adolescent delinquency. For example, the Wayward Minors' Act of New York (1923) provides that a person sixteen to twenty-one years old who is a habitual drinker or drug addict, who associates regularly with undesirable persons or frequents houses of prostitution, may be deemed a wayward minor. This Act was intended as an aid to parents with incorrigible children who had passed the upper age limit of the state's juvenile court jurisdiction. Another adolescents' court in New York City, created in 1936, is a part of the felony court of the Borough of Queens. The Wayward Minors' Court, with city-wide jurisdiction over girls sixteen to twenty-one years of age, was at first a part of the Women's Court; since 1945, officially known as the Girls' Term, it has functioned independently.

Another type of agency working with adolescents is the youth authority. The youth authority program integrates under one governmental agency the several aspects of the treatment process: diagnosis and classification, institutional treatment, parole and delinquency prevention through community organization. California has been in the vanguard in the establishment of youth authorities in the United States. The first boy placed under care of the Authority was received at the clinic in 1942; on its eighth anniversary (January, 1950), the California Youth Authority had cared for some thirteen thousand youths in its schools and camps. The success of this venture is suggested by the fact that the increase in delinquency is less than the population increase of the state.

Public Law 865, the Federal Youth Corrections Act—"to provide a system for the treatment and rehabilitation of youth offenders" and "to improve the administration of criminal justice"—was enacted by the Eighty-first Congress and approved by the President on September 30, 1950. This legislation was the culmination of ten years' work by the Judicial Conference of the United States and its Committee on Punishment for Crime to provide the means and methods of training and treatment for young offenders. The Federal Youth Corrections Act has been called the most forward step in law enforcement history. The Act defines a youth as a person under twenty-two years of age, and gives the courts greater discretion and new alternatives for dealing with him. It makes the Bureau of Prisons responsible for establishing classification centers, providing diversified institutional and treatment facilities, public or private, retraining and reeducation, and recommending to the Youth Division of the Parole Board the release of youths ready to return to their communities. Moreover, it is now possible to experiment with furloughing youthful prisoners who, without prejudice, can reenter the institution by choice or by necessity. Apparently a good many federal judges are looking forward to implementing this authority.

IMPLICATIONS FOR OTHER COURTS

The juvenile court idea not only has expanded to include youth of older years but also has influenced the treatment of many kinds of "family" cases including those pertaining to domestic relations, legal custody, adoption, illegitimacy, and related problems. Certain characteristics of juvenile court philosophy are singularly applicable to the procedure in family cases. The juvenile court is nonlegalistic, has considerable flexibility, and is distinguished by informal procedure. Its judge enjoys powers of broad discretion. It is both a judicial and administrative agency. The juvenile court makes intensive use of the social sciences in its search for causation of juvenile misconduct, neglect, and dependency, and in its aim of rehabilitating the child, if possible, within the family itself.

The juvenile court also has had some impact on criminal justice administration. This influence may be particularly observed in the utilization of presentence investigation and the widened use of probation. Superior court judges are realizing, more and more, the desirability of knowing something about the defendant besides the grand jury indictment. It is hoped that in the years ahead additional characteristics of the juvenile court, such as the lack of formalism, the by-passing of "crime" and "convict" labels, the utilization of social science, and the wider and more societal conception of moral responsibility, will be adopted by the adult criminal courts.

As Tappan so well points out, however, a note of caution is in order. There has been a tendency to exaggerate the contrasts between juvenile court procedures, pictured in glowing terms, and those of the criminal court system, viewed in a very critical and quite inaccurate light. In many places, especially in rural counties, juvenile courts do not approach adequate standards. Children's cases are handled much like other cases except for the proceedings' relative privacy and the fact that special attention is given to the allegations of the complainant-parent or police officer and to their common demands for the child's commitment. In urban areas as well there is great variation in the courts' conduct, much more so than in the criminal courts. This diversity is a reflection of the failure thus far to develop any firm consensus as to desirable

goals and methods in dealing with children and adolescents.[2] The actual procedures used by juvenile courts will be discussed in subsequent chapters.

READINGS

This chapter's subject matter is augmented by John Otto Reinemann, whose
article, "The Expansion of the Juvenile Court Idea," treats in detail four developments that have moved the juvenile court from its original relatively
limited functions to its present position as a flexible agency of the community.

While the Youth Correction Authority Act was an important step forward
in the alleviation of problems of delinquent children, it is not, of course, an
ideal legal arrangement. Some of the Act's inherent defects and possible
solutions are suggested by John F. Perkins in "Defect in the Youth Correction
Authority Act."

George W. Smyth in "The Juvenile Court and Delinquent Parents," shows
that the problems of children and parents are inseparable and that juvenile
courts should concern themselves with the implications involved. Various
types of delinquent parents are described. The thesis defended is that much
delinquency can be prevented through the alleviation of neglect.

In "Placement from the Child's Viewpoint" Leontine R. Young points out
that too often adults view delinquency from the practical vantage point of
the grownup, which blinds them to the enormous gulf dividing that vantage
point from the child's actual terror, pain, and confusion.

Michael S. Precker in "The Treatment of Juvenile Offenders in Murder
Cases" analyzes the sharp conflict between the conservative forces of established
law, as exemplified in judicial decisions, and the progressive dynamism inherent
in the program of social scientists, as evidenced in the extension of legislation
in behalf of juvenile offenders. For the most part, however, the states have
taken a position which straddles the issue as to the treatment of juvenile
offenders in murder cases.

The establishment of a state children's court does not solve all juvenile
problems; but, according to Sol Rubin in his article, "State Juvenile Court:
A New Standard," it does provide the best framework for the attainment of
high standards in all phases of juvenile court action. More state juvenile courts
may be anticipated within the next few years.

There is definite need for individualized justice, particularly in the cases of
youthful offenders who have not attained their majority. In "Boys' Court:
Individualized Justice for the Youthful Offender," J. M. Braude discusses the
Boys' Court of Chicago which was planned to handle the problems of boys
who had passed the juvenile court age of seventeen but were still under their
legal majority of twenty-one years. Judge Braude claims that this court has
been successful since its inception in 1914.

In one of the best articles written on the problems of juvenile courts "Most
Courts Have to Be Substandard!" Lowell Juilliard Carr discloses the basic
reasons why most of these tribunals are substandard. For example, small-town

---

[2] Paul W. Tappan, *Juvenile Delinquency* (New York: McGraw-Hill Book Co., 1949),
pp. 179, 180.

juvenile courts usually do not have the services of psychiatrists, and, in fact, are unfamiliar with such modern aids. Moreover, most communities are too poor to afford a juvenile court.

In "The Juvenile Court Today," Katharine F. Lenroot emphasizes problems requiring special consideration. The court's success is intimately related to the adequate treatment resources outside the court.

The Expansion of the Juvenile Court Idea*

By John Otto Reinemann. Director of Probation, Municipal Court of Philadelphia.

ANNIVERSARIES in the field of social legislation lend themselves well to stock-taking. Many articles celebrating the fiftieth return of the day on which the first juvenile court was created are dealing with the development of child care during this half-century span. These articles attempt to evaluate the contributions which the juvenile court has made to the whole child welfare program. They appraise the progress which the court itself and its closely related services—i.e., case study, classification, clinical treatment and supervision on probation—have made. Some of them are critical, because the work of the juvenile courts throughout the country has not fulfilled all the expectations of its original protagonists and its later standard-bearers. Others have allocated praise to many outstanding examples of good juvenile court practice.

There are voices heard, too, in these commemorative papers and addresses which say that the juvenile court's scope should be restricted and that other agencies should take over part of its original functions. There are strong and convincing opinions, on the other hand, which point proudly to the record of the juvenile court as the outstanding example of the new concept of "social jurisprudence," of the universal accept-

ance of the juvenile court's philosophy and practice, not only in all of the states and possessions of the Union, but by most civilized countries which adapted the American prototype to meet their own national needs and social exigencies.

The following presentation strives to highlight some of the areas of sociolegal activities which were influenced by the theory and practice of the juvenile court. The soundness of an idea, the validity of a concept, the genuineness of a belief are tested and proved by the spread of their underlying philosophy beyond its primary frame of reference. Evidence for the expansion of the juvenile court idea beyond its original scope has been specifically apparent in four developments: (1) the establishment of adolescents' courts; (2) the creation of the Youth Correction Authority and similar agencies; (3) the idea and practice of the family court; and (4) the influence of certain juvenile court methods upon procedure in general criminal courts.

Adolescents' Courts

In a few states concurrent jurisdiction has been conferred upon the juvenile court with the ordinary criminal courts either in all cases or only regarding spe-

* Reprinted from *Federal Probation*, Vol. XIII, September, 1949, pp. 34-40. Used by permission of author and publisher.

cific offenses committed by youngsters above juvenile court age but below the age of 21. However, the most significant development in this connection has been the establishment of special courts for adolescents in the three largest cities of the country.

The Wayward Minors' Act of New York State of 1923 (and later amended several times) provides that a person between the ages of 16 and 21 who is habitually addicted to the use of liquor or drugs, who habitually associates with undesirable persons, who is found in a house of prostitution, who is wilfully disobedient to the reasonable and lawful commands of a parent or guardian, or who is morally depraved or in danger of becoming morally depraved, may be deemed a wayward minor. Jurisdiction over these cases is given to the children's court (as the juvenile courts in New York State are called) and all criminal courts.

Under this act, an adolescents' court was established in Brooklyn in 1935 as part of the City Magistrates' Court, in order to deal with boys between 16 and 19 years of age. Its scope of jurisdiction, however, transcends the types of offenses enumerated in the Wayward Minors' Act. These are some of the phases of procedure:

All adolescent offenders charged with felonies or serious misdemeanors are brought to the Adolescents' Court instead of to the Felony Court. Hearings there are conducted in chambers. The arresting officer, the parents of the boy, the probation officer, an assistant district attorney, and witnesses, are the only ones present at the time of the boy's arraignment before the judge. If the boy admits his guilt or the magistrate believes him guilty after the hearing, the case is discussed with the assistant district attorney and the probation officer who had already interviewed the boy. A thorough investigation by the probation department follows, including, when necessary, a psychiatric examination. In many cases the boy is placed on probation to his parents.

Another adolescent court in New York City was created in 1936 as part of the Felony Court of the Borough of Queens. More recently the General Sessions Court of Manhattan has begun to apply the wayward minor technique to boys of the same ages as those in the Brooklyn and Queens Courts.

The Wayward Minors' Court of New York City with city-wide jurisdiction over girls 16 to 21 years of age, functions as part of the Women's Court and, since 1945, is officially known as "Girls' Term." Its jurisdiction encompasses only those types of offenses which are listed in the previously quoted Wayward Minors' Act. Its socialized procedure is characterized by the fact that defendants are not guilty but are "adjudged." There are no "convictions" but rather "adjudications" in the Wayward Minors' Court. Girls so adjudged are not fingerprinted. Upon adjudication, a wayward minor may be placed on probation for an indeterminate period of time or may be committed to an institution "duly authorized by law to receive such commitments."

Chicago, the birthplace of the juvenile court, also pioneered in the setting up of special judicial facilities for the handling of adolescents apart from older offenders. In 1914, the Boys' Court was created as one of the specialized branches of the Municipal Court of Chicago. The Boys' Court deals with misdemeanors and quasicriminal offenses, involving boys from the ages of 17 to 21, but, unlike other similar courts, it has no power to deal with such matters as waywardness, incorrigibility, or association with undesirable persons, which are not mentioned in the Criminal Code of Illinois. The Boys' Court also conducts preliminary examination in cases of felony committed by boys in this age range, holding them for action by the grand jury and possible trial by the criminal court of Cook County. Case investigations and examinations by the Social Service Department and the Psychiatric Institute, both adjuncts of the Municipal Court of Chicago, are another feature of socialized procedure employed by the Boys' Court. This court also has developed a very close and continuing co-operation with four different agencies, the Holy Name Society, the Chicago Church Federation, the Jewish Social Service Bureau, and the Colored Big Brothers Association. According to Judge J. M. Braude, of the Municipal Court of Chicago, a youthful offender—instead of being officially placed on probation—is referred to one of these organizations for supervision.

Shortly after the Chicago Boys' Court was established a similar step was taken in Philadelphia. In 1915, the Municipal Court, created 2 years before and vested with broad jurisdiction in civil, criminal, domestic relations, and juvenile matters, was given additional exclusive jurisdiction over minors above juvenile court age. The new branches of this Court, which took the name Boys' and Men's Misdemeanants' Division and Girls' and Women's Misdemeanants' Division, assumed jurisdiction in cases of minors between the ages of 16 (the upper juvenile court age limit at that time) and 21, "who shall disobey their parents' command or be found idle in the streets," or are deemed disorderly. The law defined disorderly children as those "deserting their home without good or sufficient cause, or keeping company with dissolute or vicious persons against their parents' command." Social investigation, similar to the practice employed in the juvenile court, precedes and largely guides the disposition of these cases; physical and mental examinations are given before the court hearing; probation frequently is used and medical treatment is prescribed and carried out whenever needed. Community agencies are called upon to assist.

Although the establishment of adolescents' courts represents a step in the right direction of expanding socialized procedure of juvenile courts into the higher age groups, these adolescents' courts are necessarily hybrids, embodying on the one side various but not all juvenile court aspects, and on the other side certain features of criminal procedure without, however, all the legal safeguards which the adult offender enjoys in the general criminal court. A much more adequate approach to the problem of the adolescent or youthful offender is found in the movement for the establishment of a Youth Correction Authority.

The Youth Correction Authority

In 1940 the American Law Institute, a research body devoted to the clarification and systematization of American law and composed of outstanding lawyers, judges, and professors of law and criminology, published a model law for the treatment of the adolescent offender. This model act, which was the result of careful deliberation of experts, proposed the creation of a Youth Correction Authority to be set up in each state by the legislature. Its function is to provide and administer corrective and preventive training and treatment for persons under 21 years of age at the time of their apprehension and committed to this Authority; it shall consist of three full-time members, to be appointed by the Governor for a term of office of 9 years, with a possibility of reappointment after the expiration of the term.

The late Judge Joseph N. Ulman of the Supreme Bench of Baltimore, a noted author on problems of criminal justice and a member of the committee which prepared the draft of the act, described its main features as follows:

The act provides that convicted offenders within the age group over the juvenile court age and under twenty-one shall be committed to the Youth Correction Authority for correctional treatment in all cases except those in which the trial court imposes the death penalty or life imprisonment at one end of the scale, or imposes a fine or a short term of imprisonment for minor offenses at the other end. The act provides an extended period of control by the Authority which may in exceptional cases, and subject to judicial review, continue for the life of the offender. The Authority is given wide discretion and the greatest measure of elasticity in dealing with the offender. It may release him under supervision before any period of incarceration whatever, it may limit his freedom slightly in a work camp or a supervised boarding home, or severely in a prison cell; and it may change its method of treatment from time to time and from less to more, and again to less severe forms as the exigencies of the individual case require. This plan differs from all existing practice in that it subjects the offender to continuous planned control by a single responsible administrative body instead of shifting him from one control to another. Finally, the Authority is given the right to terminate its control over the offender conditionally or unconditionally as soon as it appears that the protection of society and the welfare of the individual will be served by such termination.

In the years since publication of the Youth Correction Authority model law, the issue has left the purely theoretical stage. Four states (California, Minnesota, Wisconsin, and with certain modifications Massachusetts) have passed legislation incorporating the principles and procedures of the model act. In other legislatures, similar bills were introduced but so far failed of enactment; however, there are numerous indications that in the years to come efforts will be made by leaders in the correctional field and civic groups in many states to have such legislation put on the statute books. The Judicial Conference of the United States has fitted the plan of the Youth Correction Authority into a Federal Corrections Act for submission to Congress.

California, true to its pioneering spirit in many fields, was the first state to enact such legislation. Although the original California law of June 1941, establishing a Youth Correction Authority, drew heavily upon the model act of the American Law Institute, there were a number of important differences. One of them was the provision allowing the Authority to accept boys and girls from the juvenile courts (while the model act limited the Authority's function to youths above the juvenile court age). Another deviation from the model act was the extension of the upper age limit to 23 years at the time of apprehension; this, however, was later changed to 21 years. Unlike the model act, the California law left the power to grant probation with the courts. The name of the Authority was changed in 1943 to "Youth Authority."

The Youth Authority is headed by a board of three members appointed by the Governor; a unique feature is that two of the three members are chosen from a list of nominations prepared for the Governor by a panel consisting of the presidents of interested organizations, such as the Bar and Medical Associations of the State, the California Conference of Social Work, the California Prison Association, the Probation and Parole Officers' Association, and the Teachers' Association.

The California Youth Authority is in charge of six correctional schools and institutions, one of which is a ranch school; four permanent forestry camps; and one forestry camp open only during the summer. These institutions, schools, and camps are provided for the different age groups up to the age of majority.

A really well-functioning program of planned institutional placement stems from the services of a diagnostic center. The California Youth Authority's clinic at the Preston School of Industry serves this particular purpose and accommodates 140 youths from 15½ to 21 years of age. In addition to its diagnostic and placement functions, the Youth Authority carries on an educational campaign throughout the state, particularly in the field of positive crime prevention, and assists local agencies in an advisory capacity. It collects statistical data from all criminal courts on the number and disposition of young offenders. Parole from the institutions is also vested in the Authority. It grants parole and supervises parolees through a staff of officers attached to branch parole offices.

In Minnesota a Youth Authority was created in 1947. Called the "Youth Conservation Commission," it consisted of five persons including the director of the Division of Public Institutions, the chairman of the State Board of Parole, and three others appointed by the Governor. The district courts are committing to the Commission every person under 21 years of age convicted of a felony or gross misdemeanor who is not sentenced to life imprisonment, or imprisonment for 90 days or less, or to a fine only. The court also can place a probationer under the supervision of the Commission. A juvenile court not having a probation officer may request the Commission to investigate and accept juvenile delinquents for probation.

In the same year, Wisconsin adopted the idea of a Youth Authority by creating a "Youth Service Commission" consisting of 11 members who are appointed by the Governor with power of inquiry and the duty to make recommendations regarding the welfare of children and youth. Its operating arm is the newly established Youth Service division within the Department of Public Welfare. Wisconsin was fortunate that its Department of Public Welfare, even before the passage of the 1947 act, had at its disposal a well-integrated correctional service, including a staff and facilities for diagnosis. The law specifies that juvenile court commitments and commitments of minors where the penalty is less than life imprisonment, shall be to the Youth Service Division of the Department of Public Welfare,

which may confine the youthful offender or permit him to be at liberty under supervision, and subsequently grant a discharge. Other functions assigned to this department are crime prevention work and the performance of presentence investigation when called for by local courts.

From these examples in three states it is apparent that the basic idea of the model Youth Correction Authority Act has been considered as realistic enough to be translated into legislative acts and administrative practice. The California experiment, in particular, shows the real contribution which diagnostic services at observation and classification centers can render in the handling of delinquents. It further demonstrates that the centralization of control of a number of variegated institutional and other services makes possible the assignment of the youthful offender to the proper facilities and the transfer to another place when necessary. It abolishes the haphazard and planless commitment procedure to which the judges in many states are driven due to lack of study centers and the crazy-quilt of institutions—public as well as private—which are not co-ordinated with each other and which often are not supervised at all, or only superficially, by a central state agency. Because of its underlying philosophy of a systematic approach to the youthful offender, the idea of the Youth Correction Authority has been called "the most revolutionary step taken in American penology since the establishment of the Elmira Reformatory, and much more promising than that innovation."

The Idea of the Family Court

Not only vertically did the juvenile court idea expand, permeating, as we have seen, criminal justice procedure in adult cases but it also transcended its original scope horizontally by influencing, to a certain degree, the handling of cases dealing with all kinds of family matters. These cases concerning situations of domestic relations, legal custody, adoption, illegitimacy, and similar problems might be under the jurisdiction of the general courts or, by act of the state legislature, be assigned to courts especially created for their adjudication.

The juvenile court in some localities is closely connected with the domestic relations court; or the juvenile court, according to the laws of various states might have jurisdiction over guardianship, custody, adoption, illegitimacy, consent to marriage of minors, and annulments of marriage to minors. Probation officers, especially in smaller probation departments, have to handle not only juvenile court cases but also domestic relations matters, usually called desertion and nonsupport cases, and cases of establishment of paternity of children born out of wedlock. It is obvious that the principles and methods of juvenile court procedure are influencing the handling of all family cases, especially if they are prepared in the same probation department or in a domestic relations' court probation department operating in close proximity to the juvenile court.

In general, however, the development of special domestic relations courts, sometimes called family courts, has been much more sporadic than that of the juvenile court. Neglect to support wife and children, or desertion and nonsupport, are in many jurisdictions considered misdemeanors or summary offenses, and the begetting of a child out of wedlock (often called in the statute "fornication and bastardy") also is a criminal offense. These cases, therefore, are usually heard in the criminal courts of general jurisdiction. There is still comparatively little social service within the court machinery offered in the adjudication of these cases, although their very nature obviously would call for it. Adoption proceedings mostly take place in the probate courts, again with the emphasis on the legal phase, although in this field public and private welfare agencies play an increasingly important role and assist the courts in the preparation of these cases with regard to their social and psychological aspects.

The idea of establishing special courts with comprehensive jurisdiction in all matters concerning family and child welfare, requiring judicial disposition, has been advanced for several years by leaders in the field of law and social work, but it has been translated into practice only in a few places. Recently it received a new impetus through the National Conference on Family Life, held in Washington, D.C., in May 1948. In a report drafted by a committee of the American Bar Association for this conference, the establishment of family courts—aptly described as "socialized courts with socialized laws"—was recommended. This report was adopted by the House of Delegates of the American Bar Association which met in Seattle in 1948. Pointing to the modern juvenile court as prototype, this report said:

We suggest handling our unhappy and delinquent spouses much as we handle our delinquent children. Often their behavior is not unlike that of a delinquent child, and for much the same reasons. We would take them out of the quasicriminal divorce court and deal with them and their problems in a socialized court. When a marriage gets sick there is a cause. This cause manifests itself in the behavior, or misbehavior, of one or both spouses. Instead of determining whether a spouse has misbehaved and then "punishing" him by rewarding the aggrieved spouse with a divorce decree we would follow the general pattern of the juvenile court and endeavor to diagnose and treat, to discover the fundamental cause, then bring to bear all available resources to remove or rectify it.

The report further points out that "the proposal to have all justiciable family matters handled by one court is far from new. It has been tried and has long since passed the experimental stage. For over 30 years Cincinnati has had such a court. From the outset the soundness of the idea became more and more apparent, and soon other Ohio cities fell in line and for years the seven largest (next after Cleveland, which has an independent juvenile court) have had such integrated family courts." Other examples of family courts in existence are the Municipal Court of Philadelphia, created in 1913, and the Family Court of New Castle County (Wilmington), Delaware, established by act of 1945.

There exists a difference of opinion whether divorce cases should be included in the jurisdiction of a comprehensive family court. The previously mentioned report of the National Conference on Family Life favors the handling of divorce cases in the family court. The objection to this proposition usually is based on the argument that it would be incongruous to confer jurisdiction over divorce proceedings upon a family court which should be devoted principally to the maintenance and strengthening of family life. Another objection is that divorce cases may "take too large a part of the court's time and facilities."

But even with divorce cases being heard by courts of general jurisdiction, as is the present rule, the need for social investigation especially where children are involved, has been recognized by a number of judges in several states sitting in divorce cases. Such inroads of social aspects into the primarily legal procedure, as customarily employed in divorce actions, is another example of the expansion of juvenile court techniques into related fields.

Juvenile Court Influence on Adult Criminal Courts

We have seen that basic principles of juvenile court philosophy and practice have influenced decisively the Youth Correction Authority movement, especially in regard to the need of social and

medical diagnoses before disposition. While the scope of jurisdiction of Youth Authorities, both in theory and practice, is confined to persons below 21 years of age, the influence of the juvenile court idea has in several respects crossed the border of that age limit and has invaded the criminal justice administration in adult cases. The two most outstanding examples of this development are the presentence investigation, including the utilization of medical diagnostic facilities, and the use of probation.

Use of the presentence investigations for adult cases. The idea of individualization of justice which has found a concrete expression in the establishment of the juvenile courts also has prompted the demand for presentence investigations in adult cases, similar to the inquiries which customarily are made in cases of juvenile delinquency. Although this demand is far from universal, an ever increasing number of judges are realizing today the necessity of knowing more about the offender than what the trial with its strict rules of evidence and its exclusive limitation to the determination of guilt or innocence is likely to reveal. In order to pronounce a sentence that should serve the rehabilitation of the offender, the judge must have knowledge of the personality of the defendant, his social environment, his physical and mental make-up; he must have insight into the defendant's personal needs and, if possible, into the reason for his antisocial conduct. The presentence investigation supplies him with this information. One of the most important features of juvenile court procedure thus finds increasing recognition in the handling of adult offenders.

However, the safeguards which the law provides for the defendant in criminal trials must be respected. Therefore, information gathered through presentence investigation should be available only to the judge since the purpose of the investigation has nothing to do with the establishment of guilt or innocence and is only to be used after conviction of the accused person.

In the beginning, judges requested presentence investigations almost exclusively in cases where the granting of probation was contemplated. This is also apparent in the not too numerous statutory provisions on presentence investigation in several states.

The later development, though still quite sporadic, showed that not only in those situations where probation was a likely disposition, but also in other more serious cases, presentence investigations were considered by the judges as a vital necessity. The federal judicial system has probably gone farthest toward a more universal use of presentence investigation. The Rules of Criminal Procedure for the District Courts of the United States, adopted by the United States Supreme Court in 1946, specify that "the probation service of the court shall make a presentence investigation and report to the court before the imposition of sentence or the granting of probation unless the court otherwise directs." (Rule 32-c).

Presentence investigations are carried out by the probation departments of the local courts or, wherever they exist, by state probation departments. The compilation of social data follows quite closely the principles governing the preparation of social case studies in juvenile cases. In addition to the social investigation, the diagnoses of the offender by psychologists and psychiatrists are requested by some courts. Such facilities might be offered to the courts by clinics in hospitals and research institutions, or they might be established by the courts themselves as their own special services. An example of this type is the Behavior Clinic of the Quarter Sessions Court of Allegheny County (Pittsburgh), Pennsylvania, created in 1937 by the Board of Judges and maintained through funds supplied by the county commissioners. Another example of a presentence

clinic is the Medical Department of the Municipal Court of Philadelphia which is an integral part of this court and not only diagnoses children's cases but also adults standing trial before its criminal division and those referred by other local and federal courts in the area. There are a number of courts throughout the country utilizing similar services. Certain states are particularly well equipped along psychiatric lines, notably California, Illinois, Massachusetts, Michigan, New York, Ohio, and Pennsylvania.

Use of probation for adult offenders. Probation has its historical roots in the treatment of adults as well as juvenile offenders. As a tool of modern juvenile court procedure, however, probation has gained a much wider recognition and generally has shown a more advanced development than it has in the handling of adult cases. It has been this very development in the juvenile field that in recent years increasingly influenced the practice of probation for adult offenders. Supervision of adults on probation—though in some jurisdictions still not more than a routine "roll call" through the probationer's reporting to the probation officer in person or by mail—by now has been recognized in many progressive courts as a positive and scientific form of correctional treatment. Here, the fruitful experience of employing casework principles in the supervision of children has stimulated the use of advanced methods of guidance and counseling of adult probationers. The constructive use of authority in juvenile cases has pointed the way toward a similar approach to the adult offender. The utilization of community resources in the fields of health, family welfare, recreation and vocational guidance by the probation officer has proved of equal importance in juvenile and adult cases.

The various examples of the expansion of the juvenile court's philosophy and practice, as presented here, tend to confirm the prophetic statement of Judge

Benjamin Lindsey, one of the first protagonists of the juvenile court. More than 30 years ago he said: "The chief significance of the juvenile court move-ment is that in breaking away from the old procedure it is preparing the way for a new procedure for adults as well as for children."

Defect in the Youth Correction Authority Act*

By John F. Perkins. Justice of the Juvenile Court, Boston.

EVERY YEAR we put a large number of criminals into prison. Every year we let a large number of criminals out of prison. Every year we put back a large number we have previously let out. It seems a futile procedure.

Naturally this has evoked the criticism that the criminal law does not adequately protect the community, and our method of sentencing criminals immediately stands out as a major defect.

A Judge gives a sentence for a definite period. It may be not more than, nor less than, a certain number of years but it is fixed within limits and this fixed period need have no relation to the time necessary for the individual's rehabilitation. As a consequence men who are still dangerous get out of prison and commit new crimes, and men who are not dangerous are kept in prison, their spirit and standards destroyed, and through contact with vicious criminals they are manufactured into vicious criminals themselves.

The rule at many summer camps for boys is that no boy is allowed to go in a canoe until he has shown that he can swim a hundred yards. The non-swimmers are put into the hands of the swimming instructor, who helps each boy to learn. Some boys learn quickly, others find it slow work, and occasionally there is a boy who somehow does not seem able to learn how to swim. The present method of dealing with criminals applied to a summer camp would be this: The boys would be assigned dates in advance when they would be allowed to go in a canoe. For some the date and the ability to swim a hundred yards would coincide. For some the date set would be long after they had learned to swim. For others the date would arrive before they had learned to swim; they would go out in canoes and some of them would be drowned.

In short to attempt to determine in advance how long rehabilitation will take is a mere guess, an attempt at prophecy; and there seems no reason to prophesy when you can wait to see what happens, and then decide.

The Indeterminate Sentence

Therefore for many years various plans have been suggested to take away from the Court the power of determining the length of sentence. Advocates of these plans urge that the true function of the Court is to determine whether the law has been violated and whether the violation is sufficiently serious to make it necessary to put the offender under control. The work of correction i.e. the training and rehabilitation of the offender, they maintain, is a separate function, and should be placed in the hands of an entirely separate body, a correctional authority, to whom the court should commit the offender with-

---

* Reprinted from *The Journal of Criminal Law and Criminology* (Northwestern University School of Law), Vol. XXXIII, July–August, 1942, by John F. Perkins.

out attempting to prescribe the period during which he shall be kept under control. There is a difference of opinion as to whether the correctional authority should itself have the power to decide when an offender has sufficiently shown his fitness to return to the community, or whether the correctional authority should be required to bring him before a court and present evidence which will enable the court to determine whether he has satisfactorily demonstrated his right to be re-instated. But regardless of which of these two procedures is adopted many thoughtful people feel that by adopting one or the other of them, by taking away the Court's power to determine the period of control, we shall remove one of the most serious obstacles to the successful reform of criminals.

The present system is bad because it is inaccurate, but far more serious than its inaccuracy is the fact that it leads to injustice. Inevitably the Judge in passing sentence is influenced by the personal qualities of the prisoners; inevitably he allows this feeling to affect the length of the sentences he imposes. Furthermore, different Judges are affected differently by various crimes. One Judge is particularly severe on sex crimes and lenient on crimes of violence, and another Judge is just the opposite. So we find this universal complaint among prisoners: "X did just the same thing that I did. He got five years and I got ten." Instead of having it made clear that *they are deprived of their freedom for what they have done in the past, that their reinstatement depends on what they will do in the future and that they all start at scratch*, they see that they have been given unequal sentences for similar crimes, and not being willing to admit that their personal qualities justify discrimination, they feel that the Court's decision is purely a matter of favoritism, due to political influence or bribery.

A Merit System of Penology

Now the central and controlling fact in the correction of people is that correction is self correction, and that they have the final decision as to whether they will or will not make the necessary effort. *They* decide whether they will or they won't. *We* don't. To accomplish our purpose we must *get them to do something*, not merely *do something to them*; for if they are to correct their faults, they must do it by self-discipline and that involves systematic and persistent effort *by them*.

When men have committed crimes, when they are "outsiders" and have earned the fear and distrust of their fellowmen, it is a tough job to get their confidence, and create in them the desire to go to work to correct their faults, and the courage to face all the difficulties which confront them. It is so much easier to excuse oneself, blame some one else, and say "What's the use?" In this connection a man who used to take the histories of men committed to the Charlestown Prison told me this: "After I had examined the incoming prisoners for a year, I went to the Warden. 'I thought,' said I, 'that this was a prison for criminals.' 'What are you talking about?' said he. 'Of course it is.' " " 'No,' said I, 'I have examined every man who has come in here for a year and they all tell me that they have never done anything wrong!' "

What we are seeking for, what every one really wants is a merit system of penology. This would give criminals the chance to redeem themselves by effort and achievement. Hope is a powerful force, and if criminals realize that there is a real opportunity for them to wipe out their failures and restore themselves to good standing, many who now give up will try their best and succeed. But to be successful such a system must be fair and honestly administered. The criminals must believe in the integrity of the officials, and that if they earn their freedom, they will get it. They must believe that a man's freedom depends on himself, on his ability to meet the standard of conduct which the community requires, on his power to prove to himself and to others that he has this ability. Offenders and the public alike must get rid of the demoralizing belief that an offender's freedom depends on the whim and favor of a judge or a parole board, a belief which prevails today and for which there is far too much justification.

If a doctor is guilty of malpractice he forfeits his right to practice. He must earn his re-instatement. If a lawyer is disbarred, he must earn his re-admission to the bar. His violation of the prescribed standard is not waived or disregarded. He is not let off. That would be the equivalent of saying that he had committed no violation, or else that he personally was privileged and exempt. He must prove that he can meet the standard, that he can now succeed, where previously he has failed. He must convince others that he *will* succeed. So with those who commit crimes: they forfeit their independence and subject themselves to control. To regain their independence, they must earn it. They must demonstrate their ability to meet the required conditions. They must convince other people that they *will* meet them.

Danger Signs in Youth Correction Authority Act

Now the American Law Institute in its Youth Correction Authority Act took the first important step by taking away from the Court the power to prescribe the length of the period during which an offender shall be kept under control. But having taken this vital step forward it took two steps backward. It has removed inaccuracy but increased injustice. A merit system must be based on the principle: "By their fruits shall ye know

them." The American Law Institute has discarded this principle and in its place, has substituted the idea of a superintelligence which can decide what shall be done without needing to use an objective measure. It has gone further, and has provided that it shall act in disregard of an objective measure, and contrary to it.

Unfair discrimination. The Youth Correction Authority Act says in Section 29 (2) "The Authority shall discharge such person as soon as in its opinion there is reasonable probability that he can be given full liberty without danger to the public."

Immediately on reading this, one asks the meaning of "opinion." Is it an opinion which may reasonably be formed at once or must it be supported by objective evidence? There seems to be a difference on this point among the members of the committee who drafted the law. In Mr. Leonard Harrison's address in San Francisco, October 10, 1939, he says: "We actually propose to throw the key away after closing the door upon those offenders who *do not demonstrate* a capacity for improvement . . . we propose the greatest freedom and the earliest possible release for those who *demonstrate* that they are ready to abide by Society's rules."

On the same day at the same meeting, Judge Ulman, another member of the committee said: "It (the Authority) may dismiss him in a year, or in six months, in six days, or *at once*."

In the pamphlet, "Twenty-seven Questions and Their Answers," issued by the American Law Institute, Mr. Waite, the reporter of the committee, in his answer to Question 17, says—"Youths committed to the Authority will not necessarily be imprisoned at all; they may be discharged *at once*."

At the meeting in Washington in May 1940, when the American Law Institute adopted the Youth Correction Authority Act, I submitted the following case.

Two boys A and B steal a car, are

chased by the police, drive recklessly through the streets, try to jam the police car against the sidewalk and end in a smash-up in which an innocent bystander is killed. They are brought to Court, tried and convicted and committed to the Youth Correction Authority.

The Authority studies the boys. A is overwhelmed by what he has done, is penitent and anxious to avoid any mistake of this kind in the future. So far as anyone can see no further experience is necessary to make it safe for him to be free. B, on the other hand, is superficial and unstable. He expresses penitence, but it seems highly probable that unless his good intentions are crystallized by some form of discipline he is likely to forget them and yield to a temptation to do the same thing again.

Both boys have the same background, similar homes, and there is nothing to indicate that either is dominated by the other. Under Section 29 the Authority discharges A and keeps B under control. So A goes free, and B is sent to the Reformatory.

I asked Mr. Waite if this was a correct statement of what would be done in such a case. He said it was. Clearly, Mr. Harrison's interpretation is wrong and objective evidence is not required as a basis of the Authority's opinion. If an offender may be discharged at once, his discharge must be based on an unsupported opinion.

Here we have a law which not only permits discrimination between A and B without objective evidence, but also makes such discrimination mandatory, if the Authority forms a favorable opinion of A and an unfavorable one of B.

Let us consider for a moment how such action would work. B sees A go home while he is sent to the Reformatory. He protests: "Why should I go to the Reformatory and A get off? He was in it just as much as I was." "Oh," says the Authority, "it is not what you did that counts. It's what you are. Your act was a mere incident. You have an unstable personality. Before it will be safe to let you be at large in the community, you need corrective treatment. The public must be protected."

To which B replies: "You have no right to do this. I have learned my lesson. I will never break the law again. You say I am unstable. I say I am not unstable. I have been watching you all through your examination of me and your real reason is that you are prejudiced against Unitarians. I have as much right to say you are prejudiced as you have to say I am unstable. You cannot back up your opinion by proof of any kind. You have produced no standard of measurement to show I am different from A. What you are doing to me is absolutely unfair. You can show no evidence to justify refusing to give me the same chance that A gets."

And B would be right. Put this case to any set of boys, or school teachers, or managers of factories, or officers in the army or navy and their answer would be the same,—"It is unfair to B."

Now B is the boy the Authority is going to work with, the boy they are going to correct. And B feels that he is unfairly treated. If there is anything in the world which produces flaming resentment and antagonism, it is *unfair discrimination*. So at the very beginning of the relationship an impassable barrier is created between the boy and the Authority. Hope of inducing him to do anything except in a resentful, automatic way is gone. The chance of building the relationship and the attitude without which rehabilitation is impossible, has been destroyed. The plain fact is that we will not willingly accept any restriction of our independence without objective proof of the justice of the restriction. And if this restriction is accompanied by discrimination against us and in favor of some one else without clear-cut justification, it produces a fury that is likely to lead to serious crimes and to a bitterness almost impossible to eradicate. That is what we feel injustice is.

Fairness is the first requisite for a successful teacher, manager, officer or correction official. I have talked to great numbers of them. They all say: "If you get a reputation for being unfair, you are washed up." And here is a law put forward as a reform which not merely adopts unfair discrimination as its guiding principle, but makes it mandatory. It just won't work.

Arbitrary power. There is another principle involved in the Youth Correction Authority Act which if embodied in our law means a serious danger. In this particular Act it is so largely offset by safeguards that it is likely to escape unnoticed. But the danger is there and it is serious. It is the principle of arbitrary power; of absolutism.

Acting under its powers the Authority studies the persons committed to it, forms an opinion of the character and personal qualities of each person committed and decides whether he shall be locked up or go free, whether he shall be put in an institution or placed on probation, when he shall be paroled or transferred from one institution to another. Under this system the arrest, conviction and commitment of a violator of the law is merely a preliminary step. The test of criminality is not what a man has done. The way he is dealt with is not based on his behavior. What really determines whether a person is a criminal or not, and what shall be done with him is the *opinion* of the Authority which may be reached on any basis it sees fit. On this point it has unrestrained discretion.

Obviously this assumes that the Authority has the ability to read character and to prophesy what people are going to do, to select those who are likely to commit a crime, and those who are unlikely to commit a crime.

If this ability exists where does the logic of the situation lead us? The American Law Institute says that the objective of the Criminal Law is the protection of the public, in other words to prevent crime. If this is true are we using the ability of the Authority as effectively as we should? Under the Youth Correction Authority Act, the Authority studies only those who have already committed a crime. This is locking the door after the horse is stolen. Those whom it studies are selected by the haphazard method of arrest and conviction. If the real test of criminality is the opinion of the Authority, if the Authority has the ability to read character and foretell future behavior, why should we go through the long, expensive and inefficient process of arrest, trial, and conviction? Why not act effectively and comprehensively?

All children at eight, twelve, sixteen and from time to time thereafter should be studied and those who are likely to commit a crime taken under control. By this method we should check crime at its source, and protect the community.

I can see no escape from this conclusion if Section 29 is sound. It would, however, change the form of our government. We should replace the principle "By their fruits shall ye know them" under which we now live with the principle of an all-wise, all-powerful authority which knows what is best for us and decides accordingly.

To some people the foregoing may seem extravagant but if they had sat, as I have, at conference after conference where it has been urged that the Juvenile Court take charge of pre-delinquents they would realize it is not extravagant. The proposal was that the Court should impose its authority on Juveniles who *are going to be* delinquent. The Youth Correction Authority Act extends the idea to adolescents but limits it by safeguards. Experience has shown, however, that once the idea has gained a foothold, it spreads, and the safeguards disappear. In our zeal to improve conditions we often act like a boy who, intent on the recovery of his ball, rushes into the street directly in the path of an automobile.

Altogether the Youth Correction Authority Act has been a great disappointment. So much has been hoped from it. If it had been left simple it might have been very effective.

The Need for Standards

Suppose that instead of trying to get a penological experiment tried on a nationwide basis, an effort had been made to set up a Youth Correction Authority *with its own facilities* in one state only; and that it was provided that youths should be committed to it, in the language of an old penological report, "To be educated, reformed and made worthy of society," and that as soon as they had *demonstrated* their fitness to return to society they should be discharged. If a simple educational institution based on the merit system had been set up, if the total energy now dispersed over many states had been concentrated on getting a really first class Board of three men for the Authority, and they had been given a long term of office and allowed to work out the problem, great benefit might have resulted. The objection raised by the American Law Institute is that the merit system is impossible, that there is no standard by which conduct can be measured. Is this true? We have a standard for failure. Can't we develop one for re-instatement?

Let us take a college as an example. A number of students come there to get knowledge and training. The students have different aptitudes, and interests. Many courses are offered, but each student must select one field of concentration and make himself proficient in that. The different fields of concentration call for different kinds of ability, but the standard of achievement required in each field to earn a degree is pretty closely equivalent to the standard in all the rest.

Suppose we consider the Youth Correction Authority a College and those committed to it candidates for freedom. The College should have its own institutions, its own staff and facilities. Courses in carpentry, machine work, farming, etc., etc. would be available so that every youth would have an opportunity to develop proficiency in some form of trade if he was capable of any proficiency whatever. Discipline through pressure of work, unexpected difficulties, temptations to impulsive action could be woven into the courses. The question of equivalent standards in the various courses is undeniably difficult, but so it has been in the colleges, and it has been worked out.

Standards have been worked out for the practice of law and of medicine, for civil service, for engineering, for social work. In fact in more and more fields of human activity has the principle of standards been developed. With careful observation, with ingenuity in devising tests, with opportunities to work without supervision, it should certainly be equally possible for an Authority to decide from objective performance that men and women had shown sufficient proficiency in living with others to be allowed to return to society.

It seems ungracious, even churlish, to criticize the work of the able and devoted men who drafted the Youth Correction Authority Act. But I spent many years in the development of new machinery and I learned then the importance of working the bugs out of a new invention before manufacturing it. It is much less expensive to find mistakes in the drafting room than after the machine is built. I believe the Youth Correction Authority Act is seriously defective in its present form. In addition to the questions of principle which I have discussed other points need clarification.

Social legislation is full of pitfalls and should be subjected to the most searching scrutiny before it is adopted.

The need for improvement in our penal methods is extreme. But the extremity of a need does not put virtue into a defective remedy, and if we keep arousing enthusiasm for reforms which misfire we shall destroy enthusiasm for reforms which will work.

The Juvenile Court and Delinquent Parents[*]

By George W. Smyth. Judge, Children's Court, County of Westchester, White Plains, New York.

THE general philosophy of the juvenile court rejects the theory that we are engaged basically in the enforcement of the criminal law. Primarily these courts were created to shield children from criminal court surroundings; to bring them into new tribunals where they might be considered not as criminals, but as children in need of aid, protection, and guidance; tribunals in which a new type of individualized justice might be practiced, dependent not upon the offense committed, but upon the needs of the child; tribunals where programs of education and social work designed for the rehabilitation of homes would supplant time-dishonored sentencing of children and the further breakdown of the home.

The entire emphasis was placed upon the integration of moral training, education, social work, and physical and mental hygiene in the court or authoritative setting. A new concept appeared —the concept of a legal tribunal wedded to the social sciences; a combined socio-legal institution. We still call it a court, perhaps properly and necessarily because it represents the power of the State, and the word court conveys that meaning to the lay mind. But the juvenile court is or should be an institute of family relations with the force of the law behind it.

Into this clinic come parents and children. The purpose of the court in working with children is to endeavor to understand the problems which have caused them to become in need of the care and protection of the State, to alleviate adverse conditions as far as possible, and to bring understanding and guidance to the children who have become delinquent, as well as to those verging on delinquency because of neglect. To serve these social purposes, the court is permitted to make wide investigation before, during, and after the hearing. These investigations which are clinical in their nature, have been endorsed and approved by our highest courts. They include a broad study of the child's home and other environment, careful physical examinations, testing by the psychologist, and studies of the child and frequently of the parents by the psychiatrist in order that the court may be informed with respect to their mental attitudes and trends of thought toward their social, civic, and religious duties and responsibilities. Being thus informed, the court attempts to show the children that their conduct is harmful to themselves and society, and why it should be avoided, at the same time attempting to ameliorate the unfavorable factors in the home, and to bring the children into association with constructive character building influences, directing them to higher standards of living and personal conduct.

The same studies through which we endeavor to understand and to bring

[*] Reprinted from *Federal Probation*, Vol. XIII, March, 1949, pp. 12–17. Used by permission of author and publication.

understanding in children's cases, reveal to us the nature and extent of the contributions which the parents have made toward delinquency or neglect. They also indicate the modifications which are desirable in home surroundings and parental attitudes, in order that the children may experience, in the future, better example and guidance. While inspiring the child to seek for higher standards, we also try to teach the parents how the lack of parental guidance has combined with unfavorable elements of leadership and example outside the home, to cause the children to become in need of our care and protection.

Problems of Children and Parents Inseparable

The problems of the parents and children are inseparable. No problem of a neglected or delinquent child can be treated successfully without also considering the attitudes and actions of the parents. We find that an element of oversight, carelessness, disinterest, or ineptitude in the discharge of parental duties appears in almost every case. In some we find wilful fault such as abandonment or failure to provide support or supervision, commission of crimes such as carnal abuse and impairing morals, misconduct on the part of parents such as drunkenness or immoral personal example, and active or passive encouragement in delinquency. In any case, the basic problem for the court remains the same; namely, to alleviate the neglect and to forestall the further growth of delinquency. To that end we strive to gain the co-operation of the parents, for without it we have little chance of succeeding with the children. We need not only to open the eyes of those who slumber, but to change the thinking of those who consciously commit wrongs against children.

The only authoritative approach to the parents is through the law which confers upon the juvenile court a measure of criminal jurisdiction over parents who neglect or contribute to the delinquency of their children. Our objectives cannot be achieved through literal adherence to the statutes, but rather through persuasion, with occasional recourse to the authoritative powers we possess. All parents who contribute to the neglect or delinquency of children technically are guilty of misdemeanors and therefore subject to prosecution. Indeed, in New York the law goes so far as to provide "that a parent who omits to exercise reasonable diligence in the supervision of a child to prevent him from becoming delinquent or in need of the care and protection of the State," is guilty of a misdemeanor. The difficulty of prosecuting parents in such cases may be gleaned from the fact that no reported case under that section has appeared, although it has been on the books since 1910, except where the neglect has been wilful. The Court of Appeals, in *Cannon v. Cannon*, 287 N. Y. 425, very aptly remarked: "The law which imposes on parents the duty to support and discipline a minor child and prescribe a course of conduct designed to promote his health, education, and recreation accords to the parents a wide discretion, and in the exercise of that discretion and the performance of duties imposed by law through no choice by the parents, they are held to no higher standard of care than the measure of their own physical, mental, and financial abilities to provide for the well being of their child." The imponderables in this situation render it particularly difficult to place responsibility. On the other hand there are many cases reported in which parents have been guilty of wilful neglect or of wilfully contributing to the delinquency of their children, as distinguished from mere errors of judgment.

Method of Treating Parents

In the great majority of cases, whether based on conscious or unconscious fault, we find that if we are able to gain the confidence of the parents they will co-operate readily and willingly with those who represent the court in its endeavors to improve parental supervision and home conditions. Sometimes we encounter reluctance or failure to carry out the instructions of the court. Often the very fact that the court possesses power is sufficient to secure compliance. But in a considerable percentage we meet with ignorance, continued carelessness, or active opposition on the part of parents. It serves no useful purpose to prosecute a parent and convict him or her of the commission of a misdemeanor and to grant a suspended sentence, or to hold the threat of jail over his head, and thus try to operate through fear. We must do something more constructive than that. We must bring to these parents, whether wittingly or unwittingly at fault, a type of constructive social service which challenges our maximum ability to understand and guide human conduct and human relationships. The suspended sentence must be accompanied by probation. Whether probation is denominated casework or something else, I agree with both Professor Meeker and Miss Marilyn A. Blake who discussed the question in the June 1948 issue of *Federal Probation*. The work to be done with parents and children in these cases, involving as it does the reconstruction of human lives in the authoritative setting of the juvenile courts, is one which calls for expert skill equaling and probably exceeding that which is required in any other field of social work. Probation has been called the right arm of the juvenile court without which the court would be nothing more than one of minor criminal jurisdiction. The experience of the years has taught us how true that is, how absolutely dependent we are upon probation, and how little we can accomplish in dealing with parents except through the broadest and most competent social work backed by the

authority of the court. We speak of it as probation, and it is carried on by people called probation officers. The title is most misleading and should be changed. They should be called probation counselors, for that term is so much more truly descriptive of the attributes they should possess and the work they should do. Ideally they should have knowledge and experience in children's problems, child psychology, and the methods of solving human problems by various means. They should be sympathetic with those in misfortune and kind, yet firm when necessary, in dealing with the parents and children. They require real understanding of the physical and mental health of children and parents, and should be able to interpret and carry out the recommendations of the psychiatrist. They should acquaint themselves with the institutions and resources which are available in the community to minister to the sick and mentally ill among children and parents, to secure relief from grinding poverty, and to afford opportunities for stimulating leadership for children during their out-of-school hours. They should associate themselves with those who give spiritual leadership in the community that their clients may receive the guidance and succor which is so essential to them in their hours of trouble. All of these and many more services the probation counselor representing the court should be able to marshal for the benefit of parents as well as the children.

Those who have directed the most respected juvenile courts, where probation has reached its highest stage of development, freely admit how far short of the ideal we fall and how much still remains to be done in the way of educating probation counselors through colleges and in-service training. But despite limitations, great progress has been achieved.

Although the successful development and practice of this persuasive service enlists the co-operation of most parents, some always will remain deaf to persuasion. The law, therefore, wisely empowers the court to deal authoritatively with these recalcitrant parents. Obviously this power should never be invoked for the purpose of blind punishment. We are conducting children's courts. Our jurisdiction over adults is merely incidental to the work we do with children. We are concerned in the use of criminal law merely as an aid in salvaging the delinquent and protecting the neglected, and in prescribing such penalties as may be reasonable or necessary to right wrongs committed, and to secure compliance on the part of obdurate parents, with the general objectives of our socio-legal services. Exclusion of the offending parent from the home may be necessary in some cases and fines or imprisonment for reasonable periods in others, not as vindication, nor as a deterrent to others, but to check misconduct and to bring about reformation and permanent improvement. Probation should continue during the period of exclusion from the home and after the return of the offending spouse to the home when the period of exclusion terminates. It should also be resumed after a prison sentence terminates, in order that in either case the probation service may be constant and persistent, so long as hope remains of salvaging the individual offender or of rehabilitating the home. Thus we justify the disciplining of parents in the privacy of juvenile courts, and avoid the "lurid accounts of all the goings on" in the press, which my good friend Judge Alexander so rightly found objectionable in cases heard in open court.

Types of Delinquent Parents

Let us consider the practical application of the principles above stated:

Father who is guilty of incest. A father was found guilty of attempting immoral practices with his young daughters when he sometimes returned home drunk after they were in bed. He was placed on probation for the maximum period, ordered to leave the home and contribute a specified amount weekly to the support of the family. Thus the immoral conditions were ended, support continued, and the social service essential to both individual and family was initiated. This man is still on probation. In a similar case a few years ago, the conditions were permanently relieved and the defendant, in due time, because of the guidance he received, was restored to his family as a dependable member.

Parents who leave child at home unattended. Two college graduates were parents of a 2-year-old child. Neighbors complained that he was seen at the windows at night crying while the parents were off to the movies, having left him alone. They were prosecuted for neglect. Under probation they were helped to realize their mistake and became devoted parents.

Mother who loses three unattended children by fire. A woman lost three children in a fire because she left them unattended. She received a suspended sentence and probation. A few years later the lives of her subsequently born children were endangered in a similar manner. This time she was committed. True, the family was broken up and the children were placed. But it was a necessary step. Fortunately the reformatory, under the superintendency of one of our foremost social workers, is teaching her a great deal about parental responsibility, housekeeping, and child care. If she returns to her children eventually, all will experience the benefit derived from her stay at the institution.

Mother who refuses to send child to school. A mother stubbornly refused to send her child to school. He was placed in a foster home but she encouraged him to run away. Each time he went home she concealed him from the authorities. Finally she was charged with the misdemeanor of contributing to delinquency. Instead of a jail sentence, she, on conviction, was placed in the Psychiatric Institute and in due time emerged improved in bodily and mental health and became a firm friend of the court. Johnny continued under supervision and became a well-adjusted boy.

Mother who is alcoholic. Several mothers have been found to be alcohol addicts. Sometimes the children have been removed to foster homes; sometimes they have been left in their own homes. In either case the mother has been placed on probation, and with the aid of the psychiatric institutes or clinics, private sanitariums or Alcoholics Anonymous, improvement has been achieved in many cases. Imprisonment has been ordered only as a protection of the woman. I have never known it to effect a cure of alcoholism.

Father who lives in open adultery. Many different problems may be brought to light in one case. A 15-year-old boy who had been adjudged a juvenile delinquent because of burglary failed to respond to probation and was placed in a correctional school. Eventually he was paroled but again was brought to court a few months later on the charge of indecently exposing himself to a 9-year-old girl. Our social studies revealed that his father was then living in open adultery with a young woman in the very home he maintained for the boy; that he also had adulterous relations with the mother of a 15-year-old girl to whom he also was making improper advances; that these two adults took the child riding in his automobile, indulged in indecent language and conduct in her presence, and flaunted their improper relations before her. The girl was also before us as a neglected child because of the improper guardianship and because of budding sexual delinquency. The causal conection between the delinquency of these children and the immoral conduct of the boy's father and the girl's mother is abundantly clear.

The treatment to be attempted in each case must be molded to the accomplishment of our basic responsibility of salvaging the children through protection and guidance and through the guidance and discipline of the offending parents. Probation will play a major role, for even though it seemed advisable to remove the children, it is inevitable that they will in time return. For their sakes, as well as for the sake of other children, re-education of the adults through probation must be attempted.

Mother who has disreputable associations with other men. Mothers desert their children, usually going off with members of the opposite sex for varying periods and eventually returning. Their conduct is wilful and wrongful. Technically they are guilty. Looking beneath the surface we find unhappiness, discouragement, despair, human weaknesses, and mental or emotional unbalance. Imprisonment is not the answer. The constructive therapy of probation may help.

Father who deserts. Fathers desert their families, going off to distant points and leaving the families to be rescued through public relief. They are guilty, may be extradited, brought back, and imprisoned. But the adoption of reciprocal laws among the various states, as advocated by the State of New York (see Laws of 1947, Chapter 790) would provide a more effective remedy.

Mother who encourages daughter to engage in prostitution. Mothers with daughters use their homes for purposes of prostitution. The daughters might be taken away with consequent traumatic results. Experience proves that with the aid of the pastors and other community services the immoral conditions in the home can be eliminated and the ties of affection which exist even in such cases can be appealed to as a powerful incentive to improvement.

Parents who condone child's thefts. Not many Fagins are found (at least in the area where I work), but occasionally parents wink the other eye when children bring home stolen bicycles or other articles, and sometimes encourage them in shoplifting and other dishonest practices. I have never found it necessary to sentence a parent in such case, but through good probation counseling have succeeded in achieving the objective of the juvenile court.

Damages or Restitution

There are some forms of juvenile delinquency with which we find difficulty, either because probation seems too mild or commitment too severe, or because complete justice cannot be rendered through existing law. I refer to automobile stealing (joy riding), driving without a license, habitual truancy, and violation of Child Labor Laws. In these cases my experience proves that the parents are principally at fault and will continue to be so unless they receive a sharp lesson. I have found that charging the parent with the misdemeanor of contributing where the facts warrant such charge, and upon conviction imposing a stiff fine, is very effective. Well placed publicity concerning the fine stopped an epidemic of automobile stealing.

In cases of stealing and malicious mischief involving damage to property we find that the law does not hold the parents responsible for restitution or damages. Probably if it did the parents would be more interested in preventing such conduct, but if it only resulted in causing parents to carry insurance the injured parties would at least be able to secure restitution or damages.

Prevention of Delinquency Through Alleviating Neglect

Another effective approach to the parents of neglected and potentially delinquent children is found in many jurisdictions through the wise use of laws such as Article 3a of the Children's Court Act of the State of New York, and similar sections of the law governing the Court of Domestic Relations of the City of New York. Under these statutes the court is granted the power to hear and determine proceedings to compel the support of a child or stepchild, and the support of the wife, if pregnant, or if the support of the minor child or step-child is involved. In order to secure an award the petitioner is not required to prove that the dependent for whom support is desired would otherwise be likely to become a public charge. The amount awarded shall be such, "as justice requires having due regard to the circumstances of the respective parties." Thus we have a statute which authorizes a specialized court to grant adequate support to dependent wives and children, in a civil as distinguished from a criminal proceeding, although, as we shall see, the proceeding does at a later stage assume a quasi criminal character. This has proved to be one of the most salutary and useful of all the court's powers. Many cases are brought before us on the complaint of mothers to the effect that the defendant husbands have failed and neglected to support their wives and children in accordance with their means and the needs of the family. Our social studies in these cases reveal that nonsupport is only one of the many forms of neglect to which children in the families are exposed, ranging all the way from simple neglect to provide, to drunkenness, abuse and cruel conduct, obscene and indecent language, immoral practices, desertion, and all the ills which arise from divorce and remarriage of persons having inadequate incomes to warrant their indulging in that marital pastime. The law provides not only that orders of support may be made, but permits social service of the most complete nature, and authorizes orders of the protection to be granted setting forth conditions of behavior to be observed for a specified time, which shall be binding upon husbands or wives as circumstances may require. Such orders may direct either spouse to stay away from the home or from the other spouse or children, may permit such spouse to visit the children at stated periods, may require a husband or wife to abstain from offensive conduct against the other or against the children and to give proper attention to the care of the home, and to refrain from acts of commission or omission which tend to make the home not a proper place for the other spouse or the children. The offending spouse may be placed on probation, and these conditions may also be incorporated in the order of probation. Ample power is granted to deal with those who prove to be defiant or stubborn in their opposition to the court's efforts to improve the family situation. Undertakings for support may be required, and those who wilfully fail to obey the support order may be committed to the penitentiary for reasonable terms. At this point the proceeding acquires a somewhat quasi criminal aspect although it still continues to be regarded as a civil proceeding. Commitment or service of the sentence does not, however, terminate the liability for support, and the support order is revived and probation is resumed after the sentence has been served. Psychiatric and medical examinations are authorized and are enforceable, and, in short, the court is given complete power, within reasonable bounds, to control and rearrange the lives of the offending parent or parents in such manner that the interests of the children may be advanced, and the home cleansed of the conditions which have caused it to be an undesirable place for the children. Constructive work may be carried on with the ultimate goal of strengthening and reuniting the families wherever that may appear to be a possibility. The amounts recovered for the support of mothers and children are large, but the boon to the mothers and children in alleviating conditions inimical to the health and moral welfare of the children is greater than any financial consideration.

The principles to be observed in the treatment of these cases follow closely the methods which are employed in the other types of cases to which I have referred. After a complete social investigation including psychiatric diagnosis has been made, the most competent type of probation counseling is employed. The helpful social, educational, religious, and scientific resources which the community affords are marshaled in the manner most effective for the rehabilitation of the individual or family before the court. Understanding and sympathy are coupled with firmness and discipline.

Summary

First, the juvenile courts are concerned primarily with service to children. Limited jurisdiction is granted over adults pursuant to the criminal law for the purpose of dealing with parents who neglect or contribute to the delinquency of children.

Second, these powers should not be used principally for the purpose of vindication nor as a deterrent to others, but as an aid in securing compliance on the part of obdurate parents, with the broad objectives of the juvenile courts.

Third, imprisonment, threats and fear are neither effective nor desirable. Understanding guidance which is offered through the court and its probation counselors for the purpose of alleviating harmful conditions, and strengthening the moral and ethical concepts and conduct of both children and parents is the most constructive method of dealing with offending parents.

Fourth, it is therefore necessary that the probation service in all our courts which deal with social and moral problems involving children and parents be raised to the highest possible degree of efficiency, for the task is so great that it requires our maximum efforts.

Fifth, finally, while progress has been made in many of our courts, we must still look to our colleges and in-service training for the still greater improvements which must occur if we are to meet this challenge successfully.

Placement from the Child's Viewpoint*

By Leontine R. Young. Formerly, New York School of Social Work; Professor of Casework, School of Social Administration, The Ohio State University, Columbus.

ANY child who is compelled for whatever reason to leave his own home and family and to live in foster placement lives through an experience pregnant with pain and terror for him and potentially damaging to his personality and normal growth. It is abnormal in our society for a child to be separated for any continuing length of time from his own parents and no one knows this so well as the child himself. For him placement is a shocking and bewildering calamity, the reasons for which he usually does not understand. We may know that placement is a necessity, a tragic one, and we may know this is for him a crucial experience which, without wise help and understanding, may leave him with a backwash of suspicion, resentment, and cruel confusion. He knows only that his life has been pulled up by the roots, and two questions circle him endlessly—why and when? Why did it have to happen? When can he return to his own home? He is in a peculiarly vulnerable and helpless position, and usually the one person who can and must help him at this point is the caseworker who places him.

The Caseworker's Part

We have not always appreciated the full significance and importance of this responsibility. As adults working continuously with the process and fact of placement, we may easily minimize in our own minds its abnormality for the child and come to take it almost for granted, thus losing a basic and essential perspective for understanding its real meaning to, and impact upon, the child. As adults we find it easier to view the problems from the safe and practical vantage point of the grownup, and we may blind ourselves to the enormous gulf that here divides that vantage point from the actual terror, pain, and confusion of the child. The judge who removes a child from his own home at ten in the morning and then asks the social worker to place him by five that afternoon exhibits this blindness. The caseworker who picked up 4-year-old Tommy, without previous explanation, from one boarding home and moved him to another, was mildly surprised when he went to sleep on the way. She left him in the new foster home before he awoke, for she saw only the practical necessity of replacement, an adult consideration. She was blind to Tommy's paralyzing panic and the fact that from his side there was good reality reason for that panic; she did not see that he went to sleep because there was no other escape from a terror too great for him to face, and that when she left him to wake with total strangers, the nightmare turned into reality. She had forgotten that he was a person and had moved him like a bundle of laundry. For every caseworker preparing a child for place-

---

* Reprinted from *Social Casework*, June, 1950, pp. 250–255. Used by permission.

ment the first and most essential requisite is the ability to see the situation from the child's point of view.

There is only one source from which we can actually learn to know and understand the feelings of any child, and that is from the child himself. We need to know how to observe and how to listen if we would understand what a child is feeling and how to help him. And we need to realize that he is a person entitled to the same respect as an adult. The caseworker, who meets the child as a stranger and as the symbol of the thing he fears and dreads—placement—needs time, patience, and sensitivity if the worker is to have the opportunity to know him and hence to prepare him for what lies ahead. There are no short cuts and no compromises here. When we attempt them, the child pays the bill for our failure.

The Child's Problem

The child confronted with the fact of placement faces a dual problem: what he leaves and what he goes to. No child wants to leave his own home (with the possible exception of some adolescents) even though in many cases it seems from our eyes that the home offers him nothing but unhappiness. Bad as it may be, this home offers him the only security, the only real sense of belonging, that he has ever known. Leaving it casts him adrift in an alien and hostile world. This need to belong to someone, to have a place uniquely one's own, is a very deep and fundamental one in human nature. Adults talk a great deal about the confusion and unhappiness and insecurity of a modern world in which they do not have a clear and established place. How much greater realistically is the child's self-same need in the light of his dependency and helplessness, and, concomitantly, how much stronger his emotional necessity for security. One child in the process of replacement expressed his bitterness well, "The social workers are

the bat and I'm just the ball they sock from one place to another."

It is not strange that a child should cling so desperately to his parents despite neglect, rejection, and cruelty. Doubly bitter for him is the fact that in the majority of the cases he is not wanted by his parents. To be unwanted by one's own family is one of the cruelest and most devastating blows than can befall a human being, and placement to the child is the final, irrevocable proof of rejection. Unfortunately, in most cases the child is right in this feeling, and placement merely climaxes and translates into official action a process and a struggle of greater or less duration. What the child does not know and cannot understand is "why." It is the insistent and inevitable question for him to ask. I heard a child say in bitterness and grief and despair, "Why did this have to happen to me? Why did it have to be me instead of Johnny or Bill? What have I done that they didn't do?" Again it is not strange that almost every child answers that question in identical terms. "There must be something wrong with me. I must be so bad nobody could love me." How else could he answer it? And all too often the people around him give the same verdict in their actions if not in their words.

The child leaves his home heavy with grief and confusion, torn with anger and hate at those forces represented by the omnipotent grownups which he can neither understand nor control. He faces the future with blind panic and terror, for the future is the unknown; and nothing is quite so terrifying to anyone as the unknown, peopled as it is with creatures out of nightmares and tortured imagination. It is easy for us to miss altogether the child's terror since, knowing ourselves what a foster home is, we fail to perceive that he cannot possibly know or share our knowledge without direct experience. Words, however explicit and reassuring, are frail and feeble weapons against the terrors and fantasies that enmesh the child.

Preparation for Placement

All too often caseworkers are not clearly labeled in the child's mind as friends but rather as certain or potential enemies from whom he must withhold any open display of his emotions, even his lonely and deadly terror. More than the kindly "I am your friend and want to help you" is needed to convince a suspicious and unhappy child of that fact. Every placement worker is familiar with the quiet, obedient child who travels to the new home with little if any outward emotional reaction and who may even discuss superficial subjects with spurious cheerfulness. We have sometimes called this "adjustment" or comforted ourselves that this proves the child does not really mind. Did we look closer we would recognize shock, apathy, despair. If we, as grownups, were dropped tomorrow upon another planet with none of the familiar supports of this world, we, too, might trudge along quietly and obediently. A young man, who had been placed in an institution at the age of 6, later described how he felt in these words: "How is one to describe a 6-year-old's shock, confusion, bewilderment, and then almost apathy? I felt all choked up—couldn't cry, couldn't speak —just looking ahead, almost as if straining to see what lay before me. I was tired— of travel, of cold, of hunger, of everything, including life."

How then is the caseworker to prepare the child for the necessity of placement and to mitigate his pain and fear? Clearly, anything the worker can do depends upon ability to understand the child's feelings, to see the situation from his point of view and to prove to him that the worker is really his friend. This is possible only as the worker shares the experience step by step with him, proving by actions that the worker is trustworthy. It is very difficult for an adult to put himself into a child's shoes and, beyond perhaps a couple of toes, impossible. Hence we must take our cues from the child, knowing that only he can tell us the specific fears and worries and conflicts that are troubling him and that only he can decide finally whether or not and to what extent he will trust us. So often in our impatience we try to force or to coax the child into believing us and succeed only in driving him farther away. This decision only he can make and it is an important one, for upon it hinges much of the outcome of his ultimate acceptance or rejection of placement. It matters a great deal to his whole future adjustment whether he goes into placement alone against the world or with the support and understanding of a proven friend. No better general rule could be given any caseworker working with a troubled and unhappy child than to relax and listen and then follow the guideposts that the child himself sets up.

The Case of Tommy. Children tell us how and what they feel through actions as well as words, and the young child acts rather than talks out these feelings. Tommy, mentioned earlier, shows what can happen when we ignore what the child is trying to tell us. At the age of 3 he was taken abruptly by court order from his irresponsible and immature mother who had been neglecting him. Without warning or preparation he was placed in a temporary foster home. His mother was not permitted to see him. At first he was dazed and his reactions were those of any person suffering from severe shock. This first foster mother was a very warm, sensitive woman who understood something of what was happening to Tommy and mothered him with tenderness and patience. Gradually he began to show some spontaneity, to smile and laugh occasionally, and to give a little response to affection. His eyes were still sad and he was fearful of many things, particularly new people and places.

Then, after several months, a permanent foster home was found for him, and he was again moved abruptly. This time he screamed and wept, refused to have his coat removed when he reached the new home, and, wild with terror, sat in the middle of the floor refusing to let anyone touch him. The worker left presently, feeling that when he was alone with his new foster mother he would more quickly settle down. The new placement was not a success. This foster mother, lacking the warmth and understanding of the first, grew angry when Tommy soiled and wet, became sullen and resistant, and refused to respond to gestures of affection. And so again Tommy was moved. This time he went with the worker without protest and fell asleep on the way to the new home. When he awoke, he was alone with strangers. Truly a lost child, now Tommy withdrew into himself almost completely, his only sign of continuing rebellion the persistence of his soiling and wetting. He did not smile or laugh now and his movements were controlled and secretive, without vitality or spontaneity. His foster mother could not understand this strange, unnatural child and so Tommy was placed again.

He now had a new worker who realized what had happened. She had little time to prepare Tommy, because his foster mother wanted him moved quickly, and she was caught between two perils, the damage of another abrupt move and the rejection of the foster home. She made the best compromise possible. She spent a great deal of time with Tommy over the short span of a couple of weeks explaining over and over to him what the new home was like. She brought his mother to see him and took them out together in her car to visit the new foster home. And when Tommy was moved, she and his mother placed him together. In short, she sought to reforge those links with the past, the known from which he had been so cruelly and completely uprooted. It would be pleasant to record that she succeeded, but she did not. She came too late.

A year later, Tommy, who has remained in this foster home, has "adjusted" beautifully on the surface. He is conforming, obedient, easy to handle. Of course, he is very quiet, never laughs, rarely smiles. With other children in the home, he plays mostly by himself—quiet, mysterious games that are shared with no one. If you ask him about the past, he tells you matter-of-factly that he came directly from his own home to this home. He remembers no other foster home. Tommy has gone to live in a land where no one can follow him, and for peace he has paid the price of life. He had tried over and over again in his actions to tell us what was happening, but no one listened until too late.

The Case of Bobby. The same thing might have happened to Bobby, but he was lucky. He found adults who listened and understood. An out-of-wedlock child, he had been placed by his mother in several private boarding homes. When he was 4, she surrendered him for adoption and he came for the first time under an agency's care. Since the private boarding home wanted him removed immediately, he was placed with little preparation. However, the worker took Bobby's own mother with him, talked and played with him in the car, and explained very simply where he was going. He was quiet until they reached the foster home and then he screamed and cried. Almost immediately after his mother and the worker left, he became very quiet, submissive, and docile. His new foster parents were warm and intelligent people who understood something of Bobby's terror, and the worker helped them to understand the kind of help Bobby needed. At that time he had many problems. He had a speech defect, confused the meaning of "yes" and "no," often saying "no" when he wished to say "yes" and *vice versa*—indicating the extent of his confusion and deep anger and fear. He was too eager to please the foster parents and was very conforming. With other children he readily gave up his toys and quickly withdrew if there was any fighting or quarreling. He was afraid to put on his hat and coat and did not want to leave the house even for short trips to the store. The foster parents made few demands upon him and followed his pace. They did not take him out of the yard until he indicated he was willing to take that chance and go with the foster mother to the store. After that the family made many short trips and visits so that he could have the experience of going out and returning with them. They set up definite schedules for eating and bed and bath since regularity of routine gives some fragment of certainty and security to a fearful child.

The worker came to visit often. Always she brought a gift for Bobby and the foster parents' little girl. At first Bobby greeted the worker with a prompt "good-by" and refused even to enter the room where she was. She took her cue from Bobby, always greeted him but made no effort to break through his reserve. If he did approach closer, she immediately included him in the conversation but did not approach him. She would lay the gifts in a nearby chair and tell him he could take them whenever he wished. In short, during these first weeks she showed him she liked him and was interested in him, but she respected the fact that he had to decide how far it was safe for him to trust her. After all she had moved him once and what guarantee did Bobby have that she would not snatch him up again and take him away?

Gradually, Bobby was able to come closer to her, to accept gifts from her directly and to begin to talk to her. He remembered when she had moved him and he began to ask questions about the "black car." He talked about it as if it were a being itself, and because she listened, the worker realized that he was afraid of the car as a symbol of what had happened to him. And so she began to drive past the house when Bobby was playing outside and just wave to him so that he began to understand she and the car could pass without hurting him. Then one day she left some candy in the car and told him that he might go and get it. He hesitated for some time but just before the conclusion of the visit he asked permission of the foster mother to take his foster sister with him and the two children went to the car together and secured the candy. Since the worker remained inside the house, Bobby's fear of the car itself as a sentient being was clear. She repeated this several times until Bobby would run to the car quite confidently and freely.

With time, love, consistent protection, Bobby began to lose many of his fears, became a more active, spontaneous, normal little boy who could afford to have a personality of his own. Then the worker was able to start more direct preparation for placement in an adoptive home. She did not discuss this directly with him at first. Instead they went to lunch together and for short trips around the countryside. Several times when she was making short visits to other foster homes, Bobby went with her. He saw other children who were placed in foster homes and could then begin to discuss with the worker some of his questions about why he was placed and what had happened to him. She answered his questions simply and honestly, explaining that his mother had become very sick and had wanted him to have a mother and father who could take good care of him. She began to talk to him a little about finding this mother and father who would be wholly his own. Bobby seemed interested but not very concerned.

One day she took Bobby to lunch and the adoptive parents came by the table and spoke to her. She introduced them as friends of hers to Bobby and asked if he minded their joining the party. Bobby enjoyed them and was pleased when they invited him and the worker to lunch. Later he visited alone. The adoptive parents visited Bobby in the foster home also. Eventually he accepted an invitation to spend the night with the adoptive parents, and the next day he returned to the foster parents, saying that he was going to live for a short time with the adoptive parents. He took his clothes but carefully left his piggy bank in the boarding home. For a time both the worker and the boarding parents continued to visit Bobby and he returned once or twice to visit the boarding home. But as he put down roots in the adoptive home, his interest in both the boarding parents and the worker waned until it was only that of any normal little boy in adult visitors coming to see him and his family. Bobby had been placed without shock or fear or suffering. He had some anxious moments, but real trauma had been avoided.

Two factors had made the great difference. One, Bobby had been placed slowly at his own pace, as he was able without great anxiety and tension to accept the change from one known experience to another known situation. Throughout, the worker was a constant and steady support, a friend who shared change with him and hence robbed it of its loneliness and terror. He never faced strangers alone and he knew from their many shared experiences that the worker never let him down, never deserted him, never betrayed his trust in her. For a child who has been disappointed bitterly by adults, this consistent, continuous relationship is indispensable. There is no other way that a child can learn to trust the new except through his experience in the past that someone important and close to him is trustworthy. Without ex-periencing that, no knowledge that all adults are not cruel and rejecting of him is possible. Second, Bobby participated in this placement. He did not choose his permanent home but he was given an honest chance to accept it of his own volition. No child is capable of selecting a foster home, but only the child can make the decision of whether or not he will genuinely accept it. We have the power to place him physically even against his will and desire, but there our power ends—sometimes disastrously. We cannot make him accept that placement and use it for his own happiness. There is only one way we can help him do that —by giving him a home where he can belong and be happy and then by giving him the time, patience, and understanding which enable him to experience that knowledge for himself.

Bobby himself had made that very clear. Earlier, after about a year in the boarding home, an emergency had made it necessary for the foster parents to be gone several months. They took their own child with them, but Bobby was placed for this interval with the foster grandparents who lived close by. Bobby knew the grandparents well and seemed to make the move without difficulty and to adjust easily to living with them. When the foster parents returned, he came back to them eagerly. But this time the placement did not work. Bobby was openly unhappy and the warm, relaxed relationship he had established with them before this move was gone. The worker asked Bobby what was wrong, why he was unhappy now when he had not been before. And because Bobby loved and trusted this worker, he could tell her simply and clearly. The foster parents had gone off and left him, but they had taken his foster sister with them. How could he know now that they would not do this again? Nor did any explanation of the reality reasons convince him. For him the clear fact was that they had left him but had taken their own child. He could no longer trust them or feel that he belonged to them. When the worker asked if he would like to return to the foster grandparents, he agreed without hesitation and went happily. This time he was rejecting, not being rejected, and he could choose because there was someone to go to. It was from this home that he moved to his final placement, the adoptive home which was truly his own.

Conclusion

Only the child himself can know what placement really means to him. To help him we must first learn from him and then seek with all the resources at our command to find an answer to those needs which in fulfilment become the foundation of a healthy, happy human being.

The Treatment of Juvenile Offenders in Murder Cases*

By Michael S. Precker. Special Master of Chancery, Newark, New Jersey.

ALTHOUGH children's courts had been established in Australia in the early nineties it was not until 1899, when the State of Illinois enacted enabling legislation, that such courts were incorporated into American jurisprudence. Prior to the establishment of such courts, it had been the practice in this country to hale juvenile lawbreakers before the criminal courts and to brand them with the stigma of a criminal charge. Those who were found guilty were either punished or placed on probation. Although the theory of probation aimed at the rehabilitation of the youthful offenders and their return to society as useful, law abiding citizens, the efforts to that end were always stultified and in many instances completely frustrated by the psychological effect of their experience with the law on the impressionable minds of the young culprits.

The equitable nature of juvenile courts has been comprehensively set forth in the much quoted case of *Commonwealth of Pennsylvania v. Fisher* (213 Pa. 48, 62A. 198).

The success which attended the establishment of juvenile courts has not failed to impress politically-minded legislatures. Their response to the popularity of these courts has found expression in their attempts to broaden the jurisdiction of the courts. On the other hand, the judiciary has zealously guarded the jurisdiction of the criminal courts from the inroads of such legislation whenever the unconstitutionality of such legislation was indicated. In the main, however, the criminal courts have been shorn of their jurisdiction over youthful offenders with respect to all offenses except murder and treason. This, the question of the treatment of cases involving juveniles charged with the crime of murder, is the subject of our inquiry.

Developments in New Jersey

Nowhere, perhaps, has the jurisdictional conflict between criminal and juvenile courts been more warmly contested or more clearly resolved than in the State of New Jersey. But the courts have gone beyond the mere refusal to accept a guilty plea, for the decisions hold that evidence of such a plea may not be introduced in the trial of an accused person. Finally they have gone so far as to hold that the improper introduction of evidence of this nature constituted

* Reprinted from *The Journal of Criminal Law and Criminology* (Northwestern University School of Law), Vol. XLI, May–June, 1950, by Michael S. Precker.

sufficient grounds for the Appellate Court to declare a mistrial, notwithstanding the failure of defendant's counsel to enter an objection and exception on the record. (See *State v. Leaks*, 124 N.J.L. 216, 10A. 2d 281 N.J.S.A., 9:18–12.)

Broad considerations of the basic nature of the crime of murder having been disposed of, it may now be appropriate to turn our attention to the statute creating and defining the jurisdiction of Juvenile Courts in New Jersey.

The result in New Jersey is typical of the result in New York and Illinois and other jurisdictions when a juvenile murder case arises in spite of enlightened thinking that the juvenile delinquent should not be treated as a criminal in a criminal court.

The first thought which arises upon a reading of the opinion in the Goldberg case (*State v. Goldberg*, 124 N.J.L. 272, 11A. 2d 299) is that here is grudging admission that our judiciary realized that the benefits and constitutional advantages of the juvenile court act outweighed the constitutional disadvantages or defects, and felt constrained, therefore, to erect a barrier in cases involving the crime of murder. The opinion in this case, significantly, was written by Justice Case, who delivered the opinion also for the Court of Errors and Appeals in the Mei case (122 N.J.E. 125), and who consequently participated in the deliberations of the court on that occasion. The second thought evoked by the opinion is that the courts, although admitting the protective advantages afforded to the child by the juvenile court, "make confusion more confounded" by saying in effect: "The child needs this court to correct his erring ways, but if he errs too greatly, this court cannot open its doors to him." Dr. Ralph S. Banay, Associate Director, Research on Social Deviations, New York, commenting on the inherent contradiction in such reasoning in an article in a recent issue of *Federal Probation* entitled "Homicide among Children," makes this pertinent observation:

The apparent philosophy behind statutes concerning juvenile offenders is that a child has not reached a degree of intellectual and emotional development that would qualify him as fully responsible for his acts. The laws, however, embody an obvious contradiction; for when the offense is too obnoxious or repugnant, complete responsibility is placed upon the child and he must face the full weight of the law.

That it was the intention of the New Jersey legislature not to except the crime of murder from the jurisdiction of the juvenile court is indicated by the course of subsequent legislation. In 1943 an amendment was enacted raising the age of children under such jurisdiction from sixteen to eighteen years and adding the following provisions:

If it shall appear to the satisfaction of the court that the case of any person between the ages of sixteen and eighteen years should not be dealt with by the court, either because of the fact that the person is an habitual offender, or has been charged with an offense of a heinous nature, under circumstances which may require the imposition of a sentence rather than the disposition permitted by this chapter for the welfare of society, then the court may refer such case to the prosecutor of the pleas of the county where the court is situate.

Such case will thereafter be dealt with in exactly the same manner as any other criminal case involving an adult offender.

Any offender between the ages of sixteen and eighteen years may demand a presentment and trial by jury and, in such case, shall be referred to the prosecutor of the pleas and dealt with in exactly the same manner as any other criminal case involving an adult offender. Every case so referred shall be accompanied by all documents pertaining thereto.

Although the first of the three foregoing quoted paragraphs does not mention the crime of "murder" by name, it requires but a modicum of mental acumen to appreciate that the legislature meant "murder" and was inhibited from giving utterance to it by the umbrage resulting from the Daniecki (*Ex parte*, 117 N.J.E. 527, 117A. 91) and Mei opinions. It remains to be seen whether, in view of the clear legislative intent as expressed in the amendment, the New Jersey courts will hereafter modify their position with respect to the jurisdiction of juvenile courts in murder cases, or if they will continue to hold fast to a philosophy which attempts to justify an untenable position.

Developments in New York

In what way, if any, the courts of New Jersey have been influenced by decisions in the sister state across the Hudson is difficult to say, because there is virtually no reference to the New York precedents in the cases we have thus far considered. This may stem from the fact that there is no uniformity in the enabling legislation on the subject, such as may be found in the statutes of the several states on other subjects. The Children's Court Act of the State of New York was enacted pursuant to the provision of the state constitution that "the Legislature may establish Children's Courts and may confer upon them such jurisdiction as may be necessary for the correction, protection, guardianship and disposition of delinquent, neglected or dependent minors." The Children's Court Acts give the Children's Courts exclusive jurisdiction to hear and determine the cases of children under the age of sixteen years who are charged with juvenile delinquency. The extent of this jurisdiction has been lucidly set forth in the case of *People v. Murch* (263 N.Y. 285, 189 N.E. 220) as follows:

The legislative history of those sections, as well as the unmistakable implications of the language used, show a clear intent to remove from the category of crime any and all lawbreaking acts committed by a child between the ages of seven and sixteen years, except those punishable by death or life imprisonment. The conclusive presumption of incapacity which has always existed in the case of a child under seven years of age is, as to those acts, now applied to a child between the stated ages . . . The result is that the only crimes which a child under sixteen years of age is capable of committing are treason, murder in the first degree and murder in the second degree; and that as to those crimes alone, in the case of such a child, have the criminal courts jurisdiction.

Since the decision just quoted rested largely on the previous decision of the New York Court of Appeals in the case of *People v. Roper* (229 N.Y. 170, 181 N.E. 88), it will be helpful to quote briefly from the opinion of Lehman, J., in the latter case:

Upon the trial of a child under the age of sixteen, the participation of a child in a robbery or at least in a robbery in the second or third degrees, would not establish the guilt of a felony, but only of a minor offense characterized as juvenile delinquency. Hence, it is plain that the defendant's conviction rests upon no finding of guilt of a felony, and thus no finding of felonious intent, and the judgment must be reversed . . . A child under sixteen can be guilty of murder in the first or second degrees where he kills a man with felonious intent, but such felonious intent is not established without both proof and finding of intent to kill or of guilt of an independent felony during which the homicide occurred.

The temper of the decisions in New York since the Roper and Murch cases has been to extend the application of the "felonious intent" philosophy even further, by the use of such expressions as "design murder." An illustration of recent judicial reasoning on this subject is the case of *People v. Porter* (54 N.Y. 2d 3), which was decided in 1945 in the King's County Court of New York, from which the following significant comments are quoted:

While all four defendants move to dismiss the indictment, the only serious question is raised by the three defendants who are under the age of 16—Porter, Washington and Skinner. It is contended on their behalf that at most this is a felony murder, and under our statutes and decisions persons under the age of 16 may not be convicted of a felony murder but only of what is often designated as a design murder i.e., with a design to effect death.

This contention is correct. It is settled law that a youth under sixteen may not be deemed guilty of any crime—but of juvenile delinquency—if he commits 'any act or omission which, if committed by an adult, would be a crime not punishable by death or life imprisonment.' Penal Law No. 2186. That being so, a murder prosecution is not warranted, nor a murder conviction justified by proof that the victim was killed while the youth was engaged in committing a felony. In other words, although an adult may be convicted of first degree murder on proof that a killing occurs in the course of a felony upon which he is engaged, a fifteen year old youth may not be so adjudged, unless there is proof that he intended to kill.

Unless there is sufficient evidence before the Grand Jury that Porter, Washington and Skinner intended to kill, the indictment against them should be dismissed.

Conclusion

In this brief survey, it has been the purpose of the writer to point up the sharp conflict between the conservative forces of established law as exemplified in the judicial decisions and the progressive dynamism inherent in the program of sociologists, as evidenced in the extension of legislation in behalf of juvenile offenders. The developments in New York as well as in New Jersey indicate how the conflict will be resolved.

It would serve no useful purpose to review at length the judicial decisions of other states, for none of them presents a judicial philosophy worthy of comment. For the most part these states have taken a position which straddles the issue as to the treatment of juvenile offenders in murder cases. To the reader, who may be interested in pursuing the examination into the subject further, it is suggested that the very recent case of *Snyder v. State*, 56 A. 2d. 485, Court of Appeals of Maryland, will bring him up to November, 1947, with a review of the pertinent decisions.

State Juvenile Court: A New Standard*

By Sol Rubin. Legal Consultant, National Probation and Parole Association, New York.

JUDGE Paul W. Alexander has stated that the juvenile court is not a court in the ordinary sense, but is more like a hospital or a clinic. The analogy is carried through the entire course of a sickness—diagnosis, hospitalization, treatment and discharge. Alice Scott Nutt, a child welfare consultant says, "The juvenile court is first and foremost a court. Its legal responsibility with respect to children, and to adults who have obligations toward them, is established specifically by law in terms of the behavior or conditions which bring individual

adults and children within the jurisdiction of the court." Its procedures, although informal, are still court procedures. Miss Nutt contrasts with the court the public welfare agency, with broad responsibilities to administer child welfare activities, but without power to impose obligations on individuals or to enforce orders.

Thus the juvenile court is pulled or pushed in two directions. Although both the judge and the child welfare specialist stress the importance of nonjudicial, administrative processes in providing social

* Reprinted from *Focus*, Vol. 30, July, 1951, pp. 103–107. Used by permission.

services to children, they disagree about the nature and functions of the juvenile court.

The juvenile court concept was given another going-over by the Committee on the Standard Juvenile Court Act of the National Probation and Parole Association. The first edition of the Standard Act was published in 1925 by the Association. Revised editions were published in 1927, 1933 and 1943. In 1949 a committee met to undertake another revision, and a fifth edition of the Standard Act, containing several important changes and a number of lesser revisions, was published.

Is it surprising that the juvenile court idea should be so malleable? It was an experiment fifty years ago and the basic idea survives—that of removing children accused of crime from the criminal courts to a specialized court geared to their needs. Conflicting views—revised views of court structure and function—are welcome signs of experimentation and growth. Our concept of the juvenile court has become, not more confused through all this history, but clearer.

Many of the standards heretofore considered desirable have been continued. Reviewing them very briefly, we note that they are: (1) exclusive jurisdiction over children, and jurisdiction over adults in children's cases; (2) private, friendly court hearings and informal, noncriminal procedure; (3) a sufficient staff of professionally trained probation officers; (4) facilities for physical examinations and for psychiatric study of problem children; (5) a well-equipped detention home or selected boarding homes for temporary care of children; (6) an efficient record and statistical system; (7) cooperation with other agencies and community support through interpretation to the public.

And there is one more requirement—a full time judge *specially qualified* for juvenile court work. The 1949 edition of the Standard Act is the first to contain provision for a statewide court established on a district basis. The most important immediate purpose of that provision is to assure special juvenile court judges for an entire state, as in Connecticut, Rhode Island and Utah. In each of these states there is a state juvenile court and a small number of full time, specially selected judges. No other judges sit in the juvenile courts in those states. But in the other forty-five states, with over three thousand counties, there are at most eighty counties with special judges, and only half of these serve full time in the juvenile court. In the other counties the judge sits part time in juvenile court by virtue of being judge of some other court. In not more than twenty counties do the ex-officio judges serve full time in the juvenile court. That is, except for the statewide courts, only two per cent of the counties in the country have full time judges, and one-third of these are not specially selected to serve in the juvenile court.

Ex-officio Judges

How well can an ex-officio judge perform in a juvenile court? Let us consider first the judge of a court with equity jurisdiction. We say that juvenile court law is rooted in equity jurisdiction. This means that the court draws on the equity principle that the child is a ward of the state, entitled to its protection, and the state assumes toward the child the position of parens patriae—guardian of persons who are not of full age or ability. But it is a far cry from the jurisprudence of a court of equity to that of a juvenile court. An equity court, like a court of law, is bound by many formalities, including all the rules of evidence. A juvenile court is informal in procedure and bound by very few rules of evidence. An equity court is concerned primarily with money and property affairs. When problems of human relationship come up in it, they are frequently solved by analogy to contractual rights. On the other hand, the juvenile court is mainly concerned with the personality and behavior of individuals; there the "remedy" —if we call it that for purposes of comparison—is not a judgment between contesting parties, but an effort to find a mode of treatment, perhaps to be continued for a lengthy period of time, to improve a personal or family or social condition. A juvenile court is *not* an equity court, although it is based on equitable principles. It is a special, new type of court. An equity judge therefore has no special experience that qualifies him as a juvenile court judge. The same is true for a court of law.

Noncriminal Proceeding

Analogy is sometimes drawn between a juvenile court proceeding and a civil proceeding. It would be more accurate to say that the juvenile court proceeding is noncriminal rather than civil. It is a special proceeding of a new kind not found in civil law. A civil proceeding in law or equity is an adversary proceeding in which a preponderance of proof decides the outcome, and the precedents guiding the court to award of damages or grant of equitable relief are well established and are reviewable by an appellate court as to the evidence and the remedy. But in the great majority of juvenile court proceedings the facts are not disputed and the "remedy," which we prefer to call the mode of treatment, is in the discretion of the judge, whose chief precedents are social casework practices.

Is the criminal court judge closer to juvenile work, better equipped to sit as judge in children's cases? Our laws go to great lengths to make clear that the juvenile proceeding is noncriminal, that an adjudication shall not be considered to have the effect of a conviction of crime. Detention homes take the place of jails, and detention principles eliminate the right to bail. There are no juries. The philosophy of our criminal courts is

based on a finding of guilt in an individual; not so in the juvenile court. The juvenile court has marked a great advance in dealing with juvenile offenses precisely because it is an attempt to break away from penal philosophy.

We could, but need not, show that a probate judge, or any other ex-officio judge, does not by virtue of his other judgeship acquire experience markedly applicable to a juvenile court. Nor should it be necessary to enlarge on the proposition that ideally a juvenile court judge should devote his full time to the office. His hearings take little time. On the other hand, the problems of children and of families in trouble involves study that can not be carried out "among other things"; it calls for much research and a good deal of creative work.

It must be recognized that there are, fortunately, some outstanding judges who were appointed from other judgeships and who serve full time as in the juvenile court. This happens in large local jurisdictions where the bench of a particular court is made up of a number of judges and where rotation of the juvenile court judgeship is kept to a minimum. By the same token, however, not only are such judges exceptional but there is no possibility of extending these exceptional judgeships outside the larger urban centers. Credit is due to those ex-officio judges who, although they serve part time in the juvenile court, are devoted to their responsibilities, are capable and conscientious, spend substantial time outside court hours on children's cases, and are careful in selecting probation officers. Yet their energies are divided. It is in fact some of these men who are the likeliest candidates for full time judgeships, as in a state juvenile court.

State District Courts

Under the 1949 Standard Act the state is divided into several districts according to population, area and other factors, and one judge is appointed for each district, which he covers on a circuit basis. By this plan we can obtain full time, specially qualified judges for an entire state. In Connecticut, in place of 169 town and city judges who heard children's cases (only two of whom were juvenile court judges), there are now three special judges and no ex-officio judges. In Rhode Island there were formerly twelve district court judges functioning ex-officio in the juvenile court. With the establishment of a state-wide court in 1944, the work was taken over by two special judges. Utah had twenty-six ex-officio juvenile court judges. The state court there now has four special full time judges and one part time judge.

Merit Appointments and Salary. The state system provides that the judge be specially selected but it does not automatically ensure his qualifications for the work. However it does provide the opportunity to establish merit appointments. The 1949 Standard Act calls for appointment by the governor from an approved list of candidates nominated by a panel of representatives of the courts, the bar and the departments of education, mental hygiene, and public welfare. In Utah the judges are appointed by the Public Welfare Commission; in Connecticut by the general assembly on nomination of the governor; in Rhode Island by the governor with the advice and consent of the senate. It is noteworthy also that in each of these states the judges' terms are longer than the governor's; in Utah and Connecticut the term is six years; in Rhode Island it is ten years.

The salary paid these judges must be sufficient to attract persons of high calibre. Outside of the largest centers of population, a special judgeship may be prohibited by the cost, which generally must be borne by the local community. A local judgeship is likely to carry a very small salary or to be limited to part time service. The state can pay better salaries to the special judges. Although there is room for improvement in this respect, the salaries of the state judges already appointed are higher than those of most locally-appointed judges, except in some of the largest cities. In Connecticut the judges receive $7500. In Rhode Island the chief judge gets $9500, the associate judge $8500. In Utah the judges are paid $4320.

Place of the Probation Officer. Does the state plan create a difficulty because of the judge's absence in another part of the circuit? Is there an advantage in the availability of an ex-officio judge? A characteristic of the juvenile court is that it has brought to the fore the probation officer as a most important part of the court. In the criminal court the probation officer is called in after conviction; in a juvenile court he is working with the problem from the beginning, before the judge knows about the case, and in fact before the proceeding is officially commenced by the filing of a petition. Only the judges in a state system travel in the circuit; the probation staff remains, for the most part, in each county or other district subdivision. In addition, the referee system may be expanded so that in certain cases the presence of the judge is not necessary to a hearing. (In the state courts mentioned this has not been found necessary.)

Suitability of State Court. To what type of state, from the point of view of population distribution, is a state court well suited? At the 1948 NPPA conference a resolution was adopted recommending state or district juvenile courts like those in Connecticut, Rhode Island and Utah. Observing that large areas of most states are still without effective juvenile courts, even where the need for an adequate separate court may be recognized, the resolution notes that "it is impractical to set up such courts in rural or less densely populated areas on a county basis because there is not sufficient population or sufficient volume of work to justify a full time qualified judge, a probation staff, clerical employees and detention facilities, with the attendant financial cost." To solve this problem the conference recommended the adoption of the state plan. The plan therefore is not limited to small states with relatively dense populations. This has already been proved in Utah.

The experience in the three states which have adopted the state system strongly supports the reasoning of this resolution. In each the adoption of the plan led to improvement not only in the special judgeships but also in the probation staffs, detention systems, and even in the use of psychiatric and other facilities.

Establishment of the state court unifies the juvenile probation service. It permits a planned distribution of probation service throughout the state on the basis of need rather than according to each community's interest and ability to afford it. In Connecticut, scattered throughout each district there are area officers staffed by resident full time probation officers and office personnel. This staff is state appointed and state supported. Utah for a time had local probation service. In 1944 all local participation was discontinued, and now all personnel, except the judges, are selected under a statewide merit system and all are paid entirely by the state. In Rhode Island also the probation staff is part of the state probation service, entirely state paid and state selected by an excellent merit system.

By contrast, in juvenile courts whose staffs depend on local maintenance, few officers are appointed under a merit system, few have civil service tenure, and many are appointed politically. With the three exceptions, only two states, Vermont and West Virginia, have state probation service for the juvenile courts. In short, introduction of the state system has meant improved standards of

probation service, and it may be added, higher salaries.

Detention. What effect does a state system have on detention? Under the state system, detention becomes a part of statewide planning. Connecticut has a statewide detention system under the control of the juvenile court. In the largest city in each of the three districts there is a receiving or detention home, supplemented by foster homes for emergency detention, particularly in out-of-city cases. The result is that Connecticut is one of the very few states which have eliminated detention in jails and police lockups.

Utah has local detention, some of it good, much of it poor. Several years ago the state tried subsidizing local detention and some improvement resulted, but not enough. The state officials recognize that the detention problem can be solved only on a statewide basis. Several years ago a bill to establish a statewide detention system fell just short of enactment, and it will undoubtedly be proposed again. Detention in Rhode Island is exclusively a state function. The state training schools are used for delinquents; the state home and school for shelter care of dependent and neglected children. Some private facilities are also used by the court. It is recognized there too that statewide planning goes hand in hand with the state juvenile court.

The Court and Other Services. There is similarly a greater use of other community facilities where the state court is established. In Rhode Island the state psychological facilities, the state psychiatrist, and the state hospitals are available. A prevention coordinator has been added to the staff to utilize all the resources of the community, assisting individuals and groups in initiating neighborhood projects. He is concerned also with public education in juvenile court work.

In Utah all children's services except in the health field were coordinated in one administrative unit in 1944. It includes not only probation service but also foster care, psychiatric and other services. The Connecticut court works closely with the Division of Child Welfare of the State Welfare Department, particularly in relation to neglected children. A uniform, well established procedure for cooperation with the schools has been developed. The State Department of Health provides psychiatric service. It is clear that such facilities are naturally and easily available for a state court, but difficult or impossible to obtain for most local courts.

Summary. The establishment of a state juvenile court does not solve all juvenile court problems. Improvement is not automatic. But it does provide the best framework for the attainment of high standards in all phases of juvenile court work. Within the next few years such courts will probably be established in several more states. By that time we shall again be revising the Standard Juvenile Court Act on the basis of new experience.

And perhaps we shall be a little closer to clarification of the differing viewpoints regarding function and philosophy.

Boys' Court: Individualized Justice for the Youthful Offender*

By Jacob M. Braude. Judge, Municipal Court of Chicago.

JUSTICE, wrote Aristotle, is nothing more than giving every man what is his due.

I know a traffic court judge who has justice worked out to a very fine science. He works from a chart which he sets before himself in the courtroom as he presides. This chart consists of a number of vertical and horizontal lines, intersecting each other to form a series of squares, like a checkerboard. At the top of the vertical columns are various figures indicating speed limits, such as "25 mph," "30 mph," "35 mph," etc. Along the left hand side, next to the horizontal lines, are the proscribed rates of speed, beginning with "21 mph" and running up to "90 mph."

A defendant appears in court, charged with going 52 miles per hour in a 35 mile-per-hour speed limit zone. The judge has only to place his pencil on the horizontal line that says "52" and then to follow that line clear across the page until it meets the vertical column

headed by the symbol "35 mph." The square in this intersection has a figure neatly written in—"$20.00 and costs." Just as neatly, the judge enters a fine—"$20.00 and costs," and the next case is called.

This next case involves another person who, purely by coincidence, is charged with going at the same rate of speed in exactly the same type of zone. The judge does not even have to look at his chart. Nor, for that matter, does he have to glance up at the defendant who has entered a plea of guilty. He merely levies a similar fine, "$20.00 and costs," and another case is disposed of.

The judge has not the slightest doubt but that he is dispensing real and exact justice. Asked if this system meets the requirements of Aristotle's definition, he would probably reply that rule by chart offers the perfect method of giving every man his due. There are many who would agree with him.

* Reprinted from *Federal Probation*, Vol. XII, June, 1948, pp. 9–14. Used by permission of author and publication.

Individualized Justice

There are, on the other hand, many others who feel that such a method does not result in the meting out of substantial justice. There are many who believe that a hard and fast mechanical—almost mathematical—system fails to take into account many of the circumstances and elements which are of the utmost importance, perhaps not in arriving at a conclusion as to innocence or guilt but, most certainly, in determining what disposition shall be made of the person involved *after* there has been a finding of guilty.

In our traffic court cases, the first defendant happens to be a middle-aged man, married, with a family of five growing children. At the time of his arrest he was driving his 1935 model Ford. He was picked up early in the morning on his way to work at an hour when the streets were deserted, creating little danger to other motorists or pedestrians. In the second case we have a single man driving a very expensive car in a congested thoroughfare during the height of traffic. Each is charged with the same violation but before the judge they stand as persons presenting two entirely different problems. "Twenty dollars and costs" might sorely tax the resources of the first defendant; the second merely whips off a bill or two from a heavy roll of money and goes on his way. The only sting he feels is the loss of time which has been occasioned by his appearance in court.

It would seem to me that a suspended fine with proper admonition might be sufficient punishment in the one case to assure the court and, for that matter, satisfy the community that the first defendant had learned his lesson. In the second case a much more substantial fine might be in order to accomplish the same end. This may be a very elementary example but I have purposely selected them to serve as concrete instances. However,

this method, in principle, seems to prevail in the entire administration of justice clear up to the most serious offense.

It is obvious that slide-rule justice, by which the punishment is made to fit the crime, does not always result in true and substantial justice, and I am happy to say that the trend today is in the direction away from the "2 x 2 is 4" method.

The tendency today is rather to make the punishment (although many of us are substituting the word "treatment" for the word "punishment") fit the individual rather than the crime itself. This tendency springs from a growing realization that individuals differ from one another and that they are frequently the product, and by-product, of the conditions which surround them and over which, too often, they have but little or no control. While environmental factors cannot be held to be completely responsible for the mistakes made by the individuals, the community cannot disclaim total liability when it tolerates conditions which provide fertile ground, and sometimes even the fertilizer, for antisocial acts which come to have criminal import.

Punishment and the Crime

There is further justification for this change in attitude. We are realizing more and more as we go along that our old methods of administering the criminal law have failed in both of its objectives: (1) the protection of society and (2) rehabilitation of the offender. For centuries we have punished people for their antisocial acts; yet, we still have crime with us, more abundant crime than ever. For years we have been sending men to the gallows, to the electric chair, and to the penitentiary; yet, drastic punishment does not seem to deter the next man from committing the same kind of offense the very next day. Unfortunately, examples set by stern courts of justice do not seem to teach us much, if anything. We seem not to learn from the mistakes of others, from the lessons taught them, nor from the punishment meted out to them.

Today, there is one man in jail for every 225 men over 16 years of age who are free. Criminologists estimate that almost 2 out of every 100 males sooner or later commit crimes serious enough to call for imprisonment but the threat of punishment hanging over our heads appears neither to disturb us nor to alter the statistical probability of the same old crimes being committed in the same old way.

Nor does punishment, once imposed, keep the offender himself from committing another crime. In the Massachusetts State Prison, 70 per cent of the inmates had previously been imprisoned. In the Eastern Penitentiary of Pennsylvania, 67 per cent of the prisoners had been convicted earlier and served time. In New York, 80 per cent of the men sentenced to prison had prior criminal records; 2,703 of them had been arrested 10,766 times. In Michigan, jail inmates consisted of 63 per cent repeaters; in Washington, D. C., 70 per cent repeaters; in Louisiana, 80 per cent repeaters. In fact, recidivism has become a static sector in crimes profile.

Present-day criminal procedure permits the court, or jury, to consider only evidence which is relevant to the alleged crime. However, the greater concern to society at large should not be the question of innocence or guilt, but rather the defendant's make-up—physical, mental, moral. Once guilt has been determined, the individual himself should become the subject of paramount importance to us; yet, unfortunately, such things as personality traits, mental stability, moral quirks, and physical defects are disregarded completely in determining what penalties should be imposed for the violation of law. Even as we move in the direction of trying to make the punishment fit the individual and not the crime, we still seem bound by tradition to give primary consideration to the crime itself.

Treatment and Rehabilitation

Tradition is not the only obstacle which stands in the way of substantial justice. Trying to determine the proper treatment to be accorded the individual requires scientific study. A judge normally comes to the bench ill-equipped by training and experience to conduct such study himself and, indeed, were he adequately equipped, he probably would not have the time nor the patience to do the job well. And, undoubtedly, what the court needs are facilities, as adjuncts to the court, to assist it in conducting these investigations and in gathering the necessary data upon which to base its ultimate decision.

Once guilt has been established, and confinement to a penal or correctional institution has been determined as the proper treatment for the offender, there still remains a major drawback in the process of rehabilitating the offender. Most of our prisons do very little to reform the inmate; to help him to adjust himself so as to take his place in the community at the end of his prison term. Some institutions make an effort, but few maintain a complete constructive program geared to indoctrinate the prisoner with the equipment necessary to make him a creditable citizen of the community. Too often, the inmate has been made worse, rather than better, by reason of his confinement. His prison experience has embittered and hardened him; it has failed to convince him that the straight and narrow leads to the happy life. Instead, he comes out having learned only one thing—to be careful the "next time" that he doesn't get caught.

The prison community should be made into a social organization devoted to training its inmates, not only in a trade, or how to make a living, but to train them in the art of normal human relationships as well. They failed in these relationships when they were outside the prison walls and they will fail again if efforts are not made to correct the deficiencies which were responsible for those failures. Thomas Mott Osborne wrote: "We do not shudder when we think of a man with a broken leg being sent to the hospital, for we know that he will not come out with two broken legs, or if he has a strained tendon that he will not come out with a compound fracture. Yet, unfortunately, that is about what we feel will happen to the morally and psychically traumatized man who is sent to prison!"

Those of us who insist on this rehabilitation are frequently the victims of severe criticism by otherwise reasonable men and women who protest that we are "mollycoddling" the criminals. These critics contend that when a man has committed a crime against society he should be made to pay the debt to society by punishment which will teach him never to sin again and if he does sin again, he must be punished over and over, each time separately for each separate sin.

Although this argument has, on the surface, a measure of cold logic, it is wholly unrealistic and impractical. If we pursue that thought to its logical conclusion, we must reconcile ourselves to the notion that once a person is convicted of a crime he should be segregated from a community and separated from it for the rest of his days. It would seem that it would be much better to do all that we can to make sure that he will not sin the second time than to punish him for having sinned the first. Is it not far better to educate him, teach him, or train him to live as a law-abiding citizen than to have to punish him for not doing so?

Institutional commitment cannot be considered a successful method of pre-

venting further crime and delinquency. Despite their incarceration, a larger proportion (30 per cent) of persons sent to institutions are rearrested than those given other forms of treatment (20 per cent), such as supervision, probation, suspended sentence, and the like.

The Boys' Court at Chicago

If punishment in and of itself is not the answer and does not afford a solution to the problem of crime, where then may we look for the answer? Boys' Court in Chicago gives us some hope that there is an answer.

"Exactly what do we mean by a Boys' Court," you ask? Chicago has had such a court since March, 1914. We have managed to have this court without any special legislation, the court having been designated as one of the specialized branches of the Municipal Court of Chicago.[1] The Boys' Court deals with cases involving boys from the ages of 17 to 21. Unlike some of the other courts throughout the country which have been patterned after it, the Chicago Boys' Court has no power to deal with such offenses as waywardness, incorrigibility, or association with undesirable persons. These categories do not appear in the Criminal Code of Illinois.

In order to bring a case into the Boys' Court, a definite criminal or quasi-criminal charge must be brought against the boy if court action is desired. (Chicago has no special court for girls over juvenile court age because, under Illinois statutes, the Juvenile Court of Cook County is given jurisdiction of girls up to the age of 18. When a girl reaches her 18th birthday the law says she becomes a woman and, thereafter, if she gets into trouble she is dealt with in the Women's

---

[1] The Municipal Court of Chicago, of which the Boys' Court is a specialized branch, is a court of record with jurisdiction in both civil and criminal cases. In criminal cases it has original and unlimited jurisdiction of all misdemeanor cases and of prosecutions for the violations of municipal ordinances. In felony cases, jurisdiction is limited to preliminary examinations. If probable cause is found, cases are held to the Grand Jury. Should indictments follow, the cases are tried thereafter in the Criminal Court of Cook County.

Court, except for the charges of felony, in which event she is brought to trial in the Felony Court.)

Seventeen is the age at which juvenile court jurisdiction of boys in Illinois comes to an end. Prior to 1914, boys over 17 who ran afoul of the law were tried in the same courts in which men were tried. In those days no adequate provisions were made for dealing with the special problems presented by boys who had passed the juvenile court age of 17 but were still under their legal majority of 21.

Jurisdiction and Procedure. Today, the Boys' Court has jurisdiction over criminal and quasi-criminal offenses committed by boys of the ages specified and conducts preliminary examinations for felony cases, holding them upon finding probable cause for action by the grand jury. If an indictment is returned, such cases are tried by the Criminal Court of Cook County. This court is composed of judges who have been assigned to that court from the Superior Court of Cook County or the Circuit Court of Cook County. The Criminal Court does not have a separate division for younger defendants. The Boys' Court is Chicago's answer to the need for a tribunal equipped to deal especially with the problems which late adolescence presents. The jurisdiction and procedure of the Boys' Court are the same as those of the other branches of the judicial system but there are certain special characteristics which distinguish it from those courts which have the usual criminal and quasi-criminal jurisdiction.

First, boys' cases are segregated from other cases so that they do not associate with older offenders. Second, a degree of specialization of judicial function results from this separation. Thus, the judge is enabled to become familiar with the special problems involved, and the accent is on the individual rather than his crime. There is still too much reshuffling in the assignment of judges.

The highly specialized nature of the work calls for much longer tenure in assignment than has been the practice. The judge in Boys' Court should be retained in that specialized division for a minimum of 2 years, with a 3 or 4 year period preferred, because the unique requirements of this particular court call for a special knowledge which is best acquired by long experience and for which there is no substitute.

Available to the judge in Boys' Court are the facilities of the Social Service Department and the Psychiatric Institute, both adjuncts of the Municipal Court of Chicago.

Philosophy and Procedure. The philosophy of the Boys' Court briefly stated is this: That, if the law curiously enough says that "every dog is entitled to at least one bite" then, certainly, every boy ought to be entitled to at least one chance and every effort is made to give to a first offender that one chance. While the facility of probation is available to court, it is used at a minimum because before one can be admitted to probation he must first be found guilty. Having been found guilty, he is stamped with a criminal record and then telling him to go out and make good is more likely to be a handicap than an order. Instead, there has been developed throughout the years an extra-legal form of probation which is called "supervision." Under the technique of supervision, the defendant is placed with any one of four different agencies which cooperate with the court but are not part of the court system. These are: The Holy Name Society, representing the Catholic group; the Chicago Church Federation, representing the Protestant group; the Jewish Social Service Bureau; and the Colored Big Brothers Organization. Each of these has developed its own special techniques. All the court asks is that these techniques be used to the best possible advantage with respect to the particular defendants assigned for supervision to their respective care.

If after the period of supervision the supervising agency reports that the defendant has made an apparent adjustment and is ready for ultimate discharge, the defendant is then officially discharged on the court records and to all intents and purposes there is no criminal record against him. This system is its own reward and works at least fairly satisfactorily as attested by the fact that of all first offenders given a chance in this manner, 72 per cent do not come back while they are still Boys' Court age and, of the 28 per cent that do return, a good many come back charged with minor or insignificant offenses.

Significance of the Age Group 17 to 21

Now, why do we need a court especially for boys between the ages of 17 and 21? There are many reasons. For one, boys within that age range commit a large proportion of America's serious crimes. Thousands of them are arrested every year, go to prison, and come out hardened criminals ready for a full-fledged career in crime. These young offenders pose a serious problem in controlling crime and protecting society. Persons from 16 to 21 constitute 50 per cent of all auto thieves, 40 per cent of all burglars, and 28 per cent of all robbers and thieves. Since this group forms over 13 per cent of the population, they double the normal quotas in robberies and thefts, treble it in burglaries, and nearly quadruple it in auto thefts. These offenders make up more than 90 per cent of all major crimes in the United States. There are more statistics, rather gruesome reading, and all of them confirm this disproportion in crime in our 17 to 21 age group.

Sometime ago, speaking before the Conference of the International Association of Chiefs of Police, the late Judge Joseph N. Ulman of the Supreme Court of Baltimore had this to say:

I do not have to tell this audience how important this group is. You know better than anyone else that the automobile thief, the burglar, the highway robber, is not an old man, not even a middle-aged man—he is a nineteen year old boy. You have seen him, you have caught him at his work, breaking into stores and dwellings, borrowing automobiles without the knowledge of their owners, reckless, swaggering, often carrying a gun, a serious menace to the public safety. And I have seen him in the court room. But worse than that, I have sentenced him and sent him away from the court room with the full knowledge that he would come back again, an even greater menace, after committing more serious crimes, because I had no power and no means to deal with him adequately and constructively. This is the great tragedy of our present haphazard criminal law administration. The young offender, the offender still in the formative period of his life, the offender who might be rehabilitated and set upon the right path— we deliberately force him into a lifetime of crime. And then we arrest him again, and try him again—and again—and again—all for no good to him, no good to his family, and no good to society.

Yes, in order to discover the answer to Judge Ulman's dilemma, we should distinguish between the boys in this age group and those criminals over 21. At least we fixed this upper limit for the time being until such time as the public is ready to accept this philosophy in relation to all offenders.

Strangely enough, the civil side of our common law has always made a distinction between a male person over 21 and a male person under 21 so we find that those under 21 are still generally legally incompetent to enter into contracts which may be enforced against them with but few possible exceptions; that they may not hold or dispose of property in their own name but may do so by means of a conservator appointed by the court; that they may not sue or be sued in their own name but must act through a guardian appointed for that purpose.

Again, the civil law since early days has recognized that a male person of 21 does not possess that degree of maturity which would qualify him to take his place as a full-fledged member of society, responsible to it for all his acts. Yet, paradoxically enough, in the absence of the specific statute, the criminal side of our law has never made any such distinction. The primary test which the criminal law makes is this: Is the person charged with the crime capable of distinguishing between right and wrong? If he is, then he should be made to pay his debt to society for the wrong he has committed. So we find, as recently as 40 or 50 years ago boys in England as young as 14 years of age being put to death for murder and in some of our Eastern states sent to prison for life. Only 3 years ago a boy of 16 was indicted for murder, tried, convicted, and sentenced to the State penitentiary where he is right now—in our own Cook County Criminal Court. And, as this is being written, there is another indictment for murder in Cook County—a boy of 13 charged with the murder of an even younger playmate—and all this in the same county that gave to our country the concept of the juvenile court.

The Youth Correction Authority

There should be a Boys' Court, or its counterpart, in every county in the country—a court established on the principle that the individual boy is far more important than the crime which he has committed. Just as individuals differ from one another in physical attributes, so they differ in personality traits. The law itself recognizes but one kind of age—the chronological age. That is the law we find mentioned in our statute books. The rule says that a 20-year-old person is a person born 20 years ago. Yet, those of us who work in this field know that a person has more than one age and that those other ages are frequently more important than his

chronological age. There is, for example, the mental age. In my own work in the Boys' Court I have had before me many boys who were 19-years-old chronologically because they were born 19 years ago but were mentally much younger—9 or 10. And while a boy may be 19 years old chronologically, because he was born 19 years ago, and 19 years old mentally, because he passes our psychometric tests on the basis which we have established as norms for 19-year-old persons, yet he may be much younger in a third kind of age which the law itself does not recognize but which must be taken into account in dealing with him if the ends of substantial justice are to be met, and this age is that which we call the physiological —or the biological—or the endocrine age. The boy may be normal mentally but his body functions may be overdeveloped or underdeveloped, a factor which may govern and control him in his behavior. These are elements which evade our slide-rule justice, but must be sought out in each particular instance.

Some 9 or 10 years ago the American Law Institute recognized the importance of this approach and, at that time, had great experience after profound research. It came forward with the proposal for the establishment of a new system of dealing with youthful offenders, presented to the various statutes for their consideration a model, or what is called a "Youth Correction Authority Act" the gist of which was that the judge was to be merely the trier of the issue of innocence or guilt. Having resolved the issue in favor of guilt there would be nothing more for him to do but to "commit the convicted defendant" to a Correction Authority which would be composed of specialists in the field of psychiatry, penology, sociology, and education, whose duty it would be to study the individual and determine his particular needs, and then prescribe a method of treatment which would have for its ultimate goal the rehabilitation of the individual with a view toward his reintegration into the community with the probability of his becoming a useful citizen thereby enhanced. But one or two statutes have thus far accepted this proposal. It is too early to predict, with any degree of certainty, what success we can expect from this new approach. From preliminary reports the indications are that progress is being made. The next 5 or 10 years will tell more of the story. In the meantime, those who think along these lines have work to do. There is much satisfaction in seeking the solution to the problem of a problem boy. It was John Hay who summed it up so well when he penned:

> I think that saving a wayward boy
> And bringing him to his own
> Is a task with much more profit
> Than sitting on a throne.

Most Courts Have to Be Substandard!*

By Lowell Juilliard Carr. Department of Sociology, University of Michigan, Ann Arbor.

FIFTY years later, when juvenile courts are functioning under the laws of all 48 states and the District of Columbia, it is easy to forget that they began essentially as "big city" courts. In 1899 Denver, where Judge Ben Lindsey held court, had a population of 133,000 and Chicago, whose needs really set the movement rolling, had more than 1,600,000. In other words, at the turn of the century when the juvenile court appeared in America it was really the juridical answer of urban child welfare workers to the needs of big city children. Today, half a century later, that is still essentially what the juvenile court remains—the juridical answer to the delinquency problems of the great city.

True, rural and small town juvenile courts now outnumber big city courts 10 to 1. Out of more than 3,000 counties under juvenile court laws in the United States only 200-odd contain cities of 50,000 or more. But mere numbers mean little. Outside of those 200-odd "big city" counties the juvenile court in its dealings with children is actually a kind of legal fiction. It has the name, it has a presiding officer—probate judge, common pleas clerk, or what-have-you—chosen without regard to his understanding of children. It has sundry sketchy documents called case records, compiled, of course, without benefit of any trained caseworkers, and sometimes not even compiled; a notebook in the judge's pocket may serve the purpose! In the eyes of the law and of the public in a couple of thousand jurisdictions that assemblage of characteristics plus some legally defined authority to deal with neglected, dependent, and delinquent children constitutes the juvenile court.

The Big City Court

Any resemblance between such a casually conducted agency and a top-notch big city court such as Judge Paul W. Alexander's in Toledo, for example, must be more or less coincidental. True, the larger city courts in Ohio operate under special statute that permits them to set up civil service regulations, thereby affording protection to their probation officers. By no means are all big city courts that fortunate. But at least they do have probation officers—paid, full-time people. The overwhelm-

---

* Reprinted from *Federal Probation*, Vol. XIII, September, 1949, pp. 29–33. Used by permission of author and publication.

ing majority of American juvenile courts have no such officers. Probation for them is a matter of "signing the book"; or of placing children "on probation to their parents"—frequently the very people who have created the mess in the first place—or of utilizing untrained amateurs whose need of ego-satisfaction frequently exceeds their understanding of childhood.

The Toledo court uses its detention home as a diagnostic clinic to determine the psychological and other causal factors behind every delinquent's trouble. The 2,000-odd small town juvenile courts not only have no clinics; many of them have no decent detention homes.

On occasion, the Toledo court has its emotionally maladjusted cases studied by a psychiatrist. Some larger courts have their own psychiatric clinics. The 2,000 small town courts don't know what a psychiatrist looks like.

There is no question about the facts. Item by item one can check down the Children's Bureau's list of characteristics of a "standard" juvenile court and find the overwhelming majority of the juvenile courts in the United States below par on every count. Their judges, their facilities, their budgets, their procedures, their records, their personnel, their attempts at treatment, their grinding philosophies—all fail to measure up. The conclusion seems inescapable: the standard juvenile court, as child welfare experts define the term, is a big city court. The little fellows simply do not qualify.

The Small Town Court

For years it has been customary for child welfare theorists to bemoan this parlous state of affairs. On occasion in textbooks, at conferences, and over the radio they even have ventured to exhort the laggard brethren to catch up with the twentieth century. The usual advice is, I believe, "to raise their standards."

To date, both exhortation and advice have signally failed to close the gap.

Nine out of ten of our juvenile courts continue so far below grade as to be practically subterranean. Explanations blaming all this on crooked politicians, rural backwardness, or public stupidity violate the scientific principle of parsimony. You don't need crooked politicians, hick voters, or the moron public to account for the facts! Simple economics is enough. Consider this interesting contrast:

In 1944, 89 juvenile courts serving areas of 100,000 or more population each reported a total of 105,105 delinquency cases, or 1,180 per court. This is an average of approximately 21 delinquency cases a week in each court. Meanwhile, during the same year, 291 juvenile courts serving areas of less than 100,000 each reported only 13,521 delinquency cases, or 46 cases per court. That averaged less than one case (0.89) in each court per week.

In other words, each week the big city courts handled 23 times as many delinquency cases as did the small town courts. That is not the important thing, however. What counts is not how much business the big city courts did, but how much business the little courts *did not* do.

How typical were those 291 small town courts of the 2,000-odd small town juvenile courts in the United States? Nobody knows. But there is no reason to believe that a court's willingness to co-operate with the Children's Bureau by supplying statistics indicates any inferiority as compared with the non-co-operating courts. In other words, there is a presumption that the 291 reporting courts in general were at least up to the average of small town courts. Quite possibly they were above the average. That means that on the basis of these reports there is no reason to believe that the unreported 2,000 or more small town courts averaged significantly higher than nine-tenths of a case each per week.

Such, then, is the volume of business

of the great majority of the small town juvenile courts of the United States.

What does it mean for maintenance of standards? How many small town juvenile courts can afford to maintain a special detention home, a child-specialist judge, a trained probation officer, a special diagnostic clinic—all to handle *one delinquent every 6 or 7 days?* It does not make sense.

The small town juvenile court simply cannot come up to big city standards; and *so long as it remains merely a small town court,* it never will. Crooked politicians and stupid voters have nothing directly to do with it. So long as rural America insists on financing its juvenile courts on a local, county basis, rural America cannot possibly meet urban court standards. Rural counties cannot possibly raise the money to pay for such standards. If they could, it would be an outright waste of public money. Six days out of 7 the high-powered specialists would be playing checkers to pass the time. The delinquency business simply is not there. County by county, rural America does not produce enough juvenile delinquents to keep its juvenile courts running at big city tempo.

The County Problem

Well, then, why take it county by county? Why not combine counties to provide enough work for one well-equipped, technically competent court in place of half a dozen or a dozen of the imitations that we have now? In Michigan, for example, out of the state's 83 counties in 1940, 35 had less than 20,000 people each, 21 less than 10,000 each, 3 less than 4,000 each, and 1 less than 2,600. What sort of county government can be supported by any group of 20,000 farmers, hunters, trappers, and woodsmen—men, women and children? What kind of juvenile court can be supported by the 887 men and women over 14 who made up the labor force of a county of 2,600 population? That

was the labor force of Oscoda County, Michigan, in 1940—887 men and women trying to maintain their own families and keep a sheriff, a judge of probate, a prosecuting attorney, and other county officials going at the same time.

Grant that these public officials were as hard working and as conscientious as any in the world. That is utterly beside the point. The point is that a little cut-over farming, logging, and forestry by 887 people simply cannot pay the bills for providing modern court facilities and full-time trained personnel. Neither do scanty population and simple living in such counties develop the volume of delinquency to justify a modern court—even if local resources could pay for it.

Yet one Oscoda County youngster ignored or mishandled, as John Dillinger seems to have been ignored or mishandled years ago in Indiana, might cost the taxpayers of Michigan 10 times the yearly budget of a modern court. (John Dillinger, the notorious Public Enemy No. 1 of the mid-thirties, went directly into big time crime without a juvenile court record.)

That, of course, is the paradox of the poor counties in scores of states: they do not produce enough delinquents to justify fully-equipped modern courts; they could not possibly pay for such courts if the business were there; and yet one case mishandled by their well-meaning but untrained officials may cost their states many times the cost of efficient service. This is the situation of rich versus poor counties in Michigan. It is also the situation in Ohio, Wisconsin, Minnesota, Kentucky, West Virginia, and dozens of other states.

In the field of criminal and civil law these disparities long since have been overcome by organizing the courts into circuits or districts. But the juvenile court everywhere has been regarded as a peculiarly intimate and local institution. Therefore, it is in the hands of local politicians who have no intention of letting any of their own powers and perquisites be reorganized out of their hands. And the public, of course, does not know what the score is.

In well over 2,000 counties in the United States nobody has ever seen a well-staffed, modern juvenile court in action. The harrassed taxpayer in these thinly populated communities simply does not know what he *isn't* getting—or how little he *does* get for what he pays.

Phases of Delinquency Control

The truth is that most of rural America is still in the first of the four phases that have marked the control of juvenile delinquency in the United States.

Predominance of face-to-face primary contacts. The first phase, common to primitive societies the world over as well as to pioneer America, is characterized by the predominance of face-to-face primary contacts; the development of "we"-feeling on the part of young people toward elders not by explicit indoctrination but by the cumulative effects of simple and necessary daily experiences in families, playgroups, and neighborhoods. Even today it is probable that the behavior of the great majority of the Nation's children is still patterned mainly by the same kinds of experiences —face-to-face living in urban and rural families and playgroups, and in small town and rural neighborhoods.

Special agencies for treating individuals. But today, unlike the situation in pioneer days, religion and the law provide less dogmatic and savage reinforcements while special agencies for salvaging deviant individuals have multiplied.

This multiplication of special agencies for treating individuals began with the growth of cities in the nineteenth century and constituted the second control phase. If the first can be called the phase of rural primary group control, the second is the phase of urban individual-treatment agencies. Symptomatic of the

beginning of this second phase was the opening of the House of Refuge on Randall's Island, New York harbor, in 1825; a juvenile prison, but indicative at least of dawning public recognition of the desirability of providing a special agency for deviant children. The reform spread. Gradually emphasis shifted from juvenile segregation and punishment to vocational training, correction, and latterly adjustment. Meanwhile adult probation was invented in Boston. States, reacting to the breakdown of local and church provisions for dependent and neglected children, established orphanages, later child-placing agencies. The Y.M.C.A. was imported from England. Shortly after the Civil War a few venturesome souls began experimenting with camping as an escape from the city. Like the Y.M.C.A., the settlement house idea spread from England. Organized recreation began to appear in cities. In 1899 Judge Ben Lindsey began to administer his court in Denver to temper justice with understanding, and in Illinois the legislature enacted the first juvenile court law. From the House of Refuge to the juvenile court the growing urban culture of the nineteenth century, without deliberately shoving primary group association aside, had been busy supplementing and buttressing it with special treatment agencies. To plug the cracks in the moral dyke, spreading as increasing impersonality swallowed the middle classes and slums engulfed the poor, social reformers invented or adapted special agency after special agency: juvenile reformatories, orphanages, settlement houses, child protective societies, playgrounds, character agencies, the juvenile court. Eventually they were to add still more character agencies, child guidance clinics, the U. S. Children's Bureau, family casework, visiting teachers, and all the other twentieth-century refinements of modern social work.

Mostly these urban agencies devoted themselves to selected individuals. Even the group work agencies worked with groups of selected children. But over and above the fact of individual selection and treatment stood the more important fact that by and large these agencies were all urban agencies; they were all located in cities, and except for the Children's Bureau which was not established until 1912, they all devoted themselves primarily to the needs of urban children. Modern child welfare work grew up, in short, mainly as *urban* welfare work. Even the juvenile courts whose jurisdictions included rural areas amounted to little, as we have seen, unless they were located in sizable cities. Throughout the nineteenth and the first half of the twentieth century rural America lay outside the social work frontier. It still does.

Inside that frontier the second phase of delinquency control thus developed as an urban, individual treatment phase. *Co-ordination of urban agencies.* With the coming of World War I a third phase began to appear—a phase characterized by the increasing co-ordination of urban agencies in many cities. This took three forms: the community chest movement spreading from Denver and Cleveland; the confidential exchange for co-ordinating actual casework of agencies; and various forms of councils and conferences. One of the latter that attracted some attention in the 1930's was the co-ordinating council. This had started in Berkeley just after World War I, had been popularized in Los Angeles a few years later, and during the thirties spread into a number of other states. A survey of state or other activities supplementing or reinforcing the juvenile courts—a survey carried on by means of a questionnaire to state welfare departments or to youth authorities in the various states in May 1948—revealed the fact that only in California was the co-ordinating council movement still an important factor in the child welfare picture. California reported 284 such councils.

State-wide programs of prevention. This survey, incidentally, brought to light evidence of the beginnings of a fourth phase of delinquency control, a phase characterized by all-inclusive state-wide programs of prevention. Like the third phase this was also a product of war—World War II. During the war California, Michigan, and New York each took definite action to supplement and strengthen the work of the juvenile courts. California established a State Youth Authority—adopted in 1947 by Minnesota and Wisconsin and in 1948 by Massachusetts. Michigan expanded its child guidance facilities to 10 clinics and set up a program of state aid under which 90 visiting teachers were employed in urban and rural areas by 1947. New York set up a State Youth Commission under a law dated to expire in 1950. The unique thing about this New York commission was that it was given real money to spend to "trigger" local expenditures on guidance clinics, local youth bureaus, and recreation programs. In its first year the Commission spent $300,000 of state money to release $500,-000 in local communities, a total of more than $800,000. In 1948 this program was working through 11 youth bureaus, 3 new traveling guidance clinics added to the state's previous 8, and through 520 recreation projects.

In all, data were obtained from 39 states in this 1948 survey. Twenty-three had set up special bodies of some kind— 5 central planning bodies; 6 co-ordinating and educational bodies; and 12 special commissions whose functions ranged from advice to the drafting of new children's codes. A widespread feeling seemed to be abroad that something needed to be done to strengthen the juvenile courts, but no state seemed to be too clear about what to do. At least no state had drafted a program that included the best points of all programs, and no states except Illinois and Ohio were spending any real money on research in delinquency. Illinois and Ohio had special agencies devoted to scientific research in this field. The rest were picking ideas out of the hat.

Certain other conclusions merged: the richer a state, the richer are likely to be the preventative services available in it. Different states are in different stages of development of supplementary services for prevention. Hence, the same services are in different stages of development in different states. Services are unevenly distributed within states. Unless something is done about this, it will be a long, long time indeed before all states are pulling their share of the load and all areas in each state are getting their share of the help. Recommendations for immediate action coming from responsible officials in some 29 states called for "next steps" rather than inclusive planning to attack causes all along the front. Most states were still groping. Only five—California, Minnesota, Wisconsin, Massachusetts, and New York—had set up central bodies to plan and provide leadership.

Obviously if the small town juvenile court is going to get the help it so plainly needs, "next steps" are hardly going to be enough. A lot of planning, reorganization, and leadership on the state level will be necessary—and most states have not even started to centralize planning and leadership! A fourth phase of delinquency control may be beginning—but it still has a long way to go.

The Juvenile Court Today*

~~~~~~

By Katharine F. Lenroot. Chief, Children's Bureau, Washington, D. C.

THE JUVENILE court movement, which began in the United States 50 years ago, represented the second of the social movements in this country designed to provide care and treatment for juvenile offenders on the basis of the child's need for protection and retraining rather than society's need for punishing crime. The first such effort, dating back over a century and a quarter, took the form of the establishment of special institutions for the reformation of young offenders.

In a report on *Courts in the United States Hearing Children's Cases*, published by the Children's Bureau 20 years after the first juvenile courts had been established, it was pointed out that the jurisdiction of the juvenile court covers neglected and, in many states, dependent or destitute children, as well as children whose conduct is in conflict with the law.

. . . It is in regard to the latter class that the juvenile court movement introduced a new legal concept to the effect that the delinquent child is not to be proceeded against as one who has committed an offense against the State for which the State must mete out punishment, but is a subject for the State's special protection, care, and guardianship in exactly the same degree as the child who is neglected or homeless.

In the same report, the main features usually considered essential to the organization of a juvenile court were listed as follows:

1. Separate hearings for children's cases.

2. Informal or chancery procedure, including the use of petition or summons.

3. Regular probation service, both for investigation and for supervisory care.

4. Detention separate from adults.

* Reprinted from *Federal Probation*, Vol. XIII, September, 1949, pp. 1–15. Used by permission of author and publication.

5. Special court and probation records, both legal and social.

6. Provision for mental and physical examinations.

Only 16 per cent of 2,034 courts from which information was obtained in the course of this study met the first, third, and fifth points listed above taken together; that is, had separate hearings, regular probation service, and social as well as legal records. Courts serving cities of 100,000 or more population had developed the primary features of special organization for children's work, though some of these courts were much in advance of others. Courts serving small towns and rural communities as a rule were poorly equipped for children's work. It was estimated that approximately 175,000 children's cases were brought before courts in the United States in 1918, including cases of delinquent, neglected, and dependent children. Of these, approximately 50,000 came before courts not adapted to the handling of children's cases.

When the first juvenile courts were established professional training for social work had not yet been started; child guidance clinics had not been thought of; child-saving and child-caring work, chiefly under private auspices, emphasized the removal of children from undesirable surroundings, chiefly for care in institutions or free foster homes, rather than the strengthening and rebuilding of family life; and public outdoor relief was thought to be pauperizing and degrading.

The pioneer juvenile court act in this country, adopted in Illinois in 1899, ended with the words:

This act shall be liberally construed to the end that its purpose may be carried out, to-wit: "That the care, custody and discipline of a child shall approximate as nearly as may be that which should be given by its parents, and in all cases where it can properly be done the child be placed in an approved family home and become a member of the family by legal adoption or otherwise."

Julia C. Lathrop used to say that the chief contribution of the juvenile court was that it "made the child visible." She said:

Important as are the immediate services of a juvenile court to the children who are daily brought before it for protection and guidance because the family protection has broken down and there is no family guidance; painstaking as are the court's methods of ascertaining the facts which account for the child's trouble, his family history, his own physical and mental state; hopeful as are the results of probation; yet the great primary service of the court is that it lifts up the truth and compels us to see the wastage of human life whose sign is the child in court.

Because of the impact of the conditions under which children brought to their attention were living, upon the conscience of judges, probation officers, advisory boards, and citizens, the juvenile courts uncovered the need for and pointed the way toward public aid to dependent children in their own homes; psychiatric, psychological, and social study of problem children; improved programs of detention care; and extension and improvement of foster-home and institutional programs. Because the juvenile court was usually the only public agency dedicated to the welfare of children in difficulty or in need, it frequently was given administrative functions in one or more of these areas of work—mothers' pension administration, for example, and foster-home care.

Juvenile court legislation has been influenced widely by the juvenile court standards adopted in 1923 and the Standard Juvenile Court Act, developed respectively by the Children's Bureau and the National Probation and Parole Association as a result of the work of special conferences and advisory committees.

The juvenile court standards recognize

the variations in conditions, resources, and judicial structure that exists among the various states. They call for broad jurisdiction in cases of children under 18 years of age requiring court action or protection because of their acts or circumstances; a judge chosen because of his special qualifications for juvenile court work, with legal training, acquaintance with social problems, and understanding of child psychology; informal court procedure and private hearings; detention kept at a minimum, outside jails and police stations, and so far as possible in private boarding homes; a well-qualified probation staff, with limitation of case loads, and definite plans for constructive work in each case; and availability of resources for individual and specialized treatment such as medical, psychological, and psychiatric services, foster family and institutional care, and recreational services and facilities; state supervision of probation work; and an adequate record system, providing for both legal and social records and for the safeguarding of these records from indiscriminate public inspection. The Standard Juvenile Court Act, based in large part on these standards, has been revised from time to time, to incorporate the provisions of various state laws found to be most effective.

Present Status of the Juvenile Court

The juvenile court movement has developed to the point where we now have legislation providing for separate juvenile courts or specialized jurisdiction and procedure for the handling of children's cases in all the 48 states and in the territories and the District of Columbia. In 1938 legislation was enacted by the Congress which provided for specialized procedure in the handling of children's cases in federal courts.

It is estimated that 275,000 children come yearly to the attention of juvenile courts as delinquents. An additional 100,000 children come to the attention

of the courts through other actions such as dependency, neglect, or custody hearings.

Juvenile court standards have been widely accepted in principle, and the standard act based upon them has been drawn upon extensively in the preparation or amendment of state laws. About 12 states incorporate nearly all the provisions of the standard act, and 7 others with advanced laws include many of its provisions. The Report on Juvenile Court Laws adopted by an advisory panel of the National Conference on Prevention and Control of Juvenile Delinquency, endorsed the Standard Juvenile Court Act and recommended that each state review its juvenile court act and use the Standard Juvenile Court Act as a basis for revision, making such modifications as may be necessary to meet local conditions and laws; and codify the laws relating to the jurisdiction or responsibility of the juvenile court.

Although great progress has been made in juvenile court legislation and administration in the past half-century, many juvenile courts operate under laws that have had little revision since their enactment nearly 50 years ago. Some of the terminology and procedures of these statutes reflect the influence of the criminal law.

By 1947, only about half of the counties in the United States, according to the Directory of Probation and Parole Officers in the United States and Canada, had probation service of some sort in juvenile cases. In many states only the large cities and populous counties had such service. Emphasis is being placed on education for social work as a prerequisite for probation service, but great variation exists in skills and professional preparation.

The importance of good intake procedures in the juvenile court is receiving increasing attention. When a case is brought before the court officially, hearings generally are conducted privately and in an informal manner. Jury trials in children's cases are rare.

It is estimated that the number of children detained each year may run as high as 300,000. Most juvenile court laws make provision for prohibiting or controlling jail detention and for establishing or using some more suitable place of care. Exceptions, however, permitting placement in jail under certain circumstances, combined with lack of more appropriate and adequate facilities in many communities, result in widespread use of this type of detention. Studies of detention made by the National Probation and Parole Association and other agencies show that children are being detained in jails, police stations, or other unsuitable places in every state of the Union. It is estimated that over 50,000 children are detained in jail every year.

The development of social casework, the mental health movement, improvement in foster care in family homes and institutions, changes in educational theory and practice, community studies and community planning, and the development of public child welfare services have greatly influenced the juvenile court movement. Extension and improvement of juvenile court services and how they may be fitted into comprehensive community and state-wide programs for children must be considered in relation to all these factors.

Problems for Special Consideration

The completion of 50 years of juvenile court work makes this an appropriate time to evaluate the present status and raise some questions regarding future development. Many questions that may be raised cannot be answered conclusively in the absence of more extensive research, observation, and experimentation. Many individuals and organizations interested in various phases of court work are trying out new practices, considering changes in legislation, experimenting in co-operative working relationships with other community agencies, and promoting the development of treatment facilities in order to enable courts to render the best possible service to their communities. In regard to juvenile delinquency cases, the juvenile court, like other agencies engaged in this field of work, must work to a great extent by the trial and error method, since our knowledge of the causation and correction of delinquency is still so incomplete.

Some of the areas concerning which there is today a marked difference of opinion, or need for further exploration, are described briefly below.

Court jurisdiction. Two aspects of jurisdiction require special consideration —the court's jurisdiction over minors, up to what age, whether exclusive or concurrent; and the court's jurisdiction over adults, especially with reference to domestic relations cases.

The juvenile court standards call for exclusive jurisdiction over minors under the age of 18 years, with continuing jurisdiction up to 21 unless the case is dismissed sooner or passes out of the jurisdiction of the court. The Standard Juvenile Court Act in its latest form calls for exclusive jurisdiction over minors under the age of 18, with provision for transfer to other courts of children 16 years of age or over charged with an offense which would be a felony if committed by an adult, and if the court after full investigation deems it contrary to the best interests of such child or of the public to retain jurisdiction; but no child under 16 years of age shall be so certified.

The majority of states (27, the District of Columbia, Alaska, and Hawaii) set 18 years as the upper age limit of original juvenile court jurisdiction in delinquency cases; 6 states set 17 years; 7 states, Puerto Rico, and the Virgin Islands, set 16 years; and 2 states set 21 years. In 6 states jurisdiction differs according to sex. The Federal Juvenile Delinquency Act applies to juveniles 17 years of age or under. Generally the court's jurisdiction is exclusive, but in some states it is concurrent or must be relinquished entirely when the offense is of a specified nature and the children of specified ages. In most states in which jurisdiction is exclusive, and in others as well, provision is made for the juvenile court to waive jurisdiction, especially in the case of an older child, and to permit the criminal court to deal with him.

The juvenile court movement was directed toward application of the principle of treatment—not punishment—to all children under the ages specified, regardless of the nature of the offense. It frequently is very difficult for public opinion to accept the fact that this principle should be applied in cases of children committing the most serious crimes. For such children, intensive treatment is especially necessary. One of the reasons for reluctance to see all such cases dealt with finally by the juvenile court is the lack of resources usually available to the court for commitment to a kind of care that may extend beyond the time when the child reaches his legal majority. Improvement in methods of dealing with unstable and psychopathic people who need long-time care and protection for their own sake as well as for the security of the community would greatly lessen opposition to entrusting full and exclusive jurisdiction in delinquency cases to the juvenile court.

The juvenile court movement led to intensified interest in proceedings relating to parental rights and obligations, the termination of marriage, non-support and desertion, custody, adoption, and guardianship. Many juvenile courts have broad jurisdiction over these types of cases; other courts are designated family or domestic relations courts and include jurisdiction over delinquent, dependent, and neglected children as well. In other communities family or domestic relations courts exist side-by-side with juvenile courts, either as a part of the same court of general jurisdiction or related to different court systems.

The juvenile court standards recommend that the juvenile court should have broad jurisdiction over children, including adoption jurisdiction and children in need of protection or custodial care by reason of mental defect or disorder; non-support or desertion of minor children; and determination of paternity and the support of children born out of wedlock. Some students of the problem have recommended that the juvenile court also have jurisdiction in divorce cases in which children are involved. The Standard Juvenile Court Act is less inclusive with reference to cases not directly focusing upon the child.

Questions have been raised concerning the desirability of extensive jurisdiction over cases in which the child himself is not in need of the care, protection, and specialized services of the juvenile court. To bring large numbers of cases in which the procedure must be criminal in nature to the juvenile court may impair the atmosphere and service of the court in respect to children's cases. On the other hand, the interests of the child should be considered in all domestic relations cases in which children are involved, and the contribution which the juvenile court can make in these cases must not be overlooked. The whole question of jurisdiction, procedure, and social service in cases pertaining to the family and the relations between parents and children is greatly in need of further study.

Geographic area. A few states—Connecticut, Rhode Island, and Utah—by the development of state courts, have attempted to meet the difficulties involved in making standard juvenile court service available to children in all parts of the state. This may be feasible in states having small geographical area, in which services to children have been developed to a considerable extent on a state-wide basis. When a state juvenile court system is contemplated by a large state, serious consideration must be given to problems of providing services relating the juvenile court to community agencies. A state or district system, as a means of giving service to rural and semirural areas, with urban or semiurban areas served by an independent court or constituting an entire district, may be one way of approaching the problem.

State consultation, or other functions relating to juvenile court and probation work, are provided for in about half the states, though the nature of this responsibility and the state agency in which it is vested vary from state to state. Funds and personnel are not always available to carry out these responsibilities to the full.

Functions and services. The questions that have been raised as to the functions and services that should be performed by a juvenile court have brought out various points of view. Many social workers look upon the court primarily as a social agency. They feel, therefore, that court policies and procedures should be similar to those of social agencies and social work practice. Frequently they fail to take into consideration that the court operates within a legal framework and is limited in what it can do. On the other hand, attorneys often feel that the courts lean too heavily upon social work theory and practice and fail to give full consideration to the legal rights of children and parents. The court is the authoritarian agency which has been established by society to protect youth as well as to protect society from its more aggressive youth. The Annual Report for 1948 Cuyahoga County Juvenile Court of Cleveland has this to say:

The juvenile court, however, represents a growth in legal theory and not a deviation from it. In any matter before the court there are legal aspects to consider as well as social ones. It has the function of protect-

ing and preserving the welfare of the community as well as helping the offender to make a satisfactory adjustment. Roscoe Pound, Dean Emeritus, Harvard Law School, states, "There is need in any legal order of keeping balance between the general security and the individual life. Everywhere in the law, account must be taken of justice, the ideal relation between men, of morals, the ideal individual development as to behavior, and security, the immediate province of the legal order. No one of these may be lost sight of." He further reminds us that the original juvenile court was "set up as a court of equity, with the administrative functions incidental to equity jurisdiction, not as a criminal court, and not, as might have happened later, as an administrative agency with incidental adjudicating functions." While the juvenile court attempts to maintain a balance between these two objectives, there has been a tendency on the part of social workers to think of the juvenile court primarily as a social agency and they are inclined to be critical and distrustful because it acts as a court.

Coincident with this wariness of the courts by social workers, there has been a guarded relationship between them and the attorneys who practice in the juvenile court. This lack of confidence exists in spite of the fact that "the first juvenile court law was drafted by a committee of a bar association, a body of socially minded lawyers, co-operating with social workers."

Ideally we might say that the plan or disposition which best meets the needs of the child is also the plan which best meets the needs of the community in its relationship with the child. The best plan for the child can be made more often when the court is in an area where every needed resource is available. Unfortunately even in progressive communities adequate resources for the care and treatment of children with problems are still lacking.

With the development of comprehensive services for children on a community-wide basis, much of the work that has been done by juvenile courts in dealing with children on an informal or unofficial basis could be dealt with by other agencies in the first place, or on referral from the court when children first come to its attention. In other words, children whose problems are not of such a nature as to require the service of an agency representing the legal authority and responsibility of the state might well be dealt with by other agencies when such other services are fully available, leaving to the court the determination of which cases coming to its attention need its service.

Relationships with agencies. In considering the future development of broad services to children the judicial function of the courts and the administrative functions of social welfare and treatment agencies should be clearly recognized. A number of courts have developed programs of foster care for children who must be removed from their homes. Most of these programs were developed in the early days when the juvenile court was practically the only resource, aside from institutional care, for the treatment of the delinquent child, and when services for dependent and neglected children were markedly inadequate.

Social services for children have been developed and expanded outside of the courts under both public and private auspices, and have been widely used by the courts. Many children who are unknown to courts need service in their own homes or need foster care, due to personal limitations, unsatisfactory family relationships, emotional disturbances or the loss of a parent. Children such as these are being referred daily to both public and private child welfare agencies for help without official court action. The basic needs of these children are similar to those of children known to courts and, therefore, the program of services needed is basically the same for both groups. As social services outside of the courts become well developed we may expect courts gradually to free themselves of programs purely ad-

ministrative in nature where the authority of the court is not needed in treatment, always maintaining the role of the court in transfer of parental rights or questions involving change of custody or guardianship.

Increasing use of local public child welfare services has helped the courts to increase the effectiveness of their own services. Child welfare workers are being called upon by many courts to make social investigations and give supervision for the court in cases of delinquency and neglect. This is especially true in areas where the court is without adequate staff or facilities. Some of the problems involved have been stated in the Children's Bureau Publication No. 327 (1949) as follows:

Child welfare workers, generally attached to the local public welfare agency, have been giving service to the juvenile courts in many rural communities. They have been making social studies prior to court action. They have been doing case work with children placed on probation. This trend may be expected to continue. For the present, it will probably be chiefly in rural areas, although there is no fundamental reason why it could not occur in urban areas.

If the relationship is to be mutually satisfactory, sound principles and clear cut policies must govern. Some of these may be suggested now; many will have to be worked out through joint experimentation.

The judge of the juvenile court and administrator of the public welfare agency, to whose staff the child welfare worker is attached, should take responsibility for agreeing upon the nature, extent, and amount of service to be made available, and the administrative arrangements under which it will be furnished. Once the obligation is assumed by the welfare agency, provisions should be made to discharge it through service adequate in quality and amount.

Some of the specific questions to be faced are: whether responsibility will be accepted by the agency for all cases coming to the court, and if not, for which cases; whether full time or part time will be given; what the responsibilities and duties will be with respect to the intake of cases from the police and others and to detention care. Under what administrative arrangements services will be furnished and from whom the worker will receive technical supervision will have to be decided also. The way in which special problems can be met, for example those relating to work with older adolescent boys, will need to be considered. Other questions to be answered relate to the status of the worker and the maintenance of case records. Should the worker be appointed as an officer of the court or retain identity as a children's worker from the public welfare agency? Should the social records kept by the worker be regarded as court or agency records and who should have access to them?

We do not yet have the answers to many of these problems. Developments in this area depend upon the leadership provided by judges and administrators of public child welfare agencies. This leadership will need to recognize that, despite the development of more adequate child welfare services under both public and private auspices, many courts still are handicapped because of the inadequacy or absence of such services. We cannot question a court's operation in the area of foster care unless these services under other auspices are or can be made adequate in amount and quality. While the basic needs of most children coming to the attention of courts are similar to those of children known to child welfare agencies, we must accept the fact that in treating the older and more aggressive youth there is a difference in the emphasis, approach, and skills required. We must admit that we have failed to develop services for older children and youth to the same degree that we have developed services for infants and younger children. The establishment of youth authorities in some states constitutes recognition of this fact.

Relationships with the police. The police department is another community agency with which the court is developing co-operative working relationships. This is especially true in view of the fact that a large proportion of the referrals to the courts are from police departments. Both police departments and courts are concerned with the protection of the community. Treatment is said to begin with apprehension. The way in which a child is handled in his first contact with the police often conditions his response to later treatment. Although the problems facing the police and courts are similar in many respects their official responsibilities are different. Effective service to children by both agencies can be achieved only when these differences in function are recognized and an integrated program adopted.

Much has been accomplished in recent years in developing sound police and court relationships. Many police departments have established special divisions called juvenile or crime prevention bureaus which handle cases involving children. These bureaus have assumed functions in relation to boys that were already being performed in girls' cases by women officers.

Personnel for these bureaus are appointed or assigned on the grounds of their special abilities in working with children and youth. The bureaus can do effective work as a screening and referral agency before resorting to court action but their work often has been questioned by both courts and social agencies. The courts have felt that some bureaus were performing judicial acts as well as carrying on an unofficial treatment program. Social agencies have questioned whether personnel with limited training could do an effective referral job. When all police officers assigned to these divisions have training similar to that of workers in other children and youth serving agencies in the community, and a clear and definitive agreement as to function is reached, then controversies and misunderstandings will disappear. Police schools have incorporated courses of training for these officers. Interpretive material has been compiled by police departments and courts as well as by other local, state, and national agencies.

Qualifications of judges and probation staff. The importance of selecting juvenile court judges in accordance with the qualifications incorporated in the juvenile court act has received a considerable amount of acceptance. In many jurisdictions, however, judges are elected or appointed on the basis of general qualifications for judicial work, and then assigned to the juvenile court which operates as a branch of a court of more general jurisdiction. Even where juvenile court judges are especially selected for this work, residence qualifications frequently limit the range of choice. It is of the utmost importance that there be general public acceptance of the importance of the office of juvenile judge and the necessity of a co-ordination of legal and social qualifications and personal characteristics that will fit him for wise and understanding service.

The probation officer has one of the most difficult jobs in the whole field of child care, calling for high personal qualifications and sound professional training. The qualifications and training of court treatment personnel are, therefore, of paramount importance. The probation officer's duty entails more than just securing a mass of facts regarding the family and the child. He must be trained to interpret and evaluate these facts in relation to the present situation facing the child and his family. The court is only one of several agencies in the community giving services to children. To carry out effectively its responsibilities to children, the court must use all the facilities in the community. Training, enabling him to make a sound diagnosis and proper referral, will make it possible for the probation officer to carry out this function much more effectively. This is recognized by a great

number of juvenile court judges. There is a constant demand by courts for persons professionally trained in the field of child welfare or one of the other functional divisions of social work. Some courts have provided field placements for students, in co-operation with schools of social work. Some have attempted partially to meet the need by developing effective in-service training programs.

The need for professional training is not a concept which has been entirely accepted. In fact many who feel that professional training is necessary have raised questions in our schools of social work in relation to the training of personnel for work in authoritarian agencies. The worker in the court faces situations which cut across the functional phases of social work. The foundation of his training, therefore, must be broad. The use of authority must be recognized and training for its effective and constructive utilization must be available. It may well be that in training programs we have overlooked or failed to understand the duties and responsibilities of the worker in an authoritarian setting. Only as our schools can develop persons with the skills necessary to do a more effective job in this field can we expect a wholehearted acceptance of professional training as a necessary qualification.

Treatment resources. The success of the work of the juvenile court is intimately related to the availability of adequate treatment resources outside the court. Such resources must include facilities for guidance and service to children in their own homes, which can be provided in part by the probation staff, but which also should include resources for family casework and child guidance through community agencies. Also required are effective resources for the treatment of children outside of their own homes, in foster homes, small study homes, or institutions. The whole area of treatment of juvenile delinquency is greatly in need of further study and of demonstrations of the ways in which the basic insecurities, frustrations, and rebellions characteristic of the delinquent child can be compensated for and overcome, and the child's energies directed into constructive channels.

Expectations for the Future

The juvenile court is still developing and changing. Some of these developments have been discussed. It is questionable, however, whether any of these newer developments have been in operation for a sufficient time to establish them with any degree of finality as indications of what we may expect in the future. The services of the juvenile courts are an integral part of the broad and long-range program necessary to promote the well-being of all children as well as the protection of certain children who have special needs. A grave responsibility rests upon all of us to cooperate in the development of the different types of specialized services to children required, and their integration in a well-rounded program which will so far as possible meet the needs of every child.

SELECTED REFERENCES

1. Tappan, Paul W., *Juvenile Delinquency* (New York: McGraw-Hill Book Co., 1949), Chapter 8: "The Juvenile Court."

The early legal roots of the juvenile court are traced back to the early rules of law. A competent discussion follows of the developments of the juvenile court in the United States. Tappan is an attorney as well as a sociologist. In a clear and interesting style are discussed procedures such as appearance, arraignment, adjournment, parole or remand, interim procedures during adjournment, hearing and adjudication and dispositions.

2. Neumeyer, Martin H., *Juvenile Delinquency in Modern Society* (New York: D. Van Nostrand Co., 1949), Chapter 13: "Juvenile Court, Probation Service, and Correctional Institutions."

3. Hartwell, Samuel W., "The Guidance Clinic and the Court," *Federal Probation*, XII, September 1948.

The relationships of the clinic officials and various juvenile court judges are considered here.

4. Teeters, Negley K., and Reinemann, John Otto, *The Challenge of Delinquency* (New York: Prentice-Hall, 1950), Chapter 10: "Expansion of the Juvenile Court Idea."

This chapter is a must for the careful student who is interested in acquiring comprehensive knowledge of the growth of the juvenile court in the United States. Meaningful information is also available on Adolescents' Courts and the Youth Correction Authority.

5. Rubin, Sol, "Changing Youth Correction Authority Concepts," *Focus*, XXIX, May 1950.

With the passage of time, a gradual departure from the model act developed by the American Law Institute has taken place. The use of the word "correction" has tended to disappear in the name of the governing body.

6. Holton, Karl, "California Youth Authority: Eight Years of Action," *Journal of Criminal Law and Criminology*, XLI, May-June 1950.

7. Phillips, Orie L., "The Federal Youth Corrections Act," *Federal Probation*, XV, March 1951.

10 PROBATION

~~~~~~

PROBATION for the juvenile offender is a form of court-disposition of the defendant following the establishment of his guilt. Although it is a nonpunitive method of treating offenders, it should not be interpreted as leniency or mercy.

Probation attempts to deal with offenders as individuals; its social principle is to keep these persons out of reformatories and with their families. It tries to prevent suffering—hence, it is not, in principle, punishment. And this, paradoxically, seems to be the basic reason why numerous officials, and even a large part of the public, oppose it. Probation is a humanitarian method of administering justice—not a gesture of leniency and mollycoddling. It is, in large measure, a counseling service which emphasizes attitudes of friendship, helpfulness and sympathy. As Sanford Bates expressed it, "Probation may be regarded as an investment in humanity . . . it encourages rather than embitters. It builds up rather than degrades. It is an investment in community protection."[1] Today probation may be defined simply as the suspension of the sentence, conditioned upon good behavior, during a period of liberty in the community. This action may be either a suspension of the *imposition* or the *execution* of the sentence. It is generally considered a substitute for imprisonment.

In deciding a case involving a child or adolescent who is not insane or feeble-minded, most juvenile or criminal courts will either (1) return him to his home *on probation*, (2) refer him to such welfare services as exist in larger cities, (3) place him in a boarding or foster home, (4) send him to a correctional house, or (5) confine him to jail. For chance offenders and for first offenders, it is generally believed, the most sensible disposition of the case is to return the child to his home on probation, under court supervision. This is also the least expensive way to administer the case. Even in a case of serious offense, probation is still less expensive than committing the child to an institution or to a jail. It has been estimated that it takes about three years to rehabilitate a serious child offender at a cost of several thousand dollars. But, it will cost society even more to retain the same child in a prison, from which he may emerge, not a reformed person, but an enemy of society, more eager than ever to "get even." Therefore few steps would be more economical—as well as beneficial on other grounds—in the improvement of the administration of criminal justice, than the wise extension of probation and the raising of the quality of probation services.

---

[1] Reported in J. Howard McGrath, "The Role of the Federal Probation Officer in Criminal Justice," *Federal Probation*, XIV, December 1950, 5.

However, for many children and youths in trouble, probation does not appear to be an appropriate practice. To return to his home and neighborhood an individual of any age who has become habituated to criminal practices or who has deep-seated maladjustments, or whose delinquent behavior springs from brutality or immorality at home or from the breakdown of satisfactory relationships in the family, or, perhaps, from membership in a neighborhood gang, may involve, as one writer stresses, a disservice to the individual himself, to society, and to the cause of probation as well.[2] But it also should be remembered that if probation is undesirable for violators in these categories, the present-day principal alternative—confinement in jail or "reformatory" or prison—may result ultimately in even greater harm to society and its members.

Unfortunately, the way probation is practiced differs in various courts and in different states; therefore it is impossible to estimate accurately the total number of children on probation in the United States. The number must be several times the number of correctional school graduates, which approximate thirty thousand a year. Lowell Juilliard Carr calculates that if one were to guess that sixty-five thousand to one hundred thousand children are placed on probation each year, it would not be an overstatement of the facts.

THE PROBATION OFFICER

The care of these numerous probationers and the administration of the probation system today are in the hands of personnel generally lacking in numbers and often handicapped by limited facilities and inadequate training. Recent years have brought considerable improvement in the standards for probation officials, but the need for trained specialists in this area remains a serious problem. And the problem is aggravated by the fact that political considerations often influence the selection of probation personnel. Moreover, under the laws of various states—and certainly in the public view—there is no general agreement concerning appropriate qualifications for the probation officer.

When juvenile courts were first created a half-century ago, many of the persons connected with them still thought partly in the language of criminal law. Consequently, for many people the title "probation officer" has come to be tinged with the aura of the criminal court, and to such an extent that the term is now entirely unsuitable for use in juvenile courts. The word "probation" does not suggest the social casework done with children in juvenile courts. Sometimes the title "probation officer" keeps good-intentioned individuals from bringing matters involving children before the juvenile court early enough to help the children. These individuals often do not want the child to have a "record." Although the juvenile court laws specifically state otherwise, many people are not convinced that a child under the supervision of a probation officer has not been convicted of some high crime or misdemeanor. This interpretation is especially likely to be made when the probation officer in charge is either named by statute or is self-described as "chief probation

---

[2] John R. Ellingston, *Protecting Our Children from Criminal Careers* (New York: Prentice-Hall, 1948), pp. 82, 83.

officer"—in the manner of "chief of police" or "chief deputy sheriff." Lately some states have changed the title of the juvenile court probation officer to "probation counselor." In Rhode Island he is "youth counselor"; in Mississippi, "director" and "counselor"; in the cities of Toledo and Cleveland, Ohio, "supervisor"; and in the District of Columbia, "director of social work."

The probation officer's duties are manifold. In California, for example, it has been brought out that the probation officer may have to locate boarding homes, supervise a detention home, and operate the county's forestry camps. He is asked to collect money from parents and guardians for the care of the wards of the court and for restitutions, fines, and court costs. He must make full reports on every child investigated and keep records of the progress and discharge of the wards of the court. To make matters worse, most of the counties in the state have very few probation officers and limited staffs for the probation program. In one instance a single probation officer was expected to supervise 140 girls, to handle the intake of all new cases (boys as well as girls), and to investigate the new girl cases, preparing on each a detailed report and a recommendation for the court. In addition, this same woman was secretary to the probation committee and, on finishing her day's work, served as night matron at a detention home. In another county in California, the probation officer carried a case load of one hundred boys and girls and an equal number of adults. The county schools frequently called upon him to act as attendance officer. He had no aides and no clerk or stenographer. Naturally, he kept no records. The National Probation Association has claimed, after years of experience studying conditions of this kind, that no officer can supervise successfully more than seventy-five cases and that to do the best work the officer should carry no more than fifty boys or forty girls!

In theory, to be sure, but hardly in practice, the probation officer is a case worker who carefully studies each child, works out a definite plan of treatment, and, by utilizing every available community resource, helps the child to solve his problems. And no doubt many, if not most, officials would like to live up to the theory of their profession. But even in some of the large cities where numerous social welfare agencies aid in probationary work, genuine case work of the ideal type is a rarity. In too many communities only general supervision service is available. In the smaller centers very little is accomplished which meets case-work standards.

For one kind of delinquent, the fact that the court has no program for follow-up or for supervision probably does no harm. The court experience itself serves as jolt enough for the individual concerned so that he is less likely to commit additional offenses. Case work for delinquents who fall into this group would be merely a waste of time and money. For the delinquent who is given another chance but who probably should have been committed to an institution (a matter that can be decided, in the last analysis, only *after* the whole record is complete), case work is also a waste of effort and dollars. Between these two extremes lies the group of delinquents who need case work and who would profit from it. One of the basic problems of every juvenile court is to select for case-work treatment delinquents from this middle group.

Unfortunately, when a child faces a judge no one knows in advance whether the child can come through without case supervision. Each judge must make the wisest decision he can in the light of the information available, his own knowledge of children, and his philosophy of life.

THE FEDERAL JUVENILE DELINQUENCY ACT

Juvenile offenders against federal law, though not numerous, have presented a special problem to federal probation officers and correctional workers because there is no provision for their handling in the penal structure of the federal government. In 1932 an attempt was made to alleviate this peculiar situation by legislation authorizing United States Attorneys to divert persons under 21 years of age to state or local courts, if these particular courts would accept jurisdiction. However, if, for one reason or another, diversion could not be effected, these young people would have to be processed through the federal courts in the same fashion as adults. Moreover, federal judges were forced to confine them with adults because there were no facilities for the confinement of youthful offenders.

In recognition of a long-established juvenile court principle—that the young offender needs specialized care and treatment—and in recognition of the fact that the federal government had not provided for the juvenile offender in its courts, the Federal Juvenile Delinquency Act became a law on June 16, 1938. This Act provides that a person under 18 years of age can be prosecuted on information rather than indictment, if he so consents in writing. He can be heard by the federal court judge in private and without jury trial at any time or place within the district of the court; he can be placed on probation or committed to any public or private agency which will segregate him from adult offenders; and he can be paroled immediately or at any time following his sentence.

The key person in administering this Act is the probation officer. Immediately upon the arrest of a juvenile, he interviews the offender, investigates his family situation, and consults the United States Attorney about the possibility of diverting the case to a local juvenile court. The probation officer's findings are made available to the Attorney and the United States Commissioner, as well as to the Federal Court, the Bureau of Prisons, and the Parole Board; the officer notifies the United States Marshal of suitable places of detention for the particular offender and arranges an early court hearing. He does not permit the youth to be fingerprinted. Finally, the probation officer makes sure that the offender is intensively supervised from the time of his arrest until the completion of his term of surveillance. No doubt the probation officer's responsibility to the juvenile offender under the Federal Juvenile Delinquency Act places upon him important and exacting duties. The procedure, however, leaves the juvenile with a conviction record.

In January, 1946, an official attempt was made to circumvent a court record for juvenile offenders. The Attorney General authorized all United States Attorneys to make use of the "deferred prosecution" procedure whenever juvenile offenders were involved in court proceedings. This authorization is sometimes referred to as the "Brooklyn Plan" because the procedure was employed as early as 1936 by the federal prosecutor and probation officer of Brooklyn, New York.

Under this plan, the United States Attorney, on the basis of a report made by the probation officer, may defer prosecution for a definite period and request the probation officer, in writing, to exercise supervision over the youth—that is, treat the offender as if he were on probation. The probation officer must submit progress reports to the United States Attorney, as well as make an appropriate recommendation at the termination of the supervision. If the report is a favorable one, the original complaint against the offender is dropped. This procedure protects the youth against the stigma of an official criminal record. Of two hundred cases supervised in Brooklyn on this deferred prosecution plan, only two violators had to be referred to the court by due process of law.[3]

The success of the Brooklyn Plan and numerous other recent advances in the probation system in the United States are encouraging signs in the treatment of juvenile delinquency. As is seen, however, serious problems remain if this promising method of coping with the young offender is to match the hopes of its founders.

READINGS

John Otto Reinemann in "Probation and the Juvenile Delinquent" analyzes probation in relation to juvenile delinquency, and its history, characteristics, significance to the courts, function of supervision, and role of probation officers. He concludes with an evaluation of probation as a modern device of correctional treatment.

James N. York in his article, "Evaluating the Everyday Work of a Probation Office," examines the work of a probation office and suggests some guideposts for self-study and improvement.

In his article, "What a Difference One Year Makes," Robert L. Noble, Jr. points up the limitations of chronological demarcation in juvenile crime.

In "The Role of the Probation Officer in the Treatment of Delinquency in Children," Hyman S. Lippman stresses the importance of utilizing services other than the court, especially when an impossible case load is being carried at the same time. In too many instances, probation officers are not in a position to take advantage of these services.

David Crystal in "Family Casework in Probation" develops the theme that case work, whether in an authoritative or voluntary setting, involves the same basic elements. Helping an individual includes some consideration of relationships within the family setting.

Henry J. Palmieri in "Probation Is Treatment" points out that while probation is treatment, not all probationers can or will respond. Probation officers must continually strive to develop and refine current methods.

Harleigh B. Trecker in "The Use of Community Agencies in Probation

---

[3] See Charles H. Z. Meyer, "A Half Century of Federal Probation and Parole," *Journal of Criminal Law and Criminology*, XLII, March–April 1952.

Work" says it is increasingly evident that prevention, treatment, and eventual control of delinquency rests with the community.

William C. Nau in his selection, "Let Them Know about It," suggests that those in the probation field could use the services of a public-relations department. Too many social categories are almost totally unaware of what probation is doing or hopes to accomplish. It may be up to the probation officer to "take the stump" and let others know about the work, for no project is more rewarding than community interpretation.

The last article, "Probation: The Art of Introducing the Probationer to a Better Way of Life," by Elizabeth R. Glover, sums up in many ways the philosophy of probation. Probation officers attempt to build up the probationer's self-respect and by precept and example to inculcate a system of ethical social values too often lacking in youthful offenders.

Miss Glover, an authority in the field of probation, will be recognized as the author of *Probation and Re-education* (Routledge Kegan Paul).

Probation and the Juvenile Delinquent[*]

By John Otto Reinemann. Director of Probation, Municipal Court of Philadelphia.

THE ESTABLISHMENT of juvenile courts, first created in Illinois half a century ago and since then introduced in all states of the Union and in its possessions, was a culmination of a movement which demanded a non-punitive but rehabilitative treatment of child offenders. But a tribunal like the juvenile court, per se, could only be the framework in which the cases of juvenile delinquents were to be handled. In order to translate into practice the underlying idea of the juvenile court, special devices were required. Probation has become one of its most important tools.

Historically, the beginnings of probation anteceded the creation of juvenile courts. In 1869 Massachusetts passed a law providing for the supervision of juvenile delinquents by a state agent. This was probably the direct outcome of the efforts and services of John Augustus, a Boston shoemaker, today recognized as the "first probation officer," who in the years 1841 to 1858 had befriended countless juvenile and other offenders.

Definition and Extent of Probation

Legally, in the case of an adult offender, probation is the suspension of sentence during a period of freedom, on condition of good behavior. In the case of a delinquent child, the juvenile court uses probation as a form of case disposition which allows the child to live at liberty in his own home or in the custody of a suitable person, be it a relative, a friend of the family, or a foster home, under supervision of an agent of the court and upon such conditions as the court determines. Socially, probation is a form of treatment administered by probation officers on a case work basis.

The juvenile court laws in the forty-eight states and the territories make provision for probation by mentioning it as one of the possible case dispositions

[*] Reprinted from *The Annals* of The American Academy of Political and Social Science, 261 (January 1949), pp. 109–119. Used by permission.

which are available to the juvenile court judge. In accordance with the noncriminal procedure of juvenile courts, some laws use the term "supervision" instead of "probation," because the word "probation" is an inadequate indication of social case work and is too strongly related to criminal court practices. However, the phrase "probation" is still preponderantly employed, both in theory and in practice.

What is the extent to which probation is being used as a proper approach to a delinquency situation? According to the "Juvenile Court Statistics for 1945," published by the United States Children's Bureau and covering almost 115,000 cases reported from 374 juvenile courts throughout the country, probation was ordered in 30 per cent of the cases.

Another publication by the Children's Bureau states:

The 20 per cent decrease from 1933 to 1945 in the number of children in institutions for delinquent children is significant also. In part it reflects the increased use of probation and parole as methods of supervision of delinquent children in the homes of the parents or other relatives or in foster-family homes.

Probation Department of Juvenile Court

The great majority of juvenile courts are organized on the basis of county units, either as separate and independent courts or as special sessions, branches, or divisions of general courts. Probation is administered by the probation department, which is an adjunct to the juvenile court and consists of one or more probation officers and other clerical personnel, according to the size and population density of the county.

The fact that the various state juvenile courts acts provide for probation does not necessarily mean that there is a complete coverage of probation service in all counties throughout the United States. The National Probation and Parole Association reports that in 1947,

out of a total of 3,071 counties, 1,610 counties did not have any such service for juveniles. In many of these counties the lack may be attributed to the comparatively small number of children referred to the court. In other instances, however, it is due to an uninformed public opinion, to penny-pinching fiscal authorities, to judges without social vision; any one of these factors or all three combined may prevent the setting up of a probation program although it is vitally needed in the particular locality.

State Participation

One of the ways of stimulating the establishment or the improvement of probation services on the local level is the active participation of state agencies in juvenile court work. Such state action might take various forms. There are only a few state-administered juvenile courts, as for instance in Connecticut, Rhode Island, and Utah. But in about half of the states, a state probation commission or a division of the state welfare department or department of correction has been given some kind of responsibility for the development and operation of probation services for children.

In California, the state Youth Authority grants probation to persons under 21 years of age committed to it by the local courts. In several states, examinations are given by state boards, commissions, or departments with the purpose of establishing eligibility lists from which probation officers are appointed locally (as for example in Indiana, Nevada, and Virgania); in others, probation officers are appointed by state agencies directly (in New Hampshire and Wyoming), or their appointment, though made locally, must be approved by a state agency (e. g. in North Carolina). In a number of states, county welfare agents, appointed by and operating under a state department of welfare or assistance, may be called upon by local juvenile court judges to render probation services. In West Virginia the Division of Child Welfare of the State Department of Public Assistance renders juvenile probation service through eight district offices, each administered by a child welfare supervisor.

In Virginia state aid is provided as a means of stimulating the establishment of probation service in local communities, by paying half of the salary of probation officers in juvenile courts in cities of over 10,000 population. In New York the Division of Probation of the State Department of Correction, headed by a director of probation, has general supervision of probation officers, both adult and juvenile, throughout the state. The director makes recommendations regarding administration of probation in children's courts, and adopts rules regarding methods and procedures in administration of probation throughout the state, except in New York City. There are also several states where the law authorizes a state agency in general terms to cooperate with the courts, to collect reports from probation officers on their case loads, or to give advisory service.

This list shows all possible varieties of state participation, from centralized administration to a merely advisory function. Unfortunately, too, as in the related fields of public health, welfare, and education, lack of funds and personnel has prevented several state departments from carrying out their assigned tasks. The new policy of the United States Children's Bureau, in effect since January 1, 1946, to collect juvenile court statistics directly from the state welfare or correction department rather than from the hundreds of local juvenile courts, has at least forced all state departments to set up some machinery for the compilation of uniform statistical data within the confines of their respective states.

The Probation Officer

The main prerequisite of a well-functioning probation program is an adequate staff. In the juvenile court, more than in any other judicial branch, the judge must rely on the work of court aides; these men and women are called probation officers, juvenile officers, or probation counselors. In the majority of instances they are appointed by the juvenile court judges, except where other provisions are made by law, as outlined before. Larger probation departments are headed by a chief probation officer.

On January 1, 1947 there were 3,681 probation officers for juveniles in the continental United States, appointed locally or as state employees. Many of them functioned in juvenile *and* adult cases, and in juvenile delinquency as well as child dependency and neglect situations. Not included in this figure were 267 Federal probation officers whose work is overwhelmingly concerned with adult offenders, since Federal offenders of juvenile court age are often supervised by local juvenile court probation officers. Not all of the 3,681 probation officers are employed full time in this capacity; the other duties of part-time probation officers may include those of sheriff, bailiff, welfare worker, clerk of the court, attendance officer, or other.

Assignments. The probation officer has two main assignments. First, prior to the court hearing, he makes social investigations covering the family and home environment, the school career, and all other pertinent data concerning the child's personality. He incorporates his findings in a report to the judge, often with his own evaluation and recommendation, so that it can be used as a guide for the disposition of the case. Second, he supervises the child who has been placed on probation by the judge; the details of this work will be presented later.

These tasks, entailing the probing and diagnosis of human behavior and the guidance of young, impressionable individuals, call for understanding and skill. Recent developments and new discoveries in the social and psychological sciences have greatly influenced the total child welfare program of which the probation service for youthful offenders constitutes a notable part. It is, therefore, more and more recognized that certain qualifications regarding educational background, training, and experience should be met by those desiring to enter the probation field.

Qualifications. A committee of the Professional Council of the National Probation and Parole Association, consisting of leading authorities in the probation and parole field, in 1945 formulated "Standards for Selection of Probation and Parole Officers," after consultation with many administrators in the correctional field throughout the country. These "Standards" suggest as minimum qualifications: a bachelor's degree from a college or university of recognized standing or its educational equivalent, with courses in the social sciences; one year of paid fulltime experience under competent supervision in an approved social agency or related field. As regards his personal qualification, a probation officer must possess a good character and a balanced personality. These traits are considered essential:

good health, physical endurance, intellectual maturity, emotional stability, integrity, tact, dependability, adaptability, resourcefulness, sincerity, humor, ability to work with others, tolerance, patience, objectivity, capacity to win confidence, respect for human personality, and genuine affection for people.

The educational qualifications are proposed as an entrance minimum for new appointees, and many probation departments strive to apply these principles when staff vacancies have to be filled. But the idea is still far from being universally adopted. Many state laws are silent regarding qualifications for probation officers; others couch them in such general terms that they can be met by any untrained person as long as he is a "discreet person of reputable character." Political influences, which as a rule have been successfully banned in the teaching profession, are still operating in the probation field and have prevented many states and local communities from adopting minimum requirements for the appointment of probation officers. As the introduction to the "Standards" emphasizes,

there are in many communities devoted and successful workers, qualified by self-education and assimilated experience, who have attained professional competence and who are in fact among our best workers. No suggestion to replace such competent workers is made, the standards refer only to the training and qualifications of future appointees.

Selection and tenure. The method of selection of probation officers is closely related to the problem of qualification. The "Standards" suggest that appointments be made from eligibility lists resulting from competitive merit examinations. As has been mentioned before, some states have set up machinery for such examinations; in others, probation officers are appointed under the general state or local civil service regulations. Various progressive courts, even without specific legal requirements, have instituted a voluntary merit system.

A necessary complement to these provisions is the guarantee of reasonable tenure. This is of particular importance in view of the preponderant number of probation officers who are appointed by local judges whose office term is usually limited by statute and who often have to engage in political campaigns for re-election.

All these considerations—concerning qualification, selection, and tenure—point in the direction of making the public, the judges or other administrative bodies, and, last but not least, the probation officers themselves aware that probation service has become a profession.

Training. In order to promote this concept, special consideration must be given the training of probation officers. This includes pre-service training and in-service training.

Training prior to the entrance into the probation career is determined by the adoption of the previously quoted educational and training requirements. The "Standards" state that "the best training for probation and parole work is in a graduate school of social work," but they realize that the previously mentioned educational requirement (Bachelor's degree or equivalent, with courses in the social sciences) is probably as much as can at present be hoped for as a minimum in many parts of the country.

There is a difference of opinion whether case work training is a good preparation for probation work or not. Walter C. Reckless, for instance, thinks that the trained probation officer should have a good foundation in criminology and in the field of corrections, both juvenile and adult. He needs to take specially organized courses in probation and parole work which can give him a specific preparation rather than a case work preparation.

He is of the opinion that the basic underpinning of probation and parole should not be case work and its allied psychiatric point of view, but rather criminology, corrections, and social psychology. Reckless considers the schools of social work and the departments of sociology as the best places for the training of probation officers, but realizes that on the one hand "our schools of social work have been reticent about including courses in penology and corrections," while on the other hand "many departments of sociology have frowned disdainfully at the prospect of offering practical training."

In-service training has in recent years come to the fore in many branches of public administration; in the correctional field, in particular, it has gained widespread recognition and realization. In-service training cannot and should not be a substitute for adequate pre-service training. It will have its greatest value for probation officers who are at present employed as such and who did not have the benefit of professional schooling, and in those situations where probation departments feel that even for newly appointed staff members, professional pre-service training should not be required. However, in-service training should not be confined to these two groups; for the well-trained staff member, too, in-service training is a necessary tool for maintaining a high standard of job performance.

Several types of in-service training programs have been successfully carried out in various parts of the country.

1. Many probation departments of juvenile courts have organized their own in-service instruction for their staff members by supervisory personnel or specially assigned instructors.

2. Another type is found, for instance, in Pennsylvania (among other states), where the State Department of Public Instruction, using partly Federal funds appropriated on the basis of the George-Deen Act, has conducted in-service training courses for correctional workers on the local and state level for the past ten years, and where the probation administrators of the various courts have availed themselves of this opportunity by enrolling their staff members in these courses.

3. A number of in-service training courses or institutes open to probation officers of the local courts have been conducted by universities, e.g. the University of California at Berkeley, the University of Southern California, the University of New Hampshire, the College of William and Mary in Virginia, the University of Minnesota and others.

Assignment of cases. The assignment of cases to the probation officer should be guided by certain rules. Girls' cases should always be assigned to women probation officers; cases of boys under 12 years of age may be handled by women probation officers, but all cases of boys above that age should be assigned to men. To assign the probation officers according to geographical districts and have them handle all cases of children living in their respective territories is the most economical method; this does not preclude the assignment of special cases, for instance of sex delinquency, to officers who, due to training and experience, might be particularly qualified for this kind of work. Theoretically at least, it is generally agreed that no more than fifty cases should be under the supervision of one probation officer at any time; actually, however, this rule is far from being generally applied in practice.

Volunteer Probation Service

Volunteer service in the probation field can take the following two forms:

1. In small towns and sparsely populated rural areas an interested lay citizen may take over the supervision of a youngster placed on probation, as a neighborly sponsor. This volunteer worker should be well selected by the probation department of the county juvenile court and should be responsible to this department. Such an arrangement makes it possible to give supervision to children living in remote parts of the county who, due to the heavy case load and geographically extensive work area of the regular probation officer, would not receive the benefits of probation service.

There is, however, a danger that the services of volunteers (and this applies also in a certain degree to the previously mentioned use of part-time probation officers) are misused by protagonists of a false economy in preventing the employment of qualified, full-time probation officers where their services are vitally needed.

2. The volunteer can render valuable service in supplementing (rather than substituting for) the work of the regular probation officer, in both large and small communities.

He might be assigned as an individual or as a member of an organization to maintain frequent contacts with a child on probation and to collaborate closely with the probation officer in charge. It is considered good policy to hold each volunteer responsible for only one or two youngsters, and the type of case must be carefully selected.

In various cities members of the Big Brother and Big Sister organizations and similar youth service agencies carry out such a program. A good example of this kind of service is provided by the Juvenile Delinquency Clinics in Fayette County, Pennsylvania. Here, in the county seat (Uniontown) and several townships, business men, clergymen, and men in the professions have banded together for the purpose of giving supervision and counsel to boys assigned to them by the juvenile court upon the recommendation of the chief probation officer, to whom these lay workers are responsible and with whom they meet for frequent consultation.

Beyond the service in individual cases there is another important asset in the utilization of volunteers in probation work; it provides a good channel to the public at large for the interpretation of the meaning of probation, the problems presented by delinquent conduct of children, and the need for community facilities for youth conservation and crime prevention.

Selection of Probationers

The juvenile court judge places a child on probation after having studied the social case history, as compiled in the probation officer's investigation report, and the recommendations by the probation officer and the court psychiatrist; he has also taken into consideration the facts disclosed and impressions gained at the court hearing. In the majority of instances he orders probation as a kind of "middle of the road" disposition. These are cases in which the simple discharge or adjustment of the case, even with a reprimand by the judge, does not seem sufficient; on the other hand, these situations do not warrant the removal of the child from his home and his commitment into the controlled environment of an institution. Within these limits lie the range and the potentialities of probation.

More positively expressed, probation should be ordered whenever the following requirements are met: The home surroundings must appear sufficiently conducive to the proper upbringing of the child, and the adjustment of the boy or girl in an atmosphere of freedom, as the ordinary community life provides it, must be feasible, with the help of the court's supervisory authority. It follows from this that probation should not be "handed out" automatically, say, in all cases in which the child has committed his first serious offense or has been brought to court for the second or third time on any delinquency charge. Nor should probation be used, as happens all too frequently, though with misgivings, only because proper institutional facilities are lacking. The selection of probation as a proper treatment must be governed by all factors which are apparent in an individual case.

Attempts have been made to establish prediction tables, based on these various factors, as a guide for probation and parole selection. But, as Sanford Bates says, "the prognostic tables should never be a substitute for executive or judicial judgment, but will be a logical means of applying the accumulated experience of the past to the important problems of the future." Pauline Young adds to this, that "each institution, department, and community needs to develop its own experience tables and not rely upon those of other groups, which may strongly reflect unique elements in their peculiar situations."

Conditions of Probation

Probation is predicated upon certain conditions. These may be general conditions applicable to all children placed on probation, or they may be especially determined by the court in the individual situation. The general conditions include obedience to parents, regular school attendance, keeping of early hours, following of instructions by the probation officer, notification to the court of changes of address, and staying away from undesirable companions and from disreputable places. Many of these conditions, often enumerated in a form letter which is given or sent to the parents, are full of negatives. In order to interpret the meaning of probation as a positive constructive measure, such a communication should include some kind of an opening and closing statement like the following sample:

WHAT DOES PROBATION MEAN?

Probation means that the court has confidence in the good character of your child.

Probation means that your child will remain in your home; you will continue to be responsible for your child.

The court through its probation officer will help you in supervising your child.

REMEMBER—everything that has been mentioned here is necessary for the WELFARE OF YOUR CHILD.

We, the Court, and you, the parents, want to see your child grow up into a fine American citizen, healthy in body, mind and spirit.

Special conditions may consist of restitution for damages, living with a relative (due to inadequacy of the parental home), attendance at a special school, affiliation with an approved recreational agency, or carrying out of medical recommendations.

Supervision of Probationers

Since probation is a treatment process, it is important that the probation officer at the beginning formulate some kind of treatment plan. In many instances, the probation officer already knows the child and his family from the investigation prior to court hearing. The probation officer should conceive his task as that of a counselor, a Big Brother or Big Sister. The probation officer will therefore strive to win the confidence of the child. In order to be successful he must also be accepted by the parents and other members of the family. Sometimes he has to break down an attitude of resistance on the part of the parents, who may consider the probation officer's interest and activity as an intrusion into their rights. He will have to interpret to them the real meaning of his assignment, namely, to help the child in his readjustment.

The probation officer must be himself convinced that his is a positive and constructive task. No conscientious probation officer will be satisfied with merely keeping the child who is under his supervision out of another conflict with the law. As Lou, in his fundamental work on *Juvenile Courts in the United States*, points out:

to be really constructive, the plan must take into account not only the weak qualities of the probationer, but also his good qualities, upon which the desired superstructure of normal conduct and character may be built. It must be based upon an understanding of all the factors of the problem of the probationer, including his personality, his habits, and reactions and the reasons for them, his mental life, his physical strength and weaknesses, the home influences, and the bearing of the school regime on the child's development.

Method and frequency of contacts. The contacts of the probation officer with a child can be established either through home visits or through reporting of the child at the office of the probation department or a specially assigned room in a neighborhood settlement house.

In the home the probation officer sees the child as a part of the family; he wins an insight into the attitude of the parents toward the child, the child's relationship to his siblings, and the physical environment of home and neighborhood. The probation officer often finds himself undertaking reconstructive work with the whole family, since the child's behavior is frequently an outcome of unstable home conditions.

The reporting by the child to the probation department office or other designated place at regular intervals has its value in affording the probation officer an opportunity to converse with the child alone, unhampered by the presence of other members of the family and the frequently crowded conditions of the home. However, this form of reporting should be restricted to boys over 12 years of age.

There is, of course, no general rule regarding the frequency of contacts. Every individual case demands a different method. Some judges emphasize the need for very frequent contacts in specific cases, by placing the youngster on "strict probation." The Committee Report on Juvenile Court Standards holds that "except in rare cases, home visits at least once every two weeks are essential to effective supervision, knowledge of the assets and liabilities of the family and correction of unfavorable conditions."

Use of community resources. One of the most important prerequisites for constructive probation work is the probation officer's intimate knowledge of the community resources. It is self-understood that the probation officer keeps himself informed of the child's progress in school. Frequent conferences are held with the principal or teacher and—in an increasing number of instances and with gratifying results—the school counselor or school social worker. School authorities are usually quite willing to co-operate with the probation department.

In the cases of older children on probation, the probation officer should assist and guide them in the choice of and preparation for a vocation. The probation officer must be familiar with existing health centers and family service agencies, and will collaborate with them. He must be fully acquainted with the various recreational and character-building groups to which he can refer his probationers. In certain cases of deep-rooted emotional disturbances he may utilize the services of child guidance clinics or similar facilities.

Use of case work principles. There has been considerable discussion regarding the use of case work principles within the authoritarian setting of the juvenile court and more particularly of probation. It is today recognized that the authority inherent in probation has a constructive role to play if it is to be used by a probation officer who is aware of his great responsibility and if it is interpreted to the probationer in an understandable way and therefore is accepted by him. The Panel Report on "Case Work-Group Work" summarizes this aspect of probation as follows:

During probation . . . case work has a contribution to make. In keeping with case work philosophy the delinquent and the probation officer must see probation as an experimental period of social adjustment. During the period, the individual must learn to live with authority. He must be helped to discover and develop his capacity to take responsibility for himself, as a member of the community, accepting its standards and rules of behavior.

The probation officer should review the progress of probation with his supervisor from time to time and should modify the original plan if necessary. If a situation develops which threatens to impede the success of probation and which calls for a change of the court's order, the probation officer has not only the right but the duty to petition the judge for an amendment of his previous decision. This may result in continuance of probation in a different environment, for instance in a relative's home, or in commitment of the youngster to a foster home or an institution.

Length and Termination of Probation

In accordance with the individualistic character of probation, its length is dependent on the needs and requirements of each case. It is today customary in most juvenile courts not to limit probation in advance as to time. It is also recognized that, with rare exceptions, short-term probation is of little value. The previously quoted Committee Report on Juvenile Court Standards recommends a general minimum probation period of from six months to one year. The average length of probation for juveniles in the Municipal Court of Philadelphia, for instance, during recent years has been ten months.

Probation can be terminated in various ways. In those cases in which a definite time limit is set, it expires automatically; otherwise it is left to the probation officer to determine when the objectives of probation are met and consequently to petition the court for the discharge of the boy or girl from probation. Violations of probation may also lead to its termination. The commitment of a new offense is considered a violation of probation per se, while non-compliance with the conditions, general or specific, attached to probation is termed a technical violation. The probation officer has considerable discretion in determining whether the child and his parents are living up to the conditions imposed. In either instance the judge may decide to continue probation or to apply stricter measures, mostly institutional commitment.

Technically, probation of a juvenile

may last until his twenty-first birthday. Most of the juvenile court laws of the various states, regardless of whether the upper juvenile court age limit is 18 (as in the majority of states) or lower or higher, contain provisions extending juvenile court jurisdiction to the age of majority, once it has attached in an individual case prior to the reaching of the upper juvenile court age limit of the respective state law.

Evaluation of Probation

Has probation been successful as a modern device of correctional treatment, especially in juvenile cases? To measure success of probation is difficult unless very detailed studies of individual cases with a follow-up over several years after termination of probation are undertaken. Otherwise, the purely negative yardstick of recidivism during the period of probation and within a certain time afterwards might be used. Austin H. MacCormick states:

Based on actual performances over a term of years, a good juvenile court and probation service, operating in a community with adequate social resources and utilizing them fully, can put as high as 90 per cent of its juvenile delinquents on probation the first time around and 50 to 75 per cent the second or third time around, and get as high as 75 to 80 per cent successes.

Summarizing the positive values of probation in juvenile cases, the follow-ing points should be stressed: It is the most individualistic form of treatment; it applies the method of social case work and uses the constructive values of authority; it leaves the child in its normal home surroundings; it enlists the help of community resources; it is not considered punitive and is therefore free of social stigma.

Recently a Sub-Committee on Probation of the Division of Social Activities of the United Nations, consisting of eleven probation administrators from various parts of the United States, met to prepare a statement on the basic principles and the application of probation for juvenile and adult offenders; this report, based on experiences in the United States, will be distributed to all member nations of the United Nations as a guide for the establishment of similar services in other countries. At the first meeting of this group, a member of the United Nations Secretariat (not a United States representative) observed that probation, both in juvenile and adult cases, has progressed farthest in the United States of America. Such a statement should not cause us to be smugly proud of our achievements, but should rather make us realize our great responsibility in providing and maintaining adequate juvenile courts and probation services everywhere in the United States on behalf of all children who require such community aids.

Evaluating the Everyday Work of a Probation Office[*]

By James N. York. Supervisor of Probation, California Youth Authority.

MANY developments in the past few years have impressed me with the fact that probation is growing up. As a profession, we not only are trying to do an acceptable job today but also are looking toward the future. Throughout the country progressive departments and active professional organizations are

---

[*] Reprinted from *Federal Probation*, Vol. XII, September, 1948, pp. 24–29. Used by permission of author and publication.

talking seriously in terms of principles and objectives, staff training and development, standards of work and personnel, evaluation of the staff and of the job being done. What is more important is that we are finding an increasing number of departments progressing beyond the stage of verbalization and stepping out into fields of accomplishment, or at least experimentation, in these areas.

Probation Progress

Probation administration is becoming more sure of itself, more imaginative, more resourceful, and is developing a realization that progress in the field demands more than a policy of adhering to historical and antiquated methods. We have every reason to continue to be proud of the traditions and background of probation and of our departments. However, when we find a department where policies and procedures have their foundations in tradition alone, we have found a probation system without vigor and basically unsound. Much valid criticism of probation can be directed toward this tendency of probation departments to grow haphazardly rather than to progress soundly through the formulation of definite and studied plans and procedures. Progress demands that we look backward but only for purposes of reference and to appraise our past mistakes. From that point, our need is for *positive* planning based on sound evaluation of our present programs and incorporating all the vision and imagination of which we are capable.

It is imperative that we in the field, particularly those in supervisory and administrative positions, possess a sincere faith in the philosophy, methodology, and potentialities of probation and be keenly aware of the objectives toward which we should be working. We must be continually on the alert for new information and seek better procedures as well as improved techniques. We must be acutely aware of the needs of proba-

tion and actively strive for the most efficacious way of filling these needs. We must keep moving toward those standards of work which spell the difference between mediocrity and real professional service. Probation will develop only as rapidly as our leadership—in fact our entire personnel—meets these qualifications and makes use of initiative and determination in seeing that probation is developed to its fullest potentiality.

When it is remembered that only six states had permissive probation legislation at the turn of the century, it still would be quite proper to say that probation is a "new" method of dealing with delinquency and crime. Fifty years is a very short period of time in the history of corrections and in many jurisdictions the operational history of probation has been *much* shorter than that half century. Accepting the fact that we are a newcomer among the professions, our progress has been disappointingly slow —slower even than is warranted by our limited knowledge of the delinquency and crime treatment. We have, of course, made progress in developing techniques, in demanding and achieving higher standards, in demonstrating to the courts and to the public the importance of an adequately staffed, well financed, efficiently administered probation system in the handling of criminal and juvenile justice. Other realms of achievement are known to all of us but we must admit that advancements have been more or less sporadic and localized rather than general.

Lip Service to Standards

This condition exists for several reasons. In the first place, as a group we have without exception sold ourselves short. Possibly because we have lacked really basic faith in the worth of sound, well-administered probation services. Possibly because, having basic faith in our convictions, it has been much of a job to be evangelistic and convert others who do not share our convictions and enthusiasm. As a professional group we have been slow in realizing that this selling job is *ours* and until we accept full responsibility for it, we cannot expect it to be even passably well done. Moreover, we have, all too often, given only lip service to certain basic principles of probation and then in the operation of our own departments have disregarded them. At conferences and institutes we have convinced each other that the probationary treatment of the delinquent youth or criminal adult calls for specialized skills of the highest degree—and yet we have done a very mediocre job of putting this principle into operation or in projecting it on to any one else, including our judges. Persons of questionable qualification as to education, background, personality, and general fitness for the work still may be employed in all too many jurisdictions as probation officers to handle the extremely difficult and technical job of bringing about readjustment or rehabilitation of probationers presenting a wide variety of complex behavior, personality, mental, and social problems. By our failure or inability to set and put into practice professionally wide standards for staff recruitment, we have given support to the general opinion that no special skills, aptitudes, or techniques are needed for probation officers.

Not only must we subscribe to and put into practice in our departments the standards about which we so freely talk, but we must also expand our interests and efforts beyond our own departments. We all should be actively working for the development of higher standards of probation and, as a result, greater respect for the profession throughout the entire state in which we are employed—in fact, throughout the whole country. This is not just altruism—it materially affects your own job, your own professional standing, your own salary. It must be remembered that what is thought of us as probation officers or of our profession frequently depends upon impressions obtained of probation where services and standards—and hence salaries —leave much to be desired. As a result, your best interests as an individual, as well as the best interests of your department will be served, not only by developing high standards of both work and personnel in your own community but also through actively working for higher standards of probation throughout the United States. Improvement in probation in any part of the country, remote as it may seem, is a forward step for *you.*

Criticism of Professional Work

Our failure to always do a job of professional caliber has also made the advancement of our profession unduly slow. We talk of "individual treatment," of "social case work," of "supervision" and then frequently permit probation to become little more than a judicial leniency lacking in all of the progressive aspects of probation. What we have called "treatment" too often has consisted of having the probationer submit routine written reports or perfunctory "check off" office calls. These processes undoubtedly are of some value when properly used, but our mistake has been to allow them to replace the more constructive methods of supervision. We must admit that high quality personnel is not required to handle such routine operations and where such methods of "supervision" are used, it is quite understandable that there is generally no public support for higher standards and better salaries for probation officers.

It has been said before that probation supervision involves more than surveillance, more than keeping probationers out of trouble. Its major aims are directed at rehabilitation, at education and re-education, at assisting the probationer in every way possible in making a satisfactory readjustment to family and community living. This is a large order requiring a deep understanding of individuals and of family relations and attitudes. It requires an ability to adjust family difficulties and personal conflicts even before their symptoms become evident to the probationer. It requires a thorough knowledge and wise use of all possible community resources for the good of the probationer. It requires real thinking, sage planning, and continuous work on the part of the probation officer. To achieve the goal of rehabilitation and to effect any appreciable and lasting improvement in conditions, habits, attitudes, and objectives, supervision must be a thoroughly sustained, affirmative, positive, planned program of individualized treatment. Anything less is an injustice to the client, the court, the community, and ourselves. In using anything less we are failing to make full use of what we know to be necessary for successful probation.

Need for Critical Appraisal

Pressure of our day-to-day work has been, to a large degree, responsible for our failure to take time to study and evaluate adequately the work of our departments. This, also, has made the development of our profession proceed more slowly than we otherwise might have hoped. A continuous program of evaluation of our methods and results must be made a regular and essential part of our probation program if we are to have sound development in administration and work performance. We must make a constant critical review of the methods which we are using and the results which we are achieving. Such appraisals will pay large dividends in facilitating our search for more effective techniques and procedures and in providing us a sound basis for personal and departmental improvements.

In discussing departmental evaluations with probation officers in California, I find the opinion generally expressed that only an outside agency such as the Na-

tional Probation and Parole Association or the California Youth Authority properly can study the work of probation departments. The California Youth Authority, in connection with its countywide surveys of youth services, conducts probation surveys at the request of probation departments, juvenile courts, and community agencies. We have completed some 28 of these studies to date and with that experience have developed what we feel is a sound technique in evaluating probation departments both as to their own operation as well as to their relationship to and effectiveness in the entire community welfare program. The probation aspect of these surveys is part of my own work so quite naturally I have particular knowledge of the methods used and problems encountered by an outside agency in evaluating the work of a probation department. However, for the good of probation it is unfortunate that probation officers generally believe that evaluation is a job for only an outsider, or a so-called "expert." My own conviction is that evaluation is a continuous process which not only can but should and must be done by the department itself.

The work done by the California Youth Authority in this State and by the National Probation and Parole Association on a national scale through their surveys and studies of probation departments is, of course, important and valuable. Those organizations can provide personnel who are not influenced by local pressures. Their staffs can approach the job with completely detached attitudes. They can avoid the emotional judgments that might be expected of a probation officer called upon to criticize his own work. A thorough knowledge of successful probation practices in other parts of the state or country furnish them with examples of good practical operations elsewhere which materially assist them in giving sound criticism of the work of the department surveyed and in making recommendations for improvements.

Outside agencies experienced at doing detailed probation studies, however, have limited availability. Organizations doing this type of work usually have surveys scheduled months ahead. Your department on the other hand needs to be evaluated now and frequently. Who, then, can and should do the job?

There always will be appraisals of your work from various sources, some qualified to judge and some lacking in knowledge and background to make any constructive suggestions. Some evaluation of your department can be expected from other agencies in the community, from the schools, peace officers, press, citizen groups, individual citizens, and members of the staff. Correctional agencies, through the reports which you submit to them are in a favorable position to weigh the good and bad in some phases of your work. Other probation and parole departments which see your reports and have contacts with your probationers are likewise in a good position to make some evaluation of the caliber of the job done by your department. Such comments and criticisms when solicited can be helpful and the starting point for departmental improvements. They should, however, constitute only a part of a more rounded self-appraisal by the department itself.

Some words of caution should be given to any probation administrator setting out to study critically his department. First, I would suggest that he obtain some advice from those who have had experience in that type of work. Second, he should ascertain the facts from what he actually sees, hears, and reads, and furthermore, he must draw his conclusions only from these facts. The findings must not be predicated upon any desires or wishes on the part of the administrator or staff nor upon any attempt to justify existing policies and operations. The facts weighed against good standards must form the basis of the survey.

Guideposts for Self-Study

Now, what are the units of measurement that can serve as guideposts in the self-study of your department. Other articles have pointed out the difficulties in developing yardsticks for measuring anything as complex as the work done by probation departments in rehabilitating delinquent and criminal personalities and in all the many other areas in which probation officers have responsibility. In some aspects of the survey the units of measurement are relatively easy to find. Properly kept statistics, for example, make the qualitative approach to evaluation relatively easy. Every department also should possess accurate data on the cost of the various phases of its operation. These two phases, important as they are, provide only a beginning for any evaluation.

We need, in addition, another instrument to measure the less tangible, more complex qualitative phases of our work. We need a yardstick that will evaluate probation in terms of its functions, objectives, policies, administrative organization, its techniques and procedures, professional qualifications of personnel, the skill, work performance and morale of its staff, its relationship to the court and the community and its success in effecting the adjustment of its probationer.

In order to make such subjective measurements we must develop and accept certain standards or principles to serve both as a measuring stick for self-evaluation and as goals for attainment. These principles should be broad concepts embodying the best known practices in the field. They should be directed toward sound administration and the quality of professional service which best enables the probation department to carry out most effectively its functions and give maximum service to the community and the offender.

I shall not give here the principles which are needed in the federal probation service or those which would guide any particular probation department. Detailed principles that would have application in any department are almost impossible to formulate due to the variations in local problems, the organization of different departments, and other factors. It will be necessary for you to establish principles which should guide your work. When you begin developing such principles or standards for your own work and begin putting them into writing, you will have taken a long step toward better service and higher standards, and will have begun building the frame of reference against which you will be able to continuously gauge your progress.

In studying the work of probation departments in California, we in the California Youth Authority have developed a set of principles as an aid in surveying the work done by probation departments. We feel that they broadly cover most of the significant points while still leaving room for application that best fits the particular department being studied. Remember that these principles were formulated for studying county probation departments in California. A few of them may not have direct application to your work but you will find that most of them have implications that are significant. You will probably find that these principles either follow the manner in which your work is now being done or could serve well as objectives in your department.

Separate Investigations. Probation is based on a thorough, individualized social investigation of each case directed toward those unique factors in the individual's life which will give greatest insight into the offender's problem, and provide most information for effecting his rehabilitation.

Presentence Reports. Written pre-sentence investigation reports are essential to the court in arriving at a decision as to the proper disposition of the case, to the probation officer in carrying out treatment, and to other agencies and institutions who later may be called upon to give specialized service. To best fulfill these objectives, information obtained from the presentence investigation, after evaluation and weighing as to its relative importance, should be prepared in a topically arranged report.

Submission of the presentence investigation report to the court in ample time before the date of hearing enables the court to read and consider more thoroughly its findings and recommendations.

Treatment Plan. Probation is an individualized treatment process requiring that a definite, meaningful, and constructive plan of supervision, adapted to the individual's needs be developed and carried out on each case. Frequent review of case progress will determine the need for revision or modification of the original plan.

Home and Community Visits. Probation work carried out through the use of purposeful home visits and field calls as a part of the supervision process offers the surest approach to the discovery and solution of the basic problems in the probationer's personality and environment.

Case Loads. Effective case supervision requires that case loads be no larger than is consistent with good casework practice, having in mind the kind of load, the experience and training of the officer, the geographical area, and other factors involved.

Personnel Recruitment. Probation work requires specialized knowledge, skills, and techniques that can best be assured to the department through a program of personnel recruitment based on standards equal to or higher than those recommended by the California Probation and Parole Association.

Plans and Procedures. Definite and studied plans and procedures must be formulated for all phases of the department's work and be given continuous critical review for effectiveness.

Administrative Officer. In order to have sound probation administration, assure maximum efficiency of personnel and other departmental resources, and achieve the operation of uniform policies and procedures, the chief probation officer must be given complete administrative responsibility for the operation of his department within the framework of policies jointly established by the probation officer and the court.

Community Resources. Efficiency in probation involves the utilization of all available community facilities and resources which can be of assistance in the planning and carrying out of casework treatment with the probationer.

Staff Training. The training of staff in the basic principles of probation and in the best methods and procedures of probation work is a major responsibility of the chief probation officer or administrative head. This function may be delegated to others but basic responsibility for training must be accepted by the administrative head of the department.

Specialized Services. Adequate medical, psychiatric, and psychological services as well as other treatment resources are essential to good probation work. Development and improvement of these needed services must receive support and impetus from the probation officer.

Personnel, Funds, and Equipment. Good probation service demands adequate funds, personnel—both professional and clerical—and equipment to carry out a thorough program of case investigation and treatment.

Community Organizations. Active participation, and leadership when necessary, in community organization and planning for youth and adult welfare is an important part of the probation officer's responsibility.

Interpretation of Program. Probation is supported by public funds and the public is entitled to frequent reports on the activity, progress, and work of the probation department as well as the aims, methods, and accomplishments of probation in general. Better understanding of the work of the probation department on the part of judges, administrative and legislative branches of government, the press, and the general public, through an effective public relations program, results in good will and in greater support for probation service of high quality.

Co-operation with Agencies. Probation is a part of a larger community welfare program, embracing the courts, schools, health and welfare departments, law-enforcement agencies, churches, recreation services, and other public and private agencies. Maximum service to the community can be achieved only through a program of full co-operation with all law-enforcement and social agencies in the area served by the probation department.

These are the principles that we in the Youth Authority have been following. We purposefully have made them broad, leaving room for application to fit individual departments and local situations. We feel that the list although not all-inclusive is basic and that no probation department can ignore them and do a truly professional job.

The Probation Survey

In the limited space of this paper it is impossible to give anything approaching the procedural details in the evaluation process. Briefly, we might summarize the six steps of any probation survey.

First, of course, is planning. Into that stage is the establishment of principles or standards and the laying out of methods of carrying on the survey.

Second, there is the statistical analysis

already mentioned. Here, in addition to obtaining information as to the volume of the work handled, you are also answering another important question: Are we compiling statistics of such a nature that we actually can analyze our work? Are these statistics comprehensive, accurate, and of real value?

The third step in the probation study involves the critical observation and analysis of the organizational setup, procedures, policies, and techniques of the department.

What we might call the fourth step is actually a part of the third, i.e., case record reading. What do the case records themselves show? Are they complete, sufficiently detailed, accurate, and sufficiently accessible to make study possible? (If not, you may be certain that they are not sufficiently complete to enable the performance of good probation work.) What do they reveal as to the quality of the presentence work? Do they indicate that constructive supervision is being carried on regularly? An objective evaluator can learn more about the actual work of his department, about its policy, procedure, and techniques in studying a few case records than he can from days of discussion with the probation officer or his deputies.

The fifth step should include contacts with agencies with whom the department must work, the courts, correctional facilities, police, schools, welfare department, and other public and private agencies. By such contacts valuable suggestions and criticisms regarding your work generally can be obtained and ways and means can be found to better coordinate our activities.

It is important that your survey have real depth. No attempt will be made here to indicate the many questions that should be asked in probing the depths of your operations and philosophies. This area already has been well covered by Mr. Karl Holton, now Director of the California Youth Authority, in his article entitled, "Yardstick for Measuring Probation," in the January-March 1943 issue of *Federal Probation*. This article might well be reviewed to refresh our thinking on the pointed questions asked by Mr. Holton in evaluating personnel practices, in determining the attitude and policies of the court and probation staff, in exploring the department's relationship to the community and in many other areas.

During the study of your department, frequently recurring questions should be: Are we aware of our inadequacies and if so, what efforts have been made and are being made for improvement? What has been our progress in the past 6 months, year, 5 years? What are the plans for the future?

The end results of evaluation should be improvement and progress. Evaluation without these objectives is of questionable value. It is relatively easy to note omissions and imperfections but it is far more difficult to evaluate progress properly and to develop succesful plans for the future. Nevertheless, many fruitful evaluations of the work of your department should be directed toward the sixth and final step of any probation survey—the development of ways and means for improved administration and operation directed toward service of higher quality to the court, the client, and the community.

What a Difference One Year Makes!*

By Robert L. Noble, Jr. United States Probation Officer, Savannah, Georgia.

J. B., A NICE APPEARING young fellow, walked into the U. S. post office of a small Southern town in 1949. Pressing the barrel of a .32 caliber revolver into the ribs of the postmistress, he demanded that she hand over what cash she had in the post office. She quickly complied, giving him $316 of postal funds, whereupon he departed without injuring or molesting her. Local law-enforcement officers were quickly notified and J. B. was apprehended a short distance from the scene of the robbery.

When arraigned before the U. S. Commissioner, J. B. pleaded guilty to armed robbery of a post office and stated he was 17 years of age.

I interviewed the defendant in the county jail, where he had been segregated from other prisoners, and at that time he signed a request for a hearing under the Federal Juvenile Delinquency Act, asserting that his birthdate was January 6, 1932 and that his birth certificate would be found on file in the office of the Ordinary (probate judge) of his home county.

A certified copy of the official birth certificate was obtained, but this gave his birthdate as January 6, 1931, rather than 1932. He was reported to the Juvenile Branch of the Bureau of Prisons as 18 years of age and accordingly could not be considered as a juvenile within the meaning of the law and the Federal Juvenile Delinquency Act.

The assistant U. S. attorney who had authorized the prosecution advised my chief probation officer that under the law it would be mandatory upon the court to impose a sentence of 25 years in the event defendant is indicted by a grand jury and is found guilty, or pleads guilty to the charge of armed robbery of a post office.

Both parents of J. B. were deceased, but he insisted that January 6, 1932 was his correct birthdate and that if the birth certificate on file in the Office of the Ordinary of his home county showed anything different, then the birth certificate was in error. In view of the fact that so much hinged on the birthdate —a mandatory sentence of 25 years if the defendant was 18 years of age against a possible minority commitment of 3 years, 7 months, and 27 days in the event 17 was the correct age—it was decided after conference with my chief probation officer and the assistant U. S. attorney, that every effort should be exhausted to determine the correct date of birth.

After making a thorough investigation I submitted my report to the assistant U. S. attorney—which to me was conclusive—that the official birth certificate was in error, and that J. B. was only 17 years of age, and hence eligible for hearing under the Federal Juvenile Delinquency Act. This report included affidavits from close relatives, information from the family Bible records, a statement from attending physician, an affidavit from the owner of property where J. B. was born, an affidavit from the father's employer at the time of J. B.'s birth, school records, local welfare agency records, and other substantiating evidence. Upon the basis of this report I recommended that the boy be given a

---

* Reprinted from *Federal Probation*, Vol. XIII, June, 1949, p. 49. Used by permission of author and publication.

hearing under the Federal Juvenile Delinquency Act.

The report was forwarded by the assistant U. S. attorney to the Attorney General at Washington, D. C. The Attorney General's office concurred in the view of the probation officer that the official birth certificate was in error, that his correct birthdate should be shown as January 3, 1932, and recommended that J. B. be given a hearing under the Federal Juvenile Delinquency Act.

When arraigned before the court J. B. was committed to the custody of the Attorney General for the period of his minority—3 years, 7 months, and 27 days. Had the official birth certificate not been questioned it would have left the court with only two alternatives—to commit him to the custody of the Attorney General for a period of 25 years, or to impose the same sentence and suspend the execution of it on probation. Since probation is not given in our court in cases of armed robbery of post office, the sentence would have been for 25 years instead of 3 years, 7 months, and 27 days.

Author's note: In a letter received from Mr. Noble in August, 1953, he states: "There is an interesting sequel to this story. J. B. was released conditionally from a federal institution after serving 3 years and 2 months of his minority sentence. In less than 2 months he committed an armed robbery for which he received a sentence of from 5 to 10 years in a state institution; two months later he committed suicide in the state prison. Thus we have a youth, who at the age of 17 was saved from a full 25-year term because he was too young, hanging himself at the age of 20, despondent because he could not make the proper adjustment in life."

The Role of the Probation Officer in the Treatment of Delinquency in Children*

By Hyman S. Lippman, M.D. Director, Amherst H. Wilder Child Guidance Clinic, St. Paul, Minnesota.

REGARDLESS of the nature of the delinquency, the major contribution in direct treatment by a probation officer will consist of forming a strong, friendly bond to the delinquent—a relationship that will let the delinquent know the probation officer is on his side, and that the probation officer believes the child is behaving in the only way he knows how. The probation officer must really believe this deeply, or the delinquent will have little use for him for, at best, it is difficult to get the aggressive delinquent to accept an adult as an ally. He has thought of the adult for too many years as an enemy who cannot be trusted. Many have been disillusioned repeatedly by adults and, though the individual delinquent senses the probation officer as his friend, he prefers to withhold significant information for a long time. If, as is occasionally the case, the probation officer is so conditioned by his own early experiences and training that he has a condemning attitude toward the delinquent's behavior, and to him, this will soon be sensed. He will not depend on what the probation officer says any more than the probation officer will rely on his remarks. As a delinquent he has had

---

* Reprinted from *Federal Probation*, Vol. XII, June, 1948, pp. 36–39. Used by permission of author and publication.

to learn to spot his friends quickly, and he will detect by a frown or sudden quietness or tenseness that the probation officer cannot accept him deeply. A sensitive probation officer may have difficulty in retaining a feeling of warmth for a boy who struck his mother who has just returned from the hospital; for an adolescent girl who got in after midnight after repeated promises and assurances this would never happen again; for an aggressive boy who tells in a convincing manner that his school work is satisfactory though the probation officer knows he has not been to school since the last interview. In this connection, the probation officer probably never will reach the stage when one of these clever delinquents will not be able to really convince him of his sincerity while he is telling a succession of lies.

To complicate matters, there are delinquents who will have no respect for the probation officer if they can outwit him. To some extent this may be due to a need to be punished and to have their aggression checked. More often, however, it is an expression of their narcissism; they form their relationships on a narcissistic basis and can only develop a tie to someone who can outsmart them. Fortunately, this group is in the minority, because underlying this behavior mechanism is considerable emotional conflict that is resistive to treatment in the hands of the most experienced therapist.

As Confidant

The probation officer may be discouraged if his success seems to end with having formed this bond of friendship with the delinquent. He is aware, through talks with the foster parents, school, and others, that a given delinquent suffered greatly as a young child; was subjected to scenes of cruelty by an alcoholic mother, and knows he was illegitimate, and yet he tells the probation officer nothing of these facts. He becomes defensive when his family is referred to and prefers to stay on a superficial level. At the same time, he looks forward to coming in, and has been more pleasant in the home and school—there has been a lessening of the delinquent behavior. The probation officer, acquainted with psychiatric literature, knows the part played by early emotional experiences in the development of delinquent behavior, is anxious to do something of "real value," and wants to discuss the early life experiences with the delinquent. The delinquent will give the kind of material the probation officer wants only when he is ready to do so (and he never may be ready)—when he is sure of him—when he is convinced the probation officer won't be critical of him or think less well of him, or can be relied upon not to repeat to the foster parents or the judge what he tells the probation officer. It is routine to assure him early in the treatment that what he tells the probation officer is in confidence, but it may be months before he is sure of this.

In some instances the delinquent talks freely from the outset. Usually, however, if this is the case, he will tell the probation officer what he has told others, and the telling will add little to the treatment. In some instances there will be a great deal of talking, much of which is intended to leave the probation officer with the feeling of trust in him, but which actually is a defense against revealing significant material.

There will be many delinquents who never will disclose traumatic experiences even after long periods of casework with them. They may continue with their delinquency, and admit this to the probation officer, but want to maintain contact with him, and so the probation officer is not justified in concluding he has not helped a delinquent because his delinquency persists. He may have checked a career in crime by his casework, but may never know this.

The interview is the chief tool of the

probation officer in his treatment work. The capacity to be relaxed and get the delinquent to relax develops only after experience. It will not develop quickly if the probation officer is working under the pressure of a big case load, or is on a staff that demands quick results. One cannot speed up casework on order without affecting the result. The delinquent, it must be recalled, has been sent to the agency; he has not come for help. He would have preferred to go on in his own way of delinquency, to have his pleasures without meeting reality. He has little interest in our taking this only adjustment he knows away from him. He has enjoyed the behavior that has furnished him an outlet for his hostility to a society that has rejected him and that he in turn has rejected. He must be wooed for a long time, in many instances, to keep the resentment down, if he is to continue trying to behave acceptably. There will be more temptations that will pull him back to delinquency than will keep him working with a social agency. Any pressure may start him off on a delinquent career if it stirs up the resentment that made him delinquent in the first place. The task of keeping the delinquent close to the probation officer is easier if he can find something tangible in the treatment that allows the delinquent to feel the probation officer is doing something for him. In the larger cities membership in a Y.M.C.A., a part time job, tutoring help, and removal from sources of unhappiness are useful.

As Counselor

After the probation officer has gained the confidence of the delinquent, he will be in a position to make those changes in the delinquent's surroundings which he believes are important. The statement is made in this manner purposely because of our interest in the individual delinquent at this point in the discussion. One can make many changes in the environment that will not touch the delinquent,

unless he is interested in seeing these changes made. The probation officer will be much further ahead in getting him to see the value of living in a foster home, before moving him. Many of our failures in foster-home placement of the older child result from the fact that everyone wants him in a foster home except the boy himself. He wants to be with his own neighborhood group, prefers his companions in school and the home that he may be able to dominate. To give him a choice early between a delinquency institution and a foster home does not help matters much, because then the foster home represents to him a method of punishment. It is a different matter if he is told later in the treatment when the probation officer's counsel means something to him, that he will be smart to get away from a neighborhood that is largely responsible for his delinquency and give foster-home placement a trial, especially if he is told that the probation officer's interest in him will continue and the probation officer expects to see him often while he is trying to make the new adjustment.

As Specialist

It may be well, also, to realize before beginning to deal with delinquents that probation officers will fail with at least half of them through no fault of their own. We often make the mistake of wanting to cure all or most of the delinquents we see. If half of them are helped we still will have done a great service to society. The reaction to the delinquent will be different if we keep this fact in mind. We will be gratified then by the number who improve rather than disillusioned by the number who fail.

In the group of those delinquents who are most likely not to respond to treatment are the mentally retarded, those with organic disease of the central nervous system, and those who are deeply conflicted emotionally. An adolescent who belongs in these groups needs special care that the probation officer alone cannot provide. This does not mean, however, that advantages of casework should not be supplied the delinquent just because the possibility of curing him is remote. Actually, intensive casework may provide the best means of diagnosis—of obtaining the information that will help decide on the need for institutionalization.

This leads to the subject of the neurotic delinquent who has been one of the chief interests of the psychiatrists dealing in problems of social psychiatry. I purposely shall avoid discussing the treatment of the underlying emotional conflicts of the neurotic delinquent, because there is little in the intensive treatment of such an individual that will be a part of casework, without the help of a psychiatrist. Such conflicts are of an unconscious nature, are deeply imbedded, and can only be brought to light by the psychiatrist trained in psychoanalytic techniques.

There are certain phases of the treatment of the neurotic delinquent, however, that can be carried on by the caseworker. First, and foremost, is again the development of a relationship that will lessen the need to vent his hostility on others and to attack himself. Psychoanalytic observations have demonstrated the presence of an excessive amount of cruelty in the neurotic delinquent who reacts to these deep drives with a feeling of guilt and a need for punishment. Most agencies have had experience with adolescents, bright enough to know better, who have managed their delinquencies—without being aware of it—in such a way that they were apprehended easily and punished. What happens in the everyday life of the delinquent is that small frustrations in the home, and in the school, stir up the more serious underlying frustration that has always been with him. To be denied the lesser things means again that they are not loved, that

they are rejected, and that their efforts to change the status quo will never get them anyplace. The probation officer must keep in mind the fact that the neurotic delinquent almost invariably comes from a family where other members, particularly the parents, are neurotic, and that there are, therefore, numberless opportunities for stirring up the feeling of hopelessness and revolt. The probation officer may be an all important person in breaking up this vicious circle. A positive tie may make it possible for the delinquent to find the kind, accepting parent in the probation officer unless the delinquent is too overwhelmed with guilt. To the delinquent it may mean that all adults are not cruel and rejecting, but it will not mean this during the first few weeks. He will have to be convinced of the probation officer's being well-meaning, and consistent, over and over again. If, and when, he can give up his need to change his own parent and accept the probation officer as a substitute, in some instances the delinquency will stop—there will be no more need for its existence.

At the same time it may be possible for the probation officer to work with the neurotic parents, at least to see that something is done for them. Sometimes it is inadvisable for the same probation officer to work with the delinquent and the parent, because of jealousies that arise and the possible needs of each to interfere with the satisfaction of the other. There are many things that can be said about the casework treatment with the family of the delinquent, but I am omitting them at this time. It is sufficient to say that unless this casework is done, the work with the individual delinquent in most instances will suffer.

To get back to the problem of direct treatment with the delinquent—the probation officer must keep in mind the fact that in most instances the delinquent is suffering from feelings of inferiority. These grow out of his school failure and his rejection in the home and community. The school failure has resulted from a lack of motivation and the development of poor work habits, since school work is hard work and the child does not work unless he is making somebody happy through his work. This feeling of loyalty is usually lacking in these delinquents. Sometimes the feeling of inferiority comes from a feeling of guilt related to masturbation and other sexual practices. The delinquent may be sensitive about an alcoholic father, or psychotic parent.

Anything that will strengthen the ego of the delinquent will lessen his feeling of inferiority and in turn make him feel more secure. The biggest ego boost will come from the realization that he is good enough, and worthy enough to be accepted by the probation officer. If the probation officer can get the delinquent's permission to go to his school, talk to his principal and teachers, the probation officer may be able to arrange the delinquent's schedule in a way that will make it possible for him to enjoy school. Perhaps he can change his school or be allowed to drop one of his subjects. The probation officer may even motivate him to study for the first time in his life. He may be able to get the school to help him in his attempts to change the delinquent's attitude toward school and life.

To sum up, one of the probation officer's main functions will be to check anything that emotionally disturbs the delinquent. He will have to search carefully among the various situations to which the delinquent is exposed and reduce friction wherever possible. In the home, he may locate favoritism for another child, an overly critical father, a nagging, rejecting aunt. These influences will have to be controlled or the irritation will continue daily—hourly—and keep the boy in a state of turmoil with a need to fight back either to punish or in an attempt to reduce the tension. In the school, he may be trying to do 7th

grade work though only able to do 5th grade work; or he may be able to do 7th grade work well, but be totally deficient in reading. These failures to compete successfully with his fellow students can cause more or less continuous unrest. Or he may be picked on by several older boys, or under the influence of an older sexual pervert whom he fears, and feel guilty and ashamed of this behavior. These and many more precipitating factors may keep him in a state of conflict or rebellion which invites the many forms of behavior that neurotic delinquency assumes. This does not mean that there is a lesser need than always to get at the underlying unconscious factors also, but this is not the function of the probation officer.

Perhaps the probation officer will be fortunate enough to get him to discuss spontaneously his preoccupation with sexual problems and anxiety about what will happen because of his masturbation. The probation officer's assurance that masturbation does not cause insanity, and his continued acceptance of him in spite of his behavior, may go a long way towards relieving the delinquent of tension and worry. The prevailing attitude in all his contacts with him must be one of optimism, and this must persist when the probation officer fails and the boy is sent to an institution. The probation officer's interest in his welfare must continue so that his relationship can be re-established when he leaves the institution.

As Administrator

Demands for quick decisions present themselves more often in dealing with young delinquents than with other child welfare problems. Pressure is applied to get immediate action because the community wants to be rid of the delinquent's hostility and aggression. It would be unfortunate if the probation officer yielded to this pressure and formulated a plan before he knew all the important contributing factors. One learns by experience that there are few real emergent situations that cannot wait long enough to permit thorough study—without which needless errors are made. To deal intelligently with each child, so that a diagnosis of the child, and of the total situation in which the child finds himself, can be established, requires a limitation of cases assigned to the individual workers. There are few probation officers who can handle successfully a case load of more than 30 or 40 young delinquents, and when one hears that a probation officer is dealing with 100 to 150 juvenile delinquents, the conclusion must be reached that most of the cases are inactive, or the work is of a superficial nature.

I purposely have emphasized what a probation officer can do with young delinquents, independent of the help he can receive from a child guidance clinic or an out-patient psychiatric department in a hospital, because so many probation officers are not in a position to take advantage of these services.

Family Casework in Probation*

~~~~~~

By David Crystal. Executive Director, Jewish Social Service Bureau, Rochester, New York.

IT IS A PLATITUDE to state that the family has been the basic unit of our society. To question its validity as a social institution is to question our whole sense of values —moral, social, and religious. It is perhaps not so well recognized that this basic unit of human beings living together is not a product of enlightened civilization but has existed from time immemorial. The anthropologist can confirm for the sociologist and psychologist that this form of human organization is traceable to the earliest known data about the human race. Whatever we may say about the necessities which created this form of organization—economic, social, self-preservative—from the study of early primitive society we are forced to the conclusion that there was something beyond external pressure in the environment that induced the creation of the family. If this were not so in varying climate and under varying cultural conditions, we should have witnessed a completely different development from that of the family and, therefore, we are forced to the conclusion that there is some deep instinctual impulse in the human breast that tends toward the kind of social organization which we know as the family.

In retrospect, it is difficult for us to conceive of a kind of human being that would be recognizable if he were not reared in this kind of organization. Everything we know about human character and human personality is a result of our exploration of the various subtle influences interacting upon human beings in their relationships one to another as members of a family. It is important for us to recognize as axiomatic that the family is a caldron within which human character and human personality are brewed. We well might ask ourselves the pertinent question as to the significance of the current social crisis through which we are living in its deepest human terms. What happens to human character and human personality when the statistics for divorce and broken homes continue to rise if these basic impulses that tend toward family cohesion now appear to be deflected from their course? What

* Reprinted from *Federal Probation*, Vol. XIII, December, 1949, pp. 47-53. Used by permission of author and publication.

can we expect of moral values, of social values, of mental health in the future? I do not pretend to know the answers to these questions, but I stress that since all of our knowledge of behavior stems from family living, it is important, as we address ourselves to problems individually, to determine where the distortion in family life took place, whether it is remediable, whether it is possible to treat an individual *invacuo;* i.e., without reference to past experience in a family constellation.

Role of the Family

In the professional field of social work it is almost impossible to speak of treating an individual without implicitly recognizing that we are treating a family. Even when a person is completely unattached and has no living relatives and requires service toward a better behavior adjustment, we still treat him in relation to his family in the past. We cannot isolate a single experience or a single relationship and consider it uniquely. Every human relationship is a telescoped image of a series of past relationships— that is to say that the person who has difficulty in relating to people of the opposite sex has not developed this system as a consequence of current relationships. To understand the why of his feeling and his attitudes, one must see him in relation to his whole developmental past. His relationship and problem will carry lights and shadows of relationships in his primary family unit—toward sisters, toward a mother basically, and later toward companions, and toward teachers. To expect a person to give up a system of attitudes only because he recognizes it to be a deviant from the norm is to require an effort of will that is humanly impossible of achievement. It is not a question of what is wrong and what is right, what is normal and what is abnormal, nor is it a question of choices between these various opposites. It is a question of capacity not only to recog-

nize, but to understand, and in understanding and feeling, to change. This is a basic consideration in any field involving treatment of human beings. It is a basic consideration in the field of psychology and the various social services of which probation and parole is an integral part.

Family Casework Concepts and Probation and Parole

You may ask what application all this has to a field of work which is determined by a legal system. How can we contrast or utilize the concepts of family casework with the field of probation and parole?

The field of family casework has certain basic assumptions which on the surface do not seem to resemble those in the field of probation. In family casework, the client has the right to accept or reject service; he has the choice of coming for service on his own volition or repudiating it completely. With this as an initial assumption, the family caseworker has an opportunity to test the willingness of the client either to change his situation or to hold on to it. Is this true of probation and parole? Obviously not. In family casework we speak of the nonjudgmental attitude of the worker toward the client. It is not the caseworker's right to determine what is good for the client and what is not good for the client. It is for the client to determine this for himself. His is the final decision. Is this true of probation and parole? On the surface it seems as if it is not.

In family casework there is what is known as a mutual participation planned on a democratic basis. At any point either one or the other, that is, the client or the worker, may terminate the relationship if this basic consideration fails to obtain. Is this true in probation and parole? I raise these questions because I speak of family casework as being generic; that it is a technique and a philosophy which is applicable in any of the various functional fields—child welfare, youth service, foster home placement, adoptions, etc.

If what I have said above is true, is it also generic in a field where authority is implicit in function? For no one can deny that the probation officer begins at the point where authority is exercised. He is the symbol of authority, the authority of the law, of society, and of the community. We might even be tempted to say that all the foregoing considerations of family casework are inapplicable in the field of probation and parole, but I do not think so in reality.

I raise this question. If we recognize that the probation officer is a symbol of authority, is this the same as saying that he must be authoritative or authoritarian in his approach? Is there a difference between the function of his agency and the manner in which he discharges his function? I believe we have two concepts here which we must clarify for ourselves if we are to understand how people in conflict with the law can be helped by the technique of casework. We must ask ourselves whether the approach and the function of the agency are identical. If so, we must assume that the probation officer is judgmental, that he agrees completely with the sentence imposed upon the probationer, that he has been a part in determining the conditions under which the probationer shall live. This is the same thing as saying that the social worker in a voluntary agency is the same as the board of directors, that he has determined the policy, that he has set the limitations of the agency, and this obviously is not true. The social worker in a voluntary agency may or may not agree with a particular policy of that agency, yet if he is to work in that particular setting, he is obliged to accept it as a social reality until changed. It is not his to change. In like manner, the probation officer may or may not agree with the kind of justice that has been meted out to a particular probationer. Yet his function is to carry out conditions that were determined by a higher authority. If his feeling is so deep-seated that he cannot do this conscientiously, his choice is to leave the agency.

Form of Authority

In all areas of human endeavor it is perhaps impossible to find an identity of agreement between a job that is to be done and the worker who must do it. Nevertheless, functions have to be discharged and this is a reality to which all of us in every area of human endeavor must inevitably bow. What I am trying to say is that implicit in everything we do is a form of authority; that authority permeates all of social reality and that all of us must come to grips with it. If we can separate, therefore, the existence of authority as a common and basic part of living and accept it as something to which we must relate, then we can accept the fact that the probation officer can feel perfectly comfortable about accepting a social reality that has been determined both for him and his client, and for which he has no redress. This is a common bond uniting probation officer and probationer and within this bond and this area it is possible to utilize the basic concepts of casework, which involve a nonjudgmental attitude on the part of the worker, an understanding of the total personality of the client, mutual participation of client and worker in a common effort and, finally, the individual choice of the client either to accept or reject service, in much the same manner as the client who goes to a voluntary agency requesting help must accept the limitations within that particular agency's policy, must relate to these limitations, or choose to do without service with whatever consequences that may entail. A client who goes to a voluntary agency, although he is free to choose or reject the specific help, must come to grips with the limitations of that particular agency for it is as he feels the agency's limitations that it becomes real to him.

He is then free either to relate or to do without service. In the case of relief, this alternative may involve stark destitution; in the case of marital adjustment, a possible breakup of family; in the case of behavior difficulty, the risk of an outbreak of impulses that result in delinquency. In the authoritative agency, although the client may not be free to reject the service of the agency by voluntarily leaving it, he may just as surely reject the help it has to offer, unless he can come to grips with the realities which are implicit in probation and the limitations of the service. Once the basic factor of what the agency really represents is acceptable to both probationer and probation officer, the probation officer can be nonjudgmental in allowing the probationer to risk the consequence of not using the service. Let us take a case from a voluntary agency to contrast or parallel the differences between a voluntary and authoritative agency.

Voluntary Agency. The father of a 15-year-old boy telephones the agency asking for an appointment immediately. We shall call him Mr. S. In the interview situation he asks for help presenting the situation as follows: "My boy is a problem, and my wife and I are at our wits' end. Jerry, my son, last week stole $30 from a drug store where he has part-time employment, took an aeroplane for Syracuse, and we did not hear from him for 3 days. Yesterday, a friend in Syracuse telephoned at my son's request. Now he is coming home and I want you to straighten him out."

Here boldly is the request to a voluntary agency. What is the man asking for? Where is the problem? Is there a similarity here between a request for correction from a voluntary agency and the request of an authoritative agency? Under identical conditions, the parent might have come to a children's court and asked for treatment of his son. A dissocial act had been committed. No

charge, however, had been filed by the employer. When I asked Mr. S. how he thought I might straighten the boy out, he said: "Scare the pants off him. I've tried it but it doesn't work; maybe he'll listen to you. I can't do anything with him." Tentatively, I explained that I had no authority to compel the boy even to see me and this could be done only by the boy's being aware of Mr. S.'s complaint and his choice to come, or his father's use of authority in insisting that he come; the alternative was to seek help from children's court. The man reacted strongly to taking such responsibility. "But he will hate me for telling. I can't do that. Can't you pretend to have heard about it and call him as a friend, thus helping me out of it."

Does this attitude sound familiar to you? Note how a single incident in family living mirrors for us a clear-cut design in the family relationships. With this slice of current experience, we are in a position to make a diagnosis of not a boy's problem but a family problem. Though we have a descriptive statement of a child's behavior within a limited period of time, under specific circumstances, with a given social system, we know that the pathology is not localized to the boy. Treatment involves the family, and it would be a mistake for the worker not to treat immediately this attitude of the father and its reflection as a component in the boy's behavior. As the father distorts reality to protect himself from painful experience, so the boy, too, may be forgiven for distorting his reality to protect himself from painful experience. The ensuing interview with this man was focused on this current attitude as a condensation of all his attitudes in the past toward his son; it was made clear that until he recognized what existed; namely, a dissocial act, and related to it, his boy could not be expected to have a superior reality sense or more mature judgment than his father. Note also the dynamics in beginning with a single overt act, and how it evokes feeling and a need to deny the authoritative role of the father by delegating it to a social worker. Note also how the single act of asking outside intercession justifiably raises the fear of a change in the relationship of one person to another in the family constellation. For the father to take a stand with direct action naturally provokes a defense and a reaction in the boy which, for better or for worse, may set in motion a set of factors that may later alter the status quo of this family's way of functioning.

Authoritarian Agency. Does this happen in probation and parole? When a member of a family becomes the complainant against another, does this single overt act alter, modify, change, or charge the psychological atmosphere of the family? Can the outraged wife who charges her husband with nonsupport by enlisting the aid of a social agency not be affected by the set of reactions this will induce in her husband? How will the social worker, whether probation officer or caseworker in a family agency, relate to this situation? Does the complainant understand the risks which inhere in the decision to ask help from an outside source in the hope of achieving a more positive way of family living? When he or she understands is he or she willing then to assume responsibility for treatment by accepting all of the risks, with no guarantee ahead of time, of successful outcome? In the case cited before, this complainant came to a voluntary agency before the introduction of a new person. As in many instances, a complainant may consult the court's social services before taking actual legal action. But, in any case, we must accept and focus initially on the meaning of any act not only to the person guilty of the transgression, but to every other member of the family affected by the act and the complaint. Until the family understands that the social worker is neither mother, father, brother nor sister, but a

person who has been either invited or required by law to work on a problem affecting in diverse ways mother, father, sister and brother, the possibility of constructive beginning does not exist. From the foregoing you undoubtedly will see similarities in cases of your agencies, particularly at the intake desk, and those of the private family agency.

Now what about the case where probation officer or social worker enters the situation only after a court decision has been rendered, having at hand only the bare facts of law violation that leads to court conviction? Here, too, there is a psychological climate to which worker and offender and family must be exposed and, depending on the nature of the offense and the personalities of the family, the temperature will range with alternating cold hostility to humid and guilt-laden overprotection and sentimentality. How often the guilt-feelings of the complainant now become transmuted to hostility toward the judge for the severity of the sentence. How often the probation officer is seen in the role of executioner by both offender and family and how often family is seen by offender as having cruelly rejected and virtually adopted the probation officer as the adequate, responsible son or as the idealized projection of what a father, or husband should be.

The probation officer or probationer, therefore, becomes in a psychological sense, a member of the family and unless this mantle which is unsought but nevertheless psychologically thrown over him is not gently and patiently removed, a real danger exists that the family's distorted relationships will deteriorate into a ridiculous caricature.

Interpreting the Worker's Role

How then can the representative of an agency, whether probation officer or caseworker from a voluntary agency, avoid becoming either antagonist, to be feared or hated, or pseudofamily member to be looked at as substitute for an errant member? This is a problem which in family casework is fundamental for all types and kinds of family service. For the relief worker who at intake accepts the wife's plea for assistance without involving husband, the very act of giving displaces the husband; for the caseworker counseling an adolescent without the parents' knowledge or consent, the caseworker displaces mother or father; for the worker seeing only one partner to a marital conflict, the danger exists of arousing resentment in the other at the unconscious meaning of preference for another mate. So, too, an identity exists in authoritative settings of probation officer being caught in the trap regarding a problem as individual rather than family, and thus negating, even before beginning, effective casework.

The answer lies, I believe, in a clear and definite understanding of the worker's role in relation to the function of the agency and his ability to define for his client why he is there, what he represents, how he will function, what the agency rules are to which he is bound. When this is accomplished, the client must choose either to accept or reject the services offered. This is what I mean by limitation of the agency which constitutes the common plank on which worker and client may stand.

Is this accomplished by a lecture from the worker, or by handing a printed set of rules to the client or probationer, which after listening to or reading he is free to reject? Is this what we mean by free choice? Obviously you will accuse me of oversimplification if I take this view, and you will, of course, be right.

No, free choice presupposes clear understanding of alternatives, and clear understanding presupposes the absence of emotional prejudice. Casework begins only when the interpretation of worker's role to the client is done with sensitivity to the possible emotional baggage which burdens the client's visit to the worker. Why he, the client, is there is a weighty parcel in that baggage and must be removed with the client expressing his feelings about that parcel. And as he expresses his opinions and feelings, every disguise known to man to protect himself from immediate discomfort may be used. Blame on others, blame on society and family, blame on self in an excessive mood of self-abasement, complete compliance with absence of feeling, wordy hostility or silent sullenness, complete repudiation of the act or of the self, or complete silence and withdrawal, or the façade of complete acceptance of his act and willingness to do penance, to change immediately.

These are, as I said before, psychic inventions to protect the client from facing honestly the pain of his current situation, and the caseworker or probation officer not only must be sensitive to these but ready to acknowledge that his presence evokes these attitudes not because he is caseworker or probation officer, but because he represents somebody or something else in the past of the client and is being endowed by the client with attitudes that exist in the mind of the client, but not actually in the person of the worker. This simple principle involving *relationship* is the core of all casework, counseling, and psychotherapy, and until we understand it an attempt to clarify the relationship in its true perspective, we have no right to speak of the client having made a choice freely. Thus, I believe, we are justified in saying that the recidivist does not deliberately choose this way of life; his freedom of choice is circumscribed and burdened by the baggage of emotional prejudice. Neither are we justified in saying that every case failure is a failure of the worker to achieve relationship because of lack of competence. If it were so, we all should stand indicted as social workers and request probation officers for ourselves. The problem is not that simple. But I repeat, our initial obligation is to recognize with the client that the fact of his presence in a social agency whether authoritative or voluntary, is a *new experience* for him; that in being new and different it carries overtones of fear; that his feelings about how he got there and why he should continue need opportunity for ventilation; that he has a past self that reflects itself in the present and that part of the self bears upon forming a relationship with the worker; and that finally both worker and client are bound by agency limitation and scope. In the client's ability to meet, adjust, accept, understand these conditions, he gives us an indication of his capacity to meet the larger limitations of community and society.

Basic Concepts

Casework is, indeed, generic to all settings where the helping process is at work. Fundamental principles are the same, whether in an authoritative or voluntary agency.

We must attempt to translate some of these basic concepts into specific case treatment. In practical terms, the *beginning* or intake process with the probationer becomes crucial and may set the tone for the subsequent contact. It may indeed be so decisive as to have predictive value for the outcome. At intake, then, the following items comprise the social frame of reference:

1. How does the client regard this experience?
   a. Does he express feeling and attitudes regarding this current experience—hostile, compliant, apathetic, or mixed?
   b. Toward whom are these feelings and attitudes primarily directed—society, friends, members of family, or probation officer?
2. How does the worker regard his role?
   a. As the agent of righteous law and order who lectures the client?
   b. As the symbol of potential punishment in terms of the client's failure?
3. How and by what process can client and worker find a common basis for mutual working together?

In short, when these various elements are used in the interview situation, there is an emerging sense of rapport that tends to strip two opposing symbols of their outer trappings of offender and police agent and substitute instead a person in difficulty with all the conditioning of a past reflected in his present, and a counselor with background and experience who can be of service provided the client wishes it. I can conceive of this beginning process as the most complicated part of casework treatment and one that rarely accomplishes the objective of rapport in the space of one interview.

Focus of Casework in a Probation Case

As with the probationer for whom this experience with probation is fraught with emotions of fear, anger, uncertainty, and rejection, so with other members of the family this new fact in the routine of family functioning induces a different set of attitudes and feelings and we must, therefore, include the whole family in the treatment process. Clearly the focus of casework in a probation case is this:

1. How does the probation officer help the probationer accept the conditions of his current reality?
2. How does and can the family relate to the probationer in terms of the new experience?
   a. Can they express honestly their feelings of guilt, of anticipated reprisal, of uncertainty about the impact this will have on their future lives?
   b. Will they require special help from a worker other than the probation officer, in a different kind of agency in the community? Can they now or later accept the need for help?
   c. Is the total responsibility for

change to be lodged exclusively on the offender, or can the family see change as a reaction not to one but multiple causes and that they too are part of the change, externally and internally, by their physical presence and concrete offering of shelter and food and job and by the attitude with which these visible and tangible things about the family are given?

Value of Authority as a Treatment Adjunct

I recall a case of a 16-year-old lad who was referred to a family agency. His case illustrates this point and also points up the value of authority as a treatment adjunct:

Johnny's mother appeared at the intake desk at Children's Court asking for help. She was obviously distraught and confused and explained that her son, Johnny, age 16, was the reason for her coming. Johnny had left home over 2 weeks ago following a violent quarrel with his father. She knew that Johnny was living at the home of a girl-friend, and that the girl-friend's mother was either wittingly or unwittingly encouraging his staying away from home. From Johnny's sister, who saw Johnny at school, he had been quoted as saying, "I'll never return." Pleas, letters, telephone calls, a personal visit by mother met with the same adamant and defiant attitude on the part of the boy.

The court worker after listening to this story and identifying with the natural sense of hurt of the mother, pointed out certain alternatives, one of which involved court action against the boy and the other an opportunity to attempt working out a solution through a local family agency. The worker discussed with this woman her feelings in relation to court action, leaving the way open for her return, should the other alternative not work out. The woman accepted the referral to the family service agency. At the family agency both father and mother appeared together, and on their own mutual impulse. They were seen together. The mother's story follows:

A month before this incident, the mother had been confined at the hospital and upon returning home with the new baby had felt tired and weak. The whole family had been solicitous and eager for her recovery and had urged her to take the baby with her for vacation at a sister's home in a neighboring city. Johnny had been particularly devoted and had always been extremely close to her. Never before had there been an untoward incident on Johnny's part. While she was gone this thing happened. She cannot understand why Johnny would want to hurt her so deeply, since he has always been so devoted to her. She wept as she said, "I want my boy back" and was full of resentment at the girl-friend's mother who with a word could easily accomplish this.

The father, who seemed quite adequate and protective of his wife, picked up the story at this point, focusing entirely upon "that snotty woman who thinks she's too good for us. She's filling Johnny's head full of stories that he's different and we're not good enough for him." He emphasized that "he didn't know about modern ideas" but he was the kid's father and Johnny was going to come home or he would do something terrible.

It was evident that the father was enraged because he felt guilty and defensive and it was possible to see that the mother's gentleness and protectiveness was counterbalanced by a father who had rigid ideas and attitudes and was capable of explosively direct and violent action.

The worker felt it necessary to help both focus on the nature of their request and what the agency could or could not do. Recognizing with both parents that Johnny's action amounted to a complete repudiation of them, the worker reviewed with them their rights as parents under the law and discussed with them why they had not chosen to exercise that right through the court. The mother and father verbalized freely their fear that such action would only risk adding fuel to Johnny's resentment and his coming back might lead to a more serious break with the family. Because authority, in itself, could not dam up resentment, because the parents wanted to re-establish not only physical family cohesion, but emotional cohesion as well, the counseling services of the agency were being sought. The focus of service then was the following:

1. What in Mr. and Mrs. J. contributed to this break, and were Mr. and Mrs. J. willing to be seen around this problem as a necessary precondition to the boy's wanting to stay once he returned, and

2. How does Johnny account for his behavior and how can Johnny be reached on a voluntary basis?

In the ensuing weeks contact was maintained with the parents and discussion centered around their past relationship to Johnny. While this area was being explored, there was a simultaneous effort to reach the boy. Ultimately the parents were able to understand both the events and attitudes which led to Johnny's outbreak and in consequence were able to face the risks of court action if no other way was possible. It was not possible to make contact with Johnny in any other way and on the basis of a conference with the Children's Court, it was decided to take court action.

Service to the parents had consisted in helping them see Johnny at this point in time in relation to their attitudes and this service was successful. How to help Johnny see himself in relation to his parents and a changed atmosphere was the problem. At the court hearing Johnny was sullen, defensive, brimming with hostility, but a wise judge, with all the facts and thinking of a court worker and family worker, provided the necessary opportunity for Johnny to think through the problem. Temporarily depriving both parents and the woman who shielded Johnny of their authority or their will to affect Johnny's immediate future, he frankly told Johnny he was to be referred to the detention home until the judge and Johnny could understand each other.

The judge, a wise and fatherly person, gave Johnny the opportunity to discuss his feelings. With social service data as background, the judge used his authority not to issue a command for Johnny's future behavior or for the parents, but to let Johnny decide what was wrong and how and what he could do to effect a change. After 3 weeks Johnny wanted to and did return home, not in defeat, not in resignation, but because he knew that what he wanted and what his parents wanted were not irreconcilable but that to achieve what he wanted involved change on both sides. Six weeks after this, the family worker was visited by the parents who reported that the family was functioning in balance and expressed appreciation.

I have cited the above to illustrate briefly the theme of this talk; namely, that casework, whether in an authoritative or voluntary setting, involves the same basic elements; that helping an individual involves consideration of relationships within the family setting; that behavior at a given point of time reflects a past that must be understood; and that the role of caseworker or probation officer is one of giving service within the limits and function of a particular social setting which for both probationer and probation officer is the underpinning for working out a chosen form of adjustment.

Probation Is Treatment*

By Henry J. Palmieri. Formerly Chief Probation Officer, Juvenile and Domestic Relations Court, Richmond; Director of Social Services of the Juvenile Court of the District of Columbia.

SEVENTEEN-YEAR-OLD Gerald had a step-mother. His mother had been dead three years. Together with his 30-year-old stepbrother, he was caught after several "jobs" involving breaking into freight cars and stealing. The stepbrother was sentenced 10 to 20 years in the state penitentiary. Gerald may have gotten probation, but because he was defiant and would not tell where he "unloaded" the stolen goods, he was given an 18-month jail sentence "to teach him a lesson and give him time to think things over."

This was Gerald's first jail sentence and he could not take it. He went through the ordinary "reception" procedures of the jail. His head was clipped. His first night was especially a hard one for him to take. According to the account of his cellmate, Gerald, that first night, sobbed into his straw pillow and whispered, "Please, mother."

How did Gerald make out in his "first stretch"? Let's read what his old-timer cellmate said:

For a month Gerald cleaned his cell for a half hour every morning and then walked around the prison yard. Lots of interesting fellows. All of them had made big money in a lot of different rackets. Many of them had been in many jails. What's eighteen months? You could do that standing on your ear! If you go into the rackets you gotta expect to fall once in awhile. That's part of the game.

Some of them read books but Gerald couldn't get interested in books. He liked to work with machinery. Wished he could learn to be a machinist. He would like to do a little work but there wasn't any work except in the kitchen and the laundry and that was done by the colored prisoners. All you could do was clean your cell for a half hour every day. Then you went out to the yard and talked. But you heard the same talk over and over. All about how to stick up a guy or a store. All about how to break into a house.

Soon Gerald got tired of listening and didn't go into the yard anymore. Some of the older cons talked rotten. It made him sick. He stayed in his cell and the cons would shout at him: "Yah can't take it, eh? Why don't you get a rope and hang up?"

One day Gerald beat up an older con with a broom handle. Gerald wouldn't tell the warden why. He got thirty days in solitary.

He never came back to the cell across from mine. He proved that he couldn't take it. After ten days in solitary on bread and water he hung up.

I wasn't as sorry about Gerald as I might have been. It might have been worse for him if he had accepted jail life; if he had been willing to drink up the flood of instruction on how to make money without working, to take chances on more jail stretches where you had nothing to do and had to cover yourself up with the habit of idleness. He might have been willing to learn how to live with his mind closed to all decency, grabbing what he wanted no matter to whom it might belong. Gerald couldn't accept that prospect and he couldn't see the end of his eighteen months. That is an eternity to a kid seventeen years old.

I don't know what would have happened if the judge had put Gerald on probation. Maybe the probation officer would have discovered that Gerald liked to work with

* Reprinted from *Federal Probation*, Vol. XIII, June, 1949, pp. 20–22. Used by permission of author and publication.

machinery. He might have helped him develop that talent. Maybe after some probation Gerald would have become a decent and useful citizen. I don't know. At any rate, he won't menace society any more.

Had Gerald been given a chance on probation, with adequate help to meet his needs, he might have been saved and made a useful member of society. He might have failed as a probationer, but is this not a calculated risk that must be taken into account? Failure to try something positive—in this case, probation—deprived Gerald of a chance to redeem himself. It is for this kind of boy—and thousands like him—that social welfare agencies must function. Probation is the arm of the court that should reach out and do the job. Because of his knowledge of legal structure and his close relationship to the court, the probation officer can best help these individuals to achieve a better and fuller life.

Obviously, the inference drawn from Gerald's sad plight is that there should have been a more progressive and understanding handling of his case. All sentences should be based on a careful study of the probation officer's report. The report should include a comprehensive summary of the personality make-up of the offender and his problems and needs. No stone should be left unturned in this search for the hidden causes underlying behavior—good or bad. Every available agency should be utilized in this process of finding out all we can about the accused. When this is accomplished, then we may know how to handle a given situation. Had these steps been followed in Gerald's case, in all likelihood he would have been placed under the supervision of an understanding and helpful probation officer.

Use of Community Resources

Probation, like other casework services, must make use of community resources. Community agencies can be used most effectively by the probation officer in his treatment efforts. Take, for example, the case of 8-year-old Joe, who had been troublesome since the age of 5. He had given his family, especially his father, a difficult time. In despair, because of the many complaints made by neighbors to the Society for the Prevention of Cruelty to Children, the father finally sought the assistance of a child-placing agency. This agency referred the boy to a psychiatric clinic for study and help.

When interviewed by the psychologist at the clinic, the father related that the boy had done almost everything a child should not do. Before he started school he stole from home, from neighbors, and from relatives. After he started school, he brought home many articles belonging to others. He became unruly, began to truant, was expelled from school, and subsequently was referred to the court.

A study of the boy disclosed many deep-seated problems. For example, his father could not accept nor understand the subtle difficulties of a growing and developing boy. He failed to give Joe the understanding and help that was needed during the early formative years when Joe first gave expression to feelings of conflict by stealing at home and from the neighbors.

The social history reflects a long history of failure in school. He remained in the 1st grade for 2 years, largely because of his behavior. In the 2nd grade, he spilled ink, was destructive, and was unable to concentrate for more than 5 minutes. He finally was expelled because of his bad influence.

The clinic to which Joe's case had been referred by the child-placing agency arranged to discuss the case at a staff conference. The outlook and recommendations were formulated as follows:

Although the boy had a well meaning family, there had been no appreciation of the essential trouble in his case, and even if there now were better understanding, it was practically impossible for him to do well in the neighborhood situation. It was urgent that he be placed elsewhere, preferably in a private home, and that full confidence be established with him. His reticences of the past were quite unnecessary. Judging by experiences with other boys who had similar difficulties, the case appeared hopeful, but prolonged observation and careful treatment were necessary. An institution was not recommended because there he would hardly receive the individual understanding that he needed; it was hoped the stigma of commitment could be avoided.

Joe was placed in a foster home. He was involved in numerous difficult situations which, to a certain extent, reflected his previous behavior pattern.

To meet changing needs as he progressed under the guidance and influence of the foster-home worker and the clinic, Joe was placed in different foster homes. In none of these home situations was his behavior completely satisfactory. However, at 17, after several foster-home placements and continued diagnostic study, Joe is reported in the case history to be a large, strong, mature, and a rather fine looking person, appearing to be all of 20. He was living with a foster family and receiving his training at a junior college where he specialized in mechanical subjects. He was largely self-supporting.

Joe's case illustrates the effective use of community resources and the possibilities of the dynamic approach in probation work.

Use of Specialists

As already pointed out, not all cases coming to the attention of the court and the probation department will respond favorably. Often a probation officer will find a case presenting such acute signs of disturbance that he must, without psychiatric help, let "sleeping dogs lie."

For example, a boy of 16, mannerly and neat in appearance, was arrested and held for stealing a suitcase. His commitment was suspended until a study could be made. A clinical interview revealed average intelligence and a good physique. He began stealing at 8. When he was 10 he told his father that there was something, he did not know what, that drove him to stealing. He insisted on being sent to a training school. This was done. He was paroled and quickly was involved in more trouble. Some years later he married, had children, and was doing well in business when he resorted, again, to stealing money and cars. He could not explain his conduct. He deserted his family, entered the Navy under an alias, and shortly after deserted the service. He was arrested on charges of larceny and was sentenced to a Naval place of confinement from which he escaped and became involved in more trouble. Later, he was arrested for burglary and was committed to a penitentiary where his conduct was exemplary.

A few days before he was to be released from prison, and after he had written joyously about it to his parents, he escaped. His life history is a story of arrests, incarcerations, and punitive and kindly treatment. In his case everything was tried. Nothing seemed to work. He was the type of person which a probation officer should not attempt to handle without the expert help of psychiatric service. The fact that the client was unable to explain his behavior, and that he felt the need for punishment, indicated that he was not of the common garden variety and that he was so tangled up and so emotionally involved that he required the assistance of specialists in behavior.

Conclusion

Probation as a method of treatment and prevention is no longer an ideal; it is a reality. In serving the people coming before them, courts in their day-to-day work must apply the most positive features of probation. They must stand side by side, with all other co-operating agencies, in their unrelenting efforts to help individuals and families carry their load more adequately and to take their rightful place in the life of the community.

We, in probation, must ever seek to develop and refine our methods. Good as they now may be, they must be constantly improved if we are to cope with the misunderstanding, ignorance, fear, anxiety, and insecurity which exist in our complex society.

The Use of Community Agencies in Probation Work*

By Harleigh B. Trecker, Dean, School of Social Work, University of Connecticut at Hartford.

FEW probation workers make full or even adequate use of the community resources at their disposal. Yet probation workers are quick to admit that they cannot do their best work unless they make use of everything available. This state of affairs implies both a wish to use resources and a need to become more skilled in so doing. In this article we explore what is involved in improving interagency relationships on behalf of better service for the individual.

A casual and random compilation of the major findings and recommendations from recent conferences and study groups in the area of delinquency control indicates:

1. A wide range of agencies and programs are available to render service to the multiple needs of persons who have social adjustment problems.

2. More effective co-ordination of these agencies must be arranged, so that their maximum energies will be mobilized and brought to bear systematically and continuously in behalf of the people with whom they work.

3. Many persons being served by one agency need additional help from one or several other agencies. The complex organization of social welfare resources makes it difficult, and in some cases impossible, for people to utilize available programs without help from professional workers.

Communities vary markedly in both the extent and quality of resources available to probation workers. Some communities have excellent school, recreational programs, health services and facilities, and mental hygiene resources. Other communities are woefully short on such basic services. Community organization workers in delinquency control have rightly centered attention on these gaps and lacks. It is generally the function of social welfare planning bodies to deal with these needs for facility expansion. In the meantime, probation workers must concentrate on the wise usage of what they have. This article deliberately focuses attention upon communities where there are agency resources to be utilized. In those instances where resources are lacking, it is granted that the community organizational problem is different and should be dealt with in another way.

The question is often raised, "Why don't social agencies co-operate?" The answer must be phrased in another manner: Social agencies are composed of people. The real question is, "Why don't the staff workers co-operate and make better use of one another?" Among the reasons given are: heavy work loads and lack of time to familiarize one's self with available program. Perhaps a more fundamental reason is the basic organization of social welfare resources. These re-

* Reprinted from *Federal Probation*, Vol. XI, October–December, 1947, pp. 21–24. Used by permission of author and publication.

sources have become increasingly specialized. Greater attention is being placed on agency function. As specialized agency function becomes established, the pattern of service becomes more defined and the separate agencies are required to work on problems of interagency co-operation.

A solution to the problems brought by specialization lies, not in an attempt to turn back the tide, but rather in our efforts to adjust and make use of the specialized programs we have. One approach is that of case-by-case referral. It seems to offer exceptionally bright possibilities when prosecuted with skill and purpose.

Referral

Referral in social work is the process of helping an individual with whom you are working to become related to another resource. This resource may be a worker within your own agency, or in another agency. The referral is made for the purpose of providing specific additional service. When we designate the referral as a process, we imply that it has a beginning and an ending. It begins when the probation worker and the individual recognize the need for supplementary help from another worker. Following this, we have joint exploration of available resources, and preliminary selection of the specific agency or program. It is then necessary to arrange a conference with the receiving agency, and then the actual referral can be planned.

A great deal is involved in preparing the individual for the actual appointment. When the individual and the receiving agency have come together, it is necessary to arrange a follow-up conference between the worker in the initiating agency and the worker in the receiving agency. We are here discussing referrals which originate as a part of the probation supervision and rehabilitation process wherein the probation worker

expects to retain primary responsibility for the case. The referral resource is thus supplementary. What we have in mind can be illustrated by several brief case situations.

Gary P. Gary, age 13, was the leader of a small group of boys involved in minor stealing episodes. Together with other boys, he entered a school and removed a clock from the wall and was placed on probation. Probation worker found him to be an attractive youngster with a pleasant personality. Mental tests indicated an IQ of 132. Gary is an only child who lives with his father who is almost 60 years of age. His mother died when he was an infant. His father has been both a father and mother to him and seems to enjoy the responsibility. The father works as a machinist on the night shift. He owns his home and an adjoining apartment which he rents to a family which is supposed to supervise Gary when the father is away.

The worker discovered that Gary had few friends and few outside interests. He said he would like to join a recreational group but his father discouraged him. The worker talked with Mr. P., who expressed an interest, but was unable to commit himself. Later, arrangements were made for Gary to go to a summer camp for a 10-day period. The father agreed but, at the last minute, changed his mind and refused to let Gary go. Gary has never attended church regularly except for a short time a year ago when his father allowed him to attend a downtown cathedral with an aunt. In discussing this experience, he said: "That was one church that I really like to attend. I was a big shot down there. I was one of the candle boys. But my Dad made me quit going." Mr. P. had quarreled with the aunt.

Gary's routine, at the present time, consists of doing the housework, preparing meals for himself and his father, and taking care of the yard. He has a set of machinist's tools and books. He spends most of his time reading or working on mechanical problems. He is attending a junior high school regularly, but has no friends.

It is obvious that Gary needs group experience outside of his limited home. Referral to a recreational agency will require careful planning and interpretation with Gary's father. The proposed summer camp placement was too much separation for the father to accept. It will be necessary to begin on a simple level—perhaps single recreational events —even before attempting to help Gary establish a good relationship with a group of his own age. Gary must have the support of his father in whatever he does so the focus of the worker will be more in this direction. The recreational agency worker will need to understand the situation and be prepared to work with Gary. The boy may make several attempts before he actually succeeds in becoming a part of a group. An apparent lead is his interest in tools and machinery. Initial contact might be made on this interest basis, thus tending to support the father and son simultaneously. Merely sending Gary to a recreational agency will not succeed. For many years he has been confined to social isolation. It will take a period of time to help him beyond this.

Tony M. Probation worker observed Tony, recently placed on probation, participating in a ball game on the school playground. It was noticed that the other boys did not choose him for their team. The worker asked several of the boys why this was the case. Their replies ranged from "dumb" to "blind." The worker observed Tony closely; saw that he squinted continuously, often threw the ball far short of his objective, frequently swung on seemingly good pitches with good co-ordination but poor results. When the worker saw Tony alone, he asked him to read some of the rules from the rule book. Tony held the book very close to his face.

Perhaps Tony, age 12, needed an eye examination. The worker asked Tony if he could call at home the next day and talk with his mother regarding the eye examination. He thought that Tony should have his eyes examined by a doctor. The mother was interested in having the examination made and inquired about the cost. It was explained that there was a 50-cent registration for the clinic. Glasses, if needed, would be free for boys under 18. An appointment was made and the mother took Tony to the clinic. The examination proved the need for glasses, which were provided, and after two fittings Tony seemed quite comfortable in wearing them. He improved in school, also in physical co-ordination. His school, neighborhood, and play group adjustment was much better with sight correction.

Here the worker's alert observation uncovered a need which, when met, made a great deal of difference to the boy. His knowledge of the clinic's services, hours, and fees, and his help in arranging the appointment were important factors in making the referral.

Vincent R. Vincent R., age 15, was placed on probation after entering a garage from which he took model airplanes, motors and parts, a rifle, some batteries, and a few tools. He was alone and simply remarked that he wanted the model airplane parts because he liked to build them. He is shy and withdrawn and had always been "well behaved." He has no brothers or sisters. His mother deserted a few months previously, and shortly after this his paternal grandmother came to the house to manage for his father and Vincent. The grandmother is nearing 60 years of age and has not been used to children for a long time. Vincent and the grandmother do not get along well.

Vincent's father is a factory foreman. His income is adequate. He owns his home which is comfortable. The worker tried to talk with the father about his son, but the conversation centered more on Mr. R.'s feelings about his wife who had left him. The father said that he would like a psychological test and a psychiatric examination for the boy. He did not feel that he could take Vincent to a private psychiatrist, so the worker suggested that arrangements might be made through the child guidance clinic or some other suitable organization. It was suggested that the father get in touch with the Family Service Association and discuss the general family problem with the social worker. The social worker would be able to interpret the available resources, including psychiatric if they seemed needed, and help the father make arrangements with Vincent. The father agreed to do this, and family agency worker called at the home upon his request. Since there was a waiting list for the clinic, the caseworker from the Family Service Association offered to work with the family and help them determine what was needed. The probation officer and caseworker conferred. It was agreed that the family agency representative would take primary responsibility for working with Vincent's father, and the probation officer would work with Vincent for the immediate present. A date was set for a follow-up conference.

The probation officer made a wise judgment in referring this case to the family agency worker. Factors which stand out include: (1) the recent desertion of the mother; (2) the change in the home resulting from this desertion and the coming of the grandmother; (3) Vincent's father's need to understand what is happening to him; and (4) the father's wish for psychiatric help which may or may not be needed. The family agency worker in this involved situation should be able to work along with the father at a pace which will be geared to the realities of the problem. Mr. R.'s readiness to accept help and his eager-

ness to invite the agency to be of service to him made it possible for the probation officer to put in motion a casework process which may require a sustained period of time.

Resources Available for Referral

A probation worker trainee, upon completion of a study of his community, remarked: "I have lived in my community 30 years, but have never really known it." Planned study of this community had helped him get a clearer focus and a deeper understanding of available resources. Sometimes we think we know our community because we have been in it for a long time. Unfortunately, our general familiarity with it tends to blind us to specific agencies and to the changes that are always going on. As a prerequisite to successful referral use of agencies, probation workers must maintain a "perpetual inventory" of what is available.

The kinds of agencies which we should know about will depend upon the type of case load we carry. In general, educational, recreational, health, and social welfare services should occupy a prominent place in the inventory. One group of students worked out a face sheet form on which they recorded basic data about each agency available to them and their clients. They systematically put down the name, address, and telephone of the agency. They recorded the hours of service, the name of the director, and the geographic area served. They made note of the fees, if any, and catalogued the types of service given and the eligibility requirements for service. They added a brief statement of function or program, and they closed the face sheet with the names of contact workers in the agencies. This made it possible for them to organize in an efficient manner specific data which would help them know where to turn with the difficult problems they faced.

Getting information of this kind and keeping it up to date requires persistent attention. Workers can make individual calls on agencies. This is undoubtedly the best approach. Where several workers are on a staff, they can pool their information about available programs. It is possible to circulate notices of changes as they occur so each worker can keep his material current.

Referral Suggestions

In discussing referral with a number of workers and agencies, and in analyzing a series of cases, the following suggestions were pointed out to be helpful:

1. The referral must always be individualized. Each referral is different. It should grow out of the study of the individual and his needs.

2. The purpose of the referral should be clearly understood by the worker, the individual being referred, and the receiving agency. This means referral is an integral and inherent part of the treatment process. The worker must take sufficient time in conference with the individual and with the receiving agency to define the reason for the referral and to anticipate results. Referral is thus a means to an end. Its ultimate purpose is seen as bringing about better service for the client.

3. To be most effective, referrals should be personalized. When the worker knows the purpose, function, procedures, and personnel of the agency to which the individual is being referred, he can interpret all of this to the person and make referral easier and less threatening. Experience has proved that it is far more effective to make a referral to a worker in the receiving agency by name, at a stated time, and with a written note of introduction.

4. Preparation of the individual for referral and preparation of the agency to receive the individual is very important. In giving general interpretation of the receiving agency, the worker should

avoid committing the receiving agency to any specific service because they will have to make their own diagnosis and then determine what they can do. The worker should interpret the individual being referred to the receiving agency, and should share orally, or in writing, pertinent information required by the receiving agency. The referring worker should avoid asking the receiving agency for any special privilege or deviation from established policies, procedures, and routines.

5. Immediately after referral has been made, the follow-up process should begin. The initiating worker should seek to establish co-operative relationships with the receiving agency. They should determine mutual and independent responsibility, what kind of reports they will exchange, and how frequently they should have conferences to discuss the case.

Summary

It is increasingly evident that prevention, treatment, and eventual control of delinquency rests with the community. The cooperative, inter-agency approach on a case by case referral basis will do much to weave together our network of community resources. The results will be demonstrated not only in improved services for individuals, important as this is, but also in more effective community organization. When professional workers accept the fact of their own limitations and begin to use community resources to the full, they actually build professional practice beyond the specialized level to the level of integration. It is to be hoped that many workers will study the referral process and keep records, so that we may become more exacting and skillful in helping people use other agencies. All of us, at one time or another, need some help from community resources. Not enough of us know where to go, how to ask, or how to accept service. When we receive skillful guidance at this point, we are strengthened and the community is strengthened. "Know what we have and use what we know" may well become a slogan for workers in probation and allied fields.

Let Them Know About It*

By William C. Nau. Chief Probation Officer, United States District Court, Western District, Greenville, South Carolina.

To JOHN PUBLIC and Mr. Average Citizen a federal probation and parole officer is a cross between a "revenooer" and a G-man and all law violators who unwittingly and unwisely steal from a post office or from Uncle Sam himself are destined for Alcatraz or Atlanta. When a newspaper reporter making his regular rounds in the federal building learned that a clerk, who stepped out of her office leaving her pocketbook unprotected, had been robbed of $50, he wrote a story that forcibly pointed out that this theft constituted a federal offense and the offender could be committed to Alcatraz or Leavenworth. For this reporter to go into the matter of federal court procedure and the sentencing to the custody of the Attorney General is more than we have a right to expect. The Alcatraz angle makes too good a story. Likewise, for the average newspaper reader to understand that probation and parole are not synonymous, without considerable explanation and interpretation, is more than we can expect, for sometimes even judges confuse the terms. At a recent state probation and parole institute, a state judge spoke of "paroling" defendants throughout his address when what he really meant was placing them on probation.

Through the Press

The probation officer has a responsibility for interpreting his work to the community through the medium of the press and the speaker's platform. Everyone is interested in delinquency and crime, but the radio-listening and movie-going public is usually given either an inadequate or distorted picture of probation, parole, and prisons. Greenville, South Carolina, a city of 75,000 people, with a metropolitan population of around 118,000, has an unusually co-operative and sympathetic press. The morning paper is circulated over the 12 counties that comprise the territory covered by the Western District probation office. Reporters are assigned a regular beat in the federal building, and they are avid for stories from the probation office. Although they cannot be furnished news items daily which have reader interest, their eagerness and patience can be rewarded with occasional releases that make good feature material.

"Uncle Sam Is Served Well by Probationers in World War II," was the front-page headline on a news story in 1946. That 167 men who had offended Uncle Sam should distinguish themselves by serving him in time of war made good human interest reading. The reporter played up their decorations, ribbons, citations, and battle stars. The Presidential pardon that rewarded their service was newsworthy. Of course, the success stories and the annual reports are periodically reported by the press in feature stories of interest, but for a

* Reprinted from *Federal Probation*, Vol. XV, September, 1951, pp. 35–38. Used by permission of author and publication.

thorough presentation of probation, parole, and prisons to the reading public only a series of carefully prepared feature articles written by an experienced newspaperman can adequately cover the three "P's."

The idea for such a series originated at a social gathering when Federal Judge C. C. Wyche, Roger C. Peace, newspaper publisher and former United States Senator, and William F. Gaines, city editor of the *Greenville News*, were discussing crime among youthful offenders. The judge cited figures on the number of defendants placed on probation in federal court and the small percentage of violations. He was explaining his policy of taking each case on its own merits in deciding on the proper sentence. The publisher, obviously impressed by the possibility of a good story, said to his city editor, "Bill, how about writing a feature story on federal probation? Go to Washington if necessary and interview Dick Chappell." After making a thorough study of various articles selected for him by the local federal probation office, the city editor prepared questionnaires not only for the chief of probation but for Judge Wyche; Henry P. Chandler, director of the Administrative Office; James V. Bennett, director of the Bureau of Prisons; and Victor H. Evjen, assistant chief of probation. A day's supervision trip with the probation officer gave him much live, first-hand material.

These feature articles appeared on the front page of the morning paper for 8 consecutive days, the first time that interpretative material of this nature had ever rated such front page prominence. The public response was heartening. A woman addressed a postcard to the editor commenting on the series. She wrote, "Probation is putting Christ to work in everyday living." One day the editor stopped at the fire department for a chat with some of the firemen. They began to discuss probation and parole and the series of articles he had written. They talked for over an hour. Said City Editor Gaines, "I was surprised to see the number and type of people who read those articles. They were people who ordinarily just read crime news and are scared off by interpretative features." Reprints of the series were made later in Washington and mailed to all federal judges, federal and state probation workers throughout the United States, and to all civic women's clubs in the State of South Carolina.

While this series was being published friends, acquaintances, officers, businessmen, and others remarked to the probation officer, "Well, for the first time I really understand what you do in your work." Some thought we raided stills. Others believed we dealt only with juveniles. The volume of misinformation cleared up was most gratifying.

The series had a humorous side, too. A probationer in a neighboring county wrote the probation officer, "I seen the piece you had in the *Greenville News* Sunday and I sure would not do anything to get back in trouble." The reaction was state-wide. A member of the State Probation and Parole Board asked the publisher to do a similar series on state probation and parole, and this was done at a later date.

From the Rostrum

The speaker's platform offers an equal opportunity for interpretation. Like chain reaction the results are far-reaching. Participation in a forum at a Methodist youth rally resulted in an invitation to address a Rotary Club 50 miles away. As Frederick Ward, Jr., has written in *Federal Probation*, the probation officer "must see, listen, learn, labor, join, meet, and speak; in short, everything but smell."

Belonging to a civic club provided one entering wedge. As program chairman, the probation officer arranged a forum on crime prevention. The panel included the county sheriff, an FBI agent, a representative of the police department, and the chief probation officer of the children's court, with the federal probation officer as moderator. Another service club 15 miles away requested that a similar program be brought to their meeting.

Even a police-school program featuring talks on how to apprehend criminals has a place for the probation officer. The chain reaction spreads. Sunday school classes, churches, women's clubs, PTA groups, and social work gatherings want to hear about probation and parole. In an address before a local ministerial association on the responsibilities of the clergy in correctional work, the lack of follow-up after the usual jail conversion was cited. A woman reporter covering this meeting capitalized on this statement with a story bearing an inside streamer, "Jail Conversions Are Not Lasting, Nau Tells Pastors." She did absorb and report the principal point of the talk, that ministers in general indulge in too much wishful thinking where jail conversions are concerned and that they should follow up their jail experiences with an interest in the offender after he has been released from custody. One of the ministers present came to the probation officer later interceding in behalf of a defendant who was awaiting sentence for violation of the Dyer Act. His interest in him continued after the offender was sentenced to a federal reformatory and he later served as his parole adviser. His frequent trips to the office relating to the prisoner's plan to reunite with his estranged wife upon release indicated his genuine interest in the man and his family. He was carrying out the principle of the lost sheep.

Although probation officers are not necessarily salesmen, missionaries, or public relations experts, they should feel the urge not only to explain and interpret but to participate in community activities affecting their work. Frank

Luther Mott, dean of the School of Journalism at the University of Missouri, in an article in *Delinquency and the Community in Wartime*, writes:

Probation officers ought to make the best public relations men in the world. For the very qualities which they need most in their work are the qualities which make good public relations. First, common sense—there is nothing better for meeting the problems that come up in connection with press and public. Second, patience and an equable temper—anger enlarges a rift to a chasm irreparably. Third, a co-operative spirit. Getting the other fellow's point of view, understanding his problems, sympathizing with his efforts—these attitudes are essential to both the probation officer and the public relations man.

Probation and parole can be interpreted in a variety of ways so as to hold interest for almost any group. An invitation to speak at a meeting of Negro church women was accepted and proved to be one of the most responsive audiences ever to hear the probation officer's ideas on present day methods of dealing with offenders and the "crime doesn't pay" theme. The audience punctuated the speaker's remarks with loud "amen's," listening intently to every word.

The average audience is composed of people who believe that a federal offense by its very nature calls for a heavier sentence than a state offense. "The federal men got him now. He's a goner," is a remark frequently heard. Without utterly destroying their illusions about the relative seriousness of federal and state violations, the speaker may trace the history of crime and punishment showing the change from the "eye for an eye, tooth for a tooth" philosophy of the Old Testament days to the present idea of individualized justice as illustrated in the use of the presentence investigation, probation, and parole. "If a son is stubborn and rebellious, a glutton and a drunkard, take him before the elders of the city, and stone him to death." Any audience, no matter how vindictive or punitive, agrees that such treatment of juvenile or adolescent delinquents as written in the Book of Deuteronomy was brutally harsh and inhuman. "If a man hath 100 sheep and one goeth astray, doth he not leave the 90 and 9 and go into the mountains to seek the one who went astray? And if it be that he finds him doth he not rejoice more over the one sheep than over the 90 and 9 that went not astray?" The philosophy of the Master Reformer has a great appeal and the contrast between these two pronouncements on how to proceed with those who stray from the straight and narrow are striking.

The story of the prodigal son strikes a responsive chord in any parent's heart. In our city it has been said over and over by outstanding church, business, and civic leaders that if the court salvages one child or youth or adult its existence is justified. A prominent civic leader promoting the mental hygiene clinic said, "If we save one mentally ill person from insanity and commitment to the state hospital our clinic will have been justified." That is the Christian viewpoint expressed by the leaders of the community. The origin of probation in 1841 with John Augustus bailing out a drunk man in Boston provides the historical background; and the story of the beginning of parole in the sixteenth century when English law provided for the banishment "beyond the seas of rogues who appeared to be dangerous," offers a starting point for the history of parole.

Through Churches, Schools, and Civic Clubs

A willingness to serve as speaker often results in the probation officer being drafted to serve on committees or with groups promoting movements of civic and professional interest. A sustained interest in the proposed local mental hygiene clinic was rewarded with the consummation of plans for a clinic. This clinic, which brought to our city its first psychiatrist, will certainly be an asset to the court in the event that future offenders require diagnosis or treatment. The groundwork for such a clinic was being laid when invitations to speak to the Inter-Civic-Club Council, to service clubs, and other groups were accepted.

A civic club interest culminated in the development of two Sunday school basketball leagues providing supervised recreation for several hundred boys. The idea of prevention of juvenile delinquency was not paramount in this project, but the proposal of such a league by a probation officer was greeted with enthusiasm and a financial outlay of $750 a year.

When a young adult Sunday school class was studying the church's program for combating social problems, the probation officer was asked to talk to the class on probation and parole. The speaker was requested to return the following Sunday to continue the discussion. At least one member of the class began seriously to consider going into correctional work.

The wife of a probationer, a teacher in a nearby high school, asked the probation officer to talk in the school auditorium to a group of several hundred boys and girls. Her oldest son, who was beginning to show delinquent tendencies, was one of the students present. This provided another opportunity to interpret probation and parole, but more than that to talk to a group of impressionable listeners about some of the causes and effects of crime and delinquency. The probation officer does not realize the effect of such talks until he meets one of his listeners months or years later and is remembered as the one who talked in his school. The listener can usually tell him what he said too!

Whenever a probation officer is invited to speak before a group of business men at a luncheon, there is an opportunity to conscript potential parole advisers or sponsors. A careful explanation of the duties and responsibilities of an adviser or sponsor and the opportunity it affords him to be of service prepares him for that role if he is called upon to serve either by a member of an inmate's family or by the probation officer. The editor of the Greenville Lion's Club publication, *The Lion's Tale*, printed this appeal from the federal probation officer:

There is a great need in probation and parole work for the assistance of lay leaders as parole advisers and in the providing of employment for people under probation or parole supervision. The Exchange Clubs have adopted as a national program the sponsorship of youthful parolees, a sort of Big Brother plan, and it is my belief that all service club members should be concerned about our delinquent youth and adult offenders. I know that the men in our Lion's Club are always responsive to any plea for their support and assistance in any worthwhile program, and I am therefore asking you to run this letter in the bulletin so that any interested members can let me know that they would be willing to serve as advisers or employers upon my recommendation of a person under supervision.

Shortly after this letter was published the probation officer was asked to address his own club of 250 members to elaborate further on the letter printed in the bulletin.

Through Social Work Groups

The probation officer's effectiveness in interpreting his work may not be limited to his own judicial district. He is called upon to appear on programs at state and regional social work and probation conferences. The contacts made at these meetings are invaluable in utilizing community resources in planning for probationers and parolees. A telephone call from the Traveler's Aid Society concerning a releasee from a federal reformatory who arrived in the city by mistake resulted in a speedy contact with the institution and facili-

tated arrangements for his rerouting to his proper destination. A call from the probation officer to the Traveler's Aid office to furnish transportation for a client results in equally swift action. Such co-operation is facilitated by good public relations. A man released on parole comes to the office with no place to spend the night; the Salvation Army responds to the emergency on the recommendation of the probation officer. A probationer's wife is going to have a baby; his inadequate income precludes hospital care. A call to the county investigator quickly classified the expectant mother as a charity patient. The probation officer rubs noses with these fellow workers at community council meetings. He serves on committees with them. He establishes relationships which become real assets and resources as he studies his probationer's problems and seeks answers and solutions in the community. The probation officer cannot live to himself, alone.

Conclusion

In short, no project is more rewarding to the probation officer than community interpretation. Some may understandably raise the question as to how much time can be allowed for this extracurricular activity. How many engagements can be accepted and how many speeches prepared? Will one speech serve for several engagements? One talk can be varied endlessly by a change of case histories to illustrate the techniques and objectives of the federal probation system. The probation office files are crammed with stories which rival "Mr. District Attorney" and "This Is Your FBI" in human interest and universal appeal, if not in excitement. "Rehabilitation" becomes more than just an overworked word if the probation officer can cite the case of a man who learned a profitable vocation while serving a federal sentence; or of a doctor returned from Lexington who began life again in a different environment in a small town where his services were much needed; or a widow, who after being placed on probation, was able to secure the advice and welfare services she needed to provide the necessities of life for her family by legitimate means.

Regardless of the extra work involved in interpretation, the probation officer will not begrudge the time spent this way, but will take increasing pride in being a part of one of the Government's most idealistic systems, the federal probation and parole system, and he will welcome every opportunity to promote its rightful prestige and to help integrate it as an essential and significant factor in the community's march of progress.

Probation: The Art of Introducing the Probationer to a Better Way of Life*

By Elizabeth R. Glover. Formerly Deputy Principal Probation Officer for London, England.

PROBATION was undoubtedly first envisaged as a means of saving people from the degrading effects of a prison sentence. It was assumed that the more decent type of offender would naturally realize that he had merited punishment and be deeply moved by penitence and gratitude if, instead of this, society gave him a chance to make amends. But we now question this assumption on several grounds. First, offenders cannot be classed into black and white. They, like everyone else, are a mixture of good and bad qualities. They can be generous and unreliable, loyal and unscrupulous, competent, and self-seeking, well-intentioned and impulsive, at one and the same time, making them admirable people in some respects, unsatisfactory in others. Secondly, offenders are not commonly humble enough to admit that they have merited the condemnation of public opinion. Few of us are, when we meet criticism. They are more likely to think they have just had the bad luck to be found out, and so to be moved by self-pity or self-justification rather than by penitence or gratitude. And thirdly, is it really so easy to change one's nature overnight, by an act of will? Can an irresponsible, neurotic, or egotistical person become suddenly reliable, stable, or altruistic by deciding it would be a good thing if he did? Human nature is not as simple as this. We can only respond to the present situation with our present mental and emotional apparatus. We can only become a different kind of person by developing a new set of mental and moral muscles, and this takes time and outside stimulus.

We have now come to see that instead of having the negative function of saving the offender from a worse fate, or teaching him not to do this again, probation has assumed a positive one, introducing him to a better way of life. It is on this therapeutic aspect of probation that I propose to dwell in these few pages. What can the officer do—and how does he set about it—to build up in the offender a new mentality and outlook?

Basic Principles of Treatment

To begin with there are certain principles of treatment which I should like to stress as basic to any constructive "casework."

Treatment based on consent of offender. In the first place, I believe that

* Reprinted from *Federal Probation*, Vol. XV, September, 1951, pp. 8–12. Used by permission of author and publication.

freedom is the essence of morality. No power on earth can compel another to be good. One may forcibly restrain another from doing actual harm, but goodness lies in a man's heart and thoughts, and only if a right action is his freely chosen wish is it a moral one. A boy, for instance, who does not help himself to someone else's tools because he knows his mentor is watching is not on that account an honest boy. He is honest, if seeing the tools, and wanting them very badly, preceiving that no one is about and he is unlikely to be found out, yet reflects to himself that they are not his to take, and of his own preference or volition, refrains from touching them. Hence in England no probation order can be made for offenders over the age of 14 without the consent of the offender. This means that an offender can decline to accept the conditions of a probation order and in that case none can be made. This does occasionally happen, but we believe the principle that probation must be based on the consent and good will of the offender is a sound one.

Treatment planned for the individual. Second, any treatment must be individually planned. There can be no general pattern or rule of thumb method such as a recruit expects when he joins the Army—one routine to which all must comply. Each probationer must have highly individual treatment, devised to meet his own individual situation and temperament.

Treatment planned around offender's own situation. Third, treatment must be planned around the offender in his total situation, in relation to the family or group of which he is a member. Man is not an isolated entity, but a member of society, and life consists in relationships. His very offence indicates that he has failed in human relationships. Any treatment therefore must seek to strengthen and improve these. The great weakness of prison treatment is that it divorces a man from his natural environment. The

evidence of psychologists is most emphatic on this point. They say, with increasing unanimity, that disorders of behaviour are nearly always brought about by unhappy or defective human relationships. Probation treatment will only be effective then if it aims at helping the offender to accept and adjust himself to his fellows.

Treatment planned to redirect offender's emotions. Fourth, of all the factors which go to make up human personality, I believe the emotional ones are the central and the most cogent. "All the motives which govern and drive our lives are emotional," says an English philosopher, John Macmurray. "Love and hate, anger and fear, curiosity and joy are the springs of all that is most noble and most detestable in the history of men and nations." Love is the greatest of all the emotions in the making of a stable character. Psychologists tell us that it is absolutely essential to the human spirit both to love, and to know itself loved. One has only to survey our acquaintances to see that the most balanced persons are those who enjoy the happiest family life. It is when we begin to love another that we learn naturally and spontaneously, not by an effort of will, generosity, tolerance, responsibility, and courage. Moreover, when we love another we do not lightly destroy his peace of mind or his belief in us by doing what would horrify or disappoint him. Thus we learn to modify our own inclinations and wishes, and so to grow the mental and moral muscles necessary to a stable and upright character. Love is the basis of our moral standards, and so the art of the probation officer lies in arousing and redirecting the emotions of his charge.

Application of Principles to Common Situations

Let us now apply these principles to some of the common situations met with in probation in order to see how an offender can be helped along these lines to a better way of life.

In a great many cases enquiries reveal that the young delinquent is either unwanted at home or has no real home. To settle such a youngster down and turn him into a more reliable person it is essential to find him someone who will love him and whom he himself will love in turn. There must be warm, close, permanent ties of mutual obligation and affection if you want a stable character. What can be done, then, for an unwanted or homeless youngster?

Part played by relatives. There are several possibilities. First of all it is worth seeking around for any relatives. Sometimes it appears that there is a married sister, an uncle, a "granny" somewhere. The relative should always be visited first by the officer, or by his colleague if the relative lives elsewhere. One wants to discover whether this person has any maternal or paternal feelings, understands the needs of young people, and what, if anything, he or she is prepared to do. They may be quite concerned, but unable to do much. Occasionally they are able to offer a real home, but they are sometimes totally unsuited to help the youngster, and it is because of the possibility of disappointment that the officer should make a reconnaissance first.

Part played by foster parents. Next best to a relative is a really good landlady or foster-mother. The best landladies for young delinquents are married women in their forties or fifties who have already reared their own children successfully. Such women are by this time highly experienced in the vagaries of adolescence and often still have a strong maternal instinct seeking some new outlet, now that their own children are beginning to leave home. If once a woman of this sort gets really interested in an offender she will never give him up, and it is just this persistent forbearance and personal mothering, through bad times and good, that the most difficult

young people need. It is important, of course, that her husband should also be a willing party to the business, and both must be interviewed before any placement is made. The secret of success here lies in preparing the prospective landlady (or relative) for the difficulties they are bound to meet, and in helping them by constant visits and an easy relationship to cope with these as they arise. They must know what the youngster's failings are, be prepared for trouble, and know beforehand the kind of line to take. I cannot emphasize too strongly here two points.

First, troubles *do* arise. The settlement of an irresponsible, wayward, homeless youngster with a kindly, motherly woman who showers upon him her protective good will, does *not* have the idyllic, automatic consequences which our romanticists would have us believe. There always is a stormy patch, and sometimes a prolonged one. The woman and her husband must be prepared for this.

The second point is that contrary to the belief of our sceptics, there *are* couples who are prepared to undertake the responsibilities with their eyes open. And where they take it on and go through with it they are more successful than any other method I know. I know in my own experience both girl and boy delinquents who, after a very unsatisfactory beginning, after straining the good will of everyone who tried to help them—particularly their longsuffering landladies—did at last make good, and stay good. I know young people who made their home with the landladies to whom they went on probation, for 6, 8, even 10 years, settling down and becoming acceptable members of the family until marriage or national service called them away elsewhere. Sometimes it is not the relative or landlady herself who works the miracle, but a member of her family. Many an adolescent girl has been greatly helped by the tiny grandchild of the woman with whom she has been put to lodge. This child is someone for her to love and fuss over, take out, sit on her knee, bathe, put to bed, and so forth, and who in return will love her back in the openly affectionate way of small children. For this reason, where all efforts to find a home substitute have failed, girls may be helped by being found jobs with children; and plenty of tiny children need loving nurses.

Part played by friends. Now another important need: Friends. Some delinquents have bad friends, like the gangsters. More, in my experience, have *no* friends (but I have worked mostly with girls and women). Let us have a look at these two groups in turn.

First the gangsters. It is not enough to separate the members of the gang. The leader still retains his gifts of leadership, which society needs, and if these are not made use of and redirected into socially acceptable channels, there is danger he may continue to lead rebels against law and order. The underlings have shown their capacity to follow. Society also needs people who can carry out instructions and work loyally by a prearranged plan (who can co-operate in other words), but an undiscriminating follower is as dangerous socially as an unscrupulous leader. It is not enough to separate the followers. They must be helped to develop powers of judgment and the strength of character to use these, while attempts will have to be made to inspire the leader with new ideals and ambitions. This, I maintain, will only be done through his emotions.

Next the solitary people. These are wrapped up in themselves leading lonely, inhibited lives, detached from reality. The basis of happy, easy, human relationships, I believe, is self-confidence. These people are unsociable because they have no self-confidence. They feel inadequate and uneasy with other people. It is therefore worse than useless to try and push

these unfortunate youngsters into a youth club. To see so many other hearty happy people all taking each other for granted and ragging each other is to impress upon them all the more that they are not like that and to make them feel misfits. It will increase their lack of self-confidence, rather than lessen it, however friendly the club members or leader may try to be to the newcomer. No, one must travel much more slowly than that. Probation, being absolutely individual treatment, is an admirable instrument for helping these people. Week after week, month after month even, if for only a few minutes, the probationer will have all to himself the undivided attention of the probation officer.

The Aim of the Probation Officer

The officer's aim here is to build up the probationer's self-respect. The officer concerns himself with the delinquent's health, welfare, new clothes and hair styles, prospects, fortunes—all intimate matters about which no one has ever troubled before. The officer listens —and lonely people have rarely had an audience before—and it is warming. The range of conversation widens as the weeks go by. New films are discussed, books, public people, questions of the day, and broadcasts—on terms of equality. The officer seems to regard the probationer as a normal, reasonable, sensible kind of person with ideas worth listening to; and so the inhibited probationer begins to expand a bit. He enjoys his weekly interview, looks forward to it, and leaves feeling set up and more assured. In short, he begins to enjoy conversation and company. This is the first stage and it may take months.

The next stage is to enlarge the circle and introduce new people, gradually. This can sometimes be done through a hobby. If during this time the probationer has been developing a new hobby, under the interest and encouragement of the officer (stamp collecting, perhaps, rabbit-keeping, music), the new friend or friends might well be people interested in the same line, and then the common interest is there to lessen any feeling of self-consciousness or insecurity. Sometimes the officer may ask the probationer to help him with some project at which he knows there will be other kindly disposed persons, ready to take an interest in his lonely protégé. It may be a carol singing party in aid of the local hospital, or some church theatricals, or to steward at a public meeting. The probationer will feel set up at being asked to help. That is much more enhancing to self-respect than being the object of help. He will enjoy being important. In some such ways as these the officer may be able, over the course of a year or two, to provide his solitary probationers with one or two good friends, or with a budding capacity to make friends. This will make all the difference to his future reliability.

The Place of Ethical Training

Family ties and good friends are necessary to stable character, but to achieve them, as well as to retain them, something else is necessary. This might be termed ethical training. I mean a training in responsibility, a recognition that happy human relationships depend upon give as well as take, and involve pain as well as joy. Most normal people learn this in the nursery. The small child in a happy family experiences love first as the recipient of their admiration and delight in him, and then in his own first overtures and expressions of love to them. He begins planning little presents and surprises for those he loves. He learns to modify his own wishes in deference to others. He is disturbed and unhappy when he sees those whom he loves upset or ill or in trouble. Thus he comes to learn that love is a two-way emotion. Many children nowadays are utterly neglected in this early training. They have never been taught to con-

sider other people, nor the reasons for having and obeying rules. All young people want to be a success, but a great many simply do not know because they have never been told that inconsiderate, irresponsible behaviour is wrong because it makes life more difficult or unpleasant for other people, and that it is unkind. Most delinquents are quite unaccustomed to thinking of anyone but themselves. To be really effective, then, probation must help the delinquent to see and accept his duties and responsibilities towards other people. How is this done?

It is done through the same medium as other aspects of character training, through the weekly interview, and on the same principle, slowly, imperceptibly, indirectly, over the course of a long time, approached now from one angle, now from another. For instance, films and novels often are discussed, and at once an ethical judgment has to be made. "*Ought* the hero to have done what he did?" "Why not?" "Well, but there were other people to consider. . . ." The youngster comes away with new ideas of right and wrong percolating in his head. Then one day he opens out to his probation officer about a family row. The officer discusses this objectively. What is the *right* thing to do? It will be found if one has any serious, intimate conversation with young people that they have a code by which they are very ready to judge other people's conduct, particularly as it affects them. Thus most young people declare hotly that they think unkindness is the worst sin, or hypocrisy because (though they probably are not aware of the reason) they think other people have been unkind or hypocritical to them. But once they have enunciated this, and they easily do, one can take it as their own code and help them to judge their own conduct by it. "But was that a kind thing to do? I thought you believed people should not be unkind . . . ," one can ask, if one is discussing some parental or school complaint of unrealiability or bad conduct. Adolescents often get very critical of their parents and will sometimes open out on the subject of parental friction to their probation officer. And this in turn may lead on to a discussion of what happy marriage involves. It is important to engineers to talk on this subject with adolescents who want to get married and to be happy. They should be told that happy human relationships depend upon the amount of time and trouble one gives to understanding the other, and trying to accommodate one's own preferences to those of the other. Thus, ethical training on probation must be of the suggestive type, a continual presentation of new aspects of right and wrong, in terms of human relationships, for which numberless opportunities will occur if any freedom of intimacy is achieved between officer and charge. One must try to attune their minds to appraising qualities of character, and accepting the fact that

the desirable ones do not just grow; they demand self-discipline, continually renewed self-discipline and self-sacrifice.

Ultimately it is to be hoped that they will come to realize their need of Divine help and forgiveness, in this baffling effort, and so achieve a realistic approach to religion.

Thus probation is not a matter of devising excellent plans of recovery and handing them out to a compliant probationer and to the officials of our various social services to work upon. It is rather the art of awakening his own aspirations for a different way of life, and then supporting and backing him up as he falteringly sets out to achieve this end. One can only do this by showing him something better, something more attractive than he had before, by introducing him to the deeper satisfactions of life, and these come ultimately from actual experience of the comfort and stimulus of happy human relationships.

SELECTED REFERENCES

1. Ross, Frank A., "A Lawyer Looks at Probation," *Federal Probation*, XV, December 1951.

An interesting, provocative analysis of probation from the legal point of view.

2. Chute, Charles L., *Yearbook* (New York: National Probation and Parole Association, 1941), "The Development of Probation," pp. 29–40.

An authority on probation traces the early growth of probation in the United States.

3. Tappan, Paul W., *Juvenile Delinquency* (New York: McGraw-Hill Book Co., 1949), Chapter 13: "Probation."

A first-rate discussion of probation with its many ramifications. Tappan makes a detailed analysis of the specific tasks of probation as well as professionalization in probation. The chapter concludes with an evaluation of the probation system.

4. Grinnel, Frank W., *Yearbook* (New York: National Probation and Parole Association, 1941), "The Common Law Background of Probation," pp. 23–29.

For an interesting account of probation as it relates to common law precepts, this selection well deserves the attention of those interested in the legal background that made the concept of probation a living reality today.

11 THE CORRECTIONAL INSTITUTION

REFORM schools or their equivalents have a moderately long history. It begins with the opening of the New York House of Refuge on January 1, 1825. The founders of this House envisaged the institution as a "prison, manufactory and school." The next year Boston inaugurated a similar type of institution, and Philadelphia followed in 1828. These three institutions for juvenile delinquents were the only ones of their kind until a municipal boys' reformatory was established in New Orleans in 1845. In 1847 the first state reform school for boys was founded in Westboro, Massachusetts, and later came to be known as the Lyman School for Boys. The first girls' industrial school in the United States was established in Lancaster, Massachusetts. At first, an institution of this type was called a "house of refuge." Later to remove all doubt about the purpose, the name was changed to "reform school"—a label carrying with it a definite stigma for the inmates of the institution. In an effort to remove the stigma of the name and since trade-training was often part of the school program, various authorities adopted the name "industrial school." However, this name also developed invidious overtones, and the later usage of "house of correction" did little to help the situation. Finally, these schools were named for persons or locations in an effort to avoid an unhappy connotation.

But name-changing has not greatly affected the "reform school" image commonly held by inside inmate and outside public alike. In fact, many people consider correctional institutions as places where dangerous offenders are kept out of circulation temporarily rather than as rehabilitation agencies. That there is some measure of justification for the former view is seen when the results of rehabilitative efforts are examined.

DOES THE CORRECTIONAL INSTITUTION "CORRECT"?

The crucial test of the success of a reformatory, of course, is its ability to rehabilitate its charges. That this goal is not being met in any large degree is evidenced by the fact that there are between 65 and 85 per cent rehabilitative failures among the former inmates who have spent time in reformatories and industrial or "training" schools. An extensive study of the situation, undertaken by the Gluecks in the 1930's, which reported the careers of inmates of the Massachusetts Reformatory for more than fifteen years after their discharge from the institution, revealed that only 22.6 per cent of these young people refrained from criminal activities during the post-institutional period.[1]

---

[1] Sheldon and Eleanor Glueck, *Later Criminal Careers* (New York: The Commonwealth Fund, 1937), pp. 75, 76.

This finding is consistent with those concerning the crime careers of reformatory graduates in many states. For example, one authority relates the story of 250 boys discharged in 1929 from California's Preston School of Industry, whose after careers could be traced. By 1939, 60 per cent of these boys had been arrested one or more times and 47 per cent had been sentenced to state prisons. Moreover, the 250 were not the least promising inmates discharged from Preston, but presumably the most promising, for the administration had granted them all either honorable discharges or the governor's diploma of honor.[2] These findings and the similar conclusions of many other investigations may constitute, in part, an indictment of correctional institutions. More significantly, perhaps, they raise the question of the severe handicaps that reformatories face.

For there seems to be no way to avoid the admission that prisons for children, like those for adults, continue to be effective schools for crime. One reason, as Ellingston has pointed out, is that they must accept whatever commitments the judges send them. They must take first offenders and experienced gangsters, boys going through the emotional upheaval of adolescence, runaways, truants, disobedient children, and confine them with burglars, muggers, arsonists, rapists, and even killers. Institutions must accept youths ranging from the feebleminded to the brilliant. They must take sex deviates, perverts, drug addicts, and alcoholics. They must take the highly intelligent though dangerous abnormal personalities as well as the essentially normal youths; the innocent and immature along with the degenerate; the bully and the weakling. To complicate this situation, many institutions, though very large, are perennially overcrowded—forced to pack double-decker bunks into dormitories and two boys in a single room.

Unless care is exercised, almost any child can be sent to the reform school whether his offense is serious or not. The case is related of one unimaginative social worker and judge who assigned a child to the Illinois Geneva Training School for Girls because of truancy. Her history revealed that she had lost her hair following an influenza attack. Being poor, she had to accept a coarse flaxen wig, the type one sees in a hairdresser's window. She wore this when she returned to school and was ridiculed unmercifully by other schoolmates—the important reason for her truancy. Another unfortunate "delinquent" girl's "crime" was simply that her own mother had deserted her. Not knowing what to do with her, the local officials had solved their problem by sending her to a reform school.[3] These are extreme cases, no doubt, but they point up the need for cautious and wise policy in the assignment of youth to correctional institutions. When the on-going practices of the reformatories themselves are examined further reasons why they are often breeders of crime are revealed.

REFORM SCHOOL PRACTICES

One predominant reason for the failure of these juvenile institutions to rehabilitate youth is the continuance of traditional punitive motives and methods,

---

[2] As cited in John R. Ellingston, *Protecting Our Children from Criminal Careers* (New York: Prentice-Hall, 1948), p. 84.

[3] Cases reported in Florence Monahan, *Women in Crime* (New York: Ives Washburn, 1941), pp. 111–113.

which seem to produce only more hostile and aggressive responses from most boys and girls. While it may be true that correctional incarceration, however elaborate and refined its program, can scarcely avoid a large admixture of punishment, children are still often subjected to severe disciplinary methods even for petty infractions of the multiplicity of rules. The consequence is a training in hate, bitterness, and vindictiveness. These sentiments are enhanced by the use of the still somewhat prevalent methods of corporal punishment found in many institutions. Such punishments include, for example, the "bends," the "squats," and "standing on lines" which some inmates are forced to do for inordinate periods of time, and whippings and strappings administered by the custodial staff. There are still reformatories that employ bloodhounds and offer rewards for the capture of escapees.

Reform schools for boys have a black record of stupidity, gross brutality, and human tragedy, and largely because of the practice of sadistic punishments. Their attempts at "vocational rehabilitation" are sometimes accompanied by paddles, shaved heads, prolonged icy showers, whips, and blackjacks, and other such procedures which are supposed to inculcate in boys the principles of "democracy." One authoritative writer cites the case of the Whittier School (Fred C. Nelles School) in California, once called the "showplace of the nation" in the juvenile correctional field, which maintained for older boys a "discipline cottage" with solitary cells—no bed, table, chair or light—where boys could find means to hang themselves, as two did in 1940. The same writer describes the Iowa Training School's coal pile where in August, 1945, a seventeen-year-old boy undergoing discipline collapsed and died. The administration ascribed his death to heat prostration, but the coroner attributed it to "a blow on the head." A few days later 175 of the 565 inmates ran away, some shouting "I'm not going to stay here and be killed."[4] Again these are extreme and, by no means, daily occurrences. But they do provide evidence of grave conditions and outmoded practices in correctional institutions.

In some reform schools a strong emphasis is given to *outward* cleanliness and neatness: the walks, lawn, windows, and trees are kept very well. But life inside the walls, marked by the monotony characteristic of institutions for the care of segregated persons, reveals a wide range of unhappy practices. One journalist who has investigated the institutional way of life in reformatories reports that monotony may be varied with hydrotherapy (playing a 70-pound fire hose on the backs of nude boys trapped at the side of a brick wall) or "flying home" (a well-placed kick which shocks the nervous system and lifts the boys off the floor) or "rag-sniffing" (the boys sink their noses into rags soaked in gasoline, kerosene, or shoe polish, which makes them dizzy and causes them to vomit).[5] According to other reporters, ingenious forms of punishment include brick-counting (the child stands erect with his eyes turned up to the ceiling); line toeing (the child stands erect and silent, with both hands upraised); rice-polishing (the boy crawls on his knees across a floor covered with rice grains,

---

[4] Cases cited in Ellingston, *op. cit.*, pp. 86, 87.
[5] Albert Deutsch, "Is This Reform?" *Woman's Home Companion*, March 1948, p. 30.

inducing bleeding); post-walking (the boy marches between or around posts for hours, sometimes carrying a 40-pound bag); and runaway-pills (the captured runaways are dosed with laxatives to "help them run").[6]

The Jacksonville (Florida) *Times-Union* in its January 12, 1952, issue reported on an investigation of the Arizona Industrial School for Boys and revealed that an attendant kicked a boy in the face for not moving fast enough. The report also noted that boys were whipped with pieces of fanbelts, doubled ropes, and bicycle tires, or forced to walk barefooted across the desert from Wilcox, some thirty miles away.

Practices such as these are fairly prevalent in reformatories for boys. Some of them are found in institutions for the care of girls as well, along with the persistent conditions of monotony and enforced isolation. However, there seems to have been considerable improvement in girls' reform schools in recent years. For example, the inmates at Ventura, California, no longer have shaved heads; neither are they forbidden to talk to one another, as was once the case. By way of punishment, spankings are not now permitted; solitary confinement is no longer prescribed at the least provocation; and girls are not forced to parade naked before the inmates (a practice followed by at least one state reform school and reported in the press). Corporal punishment, meted out at Claremont, the Indiana girls' school, is not nowadays officially permitted in most schools.

Large inroads are being made here and there to eliminate old-fashioned "remedies" in schools for boys as well as for girls. And conspicuous improvements in physical architecture, diet, recreational facilities, and in medical and educational provisions have been made. But big problems remain, most of them the inevitable consequence of enforced segregation. The feeling of incarceration—the more extreme among members of a society that accents individual freedom; the extended boredom; the constant contact with teachers of crime and the regrettable lessons learned thereby; the frustrated social and sexual life and the consequent ubiquitous homosexuality—practiced by both boys and girls; the persistent conflict between "keepers" and inmates—these remain chief marks of what are often thought of as "junior prisons."

REFORM SCHOOL SUPERINTENDENTS

Reform school superintendents, to a very large extent, are "the law" in their own institutions. It is the unusual superintendent who escapes the "institutionalization" that seems inevitable to most of those identified with reform schools or prisons. And as authority trickles downward from the top, the point of view of the superintendent is generally absorbed by the subordinate staffs.

The attitudes and "philosophies" of some institutional officials have been reported by Albert Deutsch. He found one superintendent, the official responsible for teaching American citizenship to his charges, who said to an investigator: "Those boys are going to tell you a pack of lies. I wouldn't trust any of them on a stack of Bibles. They're just a bad lot!" When the same superintendent was

---

[6] Negley K. Teeters and John Otto Reinemann, *The Challenge of Delinquency* (New York: Prentice-Hall, 1950), p. 461.

asked if the reformatory had a psychiatrist available, he replied, "We don't need any of those fellows here. We need practical men." At another institution Deutsch found "Cottage Parents" who were often embittered failures, refugees from the normal community, misfits, alcoholics, political hacks. One former undertaker's assistant said, "Apartments are hard to get, so I moved in here."[7] The conclusion should not be drawn, of course, that all reformatory officials are so lacking in an informed and professional viewpoint—a viewpoint increasingly found. But it should not be forgotten that cases such as those reported above are by no means rare at the present time.

In the course of time, superintendents are apt to leave an indelible impression on the staff and on the structure of the institution itself. An interesting case is seen in the Geneva Training School for Girls, the first superintendent of which was Ophelia Amigh, who reputedly supervised the institution very capably for seventeen years in the earlier days of "iron discipline" with the help of a staff of "Aunties"—as matrons were called in the 1890's. The ways of the "Aunties" and of Mrs. Amigh had by no means disappeared when Florence Monahan came to the Geneva School in 1932 to superintend, presumably, a modern and liberal institution. The "Aunties" were continuing to carry out the original policies of Mrs. Amigh: ignoring dietary problems, imposing strict discipline, even imposing decades-old uniforms on the inmates. Substituting reforms under such tradition-supported conditions, as the new superintendent learned, is not easy.[8] Another case illustrating the pervasiveness of those in charge was observed when the California Youth Authority appointed new superintendents with long experience in the probation field to take charge of the Nelles School at Whittier in 1942 and of the Preston School of Industry in 1945. Both of the new superintendents met open resistance to any change from some staff members who reportedly said, "We've worked with these boys a long time. They're tough and the only way to handle them is to keep them cowed."[9]

Resistance to change is brought about in part, then, by the supervising authorities. The authorities—superintendents and lesser officials—in turn often help to strengthen the frequently found "institutionalism" that constitutes such a high barrier to needed reforms. For as superintendents and their staffs become accustomed to procedures that "work" these tend to become routine. This typical mark of bureaucratization, which is found in all formal organizations, in some measure lessens the officials' capacity to see new situations realistically, to improvise, to experiment, to meet newcomers as distinctive personalities.

And the superintendent's own personality often plays an important role in determining the practices and policies of the institution. If he is susceptible—as so many people are—to the temptation to domination, his official situation gives him almost free reign. For he has very large powers, usually supported by wide official authority, over the human beings committed to the institution in his charge. And it may be argued, as Ellingston puts it, that the less competent the superintendent, the more likely he is to find compensation in the abuse of

[7] Deutsch, op. cit., pp. 35, 36.

[8] Monahan, op. cit., pp. 114–117.

[9] As cited in Ellingston, op. cit., pp. 130, 131.

his power and to build up his own ego at the expense of the inmates who are not in a position to resist effectively.

There is always danger in power, to be sure. But the professionally qualified, emotionally stable, and imaginative superintendent will strive to avoid the temptations of his office and work to enhance the lives of the members of the segregated world that he supervises.

INSTITUTIONAL REFORMATION?

In 1946 there were approximately 166 schools under public auspices serving about thirty thousand delinquent children in the United States. Of these, 115 were state and national schools and fifty-one were county and municipal institutions. Despite the magnitude of the situation, the public is generally unfamiliar with the nature of the correctional institutions. What about the views of informed authorities?

Florence Monahan, a competent and successful administrator of more than twenty years' experience with girls' reform schools, sums up the situation in these words:

> The longer I live in one, the more I am impressed with the abnormal atmosphere of an institution. It is an unnatural existence. No institutional-life can take the place of family-life where the child has a chance to develop as an individual. I would rather place a child in an average dirty home, if there is love and affection there, than in the finest, cleanest institution in the country.[10]

Some support for Miss Monahan's conclusion is found in the words of J. Howard McGrath, former Attorney General of the United States:

> Imprisonment as a punishment for a juvenile delinquent has been an unequivocal failure. Reform schools are not reform schools, but crucibles wherein boil the worst instincts of humanity and where innocence vanishes and insolence takes its place. The general course is from a reform school to a reformatory, then to a prison.[11]

There is no shortage of well-meaning plans for institutional reform. If they could be put into effect, rehabilitative training might become truly rehabilitative. The attainment of this goal is seriously hampered by lack of funds, lack of personnel, little sustained public interest—except in jailbreaks and tabloid publicity and "politics" both inside and out. Some institutions experience a change of supervision with every switch in elections (as if it makes any difference to children whether they are neglected or helped by Democrats or Republicans).

On the whole there is an encouraging tendency away from punitive and toward correctional policy. Today's superintendents and staffs, although they cannot do much about the situation, are increasingly aware that children in trouble need the most expert psychological handling by specialists trained in modern techniques of case and group work. And increasingly, too, modern

---

[10] Monahan, *op. cit.*, p. 173.

[11] "The Role of the Federal Probation Officer in Criminal Justice," *Federal Probation*, XIV, December 1950, 4.

methods of reconditioning offenders are being introduced, particularly among a few denominational and private welfare projects which operate training schools in various states.

Massachusetts, New York, and Ohio, among other states, have been emulating the experience of these private but quasi-official youth centers and setting up bungalow or residence schools rather than large institutions. Unlike the latter, these schools eliminate walls and bars and other symbols of the prison. Simulating home conditions, these agencies provide a background generally more suitable to rehabilitation. With girls especially the small residence arrangement is often successful, for it provides training in domestic affairs of the very kind which may engage them in the outside world.

Approaching the conditions of the outside world is, indeed, the direction of these hopeful trends. Gradually we are learning, perhaps, that one requirement of effective rehabilitation lies in making the institutional setting of correction something other than a "junior prison."

READINGS

A forward step in reform school amelioration is the reception process as outlined by Maurice A. Harmon in "The Reception Process in a State Training School." It presages the techniques of the future in those communities eager to understand better the juvenile delinquents in their care.

One of the best state reception centers is in operation in the Elmira, New York, Reformatory. A detailed description of the legal provisions of the law establishing the Center, as well as of the functions, location, facilities, administration and program of the Center appear in a brochure entitled "Department of Correction Reception Center." The major part of the information in this publication is reprinted in the reading of the same title.

The significance of group therapy as applied to delinquents in institutions is given by Gisela Konopka, who worked on a research appointment granted by the University of Minnesota in the summer of 1948. In her article, "The Group Worker's Role in an Institution for Juvenile Delinquents," she shows the value of supplementing individual treatment with therapeutic group work. Institutions for delinquent youngsters should be staffed with teams similar to child guidance clinics.

In "If You Make the Boy Right, You Make the World Right" (an address before the National Council of Juvenile Court Judges at Pittsburgh, Pennsylvania, May 3, 1950), Associate Justice Tom C. Clark, of the Supreme Court of the United States, says that the advantages of the training school have been overestimated in their contributions to delinquency prevention and control. The ten or twelve gang associates of the neighborhood may be increased to four hundred in the reform school when the judge sentences the boy to remove him from a bad gang. The value of "sponsors" is emphasized.

Harrison Allen Dobbs raises a challenging question in his article, "Are Correctional Schools Evil or Are We?" There is a civic, and, according to this author, a *moral* obligation to develop better institutional safeguards and standards.

The Reception Process in a State Training School[*]

By Maurice A. Harmon. Supervisor, Social Service Division, Illinois State Training School for Boys, St. Charles.

As more and more training school administrations aim their programs toward treatment, it is time we rethink its meaning in such a setting. More importantly, it is time to evaluate areas inside the training school where we may begin to meet this challenge of a treatment job. One of the most strategic areas and yet perhaps one of the most neglected is the intake or reception process. If we are going to have treatment in our institutions, let us take first things first. Let us begin to treat the moment the boy comes to us, not pick him up somewhere in our program several weeks later when it is quite possible that traumatic damage has already been inflicted upon him. Treatment then is more difficult than it would have been several weeks earlier if we had begun to apply our techniques when he came in our front door.

Regardless of how a boy may appear upon his entry into a training school, he is a boy threatened by fears of what he is about to face, and in most cases he will attempt to suppress the anxiety created by his fears and his insecurity. Often he will present a tough-guy front. Medical research has shown us how many adult males were overcome by the same sort of anxiety through their first few days in training centers during World War II. If men, many of whom were making mature and successful adjustments in society, were unable to adjust to the strangeness and complexity of a training center, should we not expect adolescents, who were not making a mature and successful adjustment in society, to experience the same sort of difficulty in entering an even more awesome facility, a state training school. Moreover these boys have no chance of a medical discharge, they must stay, and they must do many other things which they find much to their displeasure. They are not permitted to succumb to an impaired ego. Realizing the terrific psychological impact that entrance into a training school has on a boy, we here at St. Charles are trying to redirect our reception process so that his anxieties will be relieved as far as possible.

Many features of our procedure are new. It needs continuous revaluation, but it is quite flexible and we are ready to change if we can do more to discover a boy's needs, help his adjustment during his first days at our institution, and promote the integration of the boy into the institution.

When a boy is brought to us by a sheriff or some other public official, he is seen as soon as possible by the supervisor of the social service division. This is a brief interview, no more than three or four minutes usually, and is chiefly just meeting and saying "hello" to the newcomer. The supervisor then introduces the boy to an intake counselor for an interview lasting from fifteen minutes to half an hour. During this interview the counselor obtains face sheet information as well as other data and attempts to answer many of the child's questions about the institution. "How many shots (inoculations) do I get here? Are we allowed to wear our own clothes? Do you have a whipping post?" Thus some of the boy's surface anxiety is relieved.

[*] Reprinted from *Focus*, Vol. 29, November, 1950, pp. 180–183. Used by permission.

In regard to face sheet information, we believe ideally in obtaining this from some source other than the subject himself. The process may not only be damaging to him, but the information is often inaccurate. However, we must continue this way until the day comes when community agencies send data to the training schools. There are times, of course, when boys are brought to the school during off-duty hours. Plans for this emergency should incorporate as much of the above procedure as possible, at least in terms of the philosophy behind the method.

The boy is taken to our reception cottage and during the next few days he goes through the routine of indoctrination. This includes medical and dental examination, visits to the barber shop, to the tailor for his clothing, the shoe shop and so forth. But sometime during that week of processing the boy is again seen by his intake counselor. This time the interview approximates an hour during which a complete social history is taken. Comparatively little emphasis is placed in the written history on the offense which brought the boy to the institution, but much is laid on those personality factors which will help the staff determine what treatment might best be prescribed for this individual. Does he seem to be immature? Is he passive? Is he effeminate? Is he withdrawn? Is he aggressive? Is he tearful? In short, we want to get to know this boy and how he feels about things. We are not as much interested in *what* his delinquency happened to be as in *why* he is a delinquent.

Other specific areas that make up the social history include his familial background, his personal history, his problem as we see it and as he sees it, and his adjustment in the reception cottage. Later during the reception process, the boy is interviewed by a chaplain of his faith, by the vocational guidance counselor, and by the psychologist who administers a battery of tests. During his third week in the reception cottage, the intake counselor again sees him, but because of the severe time limitations that our counselors face, this interview by necessity is quite short. Its purpose is to show the boy our interest in him. The counselor also talks with the cottage parents and other employees who have known him during this period. When this information from various professional members of our staff has been assembled, it is read by our psychiatrist who subsequently interviews the boy and prepares a psychiatric evaluation.

A day or two later, approximately three weeks following the boy's arrival, our diagnostic staffing is held. Present are the psychiatrist, the psychologist, the caseworker (counselor), the Protestant or the Catholic chaplain, and the supervisor of the social service division. After the social history (including a report on the reception adjustment), the psychological examination, the chaplain's report, and the psychiatric evaluation are read, the staff discusses how we may best fit this boy into our program (hoping that some day we may discuss how we can best fit our program to this particular boy. Even now we are doing this in some ways, but admittedly we still have a long way to go in that objective). Much revaluation, retooling and overhauling needs to be done in almost every institutional area first.

At this staffing we not only try to place the boy in the particular homogeneous cottage group which will best fit his needs, but we attempt to select a program which will be beneficial and at the same time satisfying to him. In all of our recommendations we try to reach a consensus, and in most instances we are successful. Often we place a boy in a program not because he is suited best academically or vocationally to it, but because the staff member working in that area might be best suited to the boy. We keep the same thing in mind in cottage placement, trying to juggle as best we can the homogeneity of the group with the personality of the cottage parent. Trained group leaders in all of our cottages would minimize our concern about acceptance of the boy in the group. Recommendations are also made as to institutional adjustment. Should the treatment theme be freedom, flexibility and permissiveness, or rather, should he have a program with consistent, definite limitation of activity? In all cases stress is on the need for warmth and understanding from every member of the staff who will work with the boy. A regular counselor will be with him throughout his stay.

Some boys are selected for individual therapy, but since our staff resources are not great in this area cases are limited to those most in need and at the same time most amenable to treatment of this type. We are in the process of establishing a group for play therapy and hope to progress in this area in the near future. By raising the quality of all the areas in the training school we hope to make the term "institutional therapy" have real significance for all of our boys and staff.

A summary of the diagnostic staffing is made by the intake counselor. The original copy goes into the boy's folder, and copies go to the various administrative divisions in the institution. This summary serves a useful purpose in preparation of the placement plan when the boy is ready for release.

Besides our daily diagnostic staff sessions, the clinic department schedules also a daily review of cases which come up at periodic intervals. It has representatives from all of our administrative divisions: cottage life, placement, academic, vocational guidance, recreation and social service. The institutional adjustment of each boy must be reviewed at least once every three months by the group, although a case may be brought up more frequently if the boy's counselor deems it necessary. Any change

affecting his program in the institution must be acted upon by review staff action. This staff must also act on all releases to the community.

After the diagnostic staff has completed its recommendations and permanent assignments, the intake counselor introduces the boy to his counselor at the reception cottage, who in turn takes him on his move from the reception cottage to his assigned cottage. Here he introduces the boy to his cottage parents and to the other boys. Later he interprets staff findings to the cottage parent. This concludes the intake process, for now the boy is ready to take his place in the regular institutional program.

As we see it, there are still inherent weaknesses in our reception process. Primarily there is need for a longer reception period, in order, among other reasons, to make the first week less crowded with so many interviews and examinations. We should do all we can that first week to allay the boy's fears about us. This might best be promoted by a program of informal recreation activities, the boy being permitted to go along without rigid controls, to relax so that he will be sold on the idea that he is going to be helped at this school rather than punished. If in those first few days we throw too much at the boy in terms of tests, examinations, fittings, we can expect to leave him gasping. Our emphasis for the first few days should be in the direction of program orientation.

We need a longer reception period because information gained from observation could then play a more important role at the diagnostic staffing. Observation takes on an even more important aspect of diagnosis when the reception period is a free and easy one. This, perhaps more than any other fact, will tell us where the boy later belongs. Conversely, if we make the reception program stuffy and rigid—just to show the boy we mean business—we cannot accurately foretell how he will act once the barrier is lifted. Such treatment will only add to his hostility.

Perhaps the chief criticism of an adequate intake or reception process is the time-consumption factor for the personnel involved. Such a program may consume the services of most of the clinic personnel, leaving little or no time for help to boys in the regular program. We must ask ourselves, are we dedicated to the treatment of these youthful offenders? If so, we must prepare them for it immediately and not fool ourselves into thinking that time stands still or that by some miracle we can help this boy later when he becomes familiar with the routine. We have been sitting by too long waiting for those miracles of institutional treatment to take place. There is no therapeutic magic. We must pick up the challenge to help these boys when they first come in our doors. We must strive for the highest standards in our intake and reception program, and then attempt one by one to bring the other areas in our institution up to that same standard.

Perhaps the best evaluation of the time spent in good intake practice was expressed in the words of a fourteen year old boy, recently admitted to us, who wrote home: "When I first arrived here they were nice to me. . . ."

The New York State Reception Center*

By New York State Department of Correction, Albany.

THE RECEPTION CENTER of the New York State Department of Correction was authorized by Chapter 554, Laws of 1945. It began operation November 1, 1945.

Legal Provisions

The law provides for the following:

1. The Center is intended for the reception and classification for purposes of confinement and treatment of male offenders between the ages of 16 and 21 years.

2. Such offenders must be

a. Convicted of an offense punishable by imprisonment in a State institution under the jurisdiction of the Department, or adjudged to be Wayward Minors or Youthful Offenders and punishable in like manner, and

b. Must have been sentenced to imprisonment in a State institution.

3. Those male offenders in the age group 16 to 21, who were not committable to an institution in this Department prior to the establishment of the Center, or an offender sentenced to death, may not be committed to the Reception Center. The first exception excludes mentally normal offenders who have reached the age of 19 and who are not convicted of a felony, since such offenders were not committable to any institution in the Department prior to the opening of the Center. In other words, Misdemeanants, Youthful Offenders, and Wayward Minors 19 or 20 years of age are not committable to the Center unless they are mentally defective.

4. The power to fix sentence is reserved to the courts. However, as was the case prior to the opening of the Center, all non-felony offenders (Misdemeanants, Wayward Minors, Youthful

* Reprinted, in part, from brochure entitled *New York State Department of Correction Reception Center: Its History, Purpose, Makeup and Program,* published by the New York State Department of Correction, August, 1950. Used by permission of the Department of Correction.

Offenders) committed to an institution in this Department automatically have indefinite sentences with no minimum and a 3-year maximum. The courts may fix a minimum and maximum sentence in felony cases committed to the Center, and do so in from 25 to 30 per cent of the felony cases.

5. The Reception Center classification staff is to make a detailed study of each offender committed to the Center and recommend to the Commissioner of Correction

a. The State correctional institution best suited to receive the offender.

b. A program of treatment and training.

c. The approximate length of treatment.

6. The court may place the offender on probation, commit to a private institution, or make other disposition; but commitment to a State institution must be to the Reception Center.

7. The staff of the Reception Center is directly responsible through the Director of the Center to the Commissioner of Correction.

Reasons for the Reception Center

The Reception Center is based on the idea that after an offender has been found guilty in court, the decision as to the place and method of treatment should be decided by specialists in the correctional field. The Reception Center represents an important step toward that basic objective of correctional institutions, namely, individualized study, treatment and training.

In the past, young male offenders 16 to 21 years of age have not been sufficiently separated so as to permit effective treatment. Part of the reason has been that there are so many committing courts and that these courts vary widely in the amount of study which they give each case and in their knowledge of institutions to which such offenders are committed. Another reason is that commitments have been very largely governed by chronological age and the offense committed. It is not surprising, therefore, that there has been great variation in the types of young men committed to the various institutions. Neither the individual offender nor society has been best served, and the institutions have been handicapped in developing a program geared to the needs of particular types of offenders.

Some courts make a careful study of each offender before reaching a decision as to his disposition. A few judges also make it their business to acquaint themselves with the programs of the various institutions to which they commit offenders. Utilizing well-staffed probation departments, available professional services, such courts work efficiently towards the best possible disposition of their cases. Unfortunately many courts do not, and probably cannot, devote the time and effort to such careful study of offenders and institutions. The establishment of the Reception Center is not a reflection on the courts, but the creation of a process to supplement the courts' directives, and frequently their desires, where the time, money, or highly qualified specialists are not available for the required study in local communities.

Functions of the Reception Center

The Reception Center has been established in order to afford the following advantages:

1. Insure careful study of offenders upon admission by a competent professional staff.

2. Effect segregation based on scientific methods permitting greater specialization of institutional programs. It goes without saying that, in order for a reception center to be most effective, there must be a sufficient number and variety of institutions, with specific institutions designated to receive particular types of inmates.

3. Recommend treatment based upon

the careful study of the individual inmate at the time of commitment in the correction system. This relieves the holding institution from a considerable portion of initial classification work and provides it with a carefully thought out plan of treatment which should be followed as completely as the institutional facilities will permit. The staffs of the holding institutions are therefore able to devote most of their time and energy to treatment and training.

4. Provide a sound orientation program for all inmates, designed to facilitate their adjustment to institutional life and to develop attitudes which will enable them to make the most of opportunities offered in the institution in preparing for eventual adjustment in a free community. The first few weeks and months of an inmate's stay in an institution are extremely important. During this time, he should develop an understanding of what his stay in the institution can mean to him and that it is to his interests to make the most of his opportunities. In other words, unless he early develops the idea that he should "make time serve him," it is not likely that he will ever make such a decision.

5. Assist in the improvement of institutional programs based on the close study of inmate characteristics and needs made at the Reception Center. The Reception Center is in a position to concentrate on the central problems of inmates and the types of treatment needed. Such study should reveal the need for additional specialized institutions not provided in the state system, and also the need for additional or improved treatment facilities in existing institutions.

6. Carry on the development of research concerning the causes and treatment of delinquency.

Location and Physical Facilities

The Reception Center occupies a unit of Elmira Reformatory paralleling 375 feet of the north wall and including 132 feet of the east side or front of the Reformatory. The large cell block contains 352 outside cells; these are arranged in four tiers, 88 cells to a tier, with 44 cells on either side of each tier. The cellblock itself opens into the Reformatory auditorium at the far end, thereby providing easy access to the auditorium for motion pictures and Protestant religious services. Catholic services are held in the Reformatory Catholic chapel. The front end of the cellblock opens on one side into the yard between the Reception Center cellblock and D Block of the Reformatory, thereby providing an outdoor recreation area 390 by 80 feet. In addition to the large cellblock, there is a small cellblock (B Block) which originally contained 64 inside cells. Nineteen of these cells have been removed or taken over for storeroom, employees' toilets, and other purposes, leaving 45 cells for additional inmate housing. Seven cells on the lower tier of B Block are now used for segregation purposes and 14 on the upper tier next to the medical unit are used for an infirmary. There is, therefore, over-all regular housing accommodation for 376 inmates.

In addition to the cellblocks, there are six areas, each about 50 feet by 50 feet, which have been altered to provide the necessary offices and space for program activities. These areas house the following facilities:

1. Business and administrative offices; board room

2. Medical unit including examination room, drug room, and laboratory; the chaplains' offices; the parole office

3. Exploratory vocational shop

4. Recreational room

5. Psychological and psychiatric unit

6. Classrooms, testing and orientation room

The ground floor has been altered to include front entrance, key room, visiting room, receiving and package room, clothing room, shower room, and barber shop.

The Reception Center is, therefore, self-sufficient except for the following facilities and services which are provided by Elmira Reformatory:

1. Kitchen and messhall. Reception Center inmates eat at different times than Reformatory inmates.
2. Laundry.
3. Maintenance and repairs.
4. Hospital,—for serious illness and emergency cases only. All physical examinations and treatment for minor illnesses are handled in the Reception Center. There are rarely more than one or two Reception Center inmates in the Elmira Reformatory hospital.
5. Utilities,—power, light, heat, and water.

Administration of the Center

Although located at the Elmira Reformatory, the Reception Center is an entirely separate institution as far as administration and population are concerned. The director of the Center is responsible only to the Commissioner of Correction. Separate appropriations are made for the Center's operation and maintenance. The populations of the two institutions are kept entirely separate.

Time Spent at the Center

The law does not specify the length of time which an inmate may be held at the center. In practice, inmates are held about 75 days before transfer. This period includes about two weeks of reception and orientation, six weeks in the observation and study program, and from one to two weeks awaiting transfer. A few inmates, particularly those with very low intelligence, and tubercular cases are sometimes transferred in less than 75 days. Difficult cases, particularly seriously disturbed personality problems, are occasionally held longer than the usual time for more extensive study.

No one can be paroled from the Center nor is anyone held at the Center throughout his sentence.

Organizational Plan

There are at all times eight groups at the Center: one in reception, six in various stages of the program, and one waiting transfer. The inmates received each week constitute a group (except as indicated below) and proceed through the program activities together, although the staff study concentrates at all times on the individual. The size of the groups must depend a good deal on the intake, over which the Center has no control. At present, no more than 25 are being started through the program each week. When more than 25 are received in one week, the excess is held over in the hope that the following week's intake will be less than 25, thereby permitting inclusion of the "holdovers."

Program

The program at the Reception Center consists of three definite phases: Reception-Orientation-Group Testing; Study and Observation; Classification.

Reception, Orientation, Group-Testing. This is a vital period in the lives of most inmates, since it is during this period that impressions are formed, information given that frequently affects future institutional adjustment, and to some degree, ultimate rehabilitation. A poor start is costly to the inmates and institutions alike. For this reason, the Reception Center makes a concentrated effort to receive men in a way that will encourage their cooperation. New men are organized into a reception company and kept together as a unit in charge of two officers who supervise all of their activities. These include recreation, military drill, instructions in rules and regulations, personal hygiene, and care of cells. They quickly learn that the Reception Center has definite objectives, high standards and a sincere interest in the welfare of each man.

Many procedures must be completed during this period of from one to two weeks in order that the inmates may be ready to enter the scheduled activities program on time. These preliminary procedures include:

1. Reception, cell assignments, physical check
2. Shower and barber
3. Clothing and supply issue
4. First letter
5. Group orientation meetings
   a. The Center—director
   b. Living in an Institution—assistant director
   c. Parole—supervising parole officer
   d. Rules and Regulations—company officers
6. Finger prints, picture, and Division of Criminal Identification card
7. Blotter sheet
8. Complete physical examinations
9. Initial interview—chaplains
10. Initial interview—parole officer
11. Group tests—psychologists—three half-days
12. Orientation—reception company officer
    a. Care of cell, cleanliness of person, conduct, basic military.

These procedures must all be completed between the time the inmate arrives and the second Monday thereafter.

Early in the reception period, the men are put through the usual identification routine. After this is completed, they are given a complete physical and medical examination.

They are now ready to enter a part of the reception-orientation period that will prepare them for the testing and study-observation program. This part of the orientation includes an initial interview with his chaplain in order to acquaint him with his spiritual advisor. It also gives the chaplains the opportunity to become acquainted with the men early in their stay and to learn something of their problems. The chaplains see them several times before the completion of the program.

A parole officer conducts a group orientation session to explain parole and answer questions concerning preparation for and rules on parole. Representatives from the Division of Parole assigned to the Reception Center also interview each man to establish early contact for the Division of Parole and also learn of any sources of information that may be contacted for material to help in the study of the case. The parole officer also requests investigations by the Executive Division of Parole in cases where there are no probation reports or where the probation reports are inadequate for a thorough appraisal of the social background. This service has proven to be very effective and the material gathered by the parole investigators has been of high quality. The parole officer also prepares a summary of the delinquent and social history, including material from the interview, which serves both the Center staff and Parole.

As a part of the orientation program, the director and assistant director meet with each reception company. In these meetings, the inmates are informed of the responsibilities of the Center and the responsibilities of the inmates in the Reception Center program. Rules and regulations are thoroughly explained, and the best way of living in an institution is stressed.

In the final three afternoons of the reception-orientation period, the inmates are turned over to the psychologists for group testing. In this first phase of the psychologists' work, standard tests and questionnaires are administered in the areas of intelligence quotient, educational achievement, vocational aptitudes, vocational interests, personality. The lengthy, and for some inmates, rather arduous sessions are admittedly not ideal, but are required in order that at least tentative data be supplied to other staff members as early as possible. The proposed added week would alleviate this situation, at least in part.

The two company officers who will

supervise the group throughout the program part of their stay meet with the company to explain what is expected in the custodial situation.

Study and Observation Program. During this period the program of study and observation of the individual is intensified and expanded. This phase of the program, in addition to numerous individual interviews, includes: two classes per week in general education, each class meeting for two hours; vocational try-out shop, meeting four hours weekly; supervised recreation and physical education, meeting four hours weekly; and work periods and military drill which consume about six hours weekly.

Early in the study and observation program, the *psychologists* supplement the group tests by individual interview and in many cases by individual testing. Individual tests are given whenever the group test scores are low or widely divergent or at variance with the examiner's impression, or when anything in the inmate's history or abilities or present behavior suggests that more definitive determination is desirable. A few cases are also given more intensive study at the request of other staff members. The material employed may vary from one or two brief tests to complete batteries of both verbal and non-verbal nature, and is selected not only for value in attaining more refined measurement, but also for the light it throws on personality structure. Some use of projective techniques has been made. Time is not available for as complete psychological study as would be desirable for many cases.

Psychiatric services play a most important part in the operation of the Center, not only from the point of view of those functions usually considered in the realm of psychiatry, but also from the point of view of maintaining high standards in safety, security, and custody. When inmates are received at the Center, the various individuals who come in contact with them first have been trained and instructed to observe carefully any indications of peculiar or abnormal behavior. The probation and other reports are also examined to ascertain such factors as previous head injuries, confinements in mental hospitals, epilepsy, homosexual activities, and similar facts. This combination of observation and examination of records reveals those individuals who need to be referred immediately to the psychiatrist. Such cases continue to be under the general observation of the psychiatrist during their entire stay in the Center. Members of the staff, including custodial officers, are informed concerning these cases. Thus if difficulties are encountered in handling such inmates or if abnormal behavior occurs, therapy can be undertaken promptly.

The final psychiatric examination of all inmates is made usually during the latter part of their participation in the program. By this time, considerable data is available, including the social history, staff observations, medical report, and psychological data. An accurate and comprehensive evaluation of the boy's personality is extremely important in the determination of the institution to which the inmate is to be transferred, the type of program he should follow, and the probability that he can learn to make a successful adjustment. More than one interview is frequently required to arrive at a sound diagnosis, and in especially difficult cases, the psychiatrist, psychologist, and other staff members hold special conferences in an attempt to resolve the various problems presented.

The electroencephalograph is used in those cases in which there is indication of epilepsy or brain trauma. This makes possible clarification of clinical diagnoses, as well as occasionally revealing things which might otherwise not become apparent.

The *general education* program works

toward two major objectives. One is diagnostic, designed to ascertain educational strengths and weaknesses and to recommend suitable educational programs for each person. The other objective deals with goals and attitudes. The methods used are designed to encourage the individual to talk out his problems, to lead him to recognize desirable goals and ways of reaching them, and to develop an understanding of and a desire to take advantage of the opportunities that lie ahead.

The general education program attempts to have each man enter the next institution with an understanding of his past school experiences and how they have affected his present attitudes toward education, and with an acceptable educational plan. The general education program of the Center should also develop in each individual confidence that he can carry his plan out because he knows that his potentialities, his personality manifestation, and educational needs are understood.

The final report of the general education supervisors attempts to make clear to the personnel in the next institutions the educational potentialities of each inmate, through an evaluation of his performance in the learning situation, his group reactions, and diagnostic analysis of needs in the basic skills. The report also indicates the starting point and the desired ultimate goals, together with suggestions as to methods.

The procedures used by the general education supervisors include:

1. Discussion techniques
2. Visual aids having social content to stimulate thinking and reactions concerning home and family, delinquency, social adjustment, and personal goals
3. Analysis of test results, and supplementary testing
4. Personal interviews
5. Study of case history

Correspondence with school authorities is carried on in a good many cases to obtain additional information as to the educational history and especially to secure transcripts in those cases where a boy has completed part of a high school program. Other Reception Center staff findings, particularly those of the psychologists, are utilized.

Classes provide opportunities to evaluate the teacher-pupil relationship, and to try out different approaches. These classes also aid in evaluating major weaknesses and strengths in basic skills, as well as the rate of progress to be expected and the relationship between expressed interests and perseverance. Lesson assignments are not made, but opportunities are given for the inmate to correct his weaknesses and study on his own. Psychometrics are used to determine discrepancies between present performance levels and estimated optimum levels.

Group activities are carried on, using the principles of nondirective and permissive approaches to achieve frank expression of feeling and attitudes. The individual talks out his problems, receives the reactions of his group, tries for status, and in other ways reveals his feelings concerning education, social values, and problems of adjustment. Furthermore, it is possible through this method to estimate the degree to which he can control basic hostility, aggression, or shyness because of his desire to succeed in the group. In this atmosphere some direction is used to help the individual begin a re-evaluation of his ideas about himself, his problems, and social institutions. Individual interviews are used to evaluate his sincerity and the meaning of his group reactions and attitudes. During these interviews an acceptable education program is worked out with him.

The general education report includes the salient points in the boy's educational background; sets forth his educational status, needs, and potentialities, delineates his reactions and attitudes towards self-improvement. Specific educational recommendations are made.

The main general education recommendations include the following:

1. Train for literacy
2. Remedial education
3. Refresher work
4. Social education
5. Cell study in a particular area
6. Regents 8th
7. Regents high school
8. Commercial education
9. Related technical training

Specific recommendations in the social education field indicate the attitudes and social and ethical concepts which require most attention in the individual case.

The *vocational program* at the Center is primarily a tryout and vocational counseling service. The major objectives of this phase of the study program are:

1. To acquaint inmates with the opportunities available to them in the other institutions.

2. To determine the abilities of each inmate to handle tools, to follow directions, to maintain sustained effort, and to get along with others on a job.

3. To help each inmate to plan a vocational program which he can handle, which he believes in, which can be followed in the next institution, and which appears to lead to definite outcomes in the boy's development and employability after release.

The two supervisors share the job, each taking full responsibility for alternate companies. Each company is scheduled for two 2-hour periods in the shop weekly. During the first week the company is briefed on the purposes of the shop, opportunities in the other institutions, shop rules, and procedures. Each inmate is given written material covering the more important aspects of vocational planning and a list of training activities available in the other institutions. Along with this he is given a questionnaire, used to determine his vocational interests and his preference in regard

to the activities available in the Center shop. This is used in making the inmate's initial assignment. Each inmate is expected to work in at least two areas. At the present time the tryout areas available in the shop are: auto, plumbing, sheet metal, wood, electricity, machine shop, art, printing, and welding. A record is kept of each inmate's accomplishments and an estimate, based on observation, is made of his ability and attitude. During the last two weeks of a company's six weeks in the program, reports are written on each inmate. These include a digest of pertinent facts from observations, and from the case history, such as educational achievement, work record, job possibilities. An interview is held with each inmate during this period, prior to the completion of his report, even though several interviews may have been held previously. On hand at the time of final interview are the psychometric results, data from the case history, and shop observations.

The final vocational report contains the following:

1. Inmate's school attainment and trade training received, his adjustment when he left school, any previous institution, his adjustment and training

2. Work history and available characterizations of inmate by former employers

3. Vocational preference indicated when he entered the program, what he did in the shop, how he did it, how he got along

4. Significant elements of the final interview

5. Discussion of inmate's vocational assets and liabilities, degree of initiative and dependability, and prognosis of his vocational adjustment

6. Summary

7. Recommendations and alternative

Every effort is made to help the inmate make a choice of a vocational program rather than to write a prescription.

The *physical education and recreation*

program at the Reception Center is devoted to the evaluation of each boy's leisure-time interests, attitudes and abilities. This evaluation is made by placing the boy in different play situations and observing his reactions. These observations serve as a guide to the supervisor in recommending a suitable program for the individual after he is transferred to another institution.

An orientation period is given when a new company enters the program. The supervisor outlines the purpose of the physical education classes and recreation periods. The values of a supervised and well-rounded program of activities and of proper leisure-time activities are stressed. A questionnaire is filled out by each boy, pertaining to his personal leisure-time activities, noting sports, hobbies, leisure-time clubs or groups, etc. The few boys in each group who cannot properly fill out this questionnaire are interviewed immediately by the supervisor.

Boys who are physically fit are expected to take an active part in the physical education and recreation program. Each boy attends one physical education class each day during his time in the regular program and is placed for a time in a group activity program so as to observe and evaluate behavior in a group play situation. Calisthenics and a partial physical efficiency test taken from the West Point Physical Efficiency Tests are administered to each boy. In this way, muscular coordination and physical weaknesses are observed.

The boys are allowed to gravitate toward the activity which most interests them. The aggressive type usually prefers individual contest activities like boxing and wrestling, which project their personality and give them a feeling of satisfaction. A large percentage of the population participates in the non-contact individual and group activities, such as handball, volleyball, softball, table tennis, crossbar, and tumbling.

The physical education supervisor uses a work sheet with the boy's picture attached to record his findings on the boy from observation and working with him in the program. The main points of interest on this sheet are the results of the physical efficiency tests, the extent of participation and ability in the various activities in the program, and the attitude and personality picture of the boy during his stay in the program. A report is then prepared, based on the work sheet and observation of the boy in the program.

The recommendation of the physical training supervisor indicates to the recreation worker in the receiving institution the type of program that may assist a particular individual. Summarized below are the major types of recommendations made and the reasons for them.

a. Regular physical training program

A boy who is active and interested in physical activities and sports, cooperative, a good mixer in a group situation, and has some athletic ability. He has assumed a good attitude in the program and should adjust.

b. A program of group games with emphasis on fundamentals

A boy who is timid or shy because of his lack of ability in sports activities. One who would rather play individual non-contact games. Probably a boy with a rural background who participated very little in sports while not incarcerated. He should, with proper motivation, be placed in a group situation.

c. Supervised team games

A boy who has good ability in competitive team games. He has a knowledge of the rules, but he is inclined to argue and become overly aggressive if the situation arises. His attitude *toward* the program is good, but his attitude *in* the program is poor.

d. Medical excuses

Are referred to the physical training

supervisor for further evaluation by the institution physician before an activity program is set-up.

e. Interview with physical training supervisor

A boy who is hard to reach. One who has never taken part in physical activities and states that he is not interested. His attitude *in* the program may be conforming, but his attitude *toward* the program is poor. Occasionally such cases require psychiatric evaluation to determine the advisability of an active recreational program.

f. A program of corrective exercises to help this boy's physical development, muscular and postural defects.

A *company officer* plan carries on the study and observation in the custodial phase of the program. The custodial staff not only maintains custody and discipline, but also makes direct contributions to the study of the inmate through this plan. Each company is in charge of the same two officers for the entire working day during the full period of study and observation. In addition to their duties in connection with institutional operation, the company officers study and observe each man in the company, especially with reference to his response to orders and authority, care of self and cell, type of supervision needed, attitudes toward work and his relationships to inmates and officers. The company officers are particularly watchful for peculiarities and for signs of personality difficulties.

When the company is first assigned to these officers, they study the probation reports and other material so that they have information in regard to each inmate in their group. As the company progresses through the program, the officers counsel with each inmate in regard to his adjustment, confer with various members of the staff with regard to special problem cases, and record the results of their observations.

Each company has work periods each day, devoted largely to cleaning and other maintenance activities. The company officers, therefore, have some opportunity to evaluate the energy, initiative, and perseverance shown by the inmate as well as his capacity to go ahead with a job with or without close supervision. Each company also devotes some time to military drill, although after the reception period, this amounts only to about one hour per week. Other periods are devoted to free recreation, either in the yard or at tables on the flats. The company officers also accompany their group to the various program activities. They have, therefore, an excellent opportunity to observe the attitudes and reactions of the inmates in several types of situations.

The company officers, at the end of the period, submit a report incorporating the results of their observations of each man, which becomes a part of the Reception Center report. The officers also note in their reports previous escapes or attempts to escape, any evidence of assaultiveness either in the past or during the stay at the Center, any homosexual tendencies, and other items which are of particular interest in the custodial situation. The officers participate in the staff meeting at the time their particular group is being considered.

The *religious program* is composed of religious services and study and counseling by the chaplains. The chaplains strive to see each boy at least three times during his stay at the Center. In many cases, additional interviews are held, either because of special problems or because of the request of the inmate himself to talk with the chaplain. The chaplain also talks with the parents and relatives who visit the inmates. The chaplain evaluates the boy's religious background and training and the extent to which religion plays a part in his life. Every attempt is made also to prepare the boy to progress in his observation of his religious obligations at the next institution as well as to respond to continued counseling and guidance.

The *senior social worker* evaluates the family and environmental situation out of which the inmate came and into which he will probably return; handles special problems of inmates revealed in the probation reports, inmate correspondence, referred by other members of the staff, or brought to the social worker by the inmate himself; and coordinates the reporting procedures on inmates, particularly with regard to special features of each case. The special problems which most frequently arise involve relationship with inmate and his family, girl friends, finding suitable outside contacts for inmates who have no parents or relatives, assisting with welfare of families, adjusting difficulties due to social and personality factors, etc. Relatives visiting inmates are interviewed by the senior social worker.

The *medical department* makes two complete physical examinations and two check-ups during a boy's stay at the Center. A check is made at the time the inmate is received; a complete physical examination is given within a very few days after reception; a complete check-up is made prior to the board presentation of the case; and a final check-up is made prior to the transfer. In addition to supervising the health of the inmates during their stay, the medical department at the Center evaluates the physical condition of the inmate, noting any special handicaps, need for surgical or other medical treatment, and makes a detailed study of any abnormal physical condition. The policy is to postpone the correction of physical defects until after transfer to the next institution, except in emergency cases. One exception to this policy is the recent development which will make it possible to examine and provide glasses for those boys whose vision is so limited as to be a definite handicap in their participation in a training and treatment program.

Classification. The culmination of the Reception Center study program is the meeting each week when the staff assembles in case conference to review and discuss each inmate and to prepare final recommendations. Each staff member presents his findings, and these are discussed to bring into sharp focus a picture of the inmate, the problems he presents, his assets, liabilities, needs, and potentialities. Following the completion of the study program, all staff members supervising and working with the group to be considered submit their reports. These reports go together to make a 12-to-15 page summary. Attending the staff board are all the staff members who have worked with the particular group under consideration. At each meeting there are, therefore, the following: a psychologist, psychiatrist, physician, general education supervisor, company officers, chaplains, senior social worker, parole officer, the assistant director, and the director. The findings in each case are discussed in detail, and full and free discussion takes place. In addition to the detailed findings and recommendations in each area, concerted effort is made to determine what appear to be the most outstanding problems in each case and to point up these problems for special attention at the next institution, together with suggestions for possible solutions. After discussion, a vote is taken to determine to which institution the inmate should be transferred.

Following the board meeting, the entire report, together with recommendations, is forwarded to the Commissioner of Correction for his approval or revision. When these recommendations are approved, the inmates are transferred to the designated institutions and two copies of the Reception Center report are forwarded with the inmate.

Reception Center Report

The Reception Center composite study consists of nine sections. These are: 1) medical, 2) psychiatric, 3) psychological, 4) general education, 5) vocational education, 6) physical education, 7) chaplain's, 8) custodial and 9) inmate's cumulative chronological record.

In each of these, salient factors pertaining to the inmate with respect to the area of work involved are set forth, and appropriate recommendations made, to serve as a guide for the personnel at the receiving institutions. It is believed the over-all picture presented by these combined reports offers significant data which, if employed in handling the inmate at the holding institution, should result in definite progress toward his adjustment in free society.

The over-all report prepared at the Center on each inmate includes more than the various Center area reports listed above and constitutes the beginning of the cumulative chronological record which is carried on throughout the inmate's institutional stay and on parole. The form of this cumulative record is a comparatively recent development, and represents a joint enterprise of the Department of Correction and the Division of Parole in the Executive Department. It consists of:

1. Reception Center transfer recommendation and Commissioner's approval, legal and medical data;

2. Summary of delinquent and social history and of the parole officer's interview with the inmate;

3. Summaries of the reports of the individual staff members of the Reception Center;

4. Recommendations of the Reception Center in each area of investigation;

5. Complete Reception Center reports listed above;

6. Chronological record.

The parole officers assigned to the Reception Center are responsible for the compilation of Part 2 mentioned above. The whole chronological report, beginning at the Center and continued in the next institution and on parole, represents real progress in coordinating the work of the Department of Correction and the Division of Parole in the treatment of each inmate and in implementing the generally accepted and sound concept that "parole begins when the inmate enters the institution and correction ends with successful adjustment in the community." In the Reception Center, this cumulative chronological record can be developed only to the extent that information with respect to the inmate is immediately available. Additional information about the inmate will be secured through subsequent investigations made by the Division of Parole and through experience with the inmate in the holding institution. The process of recording all information chronologically in one running record builds up a body of significant data by the time the inmate appears before the Board of Parole. This comprehensive record provides an excellent basis for evaluating the possibilities of successful adjustment in free society and sets forth specific problems needing particular attention on the part of the supervising parole officer. This record is also of great value to the institution in initial programing and periodic evaluations. Of great importance in this chronological record are interpretative statements concerning the accomplishment, progress, general reaction, and attitudes displayed by the inmate during his stay in the holding institution. The continuation of this record started at the Reception Center is an important function of the service units in the various institutions.

Post-Board Interviews

Subsequent to the staff meeting, each inmate considered at the meeting is assigned to a particular member of the staff for follow-up interview. In this interview, the findings of the Reception Center are pointed up for the inmate and interpreted for him in terms of efforts which he must make if he is to achieve the status of a self-supporting and responsible citizen. The program which has been recommended is also clarified for the inmate to make sure that he understands the various plans for treatment and training which he has discussed previously with various staff members. Inmates are told where they are to be transferred, but not when. Reports from other institutions indicate that most inmates, upon reaching the institution to which they are transferred, are prepared to start on a specific program and evidence a desire to make definite progress.

On the custodial staff of the Reception Center are officers from practically every other institution in the Department of Correction. Each inmate considered at the staff meeting is therefore also assigned to a custodial officer who has worked in the institution to which the inmate has been recommended. This officer explains to the inmate the operation of the institution as he knows it, physical facilities, discipline procedures, and other pertinent factual information. The inmate therefore leaves the Reception Center with some idea of the institution to which he is being transferred. Comments received from the holding institutions indicate that this practice has considerable merit. It facilitates the process of orientation in the holding institution and thus makes it possible for the inmate to get into a training and treatment program earlier than might otherwise be normally expected.

Transfer Possibilities

The decision as to where an offender shall be transferred from the Reception Center is entirely within the jurisdiction of the Department of Correction, and any offender may be sent to any institution in the Department regardless of the offense or of the sentence, with the single exception that only felons may be sent to a State prison.

The Center has the following transfer possibilities available:

1. Three reformatory-type institutions
2. Institution for male defective delinquents (for mental defectives with I.Q. of 70 or below)
3. Correctional institution (for offenders of borderline intelligence, approximately I.Q. of 70 to 80)
4. Two institutions for mentally ill delinquents
5. Six maximum-security state prisons (Transferees are all felony cases and are usually those who have a long delinquent history, those with long minimum sentences, those who have served terms in several other institutions, and/or are less hopeful or are considered to be dangerous. In those cases where the needs of the individual call for specialized services or training programs available in some but not all State prisons, the Center recommends a specific prison. In most cases, transfer to "State Prison" is recommended without designation and the particular prison is specified by the central office of the Department of Correction.)
6. Medical transfers
7. Department of Social Welfare

Transfer of special cases of boys who are so immature, even though they are 16 years of age or over, that they are not suitable for institutions in the Department of Correction must be approved by the Commissioners of Correction, Social Welfare and Mental Hygiene.

Clerical and Stenographic Work

The clerical and office work required at the Reception Center is, in some respects, unique as compared to similar work in regular correctional institutions. This is because the Center, in addition to being a correctional institution receiving the largest number of prisoners in a given period from the various courts, is also a classification and diagnostic unit.

It is necessary to handle a tremendous

amount of legal matters with the various courts throughout the State regarding commitments and legalities. It should be borne in mind that the Center receives Misdemeanants, Wayward Minors, Youthful Offenders, Felons, and some other types of commitment cases, including Mental Defectives in our age group.

As a receiving institution, it is necessary to compile the various records and forms required by various agencies and this Department, including fingerprints, blotter sheets, etc.

In addition to receiving duties, the institution has to provide for its maintenance, personal service, and business operations the same as any other institution.

In regard to the classification clerical work, a 12-page (8 copy set) Reception Center report is prepared for each prisoner received (about 1250 per year). This report is made as a result of the findings of the following staff: medical, psychologists, psychiatrists, recreational supervisor, general education supervisors, vocational education supervisors, and custodial. It takes a clerical force of 15 employees working at maximum effort to effect the clerical requirements at the Center.

Personnel

The present personnel provided for the Center to accomplish the program set forth above is as follows:

Director, assistant director, senior physician, 2 graduate nurses, 2 associate clinical psychiatrists, 2 senior psychologists, psychologist, psychology intern.

3 correction institution education supervisors (academic), 3 correction institution education supervisors (vocational), 2 correction institution education supervisors (recreational), 2 resident chaplains, senior social worker, lieutenant, 4 sergeants, 38 prison guards.

Identification officer, head clerk, principal account clerk, senior clerk, clerk, 3 senior stenographers, 5 stenographers, 2 typists, chauffeur.

Some persons who have visited the Center have expressed surprise at the scope of the physical set-up and the personnel provided as well as the comprehensive program carried on. Apparently it is larger and more extensive than most people realize. It is by no means too large. The intake has been so heavy that it has strained both the physical facilities and the staff to carry out the functions of the Center adequately.

Cooperation of the Courts and Probation Departments

The establishment of the Reception Center brought about considerable change with respect to the courts' committing to a particular institution, since all commitments in this age group are required to be made to the Reception Center. In spite of this modification, as far as can be determined, the Reception Center has been well received by the majority of the courts of the State, many of which have indicated that they appreciate the service which the Reception Center is rendering. Intensive effort has been made to acquaint the courts with the purposes of the Reception Center through direct visitation. Many of the courts of the State have been thus contacted, particularly those from which most of the Center's intake is received. The result has been the establishment of a mutual understanding and a friendly spirit of cooperation. The probation departments of the various counties have likewise been contacted with resultant similar beneficial results. The quality of the probation reports received from the probation departments is highly important in the work of the Reception Center, and their cooperation is deeply appreciated.

The Group Worker's Role in an Institution for Juvenile Delinquents*

By Gisela Konopka. School of Social Work, University of Minnesota.

IN THE SUMMER of 1948 the University of Minnesota gave me a research appointment to study the contribution that a trained group worker can make in an institution for juvenile delinquents. In many out-patient settings, such as child guidance clinics, we have realized in the past years the value of supplementing individual treatment with therapeutic group work. We have a beginning of the use of this method in several psychiatric hospitals, but we have thus far badly neglected the institutions for delinquent youngsters. Our "training schools," or whatever name is given to them, are in most cases "detention facilities."

The establishment of youth commissions in different parts of the country is a step forward in recognizing the youthful offender as a person in need of help rather than punishment. In 1948 Minnesota created its Youth Commission and the first reception centers under its auspices with the explicit purpose of helping in "diagnosis and treatment of the juvenile delinquent." Because of lack of funds, those reception centers were established in the existing state training schools, used the existing staff, and in many ways had to conform to the routine of the training schools. Such a reception center was used for the experiment.

The Routine Day

At the time of my arrival about 70 boys were living in the cottage. It was a quickly changing group. New boys were continually brought in, and others were left after the Youth Commission had made a decision regarding further plans. The boys were sent to the training school, put on probation at home, or sent to a foster home.

It is easily understood that the atmosphere in the reception center, therefore, was filled with anxiety, extreme insecurity, defiance, and real fear. Here youngsters lived together in a strange environment after having been pulled out of their home environment usually after a difficult encounter with police, jails, and court. A routine day in the institution and at the reception center follows:

The boys got up at 6:00 o'clock, made their beds, had breakfast. To avoid contact with the boys regularly committed to the training school, meals were taken in the large dining room before the other boys came in. The boys always marched in formation from one building to another.

After breakfast some of the boys helped with cleaning, while others were in the basement—this was the shower and locker room in which the boys were asked to stay when they were not on duty. From about 9:00 to 11:00 a.m. they did some chores such as cleaning up the grounds, cutting beans for canning, etc. After 11:00 a.m. they were again in the basement for about a half hour to clean up for the noon meal. After the noon meal they were in the basement, and at 1:00 o'clock they marched to the library of the training school.

The library is a very pleasant room

---

* Reprinted from *Federal Probation*, Vol. XV, June, 1951, pp. 15–23. Used by permission of author and publication.

with a great variety of books and some handicraft material. The boys chose their books and were allowed to take out books. During this hour they sat around tables and on the floor. At 2:00 o'clock the boys had gym if no other work had to be done. From 3:00 to 5:00 the boys were either in the basement or outside on the playground, usually playing ball-games. At around 5:00 o'clock they had supper. After this they returned to the basement or played for about an hour out-of-doors and then went to bed. They were allowed to listen to the radio or to read for about an hour. They slept in large locked dormitories.

This routine was sometimes interrupted by a visit from their families, by a visit to the hospital for a check-up, or by conferences with the caseworker, the probation officer, or the visiting psychiatrist. The boys never crossed the campus by themselves without a guard except for a few boys who had the confidence of the staff and who could be recognized by wearing a special belt. Strict conformity was required. Punishment consisted mainly of "standing on line." The boys would stand with crossed arms, not being allowed to sit down, or speak, or do anything else. Often the whole "company" had to stand "on line," if one of the boys had done something more serious such as running away. Punishment sometimes consisted in beating but this was definitely forbidden by the management of the training school and the Youth Commission, and members of staff were continually admonished to "keep hands off."

This quite drab routine was livened up by the human attitude of some of the staff members and the sincere efforts of the supervisor to create a more therapeutic atmosphere.

Reaction to Routine

I think it is self-evident that such strict routine does little to relieve anxiety and therefore open the way to any kind of treatment. It also makes diagnosis almost impossible. It struck me that not only aggressive but also withdrawn behavior was repressed this way. Conforming meant to act exactly the way everyone else acted and the way it was safest to live through this experience without being punished or prolonging the stay. There was no room for self-determination, and little room for showing anything of the true self. It seems to me that this basically explains so many of our failures with youngsters who behaved so well in the protected setting, but fell back into delinquency the moment they left the institution. Not only did they not receive help, but they were never allowed to show their real self. There simply was no way for them to act the way they really felt and, therefore, no way was open for the observer to see them and to give help.

To make diagnosis possible we must find a way to create a climate that allows the youngster to express his likes and dislikes, his fears and wishes, his resentment and his affection. That means that the experience of being segregated from the rest of the community, from his friends, his gang, and his usual environment must change into an experience of acceptance by contemporaries and adults, by some belief in one's own value and own strength. Certainly each delinquent is different and there are individual problems, but we must realize that in forcing them to live together we have created for them a group situation which must be used in the most skillful way to help toward better adjustment.

In addition to the fact that there is a given group situation we know that the group means a great deal to the adolescent. John R. Ellingston has said:

"To earn the right to belong he (the child) will adopt whatever code of behavior the gang or group prescribes regardless of how much it conflicts with society."

Since we could conduct the experiment

for one month only, we were sure that no final results could be achieved. All we could do was to try the value of a method that takes into account the understanding of individual and group behavior, that allows for a large amount of freedom and that is based on respect for the individual.

Detailed process records were kept and I want to present a few of them.

Selection of a Natural Subgroup for Experiment

It was clear that individual attention could not be given in a group of 70 boys. The group had to be broken down into smaller groups. How should this be done? We knew from previous experience how important good grouping is for purposes of therapy. Little was known about the individual boy. There was usually only a juvenile court record giving the reason for detention, but nothing else. In a few cases there was a case history available at the time of arrival. Some knowledge of the boy was gained through an initial interview by the caseworker and in some instances psychological examinations had been given. The grouping therefore could not be done very systematically. The group worker decided to observe the boys for one day, get acquainted with them, and choose a natural subgroup as the core of the group with which she would work.

Here is the record of this first contact.

Arrived at reception center around 1:30 p.m. The boys, about 60 of them, were scattered over the playground waiting for visitors. The first Sunday of each month is visiting day.

Supervisor introduced W. (worker) first to Arne. . . . Told him that W. would be around for the month of August and probably later would take on a group of boys but that W. would like to know all the boys if possible. Several boys sitting close by were interested and volunteered their names. One of them, Ralph, said his name only when another nudged him, and seemed quite disgruntled. Supervisor also

introduced W. to Bob who during the rest of the day kept very close to W. We kidded first some about names and how hard they are, etc., to become a little acquainted with each other. More and more boys crowded around. They spontaneously told from where they came.

Bob very quickly related to W. and was apparently hungry for such contact. He said sadly that nobody would come for him. His parents are divorced and, "I am on my own since I was 6 months old." He said if somebody only cared for him he might not be here now, and "if they would let us little kids work." He is "in" for "armed robbery." W. said that he did not look terribly "tough" and he said he wished now he had not done it. He hoped he would get into a boarding home. He repeated twice, "Miss S. thinks this is not the place for me." He pointed several boys out to W. and took his task to "introduce" W. very seriously.

Ralph was sitting on the bench, often staring into space as if he hardly saw anyone. Some boys teased him, said he was telling on others. Ralph said, "Nobody likes me here, they say one of the boys was sent to the training school because I told on him." Bob said with feeling, "I like you, Ralph, and he would have been sent there anyway."

Some other boys came to the bench. They asked what W. would do, whether W. would go with her group off the grounds. There was an apparent interest in something "new." A handsome boy with the name of Ted joined the group several times. He was lively, seemed something like a link between the older and the younger boys.

There was some talk about the candy some of the boys were getting and how some would not want to share and how they just take the candy away from them. There was much mentioning of the "Commission" and how they wanted to get before it and know what would happen to them.

Each boy also mentioned that three boys had "drifted" (run away) the previous day. They said that because of this they will have to stand in line all day for 15 days with hands folded and were not allowed to play with the exception of Sunday and when they worked. They said that one boy wanted to sit down but the attendant hit him. Mr. N. is smarter, they said. When he had to leave he said that they could sit down, because he knew that they would do it anyhow when they were alone.

W. caught a ball of one of the boys and soon about six of the younger boys and one older one (about 17) and W. were engaged in a long and fast ball game. One of the boys, Ferd, was especially intent on making W. lose. It was clear that he enjoyed trying to defeat an adult, but that he could do it in an almost friendly, acceptable way. A young blond boy, Walter, sat restlessly and dejectedly around saying sadly that nobody came for him. W. told him that it was only 3 o'clock and there might be a good chance that they yet might come. He suggested that he join the game. He did so, and while we laughed and ran and caught the ball he forgot the time and was happily surprised when his family finally arrived.

At around 4 o'clock the boys went inside. Two boys, Al and Leo, were on duty with the visitors. Both of them gave the impression of being especially friendly, sensitive boys. Al told W. that he really is on probation but it might take a long time until they find a farm where he can be. He would like to do farming. He said, "The hardest thing is to tell people that the time is up for a visit, but you have to do it." The other boy, Leo, asked W. with great interest and intelligence what W. would do. He said it would be good if somebody is around who can make things a bit more pleasant— "Sometimes you don't know *what* to do." Then he added, "I saw you playing with the kids. You are the first adult I have seen playing with them."

W. went downstairs where the boys stay about an hour before supper. It is a large empty room with benches at the walls. The older boys were in one group together smoking and talking. Some of the older boys sat in smaller groups playing cards. The younger ones sat around doing nothing, as far as W. could see. Only Ralph was working on some handicraft.

W. sat down beside Ralph on one side and Harry, the only colored boy in the whole group. On the playground the boys had pointed Harry out to W. and had said that he can get "real mad." W. wondered whether that does not happen to anybody once in a while and that started Bob out to tell how he got mad at the county school

and threw a billiard ball and others told how they got mad. W. asked Harry whether he had had any visitors and he said that he did, and that he hoped to go home soon. He says everything with a solemn, hesitant manner. Arne came over and was very affectionate with several of the boys sitting on their laps and holding them.

The boys said that they were not allowed to have a show this week because of the drifters. W. wondered whether they might like to put on their own show some time, and they seemed very enthusiastic. They wondered whether they could use the auditorium.

This time and the place seemed especially boring. We talked about other things to do, such as clay work, and everything was taken up with enthusiasm. W. had some pieces of paper and a pencil in her pocketbook and started some writing games. W. never thought that one could make such a hit. Harry, Bob, Ted, and Ralph played very intensely. If W. had had more paper many would have played. Bob showed a considerable amount of intelligence and skill in the games, Harry and Ted were average, Ralph was slow but wanted badly to be in on it. When W. told stories and drew pictures he became especially interested and tried to imitate more as a smaller child would do. In this group activity was also the youngest boy, Ed. He kept more by himself than some of the others.

While many boys stood around there was again talk about hearings before the Commission. Several mentioned their birthdays. Leo said, "A sad place to celebrate your birthday."

(W. wonders whether birthdays should not be celebrated somehow? They mean a lot to boys.)

There was again talk about W.'s "group." Several of the boys, Harry, Bob, Ralph, Ferd and an older boy, begged W. to take them into the group. W. said that we did not have to decide right away anyhow.

The boys went to supper.

W. met the boys after supper on the playground. A whole bunch greeted W. right away, stood around ready to talk or to do something. It was obvious that they waited for some initiative coming from W. W. wondered who knew a good game. The same boy who had spoken so intelligently about the need of doing something suggested a running game, and about 10 boys and W. played this game with a lot of laughter until W. was exhausted.

W. taught them a new game that is played sitting down. Bob and Ralph showed again their great need for attention, because they always wanted to be "it." Interestingly enough, the other boys seemed very tolerant of this need.

Several of the boys questioned whether W. would be around.

We see in this record the group worker using several principles of group work:

1. Start where your group is. To do this you must know where your group is and you must learn to know the members of your group as quickly as possible. We see the observation and the detailed recording of each boy who stands out as an individual. There is emphasis on observation of nonverbal material, so important in children, as in the case of Ralph "staring into space," Ferd's way of playing a game, or Arne's being affectionate with other boys.

2. Establish an informal, relaxed, friendly relationship. The group worker —and here he differs in his role often from the caseworker and psychiatrist— works indirectly with the problem of the group member. His contribution to an all-around treatment situation lies in working with the strength of the client, with the part that is healthy, making him feel comfortable in the knowledge that there *is* something healthy in him, that he is in some ways *not* different from other people. The group worker is at the same time aware of the sickness, too, and might at times work with it, but his specific task is to relax the emotionally upset person. We see this informal approach in the kidding about names, the spontaneous ball game *in which the worker takes part,* the running game, the sitting down with the boys in a place they especially dislike, such as the basement.

3. Use material or some kind of program as a helpful means to better mental health. Program is an important tool in group activity therapy. We see a begining here in drawing Walter into the game to help him overcome his fear of rejection by his family, and in the writing game in the basement.

The Group Meetings

A group of about 15 boys was formed, most of them around the age of 14 and 15 years. The reasons for their referral to the Youth Commission were various. In most cases it was their second or third "offense" which had brought them to the reception center. In most cases the "offense" consisted of stealing.

At the beginning of the group meetings, the boys showed the same conforming behavior that was requested of them in the institution. These meetings lasted 2 hours in the morning and 2 hours in the afternoon. Very soon the "group climate" changed. There were fights among the boys and reconciliations; complaints against treatment received; initiative in asking for some specific work; etc.

In this loosening-up process some of the boys showed considerable fear of this greater freedom. For the first time they were able to show their insecurity. They needed to make a greater effort when they had to make their own decisions, instead of doing what they were told. It was necessary to give them support and reassurance, while continuing to encourage them to express their feelings. Now individuals with their strengths and weaknesses emerged.

Leadership. Ray, for instance, a 14-year-old, handsome, strong boy was known to all the attendants only as an insignificant, rather conforming boy who caused "no trouble." In this group Ray showed more and more the qualities of a gang leader. Other boys followed him willingly even if he handled them roughly. He was often charming toward adults and youngsters alike, but he also showed a mocking attitude as if he wanted to say that really nobody mattered much. He showed little concern for anybody. Some of his remarks directed at other boys were cruel, yet the boys never challenged him. At the same time Ray showed a real talent for drawing which he hid first behind a great deal of smearing, until he felt more secure. Slowly he drew excellent cartoons and did some very good clay modeling.

The important point is that under the restricting circumstances in the institution Ray could not be seen the way he really was. There was also no way to help him to turn some of the strength that made him a gang leader into more constructive use.

The help given to him in the group had to be threefold. He had to learn (1) that he could gain recognition for a more acceptable kind of behavior; (2) to gain confidence in at least one adult; and (3) that he could continue being respected by his contemporaries even if he was not abusing them. Point one was partially satisfied by the recognition he got through his drawing and also through his skill in games. On point two I would like to quote from the record:

There was a scuffle around the pool table. W. had assigned Ralph to play, not realizing that it was not yet his turn. Ray had pushed him. Ralph sat on a chair doubled up as in agony and crying. Ray said he is a cry baby. W. said he might be really hurt and what was it all about? The boy explained and W. said to Ray that it was really her fault, was it not, and next time he should hit W. for that, not the other boy. His face looked blank, then he smiled—for the first time, W. thought, warmly without his usual irony—and said twice, "I am sorry, Ralph."

Ray was startled by an adult accepting the responsibility for a mistake made and this was the beginning of some change in him. On point three, the boys had talked once about elections. I quote again from the record.

Ray clamored for the election. W. suggested that we could at least start it and go on tomorrow. W. wondered whether he would write down the different offices. He did, asked a lot about spelling.

W. tried to call the boys together and calm them, which seemed like an impossible task. Ray again became the leader in the rough way of the gang leader who knows "how to handle them." He would pull boys and push little Ed into the circle. Ed hit back, etc. Arne sulked in a corner, said that he did not want any office anyway.

Ray suggested: one mayor, one judge, two policemen, three from the jury, one probation officer and one sheriff. The list of "government" officials certainly is indicative.

W. asked who wanted to run for mayor. Ray and Charles volunteered. When asked about election speeches, Ray became tongue-tied, murmured about giving good government and sending the kids to the judges and probation. Charles was less embarrassed, said that he would run the city well.

After the voting the record continues:

Only a short time after every boy had started "office," Ray made definite positive contribution to the group. As the mayor, he started to count his "citizens" which helped to check on the presence of everybody. Yet he did this in a friendly, nonauthoritarian manner.

Here we see the beginning of a change from the rough gang leader to a real leadership personality.

The gang leader plays a great role in the whole formation of juvenile gangs. If we can learn how to recognize and work with him, we will be a great step forward in our work with delinquents. For much too long a time we have only isolated or disregarded the gang leader.

After some time of observation in the group the group worker pointed out in her summary of Ray to the Youth Commission his leadership potentialities and suggested a closer relationship with a man since it seemed that he needed the identification with a strong male person.

The case history, received later, bore out this tentative diagnosis. When Ray was 7 years old his parents were divorced and he stayed with his mother and three siblings. His father remarried, but soon moved with his second family into the house of the first family.

The case history shows in the following years constant disorganization of the family. Father deserted, returned, deserted again, etc. Ray was sent away to relatives, was called back and sent away again. He finally burglarized a school, was put on probation, but broke probation by stealing several cars. The case history points out the lack of identification with a father person.

Emotional Difficulties. Group workers who work in neighborhood houses and other youth serving agencies are constantly in the position of working with emotional difficulties in children without the benefit of case histories. Clues come from individual behavior and relationship to the group. This skill will be needed badly in our institutions since we cannot expect to receive good case histories in each case because of lack of professional personnel in the communities from where the youngsters come and often work must be begun with a youngster a long time before case histories can be received.

Because of lack of time and space this paper cannot go more into all the aspects of working out inter-relationships in the groups. One question that is often asked is how difficult situations among easily excitable youngsters can be handled. Again most training schools will ask for restrictions and punishment when fights occur. To this question there is no general answer, but only the application of a general principle; even the difficult situation must be handled from the point of view of treatment, and not of retaliation.

The worker being with a group of youngsters under the trying circumstances of confinement in an institution must understand that often tempers flare up because of the close living together, the anxiety, and the accumulation of many unstable youngsters in one place. The freer the atmosphere the less conflict there will be. In many instances the worker will "feel" the rising conflict before it breaks out, and may open up channels early enough so that it does not turn into a tempest. Yet outbursts will not always be avoided. I am quoting from the record to give an example of such an incident:

. . . It was a hot day and the wind was blowing without any relief. This weather seems to make itself felt with everyone. The boys were restless.

Things went all right until Ed and Larry got into a fight. Both boys had no self control, but Larry had a real fit and was dangerous. He threw stones, took the scissors or a large pole. He is not very fast so W. could get hold of him. W. held his two arms, talking in a soothing voice until he relaxed under her hands. The difficulty was that Ed did not let him alone but provoked him. Larry's rage mounted again, and beside physical force he used terrible language. Again he reacted upon the holding and the soothing words like somebody coming out of a trance. He then lay down on the ground, perfectly exhausted, sweat standing on his brows. When he was rested a little W. asked him whether he wanted to draw and write out all his anger. He was perfectly willing to do this. Ed immediately asked for paper too.

The important point in this situation is that despite his tantrum the boy felt that the worker was not angry at him. The worker did not let him "just release," which is one of the dangerous concepts in therapeutic work, when it is carried to the extreme. She certainly limited him, but he could feel at the same time that she was not fighting him. We must also know that this event did not occur in a vacuum. The worker was not alone with those two boys. Fifteen other boys were present. Yet the fight was not carried over to the others. If the worker had reacted with violence, I am convinced that this would have involved violent reactions from others in the group. This way the conflict was isolated.

The Discussion Groups

Besides those activity meetings, discussion groups with a smaller number of boys were conducted. In the discussion groups the focus was on a very tangible problem. Indirectly this helped the boys to realize something about themselves, and their own reactions to their environment.

The first discussion group (Group 1) consisted of five boys, 14 years of age, who had their hearing before the Youth Commission and were told that they would go on probation the moment suitable placement was found for them. All four boys knew the worker through the informal activity meetings and therefore felt free in her presence.

The second discussion group (Group 2) consisted of four boys, 15 years of age, who had only recently come to the reception center and who seemed most disturbed, bitter and forlorn. These boys knew the worker from at least one meeting in the activity group. This method of introducing seems especially helpful to me since otherwise discussions often are strained and the boys need a much longer time to feel free and confident.

Group 1. Here is the record of the second discussion meeting with the first group of boys:

W. wondered whether there were other difficulties they would have to face after leaving the Center. Arne said it would be the people at home who would ask so many questions, where they had been, etc. Bob, Dale, and Walter were reasonably sure that they would not get into the same environment, but they all agreed that people might ask them at the new place too and anyhow, they hoped to visit at home. They all agreed that it was a tough problem to face people.

W. asked, "Why?" Bob slowly said, "Because it is a disgrace." Harry added, "It is, and they always think that it is your mother's fault." Arne said, "I have older brothers and they feel disgraced."

Worker: Let us think for a moment what that means. What is really the disgrace? To be here?
Dale: Oh, really the things we have done, but people think differently.

W. suggested to stick first to what we thought. Walter said that this was really a place which wanted to help them to get along better. W. said that they knew that this was not a jail. They understood, they said, but Arne said with feeling that they were closed up anyhow and beaten, and people don't always understand. W. suggested to the boys that this time we should stick to our difficulties and talk about the problems we would have when leaving here.

Arne: Yes, let's do that. Now, for instance, there is a man in a drugstore at the corner. I don't know whether he likes me and is interested in me or if he is mean and wants to tease me. Every time I come back he right away asks me where I have been, why I went there, etc. It makes me mad.
Worker: What do you answer, Arne?
Arne: It is none of your business.
Walter: Well, that will make him really mad at you.
Worker: What would you answer, Walter?
Walter: I was at the Y.C.C. because I got into trouble and now I know better and will get along.
Worker: What do the others think?
Harry: That won't make him so mad, but he will ask more.
Worker: Let's think for a moment why the man and others might ask such questions.
Arne: He wants to know.
Dale: He is jealous.
        The others laugh, "What should he be jealous about?"
Dale: I can't explain, it just seems to me. . . .

Worker:	Maybe Dale has something there —wait a minute. And what do others think?
Bob:	He is curious.
	The others agreed with the latter.
Worker:	Have you ever seen what people do when they see a soldier coming home with one arm?
Bob:	Sure, they always ask questions. And the soldier might not want to talk about it either.
Arne:	They are not really mean, they are just curious.
Worker:	Sure, see, people are that way. Your drugstore man probably too. And a friendly answer does help. But what about Dale? He said jealous. You know people always like to get some attention and you boys get it, even if it is not pleasant. The man probably does not know it, but maybe he likes some attention too.
Bob:	So it is better to give some friendly, steady answer.
Worker:	Do you think you boys can try now?
Arne:	I think I can, but it is tougher with the kids. They really tease you.
Harry:	Sure, they make you feel miserable. They ask, where have you been, what did you do? What do they do to you? Do they beat you? Do you get enough to eat? Tell us all about it.
Arne:	Harry knows; Harry went through it once.
Worker:	Why do you think the boys ask?
Dale & Bob:	Oh, they are curious too.
Arne:	And it sounds exciting.
Worker:	Sure, they like adventure and it is like an adventure story to them. What do you do when they tease you?
Arne:	Oh, I get mad, really mad.
Walter:	That won't help, Arne.
Worker:	Let's try it. One of you teases the other and he answers. (The boys all refused to be the teaser, fearing the other would really get mad at him.)
Worker:	O.K., I will tease Arne and he will answer.

W. does not recall this game verbally, but she repeated the things the boys had said, such as where have you been and you good-for-nothing, etc. Arne always answered defiantly, getting more and more angry until he got to a "you . . . you . . ." W. stopped at this point and asked what would come next? They all shouted that now a fight would come. One of them added, "and being on probation, that might end badly for you, Arne."

W. asked whether someone else would like to try. Walter was willing. This time Arne was the teaser. This dramatization was unusually realistic. Arne used every mean device. After he had asked the usual questions, he started with a dry "Well, you won't go straight. Started little and you will get worse. You will end in the penitentiary anyhow."

Walter stuck with an amazing calm to his guns. He always answered clearly. He gave a good interpretation of Y.C.C. He said he *tried* to go straight. On the penitentiary attack he said, "Maybe, but I will try not to." At another point he said, "I have been out for three weeks and I am still all right" after Arne had attacked him with, "I bet you can't go straight for three days."

Arne:	Oh, three weeks. Your parents probably kept you at home all the time. You are only good when you are in bed.
Walter:	I went to school, didn't I?
Arne:	Your poor mother—What she has to take!
Walter:	We are getting along all right now.

W. stopped the dramatic play at this point. The others discussed it, saying that it was helpful to get it so clearly. They would try to act as Walter in the play. W. said that she knew it would be harder when the teasing was real, but she hoped it helped to have thought it through a little and maybe, in the middle of the teasing, they might remember our discussion.

Preceding these discussions there was often first an outburst about conditions in the institution. This was very helpful because it made the boys free to come back to discuss their own difficulties. A preparation for "life outside" seems to me especially important. We have had a great deal of literature about the returning soldier and how to help him make the change from a confined life with many restrictions and constant living with many men to a civilian life, but we have not given much thought to the youngster who has spent a short or a long time under even more restricted circumstances at a very impressionable age. We send him out "on probation" without preparing him for all the difficulties he will encounter. One interview certainly may not help. One group discussion alone will not give much help either. Yet it is a beginning of their knowing that they are not alone in facing the difficult problem of returning to an often hostile environment.

Group 2. The beginning of the discussion with the new boys was more difficult, because they did not know the worker so well. I quote from the first record:

The group sat outside around the table and W. told the boys that she has asked them to come for an hour discussion because she thought they had a lot of questions on their mind. W. said that we could be very frank with each other here, that the more openly we discussed things the more helpful it would be. After today they could decide themselves whether they wanted more of this.

Gus started the ball rolling by asking what W.'s group was all about. W. explained in as simple terms as possible that we thought it helpful not to have the large group together all of the time; that W. also had found that it was good to have a few hours where the boys could decide on their own activity, make some of their own decisions. They would have to do this later on too. W. asked them whether they would like to do something specific. W. would try to provide it, if possible. Suggestions came fast from all five of the boys, mainly in terms of handicraft. Lastex work and making rings out of plastic were on the top of the list. W. was interested in the real need for such work that was expressed. W. asked whether there were other things in which they needed help. Roy said hesitantly that he would like to know what "YCC" meant, why they were here. Herb joined in, said he did not understand the whole thing. W. asked whether anyone had explained to them the Youth Commission set-up. Their faces were blank. Had the judges not told them? W. asked each one what the judge had said when he had suggested their coming to the YCC Reception Center. The answers can be summarized by Herb's answer: "He looked at some magazines and he looked at a big book and he said, YCC, and I was brought here."

(It was perfectly possible that the judges gave a much more detailed explanation. It only shows how upset the boys are at this point and how more often they need information.)

W. explained that Youth Commission means how the new law tries to help youngsters like them, how this is just a period of trying to learn to know them and then make a decision as to what would be best for them. Roger and Herb asked why, since this was not a punishment, they were allowed to be beaten by the attendants and why they were constantly locked in and watched. The others joined in on this, said how terrifying the locking in at night was especially. W. said that beating was not allowed, that they should let Miss S. know when it happened. The locking up, W. said, is mainly because of the fear that some would run away. W. said that she and everybody else working here do not think that everything is perfect, but that W. thought they were old and intelligent enough to know that things do not always work the best way. W. explained how young YCC was, explained about the lack of funds. It was interesting that the boys listened attentively, sometimes nodding assent.

Joe suddenly said in a bitter tone of voice that the whole thing was nonsense anyhow, they would all go to the Training School, and even if they are put on probation they all would be back some day. W. asked Joe why he thought this. In the same bitter tone he said that they all were no good anyhow, that they will do the same things they did before, he knows. He will do it too. (Joe's bitterness was pathetic. He is one of the most intelligent boys and apparently very hurt. He needs much help.)

The other boys, especially Herb, objected, "No, we will not do it again."

Gus: Sometimes you do those things because you had a raw deal.

Worker: Hm, there *are* reasons why we do these things. What happened to you, Gus?

Gus: Well, everything would be O.K. now, I would have a new family if I had not been caught. You know, I ran away from Boy's Town and I got along all right. I slept on the roofs and I met Arthur in a movie. Arthur is such a swell boy. And he took me home and his family would have adopted me.

Worker: Do you know anything about your parents, Gus?

Gus: (Apparently relieved that he can talk more about himself, pouring out his whole story) No, I don't know my father. But I have a mother, I have a mother. But I lived in a convent. And the Sisters said I had set fire, but I did not. I wished they don't say things. I did not set the fire. I ran away from the convent and later I ran away from Boy's Town.

Roger: He did have a raw deal. He has no parents. I have parents. I did not have a raw deal, but I stole a car. Lots of boys do, only I got caught.

Worker: If you were not caught, then the car stealing would be all right, Roger?

Roger: I don't know.

Worker: Would you like it if you had a car that somebody stole from you?

Joe: I would, if I had insurance. I would be glad if somebody stole it.

Herb: You are crazy, Joe. He might have to go somewhere fast and the car is gone. And it is wrong anyhow. You should not steal. (Here Roy, who usually was very quiet, nodded.)

Herb: I surely will never take a car again. Only I am so worried about my mother. She had in-

tended to move to California and now she can't because I am here. What will happen to us?

The third meeting shows how they have relaxed more and how they gain some insight.

Roger: I stole a car. Funny, all of us have taken a car or so. Most kids would not be here if it were not for cars.

Worker: That *is* interesting, Roger, is it not? It would help us to understand why we do this. When did you start thinking of taking a car?

This question was put to all four boys and they all said about when they were 13 years old.

During all this Roy sat silently, looking very unhappy. He said he would never tell why he came here. W. said this was all right. Did he want to leave the group? No, he wanted to stay, but he did not want to talk. He was told that this was all right.

W. said to the boys that it was interesting that they all started around the same age. They nodded thoughtfully. W. then explained in very simple terms about adolescence, without using the word. W. said that at that age both boys and girls get somewhat restless. Things change. They are not really children anymore. And because they are restless, they want to do a lot of things, "and go fast" added Roger. W. said he had hit it on the head. And going fast and having adventure was now connected with cars. W. said that it might be, also, that they wanted to impress a girl. Herb said with astonishment, "How did *you* know?" W. said it was not so unusual, we all, at that age, like to impress the other sex. Herb said the girls want a fellow with a car, and he felt so lonely. He again mentioned his parents' divorce. W. said that she knew it was hard feeling lonely. Gus said he was all alone, but he wanted to find a girl who did not need a car to love him (he said this very seriously) and Roger said he knew one who did not mind a fellow without a car, but he felt sometimes alone too. Joe said it was tough when your father is dead. . . .

These boys who usually pretend being

"tough," especially Joe and Roger, could now frankly admit that they often felt lonely and scared.

W. said that being lonely makes you do things sometimes which you later regret. Maybe we could help find things and people who help you over such times. Herb said, maybe these days had helped him a little, he understood things better. He added, "And I will go back to my mother. I know now that I can't have both of my parents."

Conclusions Drawn from Experiment

We were able to draw some conclusions from this experiment:

1. There is the need of a person, or several persons, on the staff of an institution who can handle a group situation in an informal, releasing way; who understands enough about dynamics of individual behavior to react in a therapeutic way; who understands the meaning of behavior; and who is able to make an intelligent report to other professional people on the staff.

2. We recognized that the more rigid the group climate, the less hope there is for accurate diagnosis.

3. We learned something about spontaneous grouping, knowledge of which is greatly needed to do better group work. Some of the principles of grouping we observed are:

(a) The more rigid the group climate, the smaller the group cohesion. In the rigid climate we find a great deal of fighting, "telling on each other," distrust. The more relaxed the group climate the more real "esprit de corps." There was genuine "we-feeling" in the selected group of boys.

(b) Spontaneous grouping did not occur according to the clinical difficulty of the boys, but more according to social maturity. Age was important mainly in terms of status. Being older meant being stronger; having had more adventures;

being allowed to smoke, knowing girls. Similar reactions toward the adult created subgroups. The boys who were more secure with adults than others formed a definite subgroup.

4. We learned that, as in most groups, work with the indigenous leader is important. Only in the presence of an accepting adult will this leader reveal himself. Help in working with him comes from direct work with him and from strengthening the rest of the group members so that they are able to get along without depending on him.

5. Group discussions are most helpful when they are preceded by some informal group meeting with the worker. The great contribution of the informal group meetings lies in their relaxing influence, in the feeling transmitted to the youngsters that they are not *all* bad, not *all* different from any other youngster in society. It is a strengthening of the ego by strengthening the *healthy* parts of it. In the group discussion the youngster is forced to focus on his problem. He will do it more frankly and with greater security in the presence of an adult with whom he has had a pleasant contact.

Institutions for delinquent youngsters should be staffed with teams similar to child guidance clinics. Since the youngsters live in close group associations the professional group worker is an essential part of this team. For too long a time we have either neglected our institutions for delinquents, or we have thought that an hour interview of an expert will help the youngsters. Professional services of psychiatrists, psychologists, caseworkers are indispensable, but they will be lost if the people who work daily and hourly with the boys are not directed toward the basic therapeutic aim of restoring in the youth a feeling of self-respect and a warmth toward other human beings.

If You Make the Boy Right, You Make the World Right*

By The Honorable Tom C. Clark. Justice, Supreme Court of the United States.

THE CREATION of the juvenile court marked the turning point in our recognition of the needs of children before the law. We realize that young people should be treated differently from adult offenders if their welfare is to be protected on the one hand, and the community adequately safeguarded on the other. I am sure that as much as we desire to protect and assist the child, we do not intend that he should be shielded from responsibility for the consequences of his acts. The welfare of the community cannot be separated from the welfare of the child, and it is the court's obligation to take such action in each case as will best promote the interest of the child and at the same time the broad interests of the community. For this reason the broad social effects of the juvenile court where the offending boy or girl first meets the law outrank in significance those of any other branch of our judicial system.

The juvenile court, fortunately, is a court with sufficient breadth of authority to handle each case in accordance with the young person's needs, a court that is not bound by the usual legal technicalities nor a court that is sought to be influenced by long-winded oratory. However, this informality should not be used to transform the juvenile court into a nursery, nor its hearings into a field day for professional workers. I think we can reach the point of professional absurdity. Your court is one of law, it is not an administrative agency. It is entitled to the prestige and dignity of a court of law. If it does not enjoy this respect, the fault

lies with the court itself. And we must remember that particular emphasis must be placed upon the safeguarding of basic constitutional guarantees. Our Constitution—and its protection—extends to boys and girls. Your courts must be eternally vigilant to protect their human rights and human dignity, their individuality, and the basic civil rights that every American enjoys.

Effect of Training School

During the time I was Attorney General I had occasion from time to time to look into the functioning of some of the juvenile courts and to determine how well our federal juvenile delinquency procedure worked. You will remember our conference on this topic in Washington, which was attended by several hundred experts, including many of the judges here. At that time there were over 600 boys in our training school in Washington. I gained the impression that some juvenile courts and some federal courts were too frequently using their power to commit young people to training schools. I tried to bring home to our district attorneys and federal probation officers the desirability of trying some method of disposing of a case other than by bringing the young person into court and formally charging him and giving him a record. We introduced the Brooklyn Plan on a national scale. As a result of our activities, we reduced the number of cases coming into federal courts from approximately 3,500 a year when I took office as Attorney General in 1945 to about 2,000 last year. And the

* Reprinted from *Federal Probation*, Vol. XIV, December, 1950, pp. 10–12. Used by permission of author and publication.

population of the Training School was down to less than 250. Of course, I do not want to criticize our training schools, but from my experience and knowledge of them I feel that at best they afford a poor disposition of a case. Certainly the training school is not a panacea for all the ills of delinquency. There are some, you know, who regard commitment to a training school as the only appropriate disposition of a juvenile offender. There are those, on the other hand, who think that no child should ever be placed in an institution.

From my personal experience with the programs of training schools, I am convinced that in the main the juvenile courts have grossly overestimated the contributions which such institutions can make to delinquency prevention and control. I characterize them as often being graduate schools to crime. Of course there are exceptions, but in my experience they are not in large numbers. As you know better than I, some children are sent to the training schools for educational purposes, and others for the teaching of a trade, while most commitments are made because the child has a poor home or bad associates. There is scarcely a training school in the United States which does not include in its population a group of children who are committed because no more suitable place has been provided or has been found for them. Thus, the mentally retarded are housed with those of normal capacities; the emotionally disturbed, the mentally and chronically ill, the physically handicapped are placed in the same program as the "normal" youth who is a behavior problem.

The judge who commits a boy to a school to remove him from a bad gang must realize that instead of a gang of, say, four, the child may come to have 400 such associates. The judge who commits a boy because he has an impossible home situation must recognize that the youth will not be in a normal environment while in the school. And as to academic education, more adequate schools are usually available to children in the community than in the average institution. Moreover, it is a serious indictment of our school system if a boy must be sent to a training school to obtain vocational training. Finally, as to discipline, I have little confidence that discipline in the sense in which it is usually used will carry over into community life. A boy may continue to say "yes, sir" and "no, sir" long after he has left a training school, yet retain the motivations which prompted him to steal a car in the first place.

These observations, while I am sure they are not particularly new to any of you, will serve to underline what I regard to be among the primary responsibilities of a sound juvenile court.

Effect of Sponsorship

You juvenile court judges must also be salesmen, educating the community as to its shortcomings and its needs; pointing out its breeding places of delinquency and the cure for them. One resource of the community that I found not to have been used extensively was the private citizen and the service clubs. We found both to be most helpful in our federal program.

When I first began to visit the National Training School for Boys in Washington, I was impressed by one fact above all others—the boys in that school were hungry for friendship. They wanted to feel that someone other than those responsible for their safekeeping and training was interested in them. It was the recognition of this fact that led me to take an active part in promoting what we call our sponsorship program. We enlisted the interest of citizens in all walks of life in the idea of giving a little of their time to individual boys. We asked them if they would be willing to go to the school periodically to visit youngsters and discuss with them their problems. Slowly at first, and then in increasing numbers, the volunteers presented themselves; then a national service club and the American Legion came forward. Efforts were made to select men from these groups who had some common interests with the boys. As the relationships developed between the youngsters and their sponsors under the careful guidance of the training school staff, opportunities were provided for the boys to leave the school in company with their sponsors for an occasional trip to a ball game, to the sponsor's home for dinner, or for a sightseeing visit in town. Out of this sharing of time with the boys came something vastly more important: a sharing of mature experience and sound values. For the first time in their lives many of the boys could look for guidance and counsel to an adult male friend with a wholesome outlook upon life.

Let me give you an example of one boy:

In a few weeks, a young man whom I knew in our training school will complete his first year in one of our better known southern universities. My young friend is doing a fine job in school and we are proud of him. But we are even more proud of the fact that he has gotten on the right road because of the influence of his sponsor. When we first met this boy, he had already acquired a wealth of delinquent experience. Cynical beyond his years, he looked like anything but a hopeful prospect for future social adjustment. To the school authorities he was something of an enigma. A youngster of more than average intelligence, he seemed to respond to no aspect of the school's program. His sponsor, one of my associates in the Department of Justice, found the boy somewhat sullen and inaccessible at first, but as the weeks passed a bond of friendship and confidence grew between them. Gradually, the boy took a greater interest in the opportunities of the school. He decided to complete high school. The boy confided in his sponsor that some day he, too, would like to be an attorney. With the help of other friends, doors to the university were opened and this young man, in a new community under the guidance of a new sponsor, is on his way, thanks to the sponsorship program.

We soon learned that however important it was for youngsters to have the friendship of sponsors while at the school, it was even more important that upon their return to the community there be someone to give them continuing support and help. Their problems were brought to the attention of a number of national organizations such as the American Legion and service clubs, who for some months have been enlisting the efforts of their local chapters and units in the plan. I am hopeful that in time the program may assume nationwide proportions. It can be of great practical value to the juvenile court and I hope you will make the fullest use of it.

If You Make the Boy Right. . .

During the next 50 years, we may confidently expect that the horizons of our knowledge of human behavior will be increasingly extended. Our courts must remain constantly alert to new and significant discoveries and to find ways of relating these discoveries to their day-to-day activities in helping children. It is while working with the child of tender years that we have the greatest opportunity to mold attitudes and behavior. If we succeed we will contribute positively to the reduction of the terrible toll exacted from society by lawlessness and crime.

Let me conclude by telling you a story about a boy whose father was trying to get a little rest one afternoon. The boy kept asking him when he was going to get up. The father couldn't think of anything that would keep the boy quiet for long until he remembered a jig-saw puzzle he had bought for him the day before. He had been attracted to it because it was a map of the world and he thought that his boy by putting it together could have some fun and learn some geography too. So he gave it to the boy and told him to put it together. Much to the father's amazement, the boy in a very short time brought the puzzle back to him all finished. The father couldn't understand how he had done it so quickly. Then the boy explained that he noticed the puzzle had two sides. One was the map of the world, but the other was the picture of a boy. All he did was to put the boy together properly and turn the whole puzzle over on a couple of boards and the map of the world was complete. So just remember, *if you make the boy right, you make the world right.* You can do it!

Are Correctional Schools Evil or Are We?[*]

By Harrison Allen Dobbs. Professor of Social Welfare, Louisiana State University, Baton Rouge.

PUBLIC INSTITUTIONS for the care and training of delinquent youth occupy an unsavory position in public thinking. Some of these correctional schools lately have taken a hard beating. Others get by with restricted programs or have had sufficient luck, thus far, to escape sensational exposure. Causes of this general disrest should be carefully examined. Many dire conditions can and must be prevented.

It is a social misfortune that the physical, mental, and social well-being of so many important children is jeopardized countrywide because of this unnecessary plight. We must face, with intelligence and determination, the personal and community loss it represents and recognize the threat this is to our best welfare—individually and nationally. Fortunately, many of these detrimental conditions can be materially altered.

Where Does Responsibility Rest?

Something constructive and lasting must be done to counteract such individual and group peril. Persons everywhere have a lasting stake in the grave issues confronting states in the matter of their training schools. This becomes a public issue too significant to go unattended any longer. We presently react to this social predicament like the proverbial ostrich and foolishly "bury our heads in the sand."

Citizens themselves are, on the whole, responsible for what delinquent children in these residential school programs commonly encounter. People must carry realistically the blame for the harm they do these girls and boys and set about modifying, in a concrete way, discreditable conditions. Co-operative effort should be made to wipe out this ominous situation.

The attempt to shift an obligation as socially imperative as this one to a few scapegoats is expensive and degrading. Institution superintendents, along with their staffs, carry a great deal of undeserved criticism and disfavor because "the buck" is passed to them so freely. It is high time to take a new approach and place the responsibility where it rightfully belongs. This ought to lead to better achievements.

[*] Reprinted from *Federal Probation,* Vol. XIV, December, 1950, pp. 35–41. Used by permission of author and publication.

The public is constantly kept conscious of the fact that here is an important social institution functioning poorly. Communities are informed in a dramatic way of disgraceful conditions through newspapers, broadcasts, and movies. Nevertheless, there are few people who see yet why they are guilty for not protesting vigorously the substandard care that is provided these unfortunate children. This indifference invites an unnecessary waste of human resources. It can have social consequence of immeasurable importance.

This brief article tells why citizens back home should be thoroughly awakened. Reasons are given for some institutional shortcomings. There could be a far-reaching modification of the present limitation; that is, if everyone tried intelligently to effect a genuine improvement.

Too much is said currently about what is happening. Too little is done to stop costly mistakes from getting started. Impairment of the personal and social status of these growing and developing children who should become happy and healthy citizens is a serious matter. The viewpoints expressed here stress why this correctional school problem has great moment, personally and socially, and they suggest something definite to be done about it collectively.

Is It All Failure?

Shocking events at these residential schools have broken ruthlessly into the news many times. Unruly boys have been killed by their caretakers so as to preserve the semblance of law and order. Emotionally sick girls end their life to escape intolerable institutional living. The rape of cottage mothers has been attempted and other sex violations are said to be rampant. Aggressive gangs in institutions beat to death other boys they dislike. Wanton destruction of valuable state property is heralded. Runaways are bitterly denounced, because of the additional threat they make to public safety.

Tragic incidents like these stimulate a great deal of interest. However, they also confuse and misguide social thinking and response. Real problems are likely to be lost from sight. There is, moreover, hazard in generalizing from a few particulars. It is disconcerting that so much public opinion and planning about "reform schools" stem from an emotional account of occasional gross violations.

Legislative commissions to investigate conditions are belatedly instituted. Agitated civic and church organizations pass high-sounding resolutions demanding immediate changes (usually in personnel). Strong editorials and colorful feature stories try hard to crystallize community disapproval. Sightseeing tours to correctional schools are arranged. These intend to let people experience some "inside" conditions.

Fruitful activity occasionally is instigated by this fanfare and loud trumpeting. The usefulness of this sporadic effort, however, could be enhanced; that is, if less expression were given to superficial symptoms. More energy must be spent assuring attention to the influential factors that rest inevitably underneath.

Basic causes of these hurtful institutional conditions need to be ferreted out. Psychological and sociological reasons for such happenings must be better understood and heeded generally. This seems a feasible directive. This goal will be reached, easier and more certainly, when the intrinsic worth of every child commands sufficient social respect nationally. We still value cheaply the life and welfare of American children, delinquent ones particularly.

It is important to stop and stress a special point that commonly goes unnoticed. This is the fact that a correctional school frequently does help many needy children. Personal progress is achieved there, even in the face of great odds. This change is seldom recognized, and what the school has helped the child to accomplish is little appreciated by the fickle public. Boys and girls who manage to get along satisfactorily in these institutions receive no acclaim. The hard-wrought gains they make are lost from view. Conspicuous failures usurp the stage so completely.

The probability of allowing the negatives in the correctional school picture to overshadow positives is considerable. Detrimental attitudes come from this negative kind of psychology. These lessen the likelihood of productive guidance. Positive institutional characteristics are to be found; that is, if the attempt to find them is diligently made. These must be taken hold of more consistently; and they could be usefully extended, if there were the right kind of social vision and sponsorship in every community.

It is readily forgotten that these promising traits in institutional care and training for selected children do persist. Such aspects should come into play more commonly. This would happen oftener, if they were not so outshone by the distasteful qualities that most people prefer to have emphasized. This may be for reasons of a deepset psychological kind.

What Importance Has the Over-All Quality?

The problem of correctional school care should be looked upon first as a whole. Subsequently, functional segments that claim special recognition can be evaluated separately with profit. Any one of these has enough potency to modify substantially the usefulness of any rehabilitative service. However, it should never be thought of as an independent cause, operating alone.

The crux of determining success or failure in institutions is finding out what the whole program affords. What does it mean totally to these special boys and girls? A new, greater factor is bound to appear when an institution is considered in this comprehensive manner; that is, wholly.

This composite quality has greater influence, socially and psychologically, than considering the sum one gets from calculating the limitations and strengths that separate components entail. The value of approaching social problems this holistic way recommends generous use of this method. This is so, if we are truly anxious to meet issues satisfactorily. It is infrequently done in this meaningful way.

The concept of wholes, as used here, should have a brief explanation for purpose of clarity. It happens that institutions seem better or worse to the public eye than they are empirically. One explanation is the permeating nature of the overall quality a total child-care institution imparts. This influential attribute is difficult to define and isolate. Only wholes afford it; it unavoidably affects what shall happen, favorably or unfavorably, to children who live and develop in that setting. This general impact prevails, despite specific excellencies or weaknesses that the particular parts of an institutional program engender.

It is necessary, therefore, to be aware, on the one hand, of multiple factors; and, on the other, of the whole that these uniquely beget. Both enter substantially into the "relearning for better living" activity of correctional school children. Incorrect impressions regarding the efficacy of a correctional school can arise and magnify falsely, if only one of these aspects enters into making the evaluation.

The particular *system*, or *mosaic*, that the functional segments of an institution form, has greater influence in determining treatment outcomes than do organizational parts. It is the *system* that these jointly bring into being that controls, for the most part, what happens educationally to children at state training schools.

The proper growth and development of boys and girls placed there depends mostly upon this synthetic quality. For example, a juvenile court judge makes use of the correctional school (system of services) for a particular child's training, because of this encompassing attribute. He counts on procuring social help for this needy individual because he fundamentally believes in the system. It is not because the judge has direct knowledge of its service-giving parts nor an estimation of their worth singly. It is a matter of major consequence, therefore, to pay attention to the intangible "tone" that is discovered only when wholes are examined and given attention.

When Are Appearances Deceiving?

The over-all impression that a training school for delinquent youth presents depends upon what one sees superficially, and upon what is going on far inside. However, we are influenced mostly by surface characteristics. Unless one is prodded to dig deeper, these will supply most of the material for passing judgment.

It is natural that the usual observer should view such an institution favorably. Generally, it has a pleasant physical setting. The magnitude and uniqueness of it incite admiration. In addition, there is the practical fact that visitors are usually guided by some attaché, who has the acquired skill in putting and keeping "the best foot forward."

The buildings and grounds of these residential schools are almost always kept in excellent shape. The orderliness, cleanliness, and spaciousness of the whole plant impart a favorable feeling. It seems to offer an unusually conducive environment for these particular children, most of whom are thought to be economically and culturally deprived, but still appreciative. Living in cottages, attending a modern school, having regular religious instruction, getting vocational training, profiting from the help of specialists—these cultural opportunities are hard to duplicate. One could feel that seemingly superior conditions like these might make less favored parents and communities grow envious.

Children, too, look promising and effectively disciplined. It is hard to believe that they were once court cases requiring commitment. Their manners, marching, and self-mastery call forth favorable comment. One is impressed by the apparent ease these children reveal fitting into a new kind of living situation. The impressive manner in which older youth guide and counsel those who are younger seems uncanny. The service they give compensates (so one erroneously thinks) for reported personnel shortages and the political appointees who, the public knows, find their way easily into some welfare institutions.

Careful reflection, however, brings to the front other more significant reactions. What are the basic needs of these particular children? How well are these being satisfied? Has each institutional worker the sufficiently professional competency that is required to do a successful job? Do the psychological aspects of group living affect some of these children adversely? What is the meaning and cause of the emotional undercurrents one senses in institutional living? Why are there reported so many failures to get along well after leaving these training schools? Who gives official oversight to these public institutions and how successful is the supervision? Where shall responsibility for discrepancies and their correction be vested? Such questions inevitably arise; each calls for a dependable answer.

Here is where the distinct advantage of viewing correctional schools as a whole becomes evident. More insight is possible this way; making for a better outlook. The closer a complete overview is attained, the greater the usefulness such a study will have.

Social wisdom is shown when correctional schools are considered macroscopically. This method reveals significant issues that often are hidden, even when a powerful microscopic lens is used. Therefore, it is important for all of us to "look upon the forest instead of trees" from time to time, when considering the correctional school problem.

What Can Be the Matter?

Ten assertions that pertain to the current status of correctional schools throughout this Nation have been drafted for tentative acceptance. These grow out of the writer's long connection, directly and indirectly, with this social work field. Each is subject to debate and clarification; this is the main reason for presenting them here. If they provoke reflective thinking, stimulate some research, pin down obligation, and bring even a little change in the institutional picture this article will have been well worth while.

1. It is asserted that there prevails countrywide too little respect for the worth of persons; that those who trespass, or appear unpromising, get less than the rest; and that this basic lack must be rectified.

2. It is asserted that there are too many children now in correctional schools whose problems were long neglected socially and who presently have emotional difficulties so advanced that their successful handling becomes very complicated and uncertain.

3. It is asserted that an institutional setting for delinquents is physically and emotionally unsuited for their best growth and development, except for a relatively few well-chosen ones.

4. It is asserted that the great admixture of widely differing children in a correctional school impairs individual rehabilitation and precipitates many individual and group problems; and that each institutional admission must be completely determined.

5. It is asserted that it is likely there exists nowhere a correctional school staff that is adequate, competent, and secure enough presently to carry fully its responsibility for individuals and groups.

6. It is asserted that there is presently too restricted knowledge regarding the dynamic nature of each delinquent child's behavior; and that there is urgent need for more psychological and sociological research; but at the same time, even greater demand to utilize better that which is already known scientifically.

7. It is asserted that the treatment of most children in a correctional school proceeds with scant or no biographical information, and with too limited guidance at each step; and that society would never tolerate any community or person treating physically ill children as amateurishly as it does those who are ill socially.

8. It is asserted that there is too slight tying together of all that the institutional staff tries to do in behalf of its children; and that essential service is lost, because of the lack of a co-ordinated segmentalized approach various functional departments customarily follow.

9. It is asserted that many correctional school placements for children are badly timed; that rehabilitation goals cannot possibly be realized until we learn when to start and to end it appropriately; and that convalescent care and training, for most of these children, is as crucial as their institutional experience and cannot be at all forfeited, without hazard and increased social cost.

10. It is asserted that there prevails in most correctional schools too much political domination and interference of both a direct and indirect kind; and that only slight progress can be anticipated institutionally until this poisonous influence is more completely uprooted.

How Can Change Be Started?

Any one of the 10 concepts just presented could make a suitable starting point for modifying the unfavorable status that institutional care for delinquent children now has. Moving ahead effectively in this, a single respect (hoping to change the manner and extent of the influence of that factor on the whole situation), could not help but influence what happens totally to youths being re-educated there. The system, that characterizes the particular setting, could be changed to a significant degree.

The last point of the 10, that is, the consequence of political indifference and interference, might well be the chief menace facing children countrywide in correctional schools. It is chosen as a telling example of where specific progress could be advantageously made. This does not imply that the greatest threat to their welfare are politicians themselves. On the contrary, public officials are intentionally guilty of doing harm to young state wards in few instances. It is rather what is done by them indirectly, and perhaps unconsciously, that brings about greatest handicaps.

The basic cause for costly institutional mishaps is the indifference of voters. They choose representatives and then fail to inform them adequately regarding their wishes, or do not do it at all. It can be reasonably held that the ignorance and inertia of citizens is at the root of our correctional school evil. This is what was referred to earlier when it was urged that we lodge social responsibility for this problem where it belongs. Nothing else seems as useful as doing this successfully.

Three specific illustrations are chosen to show the influential part politics plays in this matter: (1) enacting and continuing restrictive legislation; (2) insisting that some institutional staff be appointed on other than a merit-selection basis; (3) preserving institutional status quo by officially discouraging experimental activity at correctional schools in order to avert public criticism at election time. Evidence to substantiate these points is readily available.

Thoroughgoing investigation should be made sometime to determine accurately the full damage these deterring political factors do to society, and especially do to delinquent youth in publicly administered institutions. At this moment, all that can be undertaken is to scan a few highlights.

Restrictive legislation. This factor shows itself in several ways. First, and often the foremost, is the matter of providing an insufficient appropriation for operating state institutions adequately. Only rarely is a legislature disposed to supply funds for socially ill children as substantially as most communities do now for physically ill ones who require hospitalization. For example, the amount of money that is to supply a few weeks care for a child in the pediatrics ward of a Class A hospital must be stretched to last a year or more if it were to be used for the treatment of a child in the usual correctional school.

Second, statutory provisions that are enacted by legislatures to administer state schools frequently have consequential flaws. There is likely to be a plan for isolated control and direction that is scant and irregular. What is provided sometimes is placed in the hands of unqualified supervisory officials. Rarely is it legally required that there be close interdepartmental co-operation at the state capitol or locally. As a result, one finds too little functional relationship between these schools and state departments of health, education, safety, and sometimes even welfare.

Third, legislation pertaining to family and child welfare generally, and to juvenile delinquents particularly, is frequently outmoded, indecisive, and not well enforced (i.e., juvenile court laws, child labor laws, compulsory school attendance laws, institution licensing laws, etc.). Each of these, and many others, relates directly to the welfare of a great number of children. They reflect clearly the degree of social awareness that legislators and their constituents have about many welfare measures.

While there are important exceptions, it can be stated, with certainty, that there prevails countrywide far from the best social legislation and public administration pertaining to needy children. What courts, police, welfare agencies, guidance centers and such undertake and accomplish controls largely who shall go to the correctional schools. Legislative failure that shows itself in community welfare planning has a far-reaching effect that is both hurtful and expensive. This is something about which institutional staffs themselves can do little, but about which trustworthy legislators could accomplish a great deal.

Political influence on the institutional staff directly. This factor deserves careful scrutiny. It often relates, more than anything else, to the pervading inner spirit of correctional schools throughout the Nation. It is an insidious encroachment that saps, quickly and completely, much of the worth from these programs. This has many influential facets; and different ones come to the fore periodically. These appear sometimes overtly, but more in a subversive manner. The toll they exact becomes, at last, dramatically apparent and appalling.

Rather than undertaking even a brief discussion of the nature of this influence, it appears wiser to list here 10 ways in which it makes a nefarious appearance. Taken singly, each example helps explain limited local situations. Taken all together, these instances furnish a strong indictment of our social neglect to control the political component of treatment in correctional schools.

Instances where

1. An incompetent, politically appointed superintendent tries to help children and his party develop at the same time.

2. A competent superintendent tries to re-educate children with a staff, wholly or even partially selected on a political basis.

3. An incompetent, politically approved superintendent and the same kind of staff are wholly unable to cope with the complicated problems of delinquent children.

4. A competent superintendent must comply with the orders and directions of unqualified political supervisors.

5. A competent superintendent must reinstate a discharged employee for political reasons.

6. A competent superintendent has his institutional budget pared by the legislature, while other politically favored superintendents fare unreasonably well.

7. A superintendent and an important segment of the staff who have grown in their competency are replaced by novices after an election.

8. Conditions detrimental to children's welfare are planfully "white-washed" by influential political commissions or powerful officials so that the public never sees nor debates real issues.

9. An incompetent nonpolitical superintendent is retained because he has built, at great cost, "political fences."

10. A competent superintendent cannot attract new and promising personnel because of a distrust generally in public service.

Such political conditions are of great psychological and sociological moment. Are these inevitable? Must they continue? Shall delinquent children be "political footballs"? Why do citizens commonly allow this laxness? What causes hard won advances frequently to slip back? Are there civic organizations strong enough to combat these harmful conditions? Questions like these pose a genuine social challenge. They betray, also, a social weakness too persistent to overlook comfortably.

Political intimidation. This refers to an insidious power over ideas. This is often inimical to children's best growth and development in a correctional school setting. It frequently happens that progressive child-care plans must be foregone. Outside pressure is brought to bear on a forward-looking superintendent and his able assistants. Some person or group resents and resists constructive changes in the institution. This opposition often is spearheaded by a legislator or petty official. Their selfish interest is easy to solicit because here is something to capitalize on politically.

It is a concomitant of change that there should be some upset. In an institution, this expresses itself momentarily in an increased restlessness and the dissatisfaction of children and staff. The hurt and harm are oftentimes more assumed than real. Nevertheless, the condition is taken advantage of unfavorably.

Some newspapers are prone to play up these internal dissensions and extend adverse criticism even further, no matter how unreasonable it is. It is usual, and perhaps natural, that those connected with politics are especially sensitive to these complaints. They put forth great effort to hold intact an institutional status quo, if they figure that is what a vocal constituent or constituency desires. They consider it advantageous to take a reactionary stand on change and block progress for expedient reasons.

There are records of occasions where politicians directly interfered with staff planning or complained to higher supervisory officials without warrant. For example, when runaways increase in number, or disciplinary control is thought to be weak, they point condemning fingers. This is so despite the fact that it may be only a transitional phase or that which was lost is much less significant than what has been basically gained. Rather than finding out what the matter is, they immaturely criticize administrative procedures and publicly threaten official reprisals.

Minor politicians take sides, with disgruntled employees especially. They champion local tradesmen who are disappointed economically. Parents persuade them easily to intercede for their children. Institutional gossip and intrigue are welcomed by them as effective whips to use. They often prefer working backhandedly in this manner. Only rarely can one be found who will take a positive position and definitely support constructive institutional revisions.

Many a correctional school service has been totally ruined by little people acting big, and exercising unfortunately far more influence than was ever meant. Eager politicians speak louder, oftener, and with more determination than do the real friends of the correctional school and its needy children. The questionable results they get can be felt quickly and widely.

This makes substantial institutional administration extremely difficult and uncertain. It dampens group enthusiasm and curtails individual effort. Upset and sabotage by some persons who care more about their own selfish gains than they do about children do irreparable damage. It is a pity to what extent props are knocked from under hopeful experimentation in institutions by unintelligent intrusion. Political intimidation is costly to children, staff, and taxpayers. Somehow or other, it appears little minded by those of us who should be caring and interceding a lot.

Is There a Logical Inference?

A simple conclusion stands out preeminently. It is this: *we must mind our own business.* When citizen concern is honestly expressed about unhealthy conditions in institutions for the care and training of delinquent children, it is not just a busy-body intent. There is need of a serious warning. The social carelessness we frequently permit must be lessened.

We have a civic obligation to develop better institutional safeguards and standards. There must be sufficient maturity to stop name calling, rationalization, and escape. The fault is inherently ours. It is not these children; not the institutional staff; nor the politicians who are chiefly to blame for the incompetency of institutional programs. It rests on us, as citizens, because we have not been tending to our duty properly. Whether correctional school care for children will grow better or worse nationally depends, to a great extent, on whether or not we get wide enough awake socially.

A corollary of this conclusion is: *we can change conditions, if we only will.* It is immoral that a young state ward must be killed or commit suicide before citizens realize inwardly their responsibility. Whenever a correctional school is neglected, we are being evil and should be considered in direct league with those persons who are ungodly in other ways.

SELECTED REFERENCES

1. Monachesi, Elio D., "Personality Characteristics of Institutionalized and Non-Institutionalized Male Delinquents," *Journal of Criminal Law and Criminology*, XLI, July-August 1950.

Personality differences are the subject matter examined in this important survey of male delinquents.

2. Deutsch, Albert, "Is This Reform?" *Woman's Home Companion*, March 1948.

This well-known social investigator, after first-hand study of various reform schools throughout the nation, denounces the vast majority in no uncertain terms.

3. Tappan, Paul W., *Juvenile Delinquency* (New York: McGraw-Hill Book Co., 1949), Chapter 16: "Institutional Treatment: Its Deficiencies."

The major concern of this chapter is institutional commitment and the types, methods, and problems of institutions which handle the young offender.

4. Berenstein, E., *Yearbook* (New York: National Probation and Parole Association, 1940), "Release of the Child from the Institution," pp. 47–67.

A stimulating discussion of the problems attendant upon releasing the child who has served time in an institution.

12 PAROLE SUPERVISION AND SPONSORSHIP

IT HAS been reported that the first modern usage of the word "parole" in the United States was made by Dr. S. G. Howe of Boston who, in a letter to the Prison Association of New York in 1846, wrote: "I believe there are many prisoners who might be so trained as to be left upon their parole during the last period of their imprisonment with safety." The word is derived from the French word *parole* and is used in the sense of "word of honor,"—*parole d'honneur*. Although the initial parole legislation was enacted in Massachusetts in 1837, New York in 1877 was the first state to include the word "parole" in the statute.

Parole is an administrative act—a form of release granted to an inmate after he has served a portion of his sentence in a penal institution. When he is paroled he finishes serving his "time" outside prison or reformatory walls. Parole, in principle, is neither mercy nor leniency. Parole is an extension of punishment. It does not imply forgiveness and is not designed as a reward for good conduct in the institution. No inmate has the *right* to parole, and the public does not have the *right* to parole him. Obviously, parole is less expensive than incarceration, since the parolee is able to earn some money and in many cases contribute to the support of his family, thus removing both himself and family from public support.

One of the fallacies concerning parole is the view that the individual inmate achieves eligibility by his own efforts. Some judges will tell the convicted or his family that if he maintains a "good work record and good conduct record" while he is in prison, he will be eligible for parole. The fact of the matter is that most inmates become eligible for parole regardless of their records. At least 90 per cent of all prisoners make "good" records, but only approximately 30 per cent are paroled.

PAROLE AND THE YOUNG OFFENDER

Oddly enough, the first elements of parole began in the United States in colonial times as a system of indenture for juvenile delinquents. Under this early practice, young prisoners were released and placed in the employment of private citizens to whom such prisoners were legally bound. While these juveniles were not subject to supervision by the state, they were permitted to earn their final discharge from their employers. A further development occurred when state visiting agents were appointed to supervise the children and to prevent their exploitation by employers while on indenture. This system was adopted by the New York House of Refuge, founded in 1825.

In the area of juvenile delinquency, the term "parole" applies to a procedure other than the supervision of an inmate after his release from jail, reformatory, prison, or some other institution. Parole in this particular usage refers to the assignment of juvenile offenders to parents, relatives, or social agencies; and more rarely, in the case of adolescents, to boarding homes or, in rare instances, to hotels.

Juvenile parole, sometimes referred to as "after care," has for many years constituted a neglected field in the child welfare program. Little uniformity is to be found in its administration. This unevenness reflects the great differences in the regulations governing state institutions and is also partly the result of the fact that many schools and institutions for juvenile delinquents are private or semiprivate, and only in a measure subject to state regulation and supervision. The growing policy governing adult parole, a policy leading toward greater centralization in the granting and supervising of parolees on the state level, has not been adopted in the juvenile field. In view of the fact that one of the most important phases of the training program involved in institutional experience is the inmate's parole into the community and the facilitation of the offender's adjustment there, the need to improve parole procedures is evident.

PAROLE SYSTEMS AND PROBLEMS

The rapid growth of parole legislation necessitated a corresponding spread of parole systems to administer this new social technique. By 1900, parole systems of a sort had been introduced into twenty states; by 1910, thirty-two states and the federal government had adopted parole systems; and by 1922, parole was in operation in forty-four states, the Territory of Hawaii, and the federal government. Today all states have parole laws of some type.

In large part, because of this rapid development of the philosophy of parole among the forty-eight states, the various administrative parole systems present a somewhat kaleidoscopic view. According to one specialist in this field, organizations and agencies granting parole within the various states are of three types: central board, governors, and institution boards. In twenty-nine jurisdictions, central boards are vested with the power to grant parole, or so-called paroles, to inmates of state prisons and reformatories. In seventeen states the sole power to grant parole is vested in the governor, acting independently or assisted by an advisor or an advisory board. Seven states utilize institutional parole agencies.[1] Where institutions serve a rather large territory and cannot let their staff members travel to outlying counties for purposes of investigation, the granting of parole and the supervision on parole may be in the hands of the committing juvenile court. State agencies, such as the Youth Authority in California, the Youth Service Commission in Wisconsin, the Youth Service Board in Massachusetts, and the Division of Juvenile Parole Services of the Illinois Department of Welfare, are charged with the preparation and the supervision of parole of those committed to institutions in these states.

The administration of parole is beset with many problems, the most im-

---

[1] George G. Killinger in Paul W. Tappan, ed., *Contemporary Correction* (New York: McGraw-Hill Book Co., 1951), p. 362.

portant of which center in the supervisory process—the crux of the parole system (discussed on page 444). The problems are often complicated by inefficient administrative planning and inadequate staffing (some parole systems exist largely on paper). Again, many parole officers are burdened by very large case loads. And both officers and parolees are sometimes handicapped by detailed legal and administrative rules that restrict needed flexibility of operation.

Parole staffs are often of low quality because of unattractive salary scales. Competent men may not stay in parole service long for that reason. Nor are they always obtainable through Civil Service examinations. The latter, as one author stresses, do not always measure what they set out to measure; nor is it possible to determine from a written test whether an applicant has the temperament, the ability, and the personal integrity demanded in an efficient parole officer. Candidates may place high on the competitive lists and yet be very poor material, even emotionally unstable. For example, in one Civil Service examination, an applicant passed the test with flying colors only to go to prison later for dishonesty; another, at the bottom of the list, barely managed to be appointed but became one of the most valuable members of the parole staff.[2]

There are, then, serious problems in on-going parole systems: problems of personnel selection and quality, of inadequate facilities and funds, of administrative policy and practice. But these problems are by no means insurmountable. Nor should they overshadow the positive accomplishments of parole itself.

WHAT DETERMINES THE USE OF PAROLE?

In the case of adults, the two prerequisites for parole, outside of an acceptable institutional record, are the absence of detainers (that is, legal "hold orders" for other authorities) and guaranteed employment. In some states the applicant for parole must have a home, a sponsor, and a job, and these must be *bona fide*. However, many factors affect the probable fitness of a child or youth for parole or conditional liberation.

Parole boards, institutional heads, and juvenile courts are interested to receive information that will help them in arriving at a correct and intelligent decision concerning whom should be paroled. It must be determined if the applicant is capable of living in the community and remaining at liberty without violating laws. In considering an inmate's release on parole, both negative and positive considerations in each case must be appraised. References are made, if available, to the psychiatric and psychological reports worked up by the professional staffs within the institution of commitment. An analysis is made of the inmate's educational progress within the institution, his plans for the future, his maturation, his seriousness of purpose. In addition, the parole applicant's conduct during incarceration, previous offense record, military experience, past occupational history, and present attitude toward life in general are studied.

The California Authority believes the wisest course is to give selected youthful inmates a trial on parole, a procedure followed only after inmates have been in a training school for a period of time that has proved sufficient to effect a measurable change of habits in other persons with similar difficulties. Should

[2] David Dressler, *Parole Chief* (New York: The Viking Press, 1951), p. 309.

the youth fail on parole, the Authority can return him to the reform school for additional or perhaps different training. It is true that some youths who seem least favorably influenced in a training unit show, as soon as they are on parole, that they have acquired a new attitude and are now able to adjust well in the community. The California Authority has encountered difficulties in removing the idea of "doing time" from the minds of its charges, especially the older boys. Courts find them delinquent or guilty and commit them to the Youth Authority; the boys are apt to look upon the parole procedure itself as regular court sentence. At the diagnostic clinic often their first question is this: "How much time will I have to do?"

Progress has been made in some institutions in their ability to make wise selections of parolees. Improved training and treatment methods within the institution, as well as the utilization of modern methods of classification and analysis of the inmates assist the paroling authority to base its selection upon facts and performance, instead of upon whim, fancy, or "intuition."

PAROLE SUPERVISION

It was pointed out above that one of the most important phases of the whole rehabilitative process is intelligent and efficient parole supervision. And some of the handicaps facing supervisors today were noted, including inadequate staffing, large case loads, and administrative inflexibility. A more detailed consideration of supervision and its problems should form part of any serious discussion of parole.

Releasing the youth from the correctional institution and his subsequent adjustment under parole supervision should be a gradual process. A weak link in the chain of rehabilitation at the present time is the supervision of youth while on parole. There are few parole staffs which are sufficiently large or well enough trained to cope readily with the problems of the post-institutional training period. In some states parole services for children are conspicuous by their absence; upon release from the institution children must get along as best they can unsupervised. Yet the program demanded in training children while on parole, in principle, involves extensive and professional case work. Short of this principle and of the needed personnel to carry it out, alternative methods have been devised, including sponsorship.

Authorities often require a sponsor if the youth is to be released on parole. The sponsor may be a family friend, a clergyman, or other interested citizen, but he should be selected by the paroling officials with utmost care. The sponsor is no substitute for the parole officer who officially supervises the boy. In some states, in the case of adult parole, the sponsor may be accepted by the parole authorities as a substitute for the parole officer for all practical intent and purposes. In juvenile parole, the sponsor cooperates with the parole officer and seeks his advice. Since the sponsor is responsible for one individual only, he can more readily concentrate his efforts and available time than an overburdened parole officer.

Civic organizations have in recent years volunteered as sponsors of delinquent youth. In Philadelphia, Junior Chamber of Commerce members have successfully sponsored boys released from the Pennsylvania Industrial School. The National Exchange Club has undertaken a nation-wide program of supplying sponsors for boys returning home from the National Training School. One of the most recent manifestations of a service club's work in this field is that of the Kiwanis Club of Pueblo, Colorado, which reports about 90 per cent success in their sponsorship program.

Parolees fortunate enough to have officially approved sponsors are not infrequently enabled to make a satisfactory adjustment to their community. They are not only freed from the "professional-client" relationship but also removed from the multiplicity of restrictions which are imposed upon them by the parole office, where all too often the standards for the worst parolee are extended to all. With this system in full operation the authoritarian pressures inherent in formalized systems of parole would very likely tend to disappear.

Much still remains to be accomplished in the parole area. At the present time, a majority of the institutions are without psychiatric counsel, a lack that increases the work and responsibility of the parole authorities in selecting those inmates eligible for parole. Parole authorities are especially handicapped in dealing with psychopathic delinquents, the mentally retarded, and habitual "sex" cases without psychiatric aid.

Parole is also an area in need of the help of scientific knowledge. A long-range program of research could be initiated, for example, to study the behavior of released inmates over a prolonged period of time. Very little is known about the details of parole violations. Such research might form the basis of valid prediction instruments which could serve as a source of guidance in selecting parolees. On a broader scale, research would shed light on a field about which too little is known.

READINGS

In "Parole Supervision: A Case Analysis," Arthur E. Fink provides a summary of parole supervision based upon an analysis of presentence investigation reports and chronological records. The discussion of general principles to guide supervision are of special interest to those working in the field of parole.

Joseph Vogel in "Reconstructing Youth: Some Case Studies" discusses a situation of noncorrectional-school placement together with the treatment plan and successful outcome. In addition, he presents a case of foster-home placement, its treatment plan and outcome, as well as the commitment to the National Training School for Boys.

Harry E. Brager and Richard A. Chappell in their article, "Jim, Mr. Brown and You," provide valuable information for any person who is seriously considering taking on the responsibility of sponsoring a boy recently released on parole from a correctional institution. Their basic recipe for a good sponsor is "one part good heart and one part good mind."

G. Howland Shaw in "Sponsoring a Delinquent" describes sponsorship as an art and emphasizes the difficulties of adequately bridging the gap between the sponsor and the individual sponsored. It is more than a question that can be easily answered, he says "by taking the boy to a baseball game . . . or having the boy to supper in one's home," although these are ways of establishing rapport with him.

Parole Supervision: A Case Analysis[*]

By Arthur E. Fink. Dean, School of Social Work, University of North Carolina, Chapel Hill.

HENRY McGILL, age 15 at the time he was involved in violating the National Motor Vehicle Theft Act, is native born, white, and a member of the Baptist church. He had ninth grade education. On February 3, 1942, together with another youth, he stole an automobile. They transported the car to Mountainsburg, Arkansas, where they were arrested on February 4. On February 18 Henry was committed to the National Training School at Washington, D. C., for a period of 3 years. He was paroled on April 17, 1943.

Background of the Case

Previous convictions. On December 2, 1941, when Henry was 15, he was placed on probation in the . . . County juvenile court. He had been arrested in November 1941 for six car thefts which had been committed locally. Also, he had been involved during the preceding few months in six out-of-state car thefts, several of the cars having been driven interstate. It also was learned by the police that in October 1941 Henry and an associate forced entrance during the nighttime into two business places.

Prior to probation Henry had been a problem in the community since his fourteenth birthday. He was frequently truant from home and school and came to the attention of the local child guidance center. In May 1941 Henry, with two boy companions, truanted from home, went to New York State and later into Canada. Through falsifying his age,

Henry enlisted in the Canadian Army and was in active service for about 31 days. He was granted a 6-day furlough, came back to his mother's home, and then failed to return to duty.

Family background. Henry is an only child and there is some question as to his paternity. His parents separated about 3 weeks before his birth and soon afterward the mother, then 20, filed for a divorce. The father, who was 21 when Henry was born, had an exceedingly poor reputation. He was known as a bootlegger, a gambler, and had a penchant for women. When Henry was 1 year old his father was convicted of armed robbery and sentenced to the state prison. Five years later the father was paroled to the State of Arkansas and his address is unknown. It appears that the father has never seen Henry nor did he ever help with financial support.

From birth to age 15 Henry lived with his maternal grandparents. His mother also lived in the home until Henry's thirteenth birthday, at which time she remarried. The mother worked constantly outside the home and most of Henry's upbringing was left to her parents. There was constant conflict between Henry's mother and grandparents over money matters and problems of discipline and authority. Also present in the grandparents' home were several maternal aunts and uncles who resented the attention their parents were showing Henry. There is considerable evidence that the grandparents overindulged

* Reprinted from *Federal Probation*, Vol. XV, September, 1951, pp. 39–45. Used by permission of author and publication.

Henry and were exceedingly lax in discipline. Following Henry's arrest in the federal case he described his grandparents' attitude as "easy on a kid; you could get away with murder." Henry was particularly close with one of the uncles in the grandparents' home and associated with him a great deal. In 1941, when Henry was 15, the uncle was convicted of rape and armed robbery and was sentenced to the state prison. There is some evidence that the uncle helped create in Henry's mind a disrespect for law and authority.

Henry's mother remarried in 1939 and wanted to take Henry immediately into her new home. However, Henry's grandparents insisted on keeping him and during the 2 years before Henry moved into his mother's and stepfather's home, the grandparents apparently did everything possible to fill Henry's mind with prejudices and hatred toward the stepfather. In an effort to discourage Henry from moving to his mother's home the grandparents belittled his mother, telling him that if she were not a person of poor judgment she would not have married Henry's father who was "nothing but a criminal."

In 1941 Henry moved into his mother's and stepfather's home. The stepfather had previously been married and divorced and had two children by his first marriage. The older of these children was 15, the same age as Henry. The stepbrother was an excellent student and his father's pride and joy. There developed an intense rivalry between Henry and the stepbrother for attention and recognition. In this connection it appears that the stepfather did not properly understand Henry's feelings and needs. On at least one occasion the stepfather administered physical punishment to Henry who felt that he had been treated unfairly.

Education. Henry made satisfactory progress in school until he reached 9B grade at. . . . A mental test revealed that Henry had an I.Q. of 95. In the 9B grade he received three D's and one E (not passing) and had a very poor attendance record. During 9A Henry failed several courses and, according to his own statement, "broke the school record for truancy." While at this school Henry's highest grades were attained in woodshop and the mechanical trades. He received A and B grades in these courses. In October 1941 he transferred to a trade school for part-time students and delinquents. Soon after he ran away from home and subsequently did not return to school.

Health. During childhood Henry had cholera infantum, mumps, measles, scarlatina and chicken pox in fairly rapid succession. However, Henry developed into a healthy, robust child. At 16 he was large for his age, weighing 182 pounds and standing 5 feet, 10 inches tall.

Employment. Henry's work experience was limited to occasional part-time employment as a soda clerk and pinsetter. He had no formal trade training.

Interest and activities. He was interested in most sports, especially football. His hobbies were woodworking and cartooning. In general, Henry did not spend his spare time constructively. He kept poor associates, stayed out late nights, and drank occasionally.

Personality factors. Henry was an emotionally unstable youth who showed resentment toward law and authority. He displayed poor judgment and lacked insight into his personality problems. He was impulsive and lacked self-control. As the result of inner conflicts and tensions he was somewhat revengeful and easily led by others. He seemed to have difficulty in discriminating between right and wrong.

On the positive side, Henry possessed average intelligence. He showed a sense of loyalty and affection toward his mother, the grandparents, and the aunts and uncles with whom he lived for many years. He referred to his grandfather as "father" and called his aunts and uncles "brothers" and "sisters." He has good physical health and possessed mechanical ability.

Problems and Needs

The salient problem in this case appeared to be a most unsatisfactory home situation. Over a period of years Henry had been the center of much family rivalry and discord pertaining to matters of discipline and authority. He no doubt developed a feeling of frustration as the result of "being ruled over" by so many persons. He felt resentful toward his stepfather whom he believed discriminated against him in favor of his own son. It is significant that Henry's antisocial activities started at about the time that he left his grandfather's home and began living with his mother and stepfather. In the grandparents' home Henry was allowed to do "pretty much" as he pleased. The stepfather, on the other hand, was a fairly strict disciplinarian and Henry revolted against restriction on his freedom and liberty. In view of these circumstances there seemed to be a very definite need for removing Henry from this unhealthy home situation.

Henry was believed to be a little too old for foster home placement and he seemed to have no particular interest in farm work. He is a poorly disciplined youth who at the time of his arrest manifested a rather sullen and antagonistic attitude. He failed to respond to probation supervision in the local juvenile court and reverted to antisocial conduct approximately 2 months after probation began. There did not appear to be adequate local community resources which might have been utilized. The child guidance center had become interested in Henry's case but did not help him materially to effect a better adjustment. Commitment to an institution such as the National Training School in Wash-

ington, D. C., was recommended to the court. It was believed that Henry would benefit from trade training courses available at this school and from the general program of discipline and re-education.

In connection with the over-all plan of treatment, it was felt that prerelease planning should include talks with Henry's mother, stepfather, and other relatives, interpreting to them Henry's problems and needs. Unless improvement could be made in Henry's attitudes toward them and the home environment, it seemed desirable to formulate other plans of residence for parole purposes.

Comments by the Case Analyst

As the reader has ascertained from the foregoing summary Henry had a difficult beginning as a baby and an unsatisfying childhood and early adolescence up to the age when his latest escapade gets him into the hands of federal officials. It is not clear from the record whether he knew of his questioned paternity; of the kind of father (supposed?) person who was an aggressive offender; of this father person who wound up in state prison and eventually disappears from his mother's or Henry's world. Even though we are not sure of any of these we cannot deny that a growing child could have been unaffected thereby. Is it unsound to infer that there may have been conflicting feelings within this boy that may have had bearing on his development and behavior? Couple this with the fact that Henry grew up in the home of his mother's parents with all of its overindulgences and unevennesses of discipline, and in a home in which an uncle eventually lands in state prison convicted of rape and armed robbery and we get some further understanding of how rudderless these first 15 years must have been. Perhaps it is understandable, too, that the school as well as the child guidance center was of limited help when there was so little to take hold of in Henry.

What we know for certain is that on February 18, 1942 a federal judge, with the aid of his probation staff, had a decision to make that related not only to what Henry had been but, more importantly, also had a bearing on what Henry was to be during the rest of his life. In the concluding words of his presentence report the investigating officer unoptimistically remarks:

It is apparent that the juvenile is in need of strict discipline through incarceration. All efforts of the child guidance center failed in bringing about some degree of reformation. The juvenile could not be depended upon to live up to any of the conditions of probation which might be imposed.

An institution affording a trade training in woodworking would be considered as most desirable. It is felt that, if given an opportunity to learn a trade whereby he could support himself, he would adjust favorably in the future. Probation is not recommended.

The reader cannot but wonder wherein lies the magic of a prescription that bases restoration upon learning a trade. What of the effect of the previous 15 years of life experiences? Are they all corrected by the simple expedient of learning a trade? What is this other supposed magic of "strict discipline through incarceration" and what relation is it presumed to have to the foregoing 15 years? Why can we not recommend probation? Do we doubt the effectiveness of our probation skill to help a person like Henry until he has learned a trade and endured the strict discipline of incarceration? This is the question every probation officer must ask himself day in and day out, and answer honestly.

Do we think of the training school as the last resort, to be used only when nothing else is available or when we do not know where else to turn? An illustration from another area of service may

help. There was a time when it was believed that the orphanage was the last place to send a child, and to be used only as a last resort or after everything had failed. Not so, now; workers see children's institutions as having a valid place in the gamut of child welfare services and that these institutions are to be used to meet the particular needs of particular children. Should not correctional institutions for juveniles be so regarded —or deserve to be so regarded? Perhaps it is about time that such institutions were so organized, staffed, and operated that they were used because they effectively met the needs of youngsters. This is a far more constructive use and purpose than to tolerate them because there is nothing else.

Report of Supervision Progress

February 15, 1943.—"Talked at length with Henry's mother concerning parole which is to be granted on or about April 17, 1943. The mother seems anxious for Henry's return home. She mentioned that she and her second husband are separated but there is a possibility of a reconciliation. PO discussed with the mother some of the significant causes of Henry's past delinquency. It was suggested to the mother that her son must be shown considerably more understanding and affection than was formerly the case. Otherwise, Henry is likely to go back to antisocial conduct as a way of getting recognition. It was stressed that Henry must be made to feel that he is definitely wanted in the home. Also, if there is to be improvement in Henry's conduct discipline will have to be administered in a more intelligent, orderly, and reasonable manner. The mother feels that she must continue to work outside the home but said that she realizes that she must change some of her ways if she is to help her son."

One wonders whether Henry's mother might have been approached in some other way. There seems to be a note of lecturing or preaching to her, even a directive as to how she is to deal with him. Might she have been permitted to discuss how she felt about Henry and his difficulties and have been encouraged to express how she felt he could be helped in the home situation and what responsibility for himself he could reasonably be expected to take? Henry's mother undoubtedly has been through a great deal during his tempestuous years. For her to know that someone understood her as well as Henry and was ready to help could mean a good deal to her. How one dealt with her in these critical days before Henry was to come home would have much to do with how she could handle the situation when and after he arrived. It makes a difference whether the helping person—the parole officer—lectures and directs her, or whether he is understanding of her and affords her an opportunity to participate in the planning and thinking. What the parole officer says, and how he says it is very important.

This same point is involved in the interview with the mother on April 20, 1943 after Henry has returned home. What virtue is served in reviewing some of the causative factors in Henry's previous delinquency and in demanding or ordering "family unity and harmony?" Doesn't Henry's mother have a fairly adequate sense of these things, and wouldn't it be more profitable to enable her to discuss with the parole officer what she and Henry can do and will do? Isn't it really Henry and his mother who have to make a go of it, and what they themselves put into that effort will determine to a large degree its success.

February 15.—"Interviewed Mr. Robert Wilson, proposed parole adviser. He is assistant manager of the Metropolitan Life Insurance Company at. . . . He seems to be a man of good intelligence and one who would have a great deal of patience and understanding in working with a juvenile delinquent.

"Mr. Wilson has talked to subject's mother, lives near their home, and seems to know quite a little about the family back-

ground and some of Henry's problems and needs. In probation officer's judgment, Mr. Wilson will make an excellent adviser."

April 20.—"Visited the home and had a private talk with Henry's mother. She seems most happy to have her son home again. The mother notes improvement in Henry's attitude as he seems to be more mature, responsible, and considerate of others.

"During the course of conversation PO again reviewed some of the causative factors in Henry's former delinquent behavior. It was pointed out how the involved family differences acted detrimentally to Henry's adjustment, that Henry will have a very difficult time to readjust to free society, and will need all possible help, including family unity and harmony.

"Later PO talked with Henry who was not at home when PO first called. He displays a friendly, co-operative attitude. He has an opportunity to get a better job than that with the NYA which was approved for parole purposes. He requested permission to work for the Meadow Dairy Company which would pay considerably more than the NYA job. He mentioned that this proposed employer knows of his parole status. PO approved of this change in employment."

May 7.—"Called at Meadow Dairy and talked to the manager who said Henry is doing his work well and is liked by the other employees. He is now doing general labor work and earns approximately $35 a week. The manager said that he would let us know if Henry's work adjustment should become unsatisfactory."

May 7.—"Visited the home and interviewed Henry and his mother. Henry has undergone treatments for hemorrhoids. His mother is paying for the treatments which will cost about $125. Henry likes his job although at times he has to do heavy lifting which aggravates the hemorrhoid condition.

"The mother told PO that she is planning on reuniting with her estranged husband. She remarked that she will make it plain to him that unjust treatment of her son will not be tolerated.

"PO discussed with Henry the possibility of the stepfather living in the home and urged him not to be prejudiced because of past experiences. Henry said that he would be as fair and understanding of his stepfather as he possibly can be. PO encouraged Henry to consult with us at any time that he has problems or difficulties which are causing him worry and anxiety. Henry indicated that several days ago he went to the YMCA and that he would like to join the 'Y' and possibly live there. He learned that there is a long waiting list for rooms and intimated that he would appreciate PO's help in getting him into the 'Y'."

When a parole officer visits a parolee's employer does he do it with the knowledge of the parolee? Before the visit? Afterward? How does the visit to the employer, with or without knowledge of the parolee affect the nature of the parole officer-parolee relationship? Is it something for the parole officer to be aware of? In the instant situation does the parole officer discuss with Henry later that day his visit to the employer? If not—and there is no indication in the record—why not?

It seems a reasonable inference from the foregoing entries in the record that there is a helpful relationship between the probation officer and Henry. He seems able to turn to the worker when he wants him, and the worker seems to respond to these overtures of Henry's. The exchange about getting or not getting a room at the YMCA is certainly a case in point.

May 12.—"Henry came to the probation office and said that he has decided against moving to the YMCA, at least for the time being. He appears to have gained quite a little insight into his personality and difficulties; also seems sincerely desirous of wanting to make a good adjustment.

"During the interview Henry showed great admiration and respect for his parole adviser. He said that he had never met anyone who took such great interest in his welfare. The adviser visits him frequently at home and takes him to movies and boxing bouts. Henry regards his adviser as a true friend.

"Henry hopes someday to obtain a job where there is a possibility of learning a trade."

In the field notes in the case history an entry dated June 2, 1943, shows that when the parole officer called on Henry and found no one at home he talked to the next door neighbor. According to the neighbor Henry was "doing satisfactorily." This procedure raises a question about the advisability of talking with neighbors about a parolee. How does this affect the worker-parolee relationship? What can a neighbor say that will be of such help as to warrant jeopardizing the relationship that has been set up between the parole officer and Henry? Suppose the worker had secured some information—possibly harmful to Henry—from the neighbor, what use would the worker make of it?

June 27.—"Visited the office of the parole adviser who is a very socially minded person and is devoting considerable time in assisting Henry with his problems. The adviser has a wide circle of friends, some of whom own small industrial plants. PO mentioned to the adviser that Henry indicated a desire to get a job where he might eventually become a skilled worker. The adviser said that he knows one of the owners of the Central Tool & Machine Company and will present Henry's case to him."

The question naturally arises as to whether Henry isn't capable of taking up a matter like this with his parole adviser. Doesn't Henry have to learn to exercise initiative and to take responsibility for himself, and isn't the parole officer depriving him of this opportunity by his apparently well-intentioned efforts on Henry's behalf?

July 23.—"Called at home and talked with Henry who revealed that he is now working for the Central Tool & Machine Company. He is doing inspection and delivery work and has been promised the opportunity of later apprenticing as a tool and die man.

"Henry narrated that his mother and stepfather are again living together and conditions at home are very upsetting. He remarked: 'I just can't get along with my stepfather.' PO suggested to Henry that he try to get a room at the YMCA and said that he would go there personally and recommend him. Henry is now earning enough money to support himself and be financially independent of his relatives. It was pointed out to Henry that his moving from the mother's home need not lead to an entire break in their relationship. However, by living outside the home he can avoid the constant bickering which is taking place between his mother and stepfather."

July 23.—"Visited the resident secretary at the YMCA and gave him a brief history of Henry and his family problems. The secretary stated that he would make arrangements in a day or so in order that Henry can room at the YMCA. When Henry registers the various activities of the 'Y' will be explained to him and he will be urged to participate in those activities which interest him."

When the home situation was upsetting, the parole officer quite rightly suggested to Henry the possibility of a room at the YMCA. The parole officer said he would go there personally and recommend him. Here again the worker cannot forbear doing for Henry what Henry much more properly should be doing for himself. Who is going to get out of the home and who is going to live at the YMCA, the parole officer or Henry? The parole officer goes to the "Y" secretary, and eventually Henry moves in. Why couldn't Henry have initiated arrangements? A telephone call or a letter from the parole officer to the "Y" secretary after Henry might have made the step would have been sufficient, in all likelihood. When is Henry going to be allowed to make some of his own decisions?

August 1.—"Henry came to the probation office and informed us that he has moved to the YMCA. He likes living there, has met several desirable fellows his own age, and is taking advantage of the recreational and social facilities. For spare time activities Henry works out in the gym and swims. The 'Y' sponsors some dances and coeducational activities and Henry is participating in these whenever he can.

"Henry likes his job at the Central Tool & Machine Company and is looking forward to being assigned a tool and die apprenticeship, an assignment promised him as soon as he becomes more familiar with the work."

October 9.—"Visited Henry at the 'Y' and he seems to be continuing to make a satisfactory adjustment. Henry sees his mother on Sundays when he goes with her to the grandparents' for dinner. She is still living with her second husband but is planning a divorce. Henry revealed that he has visited his maternal uncle, who is in the state prison. Whenever he has gone he has been accompanied by relatives. Henry informed probation officer that he would like to enlist in the Navy. He will be 18 in August and at that time subject to the draft."

October 9.—"Went to the Navy Recruiting Office and presented Henry's case. Henry will have to have a complete unconditional discharge from parole before he can be considered for enlistment. Also he would need three character references. The Navy recruiting officer felt that Henry's juvenile delinquency record would probably prevent his acceptance as an enlistee."

Why couldn't Henry have gone to the Navy recruiting office? Did the parole officer and Henry talk this over beforehand? Whose decision was it that the worker should go?

Likewise in the following entry, December 24, why couldn't Henry have gone to get his birth certificate? Why couldn't Henry have mailed his birth certificate to the Canadian Legation? Whose birth certificate is it, whose discharge is being sought, who got himself into the Canadian Army, and who has to get himself out? These are not rhetorical questions, but go to the heart of helping another person. We are not doing another person a favor when we take over *from* him and *for* him the responsibility which alone is his. This is not to say that we deliberately make a situation difficult for another person or that we obstruct or withhold capriciously. It means that we operate on the basis of helping people to take responsibility for themselves by enabling them to perform the acts that involve taking responsibility for themselves. We need to recognize our well-intentioned and humanly understandable efforts and at the same time enable another person to whom we are professionally and helpfully related to exercise those prerogatives, responsibilities, and initiatives that are solely his.

December 24.—"Went to county clerk's office to get a birth certificate for Henry. Henry has never received a discharge from the Canadian Army and, of course, must do so before he can get into the United States Navy. PO obtained a birth certificate and will mail it to the Military Attaché, Canadian Legation, Washington, D. C.

"Visited Henry at the 'Y.' Henry continues to work on the afternoon shift at the Central Machine Company. He seems to be making an excellent adjustment.

"Henry mentioned that he still wants to enlist in the Navy. He said that if he fails in this effort he plans to volunteer his services for induction next August when he will be 18 and at that time will register for the draft.

"Henry was informed that the PO is endeavoring to get him an honorable discharge from the Canadian Army. Several of Henry's friends have gone into the service and the young man who has been his closest companion is expecting to be inducted into the Army within the next 2 months."

February 18, 1944.—"Visited Henry at his room in the 'Y.' Henry proudly told PO that he is now working as a tool and die apprentice at the Central Machine Company. He has started to buy some of the necessary tools and gauges. He reported that his employer has given him jobs of importance and also told him that he would have a job after the war ends.

"PO left a form which is to be completed by a physician for the Canadian Military Attaché with reference to Henry's discharge from the Canadian Army."

This is a helpful procedure—to permit Henry to arrange for a physician to complete the form. Shouldn't Henry have carried responsibility for some of the preceding actions—such as going to the YMCA, going to the recruiting office, getting his birth certificate, etc.?

April 14.—"Called at the 'Y' and presented Henry with a Canadian Army discharge which was received at the probation office. PO told Henry we have written the parole board for a suspension of parole supervision during military service. Henry again expressed a desire to join some branch of the service, preferably the Navy or Marines.

"Henry continues to work on the afternoon shift at the Central Machine & Tool Company. He has now bought a full set of tools which cost more than $100. Henry remarked that he hopes some day to complete high school through attending night school."

Is there any reason why the Canadian Army couldn't have sent Henry's discharge papers directly to him? Couldn't Henry have written the parole board for a suspension of parole supervision during military service? Why do all these things have to be done for him?

April 27.—"Henry came to the probation office and said that he had been to the Navy recruiting office. The Navy officials there wouldn't accept the parole suspension certificate which he presented. Rather, told Henry that he would have to have an unconditional discharge from parole. The lieutenant in charge suggested that if he were to go personally to Washington, D. C., and talk with a certain official there his application for enlistment might be approved. PO explained to Henry that the United States Board of Parole could not grant an unconditional discharge but the parole suspension certificate during period of military service was substantially the same thing."

June 12.—"Henry again called at the office and requested permission to travel to Washington, D. C. He can make arrangements with his employer for a 2-week leave of absence from work and wants to make further attempts to enlist in the Navy.

"In view of Henry's excellent adjustment up to now travel authorization was given to Washington, D. C. Henry will be back within 2 weeks and will notify probation officer upon his return."

Isn't this one situation in which Henry might have been permitted to correspond directly with the United States

Board of Parole? If the parole officer were required to write the United States Board of Parole, couldn't it have been to support and strengthen Henry's inquiry or request? Is it realistic or even fair to Henry to provide travel authorization to Washington, a distance of over a thousand miles? Wasn't this really one situation where he might have been counseled with in view of his impetuousness in rushing to Washington? The futility of his visit to the United States Board of Parole, as shown in the June 27 entry below, must certainly have been a demoralizing experience, as well as the "run around" he felt he had been given by the recruiting officials.

June 27.—"Visited Henry at the 'Y' after he had previously reported his return from Washington, D. C. Henry said that he tried to enlist in every branch of the service but was refused. While in Washington Henry called at the office of the parole executive. He feels grateful for help received there in his attempts to enlist. However, he feels that he was given the 'run around' by recruiting officials.

"During the talk with Henry he related that he will become 18 on August 31, 1944, and at that time will register for the draft and volunteer his services for immediate induction.

"Henry revealed that his mother is now divorced from her second husband. In the event Henry does not pass the necessary examinations for entrance into the Army he plans to move out of the 'Y' and live with his mother. Henry feels that she needs financial assistance from him."

August 15.—"Talked with Henry at the 'Y.' He is working regularly at the same job and apparently is confronted with no new or unusual problems.

"Later talked with the resident secretary of the 'Y.' He revealed that Henry has made an excellent adjustment at the 'Y' and has participated in various activities."

September 10.—"Henry came to the probation office and said that he is to report for induction on September 15. He will continue to work up to the day he reports for induction. Also will let PO know immedi-

ately whether he is accepted. Henry is anxious to get into the armed forces as so many of his friends have already gone into the service. He seems to bear no ill will or feeling of bitterness because of past experiences in attempting to enlist in the Navy and the Marines."

September 15.—"Henry telephoned PO that he has been inducted into the Army. He is quite elated as he wants to do his part for this Country in time of war. Henry thanked probation officer for the help given him since his return home. He will write his parole adviser and thank him.

"PO explained to Henry that if for any reason he is discharged from the Army prior to the maximum expiration date of his sentence he should report at once to this office, either in person or by mail."

August 27, 1948.—"Henry called at the probation office and showed PO his Army discharge certificate. He received an honorable discharge and served overseas for more than 18 months as a staff sergeant in an engineer's unit.

"Henry has been out of the Army for some time and is now working as a representative for a tool company in. . . . He seems to be doing well financially and is spending a couple of weeks in . . . on a vacation. He recently purchased a new Chevrolet car and was accompanied to the probation office by his mother. They were on their way to . . . where Henry's maternal uncle is now incarcerated.

"Henry has made arrangements for renting an apartment in Florida and is planning to have his mother live with him."

The reader cannot but wonder what the Army experience meant to Henry. What elements in that experience enabled Henry to stay on his feet and to come out of it confident he could make his own living and set up an apartment that would bring him and his mother together again? Was it simply the stability that some persons allege accompanies growing older? Or had the experience with his parole officer and his parole adviser prepared him for the security which the Army experience may have held for him? We do not know from the record. We may never know. It would be worth while, however, if some study could be made that would give us insight and understanding of what military experience has accomplished for probationers and parolees—and how.

A closing comment is in order. To this reviewer there seems to have been a great deal of doing *for* Henry. In a number of situations the question might well be raised as to whether the very desire of the probation officer to help didn't deprive Henry of opportunities to carry the responsibility which was rightly his. It might well be asked how Henry was to learn to make his own decisions and to act responsibly unless he actually had the opportunity to do so. Shouldn't this have been permitted him even at the risk of mistake? How else was Henry to learn for himself?

Despite these seemingly critical remarks, it is undoubtedly true that this probation officer substantially helped Henry to get stabilized from the time he was discharged from the National Training School at 16½ years to the time he entered the Army at 18 years. Especially is this service to be appreciated when we bear in mind Henry's early upset years, the lack of help in his maternal grandparents' home, the failure to get help from various community agencies including the child guidance clinic. Was the trade training the determining factor, the discipline of the National Training School, the humanness of the parole adviser, the steady and ready hand of the probation officer? Perhaps it was all of these, and who shall say in what proportion.

Within the past several years there have been a number of articles in *Federal Probation* and *Focus* bearing on the question: is probation (or parole) work social casework? To this writer there is no question but that probation (or parole) is social casework. There is no intention here to review the controversy (Ben Meeker well states the case for social casework in *Federal Probation*,

June 1948) but merely to ask: if the probation (or parole) officer is not a social caseworker, what is he? If the probation (or parole) officer does not use the knowledge and skills of the helping process, what does he use? To claim that part of the probation (or parole) officer's job is administrative or is concerned with the law, or with the use of community resources is not to deny the essential helping function that lies at the core of the job. What has been developed in the last 50 years as skill in the helping process is applicable wherever people are in trouble. It begs the question to say the offender does not come voluntarily asking for help. The skill lies in meeting the person where he is and helping him to use what capacities he has or can develop. The skill is just as usable in a courtroom, in prison, a child guidance clinic, a children's institution, or a county welfare department. The determinant is not the *where* help is offered but the *how* it is offered.

General Principles to Guide Supervision

1. One should have a full knowledge of community resources which can be utilized for helping parolees in connection with particular problems which arise.

2. A delinquent, like any other person, does not live in a vacuum. During the period of confinement, for those delinquents who are institutionalized, some prerelease work should be directed toward treatment of faulty attitudes and habits of parents. Also correcting other defective phases of the social environment. If this were done parole supervision would in most cases be more effective and successful.

3. The selection of a parole adviser is of great importance. Especially where the parolee lives in a town or city quite a little distant from the probation office. In such cases the adviser is near at hand and can be consulted frequently. An adviser who is socially minded, intelligent,

and willing to spend quite a little time with the parolee, can be of utmost help in supervision.

4. Study a case thoroughly before release as well as during supervision. So far as possible prevent problems before they occur. At least, work for a solution before they become serious. "A call in time saves nine." It is important to make frequent contacts in the early phases of supervision. As the parolee becomes better adjusted in his work, home, and social life, supervision calls as a rule can be reduced in number.

Reconstructing Youth: Some Case Studies[*]

By Joseph Vogel. Parole Officer, National Training School for Boys, Washington, D. C.; Social Worker, Federal Prison Camp, Montgomery, Alabama.

HERE ARE three case-history summaries which vividly portray the treatment resources available under the Federal Juvenile Delinquency Act, and demonstrate the latitude and flexibility of the treatment program. These cases indicate relatively successful outcomes and are significant in that they clearly illustrate, in dealing with the youthful offender, the changing attitude from one of "punishment of the offense" to one in which there is an increasing endeavor to understand the delinquent and his background, and to treat him on the basis of his individual needs.

A Case of Noncorrectional-School Placement

Arthur, 17 years old, ran away from home and worked his way southward for a distance of more than a thousand miles. When his money gave out, he forged his father's name to a check for $35 and cashed it. In Texas he stole a car and drove to another state where he was apprehended.

The father, when notified, offered payment of damages and transportation if the court would return his son on probation. This the son refused. He wrote to his father: "Unless you can learn to talk more like a father to a son than a preacher to a sinner, I don't want to hear from you." He was committed for the period of his minority, with recommendation that he be designated to an institution of the training school type.

Home Background. The family had lived 10 years in a midwest town, the center of a farming region. They had purchased a 6-room house which the mother—one of those always-busy, always-weary women—kept spotlessly clean; her husband believed less harm would be done if she spent her devotion in the house rather than on the children. He provided well; he was the only photographer in that region, a craftsman trained in his native Germany. A daughter had graduated from high school and then had gone to work in her uncle's photography shop in another city. An older son, in contrast to the spirited independent Arthur, was an easygoing lad who took nothing, not even his father's dignity, seriously.

Arthur lived most of his life in the same town, always a healthy boy. Nothing special distinguished him from the average boy. He attended church every Sunday with his parents. In school he was rated a good student. He liked to play baseball, but his hobby took most of his time—photography.

Family Relationships. Surface impres-

---

[*] Reprinted from *Federal Probation,* Vol. VI, July–September, 1942, pp. 33–37. Used by permission of author and publication.

sion indeed revealed nothing significant about boy or family, until one looked closer within the home. Then one found that spotlessness, good behavior, even choice of a hobby were achieved by the imposition of ruthless discipline. The father ruled with an ear deaf to the slightest contradiction. Even when the children grew older he did not relax; they had to account for their thoughts and activities, report home early every evening, were not permitted even the simple liberties taken for granted by other children.

Arthur ran away from home, the first time, for 2 days. When he returned, he told his father he would no longer stand for treatment fitting to a child of 5 years. The father promised to change his attitude—and thereupon began with an iron hand to change the boy's attitude. Formerly Arthur had been allowed recreation at least part of the evening; now his father kept him home "for his own good," lectured to him on European politics, held up for his admiration (to use Arthur's words) Nazi Germany.

The boy, telling his story, perhaps unconsciously distorted his father's admiration for Germany into admiration for Nazidom, so that others might better understand and even share his loathing for the tyrant. The conflict was deeper, affecting all the children. The daughter fled the situation, we have seen, by going to another city. The older brother adapted himself, his hostility taking the form of complacency which enabled him to glide through rough water. Arthur could neither adapt himself (he resembled his father somewhat) nor offer any pretext for leaving home. He had not completed his schooling; so he ran away, more than a thousand miles, and, in so doing, committed a Federal offense.

Plan of Treatment. The factors contributing toward the runaway, and toward the offense, obviously did not call for treatment with punitive implications. Any plan for returning the boy home would no doubt have resulted in aggravation rather than in correction. The sensible course seemed, rather, to remove the boy from the aggravating factor; to accomplish constructively what he had attempted destructively. In different surroundings, under a more normal type of discipline, and with an opportunity to complete high school, he could reasonably be expected to arrive at a mature adjustment of his problem.

Arrangements were made for Arthur's enrollment and board, as a Federal ward, at a noncorrectional school located in the State in which he had been sentenced. The school, in a beautiful setting amidst farmlands, was thought to be ideal for a boy who had been brought up in a rural community. Only the principal knew the special reason for Arthur's enrollment; otherwise his status was that of any other student—neither more nor less supervision—his success or failure to be measured by the prevailing standards.

Outcome. To go into detail about Arthur's school career would reveal simply a story of the average boy who gets along "all right." Following a brief spell of homesickness, a feeling of strangeness in new surroundings, he got into full stride in his studies, also participating in an athletic program. Several months later his parents visited him; then at Christmas, at the boy's request and with the permission of the Bureau, his parents sent him transportation and he made the long trip home. When Christmas vacation ended, he returned to school.

Once, too, we visited the boy, and as we strolled along the countryside he confessed he had not conquered fully the fear that, somehow, his "secret" might become known to his fellow students. So strong had been this fear at the beginning, that more than once he had been tempted to run away. What restrained him was the thought that his runaway would destroy our faith, and possibly obstruct school placement for other boys with problems similar to his own. His parting words were: "I won't let you down."

The extent to which Arthur did not let us down became fully apparent much later, in his excellent comportment, in extracurricular achievements, and in yearly averages of 94 in civics, 97 in English, 85 in chemistry, and 96 in arithmetic.

Arthur is now about to graduate from high school. His parole plans have been completed and approved. He will live with relatives in a city two hundred miles from his parents' home. He will work in his uncle's photography shop. Arthur feels confident he will be able to get along satisfactorily until the conclusion of parole. He will then be 21 years old.

A Case of Foster-Home Placement

Three boys, riding in a taxicab, struck the driver with a blackjack, forced him at gunpoint to drive to the country where they tied him to a post, then they drove off in the cab. They abandoned the car in another State, slept overnight in a barn; the next morning, after being treated to breakfast by a farmer's wife, they tied her up, ransacked the house, and drove off in her car. They were caught after holding up a filling station, but not before the youngest, a boy of 15, had threatened to shoot the arresting officer.

The two older boys were committed to a reformatory by the State, for a term of from 1 to 20 years. Walter, the 15-year-old boy, heard under the Federal Juvenile Delinquency Act, was committed to the custody of the Attorney General for his minority, a period of almost 6 years.

Home Background. Walter had been in prior difficulties. Once previously he had been committed to a State industrial school for a year. His record in the local court included theft of a bicycle, runaways from home, incorrigibility. He

was a familiar problem to the child welfare agency. A study of his background made by the United States probation officer for the presentence report revealed practically a lifelong history of rejection, abuse, and homelessness.

The mother married when she was 18. For about 5 months her husband, a contractor, worked steadily, a performance he never again repeated. When there were three children and a fourth expected, he deserted his family. Three years later he reappeared, was arrested for passing bad checks, and again on a charge of nonsupport. He deserted once more, and returned. In 17 years his wife had nine children. She died following the still birth of her tenth child. The father then deserted the children and has never been heard from again.

Walter was 5 years old then. Three of the older children married; the remainder were placed in a children's home. Shortly afterward some of the children were accepted by relatives. Walter was placed as a foster child with a Syrian family; 4 years later the family adopted him.

Family Relationships. Even before they adopted him, Walter hated his foster parents. They taught the child industriousness by keeping him busy before and after school hours with housework. They put him to work at the age of 7 in their confectionery store. The foster mother nagged and complained continuously. If the boy put a piece of candy in his mouth, she accused him of bringing about her ruin. When she found him eating a banana, she charged him with stealing. Finally, in desperation the boy ran away; he rode off on another boy's bicycle, was caught a few miles out of the city and brought back. Again he ran away, riding a freight. When he returned his parents beat him and, to keep him out of mischief, lengthened his work hours. When he ran away the third time he hitchhiked to the Chicago World Fair, where he remained several weeks. Upon his return his foster parents turned him over to his married brother.

This brother, who already had assumed responsibility for one of the younger children, had not much to offer Walter. Sensitive to the devotion shown to the other child, and feeling that he was hardly more than a stranger in this home, Walter fled. For a while he wandered aimlessly, then returned to his adoptive parents. The mother no longer cared to trouble herself over him. Since he had played truant from school, she took him to the juvenile court and he was committed, at the age of 12, to a boys' industrial school. During his entire year's stay at the school he maintained a conduct record of "A." He was found to have superior intelligence. He completed ninth grade school work, with the respect of all his teachers.

Walter was then paroled to the care of another married brother. He worked about the house a while, then was sent to the home of his brother's mother-in-law. He worked here a while, then was sent to the home of a newly married couple. After a while he was sent back to his brother. It was an Odyssey that might have been entitled: "A Boy in Quest of a Home."

He hardly had caught his breath under roof again when his brother and sister-in-law became ill. Both had to be hospitalized, and Walter, left alone, drifted about as he pleased. It was at this time he met the two older boys, one of them not long released from a reformatory. Dissatisfied with their homes the boys decided to venture West and find work—and their manner of venturing brought Walter to us with an offense aggravated by assault, kidnaping, armed robbery, and threatening to shoot a law-enforcement officer.

Placed for observation with a juvenile research bureau, Walter was described as large for his age, more mature than the average 15-year-old; a capable workman;

I.Q. 111; a feeling of rejection; at times discouraged by self-pity. The first 2 weeks he was the best boy there, then he became troublesome. Possibly he played up to the present in order to make improper use of some future opportunity. The treatment he had received at the hands of society was not conducive to a spirit of happiness and cooperation. It was believed, however, that he was a hopeful case for probation.

Plan of Treatment. In considering designation for this boy, one kept in mind his superb record at the industrial school to which 3 years previously he had been committed. Equally significant was the fact that despite misunderstanding and abuse from his adoptive parents, he had returned "home" again and again.

The probation officer, with the approval of the Bureau of Prisons, developed a foster-home placement in a small town where the boy's past was unknown. Arrangements were made to pay board through the United States marshal.

The foster parents, a middle-aged couple experienced with boys, strived, but not too noticeably, to make Walter feel completely at home. He continued with his high school education, and found odd jobs after school hours, affording him the satisfaction of buying his school supplies and clothes. During the summer vacation he worked in a dairy, saving part of his salary for a college education. People in the small town spoke highly of the boy.

Outcome. Walter's teachers considered him superior to the average student in personal appearance and in ability to meet people. He participated in extracurricular activities, played on the school basketball team, and became student assistant to the athletic coach. In 1939 and in 1940 he was elected president of the student council. In 1940 he was elected president of the Senior class. He graduated with honors in 1941.

Since Walter's past was unknown to

the community, the usual procedure in completing a parole plan was waived. His foster father was approved as employer; his foster mother, as advisor. They told the boy that as long as they had a home, he too would have a home.

Parole was granted.

On February 7, 1942, Walter enlisted in the United States Army.

A Case of Commitment to the National Training School for Boys

When George, a 16-year-old boy from the South, came to the National Training School, he gave the impression of an arrogant, conceited lad who liked to brag about his escapades. The psychiatrist's initial report observed that George's egocentricity knew no bounds; in the short time he had been in the school he had already sought out the worst elements and vied with them in defying authority.

George's offense was violation of the National Motor Vehicle Theft Act. He already had a record of delinquencies. When he was 13 he was taken to the juvenile court for injuring private property; 2 years later he was arrested for drunkenness; and the following year he was arrested for drunken driving during which he wrecked a man's car. As usual when George got into trouble he appealed to his father, and his father paid for the damages.

Home Background and Family Relationships. Both parents were responsible, reputable citizens, the family known as one of the finest in the community. The father, a liquor distributor, earned $75 a week and provided liberally for his family and for the education of his children. The oldest son worked for his father. A younger son was a Freshman at college, an outstanding football player, having earned a scholarship for his athletic ability. George was the youngest. His childhood had been happy; he had been protected from the harsher realities. When he grew older, despite his

self-sufficient attitude, he had to lean heavily on his parents when in trouble. He became involved in serious difficulties at the age of 12. The boys he picked as friends were known as "bad ones." He skipped school frequently and in the seventh grade was expelled for fighting. At 15 he already had begun smoking and drinking excessively—he boasted about it.

Plan of Treatment. George's first few months at the National Training School were marked by rebelliousness. It was difficult to explain his attitude; one could readily understand that he had been over-indulged by his parents, for he would fly into a temper when he could not have his own way. Deeper beneath the shell one also found inability to compete with his brothers (the one in college was only 2 years older), an inability for which he compensated by arrogance and viciousness. During the first few months at the school he attempted to run away three times, and once succeeded for several hours, so that it became necessary to keep him almost constantly under special supervision. The boy's disregard for orders and regulations, his disruption of morale, made it advisable after six months to consider his transfer to a different type of institution.

A thorough re-examination was made, however, to discover any reason why he *should not* be recommended for transfer. It was found that in the cabinet shop to which he had been assigned for a time, and where he had succeeded only in making a nuisance of himself, the instructor believed that George had excellent aptitude and the ability to apply his knowledge. On the basis of this rather feeble spark of promise, it was decided to make a further attempt to direct the boy's ability in the right direction.

Juveniles do not come to the Training School as ready-made craftsmen or scholars, nor very often with the experience or capacity to know what type of training would be for their best interest. A boy's program, after being initially determined by the classification committee, therefore is carefully reconsidered every 3 months. If lack of suitable progress is noted, whether in cottage life, in academic classes, or in one of the trade shops, a further period of trial or a reassignment is decided upon. The process is necessarily to a large extent experimental, and for that very reason allows for greater flexibility.

Since George expected to work for his father, after returning home, he was first assigned to school classes with emphasis on commercial subjects. He failed to show any interest, refused even to prepare his lessons. He was tried then in the cabinet shop, where his negative attitude continued. Program planning for the boy was interrupted by his frequent attempts to run away and by consequent removal from his family group to the adjustment cottage. After a 6-month period a further attempt, as noted, was made to direct the boy's abilities into constructive channels. Assignment to a building program, it was believed, would call for greater activity and cooperation, and would place upon him fuller responsibility than he had yet been allowed to assume—it would give him a chance to fulfill his boasts of doing things "in a big way." Weight was also given to the personality of the construction officer, a frank, rugged man-to-man type, which it was considered might prove compatible with the boy's dominant spirit.

Outcome. George's specific assignment was as truck driver (which called for minimum custody qualifications) and as cement mixer operator. He drove the truck for all jobs and work squads. At the end of the first month the construction foreman reported that George was making steady progress; the boy took a keen interest in his job. The next month's report went on to say that George had been promoted to head boy, that he carried out orders promptly and to the letter. And that has continued to be the general tone of George's reports: excellent workmanship, initiative and leadership, a good influence on other boys.

How do we account for the change in George? Reclassification as a treatment process unquestionably contributed toward the change. There may have been intangibles contributing. In work with human beings, unfortunately, one cannot put one's finger directly upon intangibles, nor always even on tangibles, and say: "There! That's what did it. And if it worked for this boy, it will work for other boys."

Last February George's application for parole was denied. Despite this denial, he has continued improving his record. During the past 3-month period, his ratings in the family group and in work detail have been "A." He continues gaining in skill and in leadership. The psychiatrist notes, in comparing his present impression with that of the initial interview, that George has discovered himself, developed insight, and has progressed toward stability and maturity, with extraordinary improvement in personality.

Jim, Mr. Brown, and You*

By Harry E. Brager. National Membership Director of B'nai B'rith, and Richard A. Chappell, formerly Chief of the Federal Probation Service and Editor of *Federal Probation;* Federal Parole Board.

JIM IS AN 18-year-old from Texas whose way of life led him—via jail in Oklahoma —into the National Training School for Boys in Washington, D. C. He's a kid who needed a friend badly . . . and found one.

Mr. Brown is the friend—a "nice guy" —a successful business man in Washington with a wife and two fine, grown children . . . who realized that America must mean opportunity for kids like Jim, too . . . and decided to do something about it. So he's Jim's sponsor and he's gotten other men interested in other boys.

You are in the picture because there must be found—all over the country—a lot of Mr. Browns to help the thousands of Jims who need a friend.

What kind of man makes a good sponsor? What should sponsors do—and not do? We asked Mr. Brown. Yes, and we asked Jim, too.

Selecting the Sponsor

If you're reading this, Mr. Sponsor, how do you think you shape up on the following points?

Pick men who will be able to give of their time

Mr. Brown said . . . If you don't see your boy consistently and often, you'll never reach the pal stage with him.

Jim said . . . How do I know Mr. Brown is really interested in me? Well he's a busy guy and he certainly spends a lot of time with me.

Try to match the right sponsor with the right boy

Mr. Brown said . . . I selected Jim originally because I found that he shared my interest in photography.

Jim said . . . At the beginning Mr. Brown and I got along swell because we're both camera bugs. We talked about it plenty.

Find men with an understanding of human behavior

Mr. Brown said . . . A successful sponsor must have insight. A kid in trouble is usually emotionally disturbed. You must accept that.

Jim said . . . There are lots of times when I must be bad company—quiet and kind of beat. But Mr. Brown seems to understand and doesn't mind.

Lay off the "perfectionist"

Mr. Brown said . . . There are lots of things about Jim that need changing. But who doesn't have some bad habits?

Jim said . . . Man! You should have seen my sloppy table manners. Mr. Brown didn't say anything but I learned from watching him.

Select the man who doesn't moralize

Mr. Brown said . . . I would not expect a boy like Jim to have views on life like my own. We have different backgrounds and experiences.

Jim said . . . I'm not afraid to tell Mr. Brown things. I can tell how he feels about them from his questions—but he don't preach.

---

* Reprinted from *Federal Probation*, Vol. XIII, June, 1949, pp. 46–48. Used by permission of authors and publication.

Find cheerful men—the "optimistic" type

Mr. Brown said . . . A boy like Jim must be given the feeling that he has a chance—that he can make good.

Jim said . . . I used to think the whole world was a rat race. But maybe that ain't so.

Avoid the "Casper Milquetoast" type

Mr. Brown said . . . There is no conflict between being friendly and understanding and being firm at times.

Jim said . . . Sure Mr. Brown has a mind of his own! Could you respect a guy who didn't?

Pass over the "lonely soul"

Mr. Brown said . . . The man with few friends doesn't make a good sponsor. He sometimes needs a sponsor himself.

Jim said . . . I met lots of "right guys" through Mr. Brown. He sure knows some nice people.

Select men with a reputation for following through

Mr. Brown said . . . If you start with a boy—and don't continue—you can do him a world of harm.

Jim said . . . I wasn't sure he was really my friend until I knew Mr. Brown a long time.

Select men who will stay with it when the going gets rough

Mr. Brown said . . . You can't wave a magic wand and expect all of the boy's difficulties to disappear.

Jim said . . . When that guy fired me and Mr. Brown didn't give me walking papers, it was the best feeling I ever had.

Look for men who will "accept" a boy right from the start

Mr. Brown said . . . If inwardly you feel ashamed of a boy, don't be a sponsor.

Jim said . . . I was at Mr. Brown's house for dinner the second time we met. The food was good too!

Hints to the Sponsor

During your first few meetings with the boy . . .

He'll probably be a little nervous and so will you. Don't worry about long pauses in your conversation. It happens. It's natural.

So . . . ask him a lot of questions—primarily about superficial things. You want him to do most of the talking. Your job is to draw him out. But you do want to tell him something of yourself. Intimacy is a two way street. Let him know that you too, as a boy, had problems and discouragements and that you had your "ups" and "downs."

Then, too . . . get a line on the things he likes. Is it baseball, bowling or bull sessions; sightseeing or work shop; canoeing or camping; photography or picnicking. When you know what he likes, plan on doing some of those things.

And it's a good idea to . . . let him know you have a sense of humor. But don't be surprised if he doesn't laugh too heartily. Remember, he may be shy.

Of course you want to . . . inform him of your desire to help him. But you don't want to get maudlin about it.

And a good idea at first . . . when you leave him, make a definite appointment for the next time. It'll help give him a secure feeling until he knows you so well that he won't need that kind of assurance.

After you've known him for a while . . .

You'll begin to realize that you and he are starting to hit it off pretty well. Now you're at the point when it becomes very necessary to remember that sponsorship is serious business and not merely a way to provide a boy with recreation.

At this point you're ready to . . . talk with the boy of his future plans and help him acquire definite worth-while goals in life.

And . . . you've known him long enough to start giving him praise when it's due. Remember, he needs to develop confidence. Compliment him—even for little things he does well.

Another thing to do is . . . ask his advice about things, even trivial matters. One of his important needs is to feel a sense of importance; and being asked about this or that will help him develop that feeling.

Right about now . . . the time is ripe to try to broaden the boy's horizons. You might suggest several books that you think will interest him and lend him those he seems to have a desire to read. Or you might "happen" to buy tickets to a concert. Then again you might suggest a visit to an art museum. Even your interest in some of the beauties of nature may help him broaden his horizons. But don't overdo any of these things. Don't push the boy too fast and don't try to force your cultural interests on him.

And somewhat along the same line . . . encourage him to participate in sports, join a "Y," begin a hobby, etc. . . He can gain a lot of self-confidence and learn team work in holding down second base. Besides—it's fun.

No matter what you do, remember . . . you never want to do things *for* a boy. Rather you want to do things *with* him. The boy may have a tendency to lean on you a bit too much. Don't let him. Talk things through, but remember that he must make his own decisions. Sure he'll make mistakes. But they'll be *his* mistakes and he'll profit by them.

If the boy is still in an institution or on parole . . .

There are a few additional points to keep in mind.

First . . . it'll be perfectly natural for the boy to use you as a sounding board. As he has more and more confidence in you he'll "beef" about lots of things.

Sometimes the "beefs" will be justified . . . sometimes not.

When he sounds off . . . try to help him accept a given situation and adjust himself to it. Make him see that this is not a world of blacks and whites—but of varying shades of gray.

It's bad policy to . . . criticize the training school or the probation officer in the boy's presence. When he "beefs," promise to look into the matter. Then take it up with the proper party and let the boy know you have followed through.

And please . . . don't give in to the perfectly natural impulse to try to run the training school or the probation officer. Without becoming a "yes man" try to understand their problems.

If once in a while . . . the boy asks you a question you can't answer—say "I don't know." Try to find the right answer and give it to him the next time you see him.

At all times . . .

There are a few basic truisms which —when kept in mind—will help you do the best kind of a job.

Never forget that . . . friendship is the thing the boy needs most. All else is secondary.

Real friendship demands that . . . as a sponsor, you can't be a "fair weather" friend. Visit the boy if he's sick. Help him celebrate his birthday. If he's rearrested, see him immediately. A real test of friendship is to stick to a boy through *any* kind of difficulty. Remember, many people have deserted him when he's failed in the past. When you don't, it may be the turning point for him.

You can't buy friendship . . . expensive gifts or money won't accomplish a thing. Small remembrances are fine. It's nice to give them and to get them. But don't go overboard. You'll get nowhere being a "good time Charlie."

A very important thing . . . always keep any promise you make. If you want respect, you've got to earn it.

And above all . . . don't be discouraged if you don't seem to be getting anywhere. There are bound to be failures under the happiest of circumstances. Make the effort. If, after a fair amount of time, you are convinced that things are not going right, talk it over with the parole and probation officer. Boys and sponsors sometimes just aren't matched.

If you and the boy don't "hit it off," it may be a perfectly natural thing.

Do the Best You Can

This has been an introduction to sponsorship—an activity for men of good will that pays off in a special kind of gratification. There are really no hard and fast rules. One part good heart and one part good mind is the perfect recipe for the successful sponsor.

Do the best you can. Good luck!

Sponsoring a Delinquent*

By G. Howland Shaw. Chairman, Continuing Committee, National Conference on Prevention and Control of Juvenile Delinquency, Washington, D. C.

IN LAST analysis there is nothing complicated about sponsoring a juvenile delinquent. It is simply the art by which an adult works out a constructive relationship with a youngster who has been or who is in trouble, to the mutual benefit of both the youngster and the adult. It has been called "the art of disinterested friendship" and that is exactly what it is. You, a normal and average adult, are put in touch by a competent authority with a youngster in some training school or reformatory. The two of you "click," the boy likes you, you like the boy. You get to understand each other, a relationship develops which helps the boy to grow and helps you to grow, too. The relationship is continued after the boy leaves the institution sometimes for many years. In discussing the details of this relationship we must not forget the basic simplicity of its character.

Requirements of Sponsorship Program

There are three fundamental conditions which must be observed if a sponsoring program is to be a success

rather than a detriment. First and foremost, *the sponsor must be selected with the utmost care.* By no means should everybody who would like to be a sponsor be allowed to be one. Certain types should be excluded.

First are those, for instance, who, perhaps unconsciously but none the less certainly, are trying to solve their own emotional problems at the expense of others. To an individual suffering, let us say, from feelings of inferiority of insecurity it is pleasant to have somebody—even a delinquent boy—dependent upon him. The dependence may be carried too far or be prolonged unduly to the detriment of the boy. This group is large and varied and its members often are difficult to detect except by a practiced and discerning eye. Pretty much anything having to do with juvenile delinquency in recent years unhappily has become fashionable and individuals have been known to try to capitalize on that popularity for purely selfish ends.

Then there are those trying persons

* Reprinted from *Federal Probation*, Vol. XII, December, 1948, pp. 13–15. Used by permission of author and publication.

who are always wanting to "do good" and who wander around seeking victims for their predatory kind of altruism. There are, too, the irritating extroverts who seem to feel that cheerfulness, if it is sufficiently boisterous and prolonged, can by itself solve almost any problem, personal and less personal.

Finally, there is the "gentleman and lady bountiful type." They never stop to picture how the other half lives or indeed how anybody really feels, but lavish upon their victims entertainment which is as inappropriate as it is bewildering and destructive to those who have to receive it and seem to be grateful.

All of these types are to be gently, if you will, but very firmly put aside in favor of the man or woman of maturity and well-adjusted and well-rounded life who approaches the task of sponsoring a delinquent unselfishly, seriously, objectively, and with imagination and a sense of humor.

Second and scarcely less important than careful selection of sponsors, *the sponsor should be selected to match the boy*. We are not on terms of close friendship with everybody we meet and there is no more reason why a man chosen at random should be the proper sponsor for a boy chosen with an equal lack of discrimination. If after careful consideration it develops that the selection is not turning out well the sponsor should discuss frankly with the professional supervisor the question of whether some other person could not do a better job of getting next to the boy and serving his interests. At first this is not an easy step for the sponsor to take as it implies a very objective attitude not only toward the boy but particularly toward oneself, but if the sponsor is more interested in the boy than in his own ego, such an attitude in time can become relatively easy.

And third, *the sponsor must seek professional guidance*. The sponsor is a lawyer, a businessman, a physician—in a word, from the point of view of the several disciplines which deal scientifically with human behavior, he is a layman. And the success of the relationship depends upon his constant awareness of that fact. To be sure, it is reasonable to expect that as time goes on he will acquire some degree of familiarity with professional terms and literature, but even then he is still a layman and any illusions to the contrary are certain to lead to serious consequences. The sponsor therefore must accept and seek professional guidance. The boy on placement of parole from a training school or reformatory has a social worker or a parole officer who is a professional and who is in official charge. The sponsor must co-operate fully and at all times with this social worker or parole officer. Indeed, the willingness to accept and the desire to profit from professional guidance are important guarantees of the sponsor's seriousness and competence.

Benefits of a Sponsoring Relationship

So much for the essential conditions of the success of a sponsoring program. What does the sponsoring relationship do for the boy? Many of the boys who reach our training schools and reformatories have had no experience, or a very imperfect experience of normal, happy family life. Friendship, if it exists for them at all, does so on a strictly *quid pro quo* basis. I remember carrying on a correspondence with a young man, who has spent most of his 26 years in correctional institutions, on the subject of whether there is such a thing as disinterested friendship. He said "no" and I said "yes." It took me a while to understand that there was no reason why he should believe in the existence of disinterested friendship since he had never experienced it. The sponsor supplies that kind of friendship. The boy is used to people who claim to be interested in him and who wish to help him but who are paid for what they do. He is totally unprepared for somebody who evidently likes him and who does things for him but who is not paid for it and such an experience and the questions which it arouses in the boy's mind have a very definite therapeutic value.

When I spoke of the mutual benefits of the sponsoring relationship perhaps you thought my remarks were not to be taken too literally. I was speaking in all seriousness for as I look back on the 11 years of my friendship with delinquents and youthful offenders I find it difficult to decide whether they have done more for me than I have for them. Most of us sponsors come from the more fortunate group of society and we therefore stand in need of much education as to how the other half lives. And when we are what is called successful in life it is so easy to forget the less successful and how they feel. Sharing some of the burdens of a youngster in trouble is a most effective antidote for those deficiencies and faults. Theoretically, I suppose, we all agree that good and bad are combined in all of us. It is another matter to learn that truth directly and by first hand experience with somebody whose behavior has become a matter of public concern. There are things to learn, too, about the practice of heroic virtue under the most adverse conditions—things which facilitate the drawing of comparisons unflattering to oneself. Dealing with delinquents, whether as sponsor or on the professional level, is no exact science in which a precise diagnosis is followed by an equally precise course of treatment. All of us have blundered so often and have been proved wrong so frequently that it is impossible for us to commit the great sin of complacency. There is just enough success to keep us sponsors going but never enough to carry the conviction that we are really doing a good job. There are many occasions, I think, when we feel like getting down on our knees

and asking forgiveness for our inadequacies.

Major Problems Facing a Sponsor

Let us now turn to some of the major problems which a sponsor faces in carrying on his work.

There is the very real and very difficult problem of bridging the gap between the sponsor and the boy sponsored. That is not a problem which can be easily solved by taking the boy to a baseball game which you both enjoy and it may be intensified by having the boy to supper at your house. The fact remains that you have lived all your life under circumstances which seem to the boy luxuriously comfortable. Perhaps you have never seen the inside of a cold water flat in a tenement. You don't know much, if anything at all, about economic insecurity. If you're sick you send for a doctor whose bill you know you at least can eventually pay. You can't picture how it feels to have nobody interested in you. You're successful, you're law-abiding. You're a prominent citizen. You're "good." The boy or young man you are sponsoring is none of these things and, especially if he has had a long record of trouble, he may start out by hating you or at least by distrusting you. It may take you months of patient, thoughtful effort to overcome that hatred and suspicion. In such cases I have found it helpful to talk a good deal about myself, emphasizing particularly blunders, disappointments, and discouragements. They are what bring you closer to that boy and make him feel that while you may be a "big shot" you have at least had some experiences he can understand. Incidentally, don't be disturbed if your boy thinks at first that your success has been achieved by crooked means and inquires as to what your "racket" may be.

Another hard problem facing the sponsor is to picture just how it feels to get out of training school or reformatory and start life again on the outside. Some, of course, make the transition without too much trouble, but for many the remarks of a friend of mine who himself has failed often on the outside and whose advice I had asked about another friend just released from a penal institution hold true:

I wonder just how lonesome Tommy is? I wonder just what steps he is thinking of taking to adjust himself to this new element? You can get lonesome, Mr. Shaw, lonesome as hell out there for the inside. A guy would deny it of course, but it is the truth. That feeling only comes when a guy's mind is not occupied, but it comes. If he is working in a stockroom, or an office, or a garage, it will come to him. It will come to him when the people around him start to talk of things he has only read about, not lived. When he begins to see things and realize that things don't happen as he has heard and read in books or from other guys in the bucket. When a person writes a story, the story has to be unusual to sell, when a guy tells a story, the story has to be unusual to be listened to. So for 10 years Tommy has been listening to high spots of life, and reading high spots of literature, not realizing that life is mostly existing in a routine of your own making, waiting for the unusual, and afterwards getting back to normal. . . . Anyway, Tommy is going to have to endure a lot of disillusionment, if left to go on his own hook, before he accepts that idea, or rejects it (as I did) and goes out to *make* his own life, have his share of high spots. That just won't work. We know that, but Tommy won't believe it yet.

Unless you can understand that ambivalence, unless you can feel that loneliness, unless you realize that while we profess charity we, in practice, make many exceptions, you won't get next to the boy you are sponsoring. He does a lot of strange things because he is not at home in the world in which you are so much at home that you take it for granted.

Of course, sponsors must not preach. If you are striving to make your life

what it ought to be you won't need to preach. That does not mean that you haven't an accurate knowledge of what the boy you're sponsoring has done. You must have that knowledge and you must know what it means in terms of religion, of ethics, and of law. If your boy tries to obscure the real character of his act by either skillful or less skillful lying you want to make it quite clear to him that you are not deceived. You should not as a rule take the initiative in discussing his offense or offenses, but if he initiates it you should be able to carry on the discussion objectively and unemotionally no matter how unthinkable or disgusting the offense may seem to you.

A Sponsor Never Gives Up

Finally, there is the problem which is the acid test of the sponsor and often his Waterloo. You have worked hard over some boy or young man only to see him go on to commit some offense and perhaps a very serious offense. What are you going to do? If you are a real sponsor there is only one possible answer to that question: Never give up. Don't say: "That impossible boy; he's headed straight for the penitentiary or the electric chair." Instead, ask yourself first of all: "Where did I fail?" And then in the light of the answer to that question make a fresh start.

You won't be able to take that attitude unless you really care for this possibly very unattractive youngster who has done things that shock you because perhaps you haven't dug down into yourself far enough to realize how bad you are or might be; unless you have passed on to that youngster the power to make you happy and, by the same token, to hurt you in the very depths of your being; unless, in short, he occupies a place in your heart.

There is a well-known prayer which in a few words summarized what I have been trying to say to you concerning the sponsoring of a delinquent. It is the prayer of St. Francis of Assisi, but it might well have been written for the special use of sponsors:

Lord, make me an instrument of Thy peace; where there is hatred, let me sow love; where there is doubt, faith; where there is despair, hope; where there is darkness, light; and where there is sadness, joy. O Divine Master, grant that I may not so much seek to be consoled as to console; to be understood, as to understand; to be loved, as to love; for it is in giving that we receive, it is in pardoning that we are pardoned, and it is in dying that we are born to eternal life.

SELECTED REFERENCES

1. Wise, Randolph, *Yearbook* (New York: National Probation and Parole Association, 1950), "Parole Progress," pp. 19–26.
The various meanings and uses of the concept "parole" are exemplified by Wise as well as the progress made in the past twenty-five years.

2. Carr, Lowell Juilliard, *Delinquency Control* (New York: Harper & Brothers, 1941), Chapter 7: "Finding the Children Who Need Help."
In any plan of rehabilitation, to produce a socially adjusted individual several types of needs must be met: physical, emotional, social and vocational, and the need for social orientation or guidance.

3. Hagerty, Frank W., *Yearbook* (New York: National Probation and Parole Association, 1944), "Classification and Parole Success," pp. 196–209.
The many imponderables that enter a parole-risk situation place a heavy burden on classification committees. Some failure appears to be inevitable, yet classification methods are far superior to the former guesses, hunches and whims of a parole board.

4. Bloch, Herbert A., *Disorganization: Personal and Social* (New York: Alfred A. Knopf, 1952), Chapter 12: "Social Change and the Criminal."
In this survey of crime a successful attempt is made to show the primacy of the sociological frame of reference. The separate factors which are studied in relation to crime must always be viewed in the particular social setting.

5. Vedder, Clyde B., Samuel Koenig, and Robert E. Clark, *Criminology: A Book of Readings* (New York: Dryden Press, 1953), Chapter 20: "Parole."
For the student interested in the parole process on the adult as well as the juvenile level, this chapter contains five articles reflecting informed opinion in this area.

13 COMMUNITY RESPONSIBILITY

IN THE final analysis, everyone must share part of the responsibility for the high incidence of juvenile delinquency. For delinquency cannot be effectively prevented or controlled without community action. In other words, members of the community themselves—and this includes everyone—should support agencies and programs designed to reduce and control delinquent behavior.

But "community," one may protest (and correctly), includes so much and so many: towns, villages, neighborhoods, huge cities, the nation itself. It may be answered that the community of crucial importance in this context is the *local* living area—the community the child first meets and of which he is usually an active member. Perhaps the final solution to the problem of delinquency, indeed, must be sought in the local community. Such a solution, however, if it is to be achieved in any substantial measure, calls for an all-out effort to promote and to use techniques and facilities capable of being developed in the community in which the delinquent and potentially delinquent child himself lives.

This approach is supported by a growing number of professional workers in the field. But the fruitfulness of the approach requires realistic understanding of the vast changes that have taken place in the social environment of children. The local community, especially in urban areas, is no longer firmly integrated by the interlocking primary groups of family and neighborhood. The latter once constituted the principal context of social control and of "living" in general for most people—and particularly for children. To be sure, these primary groups continue to play an important role in the life of the young, and of the young delinquent; but more and more they compete with other groups, for example, the gang and school group, and with the pressures and appeals and cultural contradictions of modern urban society. Understanding the community, then, and exploiting its resources in the fight against delinquency demand knowledge of such changes and realization of their growing influence in the lives of young people.

Delinquent behavior, as brought out in earlier chapters, is especially prevalent in neighborhoods and urban residential areas where traditional social controls are weak and where conflicts between control agencies, such as the family and school and gang, are widespread. Community institutions in these areas are limited in their capacity to meet individual and group needs. Here, too, the temptations of the "shady world" are strong. These are the local communities,

470

therefore, that require the greatest efforts and pose the largest problems for all concerned with delinquency.

PROBLEMS AND PROGRAMS IN THE LOCAL COMMUNITY

Almost any type of effective remedial program in delinquency requires the active interest and support of community leaders and leadership groups. Their enlistment is essential, both as opinion-leaders in the community itself and as avenues leading directly to the existing law-enforcement, corrective, educational, recreational, and readjustment services. As has been seen in earlier chapters of this book, the strengthening of these services should be one of the basic objectives of a realistic delinquency-control movement.

The enlistment of helpful leadership and the strengthening of community agencies, however, are not easy accomplishments. Business and professional groups in local communities, possessing leadership capable of understanding and controlling juvenile delinquency and motivated to undertake extensive programs in this direction, frequently encounter apathy and even hostility from others. Consider the case of Fayette County, Pennsylvania, the home of over two hundred thousand people drawn from many parts of the world, where a few years ago delinquency became a grave problem. The obstacles confronted by the committee of professional and business leaders created to cope with this problem are described by Ruth W. Love:

> Citizens read newspaper stories of teen-age criminals, of the activities of a "Green Hornet" gang composed of boys terrorizing the community in which it operated, of car-stripping gangs heckling automobile owners whose private garages were not excluded from the organized depredations of youth. By 1936, a group of professional and business men decided to move into action in Redstone Township where the heaviest taxes were paid by coal companies and the offenders came from homes of families that were one, never more than two, generations removed from "the old country."
>
> These men—teachers, storekeepers, salesmen—met, discussed the problem facing them and mapped a plan for making personal contacts with a juvenile delinquent. Their efforts received a cool reception from parents, many of whom spoke only sufficient English to brand the well-meaning citizens as "meddlers" and "busybodies" stirring up trouble for the children of the foreign-born. Snubbed, rebuffed, cursed were the Redstone Township men as they began their program so quietly that few outside their own district knew of the efforts to correct existing evils spawning delinquency. Discouraged, they continued to wage battle, convinced that they were "doing good" but with meager results indicating merely wishful thinking.[1]

This case illustrates the difficulties sometimes encountered which are rooted in the economic and ethnic composition of the local community—difficulties enhanced by contrasting group ways and cultural values, the significance of which, incidentally, may not have been clearly understood by the local committee itself.

Local committees, when they are formed, and professional workers in the

---

[1] Boys of Today—Citizens of Tomorrow," *Federal Probation*, XI, October–December 1947, 43. Used by permission of author.

field, must confront with regularity problems which stem from the cultural complexity, the transitional growth, and, as it is sometimes stated, the "social disorganization" of the local community. They must realize, for example, that social disorganization of the local living area may severely handicap the very best remedial efforts. This situation is brought into sharp focus by cases involving young people who, after having spent time in correctional institutions, return to their "home" neighborhoods only to find themselves once more living in a world of instability, temptation, and, perhaps, corruption. Under such conditions, the task of encouraging such youngsters to be respected and useful junior citizens may well imply the larger but crucial requirement of transforming delinquency areas into socially healthful communities.

Any such effort today must be made in local communities increasingly marked by characteristics of urbanism: functional interdependence but psychological impersonality; class and ethnic complexity and resulting barriers of social distance; ubiquitous apathy and frequent social blindness; and an ever-growing dependence on specialized agencies. All of these features of the modern urban world must be taken into account in formulating strategy against delinquency. And the last of the list, the dependency of the community on specialized agencies, is especially relevant in the present discussion.

Campaigns against delinquency that promise some success require the enlistment of many specialists and many groups, including both policy-making officials and their junior colleagues in schools, police departments, courts of law, recreational agencies, public welfare departments and private welfare agencies, and churches. For delinquency is a many-sided problem requiring a many-sided attack by the several specialized forces of the local community if gains are to be made. And, as in all effective campaigns of peace or war, there must be coordination of the various specialists and careful consideration of the tactical weapons at their disposal.

Specific plans for community-wide programs of an informed and potentially effective type, as Professor Carr has stressed, often meet resistance from misconceptions about delinquency itself, and from real or assumed threats to special interests. Proposals for improving delinquency control in the local community may arouse the opposition of taxpayers and here the interest involved is clear; of influential citizens for various reasons, often obscure; and even of social workers and other participants in the corrective field itself—if they feel slighted or left out. The latter reaction seems to be fairly common: coordination of efforts being hampered by the presumed "freezing out" of some official, say the juvenile court judge, the chief of police, or the school superintendent. On the other hand, sometimes individuals proffer assistance to programs in the interest of personal publicity and self-aggrandizement or for partisan reasons, a situation that may handicap the larger effort.[2] Partisanship among professional workers themselves in the delinquency field is by no means unknown, reflected in the zealous advocacy of this remedial program or that. Such a situation not only lessens essential cooperation but creates uneasiness and confusion

---

[2] Lowell Juilliard Carr, *Delinquency Control* (New York: Harper & Brothers, 1950), pp. 419–421.

among the nonprofessional lay participants, whose assistance is a requirement for an effective broad-gauge program.

These several obstacles to coordinated effort are prevalent, to be sure, but they are not insurmountable. In various communities throughout the country numerous individuals and agencies have been enrolled in antidelinquency campaigns, and their efforts and facilities have been brought together in integrated programs. One of the outstanding efforts of this kind has developed in recent years in California, suggestively referred to as the "community coordinating council program." This plan originated with the Berkeley Coordinating Council, organized in 1919, which established a rough model for other communities in the state. The Los Angeles program, which involved eighty-eight local councils in 1948, receives its sponsorship and overall coordination from the Los Angeles County Probation Department, Delinquency Control Division. The councils promote cooperation among agencies and institutions concerned with child welfare, study social conditions and community resources, sponsor educational programs for the public, and stimulate "social action." The results of these efforts are sufficiently impressive to convince officials and observers in California that the most powerful deterrent to delinquency is to be found in coordinated programs of this type. While this conclusion may reflect, in part, (justifiable) pride in the local effort, most authorities would agree that large-scale efforts to harness the resources of the local community are of basic importance in delinquency control.

READINGS

Fred A. Romano in his article, "Organizing a Community for Delinquency Prevention," shows how a large city can marshal its facilities to develop a workable program for the prevention and control of juvenile delinquency.

Harrison Allen Dobbs in "A New Viewpoint to the Juvenile Delinquency Problem" asks for more substantial thinking and acting about community aspects of juvenile delinquency, stressing the principles of synthesis.

Milton Lessner, whose main efforts are directed toward community organization, seeks in his article, "Controlling War-Time Juvenile Delinquency," to expose the falsehood that the blame for delinquency can be placed totally on the parents. He gives what he considers a more profound and critical analysis of the causes and prevention of war-time crimes.

According to Lowell Juilliard Carr, in "Organized Efforts in Crime Prevention," the problem of crime-proofing a community seems to run all the way from the family to the state and the national government. The immediate problem appears to be the need of more effective social action to spread widely the best practices that are now being used somewhere in every field of control.

Paul G. Cressey in "Delinquency Prevention Begins at Home" stresses that the local situation is the key to the delinquency problem. Any planning and promoting of programs for delinquency prevention can best be done in the local community—and best of all in the neighborhood itself.

Horace S. Volz in "Let's Stop Fooling Around" strongly recommends that responsible persons do something besides rationalizing delinquency and espousing theories that smack of quackery. There is too much activity running at cross purposes. What is needed is a fund of tested knowledge and a set of guiding principles conducive to an intelligent beginning against delinquency.

Organizing a Community for Delinquency Prevention[*]

By Fred A. Romano. Consultant, Chicago Area Project.

DELINQUENCY today is a familiar topic. Having served for a period as a parole agent I have been constantly in touch with the very roots of the problem. But I have also been engaged in a program together with the other adult residents in my community, in which we are attempting to work jointly toward the solution of some of the delinquency problems among our neighborhood children.

The community which I refer to is located in Chicago's near north side. It is bounded by Chicago avenue on the south, North avenue on the north, La Salle street on the east, and the north branch of the Chicago river on the west. In size the district is roughly half a mile wide and a mile long, and it has a population today of approximately 30,000 persons.

For years my community has been one of the city areas which has had consistently high rates of delinquency. It is typical in this respect of all the areas which surround the central business districts and major industrial developments in Chicago and other large American cities.

Since 1850 the neighborhood has been one of the low rent districts in Chicago. It has been a place of first immigrant settlement, successively occupied by Irish, German, Swedish, and Italian immigrants and Negroes from the South. These people came into the area because it offered them the low cost living quarters which they had to seek because of their limited financial resources. They could not afford the higher living standards which prevailed in the more desirable residential areas. As the earlier groups prospered in the economic life of the city they tended to move out of the district and were replaced by more recent immigrants.

We of the Italian community today find some consolation in the fact that the Irish, Germans, and Swedes before us experienced the problem of delinquency and crime among their children and young adults while they lived in the neighborhood. Rates of delinquency have remained relatively constant despite the successive changes in the nationality composition of the community's population. In facing our delinquency problem today we feel that we are not facing what is distinctively ours but what has confronted every group of people who ever lived in the social and economic situation of our district.

Throughout the years traditions and patterns of delinquency and crime have become established in the life of our community. These patterns and attitudes are transmitted by older boys to younger boys growing up in the district. Many children who are exposed to contacts and experiences of a delinquent nature become educated and trained in crime in the course of participating in the daily life of the neighborhood. They learn delinquency in the same fashion that children in more fortunate circumstances learn conventional forms of conduct.

* Reprinted from 1940 *Yearbook*, National Probation and Parole Association, pp. 1–12. Used by permission.

Delinquent Children Are Normal

I think many authorities will agree with me when I say that the large majority of delinquent boys in my community are normal children. They have the same native physical and mental abilities as any other children, and their delinquencies are the result of undesirable influences in the community and a lack of socially acceptable opportunities. Given the same influences and opportunities which prevail in other sections of the city, they would be as law-abiding and as conventional as children anywhere.

Delinquency careers are usually the result of a long process of education and training. Boys start out in such minor activities as junking, shoeshining and singing in taverns. They graduate into the more serious types of delinquency step by step. The course which a boy will follow depends upon the nature of his contacts and associations. A boy usually adopts the practices which are common to his particular group.

I cannot emphasize too much the suffering and sorrow which have occurred in my community as a result of delinquency and crime. It is indeed sad to see our young boys and young men in conflict with the law, incarcerated in juvenile and adult correctional institutions, and worst of all, branded by society as criminals. Our community mothers and fathers, law-abiding themselves, have lamented the fact that their children become involved in delinquency and have exerted every effort to keep them law-abiding.

In the past we have been confronted by almost insurmountable obstacles in our efforts to provide socially approved opportunities for our children. In the first place, our community has been characterized by a confusion of conflicting attitudes and standards of behavior. This has made the task of parents difficult because frequently they found their own attitudes were in conflict with the stand-

ards and practices which their children acquired in the play group, the school, and the community. Children developed interests and desires which their parents could not satisfy because of their poverty. Parents were confused and frustrated in their efforts to instill in their children the essential qualities for conventional, law-abiding life.

Society has attempted to deal with the problem through its schools, courts, correctional institutions and character building agencies. While these efforts have no doubt had their good effects, they have in many cases further added to the confusion in the neighborhood life because they have not usually been closely related to the interests and efforts of the local people. As a rule parents and local adult residents have had little opportunity to participate in the planning and promotion of the programs of these important constructive enterprises. As a result many of these services have existed apart from our neighborhood life and for the most part they have not effected basic changes in the community.

Cooperative Action

In 1935 however, our community people were called upon to take the leadership in the formulation and promotion of our own program for the improvement of our neighborhood. This invitation came to us from the Chicago Area Project, directed by Clifford R. Shaw, head of the Department of Research Sociology at the Institute for Juvenile Research. The Area Project offered to work with us in securing financial assistance if we would undertake to work together in such a program.

This was the first time that any of our group had been approached by an organization supported from outside our neighborhood. We had never been asked to help in planning and carrying on the programs of private and public agencies operating in our community. Some of these had been functioning in the neighborhood for more than thirty years. Many of us had lamented the fact that we did not have the means to do more for our neighborhood children, and we were overjoyed at the opportunity which finally had come to us.

From the beginning we have had the support of the North Side Boys' Clubs, an organization of men many of whom are residents to the east of our area. They have given us valuable financial help and a great deal of encouragement in our work. Although these men ask no credit for the work they do and are committed to the idea of letting us local people take leadership, we have always deeply appreciated their generous and sincere cooperation.

The Nucleus

In our effort to organize a community council of local adult leaders we started from a nucleus of sixty-five men between the ages of twenty-five and thirty-five who have been together for more than fifteen years in a social and athletic club known as the Owl-Indians Athletic Club. Dr. A. J. Lendino, our community dentist and for fourteen years the president of the Owl-Indians, called his group, together with some thirty other community leaders, to a meeting at Seward Park, and they listened to a full presentation by Mr. Shaw in which he pointed out the task which lay before us. At the conclusion of this meeting, we organized the North Side Civic Committee and dedicated ourselves to the work of improving our neighborhood and the influences surrounding our children.

Before telling you of the work which we have been doing the last five years I want to mention briefly the history of the Owl-Indians because we are very proud of our earlier accomplishments as boys and young men in the community in providing for our own welfare.

A group of us, about twenty in number, began as a little street corner gang during our grammar school days. We played together, fought together and attended school together. We had no name but we were closely knit together by friendship. As we grew older we played basketball at our local park, and because our members varied in weight we had two teams. One we called the Seward Park Owls, and the other the Seward Park Indians. I happened to be an Owl.

Later on, in 1923, we decided to formally organize into a social and athletic club and secure a state charter. In choosing a name we encountered difficulties because both the Owls and the Indians were loyal to their names. After five meetings on the subject we pleased both groups by naming our organization the Owl-Indians Athletic Club.

As the Owl-Indians we had a varied athletic and social program which we planned and conducted ourselves. We played baseball, basketball and many other sports. We had picnics, dances, parties and all kinds of social events. In athletics we won park championships, A.A.U. championships, church league championships, and hundreds of individual contests with teams throughout the city.

Through the years our membership increased. Young men in the neighborhood wanted to join the Owl-Indians because we had winning teams and neighborhood prestige. Our membership became community wide and broadly representative of our neighborhood. Sixteen of our members became professional men—doctors, dentists, and lawyers. Within our group we have men engaged in all types of business and industry. By participating together for a number of years we formed strong friendships and learned to understand each other and work together. This has helped us immeasurably in our North Side Civic Committee efforts.

After we had organized the Civic Committee, eighteen subcommittees were named to plan the various phases of the contemplated community program.

These committees were concerned with delinquency, education, vocational guidance, health and sanitation, civic improvement, educational tours, Boy Scouts, music, arts and crafts, athletics, camp, societies and clubs, social functions and several other activities. When these committees had been appointed we began to function as a community organization.

Creating Play Facilities

Our first undertaking was an attempt to find and create play facilities for the community children. We approached our public parks and offered our services to help in the building of a community-wide program there. We went to our local churches and within a few months had programs operating in four of them. Game rooms and handicraft shops were established in the parks, churches and in several store front centers which we obtained.

We selected approximately thirty young men from the community to serve as leaders for the children in these recreational centers. These men were chosen because they had prestige in the community and were leaders among the boys. They were chosen because we felt they possessed the qualities of constructive leadership. Since their employment they have gone through training courses where they acquire the specialized techniques of their work. Whatever we have accomplished since the inception of the program is in large measure due to the efforts and interest of these local young men who are trying to provide for the children some of the things that they themselves lacked as boys.

At Seward Park we found the building dilapidated and rundown. The roof leaked, the showers didn't work, and the whole building had been sadly neglected. The park was monopolized by one gang of boys in the immediate vicinity. These boys used the park and excluded the other neighborhood children. We were able to secure the cooperation of these older boys and open up the park facilities to all of the community. We requested improvements for the park and take pride in the fact that today we have a completely rehabilitated building comparable to any other in the city.

Gradually we have developed a year-round program of activities for boys in the district. Our basketball tournament involves forty-five teams and our softball tournament included eighty-five teams last year. Our activities include volleyball, touch-football, table games, handicrafts, kite contests, marble tournaments, roller-skate derbies, educational tours, Boy Scouting, Cubbing, camping, swimming, movies and many others. More than seventy-five per cent of the community boys between the ages of ten and seventeen participate in this program.

We are particularly proud of what we have been able to do in Scouting. Five years ago there were no Scouts in our district. Scouting was regarded by the boys as a "sissy" activity and parents were afraid it was a military program. We felt that Scouting offered a valuable program for our children and selected two young men to be our first Scoutmasters. These men knew nothing of Scouting but they soon learned. We promoted Scouting, talked in favor of it all over the neighborhood, and encouraged the boys to participate. Today we have seven troops and five Cub packs and a total Scout membership of 255 boys. Seventy Scouts are in full uniform and the program has definitely been accepted by the community parents.

Another matter of great concern to us has been our public school situation. We found one school in our community that had had a new principal almost every year for eight years. Teachers were being regularly transferred in and out of the district. School assemblies and extra-curricular activities common to schools in other sections of the city were lacking. It was evident to us that in such an unstable and restricted school situation our children would undoubtedly be handicapped. Our educational committee went to the district superintendent of schools and made recommendations as to how the schools could be improved in our neighborhood. She appointed a new principal for the school I have referred to, a man who has now been with us four years. He is interested in working with us to better the educational opportunities for our children. Since his coming to the community, his teachers have withdrawn their applications for transfers and there is a much closer relationship between the school and the community people. Each year we conduct interschool athletic recreational programs, and last spring three of our North Side Civic Committee members addressed the graduating classes in three local schools. To a large degree our committee of local residents serves now as a parent-teachers organization interpreting the needs of the community to the school and selling the school program to the community.

Other Activities

Our other committees have functioned in regard to other community problems. The vocational guidance committee has been active in searching for employment opportunities for our young men and adults. The educational committee is now busy interesting young men and women who have completed high school in preparing themselves for teaching positions in our public schools. The civic improvement committee is working to better the housing facilities in the district and has achieved a high degree of organization and cooperation among the approximately three hundred resident property owners.

Our summer camp is one of our most valuable and constructive enterprises. Using the facilities which are extended to us by the Salvation Army, we take 400 boys between the ages of ten and sixteen to camp for a week each summer. The camp is staffed by fifty volunteer leaders selected from the neighborhood. It is truly a community endeavor, planned and conducted by our community people. The importance of the camp as a means for building a closer relationship between adults and children in the community, and for introducing new interests and attitudes to the boys cannot be overemphasized.

In our efforts to improve our district we have been greatly encouraged by the fine cooperation we have received from many sources both in our neighborhood and throughout the city. In addition to aid from the Chicago Area Project, the North Side Boys' Clubs and the Institute for Juvenile Research, we have been assisted by the Chicago park district workers, the WPA, the Boy Scouts of America and many other public and private agencies. The cooperation which has been achieved is particularly valuable in our work with delinquent boys.

We make an effort to give special supervision to all of the delinquents and potential delinquents in the community. The juvenile police officers at our two local police stations and the probation officers from the juvenile court cooperate to the extent of referring official cases to us for supervision. In addition we are constantly giving special attention to boys whom we know to be on the verge of delinquency. Through the wide membership of our committee it is possible for us to make first hand intimate contact with these boys and their parents. We are able to introduce the large majority of the boys to our program activities and establish close personal relationships with them which have proved most effective in influencing their behavior.

Both the juvenile police officers and the workers from the juvenile court feel that our program has made their work more effective. Tim Keady, the juvenile officer at Hudson avenue police station, spent eight days at camp with the neighborhood boys and reported that he established a kind of relationship with them which he had been unable to achieve in his years of police work. Stuart Forward, juvenile court probation officer, makes his neighborhood headquarters in one of our recreational centers and finds that he benefits greatly by this identification with the local community's effort.

These official authorities dealing with delinquency cases in our district have told us of marked reductions in the number of boys under their care. While we do not feel that our program has gone far enough for us to make claims regarding its potentialities for delinquency prevention, we have noted great constructive changes in the behavior of a large number of our neighborhood boys. We do not hesitate to say, however, that many of our neighborhood children are now securing satisfactions through the conventionally approved activities which were formerly achieved by participation in delinquency.

A great help in our effort has been the appointment of three local men who were selected by our North Side Civic Committee to serve in important positions in relation to our community. The Chicago Council of the Boy Scouts of America has appointed one young man to their paid staff to serve as neighborhood Scout commissioner in promoting the Scout program. The Board of Compulsory Education has appointed a local man to the position of truant officer for our community schools, and we are also fortunate to have a local man as the parole agent for our district to work with us in the supervision of our juveniles and adults who are parolees from state institutions.

I cannot stress too much the value to us of having local persons in the positions of truant officer and parole agent. These men can call upon parents and other neighborhood adults for cooperation in guiding the truants and parolees under their care. We work with the truant officer and the parole agent in creating opportunities for the boys and men they supervise. The parolees and truants themselves feel that these persons understand their problems and are working to help them.

We are working with many other community problems and as new problems arise we organize to deal with them. Our accomplishments so far have given us great confidence in our ability to do much in the way of improving our district. We know that what we have already been able to achieve is only the beginning of the task which lies before us. We need employment opportunities in our district, we need wider educational opportunities, and we still need to further strengthen the degree of organization among our neighborhood people, but we know that by working together we can in time accomplish much. With the encouragement which has come we are enthusiastically dedicating ourselves to pursue our community effort for many years to come.

A New Viewpoint to the Juvenile Delinquency Problem*

By Harrison Allen Dobbs. Professor of Social Welfare, Louisiana State University, Baton Rouge

This short paper is a venture presenting a tentative lead for more substantial thinking and acting about community aspects of juvenile delinquency. It stresses

* Reprinted from *Federal Probation*, Vol. XI, October–December, 1947, pp. 18–21. Used by permission of author and publication.

the principle of synthesis, which more community leaders might profitably follow when they plan to attack personal and social disorganization of this perplexing kind. Its statements are not intended to be authoritative, and little additional is expected from them other than the stimulation of interest toward trying a genuinely experimental approach to this challenging social problem. By making the paper brief, readers are left time and energy to weigh the full meaning of what it proposes.

It must be noted that there are many reports on the subject of juvenile delinquency. These could be, and ought to be, widely known. Communities could be using, with more consistency, what these set forth. Social and biological scientists have worked diligently in this area, and they are constantly discovering truths of great moment. One who wants to learn the import of questionable behavior in children should certainly become better acquainted with these new findings. Fortunately, a great deal of literature is to be secured today from libraries and government agencies about this problem, and it will be furnished by them to inquirers with little or no cost, and with helpful guidance. If one studies carefully in this field, he must know factually there can be developed more satisfactory ways of meeting delinquency problems than those now in general use.

The present account is purposely a restricted one. Only a few salient ideas are presented. Nevertheless, these few will have great pragmatic usefulness, if they successfully focus more thinking on the concept of wholes and emphasize forcefully the need of having a total approach to delinquency situations, instead of depending, as we do so much now, on segmentalized slants. Giving that new focus, then, is the chief aim of what follows.

The Hypotheses

Costly failures, countrywide, characterize yet a major part of the social effort that communities put forth trying to prevent and treat juvenile delinquency. It seems reasonable to inquire if this is due in considerable measure to persistent cultural patterns that adhere too strictly to a microscopic rather than macroscopic penetration of such situations. Using an old analogy, the question can well be asked if we are losing sight of the forest in this social endeavor, because trees or their leaves get too much of our attention.

The use of thorough analysis in delinquency cases does have an important place. However, factorial knowledge customarily fails to provide sufficient data for giving comprehensive pictures and for answering all the queries that communities should raise. There is always more that enters into social problems than an analytical process will evidence.

That wholes are something fundamentally different and greater than the sum of parts has now become a well-established, scientific theorem. The consequential place that this idea holds in understanding juvenile delinquency more comprehensively, and in our guiding needy children more surely, ought not be lightly dismissed by anyone. It is maintained that this concept of synthesis, with the activating principles it implies, is a very promising one. When such a viewpoint enters generally into social services, the chance of communities replacing the unsatisfactory behavior of many growing children is likely to be greatly enhanced.

Seven generic hypotheses are formulated for special use here. These come out of the weltering mass of modern, helpful data concerning the nature and treatment of juvenile delinquency in our present-day culture. They have an unusual relevance and service. This is made especially so because of the distinctive mosaic they form. A functional composite results that can be brought productively into action wherever serious community attention is being given to what best welfare is for so-called "delinquent children."

Taken as a whole, counterparts like these have propitious meaning. Together they make a good philosophical foundation to underpin the suggestions this paper offers later for dealing in a definitely synthetic fashion with this urgent social issue.

It is sounder to

1. Be dynamic and experimental in our attitudes and methods when considering the relationships and misconduct of children than it is to remain static and controlled too much by traditional heritage and practice.

2. Guide boys and girls with delinquency problems when they are thought of as being integers of a large human whole, not as isolated or specialized segments nor in a definitive category of their own.

3. Make sincere effort to re-educate so-called "delinquents" for moral, thoughtful social living than it is to condition them arbitrarily to pre-determined "social adjustments."

4. Prevent delimiting mental, physical, and social characteristics, which affect growing children detrimentally, than it is to attempt treatment for morally sick children and communities.

5. Recognize and utilize the undeveloped potentialities of the total individual than it is to over stress his inherent or acquired limitations.

6. Satisfy the growth and adjustment demands of needy children by an intelligent, co-ordinated effort of the whole community than it is to attempt this through separated activities or isolated programs.

7. Establish and nurture in the local community suitable welfare and educational services for children with problems than to relinquish too much this social responsibility to some far-away person or place.

The "Musts"

With such a frame of reference regarding delinquency freshly in mind, it is opportune to offer for further speculation a second influential Gestalt—one that pertains to a body of carefully determined "musts." These, when they are acted upon conjointly constitute a certain type of total approach to national juvenile delinquency. This has a novel quality and is worth while examining closely. A truly serviceable tool that communities might use for progressing more reliably in this particular welfare field, may eventually be evolved from a preliminary blueprint of this nature.

Before proceeding, there are two of its qualities which should have special comment. In the first place, the conclusions that are listed are not looked upon as being complete or final. They are only experimental choices. If these are retained permanently as basic parts of this new instrument, each one will have to demonstrate its own unique worth. It is possible that certain omitted components may replace some of the integers now included in the framework. It may be found, on the basis of scientific inquiry, that they have less significance than calculated.

In the second place, the casual order in which these nine concomitants are listed has real psychological importance. To epitomize the lack of a consecutive relationship and to concentrate upon the complete set as an experimental system, even the numbering of them has been intentionally avoided. Thereby, the meaning of wholes gains a much greater prominence, and a new perspective is afforded.

The following "musts," once they enter more into public thinking and acting, augurs a promising new era. Children's delinquency problems will then demand and get a whole community's organized support. Then total welfare services will function fully in behalf of whole children. This is impossible now with the degree of compartmentalized attention and planning we still tolerate. Changing over to such a unified front seems a sensible way out of some of our juvenile delinquency dilemma. In the new day we must all be doing something more concrete about this complicated problem instead of talking so much of its seriousness and how it seems everybody's cause and business but our own.

As a good illustration of this prevailing community complacency, it is pointed out that, quite foolishly, we have believed that our establishing state juvenile delinquency acts and special courts would relieve us largely of other social responsibilities in this direction. It has been expected that these alone could do for us the very big job to be done.

These social institutions are, of course, important parts of a complete social service. At their best, however, they are but elements of a much more consequential whole. Activities like these must continue to serve children only limitedly, unless they are incorporated enduringly into a total concept that can supply stronger motivation and assure well-rounded methods for the prevention and treatment of such community problems. This is why the "musts" that come next have so much meaning.

We must know effectively

That delinquent behavior of children is a symbol of danger. It is generally a sign of underlying troubles. Although signs may be mentally healthy, there are underneath them consequential causes to be ferreted out. These must be sought with great intelligence and zeal, if there are to be fundamental growth changes in either the organism or his environment.

That so-called "delinquent children" are not much different than all the other boys and girls living around them. All need specific help to unlearn their bad patterns of behavior, which we as adults have selfishly taught them or have carelessly allowed them to acquire. They must be aided to learn new, better ways of growing.

That the suitable re-educating of misbehaving children is not any one person's responsibility nor that of any single discipline or agency. It is a long continued, complicated job that requires real community organization and understanding and has to have purposeful, co-operative effort. It should be a closely coordinated kind and must begin with children's unmet needs, heeded early rather than late.

That there is constant need to detect spots in localities that encourage the growth of ideas of delinquency in children. Steps must be agreed upon and taken to clear up hazardous situations and assure healthier, more growthful surroundings in many ways.

That the wise replacement of undesirable interests and activities in growing children is essential to their maturity and that each must achieve new satisfactions and goals. A child's building acceptable patterns of behaving for himself must be constantly encouraged and ably guided.

How to recognize and heed dangerous personal and group problems promptly and well, so as to save later trouble, complications, and expense. Thereby much may be added to total happiness and welfare and to national security and wealth.

That punishing and creating fear are negative, doubtful ways of aiding anyone in trouble. Developing children need especially an adult counsel and leadership which is intelligent, ideologically positive and growthful.

The necessity of helping keep all community thinking and living on a high plane for everyone who lives in it. As children are growing and developing, their personalities are affected continuously by nurture as well as by nature.

That well trained, experienced guides

who have real knowledge of delinquency problems and who possess special skills to aid children grow are constantly required everywhere. They make good use of all community resources and adapt them to serve in economical, productive ways.

The New Ideology

It is easy to understand how modified the answer to the total problem of juvenile delinquency can be when all these nine points have the opportunity to contribute collectively toward making a new, instrumental whole. Philosophically, such a pragmatic approach does something tangible and gainful to the beliefs and practices of those of us who have a social concern for the welfare of needy children. Functionally, it widens immensely the experimental quality and quantity of educational and social work processes which are to be used in their behalf.

Administratively, plans based on this suggestive blueprint, lessen schizmatic differences and strengthen the place of democratic sharing and of co-operative undertaking in solving what have been, up until now, baffling social phenomena. These have too long affected adversely the welfare of many important children and too often the social institutions to which they all belong.

Fundamental changes in community thinking and acting about this whole matter of juvenile delinquency seem especially necessary at this time. A well unified concept of an experimental nature, like the one just described, calls for further consideration and development. It may finally evince enough reliability and worth to affect the total welfare of children and communities advantageously.

When wholes rather than parts influence more the direction of social work and educational activities and determine what shall be new methods, the improvement of social resources in communities and the care of children therein can be reasonably expected. As was stated earlier, each facet of such a holistic view requires microscopic scrutiny, but before real advances can be made, much more thought and action must be given microscopically to the delinquency problem as a whole. For example, the influential fact of the oneness of organism and environment can no longer be so hazardously disregarded.

In the light of the proposal which this paper crystallizes, it is germane to ask how boys and girls who violate laws actually fare today in each reader's own community and state. What differences might there be in the philosophy and achievements of the social services for children functioning there were this new total approach carefully studied and tried? Doing it this way does have a distinctive scientific quality that partial, disassociated programs inherently lack.

It is high time for communities to accept a new ideology regarding this mooted matter of juvenile delinquency. Concepts about it that hold out firmly for including whole fields and total events have plenty of empirical proof to sustain them. For these and other reasons, it would seem that more community action nation-wide based on the ideas just presented warrants a thoroughgoing, experimental tryout.

Controlling War-Time Juvenile Delinquency*

By Milton Lessner. Project Services Advisor, San Diego Federal Housing Area.

As THE nation faces the outcome of World War II and recognizes the necessity for national unity and teamwork, grave concern is being focused upon the problem of juvenile delinquency. With unity being jeopardized as a result of youth's ambiguous place in our present struggles, juvenile delinquency becomes a national, political issue. It is essential that the energies of the people must be concentrated on winning the war. Obviously any impediments, such as the delinquencies of youth, serve to retard the progress of the war. It must be remembered that the spread of juvenile delinquency gives aid only to the enemy. Reports from the Federal Bureau of Investigation, statistics gathered by local, state, and federal probation offices, and editorials in leading newspapers reveal the damaging and distracting influence juvenile delinquency is having on a nation at war.

Factors Leading to Delinquency

In discussing the problems of maladjustments of youth with a lay-executive of the Boy Scouts of America it was his viewpoint that the total blame should be placed upon the parents. He was opposed to mothers employed in war production plants and accused them of neglecting their children. Despite the crippling effect it would have on war manpower he suggested that these women should remain in the home. To enforce this he proposed that the court punish the parents for any offense committed by their child. By suggesting to the scout executive that perhaps the problem was of such proportions that the community and the "city fathers" might assume some of the responsibilities, he merely retorted that this line of thinking was inextricably tied to the public ownership and "government interference" program. In contradistinction he preferred to keep the problem pigeonholed within the family unit. That he is a proponent of the school of "rugged individualism," now obsolete and ineffectual, goes without saying; but the fact remains that large sections of the press and the public favor such sentiments.

Aware of its seriousness an editor of the *San Francisco Chronicle* writes: "A heavy influx from many portions of the country, working in war industry with the children largely unsupervised in new surroundings, adds to the normal problem and to some extent justifies fixing blame. But it is not sufficient to blame, or to threaten to discipline parents whose children are found to be undisciplined, and dismiss the matter at that."

One cannot dismiss the subject by accusing the Boy Scout Executive of being narrowminded and superficial. On the contrary, his concepts must be analyzed and exposed as a precondition to the introduction of scientific methods applied in combating juvenile delinquency. Let us examine the facts.

To presume that juvenile delinquency is brought about only as a result of poor parent-child relationships to the exclusion of any other factors is to theorize that the family lives in a vacuum. Thus

---

*Reprinted from *The Journal of Criminal Law and Criminology* (Northwestern University School of Law), Vol. XXXV, November–December, 1944, by Milton Lessner.

it is possible to deduce that if the fault is not with the child it must be with the parents. This oversimplified explanation may be heard by quack authorities and rumor-mongers. Fixing the blame on mothers and fathers falls utterly short because it deliberately excludes some of the most fundamental social factors which strike far beyond the parents' control of the situation and are directly or indirectly contributing to the increase of child crime.

After visiting 35 counties and consulting with 156 public officials in war production areas John P. Plover, State Supervisor of Probation in California reports: "poor housing conditions, unsatisfactory school care, and neglect of recreational facilities which naturally follow abnormal population growth . . . have been prominent factors leading to delinquency in those communities."

To cite some examples: George and Henry Q., age 11 and 13 respectively, were found in a vacant house with other children by the police. They had committed some damage which finally brought them to the attention of the court. An investigation showed that the boys' step-father was in the army. The family consisting of the mother and six children occupied an old two-room frame house in the rural district. The crowded conditions in the home were not conducive to any type of play, and the lack of recreational facilities in the neighborhood prevented a normal outlet. Hence, the disparaging home conditions and the inadequate play facilities were contributing social factors over which the mother had absolutely no control.

Jimmie P., age 15, got along very well with his parents, but he was frequently absent from school without cause. His mental age was slightly below normal, and he had, more or less, reached his capacity in so far as academic work was concerned. Though he was literally "fed up" with books and theory, he rated very high in mechanical aptitude. School

facilities were limited and offered little to hold his interest. When the authorities exerted pressure on the parents to force Jimmie to attend classes, he merely ran away from home.

Jesse W., age 16, was a bright adolescent who ran away from home, forged some checks, spent the money recklessly, was involved in an automobile accident, and was finally brought to the juvenile court where a thorough investigation was made by the probation officer. It was learned that the boy's mother was a strong-willed, aggressive person who dominated her son to the extent that he was entirely dependent upon her for his decisions. Mrs. W. had stripped Jesse of any initiative until he finally rebelled by running from home. Once on his own he was at a loss to know what he should do. The above case typifies the extremely attentive and over-protective mother who never wanted her son to grow up. She disciplined him until he was the "model" boy.

Some parents are inadequate in rearing their children. This is true despite the fact that they are sincere in their effort and earnestly try to do the right thing for their children. Obviously, punishing Jesse's mother would be a worthless gesture on the part of the court.

The above are a sampling of families daily coming before the juvenile courts. Professional social workers would find these problems most familiar. Fixing the blame on parents automatically with the intent to correct the difficulties would only lead to more corruption and strain within the family. Under pressure of the authorities, parents would find it necessary to use threats and force on their children. Severe whippings and lock-ups would become justifiable measures to the parents who know of no other methods. The strain on the parent-child relationship plus the emotional wounds taking place in the child would have a critical effect on the child's development.

Enormous funds are spent yearly by

public and private agencies toward the *correction* of delinquency; but comparatively little attention and money is given to the *prevention* of youths' offenses.

The public is slow to realize that once a crime is committed the child's act is symptomatic of a personality difficulty. Administering preventive measures necessitates treatment to the maladjusted child, thus diverting him from the path of delinquency. Agencies and protective societies have been established in some cities to carry on this work, but this in itself does not suffice. Possibly the greatest challenge to the public is the establishment of social and cultural practices that will abolish the very causes of juvenile delinquency. Legislators are giving the problem serious thought.

Characteristics of "The Critical Age"

For purposes of expediency, this article will confine itself to the delinquency problem of boys between 14 and 18 years of age, categorically labelled the "critical age." Statistics on child crime show marked increase at these age levels. This is not unusual when the facts are made known.

Children want to be grown-ups. They constantly imitate and assume adult characteristics. Their basic drives toward adulthood find expression in imagination, imitation, and experimentation.

Though many in their early teen age are mentally equipped to exercise simple adult responsibilities, they are handicapped by immature physical and muscular development. They are not large and strong enough to do strenuous, manual work. However, many boys of the 14 to 18 age level have developed physically to the degree that they can perform commensurably with adults. Deprived from active participation because of state and federal legislation, adolescents must find an outlet in other directions.

Children like adults have strong feelings which reflect themselves in the type of behavior they employ. If frustrated from exercising their natural drives or inclinations, they assume the feeling that they are "different" or unacceptable to those who control adult social standards. Significantly, the frustrated boy feels that he has failed, and frequently finds his outlet in hostile feelings or acts toward, perhaps, the school, or his parents, or the police, or, even, himself. This feeling of "not belonging" is the most salient, contributing factor motivating juvenile delinquency. Methods of combatting it are varied and complex, but for the present let us analyze the feeling of "belonging."

Every child wants to be part of something. He desires to be inextricably tied-up with a group in which he plays a definite part. That group may be his family, his school, his fraternal organization, his church, or just his neighborhood buddies. He wants to feel that he is needed; further, that he can so expedite his part as to make him feel wanted and necessary to his group. He must be assured that if he should try to experiment in the form of an adventure or risk, and perhaps fail, he will not necessarily be ostracized from his group. He must know that after achieving his immediate goal he is given proper recognition by the group in the form of attention, respect, or promotion. To recapitulate on the above, there is evidence to prove that the need for adventure and recognition coupled with the need for "being wanted" when satisfied constitutes precise guarantees for the personal security of the child.

Generally speaking, the delinquent child feels insecure because in his own inimitable way he senses that he does not belong. His frustrations and hostilities make him vulnerable to unwholesome activities and influences which inevitably bring him before the juvenile court. To be explicit, let us examine a few typical cases.

Billy W., a young lad of 15 years, stole

a gun and ammunition from a farmhouse near his own home. On a subsequent date he broke into another home in his neighborhood, and took some money. Later, he entered a school building escaping with a variety of inconsequential articles that he could not possibly use. After being apprehended he could not explain his motive for stealing. When questioned, he said: "I don't know why I did it. I guess I sort of got a kick out of it."

A search into his home and school life revealed that Billy was unhappy because he received little attention both at home and in school. Though his step-father treated him "good" he still felt estranged, while his mother just took him for granted. In school his grades were below average and Billy found the competition too difficult. Because of his weak heart he could not enter into any strenuous play. The other children without any knowledge of his deficiency resented this fact. Frustrated in his efforts to succeed through normal channels Billy resorted to delinquent patterns. Stealing without being caught signified achievement and success. In his own estimation he was clever and outstanding because of his thievery. His thirst for recognition and adventure was satisfied by his achievement in overcoming the risk of being apprehended, and his ability in gaining the loot. Some of his "pals" were aware of his activities, and apparently admired him as "a kid with guts."

In view of his unstable status at home and in school Billy unknowingly felt insecure. Unable to compete with boys of his age he found himself discredited and ostracized by them. Deflated by the fact that he was not wanted, Billy endeavored to do something unusual and exceptional, so that by his achievements he would be adequately compensated, hence, his delinquent activities.

John J., 16 years old, was a chronic truant in school, and beyond the control of his parents. Regretful because of his own lack of education John's father tried to force the boy to attend school, but finally lost patience and applied to the authorities for assistance.

John was a heavy-set, strong, young man who displayed superior mechanical aptitude but was decidedly dull in academic subjects. He failed in all his courses with the exception of those requiring manual dexterity. To attend school full time was turning out to be most discouraging and humiliating to John because of his incessant failures. While his classmates succeeded in their schoolwork, John had become distraught with failures until the gap between them widened to the degree that John felt he no longer belonged.

Jesse B., a 16-year-old Negro boy, was brought before the court for frequent fights and disorder on the schoolgrounds. He was also apprehended by the police for working late at night shining shoes in a bar. He also had a long record of truancy in school. Scholastically he had failed in practically all his subjects despite the fact that he had a superior rating in intelligence. When interviewed, Jesse professed that he hated school because the "white kids" always teased and provoked him. When Jesse attended junior high school he was well accepted by the children, but his promotion to senior high school resulted in his being an unfortunate victim of racial prejudice. Suffice it to say, Jesse felt unwanted. His feeling of not belonging to the school group was evidenced by his defiance, pugnacity, and continued absence from school.

Martin F., a lame, underweight, emaciated-looking young man of 17 years was apprehended for auto theft. During the past two years he established a long juvenile court record of car thefts. It appeared that he could not resist the temptation of stealing automobiles for short rides around the town. Martin was hungry for companionship, but the children in school and in his neighborhood avoided him. Presumably his lameness and his repulsive appearance were responsible for this unfortunate relationship. As a result he became shy, taciturn, inwardly hostile, and entertained strong feelings of inferiority.

Martin F. was intrigued by automobiles. Behind the wheel he felt the power of the car under his control. Inspired by his ability to command the car was a source of enormous personal satisfaction. This single achievement compensated for many of his deficiencies in other lines. Elevated by a sense of importance as the pilot Martin felt equal to those who shunned him.

The above cases categorically illustrate that each adolescent was suffering from "feelings of not belonging." The boys typify thousands of minors brought before the juvenile court each year.

Efforts to Prevent Delinquency

Assuming for purposes of expediency that juvenile delinquency has increased noticeably during war times, it becomes essential to pry into the reasons underlying this condition.

Generally the sphere of interest of children during peace times was focussed on the family, the school, the neighborhood, and the home town. Their interests were emphatically localized and inclined to be provincial. War has extended this sphere of interests to the nation at large, and its relationship to other nations. The transfer of "Main Street" consciousness to "one world" thinking may be accounted for by the following reasons: members of the family entering the armed forces, regrouping of populations to meet war industrial needs, and the change of women's status as active participants in the war effort. These immediate and spontaneous changes have left children with a feeling of insecurity, instability, and bewilderment. Their difficulties in adjusting to such changes have been intensified by the fact that they were *not included*

as a vital auxiliary in the war effort.

Some progress had been made toward overcoming this situation. In San Diego, California the 11th Naval District has established an apprentice course for boys between the ages of 16 and 17½ years. These young men are employed forty-four hours each week on the assembly and repair of airships, and are required to study 4 hours each week under supervision in the plant with pay. The advantages listed by a naval officer are: 1. the course provides minors an opportunity to learn a trade; 2. absenteeism is discouraged on the principle that absence from the course means loss in pay; 3. it provides an incentive to advance; 4. it gives the boys the *feeling that they are directly connected with the war effort.*

The Boy Scouts of America, the Girl Scouts of America, and the Camp Fire Girls are among those youth organizations who have established a program based on war service. They gather tin, paper, and other war-essential products as well as roll bandages, knit, etc.

A Junior Fire Marshals club was recently organized by the San Diego Bureau of Fire Prevention. The youthful members are taught to be vigilant and report any potential fire hazards to the authorities.

Adolescent members of the above described organizations are doing a genuine war service. They feel very much needed and "wanted" by virtue of their part in the war effort. By directing their energies toward helping the nation win the war, they are made to feel secure. It is obviously true that their endeavors will satisfy a need for achievement, adventure, and recognition, and further, give them a "sense of belonging" to "Uncle Sam."

This, briefly, is the broad blueprint which must be flexibly applied to meet the ever-growing problem of juvenile delinquency in war times. It is essentially a community problem and demands community thinking and action. Youth must be organized on a program based on war service so that they can assume the role of junior citizens. Any serious-minded student of social problems would concur that the fullest application of the Four Freedoms translated in terms comprehensible and workable to teen-agers is the solution.

Organized Efforts in Crime Prevention*

By Lowell Juilliard Carr. Department of Sociology, University of Michigan, and Director, Michigan Child Guidance Institute.

ONE OF THE things that most forcibly strikes anyone interested in the control of crime is the fact that it is impossible to find a community in the United States in which all that we know for the control of crime is being applied at anything approaching best practice. There are plenty of communities in which you have outstanding school systems; but frequently in those communities the police departments will be only mediocre, or the juvenile courts will be second or third class, or the recreation programs will be below par, or there will be no family case work agencies, or public opinion will be indifferent to the youth problem, or clinical services for maladjusted children will be missing, or some other condition will exist that tends to lower the average crime-controlling efficiency of the community. If the police department happens to be tip-top, the schools may not be so good; and if both schools and the police are out-standing, there may be all sorts of dis-organizing factors in the community it-self that local leadership ignores. We have innumerable examples of particular agencies or particular services, brought to a high level of efficiency but surrounded by other agencies or particular services of only mediocre quality, or by conditions that are definitely making for delin-quency and crime. Nowhere can we find an example of a community that has brought all of its agencies and services to the level of best practice in each field and has at the same time a complement of such agencies and services, all the way from the discovery of the problem child in the early grades in school to the most comprehensive community organization for the reduction of risk-factors in the community.

Study of Agencies and Services

A few years ago I had to estimate the functional efficiency of the various agencies and services in 12 Michigan cities in the field of juvenile delinquency prevention. At a conservative estimate these cities, which range in size from 9,000 to 160,000 population, were func-tioning at about 30 per cent of best practice in the various fields. Later with the cooperation of the sociology de-partments in seven colleges we at-tempted the somewhat more compre-hensive evaluation of the delinquency-control readiness of some seven com-munities. We classified the various agencies and services under six heads. First, those provided for problem cases; second, those for delinquents; third, those for normal children; fourth, agen-cies and activities for increasing agency cooperation; fifth, activities reducing environmental dangers; and sixth, activi-ties for mobilizing community action. We used for this a special Delinquency Prevention Rating Form and in each city secured from 25 to 69 ratings from rep-

* Reprinted from Federal Probation, Vol. VI, July–September, 1942, pp. 49–52. Used by permission of author and publication.

resentatives of different occupational groups. Newspaper men, law-enforcement officers, and social workers gave us the ratings, which on the basis of uniformity of scores were judged to be the most reliable. That is to say, law-enforcement officers, newspaper men, and social workers generally differed less among themselves in the given community than did other occupational groups.

Two things stood out in these ratings. One was that even on the basis of its own ratings no community was doing better than 60 per cent of best practice and some communities were doing about half that well. The other thing that stood out was that each community had its own "prevention profile," so to speak. One community would be strong, for example, in its facilities for dealing with delinquents while it might be very weak in its activities for increasing agency cooperation whereas another community would rate all of its various activities more or less on the same level so that its profile more nearly approximated a straight line. Let's take three towns: for example, 54 ratings on Bloomington, Ind., gave 50 per cent of best practice; 62 ratings in Mount Clemens, Mich., gave 35 per cent of best practice; while 69 ratings in Flint, Mich., gave 60 per cent best practice. In all of these towns, as was perhaps to be expected, the agencies and services for normal children rated somewhat better than any of the agencies and services for the exceptional and delinquent child. If these results are typical—and there is no reason to think they are not—it is obvious that we have a great deal of room for improving the average delinquency-control readiness of any community upwards toward best practice; and the place to begin in each community is with those agencies and services that are the farthest away from best practice at the moment. A few years ago I would have said that the churches and the police departments were perhaps the agencies most in need of attention. But there are many signs that police departments are waking up to the need of modernizing their methods and introducing long-range, crime-prevention programs. Probably the area of greatest need at present is in the field of community organization and agency cooperation, although a general statement of this kind may mean little in a particular community.

Lines of Attack in Crime Control

Taking in a broad view of the problem of crime-control in general, both on the community and beyond the community on the State and national level, there are at least eight lines of attack, no one of which can be neglected. Some of these in turn break down into many subareas of interest.

The first line of attack would seem to be in the direction of modernizing the criminal law. At least New York State a few years ago demonstrated that old-fashioned laws were not adequate to deal with modern crime. While this probably is not the most important, nor the most urgent need, it would seem to be very real.

The second line of attack that has been emphasized, and needs to be emphasized some more as it is by the Federal Bureau of Investigation, is the strengthening and modernizing of law-enforcement agencies—urban, rural, and State. When we say "strengthening and modernizing of law-enforcement agencies" we mean a great many things that include the reduction of political influence in the police department, more adequate salaries, better personnel, better equipment, crime-prevention programs, and so on.

The third line of attack is the modernization of criminal court procedures to eliminate sources of delay and inefficiency and especially uncertainty. These are technical matters that demand the attention of progressive lawyers and judges, for conditions such as were revealed by the classic study *Criminal Justice in Cleveland* years ago are still too prevalent.

The fourth line of attack is, of course, the wider diffusion of best practice in adult probation and parole. The National Probation Association has been carrying on an educational campaign in this field for years, but conditions in many States are far behind best practice. The fifth line of attack centers on institutional treatment. Obviously, here again we have a whole technical field in which best practice as exemplified by the Federal penal system, for example, is so far ahead of average practice, especially in some of our Southern States, that it is a bit difficult to realize that both are co-existing in the twentieth century. Here, as in some other fields, the real problem is not so much how to improve best practice, but how to make best practice prevail everywhere.

The sixth line of attack would aim at those community attitudes and deviation pressures which invite crime and delinquency. There is an enormous amount of good will in American communities, an enormous amount of wishful thinking about crime prevention; there is even a formidable volume of propaganda put out by various agencies, but there is singularly little determined and intelligent organization to change attitudes and to reduce risk-factors in the places where they need to be reduced.

The seventh line of attack centers on the handling and treatment of juvenile delinquents by the juvenile courts, the juvenile probation officers, the juvenile correctional institutions. Here again it is mainly a problem of bringing average practice up closer to the few outstanding examples of best practice.

Finally, an eighth line of attack has to do with the prevention of juvenile delinquents and ultimately the prevention of criminals by (a) the discovery and treatment of maladjusted children on the predelinquent level and (b) by the removal of causes of juvenile maladjustment in homes, neighborhoods, and communities. A tremendous amount of preventive work of one kind or another is being done, but it is scattered, uncoordinated, and seldom is it inclusive enough. Interesting demonstrations of this technique, or that, are put on and sometimes are subsidized for years, but in the very area where the demonstrations are going on little or nothing usually is done about the other techniques that might be used and should be used to supplement any given technique. Thus, guidance clinics are set up, for example, and many good people sit back complacently and feel that now the problem is to be solved. Unfortunately, aside from the fact that there are never guidance clinics enough to go around, the sad truth is, of course, that merely to treat maladjusted children *after* they have become maladjusted does not remove the *causes* of the maladjustment —that is to say, the causes of the maladjustment of other children in similar situations.

If one thing has emerged from the intensive efforts of the last generation to control delinquency, it would seem to be that no one technique is enough— that even the synthesis of techniques represented by a guidance clinic is not enough, and that if we are ever to get ahead at all, we must attack the problem on as broad a front as the problem itself. No one is more conscious than I am of the fact that there are many areas in this problem of controlling human behavior about which we do not know nearly enough. There is no end in sight to the need of further scientific research and no end in sight to the need of practical research. But a great deal is known now about how to control behavior. At least we know many things that should *not* be done. Yet all about us these things are being done, and, as I said before, even a rough appraisal of a community's delinquency-control-readiness shows a discouraging lack of readiness and a discouraging irregularity in what readiness does exist. Obviously, while research goes on, the more immediate need would seem to be *social action* to bring into wider and wider use the best practices that are now being used somewhere and are proving themselves in use. Someone with a mind for maps could make a very interesting series of "isotherms of prevention." In the matter of police practice, for example, in every state these are little islands of best practice and around these varying degrees of antiquated practice. In all sorts of fields it would be no great job to date the practices that prevail in given communities. Thus, you would have police systems at the level of 1940 and other police systems at the level of 1930 and still others at the level of 1900, and so on, until in the rural constabulary you would be back somewhere in the 19th century, if not beyond.

Groups Demanding Special Attention

In the matter of delinquency prevention alone it is fairly obvious that every community faces four groups of youngsters who demand special attention. There are first, least numerous but most urgent in their need of attention, the *parolees from the juvenile correctional institutions*. Nearly everywhere these youngsters have been returned to the situations that originally produced their trouble. That hardly seems the most intelligent procedure, but it is undoubtedly the prevailing procedure.

A second group, somewhat more numerous, consists of the *probationers from the juvenile court* who are being "treated" in their own community. Outside of a few of the larger cities the level of probation service for juveniles is something of a scandal. All too frequently it amounts to mere formality, if it amounts even to that. Geographically most of America lives outside of the range of modern juvenile probation practice.

A third group of youngsters who need attention are the *problem cases in the schools*—the children who have not yet necessarily become delinquent but who are showing symptoms of emotional strain and maladjustment. We know from studies by Willard C. Olson and others that children identifiable by their teachers as problem children will turn up in the juvenile courts, or other institutions, in far higher percentages than will their companions who have no such trouble. This is no longer guesswork; it is a matter of probability. This is well known, but singularly little is being done about it. The school system that is set up to deal early enough and intelligently enough with such cases is still an exception even in our cities, and in the rural districts practically nothing is being done at all. School commissioners and superintendents tell me that this is a matter that is still receiving inadequate attention in the training of teachers in spite of the fact that E. K. Wickman demonstrated more than a decade ago that teachers were utterly unaware of the psychiatric significance of many types of behavior. So in every community, urban and rural, we have a considerable percentage of problem cases. The estimates vary but a conservative figure would be from 2 to 5 per cent of the school population at any given time. In such a State as Michigan, for example, where we have approximately a million youngsters in school, we estimate that 30,000 of these are children with problems in various stages of development. Probably one-fifth of this number, or about 6,000, have reached the stage at which the only help must lie in some expert guidance clinic. But probably the other four-fifths, or 24,000, of these 30,000 children with problems, are still in a relatively incipient stage and could be helped by common-sense readjustments on the part of teachers and parents.

But finally, in addition to parolees, probationers, and children with problems in a community there is still a fourth group, somewhat overlapping perhaps, but much larger than all these other three put together; namely, *children in high-risk situations*. A high-risk situation is a situation which on the basis of the statistics is known to produce a higher percentage of delinquents and maladjusted children than ordinary situations. For example, an emotionally disturbed home is a high-risk situation; a poverty home is a high-risk situation; a slum is a high-risk situation. No adequate enumeration of high-risk situations in any community has yet been made, but theoretically it should be possible to approximate such an enumeration. The Stamford Study, for example, of social breakdown which found approximately 4 per cent of the families of Stamford in 1936 and 1937 showing social breakdown suggests one index of high-risk situations. In Michigan it is estimated that approximately 200,000 children, perhaps one-fifth of the total number of children in our schools, are living in high-risk situations—at least they are exposed to higher-than-average risks. These include children in poverty homes, children in emotionally disturbed and broken homes, neglected gangs, children exposed to indecent literature, and so on. On the face of figures the bulk of our delinquents in Michigan seem to come from these situations of social rather than merely emotional dangers. The figures are based largely on estimates; therefore, they can be suggestive only, but at least they show this: Over a period of years, on the average, Michigan's 83 juvenile courts handled about 5,000 youngsters each year. The only one of these courts which has its own psychiatric clinic is the Wayne County Juvenile Court. In Wayne County this Court on an average refers to the clinic 10 per cent of its cases. If we were to generalize from these figures, then, it would appear that about 10 per cent of the delinquents in Michigan are clinical cases—that is, cases of obvious personality difficulties—while the other 90 per cent are children who have come out of situations of social rather than personality danger. These 500 emotionally disturbed delinquents apparently constitute about 8 or 9 per cent of the children who are estimated to be clinical cases in need of clinical treatment at the present time. The other 4,500 juvenile delinquents constitute about 2.6 per cent of the 170,000 who are estimated to be socially in danger.

Need for Effective Social Action

The problem of crimeproofing a community, then, would seem to run all the way from the family to the State and the National Government. It involves legislative reform, strengthening and modernizing law-enforcement agencies everywhere; the modernization of court procedures; the improvement of adult probation and parole procedures; the diffusion of best practice and institutional treatment; the education of communities to attack the risk-factors within them; the leveling upward of the practices of juvenile courts, juvenile probation officers, and juvenile correctional institutions; and the direction of specific programs of discovery, diagnosis, and treatment toward parolees, probationers, problem cases, and children in high-risk situations. The immediate problem, while the need of scientific research remains, would seem the need for more effective social action to spread more widely those "best practices" that are now being used somewhere in every field of control. Social action, contrary to common impression, is a technical art. The principles and practices of social action lie beyond the present discussion. But it is an art that everyone interested in crimeproofing a community should study with some care.

Delinquency Prevention Begins at Home*

By Paul G. Cressey. Director, Social Welfare Council of the Oranges and Maplewood, New Jersey.

JUVENILE delinquency occurs in the local community and the neighborhood. Efforts to prevent it can be most effective as they come to grips with the child's *own* immediate social world in his *own* community. For this reason the local situation is the key to delinquency control; any planning and promoting of programs for delinquency prevention can best be done in the local community—and best of all in the neighborhood itself.

The primacy of the local situation arises also from the fact that conditions contributing to delinquency in an individual case are always found on close inspection to be unique. Not only are the contributing factors, when objectively perceived, never exactly identical, but the subjective aspect of these factors, *i.e.*, the *true significance* of each to the child himself, and most of all, the *meaning to him* of his delinquent acts, are certain to be uniquely his own. If we hope to correct conditions, we must first be able to individualize our children in this way, and then to perceive them in their relationship to the family, the school and the play groups in the neighborhood of which they are a part. No method of delinquency prevention lends itself as readily to this as does an approach through the local community.

Effective effort means organizing the will to action of individual citizens or groups of citizens, if not the mobilizing of public opinion throughout a community. In our American society this can be best done through the indigenous leadership within the community itself. While state and federal agencies may be invaluable in supplying information, advice, and even inspiration toward action, the program is almost certain to be ineffective if it is not rooted in local leadership.

The State Program

The New Jersey state program of community services for delinquency prevention has very wisely been founded upon this principle. The report, *Two and One-half Years of State-Local Collaboration in Delinquency Prevention*, has affirmed that the "real job of delinquency prevention . . . can only be done in the community by the people themselves." The state's program, its promotional activities, its local youth surveys, its proffered services for evaluating local programs, as well as its statistical activities are tailored for service to local communities. These, together with the more general informational services and the demonstration projects of state-local collaboration described in the report indicate that noteworthy progress has been made at the state level toward providing a favorable climate for action by municipal governments and by local citizen groups. As a matter of fact the state services are so basic and so diversified it seems certain that every community, no matter how well supplied with talented local leadership and persons of the requisite professional skills, will in the end find it advantageous to avail itself of one or more of these services.

In our populous state there are not a dozen of our cities and communities which have an established and perma-

* Reprinted from *Focus*, Vol. 28, May, 1949, pp. 78–82. Used by permission.

nently staffed agency for coordination and planning in the health and welfare field. Most of these are so seriously under-financed and under-staffed that they can do but a fraction of the work confronting them if they are to keep abreast of our changing times. Then there are the 550 odd other municipalities and communities, large and small, which do not have even these planning facilities and for which the new organization, the New Jersey Citizens Conference (formed in 1947 to provide useful information to local citizen groups on methods for effective community action), offers perhaps the other chief hope. We need every service which can be helpful to us.

Community acceptance of the new state services is made infinitely easier because state-local relationships in the past have been found congenial and productive of results. Local communities note with approval that use of these services is optional, and that the decision to establish a municipal youth guidance council is also optional. The attitude and activity of representatives of the Division of Community Services for Delinquency Prevention have been in keeping with this pattern of state-local relations.

Municipal Youth Guidance Council Act

As a matter of fact, the criticisms which can be made of the state program are those that arise, not from its administration, but from shortcomings in the Municipal Youth Guidance Council Act itself. One of the most serious of these, and one which may in some communities impair relations, is that the law as written opens the way to a duplication of agencies and services in a community, and to the confusion, misunderstandings and citizen frustration which inevitably follow. Municipal youth guidance councils are expected to be coordinating agencies in the specialized field of delinquency prevention only, but their coming inevitably creates some problems

for communities having already established coordinating and social planning bodies or local agency service programs for unadjusted youth. This is notably the situation in those larger cities having councils of social agencies (or community welfare councils), all with active committees and programs on delinquency prevention or youth services. Coordination *in particular* cannot well be done at all if it is not done through one channel. In recognition of this fact citizens and local agencies in communities having established facilities for coordination and social planning are concerned at the prospect of a proliferation of these agencies.

Omissions in the Law. This prospect is the more serious because of omissions in the law. At no point does this act call attention to the possible existence of facilities having similar objectives or the desirability of reviewing community facilities to insure that coordination problems would not be complicated by establishing a youth guidance council. As a result, instances have already occurred in which local officials have established such a council without considering the possibility of duplicating services; any doubts and questions voiced by local citizens seem to have been neutralized by the prestige of the state government and its official legislation and recommendations. The Division of Community Services for Delinquency Prevention is in a position to advise against a council or to make other special recommendations, but its influence is restricted as it has no power to disapprove setting up a council *solely* because of a local duplication in agency activities.

At the time the bill was being considered, the New Jersey chapter of the American Association of Social Workers and the New Jersey Welfare Council went on record in opposition to some of its provisions. While commending the intent of the bill, the New Jersey AASW opposed it partly because it took "no cognizance of existing welfare councils and social planning bodies" and because municipal officials "might therefore contribute to a duplication and confusion of effort." The prospect that the guidance councils might conflict with and so confuse and impede the "efforts of established agencies already combating delinquency," was likewise raised by the New Jersey Welfare Council in its opposition to the bill.

Some noteworthy features of the act are its restriction of membership to a very small number and its provision requiring appointment of public officials to nearly half of these posts. Membership in the council is limited to seven; and of these seven, one each must come from the local governing body, the public school system, and the police department. Persons for the other posts are not specified. The Division of Community Services for Delinquency Prevention in a specially prepared information and instruction sheet for municipalities has listed "voluntary health and welfare agencies, councils of social agencies and other community councils" as among those local organizations whose "interests . . . are such as to make it desirable that they be considered for appointments." But it should be noted that there is no provision in the law recommending representation from autonomous coordinating bodies and voluntary social agencies, where these exist.

Adjustments within the Law. Reports from communities throughout New Jersey suggest that actual duplication of services is greatest in those communities where the council of social agencies serves a single city rather than an area of two or more municipalities. In the latter setting municipal youth guidance councils can most easily be interrelated to the work of area-wide agencies and programs. One type of accommodation is the situation in which municipal guidance councils accept some special function within the general area of serv-

ice for youth. Another is the situation in which the youth guidance council is a means for interpreting the single municipality's problems to the area council and at the same time conveying to the local officials the particular perspective and information gained by participation on the area basis. By methods such as these which effect a division of labor or make possible a liaison between the two types of councils it is at least possible to strengthen coordination rather than to weaken it by the presence of youth guidance councils in an area-wide community setting.

Successful collaboration appears to be less probable in communities where the council of social agencies is oriented to a central city. As far as I have been able to learn, the "potential conflict and misunderstanding," of which the state report makes mention, is still unresolved for these cities if the youth guidance council undertakes a coordination program. The situation can be clarified by a carefully defined division of labor between the two organizations in the field of coordination, or by a disposition on the part of the council to stress its other functions under the law. But a "potential conflict" in the coordination field will still have to be resolved by an adjustment in program or a withdrawal of one or the other service.

Unless there are special circumstances which warrant a division in the coordination function, it would seem a matter of wisdom and practical economy to direct our efforts toward strengthening the one coordination service, whichever it may be. The question is not primarily whether the youth guidance council would "duplicate or supersede the council of social agencies," but in which way the community would be better served. Certainly an attempt by both organizations to undertake a coordination and planning program in the youth welfare field would in the end seriously confuse a community situation. The rank and file of our citizens have difficulty in understanding the need for even one coordination agency; they would certainly be more confused if asked to accept the need for two. Most important however is the fact that, even at its best, sharing by two or more organizations of a field which, economically and sociologically can best be covered by one, entails additional expenditure of effort to insure "coordination among the coordinators."

I am wondering if the dissatisfaction expressed in the state report with councils of social agencies is not directed less toward their coordinating and planning machinery than toward their failure to provide a specialized referral service for unadjusted children within their own organizations, or to lead in establishing such services. The creation of a new service is the second of the two major provisions of the Municipal Youth Guidance Council Act. This law authorizes "adjustment committees" to "provide guidance and counsel to children with incipient behavior problems and to cooperate with the juvenile and domestic relations court." Those appointed to a committee are expected to be "qualified by experience and training to assist in and coordinate the efforts of police, schools and other agencies." But no objective standards for qualifications are provided; and it has been left to the state agency through its vigilance and prestige to protect children and families against abuses possible under this law.

This feature of the act has been frequently criticized because it affords no assurance as to the professional competency of those serving on adjustment committees; moreover, the fact that appointments are to be made by municipal officials causes many to question whether the most competent condidates would always be selected. There is no certainty under the law that these committees will function as referral agencies only, or as long-time study and treatment centers. But in either case, it would certainly

seem that the responsibility of working with children in trouble, of unravelling the twisted, often almost inscrutable threads of motivation of conduct in children is too great, and the opportunities too precious to be entrusted to any but the best trained workers and those most gifted in personality. There is need for greater assurance as to the personnel of the adjustment committees than can be found in the present law.

At the same time greater understanding and appreciation among social workers and councils of social agencies of the municipal youth guidance council plan and of similar movements in other states is called for. Advocates of these programs have placed their fingers on a need which is not fully met in most of our cities. As things now stand there is often no basis for even the hope that all children showing deviant behavior will be detected early and brought to the attention of those who could help. Social agencies will be alert to their own constituency, and our best schools will be concerned about problems disclosed by children in the school situation, but there is today no certainty of full coverage. Neither is there usually a plan for police to bring children quickly in touch with the particular help they may need. These are some of the problems to which youth guidance councils may be expected to devote themselves, and they are also problems in which councils of social agencies should be concerned.

Multiple Functions of Councils

It is yet too early to attempt to forecast the future of these youth councils. But even incomplete information concerning their development in this state indicates at least three distinct trends. Some are beginning to function as coordinating and planning agencies, studying needs and local facilities, and devising improvement in youth services. A second type of development is in the council whose only function has been sponsoring an "adjustment committee" which has functioned actually as a service and referral agency. A third trend is for some council members to serve as volunteers, assisting municipal officials. The council provides liaison service with out-of-town officials and organizations, and acts as advisor to police officers and others. Members may help with phases of work in which the local officials may not be particularly adept or interested.

These divergent developments seem to come from multiple functions written into the act. While set up as a coordinating body, the guidance council is expected also to function as a "board of directors" for its own service agency, the adjustment committee. This joining of a coordinating and a service function in one organization has been generally regarded as unwise and it remains to be seen whether a council can continue successfully as both. The emphasis in the law upon its role as ancillary to other organizations and officials leads quite naturally to the situation in which the council and its citizen members may function actually as assistants to the particular officials in power at the time.

It is to be regretted that restriction of membership to seven means that at least three-sevenths—nearly half—are public officials or representatives of public bodies. This provision has the important advantage that designation of school and police representatives insures inclusion of these agencies in coordination at the administrative level. But I am wondering

if the method of appointment and the limiting of the citizen membership to a maximum of four, means that guidance councils can but be expected to continue fairly "close to City Hall"—certainly seldom if ever in direct opposition to administrative policies. This has some obvious advantages, but in many communities it could have serious consequences. Conceivably the guidance council could come to be identified with one political faction rather than to be a coordinating agency serving all.

Limitation of citizen membership means also little chance to include spokesmen for the various population groupings and various currents of local opinion. As constituted at present the council can function only as an instrument for administrative coordination. It can not become a means for enlisting the indigenous leadership in our communities, although we know this is the resource and strength which we must tap if we are to succeed notably in community organization for delinquency prevention. Discovering local citizen leadership and putting it to work for delinquency prevention was the method found successful in later developments in the west coast coordinating council movement, and it is the essence of the Chicago Area Project successes. It is to be hoped that revisions of our present law will make it possible to avail ourselves of this means for strengthening the delinquency prevention movement in New Jersey.

Let's Stop Fooling Around*

By Horace S. Volz. Probation Officer, Essex County Probation Department, Newark, New Jersey.

IN 1947 IN New Jersey there were 5,046 children taken before the juvenile courts, some of these appearing on more than one occasion, many appearing for more

* Reprinted from *Federal Probation*, Vol. XII, September, 1948, pp. 18–20. Used by permission of author and publication.

than one delinquent act. Experienced students assert that this group is only a small portion of the delinquent children in the State, that many still appear "unofficially" before police courts, many more are dismissed by the police without referral to courts, and others go undetected and unapprehended. Everywhere concern is expressed among parents, school men, welfare workers and public officials regarding the behavior of children. Newspapers and periodicals devote valuable front page and editorial space to reporting and discussing the problem and the efforts being made to solve it. At a recent national conference, called by the federal government, delegates from every state in the union went to Washington to discuss the problem and to explore its implications. More recently Governor Driscoll of New Jersey, carrying out one of the recommendations of the Washington conference, called leaders in all fields dealing with youth to a 2-day conference at Trenton, N. J.

"Hit-or-Miss" Approach

Although juvenile delinquency has been a problem of society since the dawn of recorded history, the problem has become more pressing and urgent in recent times with the development of large cities, the so-called progress of our industrial economy and the increasing complexity of modern social living.

Numerous suggestions and recommendations to solve this many-sided problem are offered. An observer finds in these suggestions and recommendations much confusion and uncertainty. Unfortunately, our attack on the problem of juvenile delinquency has been about the most hit-or-miss, trial-and-error, unorganized approach that has hit this old planet since it separated from its parent Sun and itself became a juvenile. In this, the age of the studious, planned, scientific approach to all kinds of problems—military, medical, legal, industrial, edu-

cational—in the field of behavior we continue to attack with panaceas, hunches, plans of cranks, and suggestions of well-meaning but unenlightened persons. People with unbounded interest, enthusiasm, and good intentions, but without deep and accurate knowledge of the fundamental problems involved, sometimes complicate the situation through misdirected and unguided efforts. It is true that many of these "experts" have been very well meaning. However, if we could say nothing more of our military planning and leadership than that it was well-meaning, the attack on the recently defeated enemy would have failed just as miserably as our attack on delinquency is failing. The differences in the basic principles used in these two attacks are so obvious that a detailed comparison does not seem necessary, but a review of some of the diffuse, disjointed, and poorly-planned motions we go through in our efforts to control or prevent delinquency seems advisable.

We repeat what has failed over and over again. We accept unproved reports of "successful" programs. We swallow prescriptions written by unqualified "social physicians" who only too willingly assume the very great responsibility of prescribing treatment without going to the trouble of making a studied diagnosis. Yes, we even disregard the suggestions of qualified social physicians. Oh! we call them in for consultation, but when they don't give us a ready, simple answer that will do the trick quickly and, instead, begin to talk about basic causes, co-ordinated programs and long term treatment, we get impatient and turn to the fellow who offers a direct attack on the symptoms and recklessly guarantees a high percentage of cures through the use of his treatment. The New Jersey Legislative Committee, which recently made a statewide survey and study of juvenile delinquency, found these practices on all sides. Senator Van Alstyne, Chairman of that Committee, must have had to call for the assistance of skillful diplomats when he framed it in these words: "We have been tremendously impressed with the disorganized approach to the solution of the problem." That certainly is putting it mildly.

And Juvenile Delinquency Continues!

When someone riding a hobby shouts that what we need is more recreational facilities, communities rush to build more playgrounds, gyms, swimming pools, tennis courts, and base ball fields. And juvenile delinquency continues! When another panaceist yells "better housing," communities rush to construct beautiful, low-rent housing projects, with abundant recreational facilities. And juvenile delinquency continues! When another insists that unrestricted participation in street trades is a prime factor in delinquency causation, a drive is put on in this area, but still those "stubborn and determined" juveniles become delinquents! When another insists that youth canteens will control delinquency, public-spirited citizens get on the job, but youth still comes before the bar—even canteen members. When another insists that lax and inadequate police activity is responsible, special juvenile bureaus are set up. When another claims that contact with police, courts, and places of detention is not good, a drive to keep children out of the hands of police, courts, and detention homes is made. When another claims that the root of the trouble lies in the "leniency" of juvenile courts or in the inadequacy of detention homes, we begin to think in terms of more severity and bigger detention homes. Quite naturally then, we continue to have the delinquents we deserve. Then it is decided that the trouble must lie elsewhere. "Well, let's see. What could it be? Ah! that's it! Yes, sir! Absolutely! Haven't the newspapers been full of stories about the children roaming the streets late at nights? A curfew! That's what we need. That'll stop all of this de-

linquency!" And so, at 9 or 10 P.M. the bells toll, and delinquency continues to roll!

Of course, most of these activities and regulations are socially beneficial, both those which are prohibitive and those which are constructive. These things we should have anyway for all children. But, as we have seen, juveniles continue to become delinquent in spite of them. So, let us not lose our balance in the rush to get these sorely needed facilities and ascribe to any one of them powers which it does not possess. And let us not sit back in a self-satisfied way and cluck like the proud hen: "Look, look what we've done; a masterpiece of social engineering that will make juvenile delinquency 'fold up its tents like the Arabs and silently steal away'." Our practices are akin to those of the quack physician who prescribes without the benefit of careful and scientific diagnosis. They smack of the quackery demonstrated in the case of a patient who might go to several doctors with agonizing abdominal pains and receive the following kind of treatment. They made no tests nor do they study the findings of research. The first fellow just "figgers" that the pains were caused by poor diet, because he has his own ideas about diets and believes improper eating is the cause of many, many ills. So he gives the patient a diet but the pains get worse. The next doctor he goes to happens to be extremely vitamin conscious. So he prescribes vitamins and the pains get worse. The next orders more rest and fresh air and the next regular habits of elimination and still the pains get worse. Certainly none of these things are harmful and all are generally beneficial but, none had the power to cure or arrest the patient's cancer. Occasionally, and almost wholly accidentally, a cure may be stumbled on in this way. But more often there is no therapeutic action on the specific ailment, chiefly because there was no real effort to find the fundamental causes of the symptoms. I say that our handling of the problem of juvenile delinquency is that bad and even worse.

Activity at Cross Purposes

To any observer, viewing this scene, several facts stand out in bold relief. The problems facing America in respect to youth are immediate, vast, and complicated. Many fields of endeavor and phases of life are involved. But the same observer sees much confusion, considerable dissipation of effort, a great deal of activity absolutely at cross purposes, and a significant lack of co-ordination in the attack on harmful influences and the development of a broad program for the training and protection of youth. And this in the age of incipient scientific methods in the social sciences, and in the science of human behavior. This condition is due primarily to the failure of the trained and experienced to furnish leadership for the general public; to the failure of these leaders to harness the tremendous interest of our citizens; and to their failure to convince the public that the guidance of the real expert is needed here if it is needed in any field. Yet, one sometimes wonders whether even we who are engaged professionally in this field are qualified to lead. We find the old gap caused by the lag of practice behind theory and scientifically established principles. In this field, this gap is unjustifiably large. Certainly, our social scientists are far ahead of our practitioners. Very capable investigators have made sincere, intelligent, and valid efforts to diagnose and have made considerable progress in reaching the fundamental causes, as well as in the matter of prescribing treatment. But, do our practitioners use their findings? Rarely. The medical profession spends millions on research and the good practitioner makes use of these findings. We don't even make full use of the findings given us. Much less have we succeeded in helping to interpret and sell these findings to the public. Workers in the field of probation and parole are demanding professional status. Yet, they are content to go on using unprofessional methods. This must be changed radically if we really expect to be accorded status. It must be changed drastically if we hope to enjoy any degree of success in our battle against delinquency.

What are those changes? Who is to say what changes should be made? Does any one or any group know enough about human behavior to outline a plan of treatment? Certainly the writer has no grandiose ideas about his ability to do such a tremendous job and it is not his purpose to attempt to outline such a program in detail. In fact, he believes that no such program as outlined by anyone should be accepted *in toto* at this time. He believes that in order to do a sound job we must do a great deal of exploring and re-examining before we attempt to put any plan into practice.

Need for Tested Knowledge

Let us first of all gather all of the sound, scientific findings available and accept what seems to be the best diagnoses, plans of treatment, and prevention programs. Let us apply these intelligently, scientifically, and experimentally rather than with a feeling of satisfaction or a feeling that here we have the answer. Then let us continue research. After this, we must concentrate our efforts on implementing the principles established. Let us take the findings of Healy and Bronner, the Gluecks, Shaw, and many, many others, and use them rather than musings of Joe Doakes, Elmer Twitchell, and Mike McGee. Yes, there will be disagreement. Perhaps we shall have three or four schools of thought just as there is more than one school of thought in other sciences and disciplines. But, each could be sound. The sociologists doubtless would differ with the psychiatrists in emphasis. They may differ with the religionists, the recreationists, and the educationists. But, I believe they all could be very close together fundamentally. What differences there were should be sound and tenable and worthy of exploration.

One of the greatest needs is a set of guiding principles. The recommendations of the Attorney General's National Conference on Prevention and Control of Juvenile Delinquency provide a series of guideposts by which local communities may travel on the road to an effective plan. It may be that in this conference we have taken the first sound step but,

before we jump to that conclusion, let us thoroughly examine the findings and recommendations of the conference. If it is found that this conference has completed satisfactorily the first step then let us follow their recommendations. If, on the other hand, they have not completed this first step, then let us continue further efforts to complete it before we attempt to advance to the second. At long last, then, we will be in a position to make an intelligent beginning and to terminate our promiscuous stabs in the dark.

SELECTED REFERENCES

1. Neumeyer, Martin H., *Juvenile Delinquency in Modern Society* (New York: D. Van Nostrand Co., 1949), Chapter 15: "Community Organization and Methods of Research."

As a specialist in community organization, Neumeyer examines many aspects of the community in relation to delinquency control. Communities do not act unless they are stimulated and mobilized to act. The community becomes a new frame of reference, displacing former primary groupings.

2. Reiss, Albert J, Jr., "Delinquency as the Failure of Personal and Social Controls," *American Sociological Review*, XVI, April 1951.

Reiss stresses the necessity of internalized norms and rules governing behavior in conformity with the pattern of the social system.

3. Tappan, Paul W., *Juvenile Delinquency* (New York: McGraw-Hill Book Co., 1949), Chapter 18: "The Prevention of Delinquency—Through Social Institutions."

Tappan points out that community organization and planning are matters of relatively recent development in the theory and efforts of modern social work, but that they represent tremendously significant possibilities for the development of delinquency-deterring measures.

4. Carr, Lowell Juilliard, *Delinquency Control* (New York: Harper & Brothers, 1941), Chapter 13: "Community Leadership."

Carr stresses that no type of human behavior is more important in times of stress and uncertainty than community leadership. Yet the men who manage groups best seldom write books about it, and the men who write the books seldom manage groups. Leadership is a type of directive initiative.

INDEX